SEVEN CONTEMPORARY PLAYS

SELECTED AND EDITED BY

CHARLES H. WHITMAN

Professor of English
Rutgers University

HOUGHTON MIFFLIN COMPANY

BOSTON · NEW YORK · CHICAGO · DALLAS

ATLANTA · SAN FRANCISCO

The Riverside Press Cambridge

The Riverside Press
CAMBRIDGE · MASSACHUSETTS
PRINTED IN THE U.S.A.

CONTENTS

CONTENTS

PREFACE

THE drama has sometimes been referred to as the most ubiquitous and provocative of the arts. Certainly it commands at present an intelligent and widespread interest — an interest that is gradually building up a considerable body of readers of dramatic literature. It was not so long ago that current stage successes could be had only in type-written form or in the paper-covered editions of Samuel French; now, the popular plays of the current season are promptly published in attractive and permanent format to be read both by those who have witnessed the performances and by those who, by reason of the distance from the great centres, are unable to see a stage production. Some of these printed plays, it is heartening to know, have taken their place among the best sellers.

It must be confessed that a play is somewhat harder to read than a novel, in that it is written in a sort of shorthand with all the brokenness and hesitancies of ordinary speech, and hence requires a more active exercise of the imagination. One who for the first time comes to the printed play misses the help afforded by gesture, facial expression, and pantomime of the stage drama; he misses also the descriptions and explanations to which the novel has accustomed him; and he has to learn to read between the lines, to keep ever alert to every implication and subtle shade of meaning, to get inside the lives of the characters — in short, to make the play come to life on the stage of his own imagination. It may be said that to one who acquires this sort of reading technique, the reading of plays will bring a keen sense of pleasure and satisfaction — in some instances even greater than that afforded by a stage performance.

The serious study of the contemporary drama has developed immeasurably in recent years among literary clubs and college groups, and courses in this field now occupy an honored place in the curriculum of many American universities. To meet this constantly growing interest a considerable equipment in the way of handbooks, histories, and anthologies has come into being.

"Seven Contemporary Plays" was projected in the belief that there is a real need for a compact anthology of representative plays for supplementary reading in connection with the Freshman English course or with any course in which types of literature are emphasized. Various considerations have influenced the editor in the choice of material. While the personal equation must inevitably affect any selection such as this, the editor has tried not to be influenced unduly by the personal estimate.

Realizing that many contemporary plays, though effective on the stage, are dull reading and wholly lacking in literary appeal, the editor has selected seven plays which, quite apart from their dramatic qualities, possess undoubted literary merit. Two of them — "The Sunken Bell" and "Cyrano de Bergerac" — are in verse; others, notably "Riders to the Sea" are poetic in mood; all of them are distinguished by beauty of style. The ideas underlying these plays are provocative and stimulating, and lend themselves excellently to classroom discussion. Finally, the seven plays are representative of seven countries, and thus offer a substantial basis for the study of national tendencies. All of them, however, have found acceptance not only in their homeland but on the larger stage of world drama.

Because of the limitations of space it has not been possible to illustrate all types of contemporary drama, and it has therefore seemed wise to eliminate plays that are highly experimental in character. The collection, in fact, contains no example of expressionism. It is a bit too early to determine what permanent influence expressionism may have. Dramatic fashions are constantly changing, and expressionism is certainly not now so much the vogue as it was a few years ago. As a movement, and it could hardly be said to exist as a movement outside of Germany, it has apparently spent its force. Certain manifestations of expressionism are interesting, and it may ultimately prove to have made some permanent contribution to the drama of the day; at present, however, as Mr. Montrose J. Moses has pointed out, "it is more clearly defined in methods of stage production than in technique of writing."

The other important tendencies in contemporary drama — realism, naturalism, romanticism, and symbolism — are represented by splendid examples of their genres. Realism, the predominant influence in our day, is illustrated by "An Enemy of the People" and "Beyond the Horizon"; naturalism, by "Strife" and "The Cherry Orchard"; romanticism, by "Cyrano de Bergerac"; symbolism, by "The Sunken Bell." The last named play is not true to type, though, since the symbolism is not infrequently blended with realism.

The anthology is rather unique in its inclusion of a play by Ibsen. The reason usually offered for the omission is the availability of the plays by this author. Even so, it seems appropriate to include in a general anthology a typical specimen of the work of a pioneer such as Ibsen, whose influence, as a technician and as the leading exponent of the drama of ideas, has been the most potent in modern times.

It might be objected that Ibsen should not properly come under the heading "contemporary." Perhaps not, if the matter of time be the only consideration, since his first play was published over eighty years ago. The term is, however, to be liberally interpreted to cover the drama of the past one hundred years, mainly for the cogent reason advanced by Mr. Thomas H. Dickinson: "if the term contemporary has any critical meaning for our time, this meaning must go beyond the mere accidents of date and inhere in those qualities that make the theatre of our time a different theatre from any that has gone before."

It is fortunate indeed that the British drama can be represented by such a notable play as "Strife," one of the major dramas of Galsworthy, since no work of Shaw's has yet found its way into a collection of plays, and few anthologies have included examples of Barrie or Galsworthy.

The justification for the choice of plays selected for this anthology is to be found either expressed or implied in the introductions to the individual plays in the back of the book. These introductions give a brief account of the life of the author, a discussion of his qualities and of his particular contribution to the drama of his day, and a commentary on the individual play, together with a note on its production. In the appendix will be found also a complete list of the plays of the authors represented, and a bibliography that is not intended to be inclusive, but rather to present a selective list of titles, some of a general character, others dealing with individual playwrights.

It should be said that the list of plays in this volume has had the approval of teachers of English in not a few American colleges, who have been uniformly sympathetic toward the project. Their advice and assistance are hereby gratefully acknowledged. The editor wishes also to express his appreciation of the coöperation of the publishers who control the copyrights of the plays. Specific acknowledgment is given in connection with the individual plays. Finally his thanks are due to his colleague, Mr. C. Rexford Davis, who has so kindly read considerable portions of the manuscript.

C. H. W.

AN ENEMY OF THE PEOPLE

By HENRIK IBSEN

Translated by ELEANOR MARX–AVELING

CHARACTERS

DOCTOR THOMAS STOCKMANN, *medical officer of the Baths.*

MRS. STOCKMANN, *his wife.*

PETRA, *their daughter, a teacher.*

EILIF
MORTEN } *their sons, thirteen and ten years old respectively.*

PETER STOCKMANN, *the doctor's elder brother, Burgomaster* [1] *and chief of police, chairman of the Baths Committee, etc.*

MORTEN KIIL,* [2] *master tanner, Mrs. Stockmann's adoptive-father.*

HOVSTAD, *editor of the "People's Messenger."*

BILLING, *on the staff of the paper.*

HORSTER, *a ship's captain.*

ASLAKSEN, *a printer.*

Participants in a meeting of citizens: all sorts and conditions of men, some women, and a band of schoolboys.

The action passes in a town on the South Coast of Norway.

---

[1] "Burgomaster" is the most convenient substitute for "Byfogd," but "Town Clerk" would perhaps be more nearly equivalent. It is impossible to find exact counterparts in English for the different grades of the Norwegian bureaucracy.

[2] Pronounce: *Keel.*

ACT FIRST

Evening. DR. STOCKMANN'S *sitting-room; simply but neatly decorated and furnished. In the wall to the right are two doors, the further one leading to the hall, the nearer one to the Doctor's study. In the opposite wall, facing the hall door, a door leading to the other rooms of the house. Against the middle of this wall stands the stove; further forward a sofa with a mirror above it, and in front of it an oval table with a cover. On the table a lighted lamp, with a shade. In the back wall an open door leading to the dining-room, in which is seen a supper-table, with a lamp on it.*

BILLING *is seated at the supper-table, with a napkin under his chin.* MRS. STOCKMANN *is standing by the table and placing before him a dish with a large joint of roast beef. The other seats round the table are empty; the table is in disorder, as after a meal.*

MRS. STOCKMANN. If you come an hour late, Mr. Billing, you must put up with a cold supper.

BILLING (*eating*). It is excellent — really first rate.

MRS. STOCKMANN. You know how Stockmann insists on regular meal-hours ——

BILLING. Oh, I don't mind at all. I almost think I enjoy my supper more when I can sit down to it like this, alone and undisturbed.

MRS. STOCKMANN. Oh, well, if you enjoy it —— (*Listening in the direction of the hall.*) I believe this is Mr. Hovstad coming too.

BILLING. Very likely.

BURGOMASTER STOCKMANN *enters, wearing an overcoat and an official gold-laced cap, and carrying a stick.*

BURGOMASTER. Good evening, sister-in-law.

MRS. STOCKMANN (*coming forward into the sitting-room*). Oh, good evening; is it you? It is good of you to look in.

BURGOMASTER. I was just passing, and so —— (*Looks towards the drawing-room.*) Ah, I see you have company.

MRS. STOCKMANN (*rather embarrassed*).   Oh no, not at all; it's the merest chance.   (*Hurriedly.*)   Won't you sit down and have a little supper?

BURGOMASTER.   I?   No, thank you.   Good gracious! hot meat in the evening!   That wouldn't suit my digestion.

MRS. STOCKMANN.   Oh, for once in a way ——

BURGOMASTER.   No, no, — much obliged to you.   I stick to tea and bread and butter.   It's more wholesome in the long run — and rather more economical, too.

MRS. STOCKMANN (*smiling*).   You mustn't think Thomas and I are mere spendthrifts, either.

BURGOMASTER.   You are not, sister-in-law; far be it from me to say that.   (*Pointing to the Doctor's study.*)   Is he not at home?

MRS. STOCKMANN.   No, he has gone for a little turn after supper — with the boys.

BURGOMASTER.   I wonder if that is a good thing to do?   (*Listening.*) There he is, no doubt.

MRS. STOCKMANN.   No, that is not he.   (*A knock.*)   Come in!

HOVSTAD *enters from the hall.*

MRS. STOCKMANN.   Ah, it's Mr. Hovstad ——

HOVSTAD.   You must excuse me; I was detained at the printer's. Good evening, Burgomaster.

BURGOMASTER (*bowing rather stiffly*).   Mr. Hovstad?   You come on business, I presume?

HOVSTAD.   Partly.   About an article for the paper.

BURGOMASTER.   So I supposed.   I hear my brother is an extremely prolific contributor to the *People's Messenger*.

HOVSTAD.   Yes, when he wants to unburden his mind on one thing or another, he gives the *Messenger* the benefit.

MRS. STOCKMANN (*to* HOVSTAD).   But will you not ——?

(*Points to the dining-room.*)

BURGOMASTER.   Well, well, I am far from blaming him for writing for the class of readers he finds most in sympathy with him.   And, personally, I have no reason to bear your paper any ill-will, Mr. Hovstad.

HOVSTAD.   No, I should think not.

BURGOMASTER.   One may say, on the whole, that a fine spirit of mutual tolerance prevails in our town — an excellent public spirit. And that is because we have a great common interest to hold us together — an interest in which all right-minded citizens are equally concerned ——

HOVSTAD. Yes — the Baths.

BURGOMASTER. Just so. We have our magnificent new Baths. Mark my words! The whole life of the town will centre around the Baths, Mr. Hovstad. There can be no doubt of it!

MRS. STOCKMANN. That is just what Thomas says.

BURGOMASTER. How marvellously the place has developed, even in this couple of years! Money has come into circulation, and brought life and movement with it. Houses and ground-rents rise in value every day.

HOVSTAD. And there are fewer people out of work.

BURGOMASTER. That is true. There is a gratifying diminution in the burden imposed on the well-to-do classes by the poor-rates; and they will be still further lightened if only we have a really good summer this year — a rush of visitors — plenty of invalids, to give the Baths a reputation.

HOVSTAD. I hear there is every prospect of that.

BURGOMASTER. Things look most promising. Inquiries about apartments and so forth keep on pouring in.

HOVSTAD. Then the Doctor's paper will come in very opportunely.

BURGOMASTER. Has he been writing again?

HOVSTAD. This is a thing he wrote in the winter; enlarging on the virtues of the Baths, and on the excellent sanitary conditions of the town. But at that time I held it over.

BURGOMASTER. Ah — I suppose there was something not quite judicious about it?

HOVSTAD. Not at all. But I thought it better to keep it till the spring, when people are beginning to look about them, and think of their summer quarters ——

BURGOMASTER. You were right, quite right, Mr. Hovstad.

MRS. STOCKMANN. Yes, Thomas is really indefatigable where the Baths are concerned.

BURGOMASTER. It is his duty as one of the staff.

HOVSTAD. And of course he was really their creator.

BURGOMASTER. Was he? Indeed! I gather that certain persons

are of that opinion. But I should have thought that I, too, had a modest share in that undertaking.

MRS. STOCKMANN. Yes, that is what Thomas is always saying.

HOVSTAD. No one dreams of denying it, Burgomaster. You set the thing going, and put it on a practical basis; everybody knows that. I only meant that the original idea was the Doctor's.

BURGOMASTER. Yes, my brother has certainly had ideas enough in his time — worse luck! But when it comes to realising them, Mr. Hovstad, we want men of another stamp. I should have thought that in this house at any rate ——

MRS. STOCKMANN. Why, my dear brother-in-law ——

HOVSTAD. Burgomaster, how can you ——?

MRS. STOCKMANN. Do go in and have some supper, Mr. Hovstad; my husband is sure to be home directly.

HOVSTAD. Thanks; just a mouthful, perhaps.

(*He goes into the dining-room.*)

BURGOMASTER (*speaking in a low voice*). It is extraordinary how people who spring direct from the peasant class never can get over their want of tact.

MRS. STOCKMANN. But why should you care? Surely you and Thomas can share the honour, like brothers.

BURGOMASTER. Yes, one would suppose so; but it seems a share of the honour is not enough for some persons.

MRS. STOCKMANN. What nonsense! You and Thomas always get on so well together. (*Listening.*) There, I think I hear him.

(*Goes and opens the door to the hall.*)

DR. STOCKMANN (*laughing and talking loudly, without*). Here's another visitor for you, Katrina. Isn't it capital, eh? Come in, Captain Horster. Hang your coat on that peg. What! you don't wear an overcoat? Fancy, Katrina, I caught him in the street, and I could hardly get him to come in.

CAPTAIN HORSTER *enters and bows to* MRS. STOCKMANN.

DR. STOCKMANN (*in the doorway*). In with you, boys. They're famishing again! Come along, Captain Horster; you must try our roast beef ——

(*He forces* HORSTER *into the dining-room.* EILIF *and* MORTEN *follow them.*)

MRS. STOCKMANN. But, Thomas, don't you see ——

DR. STOCKMANN (*turning round in the doorway*). Oh, is that you, Peter! (*Goes up to him and holds out his hand.*) Now this is really capital.

BURGOMASTER. Unfortunately, I have only a moment to spare ——

DR. STOCKMANN. Nonsense! We shall have some toddy in a minute. You're not forgetting the toddy, Katrina?

MRS. STOCKMANN. Of course not; the water's boiling.

(*She goes into the dining-room.*)

BURGOMASTER. Toddy too ——!

DR. STOCKMANN. Yes; sit down, and let's make ourselves comfortable.

BURGOMASTER. Thanks; I never join in drinking parties.

DR. STOCKMANN. But this isn't a party.

BURGOMASTER. I don't know what else —— (*Looks towards the dining-room.*) It's extraordinary how they can get through all that food.

DR. STOCKMANN (*rubbing his hands*). Yes, doesn't it do one good to see young people eat? Always hungry! That's as it should be. They need good, solid meat to put stamina into them! It is they that have got to whip up the ferment of the future, Peter.

BURGOMASTER. May I ask what there is to be "whipped up," as you call it?

DR. STOCKMANN. You'll have to ask the young people that — when the time comes. We shan't see it, of course. Two old fogies like you and me ——

BURGOMASTER. Come, come! Surely that is a very extraordinary expression to use ——

DR. STOCKMANN. Oh, you mustn't mind my nonsense, Peter. I'm in such glorious spirits, you see. I feel so unspeakably happy in the midst of all this growing, germinating life. Isn't it a marvellous time we live in! It seems as though a whole new world were springing up around us.

BURGOMASTER. Do you really think so?

DR. STOCKMANN. Of course, you can't see it as clearly as I do. You have passed your life in the midst of it all; and that deadens the impression. But I who had to vegetate all those years in that little hole in the north, hardly ever seeing a soul that could speak a stimulating word to me — all this affects me as if I had suddenly dropped into the heart of some teeming metropolis.

BURGOMASTER. Well, metropolis ——

DR. STOCKMANN. Oh, I know well enough that things are on a small scale here, compared with many other places. But there's life here — there's promise — there's an infinity of things to work and strive for; and that is the main point. (*Calling.*) Katrina, haven't there been any letters?

MRS. STOCKMANN (*in the dining-room*). No, none at all.

DR. STOCKMANN. And then a good income, Peter! That's a thing one learns to appreciate when one has lived on starvation wages ——

BURGOMASTER. Good heavens ——!

DR. STOCKMANN. Oh, yes, I can tell you we often had hard times of it up there. And now we can live like princes! Today, for example, we had roast beef for dinner; and we've had some of it for supper too. Won't you have some? Come along — just look at it, at any rate ——

BURGOMASTER. No, no; certainly not ——

DR. STOCKMANN. Well then, look here — do you see we've bought a table-cover?

BURGOMASTER. Yes, so I observed.

DR. STOCKMANN. And a lamp-shade, too. Do you see? Katrina has been saving up for them. They make the room look comfortable, don't they? Come over here. No, no, no, not there. So — yes! Now you see how it concentrates the light ——. I really think it has quite an artistic effect. Eh?

BURGOMASTER. Yes, when one can afford such luxuries ——

DR. STOCKMANN. Oh, I can afford it now. Katrina says I make almost as much as we spend.

BURGOMASTER. Ah — almost!

DR. STOCKMANN. Besides, a man of science must live in some style. Why, I believe a mere sheriff [1] spends much more a year than I do.

BURGOMASTER. Yes, I should think so! A member of the superior magistracy ——

---

[1] *Amtmand*, the chief magistrate of an *Amt* or county; consequently a high dignitary in the official hierarchy.

DR. STOCKMANN. Well then, even a common shipowner! A man of that sort will get through many times as much ——

BURGOMASTER. That is natural, in your relative positions.

DR. STOCKMANN. And after all, Peter, I really don't squander any money. But I can't deny myself the delight of having people about me. I must have them. After living so long out of the world, I find it a necessity of life to have bright, cheerful, freedom-loving, hard-working young fellows around me — and that's what they are, all of them, that are sitting there eating so heartily. I wish you knew more of Hovstad ——

BURGOMASTER. Ah, that reminds me — Hovstad was telling me that he is going to publish another article of yours.

DR. STOCKMANN. An article of mine?

BURGOMASTER. Yes, about the Baths. An article you wrote last winter.

DR. STOCKMANN. Oh, that one! But I don't want that to appear for the present.

BURGOMASTER. Why not? It seems to me this is the very time for it.

DR. STOCKMANN. Very likely — under ordinary circumstances ——
(Crosses the room.)

BURGOMASTER (following him with his eyes). And what is unusual in the circumstances now?

DR. STOCKMANN (standing still). The fact is, Peter, I really cannot tell you just now; not this evening, at all events. There may prove to be a great deal that is unusual in the circumstances. On the other hand, there may be nothing at all. Very likely it's only my fancy.

BURGOMASTER. Upon my word, you are very enigmatical. Is there anything in the wind? Anything I am to be kept in the dark about? I should think, as Chairman of the Bath Committee ——

DR. STOCKMANN. And I should think that I —— Well, well, don't let us get our backs up, Peter.

BURGOMASTER. God forbid! I am not in the habit of "getting my back up," as you express it. But I must absolutely insist that all arrangements shall be made and carried out in a businesslike manner, and through the properly constituted authorities. I cannot be a party to crooked or underhand courses.

DR. STOCKMANN. Have *I* ever been given to crooked or underhand courses?

BURGOMASTER. At any rate you have an ingrained propensity to taking your own course. And that, in a well-ordered community is almost as inadmissible. The individual must subordinate himself to society, or, more precisely, to the authorities whose business it is to watch over the welfare of society.

DR. STOCKMANN. Maybe. But what the devil has that to do with me?

BURGOMASTER. Why this is the very thing, my dear Thomas, that it seems you will never learn. But take care; you will have to pay for it — sooner or later. Now I have warned you. Good-bye.

DR. STOCKMANN. Are you stark mad? You're on a totally wrong track ——

BURGOMASTER. I am not often on the wrong track. Moreover, I must protest against —— (*Bowing towards dining-room.*) Good-bye, sister-in-law; good-day to you, gentlemen. (*He goes.*)

MRS. STOCKMANN (*entering the sitting-room*). Has he gone?

DR. STOCKMANN. Yes, and in a fine temper, too.

MRS. STOCKMANN. Why, my dear Thomas, what have you been doing to him now?

DR. STOCKMANN. Nothing at all. He can't possibly expect me to account to him for everything — before the time comes.

MRS. STOCKMANN. What have you to account to him for?

DR. STOCKMANN. H'm; — never mind about that, Katrina. — It's very odd the postman doesn't come.

(HOVSTAD, BILLING, *and* HORSTER *have risen from table and come forward into the sitting-room.* EILIF *and* MORTEN *presently follow.*)

BILLING (*stretching himself*). Ah! Strike me dead if one doesn't feel a new man after such a meal.

HOVSTAD. The Burgomaster didn't seem in the best of tempers this evening.

DR. STOCKMANN. That's his stomach. He has a very poor digestion.

HOVSTAD. I fancy it's the staff of the *Messenger* he finds it hardest to stomach.

MRS. STOCKMANN. I thought you got on well enough with him.

HOVSTAD. Oh, yes; but it's only a sort of armistice between us.

BILLING. That's it. That word sums up the situation.

DR. STOCKMANN. We must remember that Peter is a lonely bachelor, poor devil! He has no home to be happy in; only business, business. And then all that cursëd weak tea he goes and pours down his throat! Now then, chairs round the table, boys! Katrina, shan't we have the toddy now?

MRS. STOCKMANN (going towards the dining-room). I am just getting it.

DR. STOCKMANN. And you, Captain Horster, sit beside me on the sofa. So rare a guest as you —— Sit down, gentlemen, sit down.

(The men sit round the table; MRS. STOCKMANN brings in a tray with kettle, glasses, decanters, etc.)

MRS. STOCKMANN. Here you have it: here's arrak, and this is rum, and this cognac. Now, help yourselves.

DR. STOCKMANN (taking a glass). So we will. (While the toddy is being mixed.) And now out with the cigars. Eilif, I think you know where the box is. And Morten, you may fetch my pipe. (The boys go into the room on the right.) I have a suspicion that Eilif sneaks a cigar now and then, but I pretend not to notice. (Calls.) And my smoking-cap, Morten! Katrina, can't you tell him where I left it. Ah, he's got it. (The boys bring in the things.) Now, friends, help yourselves. I stick to my pipe, you know; — this one has been on many a stormy journey with me, up there in the north. (They clink glasses.) Your health! Ah, I can tell you it's better fun to sit cosily here, safe from wind and weather.

MRS. STOCKMANN (who sits knitting). Do you sail soon, Captain Horster?

HORSTER. I hope to be ready for a start by next week.

MRS. STOCKMANN. And you're going to America?

HORSTER. Yes, that's the intention.

BILLING. But then you'll miss the election of the new Town Council.

HORSTER. Is there to be an election again?

BILLING. Didn't you know?

HORSTER. No, I don't trouble myself about those things.

BILLING. But I suppose you take an interest in public affairs?

HORSTER. No, I don't understand anything about them.

BILLING. All the same, one ought at least to vote.

HORSTER. Even those who don't understand anything about it?

BILLING. Understand? Why, what do you mean by that? Society is like a ship: every man must put his hand to the helm.

HORSTER. That may be all right on shore; but at sea it wouldn't do at all.

HOVSTAD. It's remarkable how little sailors care about public affairs as a rule.

BILLING. Most extraordinary.

DR. STOCKMANN. Sailors are like birds of passage; they are at home both in the south and in the north. So it behoves the rest of us to be all the more energetic, Mr. Hovstad. Will there be anything of public interest in the *People's Messenger* tomorrow?

HOVSTAD. Nothing of local interest. But the day after tomorrow I think of printing your article ——

DR. STOCKMANN. Oh, confound it, that article! No, you'll have to hold it over.

HOVSTAD. Really? We happen to have plenty of space, and I should say this was the very time for it ——

DR. STOCKMANN. Yes, yes, you may be right; but you must hold it over all the same. I shall explain to you by-and-by.

PETRA, *wearing a hat and cloak, and with a number of exercise-books under her arm, enters from the hall.*

PETRA. Good evening.

DR. STOCKMANN. Good evening, Petra. Is that you?

(*General greetings.* PETRA *puts her cloak, hat, and books on a chair by the door.*)

PETRA. Here you all are, enjoying yourselves, while I've been out slaving.

DR. STOCKMANN. Well then, you come and enjoy yourself too.

BILLING. May I mix you a little ——?

PETRA (*coming towards the table*). Thank you, I'd rather help myself — you always make it too strong. By the way, father, I have a letter for you. (*Goes to the chair where her things are lying.*)

DR. STOCKMANN. A letter! From whom?

PETRA (*searching in the pocket of her cloak*). I got it from the postman just as I was going out ——

DR. STOCKMANN (*rising and going towards her*). And you only bring it me now?

PETRA. I really hadn't time to run up again. Here it is.

DR. STOCKMANN (*seizing the letter*). Let me see, let me see, child, (*Reads the address.*) Yes; this is it ——!

MRS. STOCKMANN. Is it the one you have been so anxious about, Thomas?

DR. STOCKMANN. Yes, it is. I must go at once. Where shall I find a light, Katrina? Is there no lamp in my study again!

MRS. STOCKMANN. Yes — the lamp is lighted. It's on the writing-table.

DR. STOCKMANN. Good, good. Excuse me one moment ——
(*He goes into the room on the right.*)

PETRA. What can it be, mother?

MRS. STOCKMANN. I don't know. For the last few days he has been continually on the look-out for the postman.

BILLING. Probably a country patient ——

PETRA. Poor father! He'll soon have far too much to do. (*Mixes her toddy.*) Ah, this will taste good!

HOVSTAD. Have you been teaching in the night school as well today?

PETRA (*sipping from her glass*). Two hours.

BILLING. And four hours in the morning at the institute ——

PETRA (*sitting down by the table*). Five hours.

MRS. STOCKMANN. And I see you have exercises to correct this evening.

PETRA. Yes, a heap of them.

HORSTER. It seems to me you have plenty to do, too.

PETRA. Yes; but I like it. You feel so delightfully tired after it.

BILLING. Do you like that?

PETRA. Yes, for then you sleep so well.

MORTEN. I say, Petra, you must be a great sinner.

PETRA. A sinner?

MORTEN. Yes, if you work so hard. Mr. Rörlund says work is a punishment for our sins.

EILIF (*contemptuously*). Bosh! What a silly you are, to believe such stuff as that.

MRS. STOCKMANN. Come come, Eilif.

BILLING (*laughing*).   Capital, capital!

HOVSTAD.   Should you not like to work so hard, Morten?

MORTEN.   No, I shouldn't.

HOVSTAD.   Then what will you do with yourself in the world?

MORTEN.   I should like to be a Viking.

EILIF.   But then you'd have to be a heathen.

MORTEN.   Well, so I would.

BILLING.   There I agree with you, Morten!   I say just the same thing.

MRS. STOCKMANN (*making a sign to him*).   No, no, Mr. Billing, I'm sure you don't.

BILLING.   Strike me dead but I do, though.   I am a heathen, and I'm proud of it.   You'll see we shall all be heathens soon.

MORTEN.   And shall we be able to do anything we like then?

BILLING.   Well, you see, Morten ——

MRS. STOCKMANN.   Now run away, boys; I'm sure you have lessons to prepare for tomorrow.

EILIF.   You might let me stay just a little longer ——

MRS. STOCKMANN.   No, you must go too.   Be off, both of you.

(*The boys say good-night and go into the room on the left.*)

HOVSTAD.   Do you really think it can hurt the boys to hear these things?

MRS. STOCKMANN.   Well, I don't know; I don't like it.

PETRA.   Really, mother, I think you are quite wrong there.

MRS. STOCKMANN.   Perhaps.   But I don't like it — not here, at home.

PETRA.   There's no end of hypocrisy both at home and at school. At home you must hold your tongue, and at school you have to stand up and tell lies to the children.

HORSTER.   Have you to tell lies?

PETRA.   Yes; do you think we don't have to tell them many and many a thing we don't believe ourselves?

BILLING.   Ah, that's too true.

PETRA.   If only I could afford it, I should start a school myself, and things should be very different there.

BILLING.   Oh, afford it ——!

HORSTER.   If you really think of doing that, Miss Stockmann, I shall be delighted to let you have a room at my place.   You

know my father's old house is nearly empty; there's a great big
dining-room on the ground floor ——

PETRA (*laughing*). Oh, thank you very much — but I'm afraid it
won't come to anything.

HOVSTAD. No, I fancy Miss Petra is more likely to go over to
journalism. By the way, have you had time to look into the
English novel you promised to translate for us?

PETRA. Not yet. But you shall have it in good time.

DR. STOCKMANN *enters from his room, with the letter open in his hand.*

DR. STOCKMANN (*flourishing the letter*). Here's news, I can tell you,
that will waken up the town!

BILLING. News?

MRS. STOCKMANN. What news?

DR. STOCKMANN. A great discovery, Katrina!

HOVSTAD. Indeed?

MRS. STOCKMANN. Made by you?

DR. STOCKMANN. Precisely — by me! (*Walks up and down.*) Now
let them go on accusing me of fads and crack-brained notions.
But they won't dare to! Ha-ha! I tell you they won't
dare!

PETRA. Do tell us what it is, father.

DR. STOCKMANN. Well, well, give me time, and you shall hear all
about it. If only I had Peter here now! This just shows how
we men can go about forming judgments like the blindest
moles ——

HOVSTAD. What do you mean, doctor?

DR. STOCKMANN (*stopping beside the table*). Isn't it the general opinion
that our town is a healthy place?

HOVSTAD. Of course.

DR. STOCKMANN. A quite exceptionally healthy place, indeed — a
place to be warmly recommended, both to invalids and people
in health ——

MRS. STOCKMANN. My dear Thomas ——

DR. STOCKMANN. And assuredly we haven't failed to recommend
and belaud it. I've sung its praises again and again, both in the
Messenger and in pamphlets ——

HOVSTAD. Well, what then?

DR. STOCKMANN. These Baths, that we have called the pulse of the town, its vital nerve, and — and the devil knows what else ——

BILLING. "Our city's palpitating heart," I once ventured to call them in a convivial moment ——

DR. STOCKMANN. Yes, I dare say. Well — do you know what they really are, these mighty, magnificent, belauded Baths, that have cost so much money — do you know what they are?

HOVSTAD. No, what are they?

MRS. STOCKMANN. Do tell us.

DR. STOCKMANN. Simply a pestiferous hole.

PETRA. The Baths, father?

MRS. STOCKMANN (*at the same time*). Our Baths!

HOVSTAD (*also at the same time*). But, Doctor ——!

BILLING. Oh, it's incredible!

DR. STOCKMANN. I tell you the whole place is a poisonous whited-sepulchre; noxious in the highest degree! All that filth up there in the Mill Dale — the stuff that smells so horribly — taints the water in the feed-pipes of the Pump-Room; and the same accursëd poisonous refuse oozes out by the beach ——

HOVSTAD. Where the sea-baths are?

DR. STOCKMANN. Exactly.

HOVSTAD. But how are you so sure of all this, Doctor?

DR. STOCKMANN. I've investigated the whole thing as conscientiously as possible. I've long had my suspicions about it. Last year we had some extraordinary cases of illness among the patients — both typhoid and gastric attacks ——

MRS. STOCKMANN. Yes, I remember.

DR. STOCKMANN. We thought at the time that the visitors had brought the infection with them; but afterwards — last winter — I began to question that. So I set about testing the water as well as I could.

MRS. STOCKMANN. It was that you were working so hard at!

DR. STOCKMANN. Yes, you may well say I've worked, Katrina. But here, you know, I hadn't the necessary scientific appliances; so I sent samples both of our drinking water and of our sea-water to the University, for exact analysis by a chemist.

HOVSTAD. And you have received his report?

DR. STOCKMANN (*showing letter*). Here it is! And it proves beyond

dispute the presence of putrefying organic matter in the water — millions of infusoria. It's absolutely pernicious to health, whether used internally or externally.

MRS. STOCKMANN. What a blessing you found it out in time.

DR. STOCKMANN. Yes, you may well say that.

HOVSTAD. And what do you intend to do now, Doctor?

DR. STOCKMANN. Why, to set things right, of course.

HOVSTAD. You think it can be done, then?

DR. STOCKMANN. It must be done. Else the whole Baths are useless, ruined. But there's no fear. I am quite clear as to what is required.

MRS. STOCKMANN. But, my dear Thomas, why should you have made such a secret of all this?

DR. STOCKMANN. Would you have had me rush all over the town and chatter about it, before I was quite certain? No, thank you; I'm not so mad as that.

PETRA. But to us at home ——

DR. STOCKMANN. I couldn't say a word to a living soul. But to-morrow you may look in at the Badger's ——

MRS. STOCKMANN. Oh, Thomas!

DR. STOCKMANN. Well, well, at your grandfather's. The old fellow will be astonished! He thinks I'm not quite right in my head — yes, and plenty of others think the same, I've noticed. But now these good people shall see — yes, they shall see now! (*Walks up and down rubbing his hands.*) What a stir there will be in the town, Katrina! Just think of it! All the water-pipes will have to be relaid.

HOVSTAD (*rising*). All the water-pipes ——?

DR. STOCKMANN. Why, of course. The intake is too low down; it must be moved much higher up.

PETRA. So you were right, after all.

DR. STOCKMANN. Yes, do you remember, Petra? I wrote against it when they were beginning the works. But no one would listen to me then. Now, you may be sure, I shall give them my full broadside — for of course I've prepared a statement for the Directors; it has been lying ready a whole week; I've only been waiting for this report. (*Points to letter.*) But now they shall have it at once. (*Goes into his room and returns with a MS. in his hand.*) See! Four closely-written sheets! And I'll enclose the report. A newspaper, Katrina! Get me something to wrap them up in. There — that's it. Give it to — to — (*Stamps.*) — what the devil's her name? Give it to the girl, I mean, and tell her to take it at once to the Burgomaster.

(MRS. STOCKMANN *goes out with the packet through the dining-room.*)

PETRA. What do you think Uncle Peter will say, father?

DR. STOCKMANN. What should he say? He can't possibly be otherwise than pleased that so important a fact has been brought to light.

HOVSTAD. I suppose you will let me put a short announcement of your discovery in the *Messenger*.

DR. STOCKMANN. Yes, I shall be much obliged if you will.

HOVSTAD. It is highly desirable that the public should know about it as soon as possible.

DR. STOCKMANN. Yes, certainly.

MRS. STOCKMANN (*returning*). She's gone with it.

BILLING. Strike me dead if you won't be the first man in the town, Doctor!

DR. STOCKMANN (*walks up and down in high glee*). Oh, nonsense! After all, I have done no more than my duty. I've been a lucky treasure-hunter, that's all. But all the same ——

BILLING. Hovstad, don't you think the town ought to get up a torchlight procession in honour of Dr. Stockmann?

HOVSTAD. I shall certainly propose it.

BILLING. And I'll talk it over with Aslaksen.

DR. STOCKMANN. No, my dear friends; let all such claptrap alone. I won't hear of anything of the sort. And if the Directors should want to raise my salary, I won't accept it. I tell you, Katrina, I will not accept it.

MRS. STOCKMANN. You are quite right, Thomas.

PETRA (*raising her glass*). Your health, father!

HOVSTAD *and* BILLING. Your health, your health, Doctor!

HORSTER (*clinking glasses with the* DOCTOR). I hope you may have nothing but joy of your discovery.

DR. STOCKMANN. Thanks, thanks, my dear friends! I can't tell you how happy I am —! Oh, what a blessing it is to feel that you have deserved well of your native town and your fellow citizens. Hurrah, Katrina!

(*He puts both his arms round her neck, and whirls her round with him.* MRS. STOCKMANN *screams and struggles. A burst of laughter, applause, and cheers for the* DOCTOR. *The boys thrust their heads in at the door.*)

ACT SECOND

The DOCTOR'S *sitting-room. The dining-room door is closed. Morning.*

MRS. STOCKMANN (*enters from the dining-room with a sealed letter in her hand, goes to the foremost door on the right, and peeps in*). Are you there, Thomas?

DR. STOCKMANN (*within*). Yes, I have just come in. (*Enters.*) What is it?

MRS. STOCKMANN. A letter from your brother. (*Hands it to him.*)

DR. STOCKMANN. Aha, let us see. (*Opens the envelope and reads.*) "The MS. sent me is returned herewith ——" (*Reads on, mumbling to himself.*) H'm ——

MRS. STOCKMANN. Well, what does he say?

DR. STOCKMANN (*putting the paper in his pocket*). Nothing; only that he'll come up himself about midday.

MRS. STOCKMANN. Then be sure you remember to stay at home.

DR. STOCKMANN. Oh, I can easily manage that; I've finished my morning's visits.

MRS. STOCKMANN. I am very curious to know how he takes it.

DR. STOCKMANN. You'll see he won't be over-pleased that it is I that have made the discovery, and not he himself.

MRS. STOCKMANN. Ah, that's just what I'm afraid of.

DR. STOCKMANN. Of course at bottom he'll be glad. But still — Peter is damnably unwilling that anyone but himself should do anything for the good of the town.

MRS. STOCKMANN. Do you know, Thomas, I think you might stretch a point, and share the honour with him. Couldn't it appear that it was he that put you on the track ——?

DR. STOCKMANN. By all means, for aught I care. If only I can get things put straight ——

Old MORTON KIIL *puts his head in at the hall door, and asks slyly.*

MORTEN KIIL. Is it — is it true?

MRS. STOCKMANN (*going towards him*). Father — is that you?

DR. STOCKMANN. Hallo, father-in-law! Good morning, good morning.

MRS. STOCKMANN. Do come in.

MORTEN KIIL. Yes, if it's true; if not, I'm off again.

DR. STOCKMANN. If what is true?

MORTEN KIIL. This crazy business about the water-works. Now, is it true?

DR. STOCKMANN. Why, of course it is. But how came you to hear of it?

MORTEN KIIL (*coming in*). Petra looked in on her way to the school ——

DR. STOCKMANN. Oh, did she?

MORTEN KIIL. Ay, ay — and she told me —— I thought she was only making game of me; but that's not like Petra either.

DR. STOCKMANN. No, indeed; how could you think so?

MORTEN KIIL. Oh, you can never be sure of anybody. You may be made a fool of before you know where you are. So it is true, after all?

DR. STOCKMANN. Most certainly it is. Do sit down, father-in-law. (*Forces him down on the sofa.*) Now isn't it a real blessing for the town ——?

MORTEN KIIL (*suppressing his laughter*). A blessing for the town?

DR. STOCKMANN. Yes, that I made this discovery in time ——

MORTEN KIIL (*as before*). Ay, ay, ay! — Well, I could never have believed that you would play monkey-tricks with your very own brother.

DR. STOCKMANN. Monkey-tricks!

MRS. STOCKMANN. Why, father dear ——

MORTEN KIIL (*resting his hands and chin on the top of his stick and blinking slyly at the* DOCTOR). What was it again? Wasn't it that some animals had got into the water-pipes?

DR. STOCKMANN. Yes; infusorial animals.

MORTEN KIIL. And any number of these animals had got in, Petra said — whole swarms of them.

DR. STOCKMANN. Certainly; hundreds of thousands.

MORTEN KIIL. But no one can see them — isn't that it?

DR. STOCKMANN. Quite right; no one can see them.

MORTEN KIIL (*with a quiet, chuckling laugh*). I'll be damned if that isn't the best thing I've heard of you yet.

DR. STOCKMANN. What do you mean?

MORTEN KIIL. But you'll never in this world make the Burgomaster take in anything of the sort.

DR. STOCKMANN. Well, that we shall see.

MORTEN KIIL. Do you really think he'll be so crazy?

DR. STOCKMANN. I hope the whole town will be so crazy.

MORTEN KIIL. The whole town! Well, I don't say but it may. But it serves them right; it'll teach them a lesson. They wanted to be so much cleverer than we old fellows. They hounded me out of the Town Council. Yes; I tell you they hounded me out like a dog, that they did. But now it's their turn. Just you keep up the game with them, Stockmann.

DR. STOCKMANN. Yes, but, father-in-law ——

MORTEN KIIL. Keep it up, I say. (*Rising.*) If you can make the Burgomaster and his gang eat humble pie, I'll give a hundred crowns straight away to the poor.

DR. STOCKMANN. Come, that's good of you.

MORTEN KIIL. Of course I've little enough to throw away; but if you can manage that, I shall certainly remember the poor at Christmas-time, to the tune of fifty crowns.

HOVSTAD *enters from hall.*

HOVSTAD. Good morning! (*Pausing.*) Oh! I beg your pardon ——

DR. STOCKMANN. Not at all. Come in, come in.

MORTEN KIIL (*chuckling again*). He! Is he in it too?

HOVSTAD. What do you mean?

DR. STOCKMANN. Yes, of course he is.

MORTEN KIIL. I might have known it! It's to go into the papers. Ah, you're the one, Stockmann! Do you two lay your heads together; I'm off.

DR. STOCKMANN. Oh no; don't go yet, father-in-law.

MORTEN KIIL. No, I'm off now. Play them all the monkey-tricks you can think of. Deuce take me but you shan't lose by it.

(*He goes,* MRS. STOCKMANN *accompanying him.*)

DR. STOCKMANN (*laughing*). What do you think —? The old fellow doesn't believe a word of all this about the water-works.

HOVSTAD. Was that what he ——?

DR. STOCKMANN. Yes; that was what we were talking about. And I dare say you have come on the same business?

HOVSTAD. Yes. Have you a moment to spare, Doctor?

DR. STOCKMANN. As many as you like, my dear fellow.

HOVSTAD. Have you heard anything from the Burgomaster?

DR. STOCKMANN. Not yet. He'll be here presently.

HOVSTAD. I have been thinking the matter over since last evening.

DR. STOCKMANN. Well?

HOVSTAD. To you, as a doctor and a man of science, this business of the water-works appears an isolated affair. I dare say it hasn't occurred to you that a good many other things are bound up with it?

DR. STOCKMANN. Indeed! In what way? Let us sit down, my dear fellow. — No; there, on the sofa.

(HOVSTAD *sits on sofa: the* DOCTOR *in an easy-chair on the other side of the table.*)

DR. STOCKMANN. Well, so you think ——?

HOVSTAD. You said yesterday that the water is polluted by impurities in the soil.

DR. STOCKMANN. Yes, undoubtedly; the mischief comes from that poisonous swamp up in the Mill Dale.

HOVSTAD. Excuse me, Doctor, but I think it comes from a very different swamp.

DR. STOCKMANN. What swamp may that be?

HOVSTAD. The swamp in which our whole municipal life is rotting.

DR. STOCKMANN. The devil, Mr. Hovstad! What notion is this you've got hold of?

HOVSTAD. All the affairs of the town have gradually drifted into the hands of a pack of bureaucrats ——

DR. STOCKMANN. Come now, they're not all bureaucrats.

HOVSTAD. No; but those who are not are the friends and adherents of those who are. We are entirely under the thumb of a ring of wealthy men, men of old family and position in the town.

DR. STOCKMANN. Yes, but they are also men of ability and insight.

HOVSTAD. Did they show ability and insight when they laid the water-pipes where they are?

DR. STOCKMANN. No; that, of course, was a piece of stupidity. But that will be set right now.

HOVSTAD. Do you think it will go so smoothly?

DR. STOCKMANN. Well, smoothly or not, it will have to be done.

HOVSTAD. Yes, if the press exerts its influence.

DR. STOCKMANN. Not at all necessary, my dear fellow; I am sure my brother ——

HOVSTAD. Excuse me, Doctor, but I must tell you that I think of taking the matter up.

DR. STOCKMANN. In the paper?

HOVSTAD. Yes. When I took over the *People's Messenger*, I was determined to break up the ring of obstinate old blockheads who held everything in their hands.

DR. STOCKMANN. But you told me yourself what came of it. You nearly ruined the paper.

HOVSTAD. Yes, at that time we had to draw in our horns, that's true enough. The whole Bath scheme might have fallen through if these men had been sent about their business. But now the Baths are an accomplished fact, and we can get on without these august personages.

DR. STOCKMANN. Get on without them, yes; but still we owe them a great deal.

HOVSTAD. The debt shall be duly acknowledged. But a journalist of my democratic tendencies cannot let such an opportunity slip through his fingers. We must explode the tradition of official infallibility. That rubbish must be got rid of, like every other superstition.

DR. STOCKMANN. There I am with you with all my heart, Mr. Hovstad. If it's a superstition, away with it!

HOVSTAD. I should be sorry to attack the Burgomaster, as he is your brother. But I know you think with me — the truth before all other considerations.

DR. STOCKMANN. Why, of course. (*Vehemently.*) But still —! but still ——!

HOVSTAD. You mustn't think ill of me. I am neither more self-interested nor more ambitious than other men.

DR. STOCKMANN. Why, my dear fellow — who says you are?

HOVSTAD. I come of humble folk, as you know; and I have had ample opportunities of seeing what the lower classes really require. And that is to have a share in the direction of public affairs, Doctor. That is what develops ability and knowledge and self-respect ——

DR. STOCKMANN. I understand that perfectly.

HOVSTAD. Yes; and I think a journalist incurs a heavy responsibility if he lets slip a chance of helping to emancipate the downtrodden masses. I know well enough that our oligarchy will denounce me as an agitator, and so forth; but what do I care? If only my conscience is clear, I ——

DR. STOCKMANN. Just so, just so, my dear Mr. Hovstad. But still — deuce take it ——! (*A knock at the door.*) Come in!

ASLAKSEN, *the printer, appears at the door leading to the hall. He is humbly but respectably dressed in black, wears a white necktie, slightly crumpled, and has a silk hat and gloves in his hand.*

ASLAKSEN (*bowing*). I beg pardon, Doctor, for making so bold ——

DR. STOCKMANN (*rising*). Hallo! If it isn't Mr. Aslaksen!

ASLAKSEN. Yes, it's me, Doctor.

HOVSTAD (*rising*). Is it me you want, Aslaksen?

ASLAKSEN. No, not at all. I didn't know you were here. No, it's the Doctor himself ——

DR. STOCKMANN. Well, what can I do for you?

ASLAKSEN. Is it true, what Mr. Billing tells me, that you're going to get us a better set of water-works?

DR. STOCKMANN. Yes, for the Baths.

ASLAKSEN. Of course, of course. Then I just looked in to say that I'll back up the movement with all my might.

HOVSTAD (*to the* DOCTOR). You see!

DR. STOCKMANN. I'm sure I thank you heartily; but ——

ASLAKSEN. You may find it no such bad thing to have us small middle-class men at your back. We form what you may call a compact majority in the town — when we really make up our minds, that's to say. And it's always well to have the majority with you, Doctor.

DR. STOCKMANN. No doubt, no doubt; but I can't conceive that any special measures will be necessary in this case.   I should think in so clear and straightforward a matter ——

ASLAKSEN. Yes, but all the same, it can do no harm.   I know the local authorities very well — the powers that be are not over ready to adopt suggestions from outsiders.   So I think it wouldn't be amiss if we made some sort of a demonstration.

HOVSTAD. Precisely my opinion.

DR. STOCKMANN. A demonstration, you say?   But in what way would you demonstrate?

ASLAKSEN. Of course with great moderation, Doctor.   I always insist upon moderation; for moderation is a citizen's first virtue — at least that's my way of thinking.

DR. STOCKMANN. We all know that, Mr. Aslaksen.

ASLAKSEN. Yes, I think my moderation is generally recognised. And this affair of the water-works is very important for us small middle-class men.   The Baths bid fair to become, as you might say, a little gold-mine for the town.   We shall all have to live by the Baths, especially we house-owners.   So we want to support the Baths all we can; and as I am Chairman of the House-owners' Association ——

DR. STOCKMANN. Well ——?

ASLAKSEN. And as I'm an active worker for the Temperance [1] Society — of course you know, Doctor, that I'm a temperance man?

DR. STOCKMANN. To be sure, to be sure.

ASLAKSEN. Well, you'll understand that I come in contact with a great many people.   And as I'm known to be a prudent and law-abiding citizen, as you yourself remarked, Doctor, I have a certain influence in the town, and hold some power in my hands — though I say it that shouldn't.

DR. STOCKMANN. I know that very well, Mr. Aslaksen.

ASLAKSEN. Well then, you see — it would be easy for me to get up an address, if it came to a pinch.

DR. STOCKMANN. An address?

ASLAKSEN. Yes, a kind of vote of thanks to you, from the citizens of the town, for your action in a matter of such general concern. Of course it will have to be drawn up with all fitting moderation,

---

[1] "The word *mådehold*, in Norwegian, means both "moderation" and "temperance."

so as to give no offence to the authorities and parties in power. But so long as we're careful about that, no one can take it ill, I should think.

HOVSTAD. Well, even if they didn't particularly like it ——

ASLAKSEN. No, no, no; no offence to the powers that be, Mr. Hovstad. No opposition to people that can take it out of us again so easily. I've had enough of that in my time; no good ever comes of it. But no one can object to the free but temperate expression of a citizen's opinion.

DR. STOCKMANN (*shaking his hand*). I can't tell you, my dear Mr. Aslaksen, how heartily it delights me to find so much support among my fellow townsmen. I'm so happy—so happy! Come, you'll have a glass of sherry? Eh?

ASLAKSEN. No, thank you; I never touch spirituous liquors.

DR. STOCKMANN. Well, then, a glass of beer — what do you say to that?

ASLAKSEN. Thanks, not that either, Doctor. I never take anything so early in the day. And now I'll be off round the town, and talk to some of the houseowners, and prepare public opinion.

DR. STOCKMANN. It's extremely kind of you, Mr. Aslaksen; but I really cannot get it into my head that all these preparations are necessary. The affair seems to me so simple and self-evident.

ASLAKSEN. The authorities always move slowly, Doctor — God forbid I should blame them for it ——

HOVSTAD. We'll stir them up in the paper tomorrow, Aslaksen.

ASLAKSEN. No violence, Mr. Hovstad. Proceed with moderation, or you'll do nothing with them. Take my advice; I've picked up experience in the school of life. — And now I'll say good morning, Doctor. You know now that at least you have us small middle-class men behind you, solid as a wall. You have the compact majority on your side, Doctor.

DR. STOCKMANN. Many thanks, my dear Mr. Aslaksen. (*Holds out his hand.*) Good-bye, good-bye.

ASLAKSEN. Are you coming to the office, Mr. Hovstad?

HOVSTAD. I shall come on presently. I have still one or two things to arrange.

ASLAKSEN. Very well.

(*Bows and goes.* DR. STOCKMANN *accompanies him into the hall.*)

HOVSTAD (*as the* DOCTOR *re-enters*). Well, what do you say to that, Doctor? Don't you think it is high time we should give all this weak-kneed, half-hearted cowardice a good shaking up?

DR. STOCKMANN. Are you speaking of Aslaksen?

HOVSTAD. Yes, I am. He's a decent enough fellow, but he's one of those who are sunk in the swamp. And most people here are just like him; they are for ever wavering and wobbling from side to side; what with scruples and misgivings, they never dare advance a step.

DR. STOCKMANN. Yes, but Aslaksen seems to me thoroughly well-intentioned.

HOVSTAD. There is one thing I value more than good intentions, and that is an attitude of manly self-reliance.

DR. STOCKMANN. There I am quite with you.

HOVSTAD. So I am going to seize this opportunity, and try whether I can't for once put a little grit into their good intentions. The worship of authority must be rooted up in this town. This gross, inexcusable blunder of the water-works must be brought home clearly to every voter.

DR. STOCKMANN. Very well. If you think it's for the good of the community, so be it; but not till I have spoken to my brother.

HOVSTAD. At all events, I shall be writing my leader in the meantime. And if the Burgomaster won't take the matter up ——

DR. STOCKMANN. But how can you conceive his refusing?

HOVSTAD. Oh, it's not inconceivable. And then ——

DR. STOCKMANN. Well then, I promise you —; look here — in that case you may print my paper — put it in just as it is.

HOVSTAD. May I? Is that a promise?

DR. STOCKMANN (*handing him the manuscript*). There it is; take it with you. You may as well read it in any case; you can return it to me afterwards.

HOVSTAD. Very good; I shall do so. And now, good-bye, Doctor.

DR. STOCKMANN. Good-bye, good-bye. You'll see it will all go smoothly, Mr. Hovstad — as smoothly as possible.

HOVSTAD. H'm — we shall see. (*Bows and goes out through the hall.*)

DR. STOCKMANN (*going to the dining-room door and looking in*). Katrina! Hallo! are you back, Petra?

PETRA (*entering*). Yes, I've just got back from school.

MRS. STOCKMANN (*entering*). Hasn't he been here yet?

DR. STOCKMANN. Peter? No; but I have been having a long talk with Hovstad. He's quite enthusiastic about my discovery. It turns out to be of much wider import than I thought at first. So he has placed his paper at my disposal, if I should require it.

MRS. STOCKMANN. Do you think you will?

DR. STOCKMANN. Not I! But at the same time, one cannot but be proud to know that the enlightened, independent press is on one's side. And what do you think? I have had a visit from the Chairman of the House-owners' Association too.

MRS. STOCKMANN. Really? What did he want?

DR. STOCKMANN. To assure me of his support. They will all stand by me at a pinch. Katrina, do you know what I have behind me?

MRS. STOCKMANN. Behind you? No. What have you behind you?

DR. STOCKMANN. The compact majority!

MRS. STOCKMANN. Oh! Is that good for you, Thomas?

DR. STOCKMANN. Yes, indeed; I should think it was good. (*Rubbing his hands as he walks up and down.*) Great God! what a delight it is to feel oneself in such brotherly unison with one's fellow townsmen?

PETRA. And to do so much that's good and useful, father!

DR. STOCKMANN. And all for one's native town, too!

MRS. STOCKMANN. There's the bell.

DR. STOCKMANN. That must be he. (*Knock at the door.*) Come in!

Enter BURGOMASTER STOCKMANN *from the hall.*

BURGOMASTER. Good morning.

DR. STOCKMANN. I'm glad to see you, Peter.

MRS. STOCKMANN. Good morning, brother-in-law. How are you?

BURGOMASTER. Oh, thanks, so-so. (*To the* DOCTOR.) Yesterday evening, after office hours, I received from you a dissertation upon the state of the water at the Baths.

DR. STOCKMANN. Yes. Have you read it?

BURGOMASTER. I have.

DR. STOCKMANN. And what do you think of the affair?

BURGOMASTER. H'm —   (*With a sidelong glance.*)

MRS. STOCKMANN. Come, Petra.

(*She and* PETRA *go into the room on the left.*)

BURGOMASTER (*after a pause*).   Was it necessary to make all these investigations behind my back?

DR. STOCKMANN.   Yes, till I was absolutely certain, I ——

BURGOMASTER.   And are you absolutely certain now?

DR. STOCKMANN.   My paper must surely have convinced you of that.

BURGOMASTER.   Is it your intention to submit this statement to the Board of Directors, as a sort of official document?

DR. STOCKMANN.   Of course.   Something must be done in the matter, and that promptly.

BURGOMASTER.   As usual, you use very strong expressions in your statement.   Amongst other things, you say that what we offer our visitors is a slow poison.

DR. STOCKMANN.   Why, Peter, what else can it be called?   Only think — poisoned water both internally and externally!   And that to poor invalids who come to us in all confidence, and pay us handsomely to cure them!

BURGOMASTER.   And then you announce as your conclusion that we must build a sewer to carry off the alleged impurities from the Mill Dale, and must re-lay all the water-pipes.

DR. STOCKMANN.   Yes.   Can you suggest any other plan? — I know of none.

BURGOMASTER.   I found a pretext for looking in at the town engineer's this morning, and — in a half-jesting way — I mentioned these alterations as things we might possibly have to consider, at some future time.

DR. STOCKMANN.   At some future time!

BURGOMASTER.   Of course he smiled at what he thought my extravagance.   Have you taken the trouble to think what your proposed alterations would cost?   From what the engineers said, I gathered that the expenses would probably mount up to several hundred thousand crowns.

DR. STOCKMANN.   So much as that?

BURGOMASTER.   Yes.   But that is not the worst.   The work would take at least two years.

DR. STOCKMANN.   Two years!   Do you mean to say two whole years?

BURGOMASTER.   At least.   And what are we to do with the Baths in the meanwhile?   Are we to close them?   We should have no alternative.   Do you think anyone would come here, if it got abroad that the water was pestilential?

DR. STOCKMANN. But, Peter, that's precisely what it is.

BURGOMASTER. And all this now, just now, when the Baths are doing so well!   Neighbouring towns, too, are not without their claims to rank as health-resorts.   Do you think they would not at once set to work to divert the full stream of visitors to themselves? Undoubtedly they would; and we should be left stranded.   We should probably have to give up the whole costly undertaking; and so you would have ruined your native town.

DR. STOCKMANN. I — ruined ——!

BURGOMASTER. It is only through the Baths that the town has any future worth speaking of.   You surely know that as well as I do.

DR. STOCKMANN. Then what do you think should be done?

BURGOMASTER. I have not succeeded in convincing myself that the condition of the water at the Baths is as serious as your statement represents.

DR. STOCKMANN. I tell you it's if anything worse — or will be in the summer, when the hot weather sets in.

BURGOMASTER. I repeat that I believe you exaggerate greatly.   A competent physician should know what measures to take — he should be able to obviate deleterious influences, and to counteract them in case they should make themselves unmistakably felt.

DR. STOCKMANN. Indeed —?   And then —?

BURGOMASTER. The existing water-works are, once for all, a fact, and must naturally be treated as such.   But when the time comes, the Directors will probably not be indisposed to consider whether it may not be possible, without unreasonable pecuniary sacrifices, to introduce certain improvements.

DR. STOCKMANN. And do you imagine I could ever be a party to such dishonesty?

BURGOMASTER. Dishonesty?

DR. STOCKMANN. Yes, it would be dishonesty — a fraud, a lie, an absolute crime against the public, against society as a whole!

BURGOMASTER. I have not, as I before remarked, been able to convince myself that there is really any such imminent danger.

DR. STOCKMANN. You have!   You must have!   I know that my demonstration is absolutely clear and convincing.   And you understand it perfectly, Peter, only you won't admit it. It was you who insisted that both the Bath-buildings and the water-works should be placed where they now are; and it's that — it's that damned blunder that you won't confess. Pshaw! Do you think I don't see through you?

BURGOMASTER. And even if it were so? If I do watch over my re-putation with a certain anxiety, I do it for the good of the town. Without moral authority I cannot guide and direct affairs in the way I consider most conducive to the general welfare. There-. fore — and on various other grounds — it is of great moment *to* me that your statement should not be submitted to the Board of Directors. It must be kept back, for the good of the community. Later on I will bring up the matter for discussion, and we will do the best we can, quietly; but not a word, not a whisper, of this unfortunate business must come to the public ears.

DR. STOCKMANN. But it can't be prevented now, my dear Peter.

BURGOMASTER. It must and shall be prevented.

DR. STOCKMANN. It can't be, I tell you; far too many people know about it already.

BURGOMASTER. Know about it! Who? Surely not those fellows on the *People's Messenger* ——?

DR. STOCKMANN. Oh, yes; they know. The liberal, independent press will take good care that you do your duty.

BURGOMASTER (*after a short pause*). You are an amazingly reckless man, Thomas. Have not you reflected what the consequences of this may be to yourself?

DR. STOCKMANN. Consequences? — Consequences to me?

BURGOMASTER. Yes — to you and yours.

DR. STOCKMANN. What the devil do you mean?

BURGOMASTER. I believe I have always shown myself ready and willing to lend you a helping hand.

DR. STOCKMANN. Yes, you have, and I thank you for it.

BURGOMASTER. I ask for no thanks. Indeed, I was in some measure forced to act as I did — for my own sake. I always hoped I should be able to keep you a little in check, if I helped to improve your pecuniary position.

DR. STOCKMANN. What! So it was only for your own sake ——!

BURGOMASTER. In a measure, I say. It is painful for a man in an official position, when his nearest relative goes and compromises himself time after time.

DR. STOCKMANN. And you think I do that?

BURGOMASTER. Yes, unfortunately, you do, without knowing it. Yours is a turbulent, unruly, rebellious spirit. And then you have an unhappy propensity for rushing into print upon every possible and impossible occasion. You no sooner hit upon an idea than you must needs write a newspaper article or a whole pamphlet about it.

DR. STOCKMANN. Isn't it a citizen's duty, when he has conceived a new idea, to communicate it to the public!

BURGOMASTER. Oh, the public has no need for new ideas. The public gets on best with the good old recognised ideas it has already.

DR. STOCKMANN. You say that right out!

BURGOMASTER. Yes, I must speak frankly to you for once. Hitherto I have tried to avoid it, for I know how irritable you are; but now I must tell you the truth, Thomas. You have no conception how much you injure yourself by your officiousness. You complain of the authorities, ay, of the Government itself — you cry them down and maintain that you have been slighted, persecuted. But what else can you expect, with your impossible disposition?

DR. STOCKMANN. Oh, indeed! So I am impossible, am I?

BURGOMASTER. Yes, Thomas, you are an impossible man to work with. I know that from experience. You have no consideration for anyone or anything; you seem quite to forget that you have me to thank for your position as medical officer of the Baths ——

DR. STOCKMANN. It was mine by right! Mine, and no one else's! I was the first to discover the town's capabilities as a watering-place; I saw them, and, at that time, I alone. For years I fought single-handed for this idea of mine; I wrote and wrote ——

BURGOMASTER. No doubt; but then the right time had not come. Of course, in that out-of-the-world corner, you could not judge of that. As soon as the propitious moment arrived, I — and others — took the matter in hand ——

DR. STOCKMANN. Yes, and you went and bungled the whole of my glorious plan. Oh, we see now what a set of wiseacres you were!

BURGOMASTER. All *I* can see is that you are again seeking an outlet for your pugnacity. You want to make an onslaught on your superiors — that is an old habit of yours. You cannot endure any authority over you; you look askance at anyone who holds a higher post than your own; you regard him as a personal enemy — and then you care nothing what kind of weapon you use against him. But now I have shown you how much is at stake for the town, and consequently for me too. And therefore I warn you, Thomas, that I am inexorable in the demand I am about to make of you!

DR. STOCKMANN. What demand?

BURGOMASTER. As you have not had the sense to refrain from chattering to outsiders about this delicate business, which should have been kept an official secret, of course it cannot now be hushed up. All sorts of rumours will get abroad, and evil-disposed persons will invent all sorts of additions to them. It will therefore be necessary for you publicly to contradict these rumours.

DR. STOCKMANN. I ! How? I don't understand you?

BURGOMASTER. We expect that, after further investigation, you will come to the conclusion that the affair is not nearly so serious or pressing as you had at first imagined.

DR. STOCKMANN. Aha! So you expect that?

BURGOMASTER. Furthermore, we expect you to express your confidence that the Board of Directors will thoroughly and conscientiously carry out all measures for the remedying of any possible defects.

DR. STOCKMANN. Yes, but that you'll never be able to do, so long as you go on tinkering and patching. I tell you that, Peter; and it's my deepest, sincerest conviction ——

BURGOMASTER. As an official, you have no right to hold any individual conviction.

DR. STOCKMANN (*starting*). No right to ——?

BURGOMASTER. As an official, I say. In your private capacity, of course, it is another matter. But as a subordinate official of the Baths, you have no right to express any conviction at issue with that of your superiors.

DR. STOCKMANN. This is too much! I, a doctor, a man of science, have no right to ——!

BURGOMASTER. The matter in question is not a purely scientific one; it is a complex affair; it has both a technical and an economic side.

DR. STOCKMANN. What the devil do I care what it is! I will be free to speak my mind upon any subject under the sun!

BURGOMASTER. As you please — so long as it does not concern the Baths. With them we forbid you to meddle.

DR. STOCKMANN (shouts). You forbid ——! You! A set of ——

BURGOMASTER. I forbid it — I, your chief; and when I issue an order, you have simply to obey.

DR. STOCKMANN (controlling himself). Upon my word, Peter, if you weren't my brother ——

PETRA (tears open the door). Father, you shan't submit to this!

MRS. STOCKMANN (following her). Petra, Petra!

BURGOMASTER. Ah! So we have been listening!

MRS. STOCKMANN. The partition is so thin, we couldn't help ——

PETRA. I stood and listened on purpose.

BURGOMASTER. Well, on the whole, I am not sorry ——

DR. STOCKMANN (coming nearer to him). You spoke to me of forbidding and obeying ——

BURGOMASTER. You have forced me to adopt that tone.

DR. STOCKMANN. And am I to give myself the lie, in a public declaration?

BURGOMASTER. We consider it absolutely necessary that you should issue a statement in the terms indicated.

DR. STOCKMANN. And if I do not obey?

BURGOMASTER. Then we shall ourselves put forth a statement to reassure the public.

DR. STOCKMANN. Well and good; then I shall write against you. I shall stick to my point and prove that I am right, and you wrong. And what will you do then?

BURGOMASTER. Then I shall be unable to prevent your dismissal.

DR. STOCKMANN. What ——!

PETRA. Father! Dismissal!

MRS. STOCKMANN. Dismissal!

BURGOMASTER. Your dismissal from the Baths. I shall be compelled to move that notice be given you at once, and that you have henceforth no connection whatever with the Baths.

DR. STOCKMANN. You would dare to do that!

BURGOMASTER. It is you who are playing the daring game.

PETRA. Uncle, this is a shameful way to treat a man like father!

MRS. STOCKMANN. Do be quiet, Petra!

BURGOMASTER (*looking at* PETRA). Aha! We have opinions of our own already, eh? To be sure, to be sure! (*To* MRS. STOCK-MANN.) Sister-in-law, you are presumably the most rational member of this household. Use all your influence with your husband; try to make him realise what all this will involve both for his family ——

DR. STOCKMANN. My family concerns myself alone!

BURGOMASTER. —— both for his family, I say, and for the town he lives in.

DR. STOCKMANN. It is I that have the real good of the town at heart! I want to lay bare the evils that, sooner or later, must come to light. Ah! You shall see whether I love my native town.

BURGOMASTER. You, who, in your blind obstinacy, want to cut off the town's chief source of prosperity!

DR. STOCKMANN. That source is poisoned, man! Are you mad? We live by trafficking in filth and corruption! The whole of our flourishing social life is rooted in a lie!

BURGOMASTER. Idle fancies — or worse. The man who scatters broadcast such offensive insinuations against his native place must be an enemy of society.

DR. STOCKMANN (*going towards him*). You dare to ——!

MRS. STOCKMANN (*throwing herself between them*). Thomas!

PETRA (*seizing her father's arm*). Keep calm, father!

BURGOMASTER. I will not expose myself to violence. You have had your warning now. Reflect upon what is due to yourself and to your family. Good-bye. (*He goes.*)

DR. STOCKMANN (*walking up and down*). And I must put up with such treatment! In my own house, Katrina! What do you say to that!

MRS. STOCKMANN. Indeed, it's a shame and a disgrace, Thomas ——

PETRA. Oh, if I could only get hold of uncle ——!

DR. STOCKMANN. It's my own fault. I ought to have stood up against them long ago — to have shown my teeth — and used them too! — And to be called an enemy of society! Me! I won't bear it; by Heaven, I won't!

MRS. STOCKMANN. But my dear Thomas, after all, your brother has the power ——

DR. STOCKMANN. Yes, but I have the right.

MRS. STOCKMANN. Ah, yes, right, right! What good does it do to have the right, if you haven't any might?

PETRA. Oh, mother — how can you talk so?

DR. STOCKMANN. What! No good, in a free community, to have right on your side? What an absurd idea, Katrina! And besides — haven't I the free and independent press before me — and the compact majority at my back? That is might enough, I should think!

MRS. STOCKMANN. Why, good heavens, Thomas! you're surely not thinking of ——?

DR. STOCKMANN. What am I not thinking of?

MRS. STOCKMANN. —— of setting yourself up against your brother, I mean.

DR. STOCKMANN. What the devil would you have me do, if not stick to what is right and true?

PETRA. Yes, that's what I should like to know.

MRS. STOCKMANN. But it will be of no earthly use. If they won't, they won't.

DR. STOCKMANN. Ho-ho, Katrina! just wait a while, and you shall see whether I can fight my battles to the end.

MRS. STOCKMANN. Yes, to the end of getting your dismissal; that is what will happen.

DR. STOCKMANN. Well then, I shall at any rate have done my duty towards the public, towards society — I who am called an enemy of society!

MRS. STOCKMANN. But towards your family, Thomas? Towards us at home? Do you think that is doing your duty towards those who are dependent on you?

PETRA. Oh, mother, don't always think first of us.

MRS. STOCKMANN. Yes, it's easy for you to talk; you can stand alone if need be. — But remember the boys, Thomas; and think a little of yourself too, and of me ——

DR. STOCKMANN. You're surely out of your senses, Katrina! If I were to be such a pitiful coward as to knuckle under to this Peter and his confounded crew — should I ever have another happy hour in all my life?

MRS. STOCKMANN. I don't know about that; but God preserve us from the happiness we shall all of us have if you persist in defying them. There you will be again, with nothing to live on, with no regular income. I should have thought we had had enough of that in the old days. Remember them, Thomas; think of what it all means.

DR. STOCKMANN (*struggling with himself and clenching his hands*). And this is what these jacks-in-office can bring upon a free and honest man! Isn't it revolting, Katrina?

MRS. STOCKMANN. Yes, no doubt they are treating you shamefully. But God knows there's plenty of injustice one must just submit to in this world. — Here are the boys, Thomas. Look at them! What is to become of them? Oh, no, no! you can never have the heart ——

EILIF *and* MORTEN, *with school-books, have meanwhile entered.*

DR. STOCKMANN. The boys ——! (*With a sudden access of firmness and decision.*) Never, though the whole earth should crumble, will I bow my neck beneath the yoke.   (*Goes towards his room.*)

MRS. STOCKMANN (*following him*). Thomas — what are you going to do?

DR. STOCKMANN (*at the door*). I must have the right to look my boys in the face when they have grown into free men.

(*Goes into his room.*)

MRS. STOCKMANN (*bursts into tears*). Ah, God help us all!

PETRA. Father is true to the core. He will never give in!

(*The boys ask wonderingly what it all means;* PETRA *signs to them to be quiet.*)

ACT THIRD

The Editor's Room of the "People's Messenger." In the background, to the left, an entrance-door; to the right another door, with glass panes, through which can be seen the composing-room. A door in the right-hand wall. In the middle of the room a large table covered with papers, news-papers, and books. In front, on the left, a window, and by it a desk with a high stool. A couple of arm-chairs beside the table; some other chairs along the walls. The room is dingy and cheerless, the furniture shabby, the arm-chairs dirty and torn. In the composing-room are seen a few compositors at work; further back, a hand-press in operation.

HOVSTAD *is seated at the desk, writing. Presently* BILLING *enters from the right, with the* DOCTOR'S *manuscript in his hand.*

BILLING. Well, I must say ——!

HOVSTAD (*writing*). Have you read it through?

BILLING (*laying the MS. on the desk*). Yes, I should think I had.

HOVSTAD. Don't you think the Doctor comes out strong?

BILLING. Strong! Why, strike me dead if he isn't crushing! Every word falls like a — well, like a sledge-hammer.

HOVSTAD. Yes, but these fellows won't collapse at the first blow.

BILLING. True enough; but we'll keep on hammering away, blow after blow, till the whole officialdom comes crashing down. As I sat in there reading that article, I seemed to hear the revolution thundering afar.

HOVSTAD (*turning round*). Hush! Don't let Aslaksen hear that.

BILLING (*in a lower voice*). Aslaksen's a white-livered, cowardly fellow, without a spark of manhood in him. But this time you'll surely carry your point? Eh? You'll print the Doctor's paper?

HOVSTAD. Yes, if only the Burgomaster doesn't give in ——

BILLING. That would be deuced annoying.

HOVSTAD. Well, whatever happens, fortunately we can turn the situation to account. If the Burgomaster won't agree to the Doctor's proposal, he'll have all the small middle-class down upon him — all the House-owners' Association, and the rest of them. And if he does agree to it, he'll fall out with the whole crew of big shareholders in the Baths, who have hitherto been his main support ——

BILLING. Yes, of course; for no doubt they'll have to fork out a lot of money ——

HOVSTAD. You may take your oath of that.   And then, don't you see, when the ring is broken up, we'll din it into the public day by day that the Burgomaster is incompetent in every respect, and that all responsible positions in the town, the whole municipal government in short, must be entrusted to men of liberal ideas.

BILLING. Strike me dead if that isn't the square truth!   I see it — I see it: we are on the eve of a revolution!   (*A knock at the door.*)

HOVSTAD. Hush!   (*Calls.*)   Come in!

DR. STOCKMANN *enters from the back, left.*

HOVSTAD (*going towards him*).   Ah, here is the Doctor.   Well?

DR. STOCKMANN. Print away, Mr. Hovstad!

HOVSTAD. So it has come to that?

BILLING. Hurrah!

DR. STOCKMANN. Print away, I tell you.   To be sure it has come to that.   Since they will have it so, they must.   War is declared, Mr. Billing!

BILLING. War to the knife, say I!   War to the death, Doctor!

DR. STOCKMANN. This article is only the beginning.   I have four or five others sketched out in my head already.   But where do you keep Aslaksen?

BILLING (*calling into the printing-room*).   Aslasken! just come here a moment.

HOVSTAD. Four or five more articles, eh?   On the same subject?

DR. STOCKMANN. Oh, no — not at all, my dear fellow.   No; they will deal with quite different matters.   But they're all of a piece with the water-works and sewer question.   One thing leads to another.   It's just like beginning to pick at an old house, don't you know?

BILLING. Strike me dead, but that's true!   You feel you can't leave off till you've pulled the whole lumber-heap to pieces.

ASLAKSEN (*enters from the printing-room*).   Pulled to pieces!   Surely the Doctor isn't thinking of pulling the Baths to pieces?

HOVSTAD. Not at all.   Don't be alarmed.

DR. STOCKMANN. No, we were talking of something quite different.   Well, what do you think of my article, Mr. Hovstad?

HOVSTAD. I think it's simply a masterpiece ——

DR. STOCKMANN. Yes, isn't it? I'm glad you think so — very glad.

HOVSTAD. It's so clear and to the point. One doesn't in the least need to be a specialist to understand the gist of it. I am certain every intelligent man will be on your side.

ASLAKSEN. And all the prudent ones too, I hope?

BILLING. Both the prudent and imprudent — in fact, almost the whole town.

ASLAKSEN. Then I suppose we may venture to print it.

DR. STOCKMANN. I should think so!

HOVSTAD. It shall go in tomorrow.

DR. STOCKMANN. Yes, plague take it, not a day must be lost. Look here, Mr. Aslaksen, this is what I wanted to ask you: won't you take personal charge of the article?

ASLAKSEN. Certainly I will.

DR. STOCKMANN. Be as careful as if it were gold. No printers' errors; every word is important. I shall look in again presently; perhaps you'll be able to let me see a proof. — Ah! I can't tell you how I long to have the thing in print — to see it launched ——

BILLING. Yes, like a thunderbolt!

DR. STOCKMANN. —— and submitted to the judgment of every intelligent citizen. Oh, you have no idea what I have had to put up with today. I've been threatened with all sorts of things. I was to be robbed of my clearest rights as a human being ——

BILLING. What! Your rights as a human being!

DR. STOCKMANN. —— I was to humble myself, and eat the dust; I was to set my personal interests above my deepest, holiest convictions ——

BILLING. Strike me dead, but that's too outrageous.

HOVSTAD. Oh, what can you expect from that quarter?

DR. STOCKMANN. But they shall find they were mistaken in me; they shall learn that in black and white, I promise them! I shall throw myself into the breach every day in the *Messenger*, bombard them with one explosive article after another ——

ASLAKSEN. Yes, but look here ——

BILLING. Hurrah! It's war! War!

DR. STOCKMANN. I shall smite them to the earth, I shall crush them,

I shall level their entrenchments to the ground in the eyes of all right-thinking men! That's what I shall do!

ASLAKSEN. But above all things be temperate, Doctor; bombard with moderation ——

BILLING. Not at all, not at all! Don't spare the dynamite!

DR. STOCKMANN (*going on imperturbably*). For now it's no mere question of water-works and sewers, you see. No, the whole community must be purged, disinfected ——

BILLING. There sounds the word of salvation!

DR. STOCKMANN. All the old bunglers must be sent packing, you understand. And that in every possible department! Such endless vistas have opened out before me today. I am not quite clear about everything yet, but I shall see my way presently. It's young and vigorous standard-bearers we must look for, my friends; we must have new captains at all the outposts.

BILLING. Hear, hear!

DR. STOCKMANN. And if only we hold together, it will go so smoothly, so smoothly! The whole revolution will glide off the stocks just like a ship. Don't you think so?

HOVSTAD. For my part, I believe we have now every prospect of placing our municipal affairs in the right hands.

ASLAKSEN. And if only we proceed with moderation, I really don't think there can be any danger.

DR. STOCKMANN. Who the devil cares whether there's danger or not! What I do, I do in the name of truth and for conscience' sake.

HOVSTAD. You are a man to be backed up, Doctor.

ASLAKSEN. Yes, there's no doubt the Doctor is a true friend to the town; he's what I call a friend of society.

BILLING. Strike me dead if Dr. Stockmann isn't a Friend of the People, Aslaksen!

ASLAKSEN. I have no doubt the House-owners' Association will soon adopt that expression.

DR. STOCKMANN (*shaking their hands, deeply moved*). Thanks, thanks, my dear, faithful friends; it does me good to hear you. My respected brother called me something very different. Never mind! Trust me to pay him back with interest! But I must be off now to see a poor devil of a patient. I shall look in again, though. Be sure you look after the article, Mr. Aslaksen; and, whatever you do, don't leave out any of my notes of exclamation! Rather put in a few more! Well, good-bye for the present, good-bye, good-bye.

> (*Mutual salutations while they accompany him to the door. He goes out.*)

HOVSTAD. He will be invaluable to us.

ASLAKSEN. Yes, so long as he confines himself to this matter of the Baths. But if he goes further, it will scarcely be advisable to follow him.

HOVSTAD. H'm — that entirely depends on ——

BILLING. You're always so confoundedly timid, Aslaksen.

ASLAKSEN. Timid? Yes, when it's a question of attacking local authorities, I am timid, Mr. Billing; I have learnt caution in the school of experience, let me tell you. But start me on the higher politics, confront me with the Government itself, and then see if I'm timid.

BILLING. No, you're not; but that's just where your inconsistency comes in.

ASLAKSEN. The fact is, I am keenly alive to my responsibilities. If you attack the Government, you at least do society no harm; for the men attacked don't care a straw, you see — they stay where they are all the same. But local authorities can be turned out; and then we might get some incompetent set into power, to the irreparable injury both of house-owners and other people.

HOVSTAD. But the education of citizens by self-government — do you never think of that?

ASLAKSEN. When a man has solid interests to protect, he can't think of everything, Mr. Hovstad.

HOVSTAD. Then I hope I may never have solid interests to protect.

BILLING. Hear, hear!

ASLAKSEN (*smiling*). H'm! (*Points to the desk.*) Governor Stensgård sat in that editorial chair before you.

BILLING (*spitting*). Pooh! A turncoat like that!

HOVSTAD. I am no weathercock — and never will be.

ASLAKSEN. A politician should never be too sure of anything on earth, Mr. Hovstad. And as for you, Mr. Billing, you ought to take in a reef or two, I should say, now that you are applying for the secretaryship to the Town Council.

BILLING. I ——!

HOVSTAD. Is that so, Billing?

BILLING. Well, yes — but, deuce take it, you understand, I'm only doing it to spite their high-mightinesses.

ASLAKSEN. Well, that has nothing to do with me. But if I am to be accused of cowardice and inconsistency, I should just like to point out this: My political record is open to everyone. I have not changed at all, except in becoming more moderate. My heart still belongs to the people; but I don't deny that my reason inclines somewhat towards the authorities — the local ones, I mean. *(Goes into the printing-room.)*

BILLING. Don't you think we should try to get rid of him, Hovstad?

HOVSTAD. Do you know of anyone else that will pay for our paper and printing?

BILLING. What a confounded nuisance it is to have no capital!

HOVSTAD *(sitting down by the desk)*. Yes, if we only had that ——

BILLING. Suppose you applied to Dr. Stockmann?

HOVSTAD *(turning over his papers)*. What would be the good? He hasn't a rap.

BILLING. No; but he has a good man behind him — old Morten Kiil — "The Badger," as they call him.

HOVSTAD *(writing)*. Are you so sure he has money?

BILLING. Yes, strike me dead if he hasn't! And part of it must certainly go to Stockmann's family. He's bound to provide for — for the children at any rate.

HOVSTAD *(half turning)*. Are you counting on that?

BILLING. Counting? How should I be counting on it?

HOVSTAD. Best not! And that secretaryship you shouldn't count on either; for I can assure you you won't get it.

BILLING. Do you think I don't know that? A refusal is the very thing I want. Such a rebuff fires the spirit of opposition in you, gives you a fresh supply of gall, as it were; and that's just what you need in a god-forsaken hole like this, where anything really stimulating so seldom happens.

HOVSTAD *(writing)*. Yes, yes.

BILLING. Well — they shall soon hear from me! — Now I'll go and write the appeal to the House-owners' Association.

(Goes into the room on the right.)

HOVSTAD (*sits at his desk, biting his penholder, and says slowly*): H'm — so that's the way of it. — (*A knock at the door.*) Come in.

PETRA *enters from the back, left.*

HOVSTAD (*rising*). What! Is it you? Here?

PETRA. Yes; please excuse me ——

HOVSTAD (*offering her an arm-chair*). Won't you sit down?

PETRA. No, thanks; I must go again directly.

HOVSTAD. Perhaps you bring a message from your father ——?

PETRA. No, I have come on my own account. (*Takes a book from the pocket of her cloak.*) Here is that English story.

HOVSTAD. Why have you brought it back?

PETRA. Because I won't translate it.

HOVSTAD. But you promised ——

PETRA. Yes; but then I hadn't read it. I suppose you have not read it either?

HOVSTAD. No; you know I can't read English; but ——

PETRA. Exactly; and that's why I wanted to tell you that you must find something else. (*Putting the book on the table.*) This will never do for the *Messenger.*

HOVSTAD. Why not?

PETRA. Because it flies in the face of all your convictions.

HOVSTAD. Well, for that matter ——

PETRA. You don't understand me. It makes out that a supernatural power looks after the so-called good people in this world, and turns everything to their advantage at last; while all the so-called bad people are punished.

HOVSTAD. Yes, but that's all right. That's the very thing the public like.

PETRA. And would you supply the public with such stuff? You don't believe a word of it yourself. You know well enough that things do not really happen like that.

HOVSTAD. Of course not; but an editor can't always do as he likes. He has often to humour people's fancies in minor matters. After all, politics is the chief thing in life — at any rate for a newspaper; and if I want the people to follow me along the path of emancipation and progress, I mustn't scare them away. If they find a moral story like this down in the cellar,[1] they are all the more

---

[1] The reference is to the continental feuilleton at the foot of the page.

ready to take in what we tell them above — they feel themselves safer.

PETRA. For shame! You're not such a hypocrite as to set traps like that for your readers. You're not a spider.

HOVSTAD (*smiling*). Thanks for your good opinion. It's true that the idea is Billing's, not mine.

PETRA. Mr. Billing's!

HOVSTAD. Yes, at least he was talking in that strain the other day. It was Billing that was so anxious to get the story into the paper; I don't even know the book.

PETRA. But how can Mr. Billing, with his advanced views ——

HOVSTAD. Well, Billing is many-sided. He's applying for the secretaryship to the Town Council, I hear.

PETRA. I don't believe that, Mr. Hovstad. How could he descend to such a thing?

HOVSTAD. That you must ask him.

PETRA. I could never have thought it of Billing!

HOVSTAD (*looking more closely at her*). No? Is it such a surprise to you?

PETRA. Yes. And yet — perhaps not. Oh, I don't know ——

HOVSTAD. We journalists are not worth much, Miss Petra.

PETRA. Do you really say that?

HOVSTAD. I think so, now and then.

PETRA. Yes, in the little every-day squabbles — that I can understand. But now that you have taken up a great cause ——

HOVSTAD. You mean this affair of your father's?

PETRA. Of course. I should think you must feel yourself worth more than the general run of people now.

HOVSTAD. Yes, today I do feel something of the sort.

PETRA. Yes, surely you must. Oh, it's a glorious career you have chosen! To be the pioneer of unrecognised truths and new and daring ways of thought! — even, if that were all, to stand forth fearlessly in support of an injured man ——

HOVSTAD. Especially when the injured man is — I hardly know how to put it ——

PETRA. You mean when he is so upright and true?

HOVSTAD (*in a low voice*). I mean — especially when he is your father.

PETRA (*suddenly taken aback*). That?

HOVSTAD. Yes, Petra — Miss Petra.

PETRA. So that is your chief thought, is it? Not the cause itself? Not the truth? Not father's great, warm heart?

HOVSTAD. Oh, that too, of course.

PETRA. No, thank you; you said too much that time, Mr. Hovstad. Now I shall never trust you again, in anything.

HOVSTAD. Can you be so hard on me because it's mainly for your sake ——?

PETRA. What I blame you for is that you have not acted straightforwardly towards father. You have talked to him as if you cared only for the truth and the good of the community. You have trifled with both father and me. You are not the man you pretended to be. And that I will never forgive you — never.

HOVSTAD. You shouldn't say that so bitterly, Miss Petra — least of all now.

PETRA. Why not now?

HOVSTAD. Because your father cannot do without my help.

PETRA (*measuring him from head to foot*). So you are capable of that, too? Oh, shame!

HOVSTAD. No, no. I spoke without thinking. You mustn't believe that of me.

PETRA. I know what to believe. Good-bye.

ASLAKSEN *enters from printing-room, hurriedly and mysteriously.*

ASLAKSEN. What do you think, Mr. Hovstad — (*Seeing* PETRA.) Ow, that's awkward ——

PETRA. Well, there is the book. You must give it to someone else.
(*Going towards the main door.*)

HOVSTAD (*following her*). But, Miss Petra ——

PETRA. Good-bye. (*She goes.*)

ASLAKSEN. I say, Mr. Hovstad!

HOVSTAD. Well, well; what is it?

ASLAKSEN. The Burgomaster's out there, in the printing-office.

HOVSTAD. The Burgomaster?

ASLAKSEN. Yes. He wants to speak to you; he came in by the back way — he didn't want to be seen, you understand.

HOVSTAD. What can be the meaning of this? Stop, I'll go my-self——

> (*Goes towards the printing-room, opens the door, bows and invites the* BURGOMASTER *to enter.*)

HOVSTAD. Keep a look-out, Aslaksen, that no one ——

ASLAKSEN. I understand. (*Goes into the printing-room.*)

BURGOMASTER. You didn't expect to see me here, Mr. Hovstad.

HOVSTAD. No, I cannot say that I did.

BURGOMASTER (*looking about him*). You are very comfortably in-stalled here — capital quarters.

HOVSTAD. Oh ——

BURGOMASTER. And here have I come, without with your leave or by your leave, to take up your time ——

HOVSTAD. You are very welcome, Burgomaster; I am at your service. Let me take your cap and stick. (*He does so, and puts them on a chair.*) And won't you be seated?

BURGOMASTER (*sitting down by the table*). Thanks. (HOVSTAD *also sits by the table.*) I have been much — very much worried today, Mr. Hovstad.

HOVSTAD. Really? Well, I suppose with all your various duties, Burgomaster ——

BURGOMASTER. It is the Doctor that has been causing me annoy-ance today.

HOVSTAD. Indeed! The Doctor?

BURGOMASTER. He has written a sort of memorandum to the Di-rectors about some alleged shortcomings in the Baths.

HOVSTAD. Has he really?

BURGOMASTER. Yes; hasn't he told you? I thought he said ——

HOVSTAD. Oh, yes, by-the-bye, he did mention something ——

ASLAKSEN (*from the printing-office*). I've just come for the manu-script ——

HOVSTAD (*in a tone of vexation*). Oh! — there it is on the desk.

ASLAKSEN (*finding it*). All right.

BURGOMASTER. Why, that is the very thing ——

ASLASKEN. Yes, this is the Doctor's article, Burgomaster.

HOVSTED. Oh, is that what you were speaking of?

BURGOMASTER. Precisely. What do you think of it?

HOVSTAD. I have no technical knowledge of the matter, and I've only glanced through it.

BURGOMASTER. And yet you are going to print it!

HOVSTAD. I can't very well refuse a signed communication ——

ASLAKSEN. I have nothing to do with the editing of the paper, Burgomaster ——

BURGOMASTER. Of course not.

ASLAKSEN. I merely print what is placed in my hands.

BURGOMASTER. Quite right, quite right.

ASLAKSEN. So I must —— (*Goes towards the printing-room.*)

BURGOMASTER. No, stop a moment, Mr. Aslaksen. With your permission, Mr. Hovstad ——

HOVSTAD. By all means, Burgomaster.

BURGOMASTER. You are a discreet and thoughtful man, Mr. Aslaksen.

ASLAKSEN. I am glad you think so, Burgomaster.

BURGOMASTER. And a man of very wide influence.

ASLAKSEN. Well — chiefly among the lower middle-class.

BURGOMASTER. The small taxpayers form the majority — here as everywhere.

ASLAKSEN. That's very true.

BURGOMASTER. And I have no doubt that you know the general feeling among them. Am I right?

ASLAKSEN. Yes, I think I may say that I do, Burgomaster.

BURGOMASTER. Well — since our townsfolk of the poorer class appear to be so heroically eager to make sacrifices ——

ASLAKSEN. How so?

HOVSTAD. Sacrifices?

BURGOMASTER. It is a pleasing evidence of public spirit — a most pleasing evidence. I admit it is more than I should quite have expected. But, of course, you know public feeling better than I do.

ASLAKSEN. Yes, but, Burgomaster ——

BURGOMASTER. And assuredly it is no small sacrifice the town will have to make.

HOVSTAD. The town?

ASLAKSEN. But I don't understand ——. It's the Baths ——

BURGOMASTER. At a rough provisional estimate, the alterations the Doctor thinks desirable will come to two or three hundred thousand crowns.

ASLAKSEN. That's a lot of money; but ——

BURGOMASTER. Of course we shall be obliged to raise a municipal loan.

HOVSTAD (rising). You surely can't mean that the town ——?

ASLAKSEN. Would you come upon the rates? Upon the scanty savings of the lower middle-class?

BURGOMASTER. Why, my dear Mr. Aslaksen, where else are the funds to come from?

ASLAKSEN. The proprietors of the Baths must see to that.

BURGOMASTER. The proprietors are not in a position to go to any further expense.

ASLAKSEN. Are you quite sure of that, Burgomaster?

BURGOMASTER. I have positive information. So if these extensive alterations are called for, the town itself will have to bear the cost.

ASLAKSEN. Oh, plague take it all — I beg your pardon! — but this is quite another matter, Mr. Hovstad.

HOVSTAD. Yes, it certainly is.

BURGOMASTER. The worst of it is, that we shall be obliged to close the establishment for a couple of years.

HOVSTAD. To close it? Completely?

ASLAKSEN. For two years!

BURGOMASTER. Yes, the work will require that time — at least.

ASLAKSEN. But, damn it all! we can't stand that, Burgomaster. What are we house-owners to live on in the meantime?

BURGOMASTER. It's extremely difficult to say, Mr. Aslaksen. But what would you have us do? Do you think a single visitor will come here if we go about making them fancy that the water is poisoned, that the place is pestilential, that the whole town ——

ASLAKSEN. And it's all nothing but fancy?

BURGOMASTER. With the best will in the world, I have failed to convince myself that it is anything else.

ASLAKSEN. In that case it's simply inexcusable of Dr. Stockmann — I beg your pardon, Burgomaster, but ——

BURGOMASTER. I'm sorry to say you are only speaking the truth, Mr. Aslaksen. Unfortunately, my brother has always been noted for his rashness.

ASLAKSEN. And yet you want to back him up in this, Mr. Hovstad!

HOVSTAD. But who could possibly imagine that ——?

BURGOMASTER. I have drawn up a short statement of the facts, as they appear from a sober-minded standpoint; and I have intimated that any drawbacks that may possibly exist can no doubt be remedied by measures compatible with the finances of the Baths.

HOVSTAD. Have you the article with you, Burgomaster?

BURGOMASTER (*feeling in his pockets*). Yes; I brought it with me, in case you ——

ASLAKSEN (*quickly*). Plague take it, there he is!

BURGOMASTER. Who? My brother?

HOVSTAD. Where? where?

ASLAKSEN. He's coming through the composing-room.

BURGOMASTER. Most unfortunate! I don't want to meet him here, and yet there are several things I want to talk to you about.

HOVSTAD (*pointing to the door on the right*). Go in there for a moment.

BURGOMASTER. But ——?

HOVSTAD. You'll find nobody but Billing there.

ASLAKSEN. Quick, quick, Burgomaster; he's just coming.

BURGOMASTER. Very well, then. But try to get rid of him quickly.

(*He goes out by the door on the right, which* ASLAKSEN *opens, and closes behind him.*)

HOVSTAD. Pretend to be busy, Aslaksen.

(*He sits down and writes.* ASLAKSEN *turns over a heap of newspapers on a chair, right.*)

DR. STOCKMANN (*entering from the composing-room*). Here I am, back again. (*Puts down his hat and stick.*)

HOVSTAD (*writing*). Already, Doctor? Make haste with what we were speaking of, Aslaksen. We've no time to lose today.

DR. STOCKMANN (*to* ASLAKSEN). No proof yet, I hear.

ASLAKSEN (*without turning round*). No; how could you expect it?

DR. STOCKMANN. Of course not; but you understand my impatience. I can have no rest or peace until I see the thing in print.

HOVSTAD. H'm; it will take a good while yet. Don't you think so, Aslaksen?

ASLAKSEN. I'm afraid it will.

DR. STOCKMANN. All right, all right, my good friend; then I shall look in again. I'll look in twice if necessary. With so much at stake — the welfare of the whole town — one mustn't grudge a little trouble. (*Is on the point of going but stops and comes back.*) Oh, by the way — there's one other thing I must speak to you about.

HOVSTAD. Excuse me; wouldn't some other time ——?

DR. STOCKMANN. I can tell you in two words. You see it's this: when people read my article in the paper tomorrow, and find I have spent the whole winter working quietly for the good of the town ——

HOVSTAD. Yes, but, Doctor ——

DR. STOCKMANN. I know what you're going to say. You don't think it was a bit more than my duty — my simple duty as a citizen. Of course I know that, as well as you do. But you see, my fellow townsmen — good Lord! the poor souls think so much of me ——

ASLAKSEN. Yes, the townspeople have hitherto thought very highly of you, Doctor.

DR. STOCKMANN. That's exactly why I'm afraid that —. What I wanted to say was this: when all this comes to them — especially to the poorer classes — as a summons to take the affairs of the town into their own hands for the future ——

HOVSTAD (*rising*). H'm, Doctor, I won't conceal from you ——

DR. STOCKMANN. Aha! I thought there was something brewing! But I won't hear of it. If they are getting up anything of that sort ——

HOVSTAD. Of what sort?

DR. STOCKMANN. Well, anything of any sort — a procession with banners, or a banquet, or a subscription for a testimonial, or whatever it may be — you must give me your solemn promise to put a stop to it. And you too, Mr. Aslaksen; do you hear?

HOVSTAD. Excuse me, Doctor; we may as well tell you the whole truth first as last ——

MRS. STOCKMANN *enters from the back, left.*

MRS. STOCKMANN (*seeing the* DOCTOR). Ah! just as I thought.

HOVSTAD (*going towards her*). Mrs. Stockmann, too?

DR. STOCKMANN. What the devil do you want here, Katrina?

MRS. STOCKMANN. You know very well what I want.

HOVSTAD. Won't you sit down? Or perhaps ——

MRS. STOCKMANN. Thanks, please don't trouble. And you must forgive my following my husband here; remember, I am the mother of three children.

DR. STOCKMANN. Stuff and nonsense! We all know that well enough.

MRS. STOCKMANN. Well, it doesn't look as if you thought very much about your wife and children today, or you wouldn't be so ready to plunge us all into ruin.

DR. STOCKMANN. Are you quite mad, Katrina! Has a man with a wife and children no right to proclaim the truth? Has he no right to be an active and useful citizen? Has he no right to do his duty by the town he lives in?

MRS. STOCKMANN. Everything in moderation, Thomas!

ASLAKSEN. That's just what I say. Moderation in everything.

MRS. STOCKMANN. You are doing us a great wrong, Mr. Hovstad, in enticing my husband away from house and home, and befooling him in this way.

HOVSTAD. I am not befooling anyone ——

DR. STOCKMANN. Befooling! Do you think I should let myself be befooled?

MRS. STOCKMANN. Yes, that's just what you do. I know very well that you are the cleverest man in the town; but you're very easily made a fool of, Thomas. (*To* HOVSTAD.) Remember that he loses his post at the Baths if you print what he has written ——

ASLAKSEN. What!

HOVSTAD. Well now, really, Doctor ——

DR. STOCKMANN (*laughing*). Ha, ha! just let them try—! No, no, my dear, they'll think twice about that. I have the compact majority behind me, you see!

MRS. STOCKMANN. That's just the misfortune, that you should have such a horrid thing behind you.

DR. STOCKMANN. Nonsense, Katrina; — you go home and look after your house, and let me take care of society. How can you be in such a fright when you see me so confident and happy? (*Rubbing his hands and walking up and down.*) Truth and the People must win the day; you may be perfectly sure of that. Oh! I can see all our free-souled citizens standing shoulder to shoulder like a conquering army ——! (*Stopping by a chair.*) Why, what the devil is that?

ASLAKSEN (*looking at it*). Oh, Lord!

HOVSTAD (*the same*). H'm ——

DR. STOCKMANN. Why, here's the top-knot of authority!

>(*He takes the* BURGOMASTER's *official cap carefully between the tips of his fingers and holds it up.*)

MRS. STOCKMANN. The Burgomaster's cap!

DR. STOCKMANN. And here's the staff of office, too! But how in the devil's name did they ——?

HOVSTAD. Well then ——

DR. STOCKMANN. Ah, I understand! He has been here to talk you over. Ha, ha! He reckoned without his host that time! And when he caught sight of me in the printing-room — (*Bursts out laughing*) — he took to his heels, eh, Mr. Aslaksen?

ASLAKSEN (*hurriedly*). Exactly; he took to his heels, Doctor.

DR. STOCKMANN. Made off without his stick and ——. No, that won't do! Peter never left anything behind him. But where the devil have you stowed him? Ah — in here, of course. Now you shall see, Katrina!

MRS. STOCKMANN. Thomas — I implore you ——!

ASLAKSEN. Take care, Doctor!

>(DR. STOCKMANN *has put on the* BURGOMASTER's *cap and grasped his stick; he now goes up to the door, throws it open, and makes a military salute.*)

The BURGOMASTER *enters, red with anger. Behind him comes* BILLING.

BURGOMASTER. What is the meaning of these antics?

DR. STOCKMANN. Respect, my good Peter! Now, it's I that am in power in this town. (*He struts up and down.*)

MRS. STOCKMANN (*almost in tears*). Oh, Thomas!

BURGOMASTER (*following him*). Give me my cap and stick!

DR. STOCKMANN (*as before*). You may be Chief of Police, but I am Burgomaster. I am master of the whole town I tell you!

BURGOMASTER. Put down my cap, I say. Remember it is an official cap, as by law prescribed!

DR. STOCKMANN. Pshaw! Do you think the awakening lion of the democracy will let itself be scared by a gold-laced cap? There's to be a revolution in the town tomorrow, let me tell you. You threatened me with dismissal; but now *I* dismiss you — dismiss you from all your offices of trust —. You think I can't do it? — Oh, yes, I can! I have the irresistible forces of society on my side. Hovstad and Billing will thunder in the *People's Messenger*, and Aslaksen will take the field at the head of the House-owners' Association ——

ASLAKSEN. No, Doctor, I shall not.

DR. STOCKMANN. Why, of course you will ——

BURGOMASTER. Aha! Perhaps Mr. Hovstad would like to join the agitation after all?

HOVSTAD. No, Burgomaster.

ASLAKSEN. No, Mr. Hovstad isn't such a fool as to ruin both himself and the paper for the sake of a delusion.

DR. STOCKMANN (*looking about him*). What does all this mean?

HOVSTAD. You have presented your case in a false light, Doctor; therefore I am unable to give you my support.

BILLING. And after what the Burgomaster has been so kind as to explain to me, I ——

DR. STOCKMANN. In a false light! Well, I am responsible for that. Just you print my article, and I promise you I shall prove it up to the hilt.

HOVSTAD. I shall not print it. I cannot, and will not, and dare not print it.

DR. STOCKMANN. You dare not? What nonsense is this? You are editor; and I suppose it's the editor that controls a paper.

ASLAKSEN. No, it's the subscribers, Doctor.

BURGOMASTER. Fortunately.

ASLAKSEN. It's public opinion, the enlightened majority, the house-owners and all the rest. It's they who control a paper.

DR. STOCKMANN (*calmly*). And all these powers I have against me?

ASLAKSEN. Yes, you have. It would mean absolute ruin for the town if your article were inserted.

DR. STOCKMANN. So that is the way of it!

BURGOMASTER. My hat and stick!

(DR. STOCKMANN *takes off the cap and lays it on the table along with the stick.*)

BURGOMASTER (*taking them both*). Your term of office has come to an untimely end.

DR. STOCKMANN. The end is not yet. (*To* HOVSTAD.) So you are quite determined not to print my article in the *Messenger*?

HOVSTAD. Quite; for the sake of your family, if for no other reason.

MRS. STOCKMANN. Oh, be kind enough to leave his family out of the question, Mr. Hovstad.

BURGOMASTER (*takes a manuscript from his pocket*). When this appears, the public will be in possession of all necessary information; it is an authentic statement. I place it in your hands.

HOVSTAD (*taking the MS*). Good. It shall appear in due course.

DR. STOCKMANN. And not mine! You imagine you can kill me and the truth by a conspiracy of silence! But it won't be so easy as you think. Mr. Aslaksen, will you be good enough to print my article at once, as a pamphlet? I'll pay for it myself, and be my own publisher. I'll have four hundred copies — no, five — six hundred.

ASLAKSEN. No. If you offered me its weight in gold, I dare not lend my press to such a purpose, Doctor. I daren't fly in the face of public opinion. You won't get it printed anywhere in the whole town.

DR. STOCKMANN. Then give it me back.

HOVSTAD (*handing him the MS*). By all means.

DR. STOCKMANN (*taking up his hat and cane*). It shall be made public all the same. I shall read it at a great mass meeting; all my fellow citizens shall hear the voice of truth!

BURGOMASTER. Not a single society in the town would let you their hall for such a purpose.

ASLAKSEN. Not one, I'm quite certain.

BILLING. No, strike me dead if they would!

MRS. STOCKMANN. That would be too disgraceful! Why do they turn against you like this, every one of them?

DR. STOCKMANN (*irritated*). I'll tell you why. It's because in this town all the men are old women — like you. They all think of nothing but their families, not of the general good.

MRS. STOCKMANN (*taking his arm*). Then I'll show them that an — an old woman can be a man for once in a way. For now I'll stand by you, Thomas.

DR. STOCKMANN. Bravely said, Katrina! I swear by my soul and conscience the truth shall out! If they won't let me a hall, I'll hire a drum and march through the town with it; and I'll read my paper at every street corner.

BURGOMASTER. You can scarcely be such a raving lunatic as that?

DR. STOCKMANN. I am.

ASLAKSEN. You would not get a single man in the whole town to go with you.

BILLING. No, strike me dead if you would!

MRS. STOCKMANN. Don't give in, Thomas. I'll ask the boys to go with you.

DR. STOCKMANN. That's a splendid idea!

MRS. STOCKMANN. Morten will be delighted; and Eilif will go too, I dare say.

DR. STOCKMANN. Yes, and so will Petra! And you yourself, Katrina!

MRS. STOCKMANN. No, no, not I. But I'll stand at the window and watch you — that I will.

DR. STOCKMANN (*throwing his arms about her and kissing her*). Thank you for that! Now, my good sirs, we're ready for the fight! Now we shall see whether your despicable tactics can stop the mouth of the patriot who wants to purge society!

(*He and his wife go out together by the door in the back, left.*)

BURGOMASTER (*shaking his head dubiously*). Now he has turned her head too!

ACT FOURTH

A large old-fashioned room in CAPTAIN HORSTER'S *house. An open folding-door in the background leads to an anteroom. In the wall on the left are three windows. About the middle of the opposite wall is a platform, and on it a small table, two candles, a water-bottle and glass, and a bell. For the rest, the room is lighted by sconces placed between the windows. In front, on the left, is a table with a candle on it, and by it a chair. In front, to the right, a door, and near it a few chairs.*

Large assemblage of all classes of townsfolk. In the crowd are a few women and schoolboys. More and more people gradually stream in from the back until the room is quite full.

FIRST CITIZEN (*to another standing near him*). So you're here too, Lamstad?

SECOND CITIZEN. I never miss a public meeting.

A BYSTANDER. I suppose you've brought your whistle?

SECOND CITIZEN. Of course I have; haven't you?

THIRD CITIZEN. I should think so. And Skipper Evensen said he'd bring a thumping big horn.

SECOND CITIZEN. He's a good 'un, is Evensen!

(*Laughter in the group.*)

A FOURTH CITIZEN (*joining them*). I say, what's it all about? What's going on here tonight?

SECOND CITIZEN. Why, it's Dr. Stockmann that's going to lecture against the Burgomaster.

FOURTH CITIZEN. But the Burgomaster's his brother.

FIRST CITIZEN. That makes no difference. Dr. Stockmann's not afraid of him.

THIRD CITIZEN. But he's all wrong; the *People's Messenger* says so.

SECOND CITIZEN. Yes, he must be wrong this time; for neither the House-owners' Association nor the Citizens' Club would let him have a hall.

FIRST CITIZEN. They wouldn't even lend him the hall at the Baths.

SECOND CITIZEN. No, you may be sure they wouldn't.

A MAN (*in another group*). Now, who's the one to follow in this business, eh?

ANOTHER MAN (*in the same group*). Just keep your eye on Aslaksen, and do as he does.

BILLING (*with a portfolio under his arm, makes his way through the crowd*). Excuse me, gentlemen. Will you allow me to pass? I'm here to report for the *People's Messenger*. Many thanks.

(*Sits by the table on the left.*)

A WORKING-MAN. Who's he?

ANOTHER WORKING-MAN. Don't you know him? It's that fellow Billing, that writes for Aslaksen's paper.

CAPTAIN HORSTER *enters by the door in front on the right, escorting* MRS. STOCKMANN *and* PETRA. EILIF *and* MORTEN *follow them.*

HORSTER. This is where I thought you might sit; you can so easily slip out if anything should happen.

MRS. STOCKMANN. Do you think there will be any disturbance?

HORSTER. One can never tell — with such a crowd. But there's no occasion for anxiety.

MRS. STOCKMANN (*sitting down*). How kind it was of you to offer Stockmann this room.

HORSTER. Since no one else would, I ——

PETRA (*who has also seated herself*). And it was brave too, Captain Horster.

HORSTER. Oh, I don't see where the bravery comes in.

HOVSTAD *and* ASLAKSEN *enter at the same moment, but make their way through the crowd separately.*

ASLAKSEN (*going up to* HORSTER). Hasn't the Doctor come yet?

HORSTER. He's waiting in there.

(*A movement at the door in the background.*)

HOVSTAD (*to* BILLING). There's the Burgomaster! Look!

BILLING. Yes, strike me dead if he hasn't put in an appearance after all!

BURGOMASTER STOCKMANN *makes his way blandly through the meeting, bowing politely to both sides, and takes his stand by the wall on the left. Soon afterwards,* DR. STOCKMANN *enters by the door on the right. He wears a black frock coat and white necktie. Faint applause, met by a subdued hissing. Then silence.*

DR. STOCKMANN (*in a low tone*). How do you feel, Katrina?

MRS. STOCKMANN. Quite comfortable, thank you. (*In a low voice.*) Now do keep your temper, Thomas.

DR. STOCKMANN. Oh, I shall keep myself well in hand. (*Looks at his watch, ascends the platform, and bows.*) It's a quarter past the hour, so I shall begin —— (*Takes out his MS.*)

ASLAKSEN. But surely a chairman must be elected first.

DR. STOCKMANN. No, that's not at all necessary.

SEVERAL GENTLEMEN (*shouting*). Yes, yes.

BURGOMASTER. I should certainly say that a chairman ought to be elected.

DR. STOCKMANN. But I've called this meeting to give a lecture, Peter!

BURGOMASTER. Dr. Stockmann's lecture may possibly lead to differences of opinion.

SEVERAL VOICES IN THE CROWD. A chairman! A chairman!

HOVSTAD. The general voice of the meeting seems to be for a chairman!

DR. STOCKMANN (*controlling himself*). Very well then; let the meeting have its way.

ASLAKSEN. Will not the Burgomaster take the chair?

THREE GENTLEMEN (*clapping*). Bravo! Bravo!

BURGOMASTER. For reasons you will easily understand, I must decline. But, fortunately, we have among us one whom I think we can all accept. I allude to the president of the House-owners' Association, Mr. Aslaksen.

MANY VOICES. Yes, yes! Bravo Aslaksen! Hurrah for Aslaksen!

(DR. STOCKMANN *takes his MS. and descends from the platform.*)

ASLAKSEN. Since my fellow citizens repose this trust in me, I cannot refuse —— (*Applause and cheers.* ASLAKSEN *ascends the platform.*)

BILLING (*writing*). So — "Mr. Aslaksen was elected by acclamation ——"

ASLAKSEN. And now, as I have been called to the chair, I take the liberty of saying a few brief words. I am a quiet, peace-loving man; I am in favour of discreet moderation, and of — and of moderate discretion. Everyone who knows me, knows that.

MANY VOICES. Yes, yes, Aslaksen!

ASLAKSEN. I have learnt in the school of life and of experience that moderation is the virtue in which the individual citizen finds his best advantage ——

BURGOMASTER. Hear, hear!

ASLAKSEN. —— and it is discretion and moderation, too, that best serve the community. I could therefore suggest to our respected fellow citizen, who has called this meeting, that he should endeavour to keep within the bounds of moderation.

A MAN (*by the door*). Three cheers for the Temperance Society!

A VOICE. Go to the devil!

VOICES. Hush! hush!

ASLAKSEN. No interruptions, gentlemen! — Does anyone wish to offer any observations?

BURGOMASTER. Mr. Chairman!

ASLAKSEN. Burgomaster Stockmann will address the meeting.

BURGOMASTER. On account of my close relationship — of which you are probably aware — to the present medical officer of the Baths, I should have preferred not to speak here this evening. But my position as chairman of the Baths, and my care for the vital interests of this town, force me to move a resolution. I may doubtless assume that not a single citizen here present thinks it desirable that untrustworthy and exaggerated statements should get abroad as to the sanitary condition of the Baths and of our town.

MANY VOICES. No, no, no! Certainly not! We protest.

BURGOMASTER. I therefore beg to move, "That this meeting declines to hear the proposed lecture or speech on the subject by the medical officer of the Baths."

DR. STOCKMANN (*flaring up*). Declines to hear ——! What do you mean?

MRS. STOCKMANN (*coughing*). H'm! h'm!

DR. STOCKMANN (*controlling himself*). So I am not to be heard?

BURGOMASTER. In my statement in the *People's Messenger* I have made the public acquainted with the essential facts, so that all well-disposed citizens can easily form their own judgment. From that statement it will be seen that the medical officer's proposal — besides amounting to a vote of censure upon the leading men of the town — at bottom only means saddling the ratepayers with an unnecessary outlay of at least a hundred thousand crowns. (*Sounds of protest and some hissing.*)

ASLAKSEN (*ringing the bell*). Order, gentlemen! I must beg leave to support the Burgomaster's resolution. I quite agree with him that there is something beneath the surface of the Doctor's agitation. In all his talk about the Baths, it is really a revolution he is aiming at; he wants to effect a redistribution of power. No one doubts the excellence of Dr. Stockmann's intentions — of course there cannot be two opinions as to that. I, too, am in favour of self-government by the people, if only it doesn't cost the rate-

payers too much.   But in this case it would do so; and therefore
I'll be hanged if — excuse me — in short, I cannot go with Dr.
Stockmann upon this occasion.   You can buy even gold too
dear; that's my opinion.   (*Loud applause on all sides.*)

HOVSTAD. I, too, feel bound to explain my attitude.   Dr. Stockmann's agitation seemed at first to find favour in several quarters, and I supported it as impartially as I could.   But it presently
appeared that we had been misled by a false representation of
the facts ——

DR. STOCKMANN. False ——!

HOVSTAD. Well, then, an untrustworthy representation.   This the
Burgomaster's report has proved.   I trust no one here present
doubts my liberal principles; the attitude of the *Messenger* on all
great political questions is well known to you all.   But I have
learned from men of judgment and experience that in purely
local matters a paper must observe a certain amount of caution.

ASLAKSEN. I entirely agree with the speaker.

HOVSTAD. And in the matter under discussion it is quite evident
that Dr. Stockmann has public opinion against him.   But,
gentlemen, what is an editor's clearest and most imperative duty?
Is it not to work in harmony with his readers?   Has he not in
some sort received a tacit mandate to further assiduously and un-
weariedly the interests of his constituents?   Or am I mistaken in
this?

MANY VOICES. No, no, no!   Hovstad is right!

HOVSTAD. It has cost me a bitter struggle to break with a man in
whose house I have of late been a frequent guest — with a man
who, up to this day, has enjoyed the unqualified goodwill of his
fellow citizens — with a man whose only, or, at any rate, whose
chief fault is that he consults his heart rather than his head.

A FEW SCATTERED VOICES. That's true!   Hurrah for Dr. Stockmann!

HOVSTAD. But my duty towards the community has constrained me
to break with him.   Then, too, there is another consideration
that impels me to oppose him, and, if possible, to block the ill-
omened path upon which he is entering: consideration for his
family ——

DR. STOCKMANN. Keep to the water-works and sewers!

HOVSTAD. —— consideration for his wife and his unprotected [1] children.

MORTEN. Is that us, mother?

MRS. STOCKMANN. Hush!

ASLAKSEN. I will now put the Burgomaster's resolution to the vote.

DR. STOCKMANN. You need not. I have no intention of saying anything this evening of all the filth at the Baths. No! You shall hear something quite different.

BURGOMASTER (*half aloud*). What next, I wonder?

A DRUNKEN MAN (*at the main entrance*). I'm a ratepayer, so I've a right to my opinion! And it's my full, firm, incomprehensible opinion that ——

SEVERAL VOICES. Silence up there!

OTHERS. He's drunk! Turn him out!

(*The drunken man is turned out.*)

DR. STOCKMANN. Can I speak?

ASLAKSEN (*ringing the bell*). Dr. Stockmann will address the meeting.

DR. STOCKMANN. A few days ago, I should have liked to see anyone venture upon such an attempt to gag me as has been made here tonight! I would have fought like a lion for my sacred rights! But now I care little enough; for now I have more important things to speak of.

(*The people crowd closer round him.* MORTEN KIIL *comes in sight among the bystanders.*

DR. STOCKMANN (*continuing*). I have been pondering a great many things during these last days — thinking such a multitude of thoughts, that at last my head was positively in a whirl ——

BURGOMASTER (*coughing*). H'm ——!

DR. STOCKMANN. But presently things seemed to straighten themselves out, and I saw them clearly in all their bearings. That is why I stand here this evening. I am about to make great revelations, my fellow citizens! I am going to announce to you a far-reaching discovery, beside which the trifling fact that our water-works are poisoned, and that our health-resort is built on pestilential ground, sinks into insignificance.

---

[1] Literally "unprovided-for."

MANY VOICES (*shouting*). Don't speak about the Baths! We won't listen to that! No more of that!

DR. STOCKMANN. I have said I would speak of the great discovery I have made within the last few days — the discovery that all our sources of spiritual life are poisoned, and that our whole society rests upon a pestilential basis of falsehood.

SEVERAL VOICES (*in astonishment and half aloud*). What's he saying?

BURGOMASTER. Such an insinuation ——!

ASLAKSEN (*with his hand on the bell*). I must call upon the speaker to moderate his expressions.

DR. STOCKMANN. I have loved my native town as dearly as any man can love the home of his childhood. I was young when I left our town, and distance, homesickness and memory threw, as it were, a glamour over the place and its people.

(Some applause and cries of approval.)

DR. STOCKMANN. Then for years I was imprisoned in a horrible hole, far away in the north. As I went about among the people scattered here and there over the stony wilderness, it seemed to me, many a time, that it would have been better for these poor famishing creatures to have had a cattle-doctor to attend them, instead of a man like me. *(Murmurs in the room.)*

BILLING (*laying down his pen*). Strike me dead if I've ever heard——!

HOVSTAD. What an insult to an estimable peasantry!

DR. STOCKMANN. Wait a moment! — I don't think anyone can reproach me with forgetting my native town up there. I sat brooding like an eider duck, and what I hatched was — the plan of the Baths. *(Applause and expressions of dissent.)*

DR. STOCKMANN. And when, at last, fate ordered things so happily that I could come home again — then, fellow citizens, it seemed to me that I hadn't another desire in the world. Yes, one desire I had: an eager, constant, burning desire to be of service to my birthplace, and to its people.

BURGOMASTER (*gazing into vacancy*). A strange method to select ——!

DR. STOCKMANN. So I went about revelling in my happy illusions. But yesterday morning — no, it was really two nights ago — my mind's eyes were opened wide, and the first thing I saw was the colossal stupidity of the authorities ——

(Noise, cries, and laughter. MRS. STOCKMANN coughs repeatedly.)

BURGOMASTER. Mr. Chairman!

ASLAKSEN (*ringing his bell*). In virtue of my position ——!

DR. STOCKMANN. It's petty to catch me up on a word, Mr. Aslaksen! I only mean that I became alive to the extraordinary muddle our leading men had been guilty of, down at the Baths. I cannot for the life of me abide leading men — I've seen enough of them in my time. They are like goats in a young plantation: they do harm at every point; they block the path of a free man wherever he turns — and I should be glad if we could exterminate them like other noxious animals —— (*Uproar in the room.*)

BURGOMASTER. Mr. Chairman, are such expressions permissible?

ASLAKSEN (*with his hand on the bell*). Dr. Stockmann ——

DR. STOCKMANN. I can't conceive how it is that I have only now seen through these gentry; for haven't I had a magnificent example before my eyes here every day — my brother Peter — slow of understanding, tenacious in prejudice ——

(*Laughter, noise, and whistling.* MRS. STOCKMANN *coughs.* ASLAKSEN *rings violently.*)

THE DRUNKEN MAN (*who has come in again*). Is it me you're alluding to? Sure enough, my name's Petersen; but devil take me if ——

ANGRY VOICES. Out with that drunken man! Turn him out!

(*The man is again turned out.*)

BURGOMASTER. Who is that person?

A BYSTANDER. I don't know him, Burgomaster.

ANOTHER. He doesn't belong to the town.

A THIRD. I believe he's a timber-dealer from ——

(*The rest is inaudible.*)

ASLAKSEN. The man was evidently intoxicated. — Continue, Dr. Stockmann; but pray endeavour to be moderate.

DR. STOCKMANN. Well, fellow citizens, I shall say no more about our leading men. If anyone imagines, from what I have just said, that it's these gentlemen I want to make short work of tonight, he is mistaken — altogether mistaken. For I cherish the comfortable conviction that these laggards, these relics of a decaying order of thought, are diligently cutting their own throats. They need no doctor to hasten their end. And it is not people of that sort that constitute the real danger to society; it is not they who are most active in poisoning the sources of our spiritual life and making a plague-spot of the ground beneath our feet; it is not they who are the most dangerous enemies of truth and freedom in our society.

CRIES FROM ALL SIDES. Who, then? Who is it? Name, name!

DR. STOCKMANN. Yes, you may be sure I shall name them! For this is the great discovery I made yesterday: (*In a louder tone.*) The most dangerous foe to truth and freedom in our midst is the compact majority. Yes, it's the confounded, compact, liberal majority — that, and nothing else! There, I've told you.

> (*Immense disturbance in the room. Most of the audience are shouting, stamping, and whistling. Several elderly gentlemen exchange furtive glances and seem to be enjoying the scene.* MRS. STOCKMANN *rises in alarm.* EILIF *and* MORTEN *advance threateningly towards the schoolboys, who are making noises.* ASLAKSEN *rings the bell and calls for order.* HOVSTAD *and* BILLING *both speak, but nothing can be heard. At last quiet is restored.*)

ASLAKSEN. I must request the speaker to withdraw his ill-considered expressions.

DR. STOCKMANN. Never, Mr. Aslaksen! For it's this very majority that robs me of my freedom, and wants to forbid me to speak the truth.

HOVSTAD. The majority always has right on its side.

BILLING. Yes, and truth too, strike me dead!

DR. STOCKMANN. The majority never has right on its side. Never, I say! That is one of the social lies that a free, thinking man is bound to rebel against. Who make up the majority in any given country? Is it the wise men or the fools? I think we must agree that the fools are in a terrible, overwhelming majority, all the wide world over. But how in the devil's name can it ever be right for the fools to rule over the wise men? (*Uproar and yells.*)

DR. STOCKMANN. Yes, yes, you can shout me down, but you cannot gainsay me. The majority has might — unhappily — but right it has not. It is I, and the few, the individuals, that are in the right. The minority is always right. (*Renewed uproar.*)

HOVSTAD. Ha, ha! Dr. Stockmann has turned aristocrat since the day before yesterday!

DR. STOCKMANN. I have said that I have no words to waste on the little, narrow-chested, short-winded crew that lie in our wake.

Pulsating life has nothing more to do with them. I am speaking of the few, the individuals among us, who have made all the new, germinating truths their own. These men stand, as it were, at the outposts, so far in the van that the compact majority has not yet reached them — and there they fight for truths that are too lately born into the world's consciousness to have won over the majority.

HOVSTAD. So the Doctor's a revolutionist now!

DR. STOCKMANN. Yes, by Heaven, I am, Mr. Hovstad! I am going to revolt against the lie that truth belongs exclusively to the majority. What sort of truths do the majority rally round? Truths so stricken in years that they are sinking into decrepitude. When a truth is so old as that, gentlemen, it's in a fair way to become a lie. *(Laughter and jeers.)*

DR. STOCKMANN. Yes, yes, you may believe me or not, as you please; but truths are by no means the wiry Methuselahs some people think them. A normally-constituted truth lives — let us say — as a rule, seventeen or eighteen years; at the outside twenty; very seldom more. And truths so patriarchal as that are always shockingly emaciated; yet it's not till then that the majority takes them up and recommends them to society as wholesome food. I can assure you there's not much nutriment in that sort of fare; you may take my word as a doctor for that. All these majority-truths are like last year's salt pork; they're like rancid, mouldy ham, producing all the moral scurvy that devastates society.

ASLAKSEN. It seems to me that the honourable speaker is wandering rather far from the subject.

BURGOMASTER. I beg to endorse the Chairman's remark.

DR. STOCKMANN. Why, you're surely mad, Peter! I'm keeping as closely to my text as I possibly can; for my text is precisely this — that the masses, the majority, this devil's own compact majority — it's that, I say, that's poisoning the sources of our spiritual life, and making a plague-spot of the ground beneath our feet.

HOVSTAD. And you make this charge against the great, independent majority, just because they have the sense to accept only certain and acknowledged truths?

DR. STOCKMANN. Ah, my dear Mr. Hovstad, don't talk about certain truths! The truths acknowledged by the masses, the multitude, were certain truths to the vanguard in our grandfathers' days. We, the vanguard of today, don't acknowledge them any longer; and I don't believe there exists any other certain truth but this — that no society can live a healthy life upon truths so old and marrowless.

HOVSTAD. But instead of all this vague talk, suppose you were to give us some specimens of these old marrowless truths that we are living upon. (*Approval from several quarters.*)

DR. STOCKMANN. Oh, I could give you no end of samples from the rubbish-heap; but, for the present, I shall keep to one acknowledged truth, which is a hideous lie at bottom, but which Mr. Hovstad, and the *Messenger*, and all adherents of the *Messenger*, live on all the same.

HOVSTAD. And that is ——?

DR. STOCKMANN. That is the doctrine you have inherited from your forefathers, and go on thoughtlessly proclaiming far and wide — the doctrine that the multitude, the vulgar herd, the masses, are the pith of the people — that they are the people — that the common man, the ignorant, undeveloped member of society, has the same right to sanction and to condemn, to counsel and to govern, as the intellectually distinguished few.

BILLING. Well, now, strike me dead ——!

HOVSTAD (*shouting at the same time*). Citizens, please note this!

ANGRY VOICES. Ho-ho! Aren't we the people? Is it only the grand folks that are to govern?

A WORKING MAN. Out with the fellow that talks like that!

OTHERS. Turn him out!

A CITIZEN (*shouting*). Blow your horn, Evensen.

(*The deep notes of a horn are heard; whistling, and terrific noise in the room.*)

DR. STOCKMANN (*when the noise has somewhat subsided*). Now do be reasonable! Can't you bear even for once in a way to hear the voice of truth? I don't ask you all to agree with me on the instant. But I certainly should have expected Mr. Hovstad to back me up, as soon as he had collected himself a bit. Mr. Hovstad sets up to be a freethinker ——

SEVERAL VOICES (*subdued and wondering*). Freethinker, did he say? What? Mr. Hovstad a freethinker?

HOVSTAD (*shouting*).   Prove it, Dr. Stockmann.   When have I said so in print?

DR. STOCKMANN (*reflecting*).   No, upon my soul, you're right there; you've never had the frankness to do that.   Well, well, I won't put you on the rack, Mr. Hovstad.   Let me be the freethinker then.   And now I'll make it clear to you all, and on scientific grounds too, that the *Messenger* is leading you shamefully by the nose, when it tells you that you, the masses, the crowd, are the true pith of the people.   I tell you that's only a newspaper lie.   The masses are nothing but the raw material that must be fashioned into a People.

(*Murmurs, laughter, and disturbance in the room.*)

DR. STOCKMANN.   Is it not so with all other living creatures?   What a difference between a cultivated and an uncultivated breed of animals!   Just look at a common barn-door hen.   What meat do you get from such a skinny carcase?   Not much, I can tell you!   And what sort of eggs does she lay?   A decent crow or raven can lay nearly as good.   Then take a cultivated Spanish or Japanese hen, or take a fine pheasant or turkey — ah! then you'll see the difference!   And now look at the dog, our near relation.   Think first of an ordinary vulgar cur — I mean one of these wretched, ragged, plebeian mongrels that haunt the gutters, and soil the sidewalks.   Then place such a mongrel by the side of a poodle-dog, descended through many generations from an aristocratic stock, who have lived on delicate food, and heard harmonious voices and music.   Do you think the brain of the poodle isn't very differently developed from that of the mongrel?   Yes, you may be sure it is!   It's well-bred poodle-pups like this that jugglers train to perform the most marvellous tricks.   A common peasant-cur could never learn anything of the sort — not if he tried till doomsday.   (*Noise and laughter are heard all round.*)

A CITIZEN (*shouting*).   Do you want to make dogs of us now?

ANOTHER MAN.   We're not animals, Doctor!

DR. STOCKMANN.   Yes, on my soul, but we are animals, my good sir!   We're one and all of us animals, whether we like it or not.   But truly there are few enough aristocratic animals among us.   Oh, there's a terrible difference between poodle-men and mongrel-men!   And the ridiculous part of it is, that Mr. Hovstad quite agrees with me so long as it's four-legged animals we're talking of ——

HOVSTAD. Oh, beasts are only beasts.

DR. STOCKMANN. Well and good — but no sooner do I apply the law to two-legged animals, than Mr. Hovstad stops short; then he daren't hold his own opinions, or think out his own thoughts; then he turns the whole principle upside down, and proclaims in the *People's Messenger* that the barn-door hen and the gutter-mongrel are precisely the finest specimens in the menagerie. But that's always the way, so long as the commonness still lingers in your system, and you haven't worked your way up to spiritual distinction.

HOVSTAD. I make no pretence to any sort of distinction. I come of simple peasant folk, and I am proud that my root should lie deep down among the common people, who are here being insulted.

WORKMEN. Hurrah for Hovstad. Hurrah! hurrah!

DR. STOCKMANN. The sort of common people I am speaking of are not found among the lower classes alone; they crawl and swarm all around us — up to the very summits of society. Just look at your own smug, respectable Burgomaster! Why, my brother Peter belongs as clearly to the common people as any man that walks on two legs —— (*Laughter and hisses.*)

BURGOMASTER. I protest against such personalities.

DR. STOCKMANN (*imperturbably*). —— and that not because, like myself, he's descended from a good-for-nothing old pirate from Pomerania, or thereabouts — for that's our ancestry ——

BURGOMASTER. An absurd tradition! Utterly groundless.

DR. STOCKMANN. —— but he is so because he thinks the thoughts and holds the opinions of his official superiors. Men who do that, belong, intellectually-speaking, to the common people; and that is why my distinguished brother Peter is at bottom so undistinguished, — and consequently so illiberal.

BURGOMASTER. Mr. Chairman ——!

HOVSTAD. So that the distinguished people in this country are the Liberals? That's quite a new light on the subject.

(*Laughter.*)

DR. STOCKMANN. Yes, that is part of my new discovery. And this, too, follows: that liberality of thought is almost precisely the same thing as morality. Therefore I say it's absolutely unpardonable of the *Messenger* to proclaim, day out, day in, the false doctrine that it's the masses, the multitude, the compact majority, that monopolise liberality and morality, — and that vice and corruption and all sorts of spiritual uncleanness ooze out of culture, as all that filth oozes down to the Baths from the Mill Dale tan-works! (*Noise and interruptions.*)

DR. STOCKMANN (*goes on imperturbably, smiling in his eagerness*). And yet this same *Messenger* can preach about elevating the masses and the multitude to a higher level of well-being! Why, deuce take it, if the *Messenger's* own doctrine holds good, the elevation of the masses would simply mean hurling them straight to perdition! But, happily, the notion that culture demoralises is nothing but an old traditional lie. No, it's stupidity, poverty, the ugliness of life, that do the devil's work! In a house that isn't aired and swept every day — my wife maintains that the floors ought to be scrubbed too, but perhaps that is going too far; — well, — in such a house, I say, within two or three years, people lose the power of thinking or acting morally. Lack of oxygen enervates the conscience. And there seems to be precious little oxygen in many and many a house in this town, since the whole compact majority is unscrupulous enough to want to found its future upon a quagmire of lies and fraud.

ASLAKSEN. I cannot allow so gross an insult to be levelled against a whole community.

A GENTLEMAN. I move that the Chairman order the speaker to sit down.

EAGER VOICES. Yes, yes! That's right! Sit down! Sit down!

DR. STOCKMANN (*flaring up*). Then I shall proclaim the truth at every street corner! I shall write to newspapers in other towns! The whole country shall know how matters stand here!

HOVSTAD. It almost seems as if the Doctor's object were to ruin the town.

DR. STOCKMANN. Yes, so well do I love my native town that I would rather ruin it than see it flourishing upon a lie.

ASLAKSEN. That's plain speaking.

(*Noise and whistling.* MRS. STOCKMANN *coughs in vain; the* DOCTOR *no longer heeds her.*)

HOVSTAD (*shouting amid the tumult*). The man who would ruin a community must be an enemy to his fellow citizens!

DR. STOCKMANN (*with growing excitement*). What does it matter if a lying community is ruined! Let it be levelled to the ground, say I! All men who live upon a lie ought to be exterminated like vermin! You'll end by poisoning the whole country; you'll bring it to such a pass that the whole country will deserve to perish. And if ever it comes to that, I shall say, from the bottom of my heart: Perish the country! Perish all its people!

A MAN (*in the crowd*). Why, he talks like a regular enemy of the people!

BILLING. Strike me dead but there spoke the people's voice!

THE WHOLE ASSEMBLY (*shouting*). Yes! yes! yes! He's an enemy of the people! He hates his country! He hates the whole people!

ASLAKSEN. Both as a citizen of this town and as a human being, I am deeply shocked at what it has been my lot to hear tonight. Dr. Stockmann has unmasked himself in a manner I should never have dreamt of. I must reluctantly subscribe to the opinion just expressed by some estimable citizens; and I think we ought to formulate this opinion in a resolution. I therefore beg to move, "That this meeting declares the medical officer of the Baths, Dr. Thomas Stockmann, to be an enemy of the people."

(*Thunders of applause and cheers. Many form a circle round the DOCTOR and hoot at him. MRS. STOCKMANN and PETRA have risen. MORTEN and EILIF fight the other school-boys, who have also been hooting. Some grown-up persons separate them.*)

DR. STOCKMANN (*to the people hooting*). Ah, fools that you are! I tell you that ——

ASLAKSEN (*ringing*). The Doctor is out of order in speaking. A formal vote must be taken; but out of consideration for personal feelings, it will be taken in writing and without names. Have you any blank paper, Mr. Billing?

BILLING. Here's both blue and white paper ——

ASLAKSEN. Capital; that will save time. Put it up into slips. That's it. (*To the meeting*). Blue means no, white means aye. I my-self will go round and collect the votes.

(*The BURGOMASTER leaves the room. ASLAKSEN and a few others go round with pieces of paper in hats.*)

A GENTLEMAN (*to* HOVSTAD). What can be the matter with the Doctor? What does it all mean?

HOVSTAD. Why, you know what a hare-brained creature he is.

ANOTHER GENTLEMAN (*to* BILLING). I say, you're often at his house. Have you ever noticed if the fellow drinks?

BILLING. Strike me dead if I know what to say. The toddy's always on the table when anyone looks in.

A THIRD GENTLEMAN. No, I should rather say he went off his head at times.

FIRST GENTLEMAN. I wonder if there's madness in the family?

BILLING. I shouldn't be surprised.

A FOURTH GENTLEMAN. No, it's pure malice. He wants to be revenged for something or other.

BILLING. He was certainly talking about a rise in his salary the other day; but he didn't get it.

ALL THE GENTLEMEN (*together*). Aha! That explains everything.

THE DRUNKEN MAN (*in the crowd*). I want a blue one, I do! And I'll have a white one too.

SEVERAL PEOPLE. There's the tipsy man again! Turn him out.

MORTEN KIIL (*approaching the* DOCTOR). Well, Stockmann, you see now what such monkey-tricks lead to?

DR. STOCKMANN. I have done my duty.

MORTEN KIIL. What was that you said about the Mill Dale tanneries?

DR. STOCKMANN. You heard what I said — that all the filth comes from them.

MORTEN KIIL. From my tannery as well?

DR. STOCKMANN. I'm sorry to say yours is the worst of all.

MORTEN KIIL. Are you going to put that in the papers, too?

DR. STOCKMANN. I can't gloze anything over.

MORTEN KIIL. This may cost you dear, Stockmann! (*He goes out.*)

A FAT GENTLEMAN (*goes up to* HORSTER, *without bowing to the ladies*). Well, Captain, so you lend your house to enemies of the people.

HORSTER. I suppose I can do as I please with my own property, Sir.

THE GENTLEMAN. Then of course you can have no objection if I follow your example?

HORSTER. What do you mean, Sir?

THE GENTLEMAN. You shall hear from me tomorrow.

(*Turns away and goes out.*)

PETRA. Wasn't that the owner of your ship, Captain Horster?

HORSTER. Yes, that was Mr. Vik.

ASLAKSEN (*with the voting papers in his hands, ascends the platform and rings*). Gentlemen! I have now to announce the result of the vote. All the voters, with one exception ——

A YOUNG GENTLEMAN. That's the tipsy man!

ASLAKSEN. With the exception of one intoxicated person, this meeting of citizens unanimously declares the medical officer of the Baths, Dr. Thomas Stockmann, to be an enemy of the people. (*Cheers and applause.*) Three cheers for our fine old municipality! (*Cheers.*) Three cheers for our able and energetic Burgomaster, who has so loyally set family prejudice aside! (*Cheers.*) The meeting is dissolved. (*He descends.*)

BILLING. Three cheers for the Chairman!

ALL. Hurrah for Aslaksen.

DR. STOCKMANN. My hat and coat, Petra. Captain, have you room for passengers to the new world?

HORSTER. For you and yours, Doctor, we'll make room.

DR. STOCKMANN (*while* PETRA *helps him to put on his coat*). Good! Come, Katrina, come, boys! (*He gives his wife his arm.*)

MRS. STOCKMANN (*in a low voice*). Thomas, dear, let us go out by the back way.

DR. STOCKMANN. No back ways, Katrina! (*In a loud voice.*) You shall hear from the enemy of the people, before he shakes the dust from his feet! I am not so forbearing as a certain person; I don't say: I forgive you, for you know not what you do.

ASLAKSEN (*shouts*). That is a blasphemous comparison, Dr. Stockmann!

BILLING. Strike me ——! This is more than a serious man can stand!

A COARSE VOICE. And he threatens us into the bargain!

ANGRY CRIES. Let's smash his windows! Duck him in the fiord!

A MAN (*in the crowd*). Blow your horn, Evensen! Blow, man, blow!

(*Horn-blowing, whistling, and wild shouting. The* DOCTOR, *with his family, goes towards the door.* HORSTER *clears the way for them.*)

ALL (*yelling after them as they go out*). Enemy of the people! Enemy of the people! Enemy of the people!

BILLING. Strike me dead if I'd care to drink toddy at Stockmann's tonight!

> (*The people throng towards the door; the shouting is taken up by others outside; from the street are heard cries of "Enemy of the people! Enemy of the people!"*)

ACT FIFTH

DR. STOCKMANN'S *Study. Bookshelves and glass cases with various collections along the walls. In the back, a door leading to the hall; in front, on the left, a door to the sitting-room. In the wall to the right are two windows, all the panes of which are smashed. In the middle of the room is the* DOCTOR'S *writing-table, covered with books and papers. The room is in disorder. It is forenoon.*

DR. STOCKMANN, *in dressing-gown, slippers, and skull-cap, is bending down and raking with an umbrella under one of the cabinets; at last he rakes out a stone.*

DR. STOCKMANN (*speaking through the sitting-room doorway*). Katrina, I've found another!

MRS. STOCKMANN (*in the sitting-room*). Oh, I'm sure you'll find plenty more.

DR. STOCKMANN (*placing the stone on a pile of others on the table*). I shall keep these stones as sacred relics. Eilif and Morten shall see them every day, and when I die they shall be heirlooms. (*Raking under the bookcase.*) Hasn't — what the devil is her name? — the girl — hasn't she been for the glazier yet?

MRS. STOCKMANN (*coming in*). Yes, but he said he didn't know whether he would be able to come today.

DR. STOCKMANN. I believe, if the truth were told, he daren't come.

MRS. STOCKMANN. Well, Randina, too, had an idea he was afraid to come, because of the neighbours. (*Speaks through the sitting-room doorway.*) What is it, Randina? — Very well. (*Goes out, and returns immediately.*) Here is a letter for you, Thomas.

DR. STOCKMANN. Let me see. (*Opens the letter and reads.*) Aha!

MRS. STOCKMANN. Who is it from?

DR. STOCKMANN. From the landlord. He gives us notice.

MRS. STOCKMANN. Is it possible? He is such a nice man ——

DR. STOCKMANN (*looking at the letter*). He daren't do otherwise, he says. He is very unwilling to do it; but he daren't do otherwise — on account of his fellow citizens — out of respect for public opinion — is in a dependent position — doesn't dare to offend certain influential men ——

MRS. STOCKMANN. There, you see, Thomas.

DR. STOCKMANN. Yes, yes, I see well enough; they are all cowards, every one of them, in this town; no one dares do anything for fear of all the rest. (*Throws the letter on the table.*) But it's all the same to us, Katrina. We will shape our course for the new world, and then ——

MRS. STOCKMANN. But are you sure this idea of going abroad is altogether wise, Thomas?

DR. STOCKMANN. Would you have me stay here, where they have pilloried me as an enemy of the people, branded me, smashed my windows! And look here, Katrina, they've torn a hole in my black trousers, too.

MRS. STOCKMANN. Oh, dear; and these are the best you have!

DR. STOCKMANN. A man should never put on his best trousers when he goes out to battle for freedom and truth. Well, I don't care so much about the trousers; them you can always patch up for me. But that the mob, the rabble, should dare to attack me, as if they were my equals — that is what I can't, for the life of me, stomach!

MRS. STOCKMANN. Yes, they have behaved abominably to you here, Thomas; but is that any reason for leaving the country altogether?

DR. STOCKMANN. Do you think the plebeians aren't just as insolent in other towns? Oh, yes, they are, my dear; it's six of one and half a dozen of the other. Well, never mind; let the curs yelp; that's not the worst; the worst is that everyone, all over the country, is the slave of his party. Not that I suppose — very likely it's no better in the free West either; the compact majority, and enlightened public opinion, and all the other devil's trash is rampant there too. But you see the conditions are larger there than here; they may kill you, but they don't slow-torture you; they don't screw up a free soul in a vice, as they do at home here. And then, if need be, you can keep out of it all. (*Walks up and down.*) If I only knew of any primeval forest, or a little South Sea island to be sold cheap ——

MRS. STOCKMANN. Yes, but the boys, Thomas.

DR. STOCKMANN (*comes to a standstill*). What an extraordinary woman you are, Katrina! Would you rather have the boys grow up in such a society as ours? Why, you could see for yourself yesterday evening that one half of the population is stark mad, and if the other half hasn't lost its wits, that's only because they are brute beasts who haven't any wits to lose.

MRS. STOCKMANN. But really, my dear Thomas, you do say such imprudent things.

DR. STOCKMANN. What! Isn't it the truth that I tell them? Don't they turn all ideas upside down? Don't they stir up right and wrong into one hotch-potch? Don't they call lies everything that I know to be the truth? But the maddest thing of all is to see crowds of grown men, calling themselves Liberals, go about persuading themselves and others that they are friends of freedom! Did you ever hear anything like it, Katrina?

MRS. STOCKMANN. Yes, yes, no doubt. But ——

PETRA *enters from the sitting-room.*

MRS. STOCKMANN. Back from school already?

PETRA. Yes; I have been dismissed.

MRS. STOCKMANN. Dismissed?

DR. STOCKMANN. You too!

PETRA. Mrs. Busk gave me notice, and so I thought it best to leave there and then.

DR. STOCKMANN. You did perfectly right!

MRS. STOCKMANN. Who could have thought Mrs. Busk was such a bad woman!

PETRA. Oh, mother, Mrs. Busk isn't bad at all; I saw clearly how sorry she was. But she dared not do otherwise, she said; and so I am dismissed.

DR. STOCKMANN (*laughing and rubbing his hands*). She dared not do otherwise — just like the rest! Oh, it's delicious.

MRS. STOCKMANN. Oh, well, after that frightful scene last night ——

PETRA. It wasn't only that. What do you think, father ——?

DR. STOCKMANN. Well?

PETRA. Mrs. Busk showed me no fewer than three letters she had received this morning ——

DR. STOCKMANN. Anonymous, of course?

PETRA. Yes.

DR. STOCKMANN. They never dare give their names, Katrina!

PETRA. And two of them stated that a gentleman who is often at our house said at the club last night that I held extremely advanced opinions upon various things ——

DR. STOCKMANN. Of course you didn't deny it.

PETRA. Of course not. You know Mrs. Busk herself is pretty advanced in her opinions when we're alone together; but now that this has come out about me, she dared not keep me on.

MRS. STOCKMANN. Someone that is often at our house, too. There, you see, Thomas, what comes of all your hospitality.

DR. STOCKMANN. We won't live any longer in such a pig-sty! Pack up as quickly as you can, Katrina; let's get away — the sooner the better.

MRS. STOCKMANN. Hush! I think there is someone in the passage. See who it is, Petra.

PETRA (opening the door). Oh, is it you, Captain Horster? Please come in.

HORSTER (from the hall). Good morning. I thought I might just look in and ask how you are.

DR. STOCKMANN (shaking his hand). Thanks; that's very good of you.

MRS. STOCKMANN. And thank you for helping us through the crowd last night, Captain Horster.

PETRA. How did you ever get home again?

HORSTER. Oh, that was all right. I am tolerably able-bodied, you know; and those fellows' bark is worse than their bite.

DR. STOCKMANN. Yes, isn't it extraordinary, this piggish cowardice? Come here, and let me show you something! Look, here are all the stones they threw in at us. Only look at them! Upon my soul there aren't more than two decent-sized lumps in the whole heap; the rest are nothing but pebbles — mere gravel. They stood down there, and yelled, and swore they'd half kill me —; but as for really doing it — no, there's mighty little fear of that in this town!

HORSTER. You may thank your stars for that this time, Doctor.

DR. STOCKMANN. So I do, of course. But it's depressing all the same; for if ever it should come to a serious national struggle, you may be sure public opinion would be for taking to its heels, and the compact majority would scamper for their lives like a flock of sheep, Captain Horster. That is what's so melancholy to think of; it grieves me to the heart. — But deuce take it — it's foolish of me to feel anything of the sort! They have called me an enemy of the people; well then, let me be an enemy of the people!

MRS. STOCKMANN. That you'll never be, Thomas.

DR. STOCKMANN. You'd better not take your oath of it, Katrina. A bad name may act like a pin-scratch in the lung. And that confounded word — I can't get rid of it; it has sunk deep into my heart; and there it lies gnawing and sucking like an acid. And no magnesia can cure me.

PETRA. Pooh; you should only laugh at them, father.

HORSTER. People will think differently yet, Doctor.

MRS. STOCKMANN. Yes, Thomas, that's as certain as that you are standing here.

DR. STOCKMANN. Yes, perhaps, when it is too late. Well, as they make their bed so they must lie! Let them go on wallowing here in their pig-sty, and learn to repent having driven a patriot into exile. When do you sail, Captain Horster?

HORSTER. Well — that's really what I came to speak to you about ——

DR. STOCKMANN. What? Anything wrong with the ship?

HORSTER. No; but the fact is, I shan't be sailing in her.

PETRA. Surely you have not been dismissed?

HORSTER (smiling). Yes, I have.

PETRA. You too!

MRS. STOCKMANN. There, you see, Thomas.

DR. STOCKMANN. And for the truth's sake! Oh, if I could possibly have imagined such a thing ——

HORSTER. You mustn't be troubled about this; I shall soon find a berth with some other company, elsewhere.

DR. STOCKMANN. And this is that man Vik! A wealthy man, independent of everyone! Faugh!

HORSTER. Oh, for that matter, he's a very well-meaning man. He said himself he would gladly have kept me on if only he dared ——

DR. STOCKMANN. But he didn't dare? Of course not!

HORSTER. It's not so easy, he said, when you belong to a party ——

DR. STOCKMANN. My gentleman has hit it there! A party is like a sausage-machine; it grinds all the brains together in one mash; and that's why we see nothing but porridge-heads and pulp-heads all around!

MRS. STOCKMANN. Now really, Thomas!

PETRA (to HORSTER). If only you hadn't seen us home, perhaps it would not have come to this.

HORSTER. I don't regret it.

PETRA (gives him her hand). Thank you for that!

HORSTER (to DR. STOCKMANN). And then, too, I wanted to tell you this: if you are really determined to go abroad, I've thought of another way ——

DR. STOCKMANN. That's good — if only we can get off quickly ——

MRS. STOCKMANN. Hush! Isn't that a knock?

PETRA. I believe it is uncle.

DR. STOCKMANN. Aha! (Calls.) Come in!

MRS. STOCKMANN. My dear Thomas, now do promise me ——

The BURGOMASTER *enters from the hall.*

BURGOMASTER (in the doorway). Oh, you are engaged. Then I'd better ——

DR. STOCKMANN. No, no; come in.

BURGOMASTER. But I wanted to speak to you alone.

MRS. STOCKMANN. We can go into the sitting-room.

HORSTER. And I shall look in again presently.

DR. STOCKMANN. No, no; go with the ladies, Captain Horster; I must hear more about ——

HORSTER. All right, then I'll wait.

(He follows MRS. STOCKMANN and PETRA into the sitting-room. The BURGOMASTER says nothing, but casts glances at the windows.)

DR. STOCKMANN. I dare say you find it rather draughty here today? Put on your cap.

BURGOMASTER. Thanks, if I may. (*Does so.*) I fancy I caught cold yesterday evening. I stood there shivering ——

DR. STOCKMANN. Really. On my soul, now, I found it quite warm enough.

BURGOMASTER. I regret that it was not in my power to prevent these nocturnal excesses.

DR. STOCKMANN. Have you anything else in particular to say to me?

BURGOMASTER (*producing a large letter*). I have this document for you from the Directors of the Baths.

DR. STOCKMANN. My dismissal?

BURGOMASTER. Yes; dated from today. (*Places the letter on the table*). We are very sorry — but frankly, we dared not do otherwise, on account of public opinion.

DR. STOCKMANN (*smiling*). Dare not? I've heard that phrase already today.

BURGOMASTER. I beg you to realise your position clearly. For the future, you cannot count upon any sort of practice in the town.

DR. STOCKMANN. Devil take the practice! But how can you be so sure of that?

BURGOMASTER. The House-owners' Association is sending round a circular from house to house, in which all well-disposed citizens are called upon not to employ you; and I dare swear that not a single head of a family will venture to refuse his signature; he simply dare not.

DR. STOCKMANN. Well, well; I don't doubt that. But what then?

BURGOMASTER. If I might advise, I would suggest that you should leave the town for a time ——

DR. STOCKMANN. Yes, I've had some such idea in my mind already.

BURGOMASTER. Good. And when you have had six months or so for mature deliberation, if you could make up your mind to acknowledge your error, with a few words of regret ——

DR. STOCKMANN. I might perhaps be reinstated, you think?

BURGOMASTER. Perhaps it's not quite out of the question.

DR. STOCKMANN. Yes, but how about public opinion? You daren't, on account of public opinion.

BURGOMASTER. Opinion is extremely variable. And, to speak

candidly, it is of the greatest importance for us to have such an admission under your own hand.

DR. STOCKMANN. Yes, I dare say it would be mightily convenient for you! But you remember what I've said to you before about such foxes' tricks!

BURGOMASTER. At that time your position was infinitely more favourable; at that time you thought you had the whole town at your back ——

DR. STOCKMANN. Yes, and now I have the whole town on my back —— (*Flaring up.*) But no — not if I had the devil and his dam on my back —! Never — never, I tell you!

BURGOMASTER. The father of a family has no right [1] to act as you are doing. You have no right to do it, Thomas.

DR. STOCKMANN. I have no right! There's only one thing in the world that a free man has no right to do; and do you know what that is?

BURGOMASTER. No.

DR. STOCKMANN. Of course not; but *I* will tell you. A free man has no right to wallow in filth like a cur; he has no right to act so that he ought to spit in his own face!

BURGOMASTER. That sounds extremely plausible; and if there were not another explanation of your obstinacy — but we all know there is ——

DR. STOCKMANN. What do you mean by that?

BURGOMASTER. You understand well enough. But as your brother, and as a man who knows the world, I warn you not to build too confidently upon prospects and expectations that may very likely come to nothing.

DR. STOCKMANN. Why, what on earth are you driving at?

BURGOMASTER. Do you really want me to believe that you are ignorant of the terms of old Morten Kiil's will?

DR. STOCKMANN. I know that the little he has is to go to a home for old and needy artisans. But what has that got to do with me?

---

[1] "Has no right" represents the Norwegian *tör ikke* — the phrase which, elsewhere in this scene, is translated "dare not." The latter rendering should perhaps have been adhered to throughout; but in this passage the Norwegian words convey a shade of meaning which is best represented by "has no right."

BURGOMASTER. To begin with, "the little he has" is no trifle. Morten Kiil is a tolerably wealthy man.

DR. STOCKMANN. I have never had the least notion of that!

BURGOMASTER. H'm — really? Then I suppose you have no notion that a not inconsiderable part of his fortune is to go to your children, you and your wife having a life-interest in it. Has he not told you that?

DR. STOCKMANN. No, I'll be hanged if he has! On the contrary, he has done nothing but grumble about being so preposterously over-taxed. But are you really sure of this, Peter?

BURGOMASTER. I have it from a thoroughly trustworthy source.

DR. STOCKMANN. Why, good heavens, then Katrina's provided for — and the children too! Oh, I must tell her —— (Calls.) Katrina, Katrina!

BURGOMASTER (holding him back). Hush! don't say anything about it yet.

MRS. STOCKMANN (opening the door). What is it?

DR. STOCKMANN. Nothing, my dear; go in again.

(MRS. STOCKMANN closes the door.)

DR. STOCKMANN (pacing up and down). Provided for! Only think — all of them provided for! And for life! After all, it's a grand thing to feel yourself secure!

BURGOMASTER. Yes, but that is just what you are not. Morten Kiil can revoke his will any day or hour he chooses.

DR. STOCKMANN. But he won't, my good Peter. The Badger is only too delighted to see me fall foul of you and your wiseacre friends.

BURGOMASTER (starts and looks searchingly at him). Aha! That throws a new light on a good many things.

DR. STOCKMANN. What things?

BURGOMASTER. So the whole affair had been a carefully-concocted intrigue. Your recklessly violent onslaught — in the name of truth — upon the leading men of the town ——

DR. STOCKMANN. Well, what of it?

BURGOMASTER. It was nothing but a preconcerted requital for that vindictive old Morten Kiil's will.

DR. STOCKMANN (almost speechless). Peter — you are the most abominable plebeian I have ever known in all my born days.

BURGOMASTER. All is over between us. Your dismissal is irrevocable — for now we have a weapon against you. (*He goes out.*)

DR. STOCKMANN. Shame! shame! shame! (*Calls.*) Katrina! The floor must be scrubbed after him! Tell her to come here with a pail — what's her name? confound it — the girl with the smudge on her nose ——

MRS. STOCKMANN (*in the sitting-room doorway*). Hush, hush, Thomas!

PETRA (*also in the doorway*). Father, here's grandfather; he wants to know if he can speak to you alone.

DR. STOCKMANN. Yes, of course he can. (*By the door.*) Come in, father-in-law.

MORTEN KIIL *enters.* DR. STOCKMANN *closes the door behind him.*

DR. STOCKMANN. Well, what is it? Sit down.

MORTEN KIIL. I won't sit down. (*Looking about him*). It looks cheerful here today, Stockmann.

DR. STOCKMANN. Yes, don't you think so?

MORTEN KIIL. Sure enough. And you've plenty of fresh air too; you've got your fill of that oxygen you were talking about yesterday. You must have a rare good conscience today, I should think.

DR. STOCKMANN. Yes, I have.

MORTEN KIIL. So I should suppose. (*Tapping himself on the breast.*) But do you know what *I* have got here?

DR. STOCKMANN. A good conscience, too, I hope.

MORTON KIIL. Pooh! No; something far better than that.

(*Takes out a large pocket-book, opens it, and shows* STOCKMANN *a bundle of papers.*)

DR. STOCKMANN (*looking at him in astonishment*). Shares in the Baths!

MORTEN KIIL. They weren't difficult to get today.

DR. STOCKMANN. And you've gone and bought these up ——?

MORTEN KIIL. All I had the money to pay for.

DR. STOCKMANN. Why, my dear sir, — just when things are in such a desperate way at the Baths ——

MORTEN KIIL. If you behave like a reasonable being, you can soon set the Baths all right again.

DR. STOCKMANN. Well, you can see for yourself I'm doing all I can. But the people of this town are mad!

MORTEN KIIL. You said yesterday that the worst filth came from my tannery. Now, if that's true, then my grandfather, and my father before me, and I myself, have for ever so many years been poisoning the town with filth, like three destroying angels. Do you think I'm going to sit quiet under such a reproach?

DR. STOCKMANN. Unfortunately, you can't help it.

MORTEN KIIL. No, thank you. I hold fast to my good name. I've heard that people call me "the Badger." A badger's a sort of a pig, I know; but I'm determined to give them the lie. I will live and die a clean man.

DR. STOCKMANN. And how will you manage that?

MORTEN KIIL. You shall make me clean, Stockmann.

DR. STOCKMANN. I!

MORTEN KIIL. Do you know what money I've used to buy these shares with? No, you can't know; but now I'll tell you. It's the money Katrina and Petra and the boys are to have after my death. For, you see, I've laid by something after all.

DR. STOCKMANN (flaring up). And you've taken Katrina's money and done this with it!

MORTEN KIIL. Yes; the whole of it is invested in the Baths now. And now I want to see if you're really so stark, staring mad, after all, Stockmann. If you go on making out that these beasts and other abominations dribble down from my tannery, it'll be just as if you were to flay broad stripes of Katrina's skin — and Petra's too, and the boys'. No decent father would ever do that — unless he were a madman.

DR. STOCKMANN (walking up and down). Yes, but I am a madman; I am a madman!

MORTEN KIIL. You surely can't be so raving, ramping mad where your wife and children are concerned.

DR. STOCKMANN (stopping in front of him). Why couldn't you have spoken to me before you went and bought all that rubbish?

MORTEN KIIL. What's done can't be undone.

DR. STOCKMANN (walking restlessly about). If only I weren't so certain about the affair ——! But I am absolutely convinced that I'm right.

MORTEN KIIL (weighing the pocket-book in his hand). If you stick to this lunacy, these aren't worth much. (Puts the book into his pocket.)

DR. STOCKMANN. But, deuce take it! surely science ought to be able to hit upon some antidote, some sort of prophylactic ——

MORTEN KIIL. Do you mean something to kill the beasts?

DR. STOCKMANN. Yes, or at least to make them harmless.

MORTEN KIIL. Couldn't you try ratsbane?

DR. STOCKMANN. Oh, nonsense, nonsense! — But since everyone declares it's nothing but fancy, why fancy let it be! Let them have it their own way! Haven't the ignorant, narrow-hearted curs reviled me as an enemy of the people? — and weren't they on the point of tearing the clothes off my back?

MORTEN KIIL. And they've smashed all your windows for you too!

DR. STOCKMANN. Yes, and then there's one's duty to one's family! I must talk that over with Katrina; such things are more in her line.

MORTEN KIIL. That's right! You just follow the advice of a sensible woman.

DR. STOCKMANN (turning upon him angrily). How could you act so preposterously! Risking Katrina's money, and putting me to this horrible torture! When I look at you, I seem to see the devil himself ——!

MORTEN KIIL. Then I'd better be off. But I must hear from you, yes or no, by two o'clock. If it's no, all the shares go to the Hospital — and that this very day.

DR. STOCKMANN. And what will Katrina get?

MORTEN KIIL. Not a rap.

(*The door leading to the hall opens.* HOVSTAD *and* ASLAKSEN *are seen outside it.*)

MORTEN KIIL. Hullo! look at these two.

DR. STOCKMANN (staring at them). What! Do you actually venture to come here?

HOVSTAD. Why, to be sure we do.

ASLAKSEN. You see, we've something to discuss with you.

MORTEN KIIL (whispers). Yes or no — by two o'clock.

ASLAKSEN (with a glance at HOVSTAD). Aha!

(MORTEN KIIL goes out.)

DR. STOCKMANN. Well, what do you want with me? Be brief.

HOVSTAD. I can quite understand that you resent our attitude at the meeting yesterday ——

DR. STOCKMANN. Your attitude, you say? Yes, it was a pretty attitude! I call it the attitude of cowards — of old women —— Shame upon you!

HOVSTAD. Call it what you will; but we could not act otherwise.

DR. STOCKMANN. You dared not, I suppose? Isn't that so?

HOVSTAD. Yes, if you like to put it so.

ASLAKSEN. But why didn't you just say a word to us beforehand? The merest hint to Mr. Hovstad or to me ——

DR. STOCKMANN. A hint? What about?

ASLAKSEN. About what was really behind it all.

DR. STOCKMANN. I don't in the least understand you?

ASLAKSEN (nods confidentially). Oh, yes, you do, Dr. Stockmann.

HOVSTAD. It's no good making a mystery of it any longer.

DR. STOCKMANN (looking from one to the other). Why, what in the devil's name ——!

ASLAKSEN. May I ask — isn't your father-in-law going about the town buying up all the Bath stock?

DR. STOCKMANN. Yes, he has been buying Bath stock today but ——

ASLAKSEN. It would have been more prudent to let somebody else do that — someone not so closely connected with you.

HOVSTAD. And then you ought not to have appeared in the matter under your own name. No one need have known that the attack on the Baths came from you. You should have taken me into your counsels, Dr. Stockmann.

DR. STOCKMANN (stares straight in front of him; a light seems to break in upon him, and he says as though thunderstruck). Is this possible? Can such things be?

ASLAKSEN (smiling). It's plain enough that they can. But they ought to be managed delicately, you understand.

HOVSTAD. And there ought to be more people in it; for the responsibility always falls more lightly when there are several to share it.

DR. STOCKMANN (calmly). In one word, gentlemen — what is it you want?

ASLAKSEN. Mr. Hovstad can best ——

HOVSTAD. No, you explain, Aslaksen.

ASLAKSEN. Well, it's this: now that we know how the matter really stands, we believe we can venture to place the *People's Messenger* at your disposal.

DR. STOCKMANN. You can venture to now, eh? But how about public opinion? Aren't you afraid of bringing down a storm upon us?

HOVSTAD. We must manage to ride out the storm.

ASLAKSEN. And you must be ready to put about quickly, Doctor. As soon as your attack has done its work ——

DR. STOCKMANN. As soon as my father-in-law and I have bought up the shares at a discount, you mean?

HOVSTAD. I presume it is mainly on scientific grounds that you want to take the management of the Baths into your own hands.

DR. STOCKMANN. Of course; it was on scientific grounds that I got the old Badger to stand in with me. And then we'll tinker up the water-works a little, and potter about a bit down at the beach, without its costing the town sixpence. That ought to do the business? Eh?

HOVSTAD. I think so — if you have the *Messenger* to back you up.

ASLAKSEN. In a free community the press is a power, Doctor.

DR. STOCKMANN. Yes, indeed; and so is public opinion. And you, Mr. Aslaksen — I suppose you will answer for the House-owners' Association?

ASLAKSEN. Both for the House-owners' Association and the Temperance Society. You may make your mind easy.

DR. STOCKMANN. But, gentlemen — really I'm quite ashamed to mention such a thing — but — what return ——?

HOVSTAD. Of course, we should prefer to give you our support for nothing. But the *Messenger* is not very firmly established; it's not getting on as it ought to; and I should be very sorry to have to stop the paper just now, when there's so much to be done in general politics.

DR. STOCKMANN. Naturally; that would be very hard for a friend of the people like you. (*Flaring up.*) But I — I am an enemy of the people! (*Striding about the room.*) Where's my stick? Where the devil is my stick?

HOVSTAD. What do you mean?

ASLAKSEN. Surely you wouldn't ——

DR. STOCKMANN (*standing still*). And suppose I don't give you a single farthing out of all my shares? You must remember we rich folk don't like parting with our money.

HOVSTAD. And you must remember that this business of the shares can be represented in two ways.

DR. STOCKMANN. Yes, you are the man for that; if I don't come to the rescue of the *Messenger*, you'll manage to put a vile complexion on the affair; you'll hunt me down, I suppose — bait me — try to throttle me as a dog throttles a hare!

HOVSTAD. That's a law of nature — every animal fights for its own subsistence.

ASLAKSEN. And must take its food where it can find it, you know.

DR. STOCKMANN. Then see if you can't find some out in the gutter; (*Striding about the room*) for now, by heaven! we shall see which is the strongest animal of us three. (*Finds his umbrella and brandishes it.*) Now, look here ——!

HOVSTAD. You surely don't mean to assault us!

ASLAKSEN. I say, be careful with that umbrella.

DR. STOCKMANN. Out at the window with you, Mr. Hovstad!

HOVSTAD (*by the hall door*). Are you utterly crazy?

DR. STOCKMANN. Out at the window, Mr. Aslaksen! Jump, I tell you! Be quick about it!

ASLAKSEN (*running round the writing-table*). Moderation, Doctor; I'm not at all strong; I can't stand much —— (*Screams.*) Help! help!

MRS. STOCKMANN, PETRA, and HORSTER enter from sitting-room.

MRS. STOCKMANN. Good heavens, Thomas! What can be the matter?

DR. STOCKMANN (*brandishing the umbrella*). Jump, I tell you! Out into the gutter!

HOVSTAD. An unprovoked assault! I call you to witness, Captain Horster. (*Rushes off through the hall.*)

ASLAKSEN (*bewildered*). If one only knew the local situation ——![1]
(*He slinks out by the sitting-room door.*)

MRS. STOCKMANN (*holding back the* DOCTOR). Now, do restrain yourself, Thomas!

DR. STOCKMANN (*throwing down the umbrella*). I'll be hanged if they haven't got off after all.

---

[1] *De lokale forholde* — the local conditions, or the circumstances of the locality, a phrase constantly in Aslaksen's mouth in *The League of Youth.* In the present context it is about equivalent to "the lie of the land."

MRS. STOCKMANN. Why, what can they have wanted with you?

DR. STOCKMANN. I'll tell you afterwards; I have other things to think of now. (*Goes to the table and writes on a visiting-card.*) Look here, Katrina: what's written here?

MRS. STOCKMANN. Three big Noes; what does that mean?

DR. STOCKMANN. That I'll tell you afterwards, too. (*Handing the card.*) There, Petra; let smudgy-face run to the Badger's with this as fast as she can. Be quick!

(PETRA *goes out through the hall with the card.*)

DR. STOCKMANN. Well, if I haven't had visits today from all the emissaries of the devil! But now I'll sharpen my pen against them till it becomes a goad; I'll dip it in gall and venom; I'll hurl my inkstand straight at their skulls.

MRS. STOCKMANN. You forget we are going away, Thomas.

PETRA *returns.*

DR. STOCKMANN. Well?

PETRA. She has gone.

DR. STOCKMANN. Good. Going away, do you say? No, I'll be damned if we do; we stay where we are, Katrina!

PETRA. Stay!

MRS. STOCKMANN. Here in the town?

DR. STOCKMANN. Yes, here; the field of battle is here; here the fight must be fought; here I will conquer! As soon as my trousers are mended, I shall go out into the town and look for a house; we must have a roof over our heads for the winter.

HORSTER. That you can have in my house.

DR. STOCKMANN. Can I?

HORSTER. Yes, there's no difficulty about that. I have room enough, and I'm hardly ever at home myself.

MRS. STOCKMANN. Oh, how kind of you, Captain Horster.

PETRA. Thank you!

DR. STOCKMANN (*shaking his hand*). Thanks, thanks! So that is off my mind. And this very day I shall set to work in earnest. Oh, there's no end of work to be done here, Katrina! It's a good thing I shall have all my time at my disposal now; for you must know I've had notice from the Baths ——

MRS. STOCKMANN (*sighing*). Oh, yes, I was expecting that.

DR. STOCKMANN. —— And now they want to take away my practice as well. But let them! The poor I shall keep anyhow — those that can't pay; and, good Lord! it's they that need me most. But by heaven! I'll make them listen to me; I'll preach to them in season and out of season, as the saying goes.

MRS. STOCKMANN. My dear Thomas, I should have thought you had learnt what good preaching does.

DR. STOCKMANN. You really are absurd, Katrina. Am I to let myself be beaten off the field by public opinion, and the compact majority, and all that sort of devilry? No, thank you! Besides, my point is so simple, so clear and straightforward. I only want to drive it into the heads of these curs that the Liberals are the craftiest foes free men have to face; that party-programmes wring the necks of all young and living truths; that considerations of expediency turn justice and morality upside down, until life here becomes simply unlivable. Come, Captain Horster, don't you think I shall be able to make the people understand that?

HORSTER. Maybe; I don't know much about these things myself.

DR. STOCKMANN. Well, you see — this is the way of it! It's the party-leaders that must be exterminated. For a party-leader is just like a wolf, you see — like a ravening wolf; he must devour a certain number of smaller animals a year, if he's to exist at all. Just look at Hovstad and Aslaksen! How many small animals they polish off — or at least mangle and maim, so that they're fit for nothing else but to be house-owners and subscribers to the *People's Messenger!* (*Sits on the edge of the table.*) Just come here, Katrina — see how bravely the sun shines today! And how the blessëd fresh spring air blows in upon me!

MRS. STOCKMANN. Yes, if only we could live on sunshine and spring air, Thomas.

DR. STOCKMANN. Well, you'll have to pinch and save to eke them out — and then we shall get on all right. That's what troubles me least. No, what does trouble me is that I don't see any man free enough and high-minded enough to dare to take up my work after me.

PETRA. Oh, don't think about that father; you have time enough before you. — Why, see, there are the boys already.

EILIF *and* MORTEN *enter from the sitting-room.*

MRS. STOCKMANN. Have you a holiday today?

MORTEN. No; but we had a fight with the other fellows in play-time ——

EILIF. That's not true; it was the other fellows that fought us.

MORTEN. Yes, and then Mr. Rörlund said we had better stop at home for a few days.

DR. STOCKMANN (*snapping his fingers and springing down from the table*). Now I have it! Now I have it, on my soul! You shall never set foot in school again!

THE BOYS. Never go to school!

MRS. STOCKMANN. Why, Thomas ——

DR. STOCKMANN. Never, I say! I shall teach you myself — that's to say, I won't teach you any mortal thing ——

MORTEN. Hurrah!

DR. STOCKMANN. —— but I shall help you to grow into free, high-minded men. — Look here, you'll have to help me, Petra.

PETRA. Yes, father, you may be sure I will.

DR. STOCKMANN. And we'll have our school in the room where they reviled me as an enemy of the people. But we must have more pupils. I must have at least a dozen boys to begin with.

MRS. STOCKMANN. You'll never get them in this town.

DR. STOCKMANN. We shall see. (*To the boys.*) Don't you know any street urchins — any regular ragamuffins ——?

MORTEN. Yes, father, I know lots!

DR. STOCKMANN. That's all right; bring me a few of them. I shall experiment with the street-curs for once in a way; there are sometimes excellent heads amongst them.

MORTEN. But what are we to do when we've grown into free and high-minded men?

DR. STOCKMANN. Drive all the wolves out to the far west, boys!

(EILIF *looks rather doubtful;* MORTEN *jumps about shouting "Hurrah!"*)

MRS. STOCKMANN. If only the wolves don't drive you out, Thomas.

DR. STOCKMANN. Are you quite mad, Katrina! Drive me out! Now that I am the strongest man in the town?

MRS. STOCKMANN. The strongest — now?

DR. STOCKMANN. Yes, I venture to say this: that now I am one of the strongest men in the whole world.

MORTEN. I say, what fun!

DR. STOCKMANN (*in a subdued voice*). Hush; you mustn't speak about it yet; but I have made a great discovery.

MRS. STOCKMANN. What, another?

DR. STOCKMANN. Yes, of course! (*Gathers them about him, and speaks confidentially.*) This is what I have discovered, you see: the strongest man in the world is he who stands most alone.

MRS. STOCKMANN (*shakes her head, smiling*). Ah, Thomas dear ——!

PETRA (*grasping his hands cheerily*). Father!

THE SUNKEN BELL

A FAIRY PLAY IN FIVE ACTS

By GERHART HAUPTMANN

Translated by CHARLES HENRY MELTZER

CHARACTERS

HEINRICH, a *bell-founder*.
MAGDA, *his wife*.
TWO CHILDREN, *boys, aged* 5 *and* 9.
THE VICAR.
THE SCHOOLMASTER.
THE BARBER.
OLD WITTIKIN.
RAUTENDELEIN, *an elfin creature*.
THE NICKELMANN, *an elemental spirit*.
THE WOOD-SPRITE.
FOUR ELVES.
TROLDS AND DWARFS.
VILLAGERS.

The scenes are laid in the mountains and in a village below.

ACT ONE

SCENE: *A fir-clad glade in the mountains. R. up stage, beneath an over-hanging rock, a hut, with practicable door and windows. L. C. an old well.*

RAUTENDELEIN *is seated on the edge of the well, combing her thick golden locks and addressing a bee which she is trying to drive away. In one hand she has a mirror.*

RAUTENDELEIN. Thou buzzing, golden wight — whence com'st
 thou here?
Thou sipper of sweets, thou little wax-maker!
Nay! Tease me not, thou sun-born good-for-naught!
Dost hear?... Begone!... 'Tis time I combed my hair
With Granny's golden comb. Should I delay,
She'll scold me when she comes. Begone, I say!
What?... Loit'ring still?... Away — away with thee!
Am I a rose bush?... Are my lips a rose?
Off to the wood with thee, beyond the brook!
There, there, my pretty bee, bloom cowslips fair,
And crocuses, and violets — thou canst suck
Thy fill of them. Dost think I jest? No. No.
Quick! Get thee home. Thou'rt not in favor here.
Thou knowest Granny's cast a spell on thee
For furnishing the Church with altar-lights.
Come! Must I speak again? Go not too far!
Hey!... Chimney! Puff some smoke across the glade,
To drive away this naughty, wilful bee.
Ho! Gander! Hither! Hither!... Hurry! Hurry!
Away! Away! (*Bee flies off.*)... At last!...

  (RAUTENDELEIN *combs her hair quietly for a moment or two.
  Then, leaning over the well, she calls down.*)

            Hey! Nickelmann!
               (*Pause.*)

He does not hear me. Well — I'll sing to myself.
  Where do I come from?... Whither go?
  Tell me — I long to know!

Did I grow as the birds of the woodland gay?
Am I a fay?
Who asks the sweet flower
That blooms in the dell,
And brightens the bower,
Its tale to tell?
Yet, oft, as I sit by my well, alone,
I sigh for the mother I ne'er have known.
But my weird I must dree —
And I'm fair to see —
A golden-haired maid of the forest free!

(*Pause.   She calls.*)

Hey! Nickelmann! Come up! 'Tis lonely here.
Granny's gone gathering fir-apples. I'm dull!...
Wilt keep me company and tell me tales?
Why then, tonight, perhaps, as a reward...
I'll creep into some farmer's yard and steal
A big, black cock for thee!... Ah, here he comes.
The silver bubbles to the surface mount!
If he should bob up now, the glass he'd break,
That such bright answer to my nod doth make.

(*Admiring her reflection in the well.*)

Godden to thee, my sweet maid o' the well!
Thy name?... Rautendelein?... Indeed! I see —
Thou'rt jealous of my beauty. Look at me.
For I, not thou, Rautendelein should be.
What didst thou answer? Didst thou dare to point
Thy finger at thy soft twin-breasts?... Nay, nay —
I'm fairer; fair as Freya. Not for naught
My hair was spun out of the sunbeams red,
To shine, in golden glory, even as the sun
Shines up at us, at noon, from out a lake.
Aha! Thou spread'st thy tresses, like a net,
All fiery-scarlet, set to catch the fishes!
Thou poor, vain, foolish, trull... There! Catch this stone.

(*Throwing pebble down the well and disturbing the reflection.*)

Thy hour is ended. Now — I'm fair alone!

Ho! Nickelmann! Come — help me pass the time! (*Calling.*)

(*The* NICKELMANN, *a water-spirit, half emerges from the well, and flops over the edge. He is streaming with water. Weeds cling to his head. He snorts like a seal, and his eyes blink as if the daylight hurt them.*)

He's here!... Ha! Ha! Ha! Ha! How dreadfully plain
He is!... Didst thou not hear me call? Dear, dear —
It makes one's flesh creep but to know him near!

THE NICKELMANN (*croaking*). Brekekekex!

RAUTENDELEIN (*mocking*). Brekekekex! Ay, ay —
It smells of springtide. Well, is that so strange?
Why — every lizard, mole, and worm, and mouse —
The veriest water-rat — had scented that.
The quail, the hare, the trout, the fly, the weeds,
Had told thee Spring was here.

THE NICKELMANN (*touchily*). Brekekekex!
Be not too nosey-wise. Dost understand?
Thou ape, thou midge, thou tomtit, irk me not!
I say, beware!... So, Quorax! Quack! Quack! Quack!

RAUTENDELEIN. If Master Uncle's cross today,
              I'll leave him all alone to play.
              And I'll go dance a ring-a-round.
              Partners a-plenty, I'll be bound,
              For pretty maidens may be found.

(*Calling.*) Heigh-a-aye!

Voice of WOOD-SPRITE (*heard without*). Heigh-a-o!

RAUTENDELEIN. My merry faun, come — dance with me, I pray!

(*Enter the* WOOD-SPRITE, *skipping comically across the glade.*)

THE WOOD-SPRITE. Nay, I'm no dancer; but I know a leap
Would make the mountain-goat with envy weep.
If that won't do for thee, I know a game
Will please thee more, my nixey. Fly with me;
I'll show thee in the woods a willow tree
All hollowed out with age, where never came
The sound of babbling brook, nor crow of cock.
There, in the shadow of some friendly rock,
I'll cut for thee, my own, the wond'rous pipe
All maids must dance to.

RAUTENDELEIN (*eluding him*).   Thanks, I'm not yet ripe
  For such as thou!   An thou must play thy pranks,
  Go — woo thy wood-wench.   She may like thy shanks!
  Or — go to thy dear partner, who — they say —
  Another baby bears thee every day;
  Except on Sundays, when, at early morn,
  Three dirty little brats to thee are born!
  Ha! Ha! Ha!
      (*She runs off into the hut, laughing.   The* WOOD-SPRITE *vainly
      pursues her and returns disconsolate.*)
THE NICKELMANN. Brekekekex! How mad the baggage seems!
  The lightning blast thee!
THE WOOD-SPRITE (*sitting*). Ay!... I'd love to tame her.
      (*He produces a short pipe and lights it by striking a match on his
      hoof.*)
THE NICKELMANN. And how go things at home?
THE WOOD-SPRITE. So so. So so.
  It's warmer here than on the hills.   You're snug.
  Up yonder the wind shrieks and howls all day;
  The swollen clouds drift damp about the peaks,
  And burst at last, like sponges, when they're squeezed.
  A foul time we have of it!
THE NICKELMANN. And is that all?
THE WOOD-SPRITE. No... Yesterday I cut
                My first spring salad.   It grew near my hut.
                This morning, early, I went out,
                And, roaming carelessly about,
                Through brush and brier,
                Then climbing higher,
                At last I reached the topmost wood.
                There I espied a hateful brood
                Of mortals, who did sweat and stew,
                And dig the earth, and marble hew.
                A curse upon their church and creed —
                Their chapels, and their clanging bells [1] —

---

[1] The sprites and dwarfs hated bells, especially church bells, as disturbers of their ancient privacy.

THE NICKELMANN. Their bread they mix with cummin-seed![1]

THE WOOD-SPRITE. They plague us in our woods and wells.

But vain is all our wrath and woe.
Beside the deep abyss 'twill grow
With tower and spire, and, overhead,
The cross that you and I do dread.
Ay!... The noisy monster was all but hung
In the lofty steeple, and soon had rung.
But I was alert! We shall never hear
That bell! It is drowned in the mere!
By cock and pie!   *(Changing tone.)*
A devil of a joke!... I stood on the brink
Of the cliff, chewing sorrel, to help me think,
As I rested against a stump of birch,
'Mid the mountain grasses, I watched the church.
When, all of a sudden, I saw the wing
Of a blood-red butterfly, trying to cling
To a stone. And I marked how it dipped, and tipped,
As if from a blossom the sweet it sipped.
I called. It fluttered, to left and to right,
Until on my hand I felt it light.
I knew the elf. It was faint with fright.
We babbled o' this,
And we babbled o' that,
Of the frogs that had spawned
Ere the day had dawned, —
We babbled and gabbled, a-much, I wis:
Then it broke
Into tears!...
I calmed its fears.
And again it spoke.
"O, they're cracking their whips,
And they gee! and they whoa!
As they drag it aloft
From the dale below.
'Tis some terrible tub, that has lost its lid,
All of iron! Will nobody rid

---

[1] Cummin-seed was obnoxious to the sprites.

Our woods of the horrible thing? 'Twould make
The bravest moss-mannikin shudder and quake.
They swear they will hang it, these foolish people,
High up in the heart of the new church steeple,
And they'll hammer, and bang, at its sides all day
To frighten good spirits of earth away!"

I hummed, and I hawed, and I said, ho, ho!
As the butterfly fell to the earth: while I
Stole off in pursuit of a herd near by.
I guzzled my fill of good milk, I trow!
Three udders ran dry. They will seek in vain
So much as a drop of it more to drain.
Then, making my way to a swirling stream,
I hid in the brush, as a sturdy team
Came snorting, and panting, along the road —
Eight nags, tugging hard at their heavy load.
We will bide our time, quoth I — and lay
Quite still in the grass, till the mighty dray
Rumbled by: — when, stealing from hedge to hedge,
And hopping and skipping from rock to rock,
I followed the fools. They had reached the edge
Of the cliff when there came — a block!
With flanks all a-quiver, and hocks a-thrill,
They hauled and they lugged at the dray until,
Worn out by the struggle to move the bell,
They had to lie down for a moment. Well —
Quoth I to myself, the Faun will play
Them a trick that will spare them more work today.
One clutch at the wheel — I had loosened a spoke —
A wrench, and a blow, and the wood-work broke.
A wobble, a crack, and the hateful bell
Rolled over — and into the gulf it fell!
And oh, how it sounded,
And clanged, as it bounded,
From crag to crag, on its downward way:
Till at last in the welcoming splash and the spray
Of the lake it was lost — for aye!

(During the WOOD-SPRITE'S *speech night has drawn near. It is now
dusk. Several times, towards the end of the narrative, faint cries for
help have been heard, coming from the wood. Enter from back,* HEINRICH.
As he approaches the hut, the WOOD-SPRITE *vanishes in the wood and
the* NICKELMANN *disappears in the well.* HEINRICH *is about thirty
years of age. His face is pale and careworn.)*

HEINRICH. Good people — open! Quick! I've lost my way!
　Help! Help! I've fallen!... I am weak... I faint!
　Will no one answer?... Help! Kind people! Help!

　　　*(He sinks on the ground, unconscious, near the hut. The sun has set
　　　— dark purple clouds hang over the hills. The wind rises.)*

(Enter from the wood, carrying a basket on her back, OLD WITTIKIN.)

WITTIKIN. Rautendel'! Come and help me with my load!
　I've too much on my shoulders. Come, I say!
　I'm scant o' breath!... Where can the girl be dawdling?

　　　　　　　　　　　　(A bat flies across the glade.)

　Ho! Stop thy gadding, flitter-mouse, and list!
　Thou'lt fill thy greedy craw quite soon enough.
　Come hither. Fly through yonder hole and see
　If she's within. Then send her quick to me!

　　　　　(Faint lightning. WITTIKIN *shakes her fist at the sky.)*

　Ay, ay, I see thee, Father Thor!... 'Twill storm!
　But give thy noisy goats not too much rope,
　And see thy great red beard gleams not too bright.
　Rautendel'! Hey! Rautendel'... Dost not hear?

　　　　　　　　　　　(A squirrel skips across the path.)

　Hey! Squirrel! Thou hast fleet and nimble feet.
　Hop thou into the hut, and, shouldst thou meet
　Rautendel', send her hither. As a treat,
　I'll give thee, for thy pains, a nut to eat!

　　　*(*WITTIKIN *sees* HEINRICH *and touches him contemptuously with
　　　her foot.)*

　What's this? A stranger? Well, well, I declare!
　And pray, what brings you here, my man, so late?
　Rautendel'!... Hey! Rautendel'! *(To* HEINRICH*).* Are you
　　dead?
　Plague take you! As if I'd not more'n enough

To worry me — what wi' the Bailiff and the Priest
Hunting me down like a mad dog. And now
I find a dead man at my door — Rautendel'!
A rare time I'd have of it, I'll be bound,
If they should find this fellow lying here.
They'd burn my house about my ears. (*To* HEINRICH.) Art
    dumb?
Ay. Ay.

    (RAUTENDELEIN *enters from hut, and looks out inquiringly.*)

            Oho! Thou'rt come at last. Look there!
We have a visitor. And what a one!
He's still enough. Go! Fetch a truss of hay,
And make a litter.
RAUTENDELEIN.   In the hut?
WITTIKIN (*grumbling*).   What next?
Nay, nay. We've no room in the hut for him.
    (*Exit into hut.* RAUTENDELEIN *follows her. She reappears a
        moment later, with an armful of hay, and is about to kneel beside
        HEINRICH, when he recovers consciousness.*)
HEINRICH. Where am I? Maiden — wilt thou answer me?
RAUTENDELEIN. Why, in the mountains.
HEINRICH.   In the mountains? Ay—
But how... and why? What brought me here tonight?
RAUTENDELEIN. Nay, gentle stranger, naught know I of that.
Why fret thyself about such trifles? See —
Here I have brought thee hay. So lay thy head
Down and take all the rest thou need'st.
HEINRICH.   Yes! Yes!
'Tis rest I need. Indeed — indeed — thou'rt right.
But rest will come to me no more, my child!
Now... tell me... what has happened?   (*Uneasily.*)
RAUTENDELEIN.   Nay, if I knew...
HEINRICH. Meseems... methinks... and... then... all ends in
    dreams.
Ay, surely, I am dreaming.
RAUTENDELEIN.   Here is milk.
Thou must drink some of it, for thou art weak.

HEINRICH (*eagerly*). Thanks, maiden. I will drink. Give me the milk.

(*He drinks from a bowl which she offers him.*)

RAUTENDELEIN (*while he drinks*). Thou art not used to mountain
    ways. Thy home

Lies in the vale below, where mortals dwell.

And, like a hunter who once fell from the cliff

While giving chase to some wild mountain fowl,

Thou hast climbed far too high. And yet... that man

Was not quite fashioned as the man thou art.

HEINRICH (*after drinking and looking ecstatically and fixedly at* RAU-
TENDELEIN). Speak on! Speak on! Thy drink was very sweet.
But sweeter still thy voice...

(*Again becoming anxious.*)

                    She said — a man

Not fashioned like myself. A better man —

And yet he fell!... Speak on, my child.

RAUTENDELEIN.   Why speak?

What can my words avail? I'll rather go

And fetch thee water from the brook, to wash

The blood and dust from off thy brow...

HEINRICH (*pleading and grasping her by the wrist.* RAUTENDELEIN
stands undecided).   Ah, stay!

And look into mine eyes with thy strange eyes.

For lo, the world, within thine eyes renewed,

So sweetly bedded, draws me back to life!

Stay, child. O stay!

RAUTENDELEIN (*uneasy*). Then... as thou wilt. And yet...

HEINRICH (*fevered and imploring*). Ah, stay with me! Thou wilt not
    leave me so?

Thou dost not dream how dear to me thou art.

O, wake me not, my child. I'll tell thee all.

I fell... Yet — no. Speak thou; for thy dear voice

Has Heaven's own music. God did give it thee.

And I will listen. Speak!... Wilt thou not speak?

Wilt thou not sing to me? Why then... I must...

I fell. I know not how — I've told thee that —

Whether the path gave way beneath my feet;

Whether 'twas willingly I fell, or no —

God wot.   Enough.   I fell into the gulf.
And then I clutched at a wild cherry tree
That grew between the rocks.   It broke — and I,   (*More fevered.*)
Still clasping a bough tightly, felt a shower
Of pale pink blossoms riot round my head;
Then swift was hurled to the abyss — and died!
And even now I'm dead.   It must be so.
Let no one wake me!

RAUTENDELEIN (*uncertainly*).   Yet thou seem'st alive!

HEINRICH.   I know — I know — what once I did not know:
That Life is Death, and only Death is Life.
I fell.   I lived — and fell.   The bell fell, too!   (*Collapsing again.*)
We two — the bell and I.   Was I the first —
To slip, and next — the bell?   Or — the reverse?
Who seeks to know?   And who could prove the truth?
And even were it proven, what care I?
Then I was living.   Now — ah, now... I'm dead.
Ah, go not yet!
        (*Tenderly.*)   My hand!... 'Tis white as milk!   (*Looks at his hand.*)
My hand!... It hangs so heavy!... It seems dead.
I cannot lift it!... Yet —   How sweet thou art!
The mere touch of thy soft hair doth bring relief,
As water of Bethesda!... Nay, do not fear!
My hand shall never harm thee — thou art holy!
Where have we met?... I surely know thy face.
Somewhere, but where, or when, I cannot tell,
I wrought for thee, and strove — in one grand Bell,
To wed the silver music of thy voice
With the warm gold of a Sun-holiday.
It should have been a master-work!... I failed.
Then wept I tears of blood.

RAUTENDELEIN.   Wept tears of blood?
I cannot follow thee.   What be these tears?

HEINRICH (*trying to raise his head*).   Thou lovely picture!... Help me
        to sit up.   (RAUTENDELEIN *stoops and supports his head.*)
Dost thou bend down to me?   Then, with love's arms,
Do thou release me from this cruel Earth,
Whereunto the hour nails me, as to a cross.

Release me! For thou canst. I know thou canst!
And, with thy tender hands, pluck off the thorns
That crown my head. No crown! Love — only Love!
(His head is slightly raised. He seems exhausted.)
Thanks! Thanks!
(Gently and in a lost kind of way as he looks at the landscape.)
Here all is beautiful! The rustling boughs
Have such a strange, full sound. The darkling arms
Of the great firs move so mysteriously.
How solemnly their heads sway to and fro!
The very soul of fairy fantasy
Sighs through the wood. It murmurs low, and then,
Still gently whisp'ring, stirs the tiny leaves.
Now it goes singing through the green wood-grass.
And now, veiled all in misty white, it nears —
It stretches out its long white hand and points
At me!... Now closer, it draws! It touches my ear...
My tongue... my eyes!... 'Tis gone! Yet thou art here!
Thou art my fantasy!... Kiss me, sweet fantasy! *(He faints.)*

RAUTENDELEIN *(half to herself)*. Thy speech is strange. I know not
what to make of 't. *(She suddenly resolves to go.)*
Lie thou, and sleep.

HEINRICH *(dreaming)*. Kiss me, sweet fantasy!

*(RAUTENDELEIN stops, and gazes at HEINRICH. The darkness
deepens. RAUTENDELEIN suddenly grows frightened and calls.)*

RAUTENDELEIN. O, grandmother!

WITTIKIN *(from within the hut)*. Well, girl?

RAUTENDELEIN. Come here! Come here!

WITTIKIN *(as above)*. Nay, come thou here, and help me make the
fire!

RAUTENDELEIN. O, Granny!

WITTIKIN. Hark'ee, wench. Dost hear me?
Come.
'Tis time we fed the goat. And then to milk it!

RAUTENDELEIN. Grandmother! Help him! Help him! He is
dying!

(Enter from hut, WITTIKIN. *She stands on the threshold, holding a milk pail in her left hand, and calls to her cat.)*

WITTIKIN. Here! Puss, Puss, Puss!

(*She looks carelessly at* HEINRICH.)

He hasn't budged, I see.

Well — mortals all must die. No help for it.
What matter? Let him be. He's better so.
Come — pussy! pussy!... Here is milk for thee —
Why, where is pussy?
Hurry, hurry, wood-folk, when I call! (*Calling.*)
Here, I've milk a-plenty for ye all!
Hurry, hurry, hurry, trold and sprite!

(Enter ten droll little TROLDS, *male and female. They bustle about the milk pail.)*

Here is bread — for everyone a bite!
Here's enough to drink, and here's to eat:
Food that dukes and earls 'ud count a treat.
Thou, go! (*To one of the* TROLDS.)
Thou art full, I trow.
For thee a sop — (*To the other* TROLDS.)
And for thee a drop —
Now enough ye've guzzled,
And off ye hop!
I'll have ye muzzled, (*They riot and shout.*)
Unless ye stop!
Nay this won't do —
Ye riotous crew!
Enough for today!
Away! Away!

(*The* TROLDS *vanish into the wood. Moonlight. The* WOOD-SPRITE *appears, seated on the rocks beyond the hut. Putting his horny hands to his mouth, he imitates the echo of a cry for help.*)

THE WOOD-SPRITE. Help! Help!

WITTIKIN. Why, what's amiss?

DISTANT VOICES (*from the wood*). Heinrich! Heinrich!

THE WOOD-SPRITE (*as above*). Help! Help!

WITTIKIN (*threateningly to the* WOOD-SPRITE). Fool, thy knavish
   antics cease!
  Leave our mountain-folk in peace!
  Ay, ay. It pleases thee to vent thy spite
  On the poor glass-workers!... Thou lov'st to bite
  Stray dogs — to lead lost travelers into fogs,
  And see them floundering in the moorland bogs.
THE WOOD-SPRITE. Granny, never heed my jests.
  Soon thou shalt have noble guests!
  Who rides on the goose's down?
  The barber, light as lather.
  Who rides on the goose's crown?
  The parson, reverend father —
  The teacher, with his cue —
  Three screech-owls — all for you!
THE VOICES (*nearer*). Heinrich!
THE WOOD-SPRITE (*as before*). Help!
WITTIKIN. Now may the lightning strike thee!
  Wouldst hang a schoolmaster about my neck,
  And eke a parson?

                    (*Shaking her fist at the* WOOD-SPRITE.)
        Thou shalt smart for this.
  I'll send thee swarming gnats, and stinging flies,
  To plague thee till thou shalt be so distraught
  Thou'lt long to hide thyself.
THE WOOD-SPRITE (*with malignant glee*). They're coming, Granny!
                          (*He disappears.*)
WITTIKIN. Well, and what then? They're no concern o' mine.
      (*To* RAUTENDELEIN, *who is gazing fixedly at* HEINRICH.)
  Into the hut! Blow out the light! To bed!
  Quick, wench!
RAUTENDELEIN (*sullen and defiant*). I won't!
WITTIKIN.   What? Disobey me?
RAUTENDELEIN.   Yes!
WITTIKIN. And why?
RAUTENDELEIN.   They'll take him from me.
WITTIKIN.   Well? What of 't?
RAUTENDELEIN. They must not take him, Granny!

WITTIKIN.   Girl, ha' done!
  And let them deal wi' him as they may list.
  Dust will to dust, and some day he must die.
  So let him die.   He'll be the better for 't.
  See how life irks him, how it rends his heart,
  Wi' pain and agony.

HEINRICH (*dreaming*).   The sun sets fast!

WITTIKIN. He never saw the Sun, girl! Let him be.
  Come.   Follow me.   Be warned, or thou wilt rue!
            (*Exit into hut.   Cries of "Heinrich! Heinrich!"   RAUTENLE-
            LEIN listens for a moment.   Then she suddenly breaks a flowery
            twig from a bough, and draws a circle with it round HEINRICH as
            she speaks the following lines.*)

RAUTENDELEIN. With the first fresh buds of Spring,
                  Lo, I draw the magic ring!
                  Safe from every harm and ill,
                  Thus thou art.   It is my will!
                  Thou art thine, and thine, and mine!
                  None may cross the mystic line!
                  Be thou youth, or man, or maid,
                  Here thou surely must be stayed!
                            (*She hides behind the trees in shadow.*)

(*Enter one after the other, from the wood, the* VICAR, *the* BARBER, *and the*
                  SCHOOLMASTER.)

THE VICAR. I see a light.

THE SCHOOLMASTER.   And I!

THE VICAR.   Where are we now?

THE BARBER. God only knows.   Again I hear that cry
  Of "Help! Help! Help!"

THE VICAR.   It is the Master's voice!

THE SCHOOLMASTER. I heard no cry.

THE BARBER.   It came from yonder height.

THE SCHOOLMASTER. If one fell up to Heaven, that might be,
  But, as a general rule, one tumbles — down:
  From cliff to vale, and not from vale to cliff.
  The Master lies — I'd stake my soul upon 't —
  Full fifty fathoms deeper: not up here.

THE BARBER. Ods bodikins!   Did you not hear him then?
  If that was not the voice of Master Heinrich,
  May I be set to shave old Rübezahl!
  As I'm a living barber, I will swear
  I heard a cry.
THE SCHOOLMASTER. Where from?
THE VICAR.   What place is this?
  Ere we continue, tell me that, my friends.
  My face is bleeding; I can hardly drag
  One foot after another.   How they do ache!
  I'll go no further.
VOICE.   Help!
THE VICAR.   Again that voice!
THE BARBER. And this time it was close to where we stand!
THE VICAR (*sitting wearily*). I'm racked with pain.   Indeed, my
        worthy friends,
  I can no more.   So leave me, in God's name.
  In truth, though you should beat me black and blue,
  You could not make me budge another step.
  I am worn out.   Alack, that this glad day
  Should end so sadly!   Who had ever thought
  Such things could happen!   And the mighty bell —
  The noblest of the Master's master-works ——!
  Thy ways, O Lord, indeed pass finding out
  And are most wonderful!
THE BARBER.   Ay, Father, ay.
  And do you wish to know what place this be?
  Well, I will tell you.   If you'll be advised,
  You'll get from hence — and that without delay.
  'Twere better far we spent the livelong night
  Bare-backed, and in a hornet's nest, than here.
  For, by the Lord, we're on the Silver Hill!
  Within a hundred steps should stand the house
  Of that accursèd witch.   So — let's away!
THE VICAR. I cannot budge.
THE SCHOOLMASTER.   Nay, come, I pray you, come.
  Worse things than witches are encountered here.
  If they were all, I should not turn a hair.

Ah, there's no wilder spot for leagues around —
A paradise of smugglers, thieves, and rogues —
A trysting-place for cut-throat murderers —
So infamous that Peter, — he who longed
To know what fear and trembling meant — might learn
Both easily — if he but came this way.

THE BARBER. Yes. One and one make two — we all know
          that.
But that is not the only thing worth knowing.
I hope, my master, you may never learn
What witchcraft means!... The hellish sluts who lurk,
Like toads in a hole, hatching their evil plots,
May send you illnesses, and plague your ox,
Make blood flow from the udders of your cows
Instead of milk, and rot your sheep with worms —
Or curse your children with unwholesome wens,
And horrible ulcers. All this they can do.

THE SCHOOLMASTER. You're wandering, Sirs. The night has
          turned your heads.
While you go babbling here of witches' games,
Your ears grow dull. Heard you not moans? By Heaven!
I see the very man we seek!

THE VICAR.   See whom?

THE SCHOOLMASTER. Why, Master Heinrich.

THE BARBER.   O, he's lost his wits!

THE VICAR. 'Twas witchcraft.

THE SCHOOLMASTER.   Nay, then two and two's not four,
But five. And that's impossible. Prate not
Of witches. For, as I do hope for Heaven,
There lies the master bell-founder himself!
Look! Now the clouds have ceased to hide the moon.
Look, gentlemen! Now! Now! Well — was I right?

THE VICAR. Indeed you were, my master.

THE BARBER.   'Tis the bell-founder!

          (*All three hurry towards* HEINRICH, *but recoil on reaching the edge
              of the magic ring.*)

THE VICAR. Oh!

THE BARBER.   Oh!

THE SCHOOLMASTER.   Oh! Oh!

RAUTENDELEIN (*becoming visible for a moment among the trees*).   Ha!
Ha! Ha! Ha! Ha! Ha!

(*She vanishes amid peals of mocking laughter. A pause.*)

THE SCHOOLMASTER (*bewildered*).   What was it?

THE BARBER.   Ay.   What was 't?

THE VICAR.   I heard a laugh!

THE SCHOOLMASTER. The bright light dazzled me.   I do believe
It's made a hole in my head as big as my fist.

THE VICAR. You heard the laughter?

THE BARBER.   Ay, and something cracked.

THE VICAR. The laughter seemed to come from every pine
That rustles round us in the growing gloom.
There!   Yonder!   Where the horn-owl hoots and flies!

THE BARBER. Didn't I tell you of these devilish folk?
O Lord, O Lord!   I warned you of their spells.
D'ye think we're safe here?   As for me, I quake —
My flesh creeps.   Curses on the hag, say I!

THE VICAR (*raising the crucifix which hangs round his neck, and moving
steadfastly towards the hut*).   You may be right.   Yet, though
the Devil himself
Dwelt here, I'd still say: Courage!   On!
Against him we will pit God's Holy Word!
Ah! never yet was Satan's craft more clear
Than when he hurled the Master and the bell
To death — God's servant and his instrument —
The bell that, from the edge of the abyss
Had sung the hymn of everlasting Love,
And Peace, and Mercy, through the firmament!
Here stand we as true soldiers of the Lord!
I'll knock!

THE BARBER. D—d—don't risk it!

THE VICAR.   Yes! I say, I'll knock!

(*He knocks at the door of the hut.*)

WITTIKIN (*from within the hut*). Who's there?

THE VICAR.   A Christian!

WITTIKIN.   Christian or no Christian,
What d'you want?

THE VICAR.   Open!

WITTIKIN (*appearing in the doorway carrying a lighted lantern*).   Well?
  What's your will?

THE VICAR.   In God's name, woman, whom thou dost not
  know ——

WITTIKIN.   Oho!   A pious opening, I declare!

THE SCHOOLMASTER.   Thou carrion-crow, how durst thou wag thy
  tongue?

The measure's full — thy time is meted out.

Thy evil life and thy accursèd deeds

Have made thee hated through the countryside.

So — an thou do not now as thou art bid —

Ere dawn the red cock [1] from thy roof shall crow —

Thy den of thieves shall flame and smoke to Heaven!

THE BARBER (*crossing himself repeatedly*).   Thou wicked cat!   I'm
  not afraid of thee!

Ay — scowl, and glare, and glower, as thou wilt!

Though thy red eyes should light upon my corpse,

They'll find the Cross before them.   Do as thou'rt bid!

THE VICAR.   I charge thee, woman, in God's holy name,

Have done with all thy devilish juggleries,

And help this man!   Here lies a child of God,

A Master, gifted with a wondrous art

That him doth honor, while it puts to shame

The damnèd companies of air and Hell.

WITTIKIN (*who has been prowling round* HEINRICH *with her lantern*)。

And what's all that to do wi' me?   Enough!

You're welcome to the creature.   Take him hence.

What harm did I to him?   For aught I care,

He may live on, till he has spent his breath.

I'll wager that won't be so very long!

Ye name him "Master," and ye love the sound

O' the big iron bells the creature makes.

Ye all are hard o' hearin', or ye'd know

There's no good in his bells.   He knows it, too.

Ah, I could tell ye, an' I would, what's wrong.

---

[1] In Germany "der rothe Hahn" is a symbol of incendiarism.

The best and worst o' them ring false. They're cracked.
There! Take the litter. Bear the man away —
The "Master," as ye call him! Master Milksop!

(*To* HEINRICH.)

Get up! Go home and help the parson preach!
Go — help the schoolmaster to birch his boys —
Go — mix the lather in the barber's shop!

(*The* BARBER *and the* SCHOOLMASTER *lift* HEINRICH *onto the litter.*)

THE VICAR. Thou wicked, scolding hag! Restrain thy tongue!
Thy way shall lead thee straight to Hell. Begone!

WITTIKIN. O, spare your sermons. I ha' heard ye preach.
I know, I know. 'Tis sinful to ha' senses.
The earth's a coffin, and the Heavens above
Are but a coffin-lid. The stars are holes;
The sun's a bigger hole in the blue sky.
The world 'ud come to grief wi'out the priests,
And God himself ye'd make a bug-a-boo!
The Lord should take a rod to ye — poor fools!
Ay, fools are ye — all, all! and nothing more!

(*She bangs open her door and goes into hut.*)

THE VICAR. Thou beldame!

THE BARBER.   For Heaven's sake — don't vex her more!
If you should goad her further, we are lost.

(*Exeunt the* VICAR, *the* SCHOOLMASTER, *and the* BARBER *into the wood, bearing away* HEINRICH *on the litter. The moon shines out, and lights up the peaceful landscape. FIRST, SECOND, and THIRD ELVES steal out of the wood one after the other and join hands in a dance.*)

FIRST ELF (*whispering*). Sister!

SECOND ELF (*as above*).   Sister!

FIRST ELF (*as above*).   White and chill
        Shines the moon across the hill.
        Over bank, and over brae,
        Queen she is, and Queen shall stay.

SECOND ELF. Whence com'st thou?

FIRST ELF.   From where the light
        In the waterfall gleams bright,

Where the glowing flood doth leap,
Roaring, down into the deep.
Then, from out the mirk and mist,
Where the foaming torrent hissed,
Past the dripping rocks and spray,
Up I swiftly made my way.

THIRD ELF (*joining them*). Sisters, is it here ye dance?

FIRST ELF. Wouldst thou join us? Quick — advance!

SECOND ELF. And whence com'st thou?

THIRD ELF.   Hark and hist!
Dance, and dance, as ye may list!
'Mid the rocky peaks forlorn
Lies the lake where I was born.
Starry gems are mirrored clear
On the face of that dark mere.
Ere the fickle moon could wane,
Up I swept my silver train.
Where the mountain breezes sigh,
Over clove and crag came I!

FOURTH ELF (*entering*). Sisters!

FIRST ELF.   Sister! Join the round!

ALL (*together*). Ring-a-ring-a-ring-around!

FOURTH ELF. From Dame Holle's flowery brae,
Secretly I stole away.

FIRST ELF. Wind and wander, in and out!

ALL (*together*). Ring-a-ring-a-round-about!

                          (*Lightning and distant thunder.*)

(*Enter suddenly, from the hut,* RAUTENDELEIN. *Clasping her hands
behind her head, she watches the dance from the doorway. The moonlight falls full on her.*)

RAUTENDELEIN. Ho, my fairies!

FIRST ELF. Hark! A cry!

SECOND ELF. Owch! My dress is all awry!

RAUTENDELEIN. Ho, ye fairies!

THIRD ELF.   O, my gown!
Flit and flutter, up and down.

RAUTENDELEIN (*joining in the dance*).

> Let me join the merry round.
> Ring-a-ring-a-ring-around!
> Silver nixey, sweetest maid,
> See how richly I'm arrayed.
> All of silver, white and rare,
> Granny wove my dress so fair.
> Thou, my fairy brown, I vow,
> Browner far am I than thou.
> And, my golden sister fair,
> I can match thee with my hair,
> Now I toss it high — behold,
> Thou hast surely no such gold.
> Now it tumbles o'er my face:
> Who can rival me in grace?

ALL (*together*).

> Wind and wander, in and out,
> Ring-a-ring-a-round-about!

RAUTENDELEIN.

> Into the gulf there fell a bell.
> Where is it lying?   Will ye tell?

ALL (*together*).

> Wind and wander, in and out,
> Ring-a-ring-a-round-about!
> Daisy and forget-me-not,
> Fairy footsteps injure not.

(*Enter the* WOOD-SPRITE, *skipping.   Thunder — this time louder.   During the following speech, a storm rages — thunder and hail.*)

THE WOOD-SPRITE.

> Daisy and forget-me-not
> Crush I in the earth to rot.
> If the moorland's all a-drip
> 'Tis because I leap, and skip!
> Now the bull doth seek his mate,
> Bellows at the stable gate.
> And the heifer, sleeping by,
> Lifts her head and lows reply.

On the stallion's warm brown hide
Every fly doth seek his bride,
While the midges dance above,
Fill the air with life and love.
See!   The ostler woos the maid!
Buss her, fool!   Dost fear the jade?
With the rotting straw for bed,
Soft and tender, lo they wed!
Hul'lo!   Hul'lo!   Heigh-o-hey!
Whisp'ring's over for today.
Done the dancing, hushed and chill,
Lusty life is master still!
Be it early, be it late,
Mews the tom-cat, mews its mate.
Nightingale, and thrush, and stork,
Hart, and hare, and hen, and hawk,
Snipe, and quail, and swan, and duck,
Crane, and pheasant, doe and buck,
Beetle, moth, and mole, and louse,
Toad, and frog, and bat, and mouse,
Bee, and gnat, and moth, and fly —
All must love, and all must die!

(*The* WOOD-SPRITE *snatches up one of the* ELVES *and carries her off into the wood.   The three other* ELVES *vanish in different directions.*   RAUTENDELEIN *remains standing alone and sad, in the middle of the glade.   The storm gradually dies away.*)

(*The* NICKELMANN *rises from the well, as before.*)

THE NICKELMANN. Brekekekex! — Brekekekex!   Hey!   Ho!
Why dost thou stand there?

RAUTENDELEIN.   Thou dear water-sprite —
Alas, I am so sad.   So sad am I!

THE NICKELMANN (*mockingly*). Brekekekex!   And which eye hurts
        thee, dear?

RAUTENDELEIN (*gaily*). The left eye.   But, perhaps, thou think'st I
        jest?

THE NICKELMANN. Ay, surely, surely.

RAUTENDELEIN (*pointing to a tear in her eye*).   Look — what can it be?

THE NICKELMANN. What dost thou mean?

RAUTENDELEIN.   Why — see what's in my eye!

THE NICKELMANN. What's in thine eye? Come — let me see it close.

RAUTENDELEIN. A warm, wet drop has fallen on my lid.

THE NICKELMANN. The deuce it has! Come nearer — let me see.

RAUTENDELEIN (*holding out the tear to him*). A tiny, pure, warm, glitt'ring, drop of dew.

There, only see!

THE NICKELMANN. By Heaven! 'Tis beautiful.

How would it please thee an I took the thing
And set it in a fine, pink shell for thee?

RAUTENDELEIN. Why, as thou wilt. I'll lay it on the edge
Of the well. What can it be?

THE NICKELMANN. A wondrous gem!

Within that little globe lies all the pain,
And all the joy the world can ever know.

'Tis called — a tear!

RAUTENDELEIN. A tear!... I must have wept.

So now at last I've learned what these tears be...
O, tell me something!

THE NICKELMANN. Come to me, dear child!

RAUTENDELEIN. Not I, forsooth. What good were that to me?

The edge of thine old well is wet and rough;
'Tis overrun with spiders, worms and — worse.
They irk me — all of them. And so dost thou.

THE NICKELMANN. Brekekekex! I grieve to hear it, dear.

RAUTENDELEIN. Another of those drops! How strange!

THE NICKELMANN. More rain!

Behold! Now Father Thor is all ablaze.
The lightnings from his beard fall soft, and blink
Like babies' eyes, setting the misty train
Of rolling clouds aglow with purple flame.
And yonder, near the grey, mark how a flight
Of ravens rushes madly through the night
To keep him company. With every flash
Their wings gleam wetter in the whirling rain.
Hark, child, how thirstily our Mother Earth
Drinks every drop! And how the trees and grass,
The flies and worms, grow glad in the quick light! (*Lightning.*)

Quorax! Now in the valley! Master! Hail!
Old Thor is kindling a rare Easter fire.
His hammer flares — twelve thousand miles it sweeps!
The church-tower totters — now the belfry cracks!
The smoke pours out!...

RAUTENDELEIN.   Enough! Enough! No more!
Come, tell me something else. I'm tired of Thor.

THE NICKELMANN. Thou saucy sparrow, thou ——. Brekekekex!
What ails the creature? When it's stroked — it pecks.
A pretty way to thank one! When you're done,
You're no bit further than ere you'd begun!
Am I not right?... Still pouting, eh?... Well, well.
What wouldst thou know?

RAUTENDELEIN.   O, nothing. Do but go!

THE NICKELMANN. Naught thou wouldst know?

RAUTENDELEIN.   Naught!

THE NICKELMANN (*imploringly*).   Then, speak thou, I pray.

RAUTENDELEIN. I long to leave you all and go away!

               (*Her eyes fill with tears and she stares into the distance.*)

THE NICKELMANN (*with anguish*). What have I done to thee?
      Where wouldst thou go?

Is it the world of men that thou wouldst know?
I warn thee, maiden. Man's a curious thing,
Who naught but woe to such as thou could bring.
Although, perchance, with ours his fate's entwined,
He is, yet is not quite, of our own kind.
His world is ours — and yet, I say beware!
Half here, he lives — half, no one could tell where!
Half he's our brother; yet, this many a day,
A foe he's been, and lost to us for aye.
Woe, woe to all who our free mountains flee
To join these mortals, hoping bliss to see!
Man's feet are in the Earth. In toil and pain
He lives his fleeting life. And yet — he's vain.
He's like a plant that in a cellar shoots,
And needs must pluck and pluck at its own roots.
So, languishing for light, he rots away,
Nor ever knows the joy of one sun-ray.

The breath of Spring that kisses the green leaf,
To sickly boughs brings death, and not relief.
Pry thou no further, but let Man alone:
Lest thou should hang about thy neck — a stone.
Man will but sadden thee with his grey skies,
And turn thy happy laugh to tears and sighs.
Thou shalt be chained unto an ancient Book.
Accurst — no more upon the Sun thou'lt look!

RAUTENDELEIN. Grandmother says thou art a learned seer.
Yet, an thou wilt but in thy waters peer,
Thou'lt see that never yet a rill did flow
But longed into the world of men to go.

THE NICKELMANN (*angrily*). Quorax! Brekekekex! **Be not so**
bold.
Hear now the words of one ten centuries old!
Let slavish streams pursue their fated way,
Work, wash, for men, and grind their corn each day,
Water their cabbages and garden stuff,
And swallow — Heav'n knows what! And now... enough!
But, O, my dear Princess Rautendelein, (*Warmly and earnestly.*)
For thee a King's chamber were none too fine.
I know a rare crown, all of crystal so green,
In a great golden hall, thou shalt wear it, my queen.
The floor and the roof are of clear blue stone,
Red coral the coffers and chests I own...

RAUTENDELEIN. And what though thy coffers of coral be wrought?
Life lived with the fishes were good for naught.
And though thy King's crown of pure sapphire should be,
Thy daughters should prink it alone with thee.
My own golden tresses are far more dear;
Their touch a caress is; my crown is — here! (*She turns to go.*)

THE NICKELMANN. Where art thou going?

RAUTENDELEIN (*airily and indifferently*). What is that to thee?

THE NICKELMANN (*sorrowfully*). Much. Much. Brekekekex!

RAUTENDELEIN. O, whither I will
Go I.

THE NICKELMANN. And whither wouldst go?

RAUTENDELEIN. Away and away!

THE NICKELMANN. Away and away?

RAUTENDELEIN (*flinging her arms aloft*).   To the world — of men!

(*She vanishes in the wood.*)

THE NICKELMANN (*terrified*). Quorax!

Quorax!   (*Whimpering*).

Quorax!   (*Softly*.)

(*Shaking his head sadly.*)

Brekekekex!

CURTAIN

ACT TWO

An old-fashioned room in the house of HEINRICH *the bell-founder. A deep recess occupies half the back wall.   In the recess is a large open fire-lace, with a chimney above it.   A copper kettle is suspended above the un-lighted fire.   The other half of the back wall, set at an angle, is lighted by a large old-fashioned window, with bottle-glass panes. Below this window, a bed. Doors R. and L.   That on the R. leads to the workshop, while that on the L. leads to the courtyard.   L. C. a table and chairs placed.   On the table: a full jug of milk, mugs, and a loaf of bread.   Near the table, a tub. The room is decorated with works by Adam Kraft, Peter Fischer, etc., con-spicuous among them a painted wooden image of Christ on the Cross.*

DISCOVERED: *Seated at the farther side of the table, and, in their Sunday best, the two* CHILDREN (*boys*) *of* HEINRICH (*aged respectively five and nine*), *with their mugs of milk before them.* MAGDA, *their mother, also in her Sunday best, enters L., with a bunch of cowslips in her hand.*

Early morning.   The light grows brighter as the action progresses.

MAGDA. See, children, what I've brought you from the fields!

Beyond the garden — a whole patch grew wild.

Now we can make ourselves look fine and gay,

In honor of your father's birthday feast.

FIRST CHILD. O, give me some!

SECOND CHILD.   And me!

MAGDA.   There!   Five for each!

And every single one they say's a key [1]

---

[1] In German the cowslip is called "Himmelschlüssel," *i.e.*, "the key of Heaven."

That opens Heaven.   Now drink your milk, my dears,
And eat your bread.   'Tis almost time to start.
The road to church, you know, is long and steep.

NEIGHBOR (*a woman looking in at the window*).   What! Up already,
     neighbor?

MAGDA (*at the window*).   Yes, indeed.
I hardly closed my eyes the livelong night.
But, 'twas not care that kept me wide-awake.
So now I'm just as fresh as if I'd slept
Sound as a dormouse.   Why, how bright it is!

NEIGHBOR.   Ay.   Ay.   You're right.

MAGDA.   You'll come with us, I hope?
Now don't say no.   You'll find it easy walking
On the road... These tiny feet
Shall lead the way, and gently mark our steps.
If you must have the truth, I long for wings:
I'm wild today with joy and eagerness!

NEIGHBOR.   And has your good-man not been home all night?

MAGDA.   What are you dreaming of?   I'll be content
If only the big bell is safely hung
In time to ring the people in to mass!
You see — the time was short.   They'd none to waste.
And as for sleeping — if the Master snatched
So much as one short wink in the wood-grass —
Why, Heaven be praised!   But, oh, what does it matter?
The work was hard: but great is the reward.
You cannot think how pure, and clear, and true,
The new bell sounds.   Just wait until you hear
Its voice ring out today from the church tower.
'Tis like a prayer, a hymn, a song of praise —
Filling the heart with comfort and with gladness.

NEIGHBOR.   No doubt, ma'am.   Yet one thing amazes me.
From my front door, as doubtless you're aware,
The church upon the hill is plainly seen.
Now — I had heard that when the bell was hung
A white flag would be hoisted from the tower.
I've seen no sign of that white flag.   Have you?

MAGDA.   O, look again.   It must be there by now.

NEIGHBOR. No, no.   It's not.

MAGDA.   Well, even were you right,
It would not frighten me.   Did you but know
The fret and toil and pain, by night and day,
It costs the Master to complete his work,
You would not wonder if the final stroke
Should be delayed a bit.   I understand.
By this time, I'll be bound, the flag is there.
Why, yes, I'm sure it is, could we but see 't.

NEIGHBOR. I can't believe it.   In the village streets
They do say something dreadful has occurred.
Dark omens, boding evil, fill the air.
But now, a farmer saw a naked witch,
Perched on a boar's back, riding through his corn.
Lifting a stone, he cast it at the hag —
Straightway his hand dropped — palsied to the knuckles!
'Tis said that all the mischievous mountain sprites
Are leagued and up in arms against the bell.
How strange you have not heard all this before!
Well — now the Bailiff's gone into the hills,
With half the village at his heels, to see...

MAGDA. The Bailiff?   Merciful God!   What can be wrong?

NEIGHBOR. Why, nothing's certain.   All may yet be well.
There — don't take on so, neighbor.   Come — be calm!
It's not so bad as that.   Now don't 'ee fret.
It seems the wagon and the bell broke down...
That's all we've heard.

MAGDA.   Pray Heav'n that be the worst!
What matters one bell more or less!... If he,
The Master, be but safe — these flowers may stay.
Yet — till we know what's happened... Here, prithee,
Take the two children...

                    (*She lifts the two* CHILDREN *through the window.*)
                              Will you?

NEIGHBOR.   Why, to be sure.

MAGDA. Thanks.   Take them home with you.   And, as for me,
Ah, I must go, as fast as go I can,
To see what may be done — to help.   For I

Must be with my dear Master — or, I die! *(Exit hurriedly.)*
(The NEIGHBOR *retires with the* CHILDREN. *Confused noise of
voices without. Then a piercing cry from* MAGDA.*)*

(Enter quickly the VICAR, *sighing, and wiping the tears from his eyes. He
looks round the room hastily, and turns down the coverlet of the bed.
Then, hurrying to the door, he meets the* SCHOOLMASTER *and the*
BARBER, *carrying* HEINRICH *in on the litter seen in Act One.* HEIN-
RICH *reclines on a rude bed of green branches.* MAGDA, *half beside
herself with anguish, follows, supported by a* MAN *and a* WOMAN.
Crowd of VILLAGERS *presses in behind* MAGDA. HEINRICH *is laid
on his own bed.)*

THE VICAR *(to* MAGDA). Bear up, my mistress! Put your trust in
    God!
  We laid him on our litter as one dead;
  Yet, on the way, he came to life again,
  And, as the doctor told us, only now,
  Hope's not yet lost.
MAGDA *(moaning).* Dear God, who speaks of hope?
  A moment since, I was so happy!... Now —
  What's come to me? What's happened? Won't you speak?
  Where are the children?
THE VICAR. Put your trust in God.
  Do but have patience, mistress. Patience and faith!
  Often — remember — in our direst need
  God's help is nearest. And, forget not this:
  Should He, of His all-wisdom, have resolved,
  In His own time, to call the Master hence,
  Still there shall be this comfort for your soul —
  Your husband goes from Earth to endless bliss.
MAGDA. Why do you speak of comfort, reverend Sir?
  Do I need comfort? Nay — he will get well.
  He must get well.
THE VICAR. So all of us do hope.
  But... should he not... God's holy will be done.
  Come now what may, the Master's fight is won.
  To serve the Lord, he fashioned his great bell.
  To serve the Lord, he scaled the mountain-heights —

Where the malignant powers of Darkness dwell,
And the Abyss defies the God of Hosts.
Serving the Lord, at last he was laid low —
Braving the hellish spirits in his path.
They feared the gospel that his bell had rung:
So leagued themselves against him, one and all,
In devilish brotherhood.   God punish them!

THE BARBER. A wonder-working woman lives hard by,
Who heals, as the Disciples healed of old,
By prayer and faith.

THE VICAR.   Let some one search for her:
And when she's found, return with her at once.

MAGDA. What's come to him?   Why do you stand and gape?
Off with you all!   You shall not stare at him
With your unfeeling eyes.   D'you hear?   Begone!
Cover him — so — with linen, lest your looks
Should shame the Master.   Now — away with you!
Get to the juggler's, if you needs must gape.
Ah, God!   What's happened?... Are ye all struck dumb?

THE SCHOOLMASTER. Truly, 'tis hard to tell just what took place.
Whether he tried to stop the bell — or what...
This much is certain: if you could but see
How deep he fell, you would go down on your knees
And thank the Lord.   For, if your husband lives,
'Tis nothing short of the miraculous!

HEINRICH (*feebly*).   Give me a little water!

MAGDA (*driving out the* VILLAGERS *quickly*).   Out you go!

THE VICAR. Go, my good people.   He has need of rest.

(VILLAGERS *withdraw*.)

If I can serve you, Mistress, why, you know
Where you may find me.

THE BARBER.   Yes, and me.

THE SCHOOLMASTER.   And me.
No.   On reflection, I'll stay here.

MAGDA.   You'll go!

HEINRICH. Give me some water!

(*The* VICAR, SCHOOLMASTER, *and* BARBER *withdraw slowly,
talking low, shaking their heads, and shrugging their shoulders.*)

MAGDA (*hastening to* HEINRICH *with water*). Heinrich, are you
   awake?

HEINRICH. I'm parched. Give me some water. Can't you hear?

MAGDA (*unable to control herself*). Nay, patience.

HEINRICH.   Magda, all too soon I'll learn
   What patience means. Bear with me yet a while.
   It will not be for long.   (*He drinks.*)
                  Thanks, Magda. Thanks.

MAGDA. Don't speak to me so strangely, Heinrich. Don't!
   I... I'm afraid.

HEINRICH (*fevered and angry*). Thou must not be afraid.
   When I am gone, thou'lt have to live alone.

MAGDA. I cannot... no, I will not... live without thee!

HEINRICH. Thy pain is childish. Torture me no more!
   It is unworthy, — for thou art a mother.
   Bethink thee what that word means, and be brave!

MAGDA. Ah, do not be so stern and harsh with me!

HEINRICH (*painfully*). The plain truth harsh and stern? Again I
   say —
   Thy place is by the bedside of thy boys.
   There lies thy joy, thy peace, thy work, thy life.
   All — all is tucked up in their fair, white sheets.
   Could it be otherwise, 'twere infamous!

MAGDA (*falling on his neck*). So help me Heav'n, I love thee far, far
   more
   Than our dear children, and myself, and all!

HEINRICH. Then woe unto ye all, too soon bereaved!
   And thrice-unhappy I, untimely doomed
   To snatch the milk and bread from your poor lips!
   Yet, on my tongue, I feel them turn to poison.
   That, too, is just!... Farewell. Thee I commend
   To one from whom none living may escape.
   Many a man has found Death's deepest shadow
   Prove but a welcome light. God grant it be!
   Give me thy hand. I've done thee many a wrong (*Tenderly.*)
   By word and deed. Often I've grieved thy heart,
   Far, far, too often. But thou wilt forgive me!
   I would have spared thee, had I but been free.

I know not what compelled me; yet I know
I could not choose but stab thee — and myself.
Forgive me, Magda!

MAGDA.   I forgive thee?   What?
If thou dost love me, Heinrich, be less sad:
Or thou wilt bring the tears back.   Rather — scold.
Thou knowest well how dear ——

HEINRICH (*painfully*).   I do not know!

MAGDA. Nay, who, but thou, did wake my woman's soul?
Till thou didst come, I was a poor, dull, clod,
Pining away beneath a cheerless sky.
Thou — thou — didst rescue me and make me live,
Fill me with joy, and set my heart in the sun.
And never did I feel thy love more sure
Than when, with thy strong hand, thou'dst draw my face
Out of the dark, and turn it towards the light.
And thou wouldst have me pardon thee!   For what?
Do I not owe thee all I love in life?

HEINRICH. Strangely entangled seems the web of souls.

MAGDA (*stroking his hair tenderly*).   If I have ever been a help to
        thee —
If I have sometimes cheered thy working hours —
If favor in thine eyes I ever found...
Bethink thee, Heinrich: I, who would have given
Thee everything — my life — the world itself —
I had but that to pay thee for thy love!

HEINRICH (*uneasily*). I'm dying.   That is best.   God means it well.
Should I live on... Come nearer, wife, and hear me.
'Tis better for us both that I should die.
Thou think'st, because we blossomed out together,
I was the sun that caused thy heart to bloom.
But that the eternal Wonder-Worker wrought,
.Who, on the wings of His chill winter-storms,
Rides through a million million woodland flowers,
Slaying them, as He passes, in their Spring!
'Tis better for us both that I should die.
See: I was cracked and ageing — all misshaped.
If the great Bell-Founder who moulded me

Tosses aside His work, I shall not mourn.
When He did hurl me down to the abyss,
After my own poor, faulty, handiwork,
I did not murmur: for my work was bad!
Good-wife — the bell that sank into the mere
Was not made for the heights — it was not fit
To wake the answering echoes of the peaks!

MAGDA. I cannot read the meaning of thy words.
A work — so highly-prized, so free from flaw,
So clear and true that, when it first rang out
Between the mighty trees from which it hung,
All marveled and exclaimed, as with one voice,
"The Master's bell sings as the Angels sing!"

HEINRICH (*fevered*). 'Twas for the valley, not the mountain-top!

MAGDA. That is not true! Hadst thou but heard, as I,
The Vicar tell the Clerk, in tones that shook,
"How gloriously 'twill sound upon the heights!"...

HEINRICH. 'Twas for the valley — not the mountain-top!
I only know 't. The Vicar does not know.
So I must die — I wish to die, my child.
For, look now: should I heal — as men would call 't —
Thanks to the art of our good village leech,
I'd be at best a botch, a crippled wretch;
And so the warm and generous draught of life —
Ofttimes I've found it bitter, ofttimes sweet,
But ever it was strong, as I did drink 't —
Would turn to a stale, flat, unsavory brew,
Thin and grown cold and sour. I'll none of it!
Let him who fancies it enjoy the draught.
Me it would only sicken and repel.
Hush! Hear me out. Though thou shouldst haply find
A doctor of such skill that he could cure me,
Giving me back my joy — nerving my hand,
Till it could turn to the old, daily task —
Even then, Magda, I were still undone.

MAGDA. For God's sake, husband, tell me what to think!
What has come over thee — a man so strong,
So blessed, so weighted down with Heaven's best gifts;

Respected, loved, of all — of all admired,
A master of thy craft!... A hundred bells
Hast thou set ringing, in a hundred towers.
They sing thy praise, with restless industry;
Pouring the deep, glad, beauty of thy soul
As from a hundred wine-cups, through the land.
At eve, the purple-red — at dawn, God's gold —
Know thee. Of both thou art become a part.
And thou — rich, rich, beyond thy greatest need —
Thou, voicing God — able to give, and give,
Rolling in happiness, where others go
Begging their daily dole of joy or bread —
Thou look'st unthankfully upon thy work!
Then, Heinrich, why must I still bear the life
That thou dost hate so?... What is life to me?
What could that be to me which thou dost scorn —
Casting it from thee, like a worthless thing!

HEINRICH. Mistake me not. Now thou thyself hast sounded.
Deeper and clearer than my loudest bells.
And many a one I've made!... I thank thee, Magda.
Yet thou shalt understand my thought. Thou must.
Listen!... The latest of my works had failed.
With anguished heart I followed where they climbed,
Shouting and cursing loudly, as the bell
Was dragged towards the peak. And then — it fell.
It fell a hundred fathoms deep, ay more,
Into the mere. There, in the mere, now lies
The last and noblest work my art could mould!
Not all my life, as I have lived it, Magda,
Had fashioned, or could fashion, aught so good.
Now I have thrown it after my bad work.
While I lie drinking the poor dregs of life,
Deep in the waters of the lake it's drowned.
I mourn not for what's lost. And then — I mourn:
Knowing this only — neither bell, nor life,
Shall evermore come back. Alas! woe's me!
My heart's desire was bound up in the tones —
The buried tones — I never more shall hear.

And now the life to which I clung so tight
Is turned to bitterness, and grief, and rue,
Madness, and gloom, confusion, pain, and gall!

. . . .

Well, let life go! The service of the valleys
Charms me no longer, and no more their peace
Calms my wild blood. Since on the peak I stood,
All that I am has longed to rise, and rise,
Cleaving the mists, until it touched the skies!
I would work wonders with the power on high:
And, since I may not work them, being so weak;
Since, even could I, with much straining, rise,
I should but fall again — I choose to die!
Youth — a new youth — I'd need, if I should live:
Out of some rare and magic mountain flower
Marvelous juices I should need to press —
Heart-health, and strength, and the mad lust of triumph,
Steeling my hand to work none yet have dreamed of!

MAGDA. O Heinrich, Heinrich, did I but know the spot
Where that thou pantest for, the Spring of Youth,
Lies hid, how gladly would these feet of mine
Wear themselves out to find it for thee! Yea,
Even though the waters which restored thy life
Should bring me death!

HEINRICH (*tormented, collapsing and delirious*). Thou dearest, truest!
... No, I will not drink!
Keep it!... The Spring is full of blood!... blood!... blood!
I will not!... No!... Leave me... and... let me... die!

(*He becomes unconscious.*)

(*Enter the* VICAR.)

THE VICAR. How goes it with the patient, mistress?
MAGDA. Ill!

Terribly ill! He's sick in every part.
Some strange, mysterious pain's consuming him.
I know not what to fear, and what to hope.

(*Hurriedly throwing a scarf over her shoulders.*)
Did you not speak of a woman who works miracles?

THE VICAR. I did.   Indeed, 'tis that has brought me back.
She lives... at most a mile away from here...
Her name... I can't recall it.   But she lives,
If I mistake not, in the pinewood... Ay...
Her name...

MAGDA.   Not Wittikin?

THE VICAR.   How can you ask!
Why, she's a wicked witch, the Devil's dam,
And she must die.   By now they're up in arms,
Eager for battle with the pestilent fiend.
With cudgels, torches, stones, they're hurrying fast
To make an end of her.   For you must know
She's charged with all the evil that afflicts us.
No.   I was thinking of ... Frau Findeklee...
A shepherd's widow... and a worthy soul...
Her husband left her an old recipe
Which, as I am assured by many here,
Has wondrous virtues.   Will you go for her?

MAGDA. Yes, yes, most reverend Sir!

THE VICAR.   You'll go at once?

(*Enter* RAUTENDELEIN, *disguised as a peasant girl, and carrying a basket
of berries in her hand.*)

MAGDA (*to* RAUTENDELEIN).   What wouldst thou, child?... Who
art thou?...

THE VICAR.   Why — 'tis Anna,
Anna — the maiden from the wayside inn.
Nay, 'twould be vain to question her.   Alas,
She's dumb.   A good girl.   Ah, she's brought some berries.

MAGDA. Come here, my child... What was't I wished to say...
Ah, yes!   This man lies sick.   When he awakes
Be near to help him.   Dost thou understand me?
Frau Findeklee... That was the name, you said?...
But, no; I cannot go.   It is too far.
If you'll stay here a moment, I am sure,
My neighbor will go for me... I'll come back.
And don't forget... O God, my heart will break!   (*Exit.*)

THE VICAR (*to* RAUTENDELEIN). Stand here, my child; or, if thou
    wilt, sit down,
Be good and do the very best thou canst.
Make thyself helpful, while they need thy help.
God will reward thee for the work thou doest.
Thou art greatly changed, dear child, since last I saw thee.
But keep thou honest — be a good, true maid —
For the dear Lord has blessed thee with much beauty.
In truth, my dear, now that I look at thee,
Thou art, yet art not, Anna. As a princess,
Stepped from the pages of some fairy book,
Thou seem'st. So quickly changed! Who would have thought
It possible! Well, well!... Thou'lt keep him cool?
He's burning! (*To* HEINRICH) May God bring thee back to
    health! (*Exit.*)

    (RAUTENDELEIN, *who till now has seemed shy and meek, changes
    suddenly and bustles about the hearth.*)

RAUTENDELEIN.

    Flickering spark in the ash of death,
    Glow with life of living breath!
    Red, red wind, thy loudest blow!
    I, as thou, did lawless grow!
       Simmer, sing, and simmer!
              (*The flame leaps up on the hearth.*)

    . . . .

    Kettle swaying left and right —
    Copper-lid, thou'rt none too light!
    Bubble, bubble, broth and brew,
    Turning all things old to new!
       Simmer, sing, and simmer!

    . . . .

    Green and tender herbs of Spring,
    In the healing draught I fling.
    Drink it sweet, and drink it hot —
    Life and youth are in the pot!
       Simmer, sing, and simmer!

    . . . .

And now to scrape the roots and fetch the water.
The cask is empty... But we need more light!

> (*She throws the window wide open.*)

A glorious day!   But there'll be wind anon.
A mighty cloud, in shape like some huge fish,
Lies on the hills.   Tomorrow it will burst;
And roystering spirits will ride madly down,
Sweeping athwart the pines, to reach the vale.
Cuckoo!   Cuckoo!... Here, too, the cuckoo calls,
And the swift swallow darts across the sky...

> (HEINRICH *has opened his eyes, and lies staring at* RAUTENDELEIN.)

But now to scrape my roots, and fetch the water.
I've much to do since I turned waiting-maid.
Thou, thou, dear flame, shalt cheer me at my work.

HEINRICH (*amazed*).   Tell me... who art thou?

RAUTENDELEIN (*quickly and unconcernedly*).   I?   Rautendelein.

HEINRICH.   Rautendelein?   I never heard that name.
Yet somewhere I have seen thee once before.
Where was it?

RAUTENDELEIN.   Why, 'twas on the mountain-side.

HEINRICH.   True.   True.   'Twas there — what time I fevered lay.
I dreamt I saw thee there... Again I dream.
At times we dream strange dreams!   See.   Here's my house.
There burns the fire upon the well-known hearth.
Here lie I, in my bed, sick unto death.
I push the window back.   There flies a swallow.
Yonder the nightingales are all at play.
Sweet scents float in — of jasmine... elder-blossom...
I see... I feel... I know... the smallest thing —
Even to the pattern of this coverlet...
Each thread... each tiny knot... I could describe —
And yet I'm dreaming.

RAUTENDELEIN.   Thou art dreaming?   Why?

HEINRICH (*in anguish*).   Because... I must be dreaming.

RAUTENDELEIN.   Art thou so sure?

HEINRICH.   Yes.   No.   Yes.   No.   I'm wandering.   Let me dream
on!
Thou askest if I am so sure.   I know not.

Ah, be it what it will: or dream, or life —
It is. I feel it, see it — thou dost live!
Real or unreal, within me or without,
Child of my brain, or whatsoe'er thou art,
Still I do love thee, for thou art thyself.
So stay with me, sweet spirit. Only stay!

RAUTENDELEIN. So long as thou shalt choose.

HEINRICH. Then ... I do dream.

RAUTENDELEIN (*familiarly*). Take care. Dost see me lift this little
foot
With the rosy heel? Thou dost? Why, that is well.
Now — here's a hazel nut. I take it — so —
Between my finger and my dainty thumb —
I set my heel on it. Crack! Now, 'tis broken.
Was that a dream?

HEINRICH. That only God can tell.

RAUTENDELEIN. Now watch me. See. I'll come quite close to
thee,
And sit upon thy bed. So. Here I am!...
Feasting away as merrily as thou wilt...
Hast thou not room enough?

HEINRICH. I've all I need.
But tell me whence thou'rt sprung and who has sent thee!
What would'st thou of a broken, suffering man,
A bundle of sorrow, drawing near the end
Of his brief pilgrimage...?

RAUTENDELEIN. I like thee.
Whence I did spring I know not — nor could tell
Whither I go. But Granny said one day
She found me lying in the moss and weeds.
A hind did give me suck. My home's the wood,
The mountain-side, the crag, the storm-swept moor —
Where the wind moans and rages, shrieks and groans,
Or purrs and mews, like some wild tiger-cat!
There thou wilt find me, whirling through the air;
There I laugh loud and shout for sheer mad joy;
Till faun and nixey, gnome and water-sprite,
Echo my joy and split their sides with laughter.

I'm spiteful when I'm vexed, and scratch and bite:
And who should anger me had best beware.
Yet — 'tis no better when I'm left alone:
For good and bad in me's all mood and impulse.
I'm thus, or thus, and change with each new whim.
But thee I am fond of... Thee I would not scratch.
And, if thou wilt, I'll stay. Yet were it best
Thou camest with me to my mountain home.
Then thou should'st see how faithfully I'd serve thee.
I'd show thee diamonds, and rubies rare,
Hid at the bottom of unfathomed deeps.
Emeralds, and topazes, and amethysts —
I'd bring thee all — I'd hang upon thy lids!
Forward, unruly, lazy, I may be;
Spiteful, rebellious, wayward, what thou wilt!
Yet thou should'st only need to blink thine eye,
And ere thou'dst time to speak, I'd nod thee — yes.
And Granny tells me...

HEINRICH.   Ah, thou dear, dear child.
Tell me, who is thy Granny?

RAUTENDELEIN.   Dost thou not know?

HEINRICH. No.

RAUTENDELEIN. Not know Granny?

HEINRICH.   No, I am a man,
And blind.

RAUTENDELEIN. Soon thou shalt see! To me is given
The power to open every eye I kiss
To the most hidden mysteries of earth
And air.

HEINRICH.   Then... kiss me!

RAUTENDELEIN.   Thou'lt keep still?

HEINRICH.   Nay, try me!

RAUTENDELEIN (kissing his eyes). Ye eyes, be opened!

HEINRICH.   Ah, thou lovely child,
Sent to enchant me in my dying hour —
Thou fragrant blossom, plucked by God's own hand
In the forgotten dawn of some dead Spring —
Thou free, fair, bud — ah, were I but that man

Who, in the morn of life, fared forth so glad —
How I would press thee to this leaping heart!
Mine eyes were blinded. Now, they're filled with light,
And, as by instinct, I divine thy world.
Ay, more and more, as I do drink thee in,
Thou dear enigma, I am sure I see.

RAUTENDELEIN. Why — look at me, then, till thine eyes are tired.

HEINRICH. How golden gleams thy hair! How dazzling bright!...
With thee for company, thou dearest dream,
Old Charon's boat becomes a bark for kings,
That spreads its purple sails to catch the sun,
Lighting it eastward on its stately way.
Feel'st thou the Western breeze that creeps behind us,
Flecking with foam from tiny waterfalls
The swelling bosom of the blue South seas,
And showering diamonds on us? Dost thou not feel it?
And we, reclining here on cloth of gold,
In blissful certitude of what must be,
Do scan the distance that divides us twain...
Thou knowest well from what!... For thou hast seen
The fair green island, where the birch bends down,
Bathing its branches in the azure flood —
Thou hearest the glad song of all Spring's choirs,
Waiting to welcome us...

RAUTENDELEIN.   Yes! Yes! I hear it!

HEINRICH (collapsing). So be it. I am ready. When I awake,
A voice shall say to me — Come thou with me.
Then fades the light!... Here now the air grows chill.
The seer dies, as the blind man had died.
But I have seen thee... seen... thee...!

RAUTENDELEIN (with incantations).
                    Master, sleep is thine!
                    When thou wakest, thou art mine.
                    Happy dreams shall dull thy pain,
                    Help to make thee whole again.
                              (She bustles about by the hearth.)
                    Hidden treasures, now grow bright!
                    In the depths ye give no light.

Glowing hounds in vain do bark,
Whine and whimper in the dark!
We, who serve him, glad will be:
For the Master sets us free!

(*Addressing* HEINRICH, *and with gestures.*)

One, two, three. A new man be!
For the future thou art free!

HEINRICH (*awaking*). What's happened to me?... From what
wondrous sleep
Am I aroused?... What is this glorious sun
That, streaming through the window, gilds my hand?
O, breath of morning! Heaven, if 'tis thy will —
If 'tis thy strength that rushes through my veins —
If, as a token of thy power, I feel
This strange, new, beating heart within my breast?
Then, should I rise again — again I'd long
To wander out into the world of life:
And wish, and strive, and hope, and dare, and do...
And do... and do...!

(RAUTENDELEIN *has meanwhile moved to L. and stands, leaning
against the wall, gazing fixedly at* HEINRICH. *A dazzling light
falls on her face. Enter* MAGDA.)

Ah, Magda. Is it thou?

MAGDA. Is he awake?

HEINRICH.   Yes, Magda. Is it thou?

MAGDA (*delightedly*). How is it with thee?

HEINRICH (*overcome with emotion*).   Well. Ah, well! I'll live!
I feel it. I shall live... Yes! I shall... live!

(*As he speaks, he gazes fixedly, not at* MAGDA, *but at* RAUTENDE-
LEIN, *who stands in an elfin attitude, looking toward him, with an
unnatural light on her face.*)

MAGDA (*overjoyed and embracing* HEINRICH, *who seems unconscious of her
presence*). He lives! He lives! O dearest Heinrich! Dearest!

CURTAIN.

ACT THREE

A deserted glass-works in the mountains, near the snow fields. L., an earthenware pipe, through which water from the natural rock runs into a natural stone trough. R., a "practicable" smith's forge, with chimney and bellows. Through the open entrance to the glass-works at back, R., is seen a mountain landscape, with peaks, moors, and dense fir-woods. Close to the entrance is a precipitous descending slope. In the roof is an outlet for the smoke. L., the rock forms a rude, pointed vault.

DISCOVERED: THE WOOD-SPRITE. *After throwing a stump on a heap of pinewood outside, he enters, reluctantly, and looks round.* THE NICKEL-MANN *rises from the water-trough, remaining immersed up to his breast.*

THE NICKELMANN. Brekekekex!   Come in!

THE WOOD-SPRITE.   Ah, there thou art!

THE NICKELMANN. Ay.   Plague upon this nasty smoke and soot!

THE WOOD-SPRITE. Have they gone out?

THE NICKELMANN.   Have who gone out?

THE WOOD-SPRITE.   Why — they.

THE NICKELMANN. Yes.   I suppose so.   Else they would be here.

THE WOOD-SPRITE. I've seen old Horny.

THE NICKELMANN.   Ugh!

THE WOOD-SPRITE.   ... With saw and axe.

THE NICKELMANN. What did he say?

THE WOOD-SPRITE.   He said... thou croakedst much.

THE NICKELMANN. Then let the booby keep his ears closed tight.

THE WOOD-SPRITE. And then he said... thou quackedst dismally.

THE NICKELMANN. I'll wring his neck for him.

THE WOOD-SPRITE.   And serve him right!

THE NICKELMANN. More necks than one I'd wring —

THE WOOD-SPRITE (*laughing*).   Accursèd wight!

He crowds us from our hills.   He hacks and hews,
Digs up our metals, sweats, and smelts, and brews.
The earth-man and the water-sprite he takes
To drag his burdens, and, to harness, breaks.
Our fairest elf's his sweetheart.   As for us,
We must stand by, and watch them — as they buss.
She steals my cherished flowers, my red-brown ores,

My gold, my precious stones, my resinous stores.
She serves him like a slave, by night and day.
'Tis him she kisses — us she keeps at bay.
Naught stands against him.   Ancient trees he fells.
The earth quakes at his tread, and all the dells
Ring with the echo of his thunderous blows.
His crimson smithy furnace glows and shines
Into the depths of my most secret mines.
What he is up to, only Satan knows!

THE NICKELMANN. Brekekekex! Hadst thou the creature slain,
A-rotting in the mere long since he had lain —
The maker of the bell, beside the bell.
And so when next I had wished to throw the stones,
The bell had been my box — the dice, his bones!

THE WOOD-SPRITE. By cock and pie! That, truly, had been well.

THE NICKELMANN. But, as it is, he's hale and strong, and works.
Each hammer-stroke my marrow thrills and irks. (*Whimpering.*)
He makes her rings, and chains, and bracelets rare —
Kisses her neck, her breast, her golden hair.

THE WOOD-SPRITE. Now, by my goaty face, thou must be crazed.
An old chap whine and whimper?   I'm amazed.
He has a fancy for the child?   What then?
'Tis plain she does not love you water-men.
Cheer up!   Although she shall not be thy bride,
The sea is deep: the earth is long and wide.
Catch some fair nixey, and your passion slake.
Live like a pacha: riot — be a rake!
Soon thou'lt be cured: and when they hie to bed,
Thou wilt not even turn to wag thy head.

THE NICKELMANN. I'll have his blood, I say!...

THE WOOD-SPRITE.   She dotes on him.
Thou'rt powerless.

THE NICKELMANN.   I'll tear him limb from limb!

THE WOOD-SPRITE. She will not have thee, and thy rage is vain.
While Granny stands his friend, thy cries of pain
Will all be wasted.   Ay, this loving pair
Is closely guarded.   Patience! and beware!

THE NICKELMANN. Patience? I hate the word!

THE WOOD-SPRITE.   Time runs on fast:
And men are men.   Their passion is soon past.

RAUTENDELEIN (*heard singing without*).

> A beetle sat in a tree!
> Zum! Zum!
> A coat all black and white had he!
> Zum! Zum!

Oho! We've company.   Godden, Godden to you. (*She enters.*)
Hast washed that gold for me, good Nickelmann?
Hast brought the pine-stumps, as I ordered thee,
Dear Goat's-Foot?... See: I bend beneath the weight
Of the rare treasures I have found today.
Oh, I'm no laggard when I set to work!
Here I have diamonds: here, crystals clear.
This little bag is filled with gold-dust.   Look!
And here is honeycomb... How warm it grows!

THE NICKELMANN. Warm days are followed by still warmer nights.

RAUTENDELEIN. Maybe.   Cold water is thine element:
So get thee whence thou cam'st, and cool thyself.

(*The* WOOD-SPRITE *laughs.*)

(*The* NICKELMANN *sinks silently down into his trough and disappears.*)

He will not stop until he's angered me.

THE WOOD-SPRITE (*still laughing*). Ods bobs!

RAUTENDELEIN.   My garter's twisted at the knee!
It cuts me.   Oh!

THE WOOD-SPRITE.   Shall I untwist it, dear?

RAUTENDELEIN. A pretty page thou'dst make!... No.   Go away.
Thou bring'st ill smells with thee... and oh, the gnats!
Why, they are swarming round thee now, in clouds.

THE WOOD-SPRITE. I love them better than the butterflies
That flap their dusty wings about thy face,
Now hanging on thy lips — now on thy hair,
Or clinging to thy hip and breast at night.

RAUTENDELEIN (*laughing*). There! That will do.   Enough!

THE WOOD-SPRITE.   A happy thought!
Give me this cart-wheel.   How did it come here?

RAUTENDELEIN. That thou couldst answer best, thou mischievous
rogue.

THE WOOD-SPRITE. Had I not broken down the dray, I trow,
    Thy falcon were not now meshed in thy net.
    So give me thanks — and let me take the thing.
    I'll have it tied with ropes, and smeared with pitch,
    And when it's lighted, I will roll it down
    The steepest hillside. Ah! That were a joke!

RAUTENDELEIN. Not for the village-folk. Their huts would flame.

THE WOOD-SPRITE. The flame of sacrifice! The red, red wind!

RAUTENDELEIN. But I'll not hear of it. So — get thee gone!

THE WOOD-SPRITE. Thou'rt in a hurry?... Must I really go?
    Then tell me first — what is the Master doing?

RAUTENDELEIN. He's working a great work!

THE WOOD-SPRITE.   Ah, yes, no doubt!
    We know how bells are cast: by day
    Ye work — at night, ye kiss and play.
    Hill pines for dale, dale pines for hill,
    Then, quick, the Master works his will:
    A bastard thing, half brute, half God —
    The pride of Earth — to Heaven a clod.
    Come to the hazelwoods with me!
    What he could be to thee, I'll be.
    To honor thee shall be my pleasure —
    Ape not the Virgin pure, my treasure!

RAUTENDELEIN. Thou beast! Thou rogue! I'll blind thy thank-
    less eyes,
    Should'st thou not cease that Master to despise
    Whose hammer, clanging through the dark, long night,
    Strikes to redeem thee!... For, without his might,
    Thou, I, and all of our unhappy race,
    Are curst, and kept beyond the pale of grace.
    Yet, stay!... Be what thou wilt, thy strength is vain.
    Here he, the Master, and his will, must reign!

THE WOOD-SPRITE. What's that to me?... My greeting to thy love.
    Some day, thou'lt see, I'll be thy turtle-dove.

                          (Exit laughing. Short pause.)

RAUTENDELEIN. What ails me?... Here the air seems close and
    warm.
    I'll hie to some cool grot beside the snow.

The dripping water, green and cold as ice,
Will soon refresh me... Today I trod on a snake,
As it lay sunning itself on a green stone.
It bit at me — up yonder by the falls.
Heigho!   How close it is!... Steps!... Hark!   Who comes?

(*Enter the* VICAR, *in mountain costume.   He pants for breath as he stands outside the door.*)

THE VICAR.   Ho!   Master Barber!   Follow me.   This way!
The road was rough.   But here I stand, at last.
Well, well.   I've come to do God's own good work.
My pains will be repaid a hundred-fold
If, like the Blessèd Shepherd, I should find
One poor, lost sheep, and bring him safely home.
So, courage!   Courage!
(*He enters.*)   Is there no one here?
                                    (*He sees* RAUTENDELEIN.)
Ah, there thou art.   I might have known as much!
RAUTENDELEIN (*pale and angry*).   What do you seek?
THE VICAR.   That thou shalt quickly learn.
Ay, soon enough, as God shall be my witness.
Give me but time to get my breath again
And dry my face a bit.   And now, my child —
I pray thee, tell me — art thou here alone?
RAUTENDELEIN.   Thou hast no right to question me!
THE VICAR.   Oho!
A pretty answer, truly.   But thou art frank —
Thou showest me thy very self at once.
So much the better.   Now my course is plain.
Thou creature!...
RAUTENDELEIN.   Man, beware!
THE VICAR (*folding his hands and approaching her*).
                            I fear thee not!
My heart is pure and true.   Thou canst not harm me.
He who did give my poor old limbs the strength
To brave thee in thy hidden mountain home
Will not forsake me now.   Thou devilish thing,
Think not to daunt me with thy scornful glance —

Waste thy infernal witchcraft not on me!

Thou — thou hast lured him hither — to thy hills!

RAUTENDELEIN. Whom?

THE VICAR. Whom?   Why, Master Heinrich.   Canst thou ask?

With magic spells, and sweet unhallowed draughts,

Thou hast witched him, till he obeys thee like a dog.

A man so upright, pious to the core;

A father and a husband!   Thou great God!

This mountain trull had but to raise her hand

And, in a trice, she had tied him to her skirts,

Dragged him away with her, where'er she pleased,

Shaming the honor of all Christendom.

RAUTENDELEIN. If I'm a robber, 'twas not thou I robbed!

THE VICAR. What! 'Tis not I thou hast robbed?   Thou insolent jade,

Not me alone, not only his wife and boys —

No — all mankind thou hast cheated of this man!

RAUTENDELEIN (*suddenly transformed and in triumph*).   Ah, look before thee!   See who comes this way!

Dost thou not hear the free and even sound

Of his firm footsteps?   Shall thy sland'rous flouts

Not even now be turned to joyous shouts?

Dost thou not feel my Balder's conqu'ring glance

Dart through thy soul, and stir thee, as the dance?

The grass his foot treads down is proud and glad.

A King draws nigh!   Thou, beggarly wretch, art sad?

Hail!   Hail!   O Master, Master!   Thee I greet!

> (*She runs to meet* HEINRICH, *and throws herself into his arms as he enters.*)

> (HEINRICH *is attired in a picturesque working costume.   In his hand he holds a hammer.   He enters hand in hand with* RAUTENDELEIN, *and recognizes the* VICAR.)

HEINRICH. Welcome!   Thrice welcome, friend!

THE VICAR.   Now God be praised!

Belovèd Master: is it yourself I see?

You, who but lately came so near to death,

Now stand before me, beaming with rude strength,

Straight as a stout young beech, and hale and well —

You, who did seem a sickly, tottering man,
Hopeless, and ageing?   What has wrought this change?
How, in a moment, has the grace of God,
With but a puff of His all-quickening breath,
Helped you to spring from your sick-bed to life,
Ready to dance, as David danced, and sing,
Praising the Lord, your Saviour and your King!

HEINRICH. 'Tis even as you say.

THE VICAR.   You are a marvel!

HEINRICH. That also is true.   In all my frame I feel
Wonders are being worked.   (*To* RAUTENDELEIN.)
                    Go thou, my dear.
The Vicar must be thirsty.   Bring some wine.

THE VICAR. I thank you.   But — I will not drink today.

HEINRICH. Go.   Bring the wine.   I'll vouch for it.   'Tis good.
Well — as you please.   I pray you, do not stand.
This is my first encounter with a friend
Since I released myself from the distress
And shame that sickness brings.   I had not hoped
To welcome you, before all others, here —
Within the narrow sphere that bounds my work.
Now am I doubly glad: for now 'tis clear
You have learned what strength, and love, and duty mean.
I see you breaking, with one resolute blow,
The murderous chains of worldly interest —
Fleeing mankind, to seek the one true God.

THE VICAR. Now, God be thanked!   You are the old, true, Heinrich
They lied, who, in the valley, had proclaimed
You were no more the man that once we knew.

HEINRICH. That man am I, and yet... another man.
Open the windows — Light and God stream in!

THE VICAR. A goodly saying.

HEINRICH.   Ay.   The best I know.

THE VICAR. I know some better.   Yet your saying's good.

HEINRICH. Then, if you are ready, give me your right hand,
I swear, by Cock and Swan and Head of Horse,
With all my soul to serve you as your friend.

I'll open to you wide the gates of Spring —
The Spring that fills my heart.

THE VICAR.   Do as you say.
'Twill not be the first time.   You know me well.

HEINRICH. I know you.   Yes.   And though I knew you not,
Yea, though a vulgar soul your face should hide,
So boundless is my craving to do good,
That I ——.   Enough.   Gold always will be gold.
And even on the souls of sycophants
Good seed's not wasted.

THE VICAR.   Master, tell me this:
What was the meaning of your curious oath?

HEINRICH. By Cock and Swan?

THE VICAR.   Ay; and by Head of Horse?

HEINRICH. I know not how the words came to my lips...
Methinks... the weathercock on your church steeple —
The horse's head upon your neighbor's roof —
The swan that soared into the bright blue sky —
Or... something else — was in my mind just then.
What does it matter?... Ah, here comes the wine.
Now, in the deepest sense of every word,
I drink to our good health... yours... thine... and mine.

THE VICAR. I thank you: and once more I wish good health
To him who has so wondrously been healed.

HEINRICH (*pacing to and fro*). Yes.   I am healed — indeed.   I feel
    it here —
Here, in my breast, that swells as I draw in
Strength and new rapture with each living breath.
It is as though the very youth of May
Gladdened my heart and streamed into my being.
I feel it in my arm — 'tis hard as steel;
And in my hand, that, as the eagle's claw,
Clutches at empty air, and shuts again,
Wild with impatience to achieve great deeds.
Saw you the sanctuary in my garden?

THE VICAR. What do you mean?

HEINRICH.   There!... 'Tis another marvel.
    Look!

THE VICAR. I see nothing.

HEINRICH. I mean yonder tree,
That seems so like a glowing evening-cloud.
For the god Freyr once rested in its boughs.
From its green branches, and from round its stem,
Comes the voluptuous hum of countless bees —
Hark how they buzz and swarm about the flowers
Eager to sip sweet draughts from every bud!
I feel that I am like that wondrous tree...
Even as he came down into those boughs,
So did the god descend into my soul,
And, in an instant, it was all a-bloom.
If any bees go thirsting, let them suck!

THE VICAR. Go on, go on, my friend. I love to listen.
You and your blossoming tree indeed may boast.
Whether your fruit shall ripen, rests with God!

HEINRICH. Surely, dear friend. Does He not order all?
He hurled me down the precipice. 'Twas He
Who raised me up and caused my life to bloom.
He made the fruit, and flowers, and all that grows.
Yet — pray that He may bless my new-born Summer!
What's germed within me's worthy of the blessing —
Worthy of ripening: really and indeed.
It is a work like none I had yet conceived;
A chime, of all the noblest metals wrought,
That, of itself, shall ring and, ringing, live.
If I but put my hand up to my ear,
Straightway I hear it sing. I close my eyes —
Form after form at once grows palpable.
Behold. What now is freely given to me,
Of old — when ye were wont to acclaim me "Master" —
In nameless agony, I vainly sought.
I was no Master then, nor was I happy.
Now am I both; I am happy and a Master!

THE VICAR. I love to hear men call you by that name.
Yet it seems strange that you yourself should do so.
For what church are you making your great work?

HEINRICH. For no church.

THE VICAR.   Then — who ordered it, my friend?

HEINRICH. He who commanded yonder pine to rise
   In strength and majesty beside the abyss!...
   But — seriously: the little church you had built
   Lies half in ruins — half it has been burned.
   So I must find a new place on the heights:
   A new place, for a new, a nobler, temple!

THE VICAR. O, Master, Master!... But, I will not argue.
   Perchance we have misunderstood each other.
   To put things plainly, what I mean is this:
   As your new work must cost so very dear...

HEINRICH. Yes. It is costly.

THE VICAR.   Such a chime as yours...

HEINRICH. Oh, call it what you will.

THE VICAR.   You said — a chime?

HEINRICH. A name I gave to that which none may name,
   Nor can, nor shall baptize, except itself.

THE VICAR. And tell me, pray — who pays you for your work?

HEINRICH. Who pays me for my work? Oh, Father! Father!
   Would you give joy to joy — add gold to gold?...
   If I so named it, and the name you love —
   Call my great work — a chime!... But 'tis a chime
   Such as no minster in the world has seen.
   Loud and majestic is its mighty voice.
   Even as the thunder of a storm it sounds,
   Rolling and crashing o'er the meads in Spring.
   Ay, in the tumult of its trumpet-tones,
   All the church-bells on earth it shall strike dumb.
   All shall be hushed, as through the sky it rings
   The glad new Gospel of the new-born light!

     .   .   .   .

   Eternal Sun! [1] Thy children, and my children,
   Know thee for Father, and proclaim thy power.
   Thou, aided by the kind and gentle rain,
   Didst raise them from the dust and give them health!
   So now — their joy triumphant they shall send

---

[1] In the German the Sun is feminine. The original passage has consequently been modified.

Singing along thy clear, bright, path to Heaven!
And now, at last, like the grey wilderness
That thou hast warmed, and mantled with thy green,
Me thou hast kindled into sacrifice!
I offer thee myself, and all I am!...
O Day of Light — when, from the marble halls
Of my fair Temple, the first waking peal
Shall shake the skies — when, from the sombre clouds
That weighed upon us through the winter night,
Rivers of jewels shall go rushing down
Into a million hands outstretched to clutch!
Then all who drooped, with a sudden power inflamed,
Shall bear their treasure homeward to their huts,
There to unfurl, at last, the silken banners,
Waiting — so long, so long — to be upraised,
And, pilgrims of the Sun, draw near the Feast!

. . . .

O, Father, that great Day!... You know the tale
Of the lost Prodigal?... It is the Sun
That bids his poor, lost, children to my Feast.
With rustling banners, see the swelling host
Draw nearer, and still nearer to my Temple.
And now the wondrous chime again rings out,
Filling the air with such sweet, passionate sound
As makes each breast to sob with rapturous pain.
It sings a song, long lost and long forgotten,
A song of home — a childlike song of Love,
Born in the waters of some fairy well —
Known to all mortals, and yet heard of none!
And as it rises, softly first, and low,
The nightingale and dove seem singing, too;
And all the ice in every human breast
Is melted, and the hate, and pain, and woe,
Stream out in tears.

. . . .

Then shall we all draw nearer to the Cross,
And, still in tears, rejoice, until at last
The dead Redeemer, by the Sun set free,

His prisoned limbs shall stir from their long sleep,
And, radiant with the joy of endless youth,
Come down, Himself a youth, into the May!

(HEINRICH'S *enthusiasm has swelled as he has spoken the fore-*
going speech, till at last it has become ecstatic. He walks to and
fro. RAUTENDELEIN, *who has been silently watching him all this*
time, showing her love and adoration by the changing expression of
her face, now approaches HEINRICH, *with tears in her eyes, kneels*
beside him, and kisses his hand. The VICAR *has listened to*
HEINRICH *with growing pain and horror. Towards the end of*
HEINRICH'S *speech he has contained himself with difficulty.*
After a brief pause he answers. At first he speaks with enforced
calm. Gradually, however, his feeling carries him away.)

THE VICAR. And now, dear Master, I have heard you out:
Now every syllable those worthy men
Had told me of your state, alas, is proved.
Yea, even to the story of this chime of bells.
I cannot tell you all the pain I feel!...
A truce to empty words! If here I stand,
'Tis not because I thirsted for your marvels.
No! 'Tis to help you in your hour of need!
HEINRICH. My need?... And so you think I am in need?
THE VICAR. Man! Man! Bestir yourself. Awake! You dream!
A dreadful dream, from which you'll surely wake
To everlasting sorrow. Should I fail
To rouse you, with God's wise and holy words,
You are lost, ay, lost for ever, Master Heinrich!
HEINRICH. I do not think so.
THE VICAR.   What saith the Good Book? [1]
"Those whom He would destroy, He first doth blind."
HEINRICH. If God so willed it — you'd resist in vain.
Yet, should I own to blindness,
Filled as I feel myself with pure, new life,
Bedded upon a glorious morning cloud,
Whence with new eyes I drink in all the heavens;
Why, then, indeed, I should deserve God's curse,
And endless Darkness.

---

[1] So it stands in the original.

THE VICAR. Master Heinrich — friend,
I am too humble to keep pace with you.
A simple man am I — a child of Earth:
The superhuman lies beyond my grasp.
But one thing I do know, though you forget,
That wrong is never right, nor evil, good.

HEINRICH. And Adam did not know so much in Eden!

THE VICAR. Fine phrases, sounding well, but meaningless.
They will not serve to cloak your deadly sin.
It grieves me sore — I would have spared you this.
You have a wife, and children...

HEINRICH. Well — what more?

THE VICAR. You shun the church, take refuge in the mountains;
This many a month you have not seen the home
Where your poor wife sits sighing, while, each day,
Your children drink their lonely mother's tears! (*A long pause.*)

HEINRICH (*with emotion*). Could I but wipe away those sorrowful
    tears,
How gladly would I do it!... But I cannot.
In my dark hours, I've digged into my soul,
Only to feel, I have no power to dry them.
I, who am now all love, in love renewed,
Out of the overflowing wealth I own,
May not fill up their cup! For, lo, my wine
Would be to them but bitter gall and venom!
Should he whose hand is as the eagle's claw
Stroke a child's sick wet cheek?... Here none but God
Could help!

THE VICAR. For this there is no name but madness,
And wicked madness. Yes. I speak the truth.
Here stand I, Master, overcome with horror
At the relentless cruelty of your heart.
Now Satan, aping God, hath dealt a blow —
Yes, I must speak my mind — a blow so dread
That even he must marvel at his triumph.
That work, Almighty God, whereof he prates —
Do I not know 't?... 'Tis the most awful crime
Ever was hatched within a heathen brain!

Far rather would I see the dreadful plagues
Wherewith the Lord once scourged rebellious Egypt
Threaten our Christendom, than watch your Temple
Rise to the glory of Beelzebub.
Awake! Arise! Come back, my son, to Christ!
It is not yet too late! Cast out this witch!
Renounce this wanton hag — ay, cast her out!
This elf, this sorceress, this cursèd sprite!
Then in a trice, the evil spell shall fade
And vanish into air. You shall be saved!

HEINRICH. What time I fevered lay, a prey to death,
    She came, and raised me up, and made me well.

THE VICAR. 'Twere better you had died — than live like this!

HEINRICH. Why, as to that, think even as you will.
    But, as for me — I took life's burden up.
    I live anew, and, till death comes, must thank
    Her who did give me life.

THE VICAR.   Now — I have done!
Too deep, yea to the neck, you are sunk in sin!
Your Hell, decked out in beauty as high Heaven,
Shall hold you fast. I will not waste more words.
Yet mark this, Master: witches make good fuel,
Even as heretics, for funeral-pyres.
Vox populi, vox Dei! Your ill deeds,
Heathen, and secret once, are now laid bare.
Horror they wake, and soon there shall come hate.
So it may happen that the storm, long-curbed,
All bounds shall overleap, and that the people
Whom you have outraged in their holiest faith,
Shall rise against you in their own defence,
And crush you ruthlessly!   *(Pause.)*

HEINRICH *(calmly)*.   And now hear me...
I fear you not!... Should they who panting lie
Dash from my hand the cup of cooling wine
I bore to them: if they would rather thirst —
Why, then, it is their will — perhaps their fate —
And none may justly charge me with their act.
I am no longer thirsty. I have drunk.

If it is fitting that, of all men, you —
Who have closed your eyes against the truth — should be
That man who now assails so hatefully
The blameless cup-bearer, and flings the mud
Of Darkness 'gainst his soul, where all is light:
Yet I am I!... What I would work, I know.
And if, ere now, full many a faulty bell
My stroke has shattered, once again will I
Swing my great hammer, for a mightier blow,
Dealt at another bell the mob has made —
Fashioned of malice, gall, and all ill things,
Last but not least among them ignorance.

THE VICAR. Then, go your way!   Farewell.   My task is done.
The hemlock of your sin no man may hope
To rid your soul of.   May God pity you!
But this remember!   There's a word named rue!
And some day, some day, as your dreams you dream,
A sudden arrow, shot from out the blue,
Shall pierce your breast!   And yet you shall not die,
Nor shall you live.   In that dread day you'll curse
All you now cherish — God, the world, your work,
Your wretched self you'll curse.   Then... think of me!

HEINRICH. Had I a fancy to paint phantoms, Vicar,
I'd be more skilful in the art than you.
The things you rave of never shall come true,
And I am guarded well against your arrow.
No more it frets me, nor my heart can shake,
Than that old bell, which in the water rolled —
Where it lies buried now, and hushed — forever!

THE VICAR. That bell shall toll again!   Then think of me!

CURTAIN

ACT FOUR

SCENE: *The glass-works as in Act Three. A rude door has been hewn out of the rocky wall, L. Through this, access is obtained to a mountain-cave. R., the open forge, with bellows and chimney. The fire is lighted. Near the forge stands an anvil.*

DISCOVERED: HEINRICH, *at the anvil, on which he is laying a bar of red-hot iron which he holds tight with his tongs. Near him stand six little* DWARFS *attired as mountaineers. The* FIRST DWARF *holds the tongs with* HEINRICH; *the* SECOND DWARF *lifts the great forge hammer and rings it down with a ringing blow on the iron. The* THIRD DWARF *works the bellows. The* FOURTH DWARF *stands motionless, intently watching the progress of the work. The* FIFTH DWARF *stands by, waiting. In his hand he holds a club, ready to strike. The* SIXTH DWARF *sits perched on the stump of a tree. On his head he wears a glittering crown. Here and there lie fragments of forged iron and castings, models and plans.*

HEINRICH (*to* SECOND DWARF). Strike hard! Strike harder! Till
    thy arm hangs limp.
Thy whimpering does not move me, thou poor sluggard —
Shouldst thou relax before the time I set,
I'll singe thy beard for thee in these red flames.

                (SECOND DWARF *throws his hammer down.*)

Oho! 'Tis as I thought. Well, wait, thou imp!
And thou shalt see I mean what I have threaten'd!

    (SECOND DWARF *struggles and screams as* HEINRICH *holds him
      over the fire.* THIRD DWARF *goes to work more busily than ever
      at the bellows.*)

FIRST DWARF (*with the tongs*). I can't hold on. My hand is stiff,
    great Master!
HEINRICH. I'm coming.   (*He turns to* SECOND DWARF.)
            Well, dost thou feel stronger now?

    (SECOND DWARF *nods reassuringly, and hammers away for dear
      life.*)

HEINRICH. By Cock and Swan! I'll have no mercy on you!

                (*He clutches the tongs again.*)

No blacksmith living could a horseshoe shape
An he should stand on trifles with such rogues.

No sooner have they struck the first good stroke
When off they'd go, and leave the rest to chance.
And as for counting on them for the zeal
That spurs an honest workman to attempt
Ten thousand miracles — why, 'twould be mad.
To work! To work! Hot iron bends — not cold!

(*To* FIRST DWARF).

What art thou at?

FIRST DWARF (*busily trying to mould the red-hot iron with his hand*).
                    I'm moulding it with my hand.

HEINRICH. Thou reckless fool. What? Hast thou lost thy wits?
Wouldst thou reduce thy clumsy paw to ashes?
Thou wretched dwarf, if thou shouldst fail me now,
What power had I?... Without thy helping art,
How could I hope to see my cherished work
Rise from the summit of my temple towers
Into the free and sunlit air of heaven?

FIRST DWARF. The iron is well forged. The hand is whole —
Deadened and numbed a little: that is all.

HEINRICH. Off to the well with thee! The Nickelmann
Will cool thy fingers with his water-weeds.

(*To the* SECOND DWARF.)

Now take the rest thou'st earned, thou lazy imp,
And make the most of it. I'll comfort seek
In the reward that comes of honest effort.

(*He picks up the newly forged iron, sits, and examines it.*)

Ah, here's rare work for you! The kindly powers
Have crowned our labor with this good result.
I am content. Methinks I have cause to be,
Since, out of shapelessness, a shape has grown,
And, out of chaos, this rare masterpiece:
Nicely proportioned — here... above... below...
Just what was needed to complete the work.

(*The* FOURTH DWARF *clambers on to a stool and whispers in*
HEINRICH'S *ear.*)

What art thou muttering, imp? Disturb me not,
Lest I should tie thy hands and feet together,
And clap a gag into thy chattering throat!

(DWARF *retreats in alarm.*)

What's out of joint in the great scheme?   What's wrong?
What irks thee?   Speak when thou art questioned, dwarf!
Never as now was I so filled with joy;
Never were heart and hand more surely one.
What art thou grumbling at?   Am I not Master?
Wouldst thou, poor hireling, dare to vie with me?
Well — out with it!   Thy meaning — Speak!   Be plain!

>   (DWARF *returns and whispers.*   HEINRICH *turns pale, sighs, rises,*
>   *and angrily lays the iron on the anvil.*)

Then may the Devil end this work himself!
I'll grow potatoes, and plant cabbages.
I'll eat and drink and sleep, and then — I'll die!

>   (FIFTH DWARF *approaches the anvil.*)

Thou, fellow, do not dare to lay thy hand on 't!
Ay, burst with fury, an thou wilt.   I care not.
And let thy hair stand straight on end — thy glance
Dart death.   Thou rogue!   Who yields but once to thee,
Or fails to hold thee tightly in his clutch,
Might just as well bow down and be thy slave,
And wait till, with thy club, thou end his pain!

>   (FIFTH DWARF *angrily shatters the iron on the anvil;* HEINRICH
>   *grinds his teeth with rage.*)

Well, well!   Run riot!   No more work tonight.
A truce to duty.   Get ye hence, ye dwarfs!
Should morning, as I hope, put fresh, new life
Into this frame of mine — I'll call ye back.
Go! — Work unbidden would avail me naught.

>   (*To* THIRD DWARF.)

Come — drop thy bellows, dwarf.   With all thy might,
Thou'dst hardly heat me a new iron tonight.

>   Away!   Away!

>   (*All the* DWARFS, *with the exception of the one with the crown,*
>   *vanish through the door L.*)

And thou, crowned King, who only once shalt speak —
Why dost thou linger?   Get thee gone, I say.
Thou wilt not speak today, nor yet tomorrow:
Heaven only knows if thou wilt ever speak!
My work!... My work!   When will it end!... I'm tired!

I love thee not, sad twilight hour, that liest
Pressed 'twixt the dying day and growing night.
Thou wringest from my nerveless hand the hammer,
Yet bring'st me not the sleep, the dreamless sleep,
That gives men rest. A heart athirst for work
Knows it must wait, and wait in idleness:
And so — in pain — it waits... for the new day.
The sun, wrapped round in purple, slowly sinks
Into the depths... and leaves us here alone.
While we, who are used to light, look helpless on,
And, stripped of everything, must yield to night.
Rags are the coverlets that cloak our sleep.
At noon we're kings... at dusk we're only beggars.

*(He throws himself on a couch and lies dreaming, with wide-open
eyes. A white mist comes in through the open door. When it
disappears, the* NICKELMANN *is discovered leaning over the edge
of the water-trough.)*

THE NICKELMANN. Quorax!... Brekekekex!... So there he lies —
This Master Earth-Worm — in his moss-grown house.
He's deaf and blind, while crookback imps do creep
Like the grey mists upon the mountain-side.
Now they uplift their shadowy hands, and threaten!
Now they go wringing them, as though in pain!
He sleeps! He does not heed the moaning pines;
The low, malignant piping of the elves
That makes the oldest fir-trees quake and thrill,
And, like a hen that flaps her foolish wings,
Beat their own boughs against their quivering flanks...!
Now, he grows chiller, as the winter-grey
Searches the marrow in his bones. And still,
Even in sleep, he toils!
Give over, fool! Thou canst not fight with God!
'Twas God that raised thee up, to prove thy strength;
And now, since thou art weak, He casts thee down!

*(*HEINRICH *tosses about and moans in his sleep.)*

Vain is thy sacrifice. For Sin is Sin.
Thou hast not wrung from God the right to change
Evil to good — or wages give to guilt.

Thou'rt foul with stains.   Thy garments reek with blood.
Now, call thou ne'er so loud, the gentle hand
That might have washed thee clean, thou'lt never see!
Black spirits gather in the hills and dales.
Soon in thine anguished ear the sound shall ring
Of the wild huntsmen and the baying hounds!
They know what game they hunt!... And now, behold!
The giant builders of the air upraise
Castles of cloud, with monstrous walls and towers.
Frowning and grim, they move against thy heights,
Eager to crush thy work, and thee, and all!

HEINRICH.   Help! Help! Rautendelein! An alp! I choke.

THE NICKELMANN. She hears thee — and she comes — but brings
no help!
Though she were Freya, and though thou wert Balder —
Though sun-tipped shafts did fill thy radiant quiver,
And ev'ry shaft that thou shouldst point went home —
Thou must be vanquished.   Hear me!

> A sunken bell in the deep mere lies,
> Under the rocks and the rolling:
> And it longs to rise —
> In the sunlight again to be tolling!
> The fishes swim in, and the fishes swim out,
> As the old bell tosses, and rolls about.
> It shudders and sways as they come and go,
> And weeping is heard, and the sound of woe.
> A muffled moan, and a throb of pain,
> Answer the swirling flood —
> For the mouth of the bell is choked with blood!
> Woe, woe, to thee, man, when it tolls again!
>   Bim!... Boom!
> The Lord save thee from thy doom!
>   Bim!... Boom!
>   Hark to the knell!
> Death is the burden of that lost bell!
>   Bim!... Boom!
> The Lord save thee from thy doom!

(*The* NICKELMANN *sinks into the well.*)

HEINRICH. Help! Help! A nightmare chokes me! Help! Help!
    Help!   (*He awakes.*)
   Where am I?... Am I living?
              (*He rubs his eyes and looks round him.*)
         No one here?

RAUTENDELEIN (*entering*). I'm here! Did'st call?

HEINRICH.   Yes! Come! Come here to me.
   Lay thy dear hand upon my forehead — so,
   And let me stroke thy hair... and feel thy heart.
   Come. Nearer. In thy train thou bring'st the scent
   Of the fresh woods and rosemary. Ah, kiss me!
   Kiss me!

RAUTENDELEIN. What ails thee, dearest?

HEINRICH.   Nothing, nothing!
   Give me a coverlet... I lay here chilled...
   Too tired to work... My heart grew faint... and then
   Dark powers of evil seemed to enter in...
   Laid hold of me, possessed me, plagued me sore,
   And tried to throttle me... But now I'm well.
   Have thou no fear, child. I'm myself again!
   Now let them come!

RAUTENDELEIN.   Who?

HEINRICH.   Why, my foes.

RAUTENDELEIN.   What foes?

HEINRICH. My nameless enemies — ay, one and all!
   I stand upon my feet, as once I stood,
   Ready to brave them, though they filled my sleep
   With crawling, creeping, cowardly terrors!

RAUTENDELEIN. Thou'rt fevered, Heinrich!

HEINRICH.   Ay, 'tis chill tonight.
   No matter. Put thy arms around me. So.

RAUTENDELEIN. Thou, dearest, dearest!

HEINRICH.   Tell me this, my child.
   Dost trust in me?

RAUTENDELEIN.   Thou Balder! Hero! God!
   I press my lips against the fair white brow
   That overhangs the clear blue of thine eyes.   (*Pause.*)

HEINRICH. So — I am all thou say'st?... I am thy Balder?

Make me believe it — make me know it, child!
Give my faint soul the rapturous joy it needs,
To nerve it to its task.   For, as the hand,
Toiling with tong and hammer, on and on,
To hew the marble and to guide the chisel,
Now bungles here, now there, yet may not halt,
And nothing, small or great, dare leave to chance,
So do we ofttimes lose our passionate faith,
Feel the heart tighten, and the eyes grow dim,
Till, in the daily round of drudging work,
The clear projection of the soul doth vanish.
For, to preserve that Heaven-sent gift is hard.
No clamp have we, no chain, to hold it fast.
'Tis as the aura that surrounds a sun,
Impalpable.   That lost, all's lost.
Defrauded now we stand, and tempted sore
To shirk the anguish that foreruns fruition.
What, in conception, seemed all ecstasy,
Now turns to sorrow.   But — enough of this.
Still straight and steady doth the smoke ascend
From my poor human sacrifice to Heaven.
Should now a Hand on high reject my gift,
Why, it may do so.   Then the priestly robe
Falls from my shoulder — by no act of mine;
While I, who erst upon the heights was set,
Must look my last on Horeb, and be dumb!
But now bring torches!   Lights!   And show thine art!
Enchantress!   Fill the winecup!   We will drink!
Ay, like the common herd of mortal men,
With resolute hands our fleeting joy we'll grip!
Our unsought leisure we will fill with life,
Not waste it, as the herd, in indolence.
We will have music!

RAUTENDELEIN.   O'er the hills I flew:
Now, as a cobweb, on the breezes drifting,
Now frolicking as a bee, or butterfly,
And darting hungrily from flower to flower.
From each and all, from every shrub and plant,

Each catch-fly, harebell, and forget-me-not,
I dragged the promise, and I forced the oath,
That bound them never to do harm to thee.
And so — the blackest elf, most bitter foe
To thee, so good and white, should vainly seek
To cut thy death-arrow! [1]

HEINRICH.   What is this arrow?
I know the spirit!... Yes, I know't!... There came
A spirit to me once, in priestly garb,
Who, threat'ning, raised his hand, the while he raved
Of some such arrow that should pierce my heart.
Who'll speed the arrow from his bow, I say?
Who — who will dare?

RAUTENDELEIN.   Why, no one, dearest. No one.
Thou'rt proof against all ill, I say — thou'rt proof.
And now, blink but thine eye, or only nod,
And gentle strains shall upward float, as mist,
Hem thee about, and, with a wall of music,
Guard thee from call of man, and toll of bell:
Yea, mock at even Loki's mischievous arts.
Make the most trifling gesture with thy hand,
These rocks shall turn to vaulted palace-halls,
Earth-men unnumbered shall buzz round, and stand
Ready to deck the floor, the walls, the board!
Yet — since by dark, fierce foes we are beset,
Wilt thou not flee into the earth with me?
There we need fear no icy giant's breath —
There the vast halls shall shine with dazzling light ——

HEINRICH. Peace, child. No more. What were thy feast to me
So long as solemn, mute, and incomplete,
My work the hour awaits, wherein its voice
Shall loudly usher in the Feast of Feasts!...
I'll have one more good look at the great structure.
So shall new fetters bind me to it fast.
Take thou a torch, and light me on my way.
Haste! Haste!... Since now I feel my nameless foes

---

[1] It was an old belief that dangerous arrows were shot down from the air by elves.

Busy at work to do me injury —
Since now the fabric's menaced at the base —
'Tis meet the Master, too, should toil — not revel.
For, should success his weary labor crown,
The secret wonder stand at last revealed,
In gems and gold expressed, and ivory,
Even to the faintest, feeblest, of its tones —
His work should live, triumphant, through the ages!
'Tis imperfection that draws down the curse,
Which, could we brave it here, we'd make a mock of.
Ay, we will make a mock of't!   (*He moves to the door and halts.*)
                                        Well, child?...
Why dost thou linger!... Have I grieved thee?
RAUTENDELEIN.   No!
   No!   No!
HEINRICH.   What ails thee?
RAUTENDELEIN.   Nothing!
HEINRICH.   Thou poor soul!
   I know what grieves thee. — Children, such as thou,
   Run lightly after the bright butterflies,
   And often, laughing, kill what most they love.
   But I am not a butterfly.   I am more.
RAUTENDELEIN. And I?   Am I a child?... No more than that?
HEINRICH. Ay, truly, thou art more!... That to forget
   Were to forget the brightness of my life.
   The dew that glistened in thy shining eyes
   Filled me with pain.   And then I pained thee, too.
   Come!   'Twas my tongue, not I, that hurt thee so.
   My heart of hearts knows naught, save only love.
   Nay — do not weep so.   See — now I am armed;
   Thou hast equipped me for the game anew.
   Lo, thou hast filled my empty hands with gold;
   Given me courage for one more last throw!
   Now I can play with Heaven!... Ah, and I feel
   So blessed, so wrapped in thy strange loveliness —
   Yet, when I, wond'ring, seek to grasp it all,
   I am baffled.   For thy charm's unsearchable.
   And then I feel how near joy's kin to pain —
   Lead on!   And light my path!

THE WOOD-SPRITE (*without*).   Holdrio!
  Up! Up! Bestir yourselves! Plague o' the dawdlers!
  The heathen temple must be laid in ashes!
  Haste, reverend Sir! Haste, Master Barber, haste!
  Here there is straw and pitch a-plenty. See!
  The Master's cuddling his fair elfin bride —
  And while he toys with her, naught else he heeds.

HEINRICH. The deadly nightshade must have made him mad.
  What art thou yelling in the night, thou rogue?
  Beware!

THE WOOD-SPRITE (*defiantly*).
      Of thee?

HEINRICH.   Ay, fool. Beware of me!
  I know the way to manage such as thou,
  I'll grab thee by thy beard, thou misshaped oaf;
  Thou shalt be shorn and stripped, and when thou'rt tamed,
  When thou hast learned to know who's master here,
  I'll make thee work and slave for me — thou goat-shank!
  What?... Neighing, eh?... Dost see this anvil, beast?
  And, here, this hammer? It is hard enough
  To beat thee to a jelly.

THE WOOD-SPRITE (*turning his back on* HEINRICH *insolently*).
        Bah! Hammer away!
  Many and many a zealot's flashing sword
  Has tickled me, ere it was turned to splinters.
  The iron on thy anvil's naught but clay,
  And, like a cow's dug, at the touch it bursts.

HEINRICH. We'll see, thou windbag, thou hobgoblin damned!
  Wert thou as ancient as the Wester wood,
  Or did thy power but match thy braggart tongue —
  I'll have thee chained, and make thee fetch and carry,
  Sweep, drudge, draw water, roll huge stones and rocks,
  And shouldst thou loiter, beast, I'll have thee flayed!

RAUTENDELEIN. Heinrich! He warns thee!

THE WOOD-SPRITE.   Ay! Go to! Go to!
  'Twill be a mad game when they drag thee hence
  And roast thee, like an ox! And I'll be by!
  But now to find the brimstone, oil, and pitch,

Wherewith to make a bonfire that shall smoke
Till daylight shall be blotted out in darkness.   (*Exit.*)

> (*Cries and murmurs of many voices heard from below,
> without.*

RAUTENDELEIN. Dost thou not hear them, Heinrich? Men are
    coming!

  Hark to their boding cries!... They are for thee!

> (*A stone flung from without strikes* RAUTENDELEIN.)

  Help, grandmother!

HEINRICH.   So that is what was meant!

I dreamt a pack of hounds did hunt me down.
The hounds I hear. The hunt has not begun!
Their yelping, truly, could not come more pat.
For, though an angel had hung down from Heaven,
All lily-laden, and, with gentle sighs,
Entreated me to steadfastness,
He had convinced me less than those fierce cries
Of the great weight and purport of my mission.
Come one, come all! What's yours I guard for you!
I'll shield you from yourselves!... That be my watchword!

> (*Exit with hammer.*)

RAUTENDELEIN (*alone and in excitement*). Help, help, Bush-Grand-
    mother! Help, Nickelmann!

> (*The* NICKELMANN *rises from the well.*)

Ah, my dear Nickelmann, I beg of you —
Bid water, quick, come streaming from the rocks,
Wave upon wave, and drive them all away!
Do! Do!

THE NICKELMANN. Brekekekex! What shall I do?

RAUTENDELEIN. Let thy wild waters sweep them to the abyss!

THE NICKELMANN. I cannot.

RAUTENDELEIN.   But thou canst, good Nickelmann!

THE NICKELMANN. And if I should — what good were that to me?

I have no cause to wish well to the Master.
He'd love to lord it over God and men.
'Twould suit me if the fools should strike him down!

RAUTENDELEIN. Oh, help him — help! Or it will be too late!

THE NICKELMANN. What wilt thou give me, dear?

RAUTENDELEIN.   I give thee?

THE NICKELMANN.   Yes.

RAUTENDELEIN. Ah, what thou wilt!

THE NICKELMANN.   Oho! Brekekekex!
  Then strip thy pretty gown from thy brown limbs,
  Take off thy crimson shoon, thy dainty cap.
  Be what thou art! Come down into my well —
  I'll spirit thee a thousand leagues away.

RAUTENDELEIN. Forsooth! How artfully he'd made his plans!
  But now I tell thee once, and once for all;
  Thou'dst better clear thy pate of all thy schemes.
  For, shouldst thou live to thrice thy hoary age —
  Shouldst thou grow old as Granny — shouldst thou forever
  Prison me close in thine own oyster shells,
  I would not look at thee!

THE NICKELMANN.   Then... he must die.

RAUTENDELEIN. Thou liest!... I'm sure of't. Thou liest! Hark!
  Ah, well thou knowest his clear-sounding voice!
  Dost think I do not see thee shrink in fear?

                (*The* NICKELMANN *disappears in the well.*)

(*Enter* HEINRICH *in triumph, and flushed with the excitement of the strife.*
                    He laughs.)

HEINRICH. They came at me like hounds, and, even as hounds,
  I drove them from me with the flaming brands!
  Great boulders then I rolled upon their heads:
  Some perished — others fled! Come — give me drink!
  War cools the breast — 'tis steeled by victory.
  The warm blood rushes through my veins. Once more
  My pulse throbs joyously. War does not tire.
  War gives a man the strength of twenty men,
  And hate and love makes new!

RAUTENDELEIN.   Here, Heinrich. Drink!

HEINRICH. Yes, give it me, my child. I am athirst
  For wine, and light, and love, and joy, and thee! (He drinks.)
  I drink to thee, thou airy elfin sprite!
  And, with this drink, again I thee do wed.
  Without thee, my invention would be clogged,

I were a prey to gloom — world-weariness.
My child, I entreat thee, do not fail me now.
Thou art the very pinion of my soul.
Fail not my soul!

RAUTENDELEIN.   Ah, do not thou fail me!

HENRICH. That God forbid!... Ho!   Music!

RAUTENDELEIN.   Hither! Hither!
Come hither, little people!   Elves and gnomes!
Come! Help us to make merry! Leave your homes!
Tune all your tiny pipes, and harps, and flutes,

                    (*Faint elfin music heard without.*)

And watch me dance responsive to your lutes!
With glowworms, gleaming emerald, lo, I deck
My waving tresses and my dainty neck.
So jeweled, and adorned with fairy light,
I'll make e'en Freya's necklace seem less bright!

HENRICH (*interrupting*). Be still!... Methought...

RAUTENDELEIN.   What?

HEINRICH.   Didst not hear it then?

RAUTENDELEIN. Hear what?

HENRICH.   Why — nothing.

RAUTENDELEIN.   Dearest, what is wrong?

HEINRICH. I know not... But, commingling with thy music...
Methought I heard... a strain... a sound...

RAUTENDELEIN.   What sound?

HEINRICH. A plaint... a tone... a long, long, buried tone...
No matter. It was nothing! Sit thou here!
Give me thy rose-red lips. From this fair cup
I'll drink forgetfulness!

> (*They kiss. Long and ecstatic pause. Then* HEINRICH *and*
> RAUTENDELEIN *move, locked in each other's arms, through the
> doorway.*)

See! Deep and cool and monstrous yawns the gulf
That parts us from the world where mortals dwell.
I am a man.   Canst understand me, child?...
Yonder I am at home... and yet a stranger —
Here I am strange... and yet I seem at home.
Canst understand?

RAUTENDELEIN. Yes!

HEINRICH. Yet thou eyest me
So wildly. Why?

RAUTENDELEIN. I'm filled with dread — with horror!

HEINRICH. With dread? Of what?

RAUTENDELEIN. Of what? I cannot tell.

HEINRICH. 'Tis nothing. Let us rest.

(HEINRICH *leads* RAUTENDELEIN *towards the doorway in the rocks,*
L. He stops suddenly, and turns towards the open country.)
Yet may the moon,
That hangs so chalky-white in yonder heavens,
Not shed the still light of her staring eyes
On what's below... may she not flood with brightness
The valley whence I rose to these lone heights!
For what lies hid beneath that pall of grey
I dare not gaze on!... Hark! Child! Didst hear nothing?

RAUTENDELEIN. Nothing! And what thou saidst was dark to me!

HEINRICH. What! Dost thou still not hear't?

RAUTENDELEIN. What should I hear? —
The night wind playing on the heath, I hear —
I hear the cawing of the carrion-kite —
I hear thee, strangely uttering strange, wild, words,
In tones that seem as though they were not thine!

HEINRICH. There! There! Below... where shines the wicked
moon!
Look! Yonder!— Where the light gleams on the waters!

RAUTENDELEIN. Nothing I see! Nothing!

HEINRICH. With thy gerfalcon eyes
Thou seest naught? Art blind? What drags its way
Slowly and painfully along... There... See!

RAUTENDELEIN. Thy fancy cheats thee!

HEINRICH. No!... It was no cheat,
As God shall pardon me!... Peace! Peace! I say!
Now it climbs over the great boulder, yonder —
Down by the footpath...

RAUTENDELEIN. Heinrich! Do not look!
I'll close the doors and rescue thee by force!

HEINRICH. No! Let me be!... I must look down! I will!

RAUTENDELEIN. See — how the fleecy clouds whirl round and round,

As in a giant cauldron, 'mid the rocks!

Weak as thou art, beware! Go not too near!

HEINRICH. I am not weak!... 'Twas fancy. Now 'tis gone!

RAUTENDELEIN. That's well! Now be once more our Lord and Master!

Shall wretched visions so undo thy strength?

No! Take thy hammer! Swing it wide and high!...

HEINRICH. Dost thou not see them, where they climb and climb?...

RAUTENDELEIN. Where?

HEINRICH. There!... Now they have reached the rocky path...

Clad only in their little shirts they come!

RAUTENDELEIN. Who come?

HEINRICH. Two little lads, with bare, white feet.

They hold an urn between them... 'Tis so heavy!

Now one, and now the other, bends his knee...

His little, baby knee, to raise it up...

RAUTENDELEIN. O, help him, mother — help him in his need!

HEINRICH. A halo shines about their tiny heads...

RAUTENDELEIN. Some will-o'-the-wisp!

HEINRICH. No!... Kneel, and clasp thy hands!

Now... see... they are coming. Now... they are here!

(*He kneels, as the phantom forms of two* CHILDREN, *barefooted and clad only in their nightgowns, ascend from below and advance painfully towards him. Between them they carry a two-handled pitcher.*)

FIRST CHILD (*faintly*). Father!

HEINRICH. My child!

FIRST CHILD. Our mother sends thee greeting.

HEINRICH. Thanks, thanks, my dear, dear lad! All's well with her?

FIRST CHILD (*slowly and sadly*). All's very well!...

(*The first faint tones of the sunken bell are heard from the depths.*)

HEINRICH. What have you brought with you?

SECOND CHILD. A pitcher.

HEINRICH. Is't for me?

SECOND CHILD. Yes, father dear.

HEINRICH. What is there in the pitcher, my dear boy?

SECOND CHILD. 'Tis something salt!...

FIRST CHILD.   ... And bitter!

SECOND CHILD.   Mother's tears!

HEINRICH. Merciful God!

RAUTENDELEIN.   What art thou staring at?

HEINRICH. At them... at them...

RAUTENDELEIN.   At whom?

HEINRICH.   Hast thou not eyes?
  At them!   (*To the* CHILDREN.)

      Where is your mother? Speak, oh, speak!

FIRST CHILD. Our mother?

HEINRICH.   Yes! Where is she!

SECOND CHILD.   With... the... lilies...
  The water-lilies...   (*The bell tolls loudly.*)

HEINRICH.   Ah! The bell!

RAUTENDELEIN.   What bell?

HEINRICH. The old, old, buried bell!... It rings! It tolls!
  Who dealt this blow at me?... I will not listen!
  Help! Help me!... Help!...

RAUTENDELEIN.   Come to your senses, Heinrich!

HEINRICH. It tolls!... God help me!... Who has dealt this blow?
  Hark, how it peals! Hark, how the buried tones
  Swell louder, louder, till they sound as thunder,
  Flooding the world!...   (*Turning to* RAUTENDELEIN.)
              I hate thee! I abhor thee!
  Back! Lest I strike thee! Hence! Thou witch! Thou trull!
  Accursèd spirit! Curst be thou and I!
  Curst be my work!... And all!... Here! Here am I!...
  I come!... I come!... Now may God pity me!...

      (*He makes an effort, rises, stumbles, rises again, and tears himself
      away.*)

                          (*The* CHILDREN *have vanished.*)

RAUTENDELEIN. Stay! Heinrich! Stay!... Woe's me! Lost!...
  Lost for aye!

CURTAIN

ACT FIVE

The fir-clad glade seen in Act One.
Time: *Between midnight and dawn.*
Discovered: *Three* Elves, *resting near the well.*

FIRST ELF. The flame glows bright!
SECOND ELF.   The wind of sacrifice —
The red, red wind — blows in the vale!
THIRD ELF.   And lo,
The dark smoke from the pine-clad peak streams down
Into the gulf!
FIRST ELF.   And, in the gulf, white clouds
Lie thickly gathered!   From the misty sea
The wond'ring herds lift up their drowsy heads,
Lowing, impatient, for their sheltered stalls!
SECOND ELF. A nightingale within the beechwood sang:
It sang and sobbed into the waning night —
Till, all a-quiver with responsive woe,
I sank upon the dewy grass and wept.
THIRD ELF. 'Tis strange!   I lay upon a spider's web.
Between the blades of meadow-grass it hung,
All woven out of marvelous purple threads,
And softer than a royal shift it clung.
I lay, and rested, while the glistening dew
Flashed up at me from the green mead below:
And so, my heavy lids did gently droop,
Until at last I slept.   When I awoke,
The light had faded in the distant west:
My bed had turned to grey.   But, in the east,
Thick clouds went up, and up, that hid the moon,
While all the rocky ridge was covered o'er
With molten metal, glowing in the night.
And, in the bloody glare that downward streamed,
Methought — 'twas strange — the fields did stir with life,
And whisp'rings, sighs, and voices low I heard
That filled the very air with wretchedness.
Ah, it was pitiful!... Then, quick, I hailed

A fire-fly, who his soft, green lamp had trimmed.
But on he flew. And so alone I lay,
Trembling with fear, and lost in wonderment.
Till, winged and gleaming as the dragon-fly,
The dearest, loveliest, of all the elves,
Who from afar his coming had proclaimed,
Rustled and fell into my waiting arms.
And, as we prattled in our cosy bed,
Warm tears were mingled with our kisses sweet,
And then he sighed, and sobbed, and pressed me tight,
Mourning for Balder... Balder, who was dead!

FIRST ELF (*rising*). The flame glows bright!

SECOND ELF (*rising*). 'Tis Balder's funeral pyre!

THIRD ELF (*who meanwhile has moved slowly to the edge of the wood*).
Balder is dead!... I'm chill! (*She vanishes.*)

FIRST ELF. A curse doth fall
Upon the land — as Balder's funeral pall!

(*Fog drifts across the glade. When it clears away the* ELVES *have vanished.*)

(*Enter* RAUTENDELEIN, *slowly and wearily descending from the hillside. She drags herself towards the well, halting to rest, sitting and rising again with an effort, on her way. When she speaks, her voice is faint and strange.*)

RAUTENDELEIN.

Whither?... Ah, whither?... I sat till late,
While the gnomes ran wild in my hall of state.
They brought me a red, red cup to drain —
And I drank it down, in pain.
For the wine I drank was blood!

.   .   .   .

And, when I had drained the last red drop,
My heart in my bosom seemed to stop:
For a hand of iron had gripped the strings —
And still with a burning pain it wrings
The heart that I long to cool!

.   .   .   .

Then a crown on my wedding-board they laid —
All of rose-red coral and silver made.

As I set it upon my brow I sighed.
Woe's me!   Now the Water-man's won his bride!
And I'll cool my burning heart!

. . . .

Three apples fell into my lap last night,
Rose-red, and gold, and white —
Wedding-gifts from my water-sprite.
I ate the white apple, and white I grew:
I ate the gold apple, and rich I grew —
And the red one last I ate!

. . . .

Pale, white, and rosy-red,
A maiden sat — and she was dead.
Now, Water-man, unbar thy gate —
I bring thee home thy dead, dead, mate.
Deep down in the cold, damp, darkness, see —
With the silver fishes I come to thee...
Ah, my poor, burnt, aching, heart!

(*She descends slowly into the well.*)

(THE WOOD-SPRITE *enters from the wood, crosses to the well, and calls down.*)

THE WOOD-SPRITE. Hey!   Holdrio!   Old frog-king!   Up with
thee!
Hey!   Holdrio!   Thou web-foot wight bewitched!
Dost thou not hear me, monster?   Art asleep?
I say, come up! — and though beside thee lay
Thy fairest water-maid, and plucked thy beard,
I'd still say, leave thy reedy bed and come!
Thou'lt not repent it: for, by cock and pie,
What I've to tell thee is worth many a night
Spent in the arms of thy most lovesick sprite.

THE NICKELMANN (*from below*). Brekekekex!

THE WOOD-SPRITE.   Up!   Leave thy weedy pool!

THE NICKELMANN (*from below*). I have no time.   Begone, thou
chattering fool!

THE WOOD-SPRITE. What?   What?   Thou toad-i'-the-hole, thou
hast no time

To spare from wallowing in thy mud and slime?
I say, I bring thee news. Didst thou not hear?
What I foretold's come true. I played the seer!
He's left her!... Now, an thou wilt but be spry,
Thou'lt haply catch thy wondrous butterfly!
A trifle jaded — ay, and something worn:
But, Lord, what care the Nickelmann and Faun?
Rare sport thou'lt find her, comrade, even now —
Ay, more than thou hadst bargained for, I'll vow.

THE NICKELMANN (*rising from the well and blinking slyly*). Forsooth!
    ... He's tired of her, the minx! And so
Thou'dst have me hang upon her skirts?... No, no!

THE WOOD-SPRITE. What?... Hast thou wearied of this beauty,
    too?
Why, then — I would her whereabouts I knew!

THE NICKELMANN. Go hunt for her!

THE WOOD-SPRITE.   I've sought her, like a dog:
Above — below, through mirk, and mist, and fog.
I've climbed where never mountain-goat had been,
And every marmot far and near I've seen.
Each falcon, glede, and finch, and rat, and snake,
I've asked for news. But none could answer make.
Woodmen I passed — around a fire they slept —
From them I stole a brand, and upward crept:
Till, grasping in my hand the burning wood,
At last before the lonely forge I stood.
And now the smoke of sacrifice ascends!
Loud roar the flames — each rafter cracks and bends!
The power the Master boasted once is fled:
For ever and for aye, 'tis past and dead!

THE NICKELMANN. I know. I know. Thy news is old and
    stale.
Hast thou disturbed me with this idle tale?
Much more I'd tell thee — ay, who tolled the bell!
And how the clapper swung that rang the knell!
Hadst thou but seen, last night, as I did see,
What ne'er before had been, nor more shall be,
The hand of a dead woman, stark and cold,

Go groping for the bell that tossed and rolled.
And hadst thou heard the bell then make reply,
Peal upon peal send thundering to the sky —
Till, like the lioness that seeks her mate,
It thrilled the Master, even as the Voice of Fate!
I saw the woman — drowned. Her long, brown hair
Floated about her face: 'twas wan with care.
And alway, when her hand the bell had found,
The awful knell did loud, and louder, sound!
I'm old, and used to many a gruesome sight:
Yet horror seized me, and — I took to flight!
Hadst thou but seen, last night, what I have seen,
Thou wouldst not fret about thine elfin quean.
So, let her flit at will, from flower to flower:
I care not, I! Her charm has lost its power.

THE WOOD-SPRITE. Ods bodikins! I care, though, for the maid.
So — each to his own taste. I want the jade.
And once I hold her panting in these arms,
'Tis little I shall reck of dead alarms!

THE NICKELMANN. Quorax! Brekekekex! Oho! I see.
So that is still the flea that's biting thee?
Well — kill it, then. Go hunt her till thou'rt spent.
Yet, though a-hunting twice ten years thou went,
Thou shouldst not have her. 'Tis for me she sighs!
She has no liking for thy goaty eyes.
A hen-pecked Water-man, alack, I'm tied
By every whim and humor of my bride.
Now fare thee well. Thou'rt free, to come, or go:
But, as for me — 'tis time I went below!

(*He disappears in the well.*)

THE WOOD-SPRITE (*calling down the well*). So sure as all the stars in
heaven do shine —
So sure as these stout shanks and horns are mine —
So sure as fishes swim and birds do fly —
A man-child in thy cradle soon shall lie!
Good-night. Sleep well! And now, be off to bed!
On! On! Through brush and brier!... The flea is dead!

(THE WOOD-SPRITE *skips off.*)

(OLD WITTIKIN *issues from the hut and takes down her shutters.*)

WITTIKIN. 'Twas time I rose. I sniff the morning air.
A pretty hurly there has been tonight. (*A cock crows.*)
Oho! I thought so. Kikereekikee!
No need to give thyself such pains for me —
Thou noisy rogue — as if we did not know
What's coming, ere such cocks as thou did crow.
Thy hen another golden egg has laid?
And soon the sun shall warm the mirky glade?
Ay. Crow thy loudest, gossip! Sing and sing!
The dawn draws near. So strut thy fill and sing.
Another day's at hand. But — here 'tis dark...
Will no mad jack-o'-lantern give me a spark?...
I'll need more light to do my work, I wis...
And, as I live, my carbuncle I miss.

(*She fumbles in her pocket and produces a carbuncle.*)
Ah, here it is.

HEINRICH (*heard without*). Rautendelein!

WITTIKIN. Ay, call her!
She'll answer thee, I wager, thou poor brawler!

HEINRICH (*without*). Rautendelein! I come. Dost thou not hear?

WITTIKIN. Thou'lt need to call her louder, man, I fear.

(HEINRICH, *worn and weary, appears on the rocks above the hut.*
He is pale and in tatters. In his right hand he holds a heavy stone,
ready to hurl it back into the depths.)

HEINRICH. Come, if you dare! Be it priest, or be it barber,
Sexton, or schoolmaster — I care not who!
The first who dares another step to take,
Shall fall and headlong plunge into the gulf!
'Twas ye who drove my wife to death, not I!
Vile rabble, witless wretches, beggars, rogues —
Who weeks together mumble idle prayers
For a lost penny! Yet, so base are ye,
That, where ye can, God's everlasting love
Ye cheat of ducats!... Liars! Hypocrites!
Like rocks ye are heaped about your nether-land,
Ringing it round, as with a dam of stone,

Lest haply God's own waters, rushing in,
Should flood your arid Hell with Paradise.
When shall the great destroyer wreck your dam?
I am not he... Alas! I am not the man!

(He drops the stone and begins to ascend.)

WITTIKIN. That way is barred. So halt! And climb no more.

HEINRICH. Woman, what burns up yonder?

WITTIKIN.   Nay, I know not.
Some man there was, I've heard, who built a thing,
Half church, half royal castle. Now — he's gone!
And, since he's left it, up it goes in flame.

(HEINRICH makes a feeble effort to press upward.)

Did I not tell thee, man, the road was barred?
He who would pass that way had need o' wings.
And thy wings have been broken.

HEINRICH.   Ah, broken or no,
I tell thee, woman, I must reach the peak!
What flames up yonder is my work — all mine!
Dost understand me?... I am he who built it.
And all I was, and all I grew to be,
Was spent on it... I can... I can... no more!

WITTIKIN *(pause)*. Halt here a while. The roads are still pitch dark.
There is a bench. Sit down and rest.

HEINRICH.   I?... Rest?...
Though thou shouldst bid me sleep on silk and down,
That heap of ruins still would draw me on.
The kiss my mother — long she's joined the dust —
Did press years since upon my fevered brow,
Would bring no blessing to me now, no peace:
'Twould sting me like a wasp.

WITTIKIN.   Ay, so it would!
Wait here a bit, man. I will bring thee wine.
I've still a sup or two.

HEINRICH.   I must not wait.
Water! I thirst! I thirst!

WITTIKIN.   Go, draw, and drink!

*(HEINRICH moves to the well, draws, sits on the edge of the well, and
drinks. A faint, sweet voice is heard from below, singing
mournfully.)*

THE VOICE (*from below*).

> Heinrich, my sweetheart, I loved thee true.
> Now thou art come to my well to woo.
> Wilt thou not go?
> Love is all woe —
> Adieu!   Adieu!

HEINRICH. Woman, what voice was that?   Speak — answer me!
  What called and sang to me in such sad tones?
  It murmured, "Heinrich!"... from the depths it came...
  And then it softly sighed, " Adieu!   Adieu!"
  Who art thou, woman?   And what place is this?
  Am I waking from some dream?... These rocks,
  Thy hut, thyself, I seem to know ye all!
  Yet all are strange.   Can that which me befell
  Have no more substance than a peal that sounds,
  And, having sounded, dies away in silence?
  Woman, who art thou?

WITTIKIN.   I?... And who art thou?

HEINRICH. Dost ask me that?... Yes!   Who am I?   God wot!
  How often have I prayed to Heaven to tell me!...
  Who am I, God!... But Heaven itself is mute.
  Yet this I do know: whatsoe'er I be,
  Hero or weakling, demi-god or beast —
  I am the outcast child of the bright Sun —
  That longs for home: all helpless now, and maimed.
  A bundle of sorrow, weeping for the Light
  That stretches out its radiant arms in vain,
  And yearns for me!... What dost thou there?

WITTIKIN. Thou'lt learn that soon enough.

HEINRICH (*rising*).   Nay, I'll begone!
  Now, with thy bloody lamplight, show me a way
  Will lead me onward, upward, to the heights!
  Once I am there, where erst I Master stood,
  Lonely I'll live — thenceforth a hermit be —
  Who neither rules, nor serves.

WITTIKIN.   I doubt it much!
  What thou would'st seek up yonder is not that.

HEINRICH. How canst thou know?

WITTIKIN.   We know what we do know.

They'd almost run thee down, my friend?...Ay, ay!
When life shines bright, like wolves ye men do act,
Rend it and torture it.   But, when death comes,
No bolder are ye than a flock of sheep,
That trembles at the wolf.   Ay, ay, 'tis true!
The herds that lead ye are but sorry carles
Who with the hounds do hunt and loudly yelp:
They do not set their hounds to hunt the wolf:
Nay, nay: their sheep they drive into its jaws!...
Thou'rt not much better than the other herds.
Thy bright life thou has torn and spurned away.
And when death fronted thee, thou wast not bold.

HEINRICH. Ah, woman, list!... I know not how it came
That I did spurn and kill my clear bright life:
And, being a Master, did my task forsake,
Like a mere 'prentice, quaking at the sound
Of my own handiwork, the bell which I
Had blessed with speech.   And yet 'tis true!   Its voice
Rang out so loud from its great iron throat,
Waking the echoes of the topmost peaks,
That, as the threatening peal did rise and swell,
It shook my soul!... Yet I was still the Master!
Ere it had shattered me who moulded it,
With this same hand, that gave it form and life,
I should have crushed and ground it into atoms.

WITTIKIN. What's past, is past: what's done, is done, for aye.
Thou'lt never win up to thy heights, I trow.
This much I'll grant: thou wast a sturdy shoot,
And mighty — yet too weak.   Though thou wast called,
Thou'st not been chosen!... Come.   Sit down beside me.

HEINRICH. Woman!   Farewell!

WITTIKIN.   Come here, and sit thee down.

Strong — yet not strong enow!
Who lives, shall life pursue.   But be thou sure,
Up yonder thou shalt find it nevermore.

HEINRICH. Then let me perish here, where now I stand!

WITTIKIN. Ay, so thou shalt.   He who has flown so high,

Into the very Light, as thou hast flown,
Must perish, if he once fall back to Earth!

HEINRICH. I know it. I have reached my journey's end.
So be it.

WITTIKIN. Yes! Thou hast reached the end!

HEINRICH. Then tell me —
Thou who dost seem to me so strangely wise —
Am I to die and nevermore set eyes
On what, with bleeding feet, I still must seek?
Thou dost not answer me?... Must I go hence —
Leave my deep night, and pass to deepest darkness —
Missing the afterglow of that lost light?
Shall I not see her once...?

WITTIKIN. Whom wouldst thou see?

HEINRICH. I would see her. Whom else?... Dost not know that?

WITTIKIN. Thou hast one wish!... It is thy last!... So — wish.

HEINRICH (*quickly*). I have wished!

WITTIKIN. Then thou shalt see her once again.

HEINRICH (*rising and ecstatically*). Ah, mother!... Why I name thee
thus, I know not...
Art thou so mighty?... Canst thou do so much?...
Once I was ready for the end, as now:
Half hoping, as each feeble breath I drew,
That it might be the last. But then she came —
And healing, like the breeze in early Spring,
Rushed through my sickly frame: and I grew well...
All of a sudden, now I feel so light,
That I could soar up to the heights again.

WITTIKIN. Too late! (HEINRICH *recoils in terror*.)
Thy heavy burdens weigh thee down:
Thy dead ones are too mighty for thee. See!
I place three goblets on the table. So.
The first I fill with white wine. In the next,
Red wine I pour: the last I fill with yellow.
Now, shouldst thou drain the first, thy vanished power
Shall be restored to thee. Shouldst drink the second,
Once more thou shalt behold the spirit bright
Whom thou hast lost. But an thou dost drink both,

Thou must drain down the last.

> (*She turns to enter the hut. On the threshold she halts and utters the next words with solemn emphasis.*)

        I say thou must!

>   (*She goes into the hut.*)

> (HEINRICH *has listened to the preceding speech like a man dazed. As* OLD WITTIKIN *leaves him, he rouses himself and sinks on a bench.*)

HEINRICH. Too late!... She said, "Too late!"... Now all is done!
O heart, that knowest all, as ne'er before:
Why dost thou question?... Messenger of Fate!
Thy fiat, as the axe, doth sharply fall,
Cutting the strand of life!... It is the end!
What's left is respite!... But I'll profit by 't.
Chill blows the wind from the abyss. The day
That yonder gleam so faintly doth forerun,
Piercing the sullen clouds with pale white shafts,
I shall not see. So many days I have lived:
Yet this one day I shall not live to see!

>   (*He raises the first goblet.*)

Come then, thou goblet, ere the horror come!
A dark drop glistens at the bottom. One!
A last one... Why, thou crone, hadst thou no more?
So be it! (*He drinks.*) And now to thee, thou second cup!

>   (*He raises the second goblet.*)

It was for thee that I did drain the first.
And, wert thou missing, thou delicious draught,
Whose fragrance tempts to madness, the carouse
Whereunto God has bid us in this world
Were all too poor, meseems — unworthy quite,
Of thee, who dost the festal board so honor.
Now I do thank thee — thus!   (*He drinks.*)
       The drink is good.

> (*A murmur as of æolian harps floats on the air while he drinks.*)
> (RAUTENDELEIN *rises slowly from the well. She looks weary and sad. She sits on the edge of the well, combing her long flowing locks. Moonlight.* RAUTENDELEIN *is pale. She sings into vacancy. Her voice is faint.*)

RAUTENDELEIN.

> All, all alone, in the pale moon-shine,
> I comb my golden hair,
>> Fair, fairest Rautendelein!
> The mists are rising, the birds take flight,
> The fires burn low in the weary night...

THE NICKELMANN (*from below*).   Rautendelein!

RAUTENDELEIN.   I'm coming!

THE NICKELMANN (*from below*).   Come at once!

RAUTENDELEIN.

> Woe, woe, is me!
> So tight I am clad,
> A maid o' the well, bewitched and so sad!

THE NICKELMANN (*from below*).   Rautendelein!

RAUTENDELEIN.   I'm coming!

THE NICKELMANN (*from below*).   Come thou now!

RAUTENDELEIN.

> I comb my hair in the moonlight clear,
> And think of the sweetheart who loved me dear.
> The blue-bells all are ringing.
> Ring they of joy?   Ring they of pain?
> Blessing and bane —
> Answers the song they are singing!
> Now down I go, to my weedy well —
> No more I may wait:
> I must join my mate —
> Farewell!   Farewell!   (*She prepares to descend.*)

Who calls so softly?

HEINRICH.   I.

RAUTENDELEIN.   Who'rt thou?

HEINRICH.   Why — I.

Do but come nearer — ah, why wouldst thou fly?

RAUTENDELEIN. I dare not come!... I know thee not.   **Away!**
For him who speaks to me, I am doomed to slay.

HEINRICH. Why torture me?   Come.   Lay thy hand in mine,
And thou shalt know me.

RAUTENDELEIN.   I have never known thee.

HEINRICH. Thou know'st me not?

RAUTENDELEIN.   No!

HEINRICH.   Thou hast never seen me?

RAUTENDELEIN. I cannot tell.

HEINRICH.   Then may God cast me off!
  I never kissed thee till thy lips complained?

RAUTENDELEIN. Never.

HEINRICH.   Thou'st never pressed thy lips to mine?

THE NICKELMANN (*from below*). Rautendelein!

RAUTENDELEIN.   I'm coming!

THE NICKELMANN.   Come. I wait!

HEINRICH. Who called to thee?

RAUTENDELEIN.   The Water-man — my mate!

HEINRICH. Thou seest my agony — the pain and strife
  That rend my soul, and eat away my life!
  Ah, torture me no longer. Set me free!

RAUTENDELEIN. Then, as thou wilt. But how?

HEINRICH.   Come close to me!

RAUTENDELEIN. I cannot come.

HEINRICH.   Thou canst not?

RAUTENDELEIN.   No. I am bound·

HEINRICH. By what?

RAUTENDELEIN (*retreating*). I must begone to join the round,
  A merry dance — and though my foot be sore,
  Soon, as I dancing go, it burns no more.
  Farewell! Farewell!

HEINRICH.   Where art thou? Stay, ah stay!

RAUTENDELEIN (*disappearing behind the well*). Lost, lost, for ever!

HEINRICH.   The goblet — quick, I say!
  There... there... the goblet!... Magda? Thou?... So pale!...
  Give me the cup. Who brings it, I will hail
  My truest friend.

RAUTENDELEIN (*reappearing*). I bring it.

HEINRICH.   Be thou blessed.

RAUTENDELEIN. Yes. I will do it. Leave the dead to rest!
                    (*She gives* HEINRICH *the goblet.*)

HEINRICH. I feel thee near me, thou dear heart of mine!

RAUTENDELEIN (*retreating*). Farewell! Farewell! I never can be
      thine!

Once I was thy true love — in May, in May —
Now all is past, for aye!...

HEINRICH.   For aye!

RAUTENDELEIN.   For aye!
Who sang thee soft to sleep with lullabies?
Who woke thee with enchanting melodies?

HEINRICH. Who, who — but thou?

RAUTENDELEIN.   Who am I?

HEINRICH.   Rautendelein!

RAUTENDELEIN. Who poured herself into thy veins, as wine?
Whom didst thou drive into the well to pine?

HEINRICH. Thee, surely thee!

RAUTENDELEIN.   Who am I?

HEINRICH.   Rautendelein!

RAUTENDELEIN. Farewell! Farewell!   *(He drinks.)*

HEINRICH.   Nay: lead me gently down.
Now comes the night — the night that all would flee.

    (RAUTENDELEIN *hastens to him, and clasps him about the knees.*)

RAUTENDELEIN (*exultingly*). The Sun is coming!

HEINRICH.   The Sun!

RAUTENDELEIN (*half-sobbing, half-rejoicing*).   Ah, Heinrich!

HEINRICH.   Thanks!

RAUTENDELEIN (*embracing* HEINRICH, *she presses her lips to his, and then gently lays him down as he dies*). Heinrich!

HEINRICH (*ecstatically*).   I hear them! 'Tis the Sun-bells' song!
The Sun... The Sun... draws near!... The Night is... long!

                              (*Dawn breaks. He dies.*)

THE CHERRY ORCHARD

A COMEDY IN FOUR ACTS

By ANTON TCHEKOV

Translated by CONSTANCE GARNETT

CHARACTERS IN THE PLAY

MADAME RANEVSKY (LYUBOV ANDREYEVNA) (*the owner of the Cherry Orchard*).

ANYA (*her daughter, aged* 17).

VARYA (*her adopted daughter, aged* 24).

GAEV (LEONID ANDREYEVITCH) (*brother of Madame Ranevsky*).

LOPAHIN (YERMOLAY ALEXEYEVITCH) (*a merchant*).

TROFIMOV (PYOTR SERGEYEVITCH) (*a student*).

SEMYONOV-PISHTCHIK (*a landowner*).

CHARLOTTA IVANOVNA (*a governess*).

EPIHODOV (SEMYON PANTALEYEVITCH) (*a clerk*).

DUNYASHA (*a maid*).

FIRS (*an old valet, aged* 87).

YASHA (*a young valet*).

A VAGRANT.

THE STATION MASTER.

A POST-OFFICE CLERK.

VISITORS, SERVANTS.

The action takes place on the estate of MADAME RANEVSKY.

ACT I

A room, which has always been called the nursery. One of the doors leads into ANYA'S *room. Dawn, sun rises during the scene. May, the cherry trees in flower, but it is cold in the garden with the frost of early morning. Windows closed.*

Enter DUNYASHA *with a candle, and* LOPAHIN *with a book in his hand.*

LOPAHIN. The train's in, thank God. What time is it?

DUNYASHA. Nearly two o'clock (*puts out the candle*). It's daylight already.

LOPAHIN. The train's late! Two hours, at least (*yawns and stretches*). I'm a pretty one; what a fool I've been. Came here on purpose to meet them at the station and dropped asleep.... Dozed off as I sat in the chair. It's annoying.... You might have waked me.

DUNYASHA. I thought you had gone (*listens*). There, I do believe they're coming!

LOPAHIN (*listens*). No, what with the luggage and one thing and another (*a pause*). Lyubov Andreyevna has been abroad five years; I don't know what she is like now.... She's a splendid woman. A good-natured, kind-hearted woman. I remember when I was a lad of fifteen, my poor father—he used to keep a little shop here in the village in those days—gave me a punch in the face with his fist and made my nose bleed. We were in the yard here, I forget what we'd come about—he had had a drop. Lyubov Andreyevna—I can see her now—she was a slim young girl then—took me to wash my face, and then brought me into this very room, into the nursery. "Don't cry, little peasant," says she, "it will be well in time for your wedding day" ...(*a pause*). Little peasant.... My father was a peasant, it's true, but here am I in a white waistcoat and brown shoes, like a pig in a bun shop. Yes, I'm a rich man, but for all my money, come to think, a peasant I was, and a peasant I am (*turns over the pages of the book*). I've been reading this book and I can't make head or tail of it. I fell asleep over it (*a pause*).

DUNYASHA. The dogs have been awake all night, they feel that the mistress is coming.

LOPAHIN. Why, what's the matter with you, Dunyasha?

DUNYASHA. My hands are all of a tremble. I feel as though I should faint.

LOPAHIN. You're a spoilt soft creature, Dunyasha. And dressed like a lady too, and your hair done up. That's not the thing. One must know one's place.

(*Enter* EPIHODOV *with a nosegay; he wears a pea-jacket and highly polished creaking topboots; he drops the nosegay as he comes in.*)

EPIHODOV (*picking up the nosegay*). Here! the gardener's sent this, says you're to put it in the dining-room (*gives* DUNYASHA *the nosegay*).

LOPAHIN. And bring me some kvass.

DUNYASHA. I will (*goes out*).

EPIHODOV. It's chilly this morning, three degrees of frost, though the cherries are all in flower. I can't say much for our climate (*sighs*). I can't. Our climate is not often propitious to the occasion. Yermolay Alexeyevitch, permit me to call your attention to the fact that I purchased myself a pair of boots the day before yesterday, and they creak, I venture to assure you, so that there's no tolerating them. What ought I to grease them with?

LOPAHIN. Oh, shut up! Don't bother me.

EPIHODOV. Every day some misfortune befalls me. I don't complain, I'm used to it, and I wear a smiling face.

(DUNYASHA *comes in, hands* LOPAHIN *the kvass.*)

EPIHODOV. I am going (*stumbles against a chair, which falls over*). There! (*as though triumphant*). There you see now, excuse the expression, an accident like that among others.... It's positively remarkable (*goes out*).

DUNYASHA. Do you know, Yermolay Alexeyevitch, I must confess, Epihodov has made me a proposal.

LOPAHIN. Ah!

DUNYASHA. I'm sure I don't know.... He's a harmless fellow, but sometimes when he begins talking, there's no making anything of it. It's all very fine and expressive, only there's no understanding it. I've a sort of liking for him too. He loves me to distraction. He's an unfortunate man; every day there's something. They tease him about it — two and twenty misfortunes they call him.

LOPAHIN (*listening*). There! I do believe they're coming.

DUNYASHA. They are coming! What's the matter with me?... I'm cold all over.

LOPAHIN. They really are coming. Let's go and meet them. Will she know me? It's five years since I saw her.

DUNYASHA (*in a flutter*). I shall drop this very minute.... Ah, I shall drop.

(*There is a sound of two carriages driving up to the house.* LOPA-HIN *and* DUNYASHA *go out quickly. The stage is left empty. A noise is heard in the adjoining rooms.* FIRS, *who has driven to meet* MADAME RANEVSKY, *crosses the stage hurriedly leaning on a stick. He is wearing old-fashioned livery and a high hat. He says something to himself, but not a word can be distinguished. The noise behind the scenes goes on increasing. A voice: "Come, let's go in here."*)

(*Enter* LYUBOV ANDREYEVNA, ANYA, *and* CHARLOTTA IVANOVNA *with a pet dog on a chain, all in travelling dresses.* VARYA *in an out-door coat with a kerchief over her head,* GAEV, SEMYONOV-PISHTCHIK, LOPAHIN, DUNYASHA *with bag and parasol, servants with other articles. All walk across the room.*)

ANYA. Let's come in here. Do you remember what room this is, mamma?

LYUBOV (*joyfully, through her tears*). The nursery!

VARYA. How cold it is, my hands are numb. (*To* LYUBOV ANDREYEVNA.) Your rooms, the white room and the lavender one, are just the same as ever, mamma.

LYUBOV. My nursery, dear delightful room.... I used to sleep here when I was little...(*cries*). And here I am, like a little child... (*kisses her brother and* VARYA, *and then her brother again*). Varya's just the same as ever, like a nun. And I knew Dunyasha (*kisses* DUNYASHA).

GAEV. The train was two hours late. What do you think of that? Is that the way to do things?

CHARLOTTA (*to* PISHTCHIK). My dog eats nuts, too.

PISHTCHIK (*wonderingly*). Fancy that!

(*They all go out except* ANYA *and* DUNYASHA.)

DUNYASHA. We've been expecting you so long (*takes* ANYA's *hat and coat*).

ANYA. I haven't slept for four nights on the journey. I feel dreadfully cold.

DUNYASHA. You set out in Lent, there was snow and frost, and now? My darling! (*laughs and kisses her*). I *have* missed you, my precious, my joy. I must tell you... I can't put it off a minute....

ANYA (*wearily*). What now?

DUNYASHA. Epihodov, the clerk, made me a proposal just after Easter.

ANYA. It's always the same thing with you... (*straightening her hair*). I've lost all my hairpins... (*she is staggering from exhaustion*).

DUNYASHA. I don't know what to think, really. He does love me, he does love me so!

ANYA (*looking towards her door, tenderly*). My own room, my windows just as though I had never gone away. I'm home! Tomorrow morning I shall get up and run into the garden.... Oh, if I could get to sleep! I haven't slept all the journey, I was so anxious and worried.

DUNYASHA. Pyotr Sergeyevitch came the day before yesterday.

ANYA (*joyfully*). Petya!

DUNYASHA. He's asleep in the bath house, he has settled in there. I'm afraid of being in their way, says he. (*Glancing at her watch.*) I was to have waked him, but Varvara Mihalovna told me not to. Don't you wake him, says she.

(*Enter* VARYA *with a bunch of keys at her waist.*)

VARYA. Dunyasha, coffee and make haste.... Mamma's asking for coffee.

DUNYASHA. This very minute (*goes out*).

VARYA. Well, thank God, you've come. You're home again (*petting her.*) My little darling has come back! My precious beauty has come back again!

ANYA. I have had a time of it!

VARYA. I can fancy.

ANYA. We set off in Holy Week — it was so cold then, and all the way Charlotta would talk and show off her tricks. What did you want to burden me with Charlotta for?

VARYA. You couldn't have travelled all alone, darling. At seventeen!

ANYA. We got to Paris at last, it was cold there — snow. I speak French shockingly. Mamma lives on the fifth floor, I went up to her and there were a lot of French people, ladies, an old priest with a book. The place smelt of tobacco and so comfortless. I felt sorry, oh! so sorry for mamma all at once, I put my arms round her neck, and hugged her and wouldn't let her go. Mamma was as kind as she could be, and she cried....

VARYA (through her tears). Don't speak of it, don't speak of it!

ANYA. She had sold her villa at Mentone, she had nothing left, nothing. I hadn't a farthing left either, we only just had enough to get here. And mamma doesn't understand! When we had dinner at the stations, she always ordered the most expensive things and gave the waiters a whole rouble. Charlotta's just the same. Yasha too must have the same as we do; it's simply awful. You know Yasha is mamma's valet now, we brought him here with us.

VARYA. Yes, I've seen the young rascal.

ANYA. Well, tell me — have you paid the arrears on the mortgage?

VARYA. How could we get the money?

ANYA. Oh, dear! Oh, dear!

VARYA. In August the place will be sold.

ANYA. My goodness!

LOPAHIN (peeps in at the door and moos like a cow). Moo! (Disappears.)

VARYA (weeping). There, that's what I could do to him (shakes her fist).

ANYA (embracing VARYA, softly). Varya, has he made you an offer? (VARYA shakes her head.) Why, but he loves you. Why is it you don't come to an understanding? What are you waiting for?

VARYA. I believe that there never will be anything between us. He has a lot to do, he has no time for me... and takes no notice of me. Bless the man, it makes me miserable to see him.... Everyone's talking of our being married, everyone's congratulating me, and all the while there's really nothing in it; it's all like a dream. (*In another tone.*) You have a new brooch like a bee.

ANYA (*mournfully*). Mamma bought it. (*Goes into her own room and in a light-hearted childish tone.*) And you know, in Paris I went up in a balloon!

VARYA. My darling's home again! My pretty is home again!

(DUNYASHA *returns with the coffee-pot and is making the coffee.*)

VARYA (*standing at the door*). All day long, darling, as I go about looking after the house, I keep dreaming all the time. If only we could marry you to a rich man, then I should feel more at rest. Then I would go off by myself on a pilgrimage to Kiev, to Moscow... and so I would spend my life going from one holy place to another.... I would go on and on.... What bliss!

ANYA. The birds are singing in the garden. What time is it?

VARYA. It must be nearly three. It's time you were asleep, darling (*going into* ANYA's *room*). What bliss!

(YASHA *enters with a rug and a travelling bag.*)

YASHA (*crosses the stage, mincingly*). May one come in here, pray?

DUNYASHA. I shouldn't have known you, Yasha. How you have changed abroad.

YASHA. H'm!... And who are you?

DUNYASHA. When you went away, I was that high (*shows distance from floor*). Dunyasha, Fyodor's daughter.... You don't remember me!

YASHA. H'm!... You're a peach!

(*Looks round and embraces her: she shrieks and drops a saucer.* YASHA *goes out hastily.*)

VARYA (*in the doorway, in a tone of vexation*). What now?

DUNYASHA (*through her tears*). I have broken a saucer.

VARYA. Well, that brings good luck.

ANYA (*coming out of her room*). We ought to prepare mamma: Petya is here.

VARYA. I told them not to wake him.

ANYA (*dreamily*). It's six years since father died. Then only a month later little brother Grisha was drowned in the river, such a **pretty** boy he was, only seven. It was more than mamma could bear, so she went away, went away without looking back (*shuddering*).... How well I understand her, if only she knew! (*A pause.*) And Petya Trofimov was Grisha's tutor, he may remind her.

(*Enter* FIRS: *he is wearing a pea-jacket and a white waistcoat.*)

FIRS (*goes up to the coffee-pot, anxiously*).   The mistress will be served here (*puts on white gloves*).   Is the coffee ready? (*Sternly to* DUNYASHA.)   Girl!   Where's the cream?

DUNYASHA. Ah, mercy on us! (*Goes out quickly.*)

FIRS (*fussing round the coffee-pot*).   Ech! you good-for-nothing! (*Muttering to himself.*)   Come back from Paris.   And the old master used to go to Paris too... horses all the way (*laughs*).

VARYA. What is it, Firs?

FIRS. What is your pleasure? (*Gleefully.*)   My lady has come home! I have lived to see her again!   Now I can die (*weeps with joy*).

(*Enter* LYUBOV ANDREYEVNA, GAEV, *and* SEMYONOV-PISHTCHIK; *the latter is in a short-waisted full coat of fine cloth, and full trousers. GAEV, as he comes in, makes a gesture with his arms and his whole body, as though he were playing billiards.*)

LYUBOV. How does it go?   Let me remember.   Cannon off the red!

GAEV. That's it — in off the white!   Why, once, sister, we used to sleep together in this very room, and now I'm fifty-one, strange as it seems.

LOPAHIN. Yes, time flies.

GAEV. What do you say?

LOPAHIN. Time, I say, flies.

GAEV. What a smell of patchouli!

ANYA. I'm going to bed.   Good-night, mamma (*kisses her mother*).

LYUBOV. My precious darling (*kisses her hands*).   Are you glad to be home?   I can't believe it.

ANYA. Good-night, uncle.

GAEV (*kissing her face and hands*).   God bless you!   How like you are to your mother! (*To his sister.*)   At her age you were just the same, Lyuba.

(ANYA *shakes hands with* LOPAHIN *and* PISHTCHIK, *then goes out, shutting the door after her.*)

LYUBOV. She's quite worn out.

PISHTCHIK. Aye, it's a long journey, to be sure.

VARYA (*to* LOPAHIN *and* PISHTCHIK). Well, gentlemen? It's three o'clock and time to say good-bye.

LYUBOV (*laughs*). You're just the same as ever, Varya (*draws her to her and kisses her*). I'll just drink my coffee and then we will all go and rest. (FIRS *puts a cushion under her feet.*) Thanks, friend. I am so fond of coffee, I drink it day and night. Thanks, dear old man (*kisses* FIRS).

VARYA. I'll just see whether all the things have been brought in (*goes out*).

LYUBOV. Can it really be me sitting here? (*Laughs.*) I want to dance about and clap my hands. (*Covers her face with her hands.*) And I could drop asleep in a moment! God knows I love my country, I love it tenderly; I couldn't look out of the window in the train, I kept crying so. (*Through her tears.*) But I must drink my coffee, though. Thank you, Firs, thanks, dear old man. I'm so glad to find you still alive.

FIRS. The day before yesterday.

GAEV. He's rather deaf.

LOPAHIN. I have to set off for Harkov directly, at five o'clock.... It is annoying! I wanted to have a look at you, and a little talk.... You are just as splendid as ever.

PISHTCHIK (*breathing heavily*). Handsomer, indeed.... Dressed in Parisian style... completely bowled me over.

LOPAHIN. Your brother, Leonid Andreyevitch here, is always saying that I'm a low-born knave, that I'm a money-grubber, but I don't care one straw for that. Let him talk. Only I do want you to believe in me as you used to. I do want your wonderful tender eyes to look at me as they used to in the old days. Merciful God! My father was a serf of your father and of your grandfather, but you — you — did so much for me once, that I've forgotten all that; I love you as though you were my kin... more than my kin.

LYUBOV. I can't sit still, I simply can't... (*jumps up and walks about in violent agitation*). This happiness is too much for me.... You may laugh at me, I know I'm silly.... My own bookcase (*kisses the bookcase*). My little table.

GAEV. Nurse died while you were away.

LYUBOV (*sits down and drinks coffee*). Yes, the Kingdom of Heaven be hers! You wrote me of her death.

GAEV. And Anastasy is dead. Squinting Petruchka has left me and is in service now with the police captain in the town (*takes a box of caramels out of his pocket and sucks one*).

PISHTCHIK. My daughter, Dashenka, wishes to be remembered to you.

LOPAHIN. I want to tell you something very pleasant and cheering (*glancing at his watch*). I'm going directly... there's no time to say much... well, I can say it in a couple of words. I needn't tell you your cherry orchard is to be sold to pay your debts; the 22nd of August is the date fixed for the sale; but don't you worry, dearest lady, you may sleep in peace, there is a way of saving it.... This is what I propose. I beg your attention! Your estate is not twenty miles from the town, the railway runs close by it, and if the cherry orchard and the land along the river bank were cut up into building plots and then let on lease for summer villas, you would make an income of at least 25,000 roubles a year out of it.

GAEV. That's all rot, if you'll excuse me.

LYUBOV. I don't quite understand you, Yermolay Alexeyevitch.

LOPAHIN. You will get a rent of at least 25 roubles a year for a three-acre plot from summer visitors, and if you say the word now, I'll bet you what you like there won't be one square foot of ground vacant by the autumn, all the plots will be taken up. I congratulate you; in fact, you are saved. It's a perfect situation with that deep river. Only, of course, it must be cleared — all the old buildings, for example, must be removed, this house too, which is really good for nothing and the old cherry orchard must be cut down.

LYUBOV. Cut down? My dear fellow, forgive me, but you don't know what you are talking about. If there is one thing interesting — remarkable indeed — in the whole province, it's just our cherry orchard.

LOPAHIN. The only thing remarkable about the orchard is that it's a very large one. There's a crop of cherries every alternate year, and then there's nothing to be done with them, no one buys them.

GAEV. This orchard is mentioned in the "Encyclopædia."

LOPAHIN (*glancing at his watch*). If we don't decide on something and don't take some steps, on the 22nd of August the cherry orchard and the whole estate too will be sold by auction. Make up your minds! There is no other way of saving it, I'll take my oath on that. No, No!

FIRS. In old days, forty or fifty years ago, they used to dry the cherries, soak them, pickle them, make jam too, and they used ——

GAEV. Be quiet, Firs.

FIRS. And they used to send the preserved cherries to Moscow and to Harkov by the waggon-load. That brought the money in! And the preserved cherries in those days were soft and juicy, sweet and fragrant.... They knew the way to do them then....

LYUBOV. And where is the recipe now?

FIRS. It's forgotten. Nobody remembers it.

PISHTCHIK (*to* LYUBOV ANDREYEVNA). What's it like in Paris? Did you eat frogs there?

LYUBOV. Oh, I ate crocodiles.

PISHTCHIK. Fancy that now!

LOPAHIN. There used to be only the gentlefolks and the peasants in the country, but now there are these summer visitors. All the towns, even the small ones, are surrounded nowadays by these summer villas. And one may say for sure, that in another twenty years there'll be many more of these people and that they'll be everywhere. At present the summer visitor only drinks tea on his verandah, but maybe he'll take to working his bit of land too, and then your cherry orchard would become happy, rich and prosperous....

GAEV (*indignant*). What rot!

(*Enter* VARYA *and* YASHA.)

VARYA. There are two telegrams for you, mamma (*takes out keys and opens an old-fashioned bookcase with a loud crack*). Here they are.

LYUBOV. From Paris (*tears the telegrams, without reading them*). I have done with Paris.

GAEV. Do you know, Lyuba, how old that bookcase is? Last week I pulled out the bottom drawer and there I found the date branded on it. The bookcase was made just a hundred years ago. What do you say to that? We might have celebrated its jubilee. Though it's an inanimate object, still it is a *book* case.

PISHTCHIK (*amazed*). A hundred years! Fancy that now.

GAEV. Yes.... It is a thing... (*feeling the bookcase*). Dear, honoured, bookcase! Hail to thee who for more than a hundred years hast served the pure ideals of good and justice; thy silent call to fruitful labour has never flagged in those hundred years, maintaining (*in tears*) in the generations of man, courage and faith in a brighter future and fostering in us ideals of good and social consciousness (*a pause*).

LOPAHIN. Yes....

LYUBOV. You are just the same as ever, Leonid.

GAEV (*a little embarrassed*). Cannon off the right into the pocket!

LOPAHIN (*looking at his watch*). Well, it's time I was off.

YASHA (*handing* LYUBOV ANDREYEVNA *medicine*). Perhaps you will take your pills now.

PISHTCHIK. You shouldn't take medicines, my dear madam... they do no harm and no good. Give them here... honoured lady (*takes the pill-box, pours the pills into the hollow of his hand, blows on them, puts them in his mouth and drinks off some kvass*). There!

LYUBOV (*in alarm*). Why, you must be out of your mind!

PISHTCHIK. I have taken all the pills.

LOPAHIN. What a glutton! (*All laugh.*)

FIRS. His honour stayed with us in Easter week, ate a gallon and a half of cucumbers... (*mutters*).

LYUBOV. What is he saying?

VARYA. He has taken to muttering like that for the last three years. We are used to it.

YASHA. His declining years!

(CHARLOTTA IVANOVNA, *a very thin, lanky figure in a white dress with a lorgnette in her belt, walks across the stage.*)

LOPAHIN. I beg your pardon, Charlotta Ivanovna, I have not had time to greet you (*tries to kiss her hand*).

CHARLOTTA (*pulling away her hand*). If I let you kiss my hand, you'll be wanting to kiss my elbow, and then my shoulder.

LOPAHIN. I've no luck today! (*All laugh.*) Charlotta Ivanovna, show us some tricks!

LYUBOV. Charlotta, do show us some tricks!

CHARLOTTA. I don't want to. I'm sleepy (*goes out*).

LOPAHIN. In three weeks' time we shall meet again (*kisses* LYUBOV ANDREYEVNA'S *hand*). Good-bye till then — I must go. (*To* GAEV.) Good-bye. (*Kisses* PISHTCHIK.) Good-bye. (*Gives his hand to* VARYA, *then to* FIRS *and* YASHA.) I don't want to go. (*To* LYUBOV ANDREYEVNA.) If you think over my plan for the villas and make up your mind, then let me know; I will lend you 50,000 roubles. Think of it seriously.

VARYA (*angrily*). Well, do go, for goodness sake.

LOPAHIN. I'm going, I'm going (*goes out*).

GAEV. Low-born knave! I beg pardon, though... Varya is going to marry him, he's Varya's fiancé.

VARYA. Don't talk nonsense, uncle.

LYUBOV. Well, Varya, I shall be delighted. He's a good man.

PISHTCHIK. He is, one must acknowledge, a most worthy man. And my Dashenka... says too that... she says... various things (*snores, but at once wakes up*). But all the same, honoured lady, could you oblige me... with a loan of 240 roubles... to pay the interest on my mortgage tomorrow?

VARYA (*dismayed*). No, no.

LYUBOV. I really haven't any money.

PISHTCHIK. It will turn up (*laughs*). I never lose hope. I thought everything was over, I was a ruined man, and lo and behold — the railway passed through my land and... they paid me for it. And something else will turn up again, if not today, then to-morrow... Dashenka'll win two hundred thousand... she's got a lottery ticket.

LYUBOV. Well, we've finished our coffee, we can go to bed.

FIRS (*brushes* GAEV, *reprovingly*). You have got on the wrong trousers again! What am I to do with you?

VARYA (*softly*). Anya's asleep. (*Softly opens the window.*) Now the sun's risen, it's not a bit cold. Look, mamma, what exquisite trees! My goodness! And the air! The starlings are singing!

GAEV (*opens another window*). The orchard is all white. You've not forgotten it, Lyuba? That long avenue that runs straight, straight as an arrow, how it shines on a moonlight night. You remember? You've not forgotten?

LYUBOV (*looking out of the window into the garden*). Oh, my childhood, my innocence! It was in this nursery I used to sleep, from here I looked out into the orchard, happiness waked with me every morning and in those days the orchard was just the same, nothing has changed (*laughs with delight*). All, all white! Oh, my orchard! After the dark gloomy autumn, and the cold winter; you are young again, and full of happiness, the heavenly angels have never left you.... If I could cast off the burden that weighs on my heart, if I could forget the past!

GAEV. H'm! and the orchard will be sold to pay our debts; it seems strange....

LYUBOV. See, our mother walking... all in white, down the avenue! (*Laughs with delight.*) It is she!

GAEV. Where?

VARYA. Oh, don't, mamma!

LYUBOV. There is no one. It was my fancy. On the right there, by the path to the arbour, there is a white tree bending like a woman....

(*Enter* TROFIMOV *wearing a shabby student's uniform and spectacles.*)

LYUBOV. What a ravishing orchard! White masses of blossom, blue sky....

TROFIMOV. Lyubov Andreyevna! (*She looks round at him.*) I will just pay my respects to you and then leave you at once (*kisses her hand warmly*). I was told to wait until morning, but I hadn't the patience to wait any longer....

(LYUBOV ANDREYEVNA *looks at him in perplexity.*)

VARYA (*through her tears*). This is Petya Trofimov.

TROFIMOV. Petya Trofimov, who was your Grisha's tutor.... Can I have changed so much?

(LYUBOV ANDREYEVNA *embraces him and weeps quietly.*)

GAEV (*in confusion*). There, there, Lyuba.

VARYA (*crying*). I told you, Petya, to wait till tomorrow.

LYUBOV. My Grisha... my boy... Grisha... my son!

VARYA. We can't help it, mamma, it is God's will.

TROFIMOV (*softly through his tears*). There... there.

LYUBOV (*weeping quietly*). My boy was lost... drowned. Why? Oh, why, dear Petya? (*More quietly.*) Anya is asleep in there.

and I'm talking loudly... making this noise.... But, Petya? Why have you grown so ugly? Why do you look so old?

TROFIMOV. A peasant-woman in the train called me a mangy-looking gentleman.

LYUBOV. You were quite a boy then, a pretty little student, and now your hair's thin — and spectacles. Are you really a student still? (*Goes towards the door.*)

TROFIMOV. I seem likely to be a perpetual student.

LYUBOV (*kisses her brother, then* VARYA). Well, go to bed.... You are older too, Leonid.

PISHTCHIK (*follows her*). I suppose it's time we were asleep.... Ugh! my gout. I'm staying the night! Lyubov Andreyevna, my dear soul, if you could... tomorrow morning... 240 roubles.

GAEV. That's always his story.

PISHTCHIK. 240 roubles... to pay the interest on my mortgage.

LYUBOV. My dear man, I have no money.

PISHTCHIK. I'll pay it back, my dear... a trifling sum.

LYUBOV. Oh, well, Leonid will give it you.... You give him the money, Leonid.

GAEV. Me give it him! Let him wait till he gets it!

LYUBOV. It can't be helped, give it him. He needs it. He'll pay it back.

(LYUBOV ANDREYEVNA, TROFIMOV, PISHTCHIK, *and* FIRS *go out.* GAEV, VARYA, *and* YASHA *remain.*)

GAEV. Sister hasn't got out of the habit of flinging away her money. (*To* YASHA.) Get away, my good fellow, you smell of the hen-house.

YASHA (*with a grin*). And you, Leonid Andreyevitch, are just the same as ever.

GAEV. What's that? (*To* VARYA.) What did he say?

VARYA (*to* YASHA). Your mother has come from the village; she has been sitting in the servants' room since yesterday, waiting to see you.

YASHA. Oh, bother her!

VARYA. For shame!

YASHA. What's the hurry? She might just as well have come to-morrow (*goes out*).

VARYA. Mamma's just the same as ever, she hasn't changed a bit. If she had her own way, she'd give away everything.

GAEV. Yes (*a pause*). If a great many remedies are suggested for some disease, it means that the disease is incurable. I keep thinking and racking my brains; I have many schemes, a great many, and that really means none. If we could only come in for a legacy with somebody, or marry our Anya to a very rich man, or we might go to Yaroslavl and try our luck with our old aunt, the Countess. She's very, very rich, you know.

VARYA (*weeps*). If God would help us.

GAEV. Don't blubber. Aunt's very rich, but she doesn't like us. First, sister married a lawyer instead of a nobleman....

(ANYA *appears in the doorway.*)

GAEV. And then her conduct, one can't call it virtuous. She is good, and kind, and nice, and I love her, but, however one allows for extenuating circumstances, there's no denying that she's an immoral woman. One feels it in her slightest gesture.

VARYA (*in a whisper*). Anya's in the doorway.

GAEV. What do you say? (*A pause.*) It's queer, there seems to be something wrong with my right eye. I don't see as well as I did. And on Thursday when I was in the district Court...

(*Enter* ANYA.)

VARYA. Why aren't you asleep, Anya?

ANYA. I can't get to sleep.

GAEV. My pet (*kisses* ANYA's *face and hands*). My child (*weeps*). You are not my niece, you are my angel, you are everything to me. Believe me, believe...

ANYA. I believe you, uncle. Everyone loves you and respects you... but, uncle dear, you must be silent... simply be silent. What were you saying just now about my mother, about your own sister? What made you say that?

GAEV. Yes, yes... (*puts his hand over his face*). Really, that was awful! My God, save me! And today I made a speech to the bookcase... so stupid! And only when I had finished, I saw how stupid it was.

VARYA. It's true, uncle, you ought to keep quiet. Don't talk, that's all.

ANYA. If you could keep from talking, it would make things easier for you, too.

GAEV. I won't speak (*kisses* ANYA's *and* VARYA's *hands*). I'll be silent. Only this is about business. On Thursday I was in the district Court; well, there was a large party of us there and we began talking of one thing and another, and this and that, and do you know, I believe that it will be possible to raise a loan on an I.O.U. to pay the arrears on the mortgage.

VARYA. If the Lord would help us!

GAEV. I'm going on Tuesday; I'll talk of it again. (*To* VARYA.) Don't blubber. (*To* ANYA.) Your mamma will talk to Lopahin; of course, he won't refuse her. And as soon as you're rested you shall go to Yaroslavl to the Countess, your great-aunt. So we shall all set to work in three directions at once, and the business is done. We shall pay off arrears, I'm convinced of it (*puts a caramel in his mouth*). I swear on my honour, I swear by anything you like, the estate shan't be sold (*excitedly*). By my own happiness, I swear it! Here's my hand on it, call me the basest, vilest of men, if I let it come to an auction! Upon my soul I swear it!

ANYA (*her equanimity has returned, she is quite happy*). How good you are, uncle, and how clever! (*Embraces her uncle.*) I'm at peace now! Quite at peace! I'm happy!

(*Enter* FIRS.)

FIRS (*reproachfully*). Leonid Andreyevitch, have you no fear of God? When are you going to bed?

GAEV. Directly, directly. You can go, Firs. I'll... yes, I will undress myself. Come, children, bye-bye. We'll go into details tomorrow, but now go to bed (*kisses* ANYA *and* VARYA). I'm a man of the eighties. They run down that period, but still I can say I have had to suffer not a little for my convictions in my life. It's not for nothing that the peasant loves me. One must know the peasant! One must know how...

ANYA. At it again, uncle!

VARYA. Uncle dear, you'd better be quiet!

FIRS (*angrily*). Leonid Andreyevitch!

GAEV. I'm coming. I'm coming. Go to bed. Potted the shot — there's a shot for you! A beauty! (*Goes out,* FIRS *hobbling after him.*)

ANYA. My mind's at rest now. I don't want to go to Yaroslavl, I don't like my great-aunt, but still my mind's at rest. Thanks to uncle (*sits down*).

VARYA. We must go to bed. I'm going. Something unpleasant happened while you were away. In the old servants' quarters there are only the old servants, as you know — Efimyushka, Polya and Yevstigney — and Karp too. They began letting stray people in to spend the night — I said nothing. But all at once I heard they had been spreading a report that I gave them nothing but pease pudding to eat. Out of stinginess, you know. ... And it was all Yevstigney's doing.... Very well, I said to myself.... If that's how it is, I thought, wait a bit. I sent for Yevstigney ... (*yawns*). He comes.... "How's this, Yevstigney," I said, "you could be such a fool as to?..." (*Looking at* ANYA.) Anitchka! (*A pause.*) She's asleep (*puts her arm round* ANYA). Come to bed... come along! (*Leads her.*) My darling has fallen asleep! Come... (*They go.*)

(*Far away beyond the orchard a shepherd plays on a pipe.* TROFIMOV *crosses the stage and, seeing* VARYA *and* ANYA, *stands still.*)

VARYA. 'Sh! asleep, asleep. Come, my own.

ANYA (*softly, half asleep*). I'm so tired. Still those bells. Uncle... dear... mamma and uncle....

VARYA. Come, my own, come along. (*They go into* ANYA'S *room.*)

TROFIMOV (*tenderly*). My sunshine! My spring.

CURTAIN.

ACT II

The open country. An old shrine, long abandoned and fallen out of the perpendicular; near it a well, large stones that have apparently once been tombstones, and an old garden seat. The road to GAEV's house is seen. On one side rise dark poplars; and there the cherry orchard begins. In the distance a row of telegraph poles and far, far away on the horizon there is faintly outlined a great town, only visible in very fine clear weather. It is near sunset. CHARLOTTA, YASHA, and DUNYASHA are sitting on the seat. EPIHODOV is standing near, playing something mournful on a guitar. All sit plunged in thought. CHARLOTTA wears an old forage cap; she has taken a gun from her shoulder and is tightening the buckle on the strap.

CHARLOTTA (*musingly*). I haven't a real passport of my own, and I don't know how old I am, and I always feel that I'm a young thing. When I was a little girl, my father and mother used to travel about to fairs and give performances — very good ones. And I used to dance *salto-mortale* and all sorts of things. And when papa and mamma died, a German lady took me and had me educated. And so I grew up and become a governess. But where I came from, and who I am, I don't know.... Who my parents were, very likely they weren't married... I don't know (*takes a cucumber out of her pocket and eats*). I know nothing at all (*a pause*). One wants to talk and has no one to talk to... I have nobody.

EPIHODOV (*plays on the guitar and sings*). "What care I for the noisy world! What care I for friends or foes!" How agreeable it is to play on the mandoline!

DUNYASHA. That's a guitar, not a mandoline (*looks in a hand-mirror and powders herself*).

EPIHODOV. To a man mad with love, it's a mandoline. (*Sings.*) "Were her heart but aglow with love's mutual flame." (YASHA *joins in.*)

CHARLOTTA. How shockingly these people sing! Foo! Like jackals!

DUNYASHA (*to* YASHA). What happiness, though, to visit foreign lands.

YASHA. Ah, yes! I rather agree with you there (*yawns, then lights a cigar*).

EPIHODOV. That's comprehensible. In foreign lands everything has long since reached full complexion.

YASHA. That's so, of course.

EPIHODOV. I'm a cultivated man, I read remarkable books of all sorts, but I can never make out the tendency I am myself precisely inclined for, whether to live or to shoot myself, speaking precisely, but nevertheless I always carry a revolver. Here it is... (*shows revolver*).

CHARLOTTA. I've had enough, and now I'm going (*puts on the gun*). Epihodov, you're a very clever fellow, and a very terrible one too, all the women must be wild about you. Br-r-r! (*Goes.*) These clever fellows are all so stupid; there's not a creature for me to speak to.... Always alone, alone, nobody belonging to me... and who I am, and why I'm on earth, I don't know (*walks away slowly*).

EPIHODOV. Speaking precisely, not touching upon other subjects, I'm bound to admit about myself, that destiny behaves mercilessly to me, as a storm to a little boat. If, let us suppose, I am mistaken, then why did I wake up this morning, to quote an example, and look round, and there on my chest was a spider of fearful magnitude... like this (*shows with both hands*). And then I take up a jug of kvass, to quench my thirst, and in it there is something in the highest degree unseemly of the nature of a cockroach (*a pause*). Have you read Buckle? (*A pause.*) I am desirous of troubling you, Dunyasha, with a couple of words.

DUNYASHA. Well, speak.

EPIHODOV. I should be desirous to speak with you alone (*sighs*).

DUNYASHA ·(*embarrassed*). Well — only bring me my mantle first. It's by the cupboard. It's rather damp here.

EPIHODOV. Certainly. I will fetch it. Now I know what I must do with my revolver (*takes guitar and goes off playing on it*).

YASHA. Two and twenty misfortunes! Between ourselves, he's a fool (*yawns*).

DUNYASHA. God grant he doesn't shoot himself! (*A pause.*) I am so nervous, I'm always in a flutter. I was a little girl when I was taken into our lady's house, and now I have quite grown out of peasant ways, and my hands are white, as white as a lady's. I'm such a delicate, sensitive creature, I'm afraid of everything. I'm so frightened. And if you deceive me, Yasha, I don't know what will become of my nerves.

YASHA (*kisses her*). You're a peach! Of course a girl must never forget herself; what I dislike more than anything is a girl being flighty in her behaviour.

DUNYASHA. I'm passionately in love with you, Yasha; you are a man of culture — you can give your opinion about anything (*a pause*).

YASHA (*yawns*). Yes, that's so. My opinion is this: if a girl loves anyone, that means that she has no principles (*a pause*). It's pleasant smoking a cigar in the open air (*listens*). Someone's coming this way... it's the gentlefolk (DUNYASHA *embraces him impulsively*). Go home, as though you had been to the river to bathe; go by that path, or else they'll meet you and suppose I have made an appointment with you here. That I can't endure.

DUNYASHA (*coughing softly*). The cigar has made my head ache... (*goes off*).

(YASHA *remains sitting near the shrine. Enter* LYUBOV ANDREYEVNA, GAEV, *and* LOPAHIN.)

LOPAHIN. You must make up your mind once for all — there's no time to lose. It's quite a simple question, you know. Will you consent to letting the land for building or not? One word in answer: Yes or no? Only one word!

LYUBOV. Who is smoking such horrible cigars here? (*Sits down*).

GAEV. Now the railway line has been brought near, it's made things very convenient (*sits down*). Here we have been over and lunched in town. Cannon off the white! I should like to go home and have a game.

LYUBOV. You have plenty of time.

LOPAHIN. Only one word! (*Beseechingly*.) Give me an answer!

GAEV (*yawning*). What do you say?

LYUBOV (*looks in her purse*). I had quite a lot of money here yesterday, and there's scarcely any left today. My poor Varya feeds us all on milk soup for the sake of economy; the old folks in the kitchen get nothing but pease pudding, while I waste my money in a senseless way (*drops purse, scattering gold pieces*). There, they have all fallen out! (*Annoyed*.)

YASHA. Allow me, I'll soon pick them up (*collects the coins*).

LYUBOV. Pray do, Yasha. And what did I go off to the town to lunch for? Your restaurant's a wretched place with its music and the tablecloth smelling of soap.... Why drink so much, Leonid? And eat so much? And talk so much? Today you talked a great deal again in the restaurant, and all so inappropriately. About the era of the 'seventies, about the decadents. And to whom? Talking to waiters about decadents!

LOPAHIN. Yes.

GAEV (*waving his hand*). I'm incorrigible; that's evident. (*Irritably to* YASHA.) Why is it you keep fidgeting about in front of us!

YASHA (*laughs*). I can't help laughing when I hear your voice.

GAEV (*to his sister*). Either I or he...

LYUBOV. Get along! Go away, Yasha.

YASHA (*gives* LYUBOV ANDREYEVNA *her purse*). Directly (*hardly able to suppress his laughter*). This minute... (*goes off*).

LOPAHIN. Deriganov, the millionaire, means to buy your estate. They say he is coming to the sale himself.

LYUBOV. Where did you hear that?

LOPAHIN. That's what they say in town.

GAEV. Our aunt in Yaroslavl has promised to send help; but when, and how much she will send, we don't know.

LOPAHIN. How much will she send? A hundred thousand? Two hundred?

LYUBOV. Oh, well!... Ten or fifteen thousand, and we must be thankful to get that.

LOPAHIN. Forgive me, but such reckless people as you are — such queer, unbusiness-like people — I never met in my life. One tells you in plain Russian your estate is going to be sold, and you seem not to understand it.

LYUBOV. What are we to do? Tell us what to do.

LOPAHIN. I do tell you every day. Every day I say the same thing. You absolutely must let the cherry orchard and the land on building leases; and do it at once, as quick as may be — the auction's close upon us! Do understand! Once make up your mind to build villas, and you can raise as much money as you like, and then you are saved.

LYUBOV. Villas and summer visitors — forgive me saying so — it's so vulgar.

GAEV. There I perfectly agree with you.

LOPAHIN. I shall sob, or scream, or fall into a fit. I can't stand it! You drive me mad! (*To* GAEV.) You're an old woman!

GAEV. What do you say?

LOPAHIN. An old woman! (*Gets up to go.*)

LYUBOV (*in dismay*). No, don't go! Do stay, my dear friend! Perhaps we shall think of something.

LOPAHIN. What is there to think of?

LYUBOV. Don't go, I entreat you! With you here it's more cheerful, anyway (*a pause*). I keep expecting something, as though the house were going to fall about our ears.

GAEV (*in profound dejection*). Potted the white! It fails — a kiss.

LYUBOV. We have been great sinners....

LOPAHIN. You have no sins to repent of.

GAEV (*puts a caramel in his mouth*). They say I've eaten up my property in caramels (*laughs*).

LYUBOV. Oh, my sins! I've always thrown my money away recklessly like a lunatic. I married a man who made nothing but debts. My husband died of champagne — he drank dreadfully. To my misery I loved another man, and immediately — it was my first punishment — the blow fell upon me, here, in the river... my boy was drowned and I went abroad — went away for ever, never to return, not to see that river again... I shut my eyes, and fled, distracted, and *he* after me... pitilessly, brutally. I bought a villa at Mentone, for *he* fell ill there, and for three years I had no rest day or night. His illness wore me out, my soul was dried up. And last year, when my villa was sold to pay my debts, I went to Paris and there he robbed me of everything and abandoned me for another woman; and I tried to poison myself.... So stupid, so shameful!... And suddenly I felt a yearning for Russia, for my country, for my little girl... (*dries her tears*). Lord, Lord, be merciful! Forgive my sins! Do not chastise me more! (*Takes a telegram out of her pocket*) I got this today from Paris. He implores forgiveness, entreats me to return (*tears up the telegram*). I fancy there is music somewhere (*listens*).

GAEV. That's our famous Jewish orchestra. You remember, four violins, a flute, and a double bass.

LYUBOV. That still in existence? We ought to send for them one evening, and give a dance.

LOPAHIN (*listens*). I can't hear.... (*Hums softly*.) "For money the Germans will turn a Russian into a Frenchman." (*Laughs*.) I did see such a piece at the theatre yesterday! It was funny!

LYUBOV. And most likely there was nothing funny in it. You shouldn't look at plays, you should look at yourselves a little oftener. How grey your lives are! How much nonsense you talk.

LOPAHIN. That's true. One may say honestly, we live a fool's life (*pause*). My father was a peasant, an idiot; he knew nothing and taught me nothing, only beat me when he was drunk, and always with his stick. In reality I am just such another blockhead and idiot. I've learnt nothing properly. I write a wretched hand. I write so that I feel ashamed before folks, like a pig.

LYUBOV. You ought to get married, my dear fellow.

LOPAHIN. Yes... that's true.

LYUBOV. You should marry our Varya, she's a good girl.

LOPAHIN. Yes.

LYUBOV. She's a good-natured girl, she's busy all day long, and what's more, she loves you. And you have liked her for ever so long.

LOPAHIN. Well? I'm not against it.... She's a good girl (*pause*).

GAEV. I've been offered a place in the bank: 6,000 roubles a year. Did you know?

LYUBOV. You would never do for that! You must stay as you are.

(*Enter* FIRS *with overcoat*.)

FIRS. Put it on, sir, it's damp.

GAEV (*putting it on*). You bother me, old fellow.

FIRS. You can't go on like this. You went away in the morning without leaving word (*looks him over*).

LYUBOV. You look older, Firs!

FIRS. What is your pleasure?

LOPAHIN. You look older, she said.

FIRS. I've had a long life. They were arranging my wedding before your papa was born...(*laughs*). I was the head footman before the emancipation came. I wouldn't consent to be set free then; I stayed on with the old master... (*a pause*). I remember what rejoicings they made and didn't know themselves what they were rejoicing over.

LOPAHIN. Those were fine old times. There was flogging anyway.

FIRS (*not hearing*). To be sure! The peasants knew their place, and the masters knew theirs; but now they're all at sixes and sevens, there's no making it out.

GAEV. Hold your tongue, Firs. I must go to town tomorrow. I have been promised an introduction to a general, who might let us have a loan.

LOPAHIN. You won't bring that off. And you won't pay your arrears, you may rest assured of that.

LYUBOV. That's all his nonsense. There is no such general.

(*Enter* TROFIMOV, ANYA, *and* VARYA.)

GAEV. Here come our girls.

ANYA. There's mamma on the seat.

LYUBOV (*tenderly*). Come here, come along. My darlings! (*Embraces* ANYA *and* VARYA.) If you only knew how I love you both. Sit beside me, there, like that. (*All sit down.*)

LOPAHIN. Our perpetual student is always with the young ladies.

TROFIMOV. That's not your business.

LOPAHIN. He'll soon be fifty, and he's still a student.

TROFIMOV. Drop your idiotic jokes.

LOPAHIN. Why are you so cross, you queer fish?

TROFIMOV. Oh, don't persist!

LOPAHIN (*laughs*). Allow me to ask you what's your idea of me?

TROFIMOV. I'll tell you my idea of you, Yermolay Alexeyevitch: you are a rich man, you'll soon be a millionaire. Well, just as in the economy of nature a wild beast is of use, who devours everything that comes in his way, so you too have your use. (*All laugh.*)

VARYA. Better tell us something about the planets, Petya.

LYUBOV. No, let us go on with the conversation we had yesterday.

TROFIMOV. What was it about?

GAEV. About pride.

TROFIMOV. We had a long conversation yesterday, but we came to no conclusion. In pride, in your sense of it, there is something mystical. Perhaps you are right from your point of view; but if one looks at it simply, without subtlety, what sort of pride can there be, what sense is there in it, if man in his physiological formation is very imperfect, if in the immense majority of cases he is coarse, dull-witted, profoundly unhappy? One must give up glorification of self. One should work, and nothing else.

GAEV. One must die in any case.

TROFIMOV. Who knows? And what does it mean — dying? Perhaps man has a hundred senses, and only the five we know are lost at death, while the other ninety-five remain alive.

LYUBOV. How clever you are, Petya!

LOPAHIN (*ironically*). Fearfully clever!

TROFIMOV. Humanity progresses, perfecting its powers. Everything that is beyond its ken now will one day become familiar and comprehensible; only we must work, we must with all our powers aid the seeker after truth. Here among us in Russia the workers are few in number as yet. The vast majority of the intellectual people I know, seek nothing, do nothing, are not fit as yet for work of any kind. They call themselves intellectual, but they treat their servants as inferiors, behave to the peasants as though they were animals, learn little, read nothing seriously, do practically nothing, only talk about science and know very little about art. They are all serious people, they all have severe faces, they all talk of weighty matters and air their theories, and yet the vast majority of us — ninety-nine per cent. — live like savages, at the least thing fly to blows and abuse, eat piggishly, sleep in filth and stuffiness, bugs everywhere, stench and damp and moral impurity. And it's clear all our fine talk is only to divert our attention and other people's. Show me where to find the crèches there's so much talk about, and the reading-rooms? They only exist in novels: in real life there are none of them. There is nothing but filth and vulgarity and Asiatic apathy. I fear and dislike very serious faces. I'm afraid of serious conversations. We should do better to be silent.

LOPAHIN. You know, I get up at five o'clock in the morning, and I work from morning to night; and I've money, my own and other people's, always passing through my hands, and I see what people

are made of all round me.   One has only to begin to do anything
to see how few honest, decent people there are.   Sometimes when
I lie awake at night, I think: "Oh! Lord, thou hast given us immense forests, boundless plains, the widest horizons, and living
here we ourselves ought really to be giants."

LYUBOV. You ask for giants!   They are no good except in story-
books; in real life they frighten us.

            (EPIHODOV *advances in the background, playing on the guitar.*)

LYUBOV (*dreamily*).   There goes Epihodov.

ANYA (*dreamily*).   There goes Epihodov.

GAEV. The sun has set, my friends.

TROFIMOV. Yes.

GAEV (*not loudly, but, as it were, declaiming*).   O nature, divine
nature, thou art bright with eternal lustre, beautiful and indif-
ferent!   Thou, whom we call mother, thou dost unite within thee
life and death!   Thou dost give life and dost destroy!

VARYA (*in a tone of supplication*).   Uncle!

ANYA. Uncle, you are at it again!

TROFIMOV. You'd much better be cannoning off the red!

GAEV. I'll hold my tongue, I will.

            (*All sit plunged in thought.   Perfect stillness.   The only thing audi-*
            ble is the muttering of FIRS.   *Suddenly there is a sound in the*
            distance, as it were from the sky — the sound of a breaking harp-
            string, mournfully dying away.)

LYUBOV. What is that?

LOPAHIN. I don't know.   Somewhere far away a bucket fallen and
broken in the pits.   But somewhere very far away.

GAEV. It might be a bird of some sort — such as a heron.

TROFIMOV. Or an owl.

LYUBOV (*shudders*).   I don't know why, but it's horrid (*a pause*).

FIRS. It was the same before the calamity — the owl hooted and the
samovar hissed all the time.

GAEV. Before what calamity?

FIRS. Before the emancipation (*a pause*).

LYUBOV. Come, my friends, let us be going; evening is falling.   (*To*
ANYA).   There are tears in your eyes.   What is it, darling? (*Em-*
braces her.)

ANYA. Nothing, mamma; it's nothing.

TROFIMOV. There is somebody coming.

(*The Wayfarer appears in a shabby white forage cap and an overcoat; he is slightly drunk.*)

WAYFARER. Allow me to inquire, can I get to the station this way?

GAEV. Yes. Go along that road.

WAYFARER. I thank you most feelingly (*coughing*). The weather is superb. (*Declaims.*) My brother, my suffering brother!... Come out to the Volga! Whose groan do you hear?... (*To* VARYA) Mademoiselle, vouchsafe a hungry Russian thirty kopeks.

(VARYA *utters a shriek of alarm.*)

LOPAHIN (*angrily*). There's a right and a wrong way of doing everything!

LYUBOV (*hurriedly*). Here, take this (*looks in her purse*). I've no silver. No matter — here's gold for you.

WAYFARER. I thank you most feelingly! (*Goes off.*) (*Laughter.*)

VARYA (*frightened*). I'm going home — I'm going... Oh, mamma, the servants have nothing to eat, and you gave him gold!

LYUBOV. There's no doing anything with me. I'm so silly! When we get home, I'll give you all I possess. Yermolay Alexeyevitch, you will lend me some more...!

LOPAHIN. I will.

LYUBOV. Come, friends, it's time to be going. And Varya, we have made a match of it for you. I congratulate you.

VARYA (*through her tears*). Mamma, that's not a joking matter.

LOPAHIN. "Ophelia, get thee to a nunnery!"

GAEV. My hands are trembling; it's a long while since I had a game of billiards.

LOPAHIN. "Ophelia! Nymph, in thy orisons be all my sins remember'd."

LYUBOV. Come, it will soon be supper-time.

VARYA. How he frightened me! My heart's simply throbbing.

LOPAHIN. Let me remind you, ladies and gentlemen: on the 22nd of August the cherry orchard will be sold. Think about that! Think about it! (*All go off, except* TROFIMOV *and* ANYA.)

ANYA (*laughing*). I'm grateful to the wayfarer! He frightened Varya and we are left alone.

TROFIMOV. Varya's afraid we shall fall in love with each other, and for days together she won't leave us. With her narrow brain she can't grasp that we are above love. To eliminate the petty and transitory which hinders us from being free and happy — that is the aim and meaning of our life. Forward! We go forward irresistibly towards the bright star that shines yonder in the distance. Forward! Do not lag behind, friends. '

ANYA (*claps her hands*). How well you speak! (*A pause.*) It is divine here today.

TROFIMOV. Yes, it's glorious weather.

ANYA. Somehow, Petya, you've made me so that I don't love the cherry orchard as I used to. I used to love it so dearly. I used to think that there was no spot on earth like our garden.

TROFIMOV. All Russia is our garden. The earth is great and beautiful — there are many beautiful places in it (*a pause*). Think only, Anya, your grandfather, and great-grandfather, and all your ancestors were slave-owners — the owners of living souls — and from every cherry in the orchard, from every leaf, from every trunk there are human creatures looking at you. Cannot you hear their voices? Oh, it is awful! Your orchard is a fearful thing, and when in the evening or at night one walks about the orchard, the old bark on the trees glimmers dimly in the dusk, and the old cherry trees seem to be dreaming of centuries gone by and tortured by fearful visions. Yes! We are at least two hundred years behind, we have really gained nothing yet, we have no definite attitude to the past, we do nothing but theorise or complain of depression or drink vodka. It is clear that to begin to live in the present we must first expiate our past, we must break with it; and we can expiate it only by suffering, by extraordinary unceasing labour. Understand that, Anya.

ANYA. The house we live in has long ceased to be our own, and I shall leave it, I give you my word.

TROFIMOV. If you have the house keys, fling them into the well and go away. Be free as the wind.

ANYA (*in ecstasy*). How beautifully you said that!

TROFIMOV. Believe me, Anya, believe me! I am not thirty yet, I am young, I am still a student, but I have gone through so much already! As soon as winter comes I am hungry, sick, careworn, poor as a beggar, and what ups and downs of fortune have I not known! And my soul was always, every minute, day and night, full of inexplicable forebodings. I have a foreboding of happiness, Anya. I see glimpses of it already.

ANYA (*pensively*). The moon is rising.

> (EPIHODOV *is heard playing still the same mournful song on the guitar. The moon rises. Somewhere near the poplars* VARYA *is looking for* ANYA *and calling* "Anya! where are you?")

TROFIMOV. Yes, the moon is rising (*a pause*). Here is happiness — here it comes! It is coming nearer and nearer; already I can hear its footsteps. And if we never see it — if we may never know it — what does it matter? Others will see it after us.

VARYA'S VOICE. Anya! Where are you?

TROFIMOV. That Varya again! (*Angrily.*) It's revolting!

ANYA. Well, let's go down to the river. It's lovely there.

TROFIMOV. Yes, let's go. (*They go.*)

VARYA'S VOICE. Anya! Anya!

CURTAIN

ACT III

A drawing-room divided by an arch from a larger drawing-room. A chandelier burning. The Jewish orchestra, the same that was mentioned in Act II, is heard playing in the ante-room. It is evening. In the larger drawing-room they are dancing the grand chain. The voice of SEMYONOV-PISHTCHIK: *"Promenade à une paire!" Then enter the drawing-room in couples first* PISHTCHIK *and* CHARLOTTA IVANOVA, *then* TROFIMOV *and* LYUBOV ANDREYEVNA, *thirdly* ANYA *with the Post-Office Clerk, fourthly* VARYA *with the Station Master, and other guests.* VARYA *is quietly weeping and wiping away her tears as she dances. In the last couple is* DUNYASHA. *They move across the drawing-room.* PISHTCHIK *shouts:* "Grand rond, balancez!" *and* "Les Cavaliers à genou et remerciez vos dames."

FIRS in a swallow-tail coat brings in seltzer water on a tray. PISHTCHIK *and* TROFIMOV *enter the drawing-room.*

PISHTCHIK. I am a full-blooded man; I have already had two

strokes. Dancing's hard work for me, but as they say, if you're in the pack, you must bark with the rest. I'm as strong, I may say, as a horse. My parent, who would have his joke — may the Kingdom of Heaven be his! — used to say about our origin that the ancient stock of the Semyonov-Pishtchiks was derived from the very horse that Caligula made a member of the senate (*sits down*). But I've no money, that's where the mischief is. A hungry dog believes in nothing but meat... (*snores, but at once wakes up*). That's like me... I can think of nothing but money.

TROFIMOV. There really is something horsy about your appearance.

PISHTCHIK. Well... a horse is a fine beast... a horse can be sold.

(*There is the sound of billiards being played in an adjoining room. VARYA appears in the arch leading to the larger drawing-room.*)

TROFIMOV (*teasing*). Madame Lopahin! Madame Lopahin!

VARYA (*angrily*). Mangy-looking gentleman!

TROFIMOV. Yes, I am a mangy-looking gentleman, and I'm proud of it!

VARYA (*pondering bitterly*). Here we have hired musicians and nothing to pay them! (*Goes out.*)

TROFIMOV (*to* PISHTCHIK). If the energy you have wasted during your lifetime in trying to find the money to pay your interest, had gone to something else, you might in the end have turned the world upside down.

PISHTCHIK. Nietzsche, the philosopher, a very great and celebrated man... of enormous intellect... says in his works, that one can make forged bank-notes.

TROFIMOV. Why, have you read Nietzsche?

PISHTCHIK. What next... Dashenka told me.... And now I am in such a position, I might just as well forge bank notes. The day after tomorrow I must pay 310 roubles — 130 I have procured (*feels in his pockets, in alarm*). The money's gone! I have lost my money! (*Through his tears.*) Where's the money? (*Gleefully.*) Why, here it is behind the lining.... It has made me hot all over.

(*Enter* LYUBOV ANDREYEVNA *and* CHARLOTTA IVANOVNA.)

LYUBOV (*hums the Lezginka*). Why is Leonid so long? What can he be doing in town? (*To* DUNYASHA.) Offer the musicians some tea.

TROFIMOV. The sale hasn't taken place, most likely.

LYUBOV. It's the wrong time to have the orchestra, and the wrong time to give a dance. Well, never mind (*sits down and hums softly.*)

CHARLOTTA (*gives* PISHTCHIK *a pack of cards*). Here's a pack of cards. Think of any card you like.

PISHTCHIK. I've thought of one.

CHARLOTTA. Shuffle the pack now. That's right. Give it here, my dear Mr. Pishtchik. Ein, zwei, drei — now look, it's in your breast pocket.

PISHTCHIK (*taking a card out of his breast pocket*). The eight of spades! Perfectly right! (*Wonderingly.*) Fancy that now!

CHARLOTTA (*holding pack of cards in her hands, to* TROFIMOV). Tell me quickly which is the top card.

TROFIMOV. Well, the queen of spades.

CHARLOTTA. It is! (*To* PISHTCHIK) Well, which card is uppermost?

PISHTCHIK. The ace of hearts.

CHARLOTTA. It is! (*claps her hands, pack of cards disappears*). Ah! what lovely weather it is today!

> (*A mysterious feminine voice which seems coming out of the floor answers her.* "Oh, yes, it's magnificent weather, madam.")

CHARLOTTA. You are my perfect ideal.

VOICE. And I greatly admire you too, madam.

STATION MASTER (*applauding*). The lady ventriloquist — bravo!

PISHTCHIK (*wonderingly*). Fancy that now! Most enchanting Charlotta Ivanovna. I'm simply in love with you.

CHARLOTTA. In love? (*Shrugging shoulders.*) What do you know of love, guter Mensch, aber schlechter Musikant.

TROFIMOV (*pats* PISHTCHIK *on the shoulder*). You dear old horse....

CHARLOTTA. Attention, please! Another trick! (*Takes a travelling rug from a chair.*) Here's a very good rug; I want to sell it (*shaking it out*). Doesn't anyone want to buy it?

PISHTCHIK (*wonderingly*). Fancy that!

CHARLOTTA. Ein, zwei, drei! (*Quickly picks up rug she has dropped; behind the rug stands* ANYA; *she makes a curtsey, runs to her mother, embraces her and runs back into the larger drawing-room amidst general enthusiasm.*)

LYUBOV (*applauds*). Bravo! Bravo!

CHARLOTTA. Now again! Ein, zwei, drei! (*Lifts up the rug; behind the rug stands* VARYA, *bowing.*)

PISHTCHIK (*wonderingly*). Fancy that now!

CHARLOTTA. That's the end (*throws the rug at* PISHTCHIK, *makes a curtsey, runs into the larger drawing-room*).

PISHTCHIK (*hurries after her*). Mischievous creature! Fancy! (*Goes out.*)

LYUBOV. And still Leonid doesn't come. I can't understand what he's doing in the town so long! Why, everything must be over by now. The estate is sold, or the sale has not taken place. Why keep us so long in suspense?

VARYA (*trying to console her*). Uncle's bought it. I feel sure of that.

TROFIMOV (*ironically*). Oh, yes!

VARYA. Great-aunt sent him an authorisation to buy it in her name, and transfer the debt. She's doing it for Anya's sake, and I'm sure God will be merciful. Uncle will buy it.

LYUBOV. My aunt in Yaroslavl sent fifteen thousand to buy the estate in her name, she doesn't trust us — but that's not enough to pay the arrears (*hides her face in her hands*). My fate is being sealed today, my fate...

TROFIMOV (*teasing* VARYA). Madame Lopahin.

VARYA (*angrily*). Perpetual student! Twice already you've been sent down from the University.

LYUBOV. Why are you angry, Varya? He's teasing you about Lopahin. Well, what of that? Marry Lopahin if you like, he's a good man, and interesting; if you don't want to, don't! No-body compels you, darling.

VARYA. I must tell you plainly, mamma, I look at the matter seriously; he's a good man, I like him.

LYUBOV. Well, marry him. I can't see what you're waiting for.

VARYA. Mamma. I can't make him an offer myself. For the last two years, everyone's been talking to me about him. Everyone talks; but he says nothing or else makes a joke. I see what it means. He's growing rich, he's absorbed in business, he has no thoughts for me. If I had money, were it ever so little, if I had only a hundred roubles, I'd throw everything up and go far away. I would go into a nunnery.

TROFIMOV. What bliss!

VARYA (*to* TROFIMOV). A student ought to have sense! (*In a soft tone with tears.*) How ugly you've grown, Petya! How old you look! (*To* LYUBOV ANDREYEVNA, *no longer crying.*) But I can't do without work, mamma; I must have something to do every minute.

(*Enter* YASHA.)

YASHA (*hardly restraining his laughter*). Epihodov has broken a billiard cue! (*Goes out.*)

VARYA. What is Epihodov doing here? Who gave him leave to play billiards? I can't make these people out. (*Goes out.*)

LYUBOV. Don't tease her, Petya. You see she has grief enough without that.

TROFIMOV. She is so very officious, meddling in what's not her business. All the summer she's given Anya and me no peace. She's afraid of a love affair between us. What's it to do with her? Besides, I have given no grounds for it. Such triviality is not in my line. We are above love!

LYUBOV. And I suppose I am beneath love. (*Very uneasily.*) Why is it Leonid's not here? If only I could know whether the estate is sold or not! It seems such an incredible calamity that I really don't know what to think. I am distracted... I shall scream in a minute... I shall do something stupid. Save me, Petya, tell me something, talk to me!

TROFIMOV. What does it matter whether the estate is sold today or not? That's all done with long ago. There's no turning back, the path is overgrown. Don't worry yourself, dear Lyubov Andreyevna. You mustn't deceive yourself; for once in your life you must face the truth!

LYUBOV. What truth? You see where the truth lies, but I seem to have lost my sight, I see nothing. You settle every great problem so boldly, but tell me, my dear boy, isn't it because you're young — because you haven't yet understood one of your problems through suffering? You look forward boldly, and isn't it that you don't see and don't expect anything dreadful because life is still hidden from your young eyes? You're bolder, more honest, deeper than we are, but think, be just a little magnanimous, have pity on me. I was born here, you know, my father and mother lived here, my grandfather lived here, I love this house. I can't conceive of life without the cherry orchard, and if it really must be sold, then sell me with the orchard (*embraces* TROFIMOV, *kisses him on the forehead*). My boy was drowned here (*weeps*). Pity me, my dear kind fellow.

TROFIMOV. You know I feel for you with all my heart.

LYUBOV. But that should have been said differently, so differently (*takes out her handkerchief, telegram falls on the floor*). My heart is so heavy today. It's so noisy here, my soul is quivering at every sound, I'm shuddering all over, but I can't go away; I'm afraid to be quiet and alone. Don't be hard on me, Petya... I love you as though you were one of ourselves. I would gladly let you marry Anya — I swear I would — only, my dear boy, you must take your degree, you do nothing — you're simply tossed by fate from place to place. That's so strange. It is, isn't it? And you must do something with your beard to make it grow somehow (*laughs*). You look so funny!

TROFIMOV (*picks up the telegram*). I've no wish to be a beauty.

LYUBOV. That's a telegram from Paris. I get one every day. One yesterday and one today. That savage creature is ill again, he's in trouble again. He begs forgiveness, beseeches me to go, and really I ought to go to Paris to see him. You look shocked, Petya. What am I to do, my dear boy, what am I to do? He is ill, he is alone and unhappy, and who'll look after him, who'll keep him from doing the wrong thing, who'll give him his medicine at the right time? And why hide it or be silent? I love him, that's clear. I love him! I love him! He's a millstone about my neck, I'm going to the bottom with him, but I love that stone and can't live without it (*presses* TROFIMOV'S *hand*). Don't think ill of me, Petya, don't tell me anything, don't tell me...

TROFIMOV (*through his tears*). For God's sake forgive my frankness: why, he robbed you!

LYUBOV. No! No! No! You mustn't speak like that (*covers her ears*).

TROFIMOV. He is a wretch! You're the only person that doesn't know it! He's a worthless creature! A despicable wretch!

LYUBOV (*getting angry, but speaking with restraint*). You're twenty-six or twenty-seven years old, but you're still a schoolboy.

TROFIMOV. Possibly.

LYUBOV. You should be a man at your age! You should understand what love means! And you ought to be in love yourself. You ought to fall in love! (*Angrily.*) Yes, yes, and it's not purity in you, you're simply a prude, a comic fool, a freak.

TROFIMOV (*in horror*). The things she's saying!

LYUBOV. I am above love! You're not above love, but simply as our Firs here says, "You are a good-for-nothing." At your age not to have a mistress!

TROFIMOV (*in horror*). This is awful! The things she is saying! (*Goes rapidly into the larger drawing-room clutching his head.*) This is awful! I can't stand it! I'm going. (*Goes off, but at once returns.*) All is over between us! (*Goes off into the ante-room.*)

LYUBOV (*shouts after him*). Petya! Wait a minute! You funny creature! I was joking! Petya! (*There is a sound of somebody running quickly downstairs and suddenly falling with a crash.* ANYA *and* VARYA *scream, but there is a sound of laughter at once.*)

LYUBOV. What has happened?

(ANYA *runs in.*)

ANYA (*laughing*). Petya's fallen downstairs! (*Runs out.*)

LYUBOV. What a queer fellow that Petya is!

(*The Station Master stands in the middle of the larger room and reads "The Magdalene," by Alexey Tolstoy. They listen to him, but before he has recited many lines strains of a waltz are heard from the ante-room and the reading is broken off. All dance.* TROFIMOV, ANYA, VARYA, *and* LYUBOV ANDREYEVNA *come in from the ante-room.*)

LYUBOV. Come, Petya — come, pure heart! I beg your pardon. Let's have a dance! (*Dances with* PETYA.)

(ANYA *and* VARYA *dance.* FIRS *comes in, puts his stick down near the side door.* YASHA *also comes into the drawing-room and looks on at the dancing.*)

YASHA. What is it, old man?

FIRS. I don't feel well. In old days we used to have generals, barons, and admirals dancing at our balls, and now we send for the post-office clerk and the station master and even they're not overanxious to come. I am getting feeble. The old master, the grandfather, used to give sealing-wax for all complaints. I have been taking sealing-wax for twenty years or more. Perhaps that's what's kept me alive.

YASHA. You bore me, old man! (*Yawns.*) It's time you were done with.

FIRS. Ach, you're a good-for-nothing! (*Mutters.*)

(TROFIMOV *and* LYUBOV ANDREYEVNA *dance in larger room and then on to the stage.*)

LYUBOV. *Merci.* I'll sit down a little (*sits down*). I'm tired.

(*Enter* ANYA.)

ANYA (*excitedly*). There's a man in the kitchen has been saying that the cherry orchard's been sold today.

LYUBOV. Sold to whom?

ANYA. He didn't say to whom. He's gone away.

(*She dances with* TROFIMOV, *and they go off into the larger room.*)

YASHA. There was an old man gossiping there, a stranger.

FIRS. Leonid Andreyevitch isn't here yet, he hasn't come back. He has his light overcoat on, *demi-saison*, he'll catch cold for sure. Ach! Foolish young things!

LYUBOV. I feel as though I should die. Go, Yasha, find out to whom it has been sold.

YASHA. But he went away long ago, the old chap (*laughs*).

LYUBOV (*with slight vexation*). What are you laughing at? What are you pleased at?

YASHA. Epihodov is so funny. He's a silly fellow, two and twenty misfortunes.

LYUBOV. Firs, if the estate is sold, where will you go?

FIRS. Where you bid me, there I'll go.

LYUBOV. Why do you look like that? Are you ill? You ought to be in bed.

FIRS. Yes (*ironically*). Me go to bed and who's to wait here? Who's to see to things without me? I'm the only one in all the house.

YASHA (*to* LYUBOV ANDREYEVNA). Lyubov Andreyevna, permit me to make a request of you; if you go back to Paris again, be so kind as to take me with you. It's positively impossible for me to stay here (*looking about him; in an undertone*). There's no need to say it, you see for yourself — an uncivilised country, the people have no

morals, and then the dullness! The food in the kitchen's abominable, and then Firs runs after one muttering all sorts of unsuitable
words.   Take me with you, please do!

(*Enter* PISHTCHIK.)

PISHTCHIK. Allow me to ask you for a waltz, my dear lady. (LYUBOV
ANDREYEVNA *goes with him.*)   Enchanting lady, I really must
borrow of you just 180 roubles (*dances*), only 180 roubles.   (*They
pass into the larger room.*)

YASHA (*hums softly*).   "Knowest thou my soul's emotion."
       (*In the larger drawing-room, a figure in a gray top hat and in check
       trousers is gesticulating and jumping about.   Shouts of "Bravo,
       Charlotta Ivanovna.")*

DUNYASHA (*she has stopped to powder herself*).   My young lady tells me
to dance.   There are plenty of gentlemen, and too few ladies,
but dancing makes me giddy and makes my heart beat.   Firs,
the post-office clerk said something to me just now that quite
took my breath away.   (*Music becomes more subdued.*)

FIRS. What did he say to you?

DUNYASHA. He said I was like a flower.

YASHA (*yawns*).   What ignorance!   (*Goes out.*)

DUNYASHA. Like a flower.   I am a girl of such delicate feelings,
I am awfully fond of soft speeches.

FIRS. Your head's being turned.

(*Enter* EPIHODOV.)

EPIHODOV. You have no desire to see me, Dunyasha.   I might be an
insect (*sighs*).   Ah! life!

DUNYASHA. What is it you want?

EPIHODOV. Undoubtedly you may be right (*sighs*).   But of course,
if one looks at it from that point of view, if I may so express myself, you have, excuse my plain speaking, reduced me to a complete state of mind.   I know my destiny.   Every day some misfortune befalls me and I have long ago grown accustomed to it, so
that I look upon my fate with a smile.   You gave me your word,
and though I ——

DUNYASHA. Let us have a talk later, I entreat you, but now leave
me in peace, for I am lost in reverie (*plays with her fan*).

EPIHODOV. I have a misfortune every day, and if I may venture to express myself, I merely smile at it, I even laugh.

(VARYA *enters from the larger drawing-room.*)

VARYA. You still have not gone, Epihodov. What a disrespectful creature you are, really! (*To* DUNYASHA.) Go along, Dunyasha! (*To* EPIHODOV.) First you play billiards and break the cue, then you go wandering about the drawing-room like a visitor!

EPIHODOV. You really cannot, if I may so express myself, call me to account like this.

VARYA. I'm not calling you to account, I'm speaking to you. You do nothing but wander from place to place and don't do your work. We keep you as a counting-house clerk, but what use you are I can't say.

EPIHODOV (*offended*). Whether I work or whether I walk, whether I eat or whether I play billiards, is a matter to be judged by persons of understanding and my elders.

VARYA. You dare to tell me that! (*Firing up.*) You dare! You mean to say I've no understanding. Begone from here! This minute!

EPIHODOV (*intimidated*). I beg you to express yourself with delicacy.

VARYA (*beside herself with anger*). This moment! get out! away! (*He goes towards the door, she following him.*) Two and twenty misfortunes! Take yourself off! Don't let me set eyes on you! (*Epihodov has gone out, behind the door his voice,* "I shall lodge a complaint against you.") What! You're coming back? (*Snatches up the stick* FIRS *has put down near the door.*) Come! Come! Come! I'll show you! What! you're coming? Then take that! (*She swings the stick, at the very moment that* LOPAHIN *comes in.*)

LOPAHIN. Very much obliged to you!

VARYA (*angrily and ironically*). I beg your pardon!

LOPAHIN. Not at all! I humbly thank you for your kind reception!

VARYA. No need of thanks for it. (*Moves away, then looks round and asks softly.*) I haven't hurt you?

LOPAHIN. Oh, no! Not at all! There's an immense bump coming up, though!

VOICES FROM LARGER ROOM. Lopahin has come! Yermolay Alexeyevitch!

PISHTCHIK. What do I see and hear? (*Kisses* LOPAHIN.) There's a whiff of cognac about you, my dear soul, and we're making merry here too!

(*Enter* LYUBOV ANDREYEVNA.)

LYUBOV. Is it you, Yermolay Alexeyevitch? Why have you been so long? Where's Leonid?

LOPAHIN. Leonid Andreyevitch arrived with me. He is coming.

LYUBOV (*in agitation*). Well! Well! Was there a sale? Speak!

LOPAHIN (*embarrassed, afraid of betraying his joy*). The sale was over at four o'clock. We missed our train — had to wait till half-past nine. (*Sighing heavily.*) Ugh! I feel a little giddy.

(*Enter* GAEV. *In his right hand he has purchases, with his left hand he is wiping away his tears.*)

LYUBOV. Well, Leonid? What news? (*Impatiently, with tears.*) Make haste, for God's sake!

GAEV (*makes her no answer, simply waves his hand. To* FIRS, *weeping*). Here, take them; there's anchovies, Kertch herrings. I have eaten nothing all day. What I have been through! (*Door into the billiard room is open. There is heard a knocking of balls and the voice of* YASHA *saying* "Eighty-seven." GAEV's *expression changes, he leaves off weeping*). I am fearfully tired. Firs, come and help me change my things (*goes to his own room across the larger drawing-room*).

PISHTCHIK. How about the sale? Tell us, do!

LYUBOV. Is the cherry orchard sold?

LOPAHIN. It is sold.

LYUBOV. Who has bought it?

LOPAHIN. I have bought it. (*A pause.* LYUBOV *is crushed; she would fall down if she were not standing near a chair and table.*)

(VARYA *takes keys from her waist-band, flings them on the floor in middle of drawing-room and goes out.*)

LOPAHIN. I have bought it! Wait a bit, ladies and gentlemen, pray. My head's a bit muddled, I can't speak (*laughs*). We came to the auction. Deriganov was there already. Leonid Andreyevitch only had 15,000 and Deriganov bid 30,000, besides the arrears, straight off. I saw how the land lay. I bid against him. I bid 40,000, he bid 45,000, I said 55, and so he went on, adding 5 thousands and I adding 10. Well... So it ended. I bid 90, and it was knocked down to me. Now the cherry orchard's mine! Mine! (*Chuckles.*) My God, the cherry orchard's mine! Tell me that I'm drunk, that I'm out of my mind, that it's all a dream (*stamps with his feet*). Don't laugh at me! If my father and my grandfather could rise from their graves and see all that has happened! How their Yermolay, ignorant, beaten Yermolay, who used to run about barefoot in winter, how that very Yermolay has bought the finest estate in the world! I have bought the estate where my father and grand-father were slaves, where they weren't even admitted into the kitchen. I am asleep, I am dreaming! It is all fancy, it is the work of your imagination plunged in the darkness of ignorance (*picks up keys, smiling fondly*). She threw away the keys; she means to show she's not the housewife now (*jingles the keys*). Well, no matter. (*The orchestra is heard tuning up.*) Hey, musicians! Play! I want to hear you. Come, all of you, and look how Yermolay Lopahin will take the axe to the cherry orchard, how the trees will fall to the ground! We will build houses on it and our grandsons and great-grandsons will see a new life springing up there. Music! Play up!

> (*Music begins to play.* LYUBOV ANDREYEVNA *has sunk into a chair and is weeping bitterly.*)

LOPAHIN (*reproachfully*). Why, why didn't you listen to me? My poor friend! Dear lady, there's no turning back now. (*With tears.*) Oh, if all this could be over, oh, if our miserable disjointed life could somehow soon be changed!

PISHTCHIK (*takes him by the arm, in an undertone*). She's weeping, let us go and leave her alone. Come (*takes him by the arm and leads him into the larger drawing-room*).

LOPAHIN. What's that? Musicians, play up! All must be as I wish it. (*With irony.*) Here comes the new master, the owner of the cherry orchard! (*Accidentally tips over a little table, almost upsetting the candelabra.*) I can pay for everything! (*Goes out with* PISCHT-CHIK. *No one remains on the stage or in the larger drawing-room except* LYUBOV, *who sits huddled up, weeping bitterly. The music plays softly.* ANYA *and* TROFIMOV *come in quickly.* ANYA *goes up to her mother and falls on her knees before her.* TROFIMOV *stands at the entrance to the larger drawing-room).*

ANYA. Mamma! Mamma, you're crying, dear, kind, good mamma! My precious! I love you! I bless you! The cherry orchard is sold, it is gone, that's true, that's true! But don't weep, mamma! Life is still before you, you have still your good, pure heart! Let us go, let us go, darling, away from here! We will make a new garden, more splendid than this one; you will see it, you will understand. And joy, quiet, deep joy, will sink into your soul like the sun at evening! And you will smile, mamma! Come, darling, let us go!

CURTAIN

ACT IV

Scene: Same as in First Act. There are neither curtains on the windows nor pictures on the walls: only a little furniture remains piled up in a corner as if for sale. There is a sense of desolation; near the outer door and in the background of the scene are packed trunks, travelling bags, etc. On the left the door is open, and from here the voices of VARYA *and* ANYA *are audible.* LOPAHIN *is standing waiting.* YASHA *is holding a tray with glasses full of champagne. In front of the stage* EPIHODOV *is tying up a box. In the background behind the scene a hum of talk from the peasants who have come to say good-bye. The voice of* GAEV: "Thanks, brothers, thanks!"*

YASHA. The peasants have come to say good-bye. In my opinion, Yermolay Alexeyevitch, the peasants are good-natured, but they don't know much about things.

(The hum of talk dies away. Enter across front of stage LYUBOV ANDREYEVNA *and* GAEV. *She is not weeping, but is pale; her face is quivering — she cannot speak.)*

GAEV. You gave them your purse, Lyuba. That won't do — that won't do!

LYUBOV. I couldn't help it! I couldn't help it!   *(Both go out.)*

LOPAHIN *(in the doorway, calls after them).* You will take a glass at parting? Please do. I didn't think to bring any from the town, and at the station I could only get one bottle. Please take a glass (*a pause*). What? You don't care for any? (*Comes away from the door.*) If I'd known, I wouldn't have bought it. Well, and I'm not going to drink it. (YASHA *carefully sets the tray down on a chair.*) You have a glass, Yasha, anyway.

YASHA. Good luck to the travellers, and luck to those that stay behind! (*Drinks.*) This champagne isn't the real thing, I can assure you.

LOPAHIN. It cost eight roubles the bottle (*a pause*). It's devilish cold here.

YASHA. They haven't heated the stove today — it's all the same since we're going (*laughs*).

LOPAHIN. What are you laughing for?

YASHA. For pleasure.

LOPAHIN. Though it's October, it's as still and sunny as though it were summer. It's just right for building! (*Looks at his watch; says in doorway.*) Take note, ladies and gentlemen, the train goes in forty-seven minutes; so you ought to start for the station in twenty minutes. You must hurry up!

(TROFIMOV *comes in from out of doors wearing a greatcoat.*)

TROFIMOV. I think it must be time to start, the horses are ready. The devil only knows what's become of my goloshes; they're lost. (*In the doorway.*) Anya! My goloshes aren't here. I can't find them.

LOPAHIN. And I'm getting off to Harkov. I am going in the same train with you. I'm spending all the winter at Harkov. I've been wasting all my time gossiping with you and fretting with no work to do. I can't get on without work. I don't know what to do with my hands, they flap about so queerly, as if they didn't belong to me.

TROFIMOV. Well, we're just going away, and you will take up your profitable labours again.

LOPAHIN. Do take a glass.

TROFIMOV. No, thanks.

LOPAHIN. Then you're going to Moscow now?

TROFIMOV. Yes. I shall see them as far as the town, and tomorrow I shall go on to Moscow.

LOPAHIN. Yes, I daresay, the professors aren't giving any lectures, they're waiting for your arrival.

TROFIMOV. That's not your business.

LOPAHIN. How many years have you been at the University?

TROFIMOV. Do think of something newer than that — that's stale and flat (*hunts for goloshes*). You know we shall most likely never see each other again, so let me give you one piece of advice at parting: don't wave your arms about — get out of the habit. And another thing, building villas, reckoning up that the summer visitors will in time become independent farmers — reckoning like that, that's not the thing to do either. After all, I am fond of you: you have fine delicate fingers like an artist, you've a fine delicate soul.

LOPAHIN (*embraces him*). Good-bye, my dear fellow. Thanks for everything. Let me give you money for the journey, if you need it.

TROFIMOV. What for? I don't need it.

LOPAHIN. Why, you haven't got a halfpenny.

TROFIMOV. Yes, I have, thank you. I got some money for a translation. Here it is in my pocket, (*anxiously*) but where can my goloshes be!

VARYA (*from the next room*). Take the nasty things! (*Flings a pair of goloshes on to the stage.*)

TROFIMOV. Why are you so cross, Varya? h'm!... but those aren't my goloshes.

LOPAHIN. I sowed three thousand acres with poppies in the spring, and now I have cleared forty thousand profit. And when my poppies were in flower, wasn't it a picture! So here, as I say, I made forty thousand, and I'm offering you a loan because I can afford to. Why turn up your nose? I am a peasant — I speak bluntly.

TROFIMOV. Your father was a peasant, mine was a chemist — and that proves absolutely nothing whatever. (LOPAHIN *takes out his pocket-book.*) Stop that — stop that. If you were to offer me two hundred thousand I wouldn't take it. I am an independent man, and everything that all of you, rich and poor alike, prize so highly and hold so dear, hasn't the slightest power over me — it's like so much fluff fluttering in the air. I can get on without you.

I can pass by you. I am strong and proud. Humanity is advancing towards the highest truth, the highest happiness, which is possible on earth, and I am in the front ranks.

LOPAHIN. Will you get there?

TROFIMOV. I shall get there (*a pause*). I shall get there, or I shall show others the way to get there.

(*In the distance is heard the stroke of an axe on a tree.*)

LOPAHIN. Good-bye, my dear fellow; it's time to be off. We turn up our noses at one another, but life is passing all the while. When I am working hard without resting, then my mind is more at ease, and it seems to me as though I too know what I exist for; but how many people there are in Russia, my dear boy, who exist, one doesn't know what for. Well, it doesn't matter. That's not what keeps things spinning. They tell me Leonid Andreyevitch has taken a situation. He is going to be a clerk at the bank — 6,000 roubles a year. Only, of course, he won't stick to it — he's too lazy.

ANYA (*in the doorway*). Mamma begs you not to let them chop down the orchard until she's gone.

TROFIMOV. Yes, really, you might have the tact (*walks out across the front of the stage*).

LOPAHIN. I'll see to it! I'll see to it! Stupid fellows! (*Goes out after him.*)

ANYA. Has Firs been taken to the hospital?

YASHA. I told them this morning. No doubt they have taken him.

ANYA (*to EPIHODOV, who passes across the drawing-room*). Semyon Pantaleyevitch, inquire, please, if Firs has been taken to the hospital.

YASHA (*in a tone of offence*). I told Yegor this morning — why ask a dozen times?

EPIHODOV. Firs is advanced in years. It's my conclusive opinion no treatment would do him good; it's time he was gathered to his fathers. And I can only envy him (*puts a trunk down on a cardboard hat-box and crushes it*). There, now, of course — I knew it would be so.

YASHA (*jeeringly*). Two and twenty misfortunes!

VARYA (*through the door*). Has Firs been taken to the hospital?

ANYA. Yes.

VARYA. Why wasn't the note for the doctor taken too?

ANYA. Oh, then, we must send it after them (*goes out*).

VARYA (*from the adjoining room*). Where's Yasha? Tell him his mother's come to say good-bye to him.

YASHA (*waves his hand*). They put me out of all patience! (DUN-YASHA *has all this time been busy about the luggage. Now, when* YASHA *is left alone, she goes up to him.*)

DUNYASHA. You might just give me one look, Yasha. You're going away. You're leaving me (*weeps and throws herself on his neck*).

YASHA. What are you crying for? (*Drinks the champagne.*) In six days I shall be in Paris again. Tomorrow we shall get into the express train and roll away in a flash. I can scarcely believe it! *Vive la France!* It doesn't suit me here — it's not the life for me; there's no doing anything. I have seen enough of the ignorance here. I have had enough of it (*drinks champagne*). What are you crying for? Behave yourself properly, and then you won't cry.

DUNYASHA (*powders her face, looking in a pocket-mirror*). Do send me a letter from Paris. You know how I loved you, Yasha — how I loved you! I am a tender creature, Yasha.

YASHA. Here they are coming!

(*Busies himself about the trunks, humming softly. Enter* LYUBOV ANDRE-YEVNA, GAEV, ANYA, *and* CHARLOTTA IVANOVNA.)

GAEV. We ought to be off. There's not much time now (*looking at* YASHA). What a smell of herrings!

LYUBOV. In ten minutes we must get into the carriage (*casts a look about the room*). Farewell, dear house, dear old home of our fathers! Winter will pass and spring will come, and then you will be no more; they will tear you down! How much those walls have seen! (*Kisses her daughter passionately.*) My treasure, how bright you look! Your eyes are sparkling like diamonds! Are you glad? Very glad?

ANYA. Very glad! A new life is beginning, mamma.

GAEV. Yes, really, everything is all right now. Before the cherry orchard was sold, we were all worried and wretched, but afterwards, when once the question was settled conclusively, irrevocably, we all felt calm and even cheerful. I am a bank clerk now — I am a financier — cannon off the red. And you, Lyuba, after all, you are looking better; there's no question of that.

LYUBOV. Yes. My nerves are better, that's true. (*Her hat and coat are handed to her.*) I'm sleeping well. Carry out my things, Yasha. It's time. (*To* ANYA.) My darling, we shall soon see each other again. I am going to Paris. I can live there on the money your Yaroslavl auntie sent us to buy the estate with — hurrah for auntie! — but that money won't last long.

ANYA. You'll come back soon, mamma, won't you? I'll be working up for my examination in the high school, and when I have passed that, I shall set to work and be a help to you. We will read all sorts of things together, mamma, won't we? (*Kisses her mother's hands.*) We will read in the autumn evenings. We'll read lots of books, and a new wonderful world will open out before us (*dreamily*). Mamma, come soon.

LYUBOV. I shall come, my precious treasure (*embraces her*).

(*Enter* LOPAHIN. CHARLOTTA *softly hums a song.*)

GAEV. Charlotta's happy; she's singing!

CHARLOTTA (*picks up a bundle like a swaddled baby*). Bye, bye, my baby. (*A baby is heard crying:* "*Ooah! ooah!*") Hush, hush, my pretty boy! (*Ooah! ooah!*) Poor little thing! (*Throws the bundle back.*) You must please find me a situation. I can't go on like this.

LOPAHIN. We'll find you one, Charlotta Ivanovna. Don't you worry yourself.

GAEV. Everyone's leaving us. Varya's going away. We have become of no use all at once.

CHARLOTTA. There's nowhere for me to be in the town. I must go away. (*Hums.*) What care I...

(*Enter* PISHTCHIK.)

LOPAHIN. The freak of nature!

PISHTCHIK (*gasping*). Oh!... let me get my breath.... I'm worn out ... my most honoured... Give me some water.

GAEV. Want some money, I suppose? Your humble servant! I'll go out of the way of temptation (*goes out*).

PISHTCHIK. It's a long while since I have been to see you... dearest lady. (*To* LOPAHIN.) You are here... glad to see you... a man of immense intellect... take... here (*gives* LOPAHIN) 400 roubles. That leaves me owing 840.

LOPAHIN (*shrugging his shoulders in amazement*). It's like a dream. Where did you get it?

PISHTCHIK. Wait a bit... I'm hot... a most extraordinary occurrence! Some Englishmen came along and found in my land some sort of white clay. (*To* LYUBOV ANDREYEVNA.) And 400 for you... most lovely... wonderful (*gives money*). The rest later (*sips water*). A young man in the train was telling me just now that a great philosopher advises jumping off a house-top. "Jump!" says he; "the whole gist of the problem lies in that." (*Wonderingly.*) Fancy that, now! Water, please!

LOPAHIN. What Englishmen?

PISHTCHIK. I have made over to them the rights to dig the clay for twenty-four years... and now, excuse me... I can't stay... I must be trotting on. I'm going to Znoikovo... to Kardamanovo.... I'm in debt all round (*sips*).... To your very good health!... I'll come in on Thursday.

LYUBOV. We are just off to the town, and tomorrow I start for abroad.

PISHTCHIK. What! (*In agitation.*) Why to the town? Oh, I see the furniture... the boxes. No matter... (*through his tears*)... no matter... men of enormous intellect... these Englishmen.... Never mind... be happy. God will succour you... no matter... everything in this world must have an end (*kisses* LYUBOV ANDREYEVNA's *hand*). If the rumour reaches you that my end has come, think of this... old horse, and say: "There once was such a man in the world... Semyonov-Pishtchik... the Kingdom of Heaven be his!"... most extraordinary weather... yes. (*Goes out in violent agitation, but at once returns and says in the doorway.*) Dashenka wishes to be remembered to you (*goes out*).

LYUBOV. Now we can start. I leave with two cares in my heart. The first is leaving Firs ill. (*Looking at her watch.*) We have still five minutes.

ANYA. Mamma, Firs has been taken to the hospital. Yasha sent him off this morning.

LYUBOV. My other anxiety is Varya. She is used to getting up early and working; and now, without work, she's like a fish out of water. She is thin and pale, and she's crying, poor dear! (*A pause.*) You are well aware, Yermolay Alexeyevitch, I dreamed of marrying her to you, and everything seemed to show that you would get married (*whispers to* ANYA *and motions to* CHARLOTTA *and both go out*). She loves you — she suits you. And I don't know — I don't know why it is you seem, as it were, to avoid each other. I can't understand it!

LOPAHIN. I don't understand it myself, I confess. It's queer somehow, altogether. If there's still time, I'm ready now at once. Let's settle it straight off, and go ahead; but without you, I feel I shan't make her an offer.

LYUBOV. That's excellent. Why, a single moment's all that's necessary. I'll call her at once.

LOPAHIN. And there's champagne all ready too (*looking into the glasses*). Empty! Someone's emptied them already. (YASHA *coughs.*) I call that greedy.

LYUBOV (*eagerly*). Capital! We will go out. Yasha, *allez!* I'll call her in. (*At the door.*) Varya, leave all that; come here. Come along! (*Goes out with* YASHA.)

LOPAHIN (*looking at his watch*). Yes.

(*A pause. Behind the door, smothered laughter and whispering, and, at last, enter* VARYA.)

VARYA (*looking a long while over the things*). It is strange, I can't find it anywhere.

LOPAHIN. What are you looking for?

VARYA. I packed it myself, and I can't remember (*a pause*).

LOPAHIN. Where are you going now, Varvara Mihailova?

VARYA. I? To the Ragulins. I have arranged to go to them to look after the house — as a housekeeper.

LOPAHIN. That's in Yashnovo? It'll be seventy miles away (*a pause*). So this is the end of life in this house!

VARYA (*looking among the things*). Where is it? Perhaps I put it in the trunk. Yes, life in this house is over — there will be no more of it.

LOPAHIN. And I'm just off to Harkov — by this next train. I've a lot of business there. I'm leaving Epihodov here, and I've taken him on.

VARYA. Really!

LOPAHIN. This time last year we had snow already, if you remember; but now it's so fine and sunny. Though it's cold, to be sure — three degrees of frost.

VARYA. I haven't looked (*a pause*). And besides, our thermometer's broken (*a pause*).

(*Voice at the door from the yard:* "Yermolay Alexeyevitch!")

LOPAHIN (*as though he had long been expecting this summons*). This minute!

(LOPAHIN *goes out quickly.* VARYA *sitting on the floor and laying her head on a bag full of clothes, sobs quietly. The door opens.* LYUBOV ANDREYEVNA *comes in cautiously.*)

LYUBOV. Well? (*A pause.*) We must be going.

VARYA (*has wiped her eyes and is no longer crying*). Yes, mamma, it's time to start. I shall have time to get to the Ragulins today, if only you're not late for the train.

LYUBOV (*in the doorway*). Anya, put your things on.

(*Enter* ANYA, *then* GAEV *and* CHARLOTTA IVANOVNA. GAEV *has on a warm coat with a hood. Servants and cabmen come in.* EPIHODOV *bustles about the luggage.*)

LYUBOV. Now we can start on our travels.

ANYA (*joyfully*). On our travels!

GAEV. My friends — my dear, my precious friends! Leaving this house for ever, can I be silent? Can I refrain from giving utterance at leave-taking to those emotions which now flood all my being?

ANYA (*supplicatingly*). Uncle!

VARYA. Uncle, you mustn't!

GAEV (*dejectedly*). Cannon and into the pocket... I'll be quiet....

(*Enter* TROFIMOV *and afterwards* LOPAHIN.)

TROFIMOV. Well, ladies and gentlemen, we must start.

LOPAHIN. Epihodov, my coat!

LYUBOV. I'll stay just one minute. It seems as though I have never seen before what the walls, what the ceilings in this house were like, and now I look at them with greediness, with such tender love.

GAEV. I remember when I was six years old sitting in that window on Trinity Day watching my father going to church.

LYUBOV. Have all the things been taken?

LOPAHIN. I think all. (*Putting on overcoat, to* EPIHODOV.) You, Epihodov, mind you see everything is right.

EPIHODOV (*in a husky voice*). Don't you trouble, Yermolay Alexeyevitch.

LOPAHIN. Why, what's wrong with your voice?

EPIHODOV. I've just had a drink of water, and I choked over something.

YASHA (*contemptuously*). The ignorance!

LYUBOV. We are going — and not a soul will be left here.

LOPAHIN. Not till the spring.

VARYA (*pulls a parasol out of a bundle, as though about to hit someone with it.* LOPAHIN *makes a gesture as though alarmed*). What is it? I didn't mean anything.

TROFIMOV. Ladies and gentlemen, let us get into the carriage. It's time. The train will be in directly.

VARYA. Petya, here they are, your goloshes, by that box. (*With tears.*) And what dirty old things they are!

TROFIMOV (*putting on his goloshes*). Let us go, friends!

GAEV (*greatly agitated, afraid of weeping*). The train — the station! Double baulk, ah!

LYUBOV. Let us go!

LOPAHIN. Are we all here? (*Locks the side-door on left.*) The things are all here. We must lock up. Let us go!

ANYA. Good-bye, home! Good-bye to the old life!

TROFIMOV. Welcome to the new life!

(TROFIMOV *goes out with* ANYA. VARYA *looks round the room and goes out slowly.* YASHA *and* CHARLOTTA IVANOVNA, *with her dog, go out.*)

LOPAHIN. Till the spring, then! Come, friends, till we meet! (*Goes out.*)

(LYUBOV ANDREYEVNA *and* GAEV *remain alone. As though they had been waiting for this, they throw themselves on each other's necks, and break into subdued smothered sobbing, afraid of being overheard.*)

GAEV (*in despair*). Sister, my sister!

LYUBOV. Oh, my orchard! — my sweet, beautiful orchard! My
life, my youth, my happiness, good-bye! good-bye!

VOICE OF ANYA (*calling gaily*). Mamma!

VOICE OF TROFIMOV (*gaily, excitedly*). Aa — oo!

LYUBOV. One last look at the walls, at the windows. My dear
mother loved to walk about this room.

GAEV. Sister, sister!

VOICE OF ANYA. Mamma!

VOICE OF TROFIMOV. Aa — oo!

LYUBOV. We are coming. (*They go out.*)

(*The stage is empty. There is the sound of the doors being locked up, then of
the carriages driving away. There is silence. In the stillness there
is the dull stroke of an axe in a tree, clanging with a mournful lonely
sound. Footsteps are heard. FIRS appears in the doorway on the right.
He is dressed as always — in a peajacket and white waistcoat, with
slippers on his feet. He is ill.*)

FIRS (*goes up to the doors, and tries the handles*). Locked! They have
gone... (*sits down on sofa*). They have forgotten me.... Never
mind... I'll sit here a bit.... I'll be bound Leonid Andreyevitch
hasn't put his fur coat on and has gone off in his thin overcoat
(*sighs anxiously*). I didn't see after him.... These young people...
(*mutters something that can't be distinguished*). Life has slipped by as
though I hadn't lived. (*Lies down.*) I'll lie down a bit....
There's no strength in you, nothing left you — all gone! Ech!
I'm good for nothing (*lies motionless*).

(*A sound is heard that seems to come from the sky, like a breaking
harp-string, dying away mournfully. All is still again, and
there is heard nothing but the strokes of the axe far away in the
orchard.*)

CURTAIN

CYRANO DE BERGERAC

By EDMOND ROSTAND

Translated by GERTRUDE HALL

DRAMATIS PERSONÆ

Cyrano de Bergerac
Christian de Neuvillette
Comte de Guiche
Ragueneau
Le Bret
Captain Carbon de Castel-Jaloux
Lignière
De Valvert
Montfleury
Bellerose
Jodelet
Cuigy
Brissaille
A Bore
A Mousquetaire
Other Mousquetaire
A Spanish Officer
A Light-Cavalry Man
A Doorkeeper
A Burgher
His Son
A Pickpocket
A Spectator
A Watchman
Bertrandou the Fifer
A Capuchin
Two Musicians
Seven Cadets
Three Marquises
Poets
Pastrycooks

Roxane
Sister Martha

LISE
THE SWEETMEAT VENDER
MOTHER MARGARET
THE DUENNA
SISTER CLAIRE
AN ACTRESS
A SOUBRETTE
A FLOWER-GIRL
PAGES

The crowd, bourgeois, marquises, mousquetaires, pickpockets, pastrycooks, poets, Gascony Cadets, players, fiddlers, pages, children, Spanish soldiers, spectators, précieuses, actresses, bourgeoises, nuns, etc.

ACT FIRST

A PLAY AT THE HOTEL DE BOURGOGNE

The great hall of the Hotel de Bourgogne, in 1640. A sort of tennis-court arranged and decorated for theatrical performances.

The hall is a long rectangle, seen obliquely, so that one side of it constitutes the background, which runs from the position of the front wing at the right, to the line of the furthest wing at the left, and forms an angle with the stage, which is equally seen obliquely.

This stage is furnished, on both sides, along the wings, with benches. The drop-curtain is composed of two tapestry hangings, which can be drawn apart. Above a harlequin cloak, the royal escutcheon. Broad steps lead from the raised platform of the stage into the house. On either side of these steps, the musicians' seats. A row of candles fills the office of footlights.

Two galleries run along the side; the lower one is divided into boxes. No seats in the pit, which is the stage proper. At the back of the pit, that is to say, at the right, in the front, a few seats raised like steps, one above the other; and, under a stairway which leads to the upper seats, and of which the lower end only is visible, a stand decked with small candelabra, jars full of flowers, flagons and glasses, dishes heaped with sweetmeats, etc.

In the centre of the background, under the box-tier, the entrance to the theatre, large door which half opens to let in the spectators. On the panels of this door, and in several corners, and above the sweetmeat stand, red playbills announcing LA CLORISE.

At the rise of the curtain, the house is nearly dark, and still empty. The chandeliers are let down in the middle of the pit, until time to light them.

The audience, arriving gradually. Cavaliers, burghers, lackeys, pages, fiddlers, etc.

A tumult of voices is heard beyond the door; enter brusquely a CAVALIER.

DOORKEEPER (*running in after him*). Not so fast! Your fifteen pence!
CAVALIER. I come in admission free!
DOORKEEPER. And why?
CAVALIER. I belong to the king's light cavalry!
DOORKEEPER (*to another* CAVALIER *who has entered*). You?

SECOND CAVALIER. I do not pay!

DOORKEEPER. But...

SECOND CAVALIER. I belong to the mousquetaires!

FIRST CAVALIER (*to the* SECOND). It does not begin before two. The floor is empty. Let us have a bout with foils.

(*They fence with foils they have brought.*)

A LACKEY (*entering*). Pst!... Flanquin!

OTHER LACKEY (*arrived a moment before*). Champagne?...

FIRST LACKEY (*taking a pack of cards from his doublet and showing it to* SECOND LACKEY). Cards. Dice. (*Sits down on the floor.*) Let us have a game.

SECOND LACKEY (*sitting down likewise*). You rascal, willingly!

FIRST LACKEY (*taking from his pocket a bit of candle which he lights and sticks on the floor*). I prigged an eyeful of my master's light!

ONE OF THE WATCH (*to a* FLOWER-GIRL, *who comes forward*). It is pleasant getting here before the lights.

(*Puts his arm around her waist.*)

ONE OF THE FENCERS (*taking a thrust*). Hit!

ONE OF THE GAMBLERS. Clubs!

THE WATCHMAN (*pursuing the girl*). A kiss!

THE FLOWER-GIRL (*repulsing him*). We shall be seen!

THE WATCHMAN (*drawing her into a dark corner*). No, we shall not!

A MAN (*sitting on the floor with others who have brought provisions*). By coming early, you get a comfortable chance to eat.

A BURGHER (*leading his son*). This should be a good place, my boy. Let us stay here.

ONE OF THE GAMBLERS. Ace wins!

A MAN (*taking a bottle from under his cloak and sitting down*). A proper toper, toping Burgundy (*drinks*), I say should tope it in Burgundy House!

THE BURGHER (*to his son*). Might one not suppose we had stumbled into some house of evil fame? (*Points with his cane at the drunkard.*) Guzzlers!... (*In breaking guard one of the fencers jostles him.*) Brawlers!... (*He falls between the gamblers.*) Gamesters!...

THE WATCHMAN (*behind him, still teasing the flower-girl*). A kiss!

THE BURGHER (*dragging his son precipitately away*). Bless my soul!... And to reflect that in this very house, my son, were given the plays of the great Rotrou!

THE YOUTH. And those of the great Corneille!

(*A band of* PAGES *holding hands rush in performing a farandole and singing.*)

PAGES. Tra la la la la la la la!...

DOORKEEPER (*severely to the* PAGES). Look, now!... you pages, you! none of your tricks!

FIRST PAGE (*with wounded dignity*). Sir!... this want of confidence... (*As soon as the doorkeeper has turned away, briskly to the* SECOND PAGE.) Have you a string about you?

SECOND PAGE. With a fish-hook at the end!

FIRST PAGE. We will sit up there and angle for wigs!

A PICKPOCKET (*surrounded by a number of individuals of dubious appearance*). Come, now, my little hopefuls, and learn your A B C's of trade. Being as you're not used to hooking...

SECOND PAGE (*shouting to other* PAGES *who have already taken seats in the upper gallery*). Ho!... Did you bring any pea-shooters?

THIRD PAGE (*from above*). Yes!... And pease!...

(*Shoots down a volley of pease.*)

THE YOUTH (*to his father*). What are we going to see?

THE BURGHER. Clorise.

THE YOUTH. By whom?

THE BURGHER. By Balthazar Baro. Ah, what a play it is!...

(*Goes toward the back on his son's arm.*)

PICKPOCKET (*to his disciples*). Particularly the lace-ruffles at the knees,... you're to snip off carefully!

A SPECTATOR (*to another, pointing toward an upper seat*). Look! On the first night of the Cid, I was perched up there!

PICKPOCKET (*with pantomimic suggestion of spiriting away*). Watches...

THE BURGHER (*coming forward again with his son*). The actors you are about to see, my son, are among the most illustrious...

PICKPOCKET (*with show of subtracting with furtive little tugs*). Pocket-handkerchiefs...

THE BURGHER. Montfleury...

SOMEBODY (*shouting from the upper gallery*). Make haste, and light the chandeliers!

THE BURGHER. Bellerose, l'Épy, the Beaupré, Jodelet...

A PAGE (*in the pit*). Ah!... Here comes the goody-seller!

THE SWEETMEAT VENDER (*appearing behind the stand*).   Oranges...
Milk... Raspberry cordial... citron-wine...

(*Hubbub at the door.*)

FALSETTO VOICE (*outside*).   Make room, ruffians!

ONE OF THE LACKEYS (*astonished*).   The marquises... in the pit!

OTHER LACKEY.   Oh, for an instant only!

(*Enter a band of foppish* YOUNG MARQUISES.)

ONE OF THE MARQUISES (*looking around the half-empty house*).   What?...
We happen in like so many linen-drapers?   Without disturbing
anybody? treading on any feet?... Too bad! too bad! too bad!
(*He finds himself near several other gentlemen, come in a moment before.*)
Cuigy, Brissaile!   (*Effusive embraces.*)

CUIGY.   We are of the faithful indeed.   We are here before the
lights.

THE MARQUIS.   Ah, do not speak of it!... It has put me in such a
humor!

OTHER MARQUIS.   Be comforted, marquis... here comes the candle-
lighter!

THE AUDIENCE (*greeting the arrival of the candle-lighter*).   Ah!...
     (*Many gather around the chandeliers while they are being lighted.   A
     few have taken seats in the galleries.*)

(LIGNIÈRE *enters, arm in arm with* CHRISTIAN DE NEUVILLETTE.
     LIGNIÈRE, *in somewhat disordered apparel, appearance of gentlemanly
     drunkard.*   CHRISTIAN, *becomingly dressed, but in clothes of a slightly
     obsolete elegance.*)

CUIGY.   Lignière!

BRISSAILLE (*laughing*).   Not tipsy yet?

LIGNIÈRE (*low to* CHRISTIAN).   Shall I present you?   (CHRISTIAN
     nods assent.)   Baron de Neuvillette...   (*Exchange of bows.*)

THE AUDIENCE (*cheering the ascent of the first lighted chandelier*).   Ah!...

CUIGY (*to* BRISSAILLE, *looking at* CHRISTIAN).   A charming head...
charming!

FIRST MARQUIS (*who has overheard*).   Pooh!...

LIGNIÈRE (*presenting* CHRISTIAN).   Messieurs de Cuigy... de Brissaille...

CHRISTIAN (*bowing*).   Delighted!...

FIRST MARQUIS (*to* SECOND). He is a pretty fellow enough, but is dressed in the fashion of some other year.

LIGNIÈRE (*to* CUIGY). Monsieur is lately arrived from Touraine.

CHRISTIAN. Yes, I have been in Paris not over twenty days. I enter the Guards tomorrow, the Cadets.

FIRST MARQUIS (*looking at those who appear in the boxes*). There comes the président Aubry!

SWEETMEAT VENDER. Oranges! Milk!

THE FIDDLERS (*tuning*). La... la...

CUIGY (*to* CHRISTIAN, *indicating the house which is filling*). A good house!...

CHRISTIAN. Yes, crowded.

FIRST MARQUIS. The whole of fashion!

> (*They give the names of the women, as, very brilliantly attired, these enter the boxes. Exchange of bows and smiles.*)

SECOND MARQUIS. Mesdames de Guéménée...

CUIGY. De Bois-Dauphin...

FIRST MARQUIS. Whom... time was!... we loved!...

BRISSAILLE. ... de Chavigny...

SECOND MARQUIS. Who still plays havoc with our hearts!

LIGNIÈRE. *Tiens!* Monsieur de Corneille has come back from Rouen!

THE YOUTH (*to his father*). The Academy is present?

THE BURGHER. Yes... I perceive more than one member of it. Yonder are Boudu, Boissat, and Cureau... Porchères, Colomby, Bourzeys, Bourdon, Arbaut... All names of which not one will be forgotten. What a beautiful thought it is!

FIRST MARQUIS. Attention! Our précieuses are coming into their seats... Barthénoide, Urimédonte, Cassandace, Félixérie...

SECOND MARQUIS. Ah, how exquisite are their surnames!... Marquis, can you tell them off, all of them?

FIRST MARQUIS. I can tell them off, all of them, marquis!

LIGNIÈRE (*drawing* CHRISTIAN *aside*). Dear fellow, I came in here to be of use to you. The lady does not come. I revert to my vice!

CHRISTIAN (*imploring*). No! No!... You who turn into ditties Town and Court, stay by me; you will be able to tell me for whom it is I am dying of love!

THE LEADER OF THE VIOLINS (*rapping on his desk with his bow*). Gentlemen!...   (*He raises his bow.*)

SWEETMEAT VENDER. Macaroons... Citronade...

(*The fiddles begin playing.*)

CHRISTIAN. I fear... oh, I fear to find that she is fanciful and intricate! I dare not speak to her, for I am of a simple wit. The language written and spoken in these days bewilders and baffles me. I am a plain soldier... shy, to boot. — She is always at the right, there, the end: the empty box.

LIGNIÈRE (*with show of leaving*). I am going.

CHRISTIAN (*still attempting to detain him*). Oh, no!... Stay, I beseech you!

LIGNIÈRE. I cannot. D'Assoucy is expecting me at the pot-house. Here is a mortal drought!

SWEETMEAT VENDER (*passing before him with a tray*). Orangeade?...

LIGNIÈRE. Ugh!

SWEETMEAT VENDER. Milk?...

LIGNIÈRE. Pah!...

SWEETMEAT VENDER. Lacrima?...

LIGNIÈRE. Stop! (*To* CHRISTIAN.) I will tarry a bit.... Let us see this lacrima?

(*Sits down at the sweetmeat stand. The* VENDER *pours him a glass of lacrima.*)

(*Shouts among the audience at the entrance of a little, merry-faced, roly-poly man.*)

AUDIENCE. Ah, Ragueneau!...

LIGNIÈRE (*to* CHRISTIAN). Ragueneau, who keeps the great cookshop.

RAGUENEAU (*attired like a pastrycook in his Sunday best, coming quickly toward* LIGNIÈRE). Monsieur, have you seen Monsieur de Cyrano?

LIGNIÈRE (*presenting* RAGUENEAU *to* CHRISTIAN). The pastrycook of poets and of players!

RAGUENEAU (*abashed*). Too much honor....

LIGNIÈRE. No modesty!... Mecænas!...

RAGUENEAU. It is true, those gentlemen are among my customers....

LIGNIÈRE. Debitors!... A considerable poet himself....

RAGUENEAU. It has been said!...

LIGNIÈRE. Daft on poetry!...

RAGUENEAU. It is true that for an ode...

LIGNIÈRE. You are willing to give at any time a tart!

RAGUENEAU. ... let. A tart-let.

LIGNIÈRE. Kind soul, he tries to cheapen his charitable acts! And for a triolet were you not known to give...?

RAGUENEAU. Rolls. Just rolls.

LIGNIÈRE (*severely*). Buttered!... And the play, you are fond of the play?

RAGUENEAU. It is with me a passion!

LIGNIÈRE. And you settle for your entrance fee with a pastry currency. Come now, among ourselves, what did you have to give today for admittance here?

RAGUENEAU. Four custards... eighteen lady-fingers. (*He looks all around.*) Monsieur de Cyrano is not here. I wonder at it.

LIGNIÈRE. And why?

RAGUENEAU. Montfleury is billed to play.

LIGNIÈRE. So it is, indeed. That ton of man will today entrance us in the part of Phœdo... Phœdo!... But what is that to Cyrano?

RAGUENEAU. Have you not heard? He interdicted Montfleury, whom he has taken in aversion, from appearing for one month upon the stage.

LIGNIÈRE (*who is at his fourth glass*). Well?

RAGUENEAU. Montfleury is billed to play.

CUIGY (*who has drawn near with his companions*). He cannot be prevented.

RAGUENEAU. He cannot?... Well, I am here to see!

FIRST MARQUIS. What is this Cyrano?

CUIGY. A crack-brain!

SECOND MARQUIS. Of quality?

CUIGY. Enough for daily uses. He is a cadet in the Guards. (*Pointing out a gentleman who is coming and going about the pit, as if in search of somebody.*) But his friend Le Bret can tell you. (*Calling.*) Le Bret!... (LE BRET *comes toward them.*) You are looking for Bergerac?

LE BRET. Yes. I am uneasy.

CUIGY. Is it not a fact that he is a most uncommon fellow?

LE BRET (*affectionately*).   The most exquisite being he is that walks beneath the moon!

RAGUENEAU.   Poet!

CUIGY.   Swordsman!

BRISSAILLE.   Physicist!

LE BRET.   Musician!

LIGNIÈRE.   And what an extraordinary aspect he presents!

RAGUENEAU.   I will not go so far as to say that I believe our grave Philippe de Champaigne will leave us a portrait of him; but, the bizarre, excessive, whimsical fellow that he is would certainly have furnished the late Jacques Callot with a type of madcap fighter for one of his masques.   Hat with triple feather, doublet with twice-triple skirt, cloak which his interminable rapier lifts up behind, with pomp, like the insolent tail of a cock; prouder than all the Artabans that Gascony ever bred, he goes about in his stiff Punchinello ruff, airing a nose.... Ah, gentlemen, what a nose is that!   One cannot look upon such a specimen of the nasigera without exclaiming, "No! truly, the man exaggerates." ... After that, one smiles, one says: "He will take it off."... But Monsieur de Bergerac never takes it off at all.

LE BRET (*shaking his head*).   He wears it always... and cuts down whoever breathes a syllable in comment.

RAGUENEAU (*proudly*).   His blade is half the shears of Fate!

FIRST MARQUIS (*shrugging his shoulders*).   He will not come!

RAGUENEAU.   He will.   I wager you a chicken à la Ragueneau.

FIRST MARQUIS (*laughing*).   Very well!

(*Murmur of admiration in the house.* ROXANE *has appeared in her box. She takes a seat in the front, her duenna at the back.* CHRISTIAN, *engaged in paying the* SWEETMEAT VENDER, *does not look.*)

SECOND MARQUIS (*uttering a series of small squeals*).   Ah, gentlemen, she is horrifically enticing!

FIRST MARQUIS.   A strawberry set in a peach, and smiling!

SECOND MARQUIS.   So fresh, that being near her, one might catch cold in his heart!

CHRISTIAN (*looks up, sees* ROXANE, *and, agitated, seizes* LIGNIÈRE *by the arm*).   That is she!

LIGNIÈRE (*looking*).   Ah, that is she!...

CHRISTIAN. Yes. Tell me at once.... Oh, I am afraid!...

LIGNIÈRE (*sipping his wine slowly*). Magdeleine Robin, surnamed Roxane Subtle. Euphuistic.

CHRISTIAN. Alack-a-day!

LIGNIÈRE. Unmarried. An orphan. A cousin of Cyrano's... the one of whom they were talking.

(*While he is speaking, a richly dressed nobleman, wearing the order of the Holy Ghost on a blue ribbon across his breast, enters* ROXANE'S *box, and, without taking a seat, talks with her a moment.*)

CHRISTIAN (*starting*). That man?...

LIGNIÈRE (*who is beginning to be tipsy, winking*). Hé! Hé! Comte de Guiche. Enamored of her. But married to the niece of Armand de Richelieu. Wishes to manage a match between Roxane and a certain sorry lord, one Monsieur de Valvert, vicomte and... easy. She does not subscribe to his views, but De Guiche is powerful: he can persecute to some purpose a simple commoner. But I have duly set forth his shady machinations in a song which... Ho! he must bear me a grudge! The end was wicked... Listen!...

    (*He rises, staggering, and lifting his glass, is about to sing.*)

CHRISTIAN. No. Good-evening.

LIGNIÈRE. You are going?...

CHRISTIAN. To find Monsieur de Valvert.

LIGNIÈRE. Have a care. You are the one who will get killed. (*Indicating* ROXANE *by a glance.*) Stay. Some one is looking...

CHRISTIAN. It is true...

    (*He remains absorbed in the contemplation of* ROXANE. *The pickpockets, seeing his abstracted air, draw nearer to him.*)

LIGNIÈRE. Ah, you are going to stay. Well, I am going. I am thirsty! And I am looked for... at all the public-houses!

         (*Exit unsteadily.*)

LE BRET (*who has made the circuit of the house, returning toward* RAGUE-NEAU, *in a tone of relief*). Cyrano is not here.

RAGUENEAU. And yet...

LE BRET. I will trust to Fortune he has not seen the announcement.

THE AUDIENCE. Begin! Begin!

ONE OF THE MARQUISES (*watching* DE GUICHE, *who comes from* ROX-ANE'S *box, and crosses the pit, surrounded by obsequious satellites, among whom the* VICOMTE DE VALVERT). Always a court about him, De Guiche!

OTHER MARQUIS. Pf!... Another Gascon!

FIRST MARQUIS. A Gascon, of the cold and supple sort. That sort succeeds. Believe me, it will be best to offer him our duty.

(*They approach* DE GUICHE.)

SECOND MARQUIS. These admirable ribbons! What color, Comte de Guiche? Should you call it Kiss-me-Sweet or... Expiring Fawn?

DE GUICHE. This shade is called Sick Spaniard.

FIRST MARQUIS. Appropriately called, for shortly, thanks to your valor, the Spaniard will be sick indeed, in Flanders!

DE GUICHE. I am going upon the stage. Are you coming? (*He walks toward the stage, followed by all the* MARQUISES *and men of quality. He turns and calls.*) Valvert, come!

CHRISTIAN (*who has been listening and watching them, starts on hearing that name*). The vicomte!... Ah, in his face... in his face I will fling my... (*He puts his hand to his pocket and finds the pickpocket's hand. He turns.*) Hein?

PICKPOCKET. Aï!

CHRISTIAN (*without letting him go*). I was looking for a glove.

PICKPOCKET (*with an abject smile*). And you found a hand. (*In a different tone, low and rapid.*) Let me go... I will tell you a secret.

CHRISTIAN (*without releasing him*). Well?

PICKPOCKET. Lignière who has just left you...

CHRISTIAN (*as above*). Yes?...

PICKPOCKET. Has not an hour to live. A song he made annoyed one of the great, and a hundred men — I am one of them — will be posted tonight...

CHRISTIAN. A hundred?... By whom?

PICKPOCKET. Honor...

CHRISTIAN (*shrugging his shoulders*). Oh!...

PICKPOCKET (*with great dignity*). Among rogues!

CHRISTIAN. Where will they be posted?

PICKPOCKET. At the Porte de Nesle, on his way home. Inform him.

CHRISTIAN (*letting him go*). But where can I find him?

PICKPOCKET. Go to all the taverns: the Golden Vat, the Pine-Apple, the Belt and Bosom, the Twin Torches, the Three Funnels, and in each one leave a scrap of writing warning him.

CHRISTIAN. Yes. I will run!... Ah, the blackguards! A hundred against one!... (*Looks lovingly toward* ROXANE.) Leave her!... (*Furiously, looking toward* VALVERT.) And him!... But Lignière must be prevented. (*Exit running.*)

> (DE GUICHE, *the* MARQUISES, *all the gentry have disappeared behind the curtain, to place themselves on the stage-seats. The pit is crowded. There is not an empty seat in the boxes or the gallery.*)

THE AUDIENCE. Begin!

A BURGHER (*whose wig goes sailing off at the end of a string held by one of the* PAGES *in the upper gallery*). My wig!

SCREAMS OF DELIGHT. He is bald!... The pages!... Well done!... Ha, ha, ha!...

THE BURGHER (*furious, shaking his fist*). Imp of Satan!...

> (*Laughter and screams, beginning very loud and decreasing suddenly. Dead silence.*)

LE BRET (*astonished*). This sudden hush?... (*One of the spectators whispers in his ear.*) Ah?...

THE SPECTATOR. I have it from a reliable quarter.

RUNNING MURMURS. Hush!... Has he come? No!... Yes, he has! ... In the box with the grating.... The cardinal!... the cardinal! ... the cardinal!...

ONE OF THE PAGES. What a shame!... Now we shall have to behave!

> (*Knocking on the stage. Complete stillness. Pause.*)

VOICE OF ONE OF THE MARQUISES (*breaking the deep silence, behind the curtain*). Snuff that candle!

OTHER MARQUIS (*thrusting his head out between the curtains*). A chair!

> (*A chair is passed from hand to hand, above the heads. The* MARQUIS *takes it and disappears, after kissing his hand repeatedly toward the boxes.*)

A SPECTATOR. Silence!

> (*Once more, the three knocks. The curtain opens. Tableau. The* MARQUISES *seated at the sides, in attitudes of languid haughtiness. The stage-setting is the faint-colored bluish sort usual in a pastoral. Four small crystal candelabra light the stage. The violins play softly.*)

LE BRET (*to* RAGUENEAU, *under breath*). Is Montfleury the first to appear?

RAGUENEAU (*likewise under breath*). Yes. The opening lines are his.

LE BRET. Cyrano is not here.

RAGUENEAU. I have lost my wager.

LE BRET. Let us be thankful. Let us be thankful.

(*A bagpipe is heard.* MONTFLEURY *appears upon the stage, enormous, in a conventional shepherd's costume, with a rose-wreathed hat set jauntily on the side of his head, breathing into a be-ribboned bagpipe.*)

THE PIT (*applauding*). Bravo, Montfleury! Montfleury!

MONTFLEURY (*after bowing, proceeds to play the part of* PHŒDO).
Happy the man who, freed from Fashion's fickle sway,
In exile self-prescribed whiles peaceful hours away;
Who when Zephyrus sighs amid the answering trees...

A VOICE (*from the middle of the pit*). Rogue! Did I not forbid you for one month?

(*Consternation. Every one looks around. Murmurs.*)

VARIOUS VOICES. *Hein?* What? What is the matter?

(*Many in the boxes rise to see.*)

CUIGY. It is he!

LE BRET (*alarmed*). Cyrano!

THE VOICE. King of the Obese! Incontinently vanish!...

THE WHOLE AUDIENCE (*indignant*). Oh!...

MONTFLEURY. But...

THE VOICE. You stop to muse upon the matter?

SEVERAL VOICES (*from the pit and the boxes*). Hush!... Enough!... Proceed, Montfleury.... Fear nothing!

MONTFLEURY (*in an unsteady voice*). Happy the man who freed from Fashion's f —...

THE VOICE (*more threatening than before*). How is this? Shall I be constrained, Man of the Monster Belly, to enforce my regulation ... regularly?

(*An arm holding a cane leaps above the level of the heads.*)

MONTFLEURY (*in a voice growing fainter and fainter*). Happy the man...

(*The cane is wildly flourished.*)

THE VOICE. Leave the stage!

THE PIT. Oh!...

MONTFLEURY (*choking*). Happy the man who freed...

CYRANO (*appears above the audience, standing upon a chair, his arms folded on his chest, his hat at a combative angle, his moustache on end, his nose terrifying).* Ah! I shall lose my temper!

(*Sensation at sight of him.*)

MONTFLEURY (*to the* MARQUISES). Messieurs, I appeal to you!

ONE OF THE MARQUISES (*languidly*). But go ahead!... Play!

CYRANO. Fat man, if you attempt it, I will dust the paint off you with this!

THE MARQUIS. Enough!

CYRANO. Let every little lordling keep silence in his seat, or I will ruffle his ribbons with my cane!

ALL THE MARQUISES (*rising*). This is too much!... Montfleury....

CYRANO. Let Montfleury go home, or stay, and, having cut his ears off, I will disembowel him!

A VOICE. But...

CYRANO. Let him go home, I said!

OTHER VOICE. But after all...

CYRANO. It is not yet done? (*With show of turning up his sleeves.*) Very well, upon that stage, as on a platter trimmed with green, you shall see me carve that mount of brawn...

MONTFLEURY (*calling up his whole dignity*). Monsieur, you cast indignity, in my person, upon the Muse!

CYRANO (*very civilly*). Monsieur, if that lady, with whom you have naught to do, had the pleasure of beholding you... just as you stand, there, like a decorated pot!... she could not live, I do protest, but she hurled her buskin at you!

THE PIT. Montfleury!... Montfleury!... Give us Baro's piece!

CYRANO (*to those shouting around him*). I beg you will show some regard for my scabbard: it is ready to give up the sword!

· (*The space around him widens.*)

THE CROWD (*backing away*). Hey... softly, there!

CYRANO (*to* MONTFLEURY). Go off!

THE CROWD (*closing again, and grumbling*). Oh!... Oh!

CYRANO (*turning suddenly*). Has somebody objections?

(*The crowd again pushes away from him.*)

A VOICE (*at the back, singing*).

Monsieur de Cyrano, one sees,
Inclines to be tyrannical;
In spite of that tyrannicle
We shall see La Clorise!

THE WHOLE AUDIENCE (*catching up the tune*).   La Clorise!   La Clorise!

CYRANO. Let me hear that song again, and I will do you all to death with my stick!

A BURGHER. Samson come back!...

CYRANO. Lend me your jaw, good man!

A LADY (*in one of the boxes*).   This is unheard of!

A MAN. It is scandalous!

A BURGHER. It is irritating, to say no more.

A PAGE. What fun it is!

THE PIT. Ksss!... Montfleury!... Cyrano!...

CYRANO. Be still!...

THE PIT (*in uproar*).   Hee-haw!... Baaaaah!... Bow-wow!... Cock-adoodledoooooo!

CYRANO. I will...

A PAGE. Meeeow!

CYRANO. I order you to hold your tongues!... I dare the floor collectively to utter another sound!... I challenge you, one and all! I will take down your names... Step forward, budding heroes! ... Each in his turn. You shall be given numbers. Come, which one of you will open the joust with me? You, monsieur? No! You? No! The first that offers is promised all the mortuary honors due the brave. Let all who wish to die hold up their hands! (*Silence.*) It is modesty that makes you shrink from the sight of my naked sword? Not a name? Not a hand? — Very good. Then I proceed. (*Turning toward the stage where* MONT-FLEURY *is waiting in terror.*) As I was saying, it is my wish to see the stage cured of this tumor. Otherwise... (*claps hand to his sword*) the lancet!

MONTFLEURY. I...

CYRANO (*gets down from his chair, and sits in the space that has become vacant around him, with the ease of one at home*).   Thrice will I clap my hands, O plenilune! At the third clap... eclipse!

THE PIT (*diverted*).   Ah!...

CYRANO (*clapping his hands*).   One!...

MONTFLEURY. I...

A VOICE (*from one of the boxes*).   Do not go!...

THE PIT. He will stay!... He will go!...

MONTFLEURY. Messieurs, I feel...

CYRANO. Two!...

MONTFLEURY. I feel it will perhaps be wiser...

CYRANO. Three!...

(MONTFLEURY *disappears, as if through a trap-door. Storm of laughter, hissing, catcalls.*)

THE HOUSE. Hoo!... Hoo!... Milksop!... Come back!...

CYRANO (*beaming, leans back in his chair and crosses his legs*). Let him come back, if he dare!

A BURGHER. The spokesman of the company!

(BELLEROSE *comes forward on the stage and bows.*)

THE BOXES. Ah, there comes Bellerose!

BELLEROSE (*with elegant bearing and diction*). Noble ladies and gentlemen...

THE PIT. No! No! Jodelet... We want Jodelet!...

JODELET (*comes forward, speaks through his nose*). Pack of swine!

THE PIT. That is right!... Well said!... Bravo!

JODELET. Don't bravo me!... The portly tragedian, whose paunch is your delight, felt sick!...

THE PIT. He is a poltroon!...

JODELET. He was obliged to leave...

THE PIT. Let him come back!

SOME. No!

OTHERS. Yes!...

A YOUTH (*to* CYRANO). But, when all is said, monsieur, what good grounds have you for hating Montfleury?

CYRANO (*amiably, sitting as before*). Young gosling, I have two, whereof each, singly, would be ample. Primo: He is an execrable actor, who bellows, and with grunts that would disgrace a water-carrier launches the verse that should go forth as if on pinions!... Secundo: is my secret.

THE OLD BURGHER (*behind* CYRANO). But without compunction you deprive us of hearing La Clorise. I am determined...

CYRANO (*turning his chair around so as to face the old gentleman; respectfully*). Venerable mule, old Baro's verses being what they are, I do it without compunction, as you say.

THE PRÉCIEUSES (*in the boxes*). Ha!... Ho!... Our own Baro!... My

dear, did you hear that? How can such a thing be said?... Ha!
... Ho!...

CYRANO (*turning his chair so as to face the boxes; gallantly*). Beautiful
creatures, do you bloom and shine, be ministers of dreams, your
smiles our anodyne. Inspire poets, but poems... spare to judge!

BELLEROSE. But the money which must be given back at the door!

CYRANO (*turning his chair to face the stage*). Bellerose, you have said
the only intelligent thing that has, as yet, been said! Far from
me to wrong by so much as a fringe the worshipful mantle of
Thespis.... (*He rises and flings a bag upon the stage.*) Catch!... and
keep quiet!

THE HOUSE (*dazzled.*) Ah!... Oh!...

JODELET (*nimbly picking up the bag, weighing it with his hand*). For such
a price, you are authorized, monsieur, to come and stop the performance every day!

THE HOUSE. Hoo!... Hoo!...

JODELET. Should we be hooted in a body!...

BELLEROSE. The house must be evacuated!

JODELET. Evacuate it!

> (*The audience begins to leave;* CYRANO *looking on with a satisfied
> air. The crowd, however, becoming interested in the following
> scene, the exodus is suspended. The women in the boxes who were
> already standing and had put on their wraps, stop to listen and end
> by resuming their seats.*)

LE BRET (*to* CYRANO). What you have done... is mad!

A BORE. Montfleury!... the eminent actor!... What a scandal!...
But the Duc de Candale is his patron!... Have you a patron,
you?

CYRANO. No!

THE BORE. You have not?

CYRANO. No!

THE BORE. What? You are not protected by some great nobleman
under the cover of whose name...

CYRANO (*exasperated*). No, I have told you twice. Must I say the
same thing thrice? No, I have no protector... (*hand on sword*)
but this will do.

THE BORE. Then, of course, you will leave town.

CYRANO. That will depend.

THE BORE. But the Duc de Candale has a long arm...

CYRANO. Not so long as mine... (*pointing to his sword*) pieced out with this!

THE BORE. But you cannot have the presumption...

CYRANO. I can, yes.

THE BORE. But...

CYRANO. And now,... face about!

THE BORE. But...

CYRANO. Face about, I say... or else, tell me why you are looking at my nose.

THE BORE (*bewildered*). I...

CYRANO (*advancing upon him*). In what is it unusual?

THE BORE (*backing*). Your worship is mistaken.

CYRANO (*same business as above*). Is it flabby and pendulous, like a proboscis?

THE BORE. I never said...

CYRANO. Or hooked like a hawk's beak?

THE BORE. I...

CYRANO. Do you discern a mole upon the tip?

THE BORE. But...

CYRANO. Or is a fly disporting himself thereon? What is there wonderful about it?

THE BORE. Oh...

CYRANO. Is it a freak of nature?

THE BORE. But I had refrained from casting so much as a glance at it!

CYRANO. And why, I pray, should you not look at it?

THE BORE. I had...

CYRANO. So it disgusts you?

THE BORE. Sir...

CYRANO. Its color strikes you as unwholesome?

THE BORE. Sir...

CYRANO. Its shape, unfortunate?

THE BORE. But far from it!

CYRANO. Then wherefore that depreciating air?... Perhaps monsieur thinks it a shade too large?

THE BORE. Indeed not. No, indeed. I think it small... small, — I should have said, minute!

CYRANO. What? How? Charge me with such a ridiculous defect? Small, my nose? Ho!...

THE BORE. Heavens!

CYRANO. Enormous, my nose!... Contemptible stutterer, snub-nosed and flat-headed, be it known to you that I am proud, proud of such an appendage! inasmuch as a great nose is properly the index of an affable, kindly, courteous man, witty, liberal, brave, such as I am! and such as you are for evermore precluded from supposing yourself, deplorable rogue! For the inglorious surface my hand encounters above your ruff, is no less devoid —
(*Strikes him.*)

THE BORE. Aï! aï!...

CYRANO. Of pride, alacrity and sweep, of perception and of gift, of heavenly spark, of sumptuousness, to sum up all, of NOSE, than that (*turns him around by the shoulders and suits the action to the word*), which stops my boot below your spine!

THE BORE (*running off*). Help! The watch!...

CYRANO. Warning to the idle who might find entertainment in my organ of smell.... And if the facetious fellow be of birth, my custom is, before I let him go, to chasten him, in front, and higher up, with steel, and not with hide!

DE GUICHE (*who has stepped down from the stage with the* MARQUISES). He is becoming tiresome!

VALVERT (*shrugging his shoulders*). It is empty bluster!

DE GUICHE. Will no one take him up?

VALVERT. No one?... Wait! I will have one of those shots at him! (*He approaches* CYRANO *who is watching him, and stops in front of him, in an attitude of silly swagger.*) Your... your nose is... errr... Your nose... is very large!

CYRANO (*gravely*). Very.

VALVERT (*laughs*). Ha!...

CYRANO (*imperturbable*). Is that all?

VALVERT. But...

CYRANO. Ah, no, young man, that is not enough! You might have said, dear me, there are a thousand things... varying the tone... For instance... here you are: — Aggressive: "I, monsieur, if I had such a nose, nothing would serve but I must cut it off!" Amicable: "It must be in your way while drinking; you ought to have a special beaker made!" Descriptive: "It is a crag!... a peak!... a promontory!... A promontory, did I say?... It is a peninsula!" Inquisitive: "What may the office be of that oblong receptacle? Is it an inkhorn or a scissor-case?" Mincing: "Do you so dote on birds, you have, fond as a father, been at pains to fit the little darlings with a roost?" Blunt: "Tell me, monsieur, you, when you smoke, is it possible you blow the vapor through your nose without a neighbor crying 'The chimney is afire'?" Anxious: "Go with caution, I beseech, lest your head, dragged over by that weight, should drag you over!" Tender: "Have a little sunshade made for it! It might get freckled!" Learned: "None but the beast, monsieur, mentioned by Aristophanes, the hippocampelephantocamelos, can have borne beneath his forehead so much cartilage and bone!" Off-hand: "What, comrade, is that sort of peg in style? Capital to hang one's hat upon!" Emphatic: "No wind can hope, O lordly nose, to give the whole of you a cold, but the Nor-Wester!" Dramatic: "It is the Red Sea when it bleeds!" Admiring: "What a sign for a perfumer's shop!" Lyrical: "Art thou a Triton, and is that thy conch?" Simple: "A monument! When is admission free?" Deferent: "Suffer, monsieur, that I should pay you my respects: that is what I call possessing a house of your own!" Rustic: "Hi, boys! Call that a nose? Ye don't gull me! It's either a prize carrot or else a stunted gourd!" Military: "Level against the cavalry!" Practical: "Will you put it up for raffle? Indubitably, sir, it will be the feature of the game!" And finally in parody of weeping Pyramus: "Behold, behold the nose that traitorously destroyed the beauty of its master! and is blushing for the same!" — That, my dear sir, or something not unlike, is what you would have said to me, had you the smallest leaven of letters or of wit; but of wit, O most pitiable of objects made by God, you never had a rudiment, and of letters, you have just those that are needed to spell "fool!" — But, had it been otherwise, and had you been possessed of the fertile fancy requisite to shower upon me, here, in this noble company, that volley of sprightly pleasantries, still should you not have delivered yourself of so much as a quarter of the tenth part of the beginning of the first.... For I let off these good things at myself, and with sufficient zest, but do not suffer another to let them off at me!

DE GUICHE (*attempting to lead away the amazed vicomte*). Let be, vicomte!

VALVERT. That insufferable haughty bearing!... A clodhopper without... without so much as gloves... who goes abroad without points... or bowknots!...

CYRANO. My foppery is of the inner man. I do not trick myself out like a popinjay, but I am more fastidious, if I am not so showy. I would not sally forth, by any chance, not washed quite clean of an affront; my conscience foggy about the eye, my honor crumpled, my nicety black-rimmed. I walk with all upon me furbished bright. I plume myself with independence and straightforwardness. It is not a handsome figure, it is my soul, I hold erect as in a brace. I go decked with exploits in place of ribbon bows. I taper to a point my wit like a moustache. And at my passage through the crowd true sayings ring like spurs!

VALVERT. But, sir...

CYRANO. I am without gloves?... a mighty matter! I only had one left, of a very ancient pair, and even that became a burden to me... I left it in somebody's face.

VALVERT. Villain, clod-poll, flat-foot, refuse of the earth!

CYRANO (*taking off his hat and bowing as if the* VICOMTE *had been introducing himself*). Ah?... And mine, Cyrano-Savinien-Hercule of Bergerac!

VALVERT (*exasperated*). Buffoon!

CYRANO (*giving a sudden cry, as if seized with a cramp*). Aï!...

VALVERT (*who had started toward the back, turning*). What is he saying now?

CYRANO (*screwing his face as if in pain*). It must have leave to stir... it has a cramp! It is bad for it to be kept still so long!

VALVERT. What is the matter?

CYRANO. My rapier prickles like a foot asleep!

VALVERT (*drawing*). So be it!

CYRANO. I shall give you a charming little hurt!

VALVERT (*contemptuous*). A poet!

CYRANO. Yes, a poet,... and to such an extent, that while we fence, I will, hop! extempore, compose you a ballade!

VALVERT. A ballade?

CYRANO. I fear you do not know what that is.

VALVERT. But...

CYRANO (*as if saying a lesson*). The ballade is composed of three stanzas of eight lines each...

VALVERT (*stamps with his feet*). Oh!...

CYRANO (*continuing*). And an envoi of four.

VALVERT. You...

CYRANO. I will with the same breath fight you and compose one. And at the last line, I will hit you.

VALVERT. Indeed you will not!

CYRANO. No?... (*Declaiming.*)

> Ballade of the duel which in Burgundy House
> Monsieur de Bergerac fought with a jackanapes.

VALVERT. And what is that, if you please?

CYRANO. That is the title.

THE AUDIENCE (*at the highest pitch of excitement*). Make room!... Good sport!... Stand aside!... Keep still!...

> (*Tableau. A ring, in the pit, of the interested; the* MARQUISES *and* OFFICERS *scattered among the* BURGHERS *and* COMMON PEOPLE. *The* PAGES *have climbed on the shoulders of various ones, the better to see. All the women are standing in the boxes. At the right,* DE GUICHE *and his attendant gentlemen. At left,* LE BRET, RAGUENEAU, CUIGY, *etc.*)

CYRANO (*closing his eyes a second*). Wait. I am settling upon the rhymes. There. I have them.

> (*In declaiming, he suits the action to the word.*)
> Of my broad felt made lighter,
> I cast my mantle broad,
> And stand, poet and fighter,
> To do and to record.
> I bow, I draw my sword...
> En garde! with steel and wit
> I play you at first abord...
> At the last line, I hit! (*They begin fencing.*)
>
> You should have been politer,
> Where had you best be gored?
> The left side or the right — ah?
> Or next your azure cord?

Or where the spleen is stored?
Or in the stomach pit?
Come we to quick accord...
At the last line, I hit!

You falter, you turn whiter?
You do so to afford
Your foe a rhyme in "iter"?...
You thrust at me — I ward —
And balance is restored.
Laridon!　Look to your spit!...
No, you shall not be floored
Before my cue to hit!　　　　(*He announces solemnly.*)

ENVOI

Prince, call upon the Lord!...
I skirmish... feint a bit...
I lunge!... I keep my word!
　　　　　(*The* VICOMTE *staggers;* CYRANO *bows.*)
At the last line, I hit!

(*Acclamations.　Applause from the boxes.　Flowers and handker-
chiefs are thrown.　The* OFFICERS *surround and congratulate*
CYRANO.　RAGUENEAU *dances with delight.　*LE BRET *is
tearfully joyous and at the same time highly troubled.　The
friends of the* VICOMTE *support him off the stage.*)

THE CROWD (*in a long shout*).　Ah!...

A LIGHT-CAVALRY MAN.　Superb!

A WOMAN.　Sweet!

RAGUENEAU.　Astounding!

A MARQUIS.　Novel!

LE BRET.　Insensate!

THE CROWD (*pressing around* CYRANO).　Congratulations!...　Well
done!...　Bravo!...

A WOMAN'S VOICE.　He is a hero!

A MOUSQUETAIRE (*striding swiftly toward* CYRANO, *with outstretched
hand*).　Monsieur, will you allow me?　It was quite, quite excellently done, and I think I know whereof I speak.　But, as a fact,
I expressed my mind before, by making a huge noise....

　　　　　　　　　　　　　　　　　　　　　(*He retires.*)

CYRANO (*to* CUIGY). Who may the gentleman be?

CUIGY. D'Artagnan.

LE BRET (*to* CYRANO, *taking his arm*). Come, I wish to talk with you.

CYRANO. Wait till the crowd has thinned. (*To* BELLEROSE.) I may remain?

BELLEROSE (*deferentially*). Why, certainly!...

(*Shouts are heard outside.*)

JODELET (*after looking*). They are hooting Montfleury.

BELLEROSE (*solemnly*). *Sic transit!* ... (*In a different tone, to the door-keeper and the candle snuffer.*) Sweep and close. Leave the lights. We shall come back, after eating, to rehearse a new farce for to-morrow.

(*Exeunt* JODELET *and* BELLEROSE, *after bowing very low to* CYRANO.)

THE DOORKEEPER (*to* CYRANO). Monsieur will not be going tc dinner?

CYRANO. I?... No. (*The doorkeeper withdraws.*)

LE BRET (*to* CYRANO). And this, because?...

CYRANO (*proudly*). Because... (*in a different tone, having seen that the doorkeeper is too far to overhear*) I have not a penny!

LE BRET (*making the motion of flinging a bag*). How is this? The bag of crowns...

CYRANO. Monthly remittance, thou lastedst but a day!

LE BRET. And to keep you the remainder of the month?...

CYRANO. Nothing is left!

LE BRET. But then, flinging that bag, what a child's prank!

CYRANO. But what a gesture!...

THE SWEETMEAT VENDER (*coughing behind her little counter*). Hm!... (*CYRANO and* LE BRET *turn toward her. She comes timidly forward.*) Monsieur, to know you have not eaten... makes my heart ache. (*Pointing to the sweetmeat-stand.*) I have there all that is needed... (*impulsively*). Help yourself!

CYRANO (*taking off his hat*). Dear child, despite my Gascon pride, which forbids that I should profit at your hand by the most in-considerable of dainties, I fear too much lest a denial should grieve you: I will accept therefore... (*He goes to the stand and selects.*) Oh, a trifle!... A grape off this... (*She proffers the bunch, he takes a single grape.*)   No... one!   This glass of water... (*She starts to pour wine into it, he stops her.*)   No... clear!   And half a macaroon.   (*He breaks in two the macaroon, and returns half.*)

LE BRET. This comes near being silly!

SWEETMEAT VENDER. Oh, you will take something more!...

CYRANO. Yes.   Your hand to kiss.

(*He kisses the hand she holds out to him, as if it were that of a princess.*)

SWEETMEAT VENDER. Monsieur, I thank you.   (*Curtseys.*)   Good-evening!   (*Exit.*)

CYRANO (*to LE BRET*). I am listening.   (*He establishes himself before the stand, sets the macaroon before him.*)   Dinner! (*does the same with the glass of water*).   Drink! (*and with the grape*).   Dessert!   (*He sits down.*)   La! let me begin!   I was as hungry as a wolf!   (*Eating.*) You were saying?

LE BRET. That if you listen to none but those great boobies and swashbucklers your judgment will become wholly perverted. Inquire, will you, of the sensible, concerning the effect produced today by your prowesses.

CYRANO (*finishing his macaroon*). Enormous!

LE BRET. The cardinal...

CYRANO (*beaming*). He was there, the cardinal?

LE BRET. Must have found what you did...

CYRANO. To a degree, original.

LE BRET. Still...

CYRANO. He is a poet.   It cannot be distasteful to him wholly that one should deal confusion to a fellow-poet's play.

LE BRET. But, seriously, you make too many enemies!

CYRANO (*biting into the grape*). How many, thereabouts, should you think I made tonight?

LE BRET. Eight and forty.   Not mentioning the women.

CYRANO. Come, tell them over!

LE BRET. Montfleury, the old merchant, De Guiche, the Vicomte, Baro, the whole Academy...

CYRANO. Enough!   You steep me in bliss!

LE BRET. But whither will the road you follow lead you?   What can your object be?

CYRANO. I was wandering aimlessly; too many roads were open...

too many resolves, too complex, allowed of being taken. I
took...

LE BRET. Which?

CYRANO. By far the simplest of them all. I decided to be, in every
matter, always, admirable!

LE BRET (*shrugging his shoulders*). That will do. — But tell me, will
you not, the motive — look, the true one! — of your dislike to
Montfleury.

CYRANO (*rising*). That old Silenus, who has not seen his knees this
many a year, still believes himself a delicate desperate danger to
the fair. And as he struts and burrs upon the stage, makes
sheep's-eyes at them with his moist frog's-eyes. And I have
hated him... oh, properly!... since the night he was so daring as
to cast his glance on her... her, who — Oh, I thought I saw a
slug crawl over a flower!

LE BRET (*amazed*). Hey? What? Is it possible?...

CYRANO (*with a bitter laugh*). That I should love? (*In a different
tone, seriously.*) I love.

LE BRET. And may one know?... You never told me...

CYRANO. Whom I love?... Come, think a little. The dream of being beloved, even by the beautiless, is made, to me, an empty
dream indeed by this good nose, my forerunner ever by a quarter
of an hour. Hence, whom should I love?... It seems superfluous
to tell you!... I love... it was inevitable!... the most beautiful
that breathes!

LE BRET. The most beautiful?...

CYRANO. No less, in the whole world! And the most resplendent,
and the most delicate of wit, and among the golden-haired...
(*with overwhelming despair*). Still the superlative!

LE BRET. Dear me, what is this fair one?

CYRANO. All unawares, a deadly snare, exquisite without concern
to be so. A snare of nature's own, a musk-rose, in which ambush
Love lies low. Who has seen her smile remembers the ineffable!
There is not a thing so common but she turns it into prettiness;
and in the merest nod or beck she can make manifest all the at-
tributes of a goddess. No, Venus! you cannot step into your iri-
descent shell, nor, Dian, you, walk through the blossoming
groves, as she steps into her chair and walks in Paris!

LE BRET. Sapristi! I understand! It is clear!

CYRANO. It is pellucid.

LE BRET. Magdeleine Robin, your cousin?

CYRANO. Yes, Roxane.

LE BRET. But, what could be better? You love her? Tell her so! You covered yourself with glory in her sight a moment since.

CYRANO. Look well at me, dear friend, and tell me how much hope you think can be justly entertained with this protuberance. Oh, I foster no illusions!... Sometimes, indeed, yes, in the violet dusk, I yield, even I! to a dreamy mood. I penetrate some garden that lies sweetening the hour. With my poor great devil of a nose I sniff the April.... And as I follow with my eyes some woman passing with some cavalier, I think how dear would I hold having to walk beside me, linked like that, slowly, in the soft moonlight, such a one! I kindle — I forget — and then... then suddenly I see the shadow of my profile upon the garden-wall!

LE BRET (touched). My friend...

CYRANO. Friend, I experience a bad half hour sometimes, in feeling so unsightly... and alone.

LE BRET (in quick sympathy, taking his hand). You weep?

CYRANO. Ah, God forbid! That? Never! No, that would be unsightly to excess! That a tear should course the whole length of this nose! Never, so long as I am accountable, shall the divine loveliness of tears be implicated with so much gross ugliness! Mark me well, nothing is so holy as are tears, nothing! and never shall it be that, rousing mirth through me, a single one of them shall seem ridiculous!

LE BRET. Come, do not despond! Love is a lottery.

CYRANO (shaking his head). No! I love Cleopatra: do I resemble Cæsar? I worship Berenice: do I put you in mind of Titus?

LE BRET. But your courage... and your wit! — The little girl who but a moment ago bestowed on you that very modest meal, her eyes, you must have seen as much, did not exactly hate you!

CYRANO (impressed). That is true!

LE BRET. You see? So then! — But Roxane herself, in following your duel, went lily-pale.

CYRANO. Lily-pale?...

LE BRET. Her mind, her heart as well, are struck with wonder! Be bold, speak to her, in order that she may...

CYRANO. Laugh in my face!... No, there is but one thing upon earth I fear.... It is that.

THE DOORKEEPER (*admitting the* DUENNA *to* CYRANO). Monsieur, you are inquired for.

CYRANO (*seeing the* DUENNA). Ah, my God!... her duenna!

THE DUENNA (*with a great curtsey*). Somebody wishes to know of her valorous cousin where one may, in private, see him.

CYRANO (*upset*). See me?

THE DUENNA (*with curtsey*). See you. There are things for your ear.

CYRANO. There are...?

THE DUENNA (*other curtsey*). Things.

CYRANO (*staggering*). Ah, my God!...

THE DUENNA. Somebody intends, tomorrow, at the earliest roses of the dawn, to hear Mass at Saint Roch.

CYRANO (*upholds himself by leaning on* LE BRET). Ah, my God!

THE DUENNA. That over, where might one step in a moment, have a little talk?

CYRANO (*losing his senses*). Where?... I... But... Ah, my God!

THE DUENNA. Expedition, if you please.

CYRANO. I am casting about...

THE DUENNA. Where?

CYRANO. At... at... at Ragueneau's... the pastrycook's.

THE DUENNA. He lodges?

CYRANO. In... In Rue... Ah, my God! my God!... St. Honoré.

THE DUENNA (*retiring*). We will be there. Do not fail. At seven.

CYRANO. I will not fail. (*Exit* DUENNA.)

CYRANO (*falling on* LE BRET'S *neck*). To me... from her... a meeting!

LE BRET. Well, your gloom is dispelled?

CYRANO. Ah, to whatever end it may be, she is aware of my existence!

LE BRET. And now you will be calm?

CYRANO (*beside himself*). Now, I shall be fulminating and frenetical! I want an army all complete to put to rout! I have ten hearts and twenty arms... I cannot now be suited with felling dwarfs

to earth.... (*At the top of his lungs.*)   Giants are what I want!
> (*During the last lines, on the stage at the back, shadowy shapes of players have been moving about.   The rehearsal has begun; the fiddlers have resumed their places.*)

A VOICE (*from the stage*).   Hey! Psst! Over there! A little lower. We are trying to rehearse!

CYRANO (*laughing*).   We are going!   (*He goes toward the back.*)

(*Through the street door, enter* CUIGY, BRISSAILLE, *several* OFFICERS *supporting* LIGNIÈRE *in a state of complete intoxication.*)

CUIGY.   Cyrano!

CYRANO.   What is this?

CUIGY.   A *turdus vinaticus* we are bringing you.

CYRANO (*recognizing him*).   Lignière! Hey, what has happened to you?

CUIGY.   He is looking for you.

BRISSAILLE.   He cannot go home.

CYRANO.   Why?

LIGNIÈRE (*in a thick voice, showing him a bit of crumpled paper*).   This note bids me beware... A hundred men against me... on account of lampoon... Grave danger threatening me... Porte de Nesle... must pass it to get home. Let me come and sleep under your roof.

CYRANO.   A hundred, did you say? — You shall sleep at home!

LIGNIÈRE (*frightened*).   But...

CYRANO (*in a terrible voice, pointing to the lighted lantern which the* DOORKEEPER *stands swinging as he listens to this scene*).   Take that lantern (LIGNIÈRE *hurriedly takes it*) and walk!... I swear to tuck you in your bed tonight myself. (*To the* OFFICERS.) You, follow at a distance. You may look on!

CUIGY.   But a hundred men...

CYRANO.   Are not one man too many for my mood tonight!
> (*The players, in their several costumes, have stepped down from the stage and come nearer.*)

LE BRET.   But why take under your especial care...

CYRANO.   Still Le Bret is not satisfied!

LE BRET.   That most commonplace of sots?

CYRANO (*slapping* LIGNIÈRE *on the shoulder*).   Because this sot, this

cask of muscatel, this hogshead of rosolio, did once upon a time a
wholly pretty thing. On leaving Mass, having seen her whom
he loved take holy-water, as the rite prescribes, he, whom the
sight of water puts to flight, ran to the holy-water bowl, and
stooping over, drank it dry....

AN ACTRESS (*in the costume of soubrette*). *Tiens*, that was nice!

CYRANO. Was it not, soubrette?

THE SOUBRETTE (*to the others*). But why are they, a hundred, all
against one poor poet?

CYRANO. Let us start! (*To the* OFFICERS.) And you, gentlemen,
when you see me attack, whatever you may suppose to be my
danger, do not stir to second me!

ANOTHER OF THE ACTRESSES (*jumping from the stage*). Oh, I will not
miss seeing this!

CYRANO. Come!

ANOTHER ACTRESS (*likewise jumping from the stage, to an elderly actor*).
Cassandre, will you not come?

CYRANO. Come, all of you! the Doctor, Isabel, Leander, all! and
you shall lend, charming fantastic swarm, an air of Italian farce
to the Spanish drama in view. Yes, you shall be a tinkling heard
above a roar, like bells about a tambourine!

ALL THE WOMEN (*in great glee*). Bravo!... Hurry!... A mantle!... A
hood!

JODELET. Let us go!

CYRANO (*to the fiddlers*). You will favor us with a tune, messieurs the
violinists!

> (*The fiddlers fall into the train. The lighted candles which fur-
> nished the footlights are seized and distributed. The procession
> becomes a torchlight procession.*)

CYRANO. Bravo! Officers, beauty in fancy dress, and, twenty steps
ahead... (*he takes the position he describes*). I, by myself, under the
feather stuck, with her own hand, by Glory, in my hat! Proud
as a Scipio trebly Nasica! — It is understood? Formal interdic-
tion to interfere with me! — We are ready? One! Two! Three!
Doorkeeper, open the door!

> (*The* DOORKEEPER *opens wide the folding door. A picturesque
> corner of Old Paris appears, bathed in moonlight.*)

CYRANO. Ah!... Paris floats in dim nocturnal mist.... The sloping

blueish roofs are washed with moonlight.... A setting, exquisite
indeed, offers itself for the scene about to be enacted.... Yonder,
under silvery vapor wreaths, like a mysterious magic mirror,
glimmers the Seine.... And you shall see what you shall see!

ALL. To the Porte de Nesle!

CYRANO (*standing on the threshold*). To the Porte de Nesle! (*Before
crossing it, he turns to the* SOUBRETTE.) Were you not asking, mademoiselle, why upon that solitary rhymester, a hundred men were
set? (*He draws his sword, and tranquilly.*) Because it was well
known he is a friend of mine! (*Exit.*)

(*To the sound of the violins, by the flickering light of the candles, the
procession* — LIGNIÈRE *staggering at the head, the* ACTRESSES
arm in arm with the OFFICERS, *the players capering behind* —
follows out into the night.)

CURTAIN

ACT SECOND

THE COOKSHOP OF POETS

RAGUENEAU'S *shop, vast kitchen at the corner of Rue St. Honoré and Rue
de l'Arbre-Sec, which can be seen at the back, through the glass door, gray in
the early dawn.*

*At the left, in front, a counter overhung by a wrought-iron canopy from
which geese, ducks, white peacocks are hanging. In large china jars, tall
nosegays composed of the simpler flowers, mainly sunflowers. On the same
side, in the middle distance, an enormous fireplace in front of which, between
huge andirons, each of which supports a small iron pot, roasting meats drip
into appropriate pans.*

*At the right, door in the front wing. In the middle distance, a staircase
leading to a loft, the interior of which is seen through open shutters; a spread
table lighted by a small Flemish candelabrum, shows it to be an eating-
room. A wooden gallery, continuing the stairway, suggests other similar
rooms to which it may lead.*

In the centre of the shop, an iron hoop — *which can be lowered by means of
a rope* — *to which large roasts are hooked.*

In the shadow, under the stairway, ovens are glowing. Copper molds and saucepans are shining; spits turning, hams swinging, pastry pyramids showing fair. It is the early beginning of the workday. Bustling of hurried scullions, portly cooks and young cook's-assistants; swarming of caps decorated with hen feathers and guinea-fowl wings. Wicker crates and broad sheets of tin are brought in loaded with brioches and tarts.

There are tables covered with meats and cakes; others, surrounded by chairs, await customers. In a corner, a smaller table, littered with papers. At the rise of the curtain, RAGUENEAU *is discovered seated at this table, writing with an inspired air, and counting upon his fingers.*

FIRST PASTRYCOOK (*bringing in a tall molded pudding*). Nougat of fruit!

SECOND PASTRYCOOK (*bringing in the dish he names*). Custard!

THIRD PASTRYCOOK (*bringing in a fowl roasted in its feathers*). Peacock!

FOURTH PASTRYCOOK (*bringing in a tray of cakes*). Mince-pies!

FIFTH PASTRYCOOK (*bringing in a deep earthen dish*). Beef stew!

RAGUENEAU (*laying down his pen, and looking up*). Daybreak already plates with silver the copper pans! Time, Ragueneau, to smother within thee the singing divinity! The hour of the lute will come anon — now is that of the ladle! (*He rises; speaking to one of the cooks.*) You, sir, be so good as to lengthen this gravy — it is too thick!

THE COOK. How much?

RAGUENEAU. Three feet. (*Goes farther.*)

THE COOK. What does he mean?

FIRST PASTRYCOOK. Let me have the tart!

SECOND PASTRYCOOK. The dumpling!

RAGUENEAU (*standing before the fireplace*). Spread thy wings, Muse, and fly further, that thy lovely eyes may not be reddened at the sordid kitchen fire! (*To one of the cooks, pointing at some small loaves of bread.*) You have improperly placed the cleft in those loaves; the cæsura belongs in the middle — between the hemistichs! (*To another of the* COOKS, *pointing at an unfinished pasty.*) This pastry palace requires a roof! (*To a young cook's apprentice, who, seated upon the floor, is putting fowls on a spit.*) And you, on that long spit, arrange, my son, in pleasing alternation, the modest pullet and the splendid turkey-cock — even as our wise Malherbe alter-

nated of old the greater with the lesser lines, and so with roasted
fowls compose a poem!

ANOTHER APPRENTICE (*coming forward with a platter covered by a napkin*).
Master, in your honor, see what I have baked.... I hope you are
pleased with it!

RAGUENEAU (*ecstatic*). A lyre!

THE APPRENTICE. Of pie-crust!

RAGUENEAU (*touched*). With candied fruits!

THE APPRENTICE. And the strings, see — of spun sugar!

RAGUENEAU (*giving him money*). Go, drink my health! (*Catching
sight of* LISE *who is entering.*) Hush! My wife!... Move on, and
hide that money. (*To* LISE, *showing her the lyre, with a constrained
air.*) Fine, is it not?

LISE. Ridiculous! (*She sets a pile of wrapping-paper on the counter.*)

RAGUENEAU. Paper bags? Good. Thanks. (*He examines them.*)
Heavens! My beloved books! The masterpieces of my friends
— dismembered — torn! — to fashion paper bags for penny
pies! — Ah, the abominable case is re-enacted of Orpheus and
the Mænads!

LISE (*drily*). And have I not an unquestionable right to make what
use I can of the sole payment ever got from your paltry scribblers
of uneven lines?

RAGUENEAU. Pismire! Forbear to insult those divine, melodious
crickets!

LISE. Before frequenting that low crew, my friend, you did not use
to call me a Mænad — no, nor yet a pismire!

RAGUENEAU. Put poems to such a use!

LISE. To that use and no other!

RAGUENEAU. If with poems you do this, I should like to know,
Madame, what you do with prose!

(*Two children have come into the shop.*)

RAGUENEAU. What can I do for you, little ones?

FIRST CHILD. Three patties.

RAGUENEAU (*waiting on them*). There you are! Beautifully browned,
and piping hot.

SECOND CHILD. Please, will you wrap them for us?

RAGUENEAU (*starting, aside*). There goes one of my bags! (*To the *children.*)   You want them wrapped, do you?   (*He takes one of the paper bags, and as he is about to put in the patties, reads.*)   "*No otherwise, Ulysses, from Penelope departing....*"   Not this one!   (*He lays it aside and takes another.   At the moment of putting in the patties, he reads.*)   "*Phœbus of the aureate locks...*"   Not that one!

(*Same business.*)

LISE (*out of patience*).   Well, what are you waiting for?

RAGUENEAU.   Here we are.   Here we are.   Here we are.   (*He takes a third bag and resigns himself.*)   The sonnet to Phyllis!... It is hard, all the same.

LISE.   It is lucky you made up your mind.   (*Shrugging her shoulders.*) Nicodemus!

(*She climbs on a chair and arranges dishes on a sideboard.*)

RAGUENEAU (*taking advantage of her back being turned, calls back the children who had already reached the door*).   Psst!... Children!   Give me back the sonnet to Phyllis, and you shall have six patties instead of three!   (*The children give back the paper bag, joyfully take the patties and exeunt.   RAGUENEAU smoothes out the crumpled paper and reads declaiming.*)   "*Phyllis!*"... Upon that charming name, a grease-spot!... "*Phyllis!*"...

(*Enter brusquely* CYRANO.)

CYRANO.   What time is it?

RAGUENEAU (*bowing with eager deference*).   Six o'clock.

CYRANO (*with emotion*).   In an hour!   (*He comes and goes in the shop.*)

RAGUENEAU (*following him*).   Bravo!   I too was witness...

CYRANO.   Of what?

RAGUENEAU.   Your fight.

CYRANO.   Which?

RAGUENEAU.   At the Hotel de Bourgogne.

CYRANO (*with disdain*).   Ah, the duel!

RAGUENEAU (*admiringly*).   Yes — the duel in rhyme.

LISE.   He can talk of nothing else.

CYRANO.   Let him!... It does no harm.

RAGUENEAU (*thrusting with a spit he has seized*).   "*At the last line, I hit!*"   "*At the last line I hit!*"— How fine that is!   (*With growing enthusiasm.*)   "*At the last line, I*" —

CYRANO. What time, Ragueneau?

RAGUENEAU (*remaining fixed in the attitude of thrusting, while he looks at the clock*). Five minutes past six. — "*I hit!*" (*He recovers from his duelling posture.*) Oh, to be able to make a ballade!

LISE (*to* CYRANO, *who in passing her counter has absentmindedly shaken hands with her*). What ails your hand?

CYRANO. Nothing. A scratch.

RAGUENEAU. You have been exposed to some danger?

CYRANO. None whatever.

LISE (*shaking her finger at him*). I fear that is a fib!

CYRANO. From the swelling of my nose? The fib in that case must have been good-sized.... (*In a different tone.*) I am expecting some one. You will leave us alone in here.

RAGUENEAU. But how can I contrive it? My poets shortly will be coming...

LISE (*ironically*). For breakfast!

CYRANO. When I sign to you, you will clear the place of them. — What time is it?

RAGUENEAU. It is ten minutes past six.

CYRANO (*seating himself nervously at* RAGUENEAU's *table and helping himself to paper*). A pen?

RAGUENEAU (*taking one from behind his ear, and offering it*). A swan's quill.

A MOUSQUETAIRE (*with enormous moustachios, enters; in a stentorian voice*). Good-morning! (LISE *goes hurriedly to him, toward the back.*)

CYRANO (*turning*). What is it?

RAGUENEAU. A friend of my wife's — a warrior — terrible, from his own report.

CYRANO (*taking up the pen again, and waving* RAGUENEAU *away*). Hush!... (*To himself.*) Write to her,... fold the letter,... hand it to her,... and make my escape.... (*Throwing down the pen.*) Coward!... But may I perish if I have the courage to speak to her,... to say a single word.... (*To* RAGUENEAU.) What time is it?

RAGUENEAU. A quarter past six.

CYRANO (*beating his breast*). A single word of all I carry here!... Whereas in writing... (*He takes up the pen again.*) Come, let us write it then, in very deed, the love-letter I have written in thought so many times, I have but to lay my soul beside my paper and copy! *(He writes.)*

(Beyond the glass door, shadowy lank hesitating shabby forms are seen moving.)

(Enter the POETS, *clad in black, with hanging hose, sadly mudsplashed.)*

LISE *(coming forward, to* RAGUENEAU*).* Here they come, your scare-crows!

FIRST POET *(entering, to* RAGUENEAU*).* Brother in art!...

SECOND POET *(shaking both* RAGUENEAU's *hands).* Dear fellow-bard....

THIRD POET. Eagle of pastrycooks, *(sniffs the air),* your eyrie smells divine!

FOURTH POET. Phœbus turned baker!

FIFTH POET. Apollo master-cook!

RAGUENEAU *(surrounded, embraced, shaken by the hand).* How at his ease a man feels at once with them!

FIRST POET. The reason we are late, is the crowd at the Porte de Nesle!

SECOND POET. Eight ugly ruffians, ripped open with the sword, lie weltering on the pavement.

CYRANO *(raising his head a second).* Eight? I thought there were only seven. *(Goes on with his letter.)*

RAGUENEAU *(to* CYRANO*).* Do you happen to know who is the hero of this event?

CYRANO *(negligently).* I?... No.

LISE *(to the* MOUSQUETAIRE*).* Do you?

THE MOUSQUETAIRE *(turning up the ends of his moustache).* Possibly!

CYRANO *(writing; from time to time he is heard murmuring a word or two).* ... "I love you..."

FIRST POET. A single man, we were told, put a whole gang to flight!

SECOND POET. Oh, it was a rare sight! The ground was littered with pikes, and cudgels...

CYRANO *(writing).* ... "Your eyes..."

THIRD POET. Hats were strewn as far as the Goldsmiths' square!

FIRST POET. Sapristi! He must have been a madman of mettle....

CYRANO *(as above).* "...your lips..."

FIRST POET. An infuriate giant, the doer of that deed!

CYRANO (*same business*). "... *but when I see you, I come near to swooning with a tender dread* ..."

SECOND POET (*snapping up a tart*). What have you lately written, Ragueneau?

CYRANO (*same business*). "... *who loves you devotedly* ..." (*In the act of signing the letter, he stops, rises, and tucks it inside his doublet.*) No need to sign it. I deliver it myself.

RAGUENEAU (*to* SECOND POET). I have rhymed a recipe.

THIRD POET (*establishing himself beside a tray of cream puffs*). Let us hear this recipe!

FOURTH POET (*examining a brioche of which he has possessed himself*). It should not wear its cap so saucily on one side... it scarcely looks well! ...   (*Bites off the top.*)

FIRST POET. See, the spice-cake there, ogling a susceptible poet with eyes of almond under citron brows! ...   (*He takes the spice cake.*)

SECOND POET. We are listening!

THIRD POET (*slightly squeezing a cream puff between his fingers*). This puff creams at the mouth.... I water!

SECOND POET (*taking a bite out of the large pastry lyre*). For once the Lyre will have filled my stomach!

RAGUENEAU (*who has made ready to recite, has coughed, adjusted his cap, struck an attitude*). A recipe in rhyme!

SECOND POET (*to* FIRST POET, *nudging him*). Is it breakfast, with you?

FIRST POET (*to* SECOND POET). And with you, is it dinner?

RAGUENEAU. *How Almond Cheese-Cakes should be made.*

> Briskly beat to lightness due,
>   Eggs, a few;
> With the eggs so beaten, beat —
> Nicely strained for this same use, —
>   Lemon-juice,
> Adding milk of almonds, sweet.
>
> With fine pastry dough, rolled flat,
>   After that,
> Line each little scalloped mold;
> Round the sides, light-fingered, spread
>   Marmalade;
> Pour the liquid eggy gold,

> Into each delicious pit;
>> Prison it
> In the oven, — and, bye and bye,
> Almond cheese-cakes will in gay
>> Blond array
> Bless your nostril and your eye!

THE POETS (*their mouths full*).   Exquisite!... Delicious!

ONE OF THE POETS (*choking*).   Humph!

> (*They go toward the back, eating.   CYRANO, who has been watching them, approaches RAGUENEAU.*)

CYRANO. While you recite your works to them, have you a notion how they stuff?

RAGUENEAU (*low, with a smile*).   Yes, I see them... without looking, lest they should be abashed.   I get a double pleasure thus from saying my verses over: I satisfy a harmless weakness of which I stand convicted, at the same time as giving those who have not fed a needed chance to feed!

CYRANO (*slapping him on the shoulder*).   You,... I like you!   (RAGUENEAU *joins his friends.   CYRANO looks after him; then, somewhat sharply.*)   Hey, Lise!   (LISE, *absorbed in tender conversation with the* MOUSQUETAIRE, *starts and comes forward toward* CYRANO.)   Is that captain... laying siege to you?

LISE (*offended*).   My eyes, sir, have ever held in respect those who meant hurt to my character....

CYRANO. For eyes so resolute... I thought yours looked a little languishing!

LISE (*choking with anger*).   But...

CYRANO (*bluntly*).   I like your husband.   Wherefore, Madame Lise, I say he shall not be sc... horned!

LISE. But...

CYRANO (*raising his voice so as to be heard by the* MOUSQUETAIRE).   A word to the wise!

> (*He bows to the* MOUSQUETAIRE, *and after looking at the clock, goes to the door at the back and stands in watch.*)

LISE (*to the* MOUSQUETAIRE, *who has simply returned* CYRANO's *bow*).   Really... I am astonished at you.... Defy him... to his face!

THE MOUSQUETAIRE. To his face, indeed!... to his face!...

> (*He quickly moves off.   LISE follows him.*)

CYRANO (*from the door at the back, signalling to* RAGUENEAU *that he should clear the room*). Pst!...

RAGUENEAU (*urging the* POETS *toward the door at the right*). We shall be much more comfortable in there....

CYRANO (*impatiently*). Pst!... Pst!...

RAGUENEAU (*driving along the* POETS). I want to read you a little thing of mine....

FIRST POET (*despairingly, his mouth full*). But the provisions....

SECOND POET. Shall not be parted from us!

(*They follow* RAGUENEAU *in procession, after making a raid on the eatables.*)

CYRANO. If I feel that there is so much as a glimmer of hope... I will out with my letter!...

(ROXANE, *masked, appears behind the glass door, followed by the* DUENNA.)

CYRANO (*instantly opening the door*). Welcome! (*Approaching the* DUENNA.) Madame, a word with you!

THE DUENNA. A dozen.

CYRANO. Are you fond of sweets?

THE DUENNA. To the point of indigestion!

CYRANO (*snatching some paper bags off the counter.*) Good. Here are two sonnets of Benserade's...

THE DUENNA. Pooh!

CYRANO. Which I fill for you with grated almond drops.

THE DUENNA (*with a different expression*). Ha!

CYRANO. Do you look with favor upon the cate they call a trifle?

THE DUENNA. I affect it out of measure, when it has whipped cream inside.

CYRANO. Six shall be yours, thrown in with a poem by Saint-Amant. And in these verses of Chapelain I place this wedge of fruit-cake, light by the side of them.... Oh! And do you like tarts... little jam ones... fresh?

THE DUENNA. I dream of them at night!

CYRANO (*loading her arms with crammed paper bags*). Do me the favor to go and eat these in the street.

THE DUENNA. But...

CYRANO (*pushing her out*). And do not come back till you have finished! (*He closes the door upon her, comes forward toward* ROXANE, *and stands, bareheaded, at a respectful distance.*) Blessed forevermore among all hours the hour in which, remembering that so lowly a being still draws breath, you were so gracious as to come to tell me... to tell me?...

ROXANE (*who has removed her mask*). First of all, that I thank you. For that churl, that coxcomb yesterday, whom you taught manners with your sword, is the one whom a great nobleman, who fancies himself in love with me...

CYRANO. De Guiche?

ROXANE (*dropping her eyes*). Has tried to force upon me as a husband.

CYRANO. Honorary? (*Bowing.*) It appears, then, that I fought, and I am glad of it, not for my graceless nose, but your thrice-beautiful eyes.

ROXANE. Further than that... I wished... But, before I can make the confession I have in mind to make, I must find in you once more the... almost brother, with whom as a child I used to play, in the park — do you remember? — by the lake!

CYRANO. I have not forgotten. Yes... you came every summer to Bergerac.

ROXANE. You used to fashion lances out of reeds...

CYRANO. The silk of the tasselled corn furnished hair for your doll...

ROXANE. It was the time of long delightful games...

CYRANO. And somewhat sour berries...

ROXANE. The time when you did everything I bade you!

CYRANO. Roxane, wearing short frocks, was known as Magdeleine.

ROXANE. Was I pretty in those days?

CYRANO. You were not ill-looking.

ROXANE. Sometimes, in your venturesome climbings you used to hurt yourself. You would come running to me, your hand bleeding. And, playing at being your mamma, I would harden my voice and say... (*She takes his hand.*) "Will you never keep out of mischief?" (*She stops short, amazed.*) Oh, it is too much! Here you have done it again! (CYRANO *tries to draw back his hand.*) No! let me look at it!... Aren't you ashamed? A great boy like you!... How did this happen, and where?

CYRANO. Oh, fun... near the Porte de Nesle.

ROXANE (*sitting down at a table and dipping her handkerchief into a glass of water*). Let me have it.

CYRANO (*sitting down too*). So prettily, so cheeringly maternal!

ROXANE. And tell me, while I wash this naughty blood away... with how many were you fighting?

CYRANO. Oh, not quite a hundred.

ROXANE. Tell me about it.

CYRANO. No. What does it matter? You tell me, you... what you were going to tell me before, and did not dare...

ROXANE (*without releasing his hand*). I do dare, now. I have breathed in courage with the perfume of the past. Oh, yes, now I dare. Here it is. There is some one whom I love.

CYRANO. Ah!...

ROXANE. Oh, he does not know it.

CYRANO. Ah!...

ROXANE. As yet....

CYRANO. Ah!...

ROXANE. But if he does not know it, he soon will.

CYRANO. Ah!...

ROXANE. A poor boy who until now has loved me timidly, from a distance, without daring to speak....

CYRANO. Ah!...

ROXANE. No, leave me your hand. It is hot, this will cool it.... But I have read his heart in his face.

CYRANO. Ah!...

ROXANE (*completing the bandaging of his hand with her small pocket-handkerchief*). And, cousin, is it not a strange coincidence — that he should serve exactly in your regiment!

CYRANO. Ah!...

ROXANE (*laughing*). Yes. He is a cadet, in the same company!

CYRANO. Ah!...

ROXANE. He bears plain on his forehead the stamp of wit, of genius! He is proud, noble, young, brave, handsome....

CYRANO (*rising, pale*). Handsome!...

ROXANE. What... what is the matter?

CYRANO. With me?... Nothing!... It is... it is... (*Showing his hand, smiling.*) You know!... It smarts a little...

ROXANE. In short, I love him. I must tell you, however, that I have never seen him save at the play.

CYRANO. Then you have never spoken to each other?

ROXANE. Only with our eyes.

CYRANO. But, then... how can you know?...

ROXANE. Oh, under the lindens of Place Royale, people will talk. A trustworthy gossip told me many things!

CYRANO. A cadet, did you say?

ROXANE. A cadet, in your company.

CYRANO. His name?

ROXANE. Baron Christian de Neuvillette.

CYRANO. What? He is not in the cadets.

ROXANE. He is! He certainly is, since morning. Captain Carbon de Castel-Jaloux.

CYRANO. And quickly, quickly, she throws away her heart!... But my poor little girl...

THE DUENNA (*opening the door at the back*). Monsieur de Bergerac, I have eaten them, every one!

CYRANO. Now read the poetry printed upon the bags! (*The* DUENNA *disappears.*) My poor child, you who can endure none but the choicest language, who savor eloquence and wit,... if he should be a barbarian!

ROXANE. No! no!... He has hair like one of D'Urfé's heroes!

CYRANO. If he had on proof as homely a wit as he has pretty hair!

ROXANE. No! No!... I can see at a single glance, his utterances are fine, pointed...

CYRANO. Ah, yes! A man's utterances are invariably like his moustache!... Still, if he *were* a ninny?...

ROXANE (*stamping with her foot*). I should die, there!

CYRANO (*after a time*). You bade me come here that you might tell me this? I scarcely see the appropriateness, madame.

ROXANE. Ah, it was because some one yesterday let death into my soul by telling me that in your company you are all Gascons,... all!

CYRANO. And that we pick a quarrel with every impudent fledgling, not Gascon, admitted by favor to our thoroughbred Gascon ranks? That is what you heard?

ROXANE. Yes, and you can imagine how distracted I am for him!

CYRANO (*in his teeth*). You well may be!

ROXANE. But I thought, yesterday, when you towered up, great and invincible, giving his due to that miscreant, standing your ground against those caitiffs, I thought "Were he but willing, he of whom all are in awe…"

CYRANO. Very well, I will protect your little baron.

ROXANE. Ah, you will… you will protect him for me?… I have always felt for you the tenderest regard!

CYRANO. Yes, yes.

ROXANE. You will be his friend?

CYRANO. I will!

ROXANE. And never shall he have to fight a duel?

CYRANO. I swear it.

ROXANE. Oh, I quite love you!… Now I must go. (*She hurriedly resumes her mask, throws a veil over her head; says absentmindedly.*) But you have not yet told me about last night's encounter. It must have been amazing!… Tell him to write to me. (*She kisses her hand to him.*) I love you dearly!

CYRANO. Yes, yes.

ROXANE. A hundred men against you?… Well, adieu. We are fast friends.

CYRANO. Yes, yes.

ROXANE. Tell him to write me!… A hundred men! You shall tell me another time. I must not linger now… A hundred men! What a heroic thing to do!

CYRANO (*bowing*). Oh, I have done better since!

> (*Exit* ROXANE. CYRANO *stands motionless, staring at the ground. Silence. The door at the right opens.* RAGUENEAU *thrusts in his head.*)

RAGUENEAU. May we come back?

CYRANO (*without moving*). Yes…

(RAGUENEAU *beckons, his friends come in again. At the same time, in the doorway at the back, appears* CARBON DE CASTEL-JALOUX, *costume of a Captain of the Guards. On seeing* CYRANO, *he gesticulates exaggeratedly by way of signal to some one out of sight.*)

CARBON DE CASTEL-JALOUX. He is here!

CYRANO (*looking up*). Captain!

CARBON DE CASTEL-JALOUX (*exultant*). Hero! We know all!… About thirty of my cadets are out there!…

CYRANO (*drawing back*). But…

CARBON DE CASTEL-JALOUX (*trying to lead him off*). Come!... You are in request!

CYRANO. No!

CARBON DE CASTEL-JALOUX. They are drinking across the way, at the Cross of the Hilt.

CYRANO. I...

CARBON DE CASTEL-JALOUX (*going to the door and shouting toward the street corner, in a voice of thunder*). The hero refuses. He is not in the humor!

A VOICE (*outside*). Ah, sandious!
> (*Tumult outside, noise of clanking swords and of boots drawing nearer.*)

CARBON DE CASTEL-JALOUX (*rubbing his hands*). Here they come, across the street....

THE CADETS (*entering the cookshop*). Mille dious!... Capdedious!... Mordious!... Pocapdedious!...

RAGUENEAU (*backing in alarm*). Messieurs, are you all natives of Gascony?

THE CADETS. All!

ONE OF THE CADETS (*to* CYRANO). Bravo!

CYRANO. Baron!

OTHER CADET (*shaking both* CYRANO's *hands*). Vivat!

CYRANO. Baron!

THIRD CADET. Let me hug you to my heart!

CYRANO. Baron!

SEVERAL GASCONS. Let us hug him!

CYRANO (*not knowing which one to answer*). Baron!... baron!... your pardon!

RAGUENEAU. Messieurs, are you all barons?

THE CADETS. All!

RAGUENEAU. Are they truly?

FIRST CADET. Our coats of arms piled up would dwindle in the clouds!

LE BRET (*entering, running to* CYRANO). They are looking for you! A crowd, gone mad as March, led by those who were with you last night.

CYRANO (*alarmed*). You never told them where to find me?...

LE BRET (*rubbing his hands*). I did.

A BURGHER (*entering, followed by a number of others*). Monsieur, the Marais is coming in a body!

> (*The street outside has filled with people. Sedan-chairs, coaches stop before the door.*)

LE BRET (*smiling, low to* CYRANO). And Roxane?

CYRANO (*quickly*). Be quiet!

THE CROWD (*outside*). Cyrano!

> (*A rabble bursts into the cookshop. Confusion. Shouting.*)

RAGUENEAU (*standing upon a table*). My shop is invaded! They are breaking everything! It is glorious!

PEOPLE (*pressing round* CYRANO). My friend... my friend....

CYRANO. I had not so many friends... yesterday!

LE BRET. This is success!

A YOUNG MARQUIS (*running toward* CYRANO, *with outstretched hands*). If you knew, my dear fellow...

CYRANO. Dear?... Fellow?... Where was it we stood sentinel together?

OTHER MARQUIS. I wish to present you, sir, to several ladies, who are outside in my coach....

CYRANO (*coldly*). But you, to me, by whom will you first be presented?

LE BRET (*astonished*). But what is the matter with you?

CYRANO. Be still!

A MAN OF LETTERS (*with an inkhorn*). Will you kindly favor me with the details of...

CYRANO. No.

LE BRET (*nudging him*). That is Theophrastus Renaudot, the inventor of the gazette.

CYRANO. Enough!

LE BRET. A sheet close packed with various information! It is an idea, they say, likely to take firm root and flourish!

A POET (*coming forward*). Monsieur...

CYRANO. Another!

THE POET. I am anxious to make a pentacrostic on your name.

SOMEBODY ELSE (*likewise approaching* CYRANO). Monsieur...

CYRANO. Enough, I say!

> (*At the gesture of impatience which* CYRANO *cannot repress, the crowd draws away.*)

(DE GUICHE *appears, escorted by officers; among them* CUIGY, BRISSAILLE, *those who followed* CYRANO *at the end of the first act.* CUIGY *hurries toward* CYRANO.)

CUIGY (*to* CYRANO). Monsieur de Guiche! (*Murmurs. Every one draws back.*) He comes at the request of the Marshal de Gaussion.

DE GUICHE (*bowing to* CYRANO). Who wishes to express his admiration for your latest exploit, the fame of which has reached him.

THE CROWD. Bravo!

CYRANO (*bowing*). The Marshal is qualified to judge of courage.

DE GUICHE. He would scarcely have believed the report, had these gentlemen not been able to swear they had seen the deed performed.

CUIGY. With our own eyes!

LE BRET (*low to* CYRANO, *who wears an abstracted air*). But...

CYRANO. Be silent!

LE BRET. You appear to be suffering...

CYRANO (*starting, and straightening himself*). Before these people?... (*His moustache bristles; he expands his chest.*) I... suffering?... You shall see!

DE GUICHE (*in whose ear* CUIGY *has been whispering*). But this is by no means the first gallant achievement marking your career. You serve in the madcap Gascon company, do you not?

CYRANO. In the cadets, yes.

ONE OF THE CADETS (*in a great voice*). Among his countrymen!

DE GUICHE (*considering the* GASCONS, *in line behind* CYRANO). Ah, ha! — All these gentlemen then of the formidable aspect, are the famous...

CARBON DE CASTEL-JALOUX. Cyrano!

CYRANO. Captain?...

CARBON DE CASTEL-JALOUX. My company, I believe, is here in total. Be so obliging as to present it to the Count.

CYRANO (*taking a step toward* DE GUICHE, *and pointing at the* CADETS).

> They are the Gascony Cadets
> Of Carbon de Castel-Jaloux;
> Famed fighters, liars, desperates,
> They are the Gascony Cadets!

All, better-born than pickpockets,
Talk couchant, rampant,... pendent, too !
They are the Gascony Cadets
Of Carbon de Castel-Jaloux!

Cat-whiskered, eyed like falconets,
Wolf-toothed and heron-legged, they hew
The rabble down that snarls and threats...
Cat-whiskered, eyed like falconets!
Great pomp of plume hides and offsets
Holes in those hats they wear askew...
Cat-whiskered, eyed like falconets,
They drive the snarling mob, and hew!

The mildest of their sobriquets
Are Crack-my-crown and Run-me-through,
Mad drunk on glory Gascon gets!
These boasters of soft sobriquets
Wherever rapier rapier whets
Are met in punctual rendezvous....
The mildest of their sobriquets
Are Crack-my-crown and Run-me-through!

They are the Gascony Cadets
That give the jealous spouse his due!
Lean forth, adorable coquettes,
They are the Gascony Cadets,
With plumes and scarfs and aigulets!
The husband gray may well look blue....
They are the Gascony Cadets
That give the jealous spouse his due!

DE GUICHE (*nonchalantly seated in an armchair which* RAGUENEAU *has hurriedly brought for him*). A gentleman provides himself to-day, by way of luxury, with a poet. May I look upon you as mine?

CYRANO. No, your lordship, as nobody's.

DE GUICHE. My uncle Richelieu yesterday found your spontaneity diverting. I shall be pleased to be of use to you with him.

LE BRET (*dazzled*). Great God!

DE GUICHE. I cannot think I am wrong in supposing that you have rhymed a tragedy?

LE BRET (*whispering to* CYRANO). My boy, your Agrippina will be played!

DE GUICHE. Take it to him....

CYRANO (*tempted and pleased*). Really...

DE GUICHE. He has taste in such matters. He will no more than, here and there, alter a word, recast a passage....

CYRANO (*whose face has instantly darkened*). Not to be considered, monsieur! My blood runs cold at the thought of a single comma added or suppressed.

DE GUICHE. On the other hand, my dear sir, when a verse finds favor with him, he pays for it handsomely.

CYRANO. He scarcely can pay me as I pay myself, when I have achieved a verse to my liking, by singing it over to myself!

DE GUICHE. You are proud.

CYRANO. You have observed it?

ONE OF THE CADETS (*coming in with a number of disreputable, draggled tattered hats threaded on his sword*). Look, Cyrano! at the remarkable feathered game we secured this morning near the Porte de Nesle! The hats of the fugitives!

CARBON DE CASTEL-JALOUX. *Spoliæ opimæ!*

ALL (*laughing*). Ha! Ha! Ha!...

CUIGY. The one who planned that military action, my word! must be proud of it today!

BRISSAILLE. Is it known who did it?

DE GUICHE. I! — (*The laughter stops short.*) They had instructions to chastise — a matter one does not attend to in person, — a drunken scribbler. (*Constrained silence.*)

THE CADET (*under breath, to* CYRANO, *indicating the hats*). What can we do with them? They are oily.... Make them into a hotch pot?

CYRANO (*taking the sword with the hats, and bowing, as he shakes them off at* DE GUICHE's *feet*). Monsieur, if you should care to return them to your friends?...

DE GUICHE (*rises, and in a curt tone*). My chair and bearers, at once. (*To* CYRANO, *violently.*) As for you, sir...

A VOICE (*in the street, shouting*).   The chairmen of Monseigneur the Comte de Guiche!

DE GUICHE (*who has recovered control over himself, with a smile*).   Have you read Don Quixote?

CYRANO. I have.   And at the name of that divine madman, I uncover...

DE GUICHE. My advice to you is to ponder...

A CHAIRMAN (*appearing at the back*).   The chair is at the door!

DE GUICHE. The chapter of the wind mills.

CYRANO (*bowing*).   Chapter thirteen.

DE GUICHE. For when a man attacks them, it often happens...

CYRANO. I have attacked, am I to infer, a thing that veers with every wind?

DE GUICHE. That one of their far-reaching canvas arms pitches him down into the mud!

CYRANO. Or up among the stars!

> (*Exit* DE GUICHE. *He is seen getting into his chair. The gentlemen withdraw whispering.* LE BRET *goes to the door with them. The crowd leaves. The* CADETS *remain seated at the right and left at tables where food and drink is brought to them.*)

CYRANO (*bowing with a derisive air to those who leave without daring to take leave of him*).   Gentlemen... gentlemen... gentlemen....

LE BRET (*coming forward, greatly distressed, lifting his hands to Heaven*).   Oh, in what a pretty pair of shoes...

CYRANO. Oh, you ... I expect you to grumble!

LE BRET. But yourself, you will agree with me that invariably to cut the throat of opportunity becomes an exaggeration ...

CYRANO. Yes.   I agree.   I do exaggerate.

LE BRET (*triumphant*).   You see, you admit it!...

CYRANO. But for the sake of principle, and of example, as well, I think it a good thing to exaggerate as I do!

LE BRET. Could you but leave apart, once in a while, your mousquetaire of a soul, fortune, undoubtedly, fame...

CYRANO. And what should a man do?   Seek some grandee, take him for a patron, and like the obscure creeper clasping a tree-trunk, and licking the bark of that which props it up, attain to height by craft instead of strength?   No, I thank you.   Dedicate, as they all do, poems to financiers?   Wear motley in the humble hope of seeing the lips of a minister distend for once in a smile not ominous of ill? No, I thank you. Eat every day a toad? Be threadbare at the belly with grovelling? Have his skin dirty soonest at the knees? Practice feats of dorsal elasticity? No, I thank you. With one hand stroke the goat while with the other he waters the cabbage? Make gifts of senna that countergifts of rhubarb may accrue, and indefatigably swing his censer in some beard? No, I thank you. Push himself from lap to lap, become a little great man in a great little circle, propel his ship with madrigals for oars and in his sails the sighs of the elderly ladies? No, I thank you. Get the good editor Sercy to print his verses at proper expense? No, I thank you. Contrive to be nominated Pope in conclaves held by imbeciles in wineshops? No, I thank you. Work to construct a name upon the basis of a sonnet, instead of constructing other sonnets? No, I thank you. Discover talent in tyros, and in them alone? Stand in terror of what gazettes may please to say, and say to himself, "At whatever cost, may I figure in the Paris Mercury!" No, I thank you. Calculate, cringe, peak, prefer making a call to a poem, — petition, solicit, apply? No, I thank you! No, I thank you! No, I thank you! But... sing, dream, laugh, loaf, be single, be free, have eyes that look squarely, a voice with a ring; wear, if he chooses, his hat hindside afore; for a yes, for a no, fight a duel or turn a ditty!... Work, without concern of fortune or of glory, to accomplish the heart's-desired journey to the moon! Put forth nothing that has not its spring in the very heart, yet, modest, say to himself, "Old man, be satisfied with blossoms, fruits, yea, leaves alone, so they be gathered in your garden and not another man's!" Then, if it happen that to some small extent he triumph, be obliged to render of the glory, to Cæsar, not one jot, but honestly appropriate it all. In short, scorning to be the parasite, the creeper, if even failing to be the oak, rise, not perchance to a great height,... but rise alone!

LE BRET. Alone? Good! but not one against all! How the devil did you contract the mania that possesses you for making enemies, always, everywhere?

CYRANO. By seeing you make friends, and smile to those same flocks of friends with a mouth that takes for model an old purse! I wish not to be troubled to return bows in the street, and I exclaim with glee, "An enemy the more!"

LE BRET. This is mental aberration!

CYRANO. I do not dispute it. I am so framed. To displease is my pleasure. I love that one should hate me. Dear friend, if you but knew how much better a man walks under the exciting fire of hostile eyes, and how amused he may become over the spots on his doublet, spattered by Envy and Cowardice!... You, the facile friendship wherewith you surround yourself, resembles those wide Italian collars, loose and easy, with a perforated pattern, in which the neck looks like a woman's. They are more comfortable, but of less high effect; for the brow not held in proud position by any constraint from them, falls to nodding this way and that.... But for me every day Hatred starches and flutes the ruff whose stiffness holds the head well in place. Every new enemy is another plait in it, adding compulsion, but adding, as well, a ray: for, similar in every point to the Spanish ruff, Hatred is a bondage,... but is a halo, too!

LE BRET (*after a pause, slipping his arm through* CYRANO's). To the hearing of all be proud and bitter,... but to me, below breath, say simply that she does not love you!

CYRANO (*sharply*). Not a word!

(CHRISTIAN *has come in and mingled with the* CADETS; *they ignore him; he has finally gone to a little table by himself, where* LISE *waits on him.*)

ONE OF THE CADETS (*seated at a table at the back, glass in hand*). Hey, Cyrano! (*Cyrano turns toward him.*) Your story!

CYRANO. Presently!

(*He goes toward the back on* LE BRET's *arm. They talk low.*)

THE CADET (*rising and coming toward the front*). The account of your fight! It will be the best lesson (*stopping in front of the table at which* CHRISTIAN *is sitting*) for this timorous novice!

CHRISTIAN (*looking up*). ...Novice?

OTHER CADET. Yes, sickly product of the North!

CHRISTIAN. Sickly?

FIRST CADET (*impressively*). Monsieur de Neuvillette, it is a good deed to warn you that there is a thing no more to be mentioned in our company than rope in the house of the hanged!

CHRISTIAN. And what is it?

OTHER CADET (*in a terrifying voice*). Look at me! (*Three times, darkly, he places his finger upon his nose.*) You have understood?

CHRISTIAN. Ah, it is the...

OTHER CADET. Silence!... Never must you so much as breathe that word, or... (*He points toward* CYRANO *at the back talking with* LE BRET.) You will have him, over there, to deal with!

OTHER CADET (*who while* CHRISTIAN *was turned toward the first, has noiselessly seated himself on the table behind him*). Two persons were lately cut off in their pride by him for talking through their noses. He thought it personal.

OTHER CADET (*in a cavernous voice, as he rises from under the table where he had slipped on all fours*). Not the remotest allusion, ever, to the fatal cartilage,... unless you fancy an early grave!

OTHER CADET. A word will do the business! What did I say?... A word?... A simple gesture! Make use of your pocket-handker-chief, you will shortly have use for your shroud!

(*Silence. All around* CHRISTIAN *watch him, with folded arms. He rises and goes to* CARBON DE CASTEL-JALOUX, *who, in conversation with an officer, affects to notice nothing.*)

CHRISTIAN. Captain!

CARBON (*turning and looking him rather contemptuously up and down*) Monsieur?

CHRISTIAN. What is the proper course for a man when he finds gentlemen of the South too boastful?

CARBON DE CASTEL-JALOUX. He must prove to them that one can be of the North, yet brave. (*He turns his back upon him.*)

CHRISTIAN. I am much obliged.

FIRST CADET (*to* CYRANO). And now, the tale of your adventure!

ALL. Yes, yes, now let us hear!

CYRANO (*coming forward among them*). My adventure? (*All draw their stools nearer, and sit around him, with craned necks.* CHRISTIAN *sits astride a chair.*) Well, then, I was marching to meet them. The moon up in the skies was shining like a silver watch, when suddenly I know not what careful watch-maker having wrapped it in a cottony cloud, there occurred the blackest imaginable night; and, the streets being nowise lighted, — *mordious* — you could see no further than...

CHRISTIAN. Your nose.

>   (*Silence. Every one slowly gets up; all look with terror at* CYRANO.
>   *He has stopped short, amazed. Pause.*)

CYRANO. Who is that man?

ONE OF THE CADETS (*low*). He joined this morning.

CYRANO (*taking a step toward* CHRISTIAN). This morning?

CARBON DE CASTEL-JALOUS (*low*). His name is Baron de Neuvill...

CYRANO (*stopping short*). Ah, very well.... (*He turns pale, then red, gives evidence of another impulse to throw himself upon* CHRISTIAN.) I ... (*He conquers it, and says in a stifled voice.*) Very well. (*He takes up his tale.*) As I was saying... (*with a burst of rage*) Mordious!... (*He continues in a natural tone*) one could not see in the very least. (*Consternation. All resume their seats, staring at one another.*) And I was walking along, reflecting that for a very insignificant rogue I was probably about to offend some great prince who would bear me a lasting grudge, that, in brief, I was about to thrust my...

CHRISTIAN. Nose...

>   (*All get up.* CHRISTIAN *has tilted his chair and is rocking on the hind legs.*)

CYRANO (*choking*). Finger... between the tree and the bark; for the aforesaid prince might be of sufficient power to trip me and throw me...

CHRISTIAN. On my nose...

CYRANO (*wipes the sweat from his brow*). But, said I, "Gascony forward! Never falter when duty prompts! Forward, Cyrano!" and, saying this, I advance — when suddenly, in the darkness, I barely avoid a blow...

CHRISTIAN. Upon the nose...

CYRANO. I ward it... and thereupon find myself...

CHRISTIAN. Nose to nose...

CYRANO (*springing toward him*). Ventre-Saint-Gris!... (*All the* GASCON *rush forward, to see;* CYRANO, *on reaching* CHRISTIAN, *controls himself and proceeds*)... with a hundred drunken brawlers, smelling...

CHRISTIAN. To the nose's limit...

CYRANO (*deathly pale, and smiling*)... of garlic and of grease. I leap forward, head lowered...

CHRISTIAN. Nose to the wind!...

CYRANO. And I charge them. I knock two breathless and run a

third through the body. One lets off at me: Paf! and I re-tort...

CHRISTIAN. Pif!

CYRANO (*exploding*). Death and damnation! Go, — all of you!

(*All the* CADETS *make for the door.*)

FIRST CADET. The tiger is roused at last!

CYRANO. All! and leave me with this man.

SECOND CADET. *Bigre!* When we see him again, it will be in the shape of mince-meat!

RAGUENEAU. Mince-meat?...

OTHER CADET. In one of your pies.

RAGUENEAU. I feel myself grow white and flabby as a table-napkin!

CARBON DE CASTEL-JALOUX. Let us go!

OTHER CADET. Not a smudge of him will be left!

OTHER CADET. What these walls are about to behold gives me gooseflesh to think upon!

OTHER CADET (*closing the door at the right*). Ghastly!... Ghastly!

(*All have left, by the back or the sides, a few up the stairway. CYRANO and CHRISTIAN remain face to face, and look at each other a moment.*)

CYRANO. Embrace me!

CHRISTIAN. Monsieur...

CYRANO. Brave fellow.

CHRISTIAN. But what does this...

CYRANO. Very brave fellow. I wish you to.

CHRISTIAN. Will you tell me?...

CYRANO. Embrace me, I am her brother.

CHRISTIAN. Whose?

CYRANO. Hers!

CHRISTIAN. What do you mean?

CYRANO. Roxane's!

CHRISTIAN (*running to him*). Heavens! You, her brother?

CYRANO. Or the same thing: her first cousin.

CHRISTIAN. And she has...

CYRANO. Told me everything!

CHRISTIAN. Does she love me?

CYRANO. Perhaps!

CHRISTIAN (*seizing his hands*). How happy I am, monsieur, to make your acquaintance!...

CYRANO. That is what I call a sudden sentiment!

CHRISTIAN. Forgive me!...

CYRANO (*looking at him, laying his hand upon his shoulder*). It is true that he is handsome, the rascal!

CHRISTIAN. If you but knew, monsieur, how greatly I admire you!...

CYRANO. But all those noses which you...

CHRISTIAN. I take them back!

CYRANO. Roxane expects a letter tonight...

CHRISTIAN. Alas!

CYRANO. What is the matter?

CHRISTIAN. I am lost if I cease to be dumb!

CYRANO. How is that?

CHRISTIAN. Alas! I am such a dunce that I could kill myself for shame!

CYRANO. But no... no.... You are surely not a dunce, if you believe you are! Besides, you scarcely attacked me like a dunce.

CHRISTIAN. Oh, it is easy to find words in mounting to the assault! Indeed, I own to a certain cheap military readiness, but when I am before women, I have not a word to say.... Yet their eyes, when I pass by, express a kindness toward me...

CYRANO. And do their hearts not express the same when you stop beside them?

CHRISTIAN. No!... for I am of those — I recognize it, and am dismayed — who do not know how to talk of love.

CYRANO. *Tiens!* ... It seems to me that if Nature had taken more pains with my shape, I should have been of those who do know how to talk of it.

CHRISTIAN. Oh, to be able to express things gracefully!

CYRANO. Oh, to be a graceful little figure of a passing mousquetaire!

CHRISTIAN. Roxane is a précieuse,... there is no chance but that I shall be a disillusion to Roxane!

CYRANO (*looking at* CHRISTIAN). If I had, to express my soul, such an interpreter!...

CHRISTIAN (*desperately*). I ought to have eloquence!...

CYRANO (*abruptly*). Eloquence I will lend you!... And you, to me,

shall lend all-conquering physical charm... and between us we
will compose a hero of romance!

CHRISTIAN. What?

CYRANO. Should you be able to say, as your own, things which I
day by day would teach you?

CHRISTIAN. You are suggesting?...

CYRANO. Roxane shall not have disillusions! Tell me, shall we win
her heart, we two as one? will you submit to feel, transmitted
from my leather doublet into your doublet stitched with silk, the
soul I wish to share?

CHRISTIAN. By Cyrano!...

CYRANO. Christian, will you?

CHRISTIAN. You frighten me!

CYRANO. Since you fear, left to yourself, to chill her heart, will you
consent, — and soon it will take fire, I vouch for it! — to con-
tribute your lips to my phrases?

CHRISTIAN. Your eyes shine!...

CYRANO. Will you?

CHRISTIAN. What, would it please you so much?

CYRANO (with rapture). It would... (remembering, and confining himself to expressing an artistic pleasure)... amuse me! It is an experiment fit surely to tempt a poet. Will you complete me, and let
me in exchange complete you? We will walk side by side: you in
full light, I in your shadow.... I will be wit to you... you, to me,
shall be good looks!

CHRISTIAN. But the letter, which should be sent to her without delay?... Never shall I be able...

CYRANO (taking from his doublet the letter written in the first part of the act).
The letter? Here it is!

CHRISTIAN. How?...

CYRANO. It only wants the address.

CHRISTIAN. I...

CYRANO. You can send it without uneasiness. It is a good letter.

CHRISTIAN. You had?...

CYRANO. You shall never find us — poets — without epistles in
our pockets to the Chlorises... of our imagining! For we are
those same that have for mistress a dream blown into the bubble
of a name! Take, — you shall convert this feigning into earnest;

I was sending forth at random these confessions and laments: you shall make the wandering birds to settle... Take it! You shall see... I was as eloquent as if I had been sincere! Take, and have done!

CHRISTIAN. But will it not need to be altered in any part?... Written without object, will it fit Roxane?

CYRANO. Like a glove!

CHRISTIAN. But...

CYRANO. Trust to the blindness of love... and vanity! Roxane will never question that it was written for her.

CHRISTIAN. Ah, my friend!

(*He throws himself into* CYRANO's *arms. They stand embraced.*)

ONE OF THE CADETS (*opening the door a very little*). Nothing more... The stillness of death... I dare not look... (*He thrusts in his head.*) What is this?

ALL THE CADETS (*entering and seeing* CYRANO *and* CHRISTIAN *locked in each other's arms*). Ah!... Oh!...

ONE OF THE CADETS. This passes bounds!   (*Consternation.*)

THE MOUSQUETAIRE (*impudent*). Ouais?

CARBON DE CASTEL-JALOUX. Our demon is waxen mild as an apostle; smitten upon one nostril, he turns the other also!

THE MOUSQUETAIRE. It is in order now to speak of his nose, is it? (*Calling* LISE, *with a swaggering air.*) Hey, Lise! now listen and look. (*Pointedly sniffing the air.*) Oh,... oh,... it is surprising!... what an odor!   (*Going to* CYRANO.)   But monsieur must have smelled it, too? Can you tell me what it is, so plain in the air?

CYRANO (*beating him*). Why, sundry blows!

(*Joyful antics of the* CADETS *in beholding* CYRANO *himself again.*)

CURTAIN

ACT THIRD

ROXANE'S KISS

A small square in the old Marais. Old-fashioned houses. Narrow streets seen in perspective. At the right, ROXANE'S *house and the wall of her garden, above which spreading tree-tops. Over the house-door, a balcony and window. A bench beside the doorstep.*

The wall is overclambered by ivy, the balcony wreathed with jasmine.

By means of the bench and projecting stones in the wall, the balcony can easily be scaled.

On the opposite side, old house in the same style of architecture, brick and stone, with entrance-door. The door-knocker is swaddled in linen.

At the rise of the curtain, the DUENNA *is seated on the bench. The window on* ROXANE'S *balcony is wide open.*

RAGUENEAU, *in a sort of livery, stands near the* DUENNA; *he is finishing the tale of his misfortunes, drying his eyes.*

RAGUENEAU. And then, she eloped with a mousquetaire! Ruined, forsaken, I was hanging myself. I had already taken leave of earth, when Monsieur de Bergerac happening along, unhanged me, and proposed me to his cousin as her steward....

THE DUENNA. But how did you fall into such disaster?

RAGUENEAU. Lise was fond of soldiers, I, of poets! Mars ate up all left over by Apollo. Under those circumstances, you conceive, the pantry soon was bare.

THE DUENNA (*rising and calling toward the open window*). Roxane, are you ready?... They are waiting for us!...

ROXANE'S VOICE (*through the window*). I am putting on my mantle!

THE DUENNA (*to* RAGUENEAU, *pointing at the door opposite*). It is over there, opposite, we are expected. At Clomire's. She holds a meeting in her little place. A disquisition upon the Softer Sentiments is to be read.

RAGUENEAU. Upon the Softer Sentiments?

THE DUENNA (*coyly*). Yes!... (*Calling toward the window.*) Roxane, you must make haste, or we shall miss the disquisition upon the Softer Sentiments!

ROXANE'S VOICE. I am coming!

(*A sound of string-instruments is heard, drawing nearer.*)

CYRANO'S VOICE (*singing in the wings*).   La! la! la! la! la!...

THE DUENNA (*surprised*).   We are to have music?

CYRANO (*enters followed by two* PAGES *with theorbos*).   I tell you it is a demi-semi-quaver!... you demi-semi-noddle!

FIRST PAGE (*ironically*).   Monsieur knows then about quavers, semi and demi?

CYRANO.   I know music, as do all Gassendi's disciples!

THE PAGE (*playing and singing*).   La! la!

CYRANO (*snatching the theorbo from him and continuing the musical phrase*). I can carry on the melody.... La, la, la, la,...

ROXANE (*appearing on the balcony*).   It is you?

CYRANO (*singing upon the tune he is continuing*).   I, indeed, who salute your lilies and present my respects to your ro-o-oses!...

ROXANE.   I am coming down!   (*She leaves the balcony.*)

THE DUENNA (*pointing at the* PAGES).   What is the meaning of these two virtuosi?

CYRANO.   A wager I won, from D'Assoucy.   We were disputing upon a question of grammar.   Yes! No! Yes! No!   Suddenly pointing at these two tall knaves, expert at clawing strings, by whom he constantly goes attended, he said, "I wager a day long of music!"   He lost.   Until therefore the next rise of the sun, I shall have dangling after me these archlute players, harmonious witnesses of all I do!... At first I liked it very well, but now it palls a little.   (*To the musicians.*)   Hey!... Go, from me, to Montfleury, and play him a pavane!... (*The* PAGES *go toward the back.   To the* DUENNA.)   I have come to inquire of Roxane, as I do every evening... (*To the* PAGES *who are leaving.*)   Play a long time... and out of tune!   (*To the* DUENNA.)... whether in the friend of her soul she can still detect no fault?

ROXANE (*coming out of the house*).   Ah, how beautiful he is, what wit he has, how deeply I love him!

CYRANO (*smiling.*)   Christian has so much wit?...

ROXANE.   Cousin, more than yourself!

CYRANO.   I grant you.

ROXANE.   There is not one alive, I truly believe, more apt at turning those pretty nothings which yet are everything.... Sometimes he is of an absent mood, his muse is wool-gathering, then, suddenly, he will say the most enchanting things!

CYRANO (*incredulous*). Come!...

ROXANE. Oh, it is too bad! Men are all alike, narrow, narrow: because he is handsome, he cannot possibly be witty!

CYRANO. So he talks of the heart in acceptable fashion?

ROXANE. Talks, cousin, is feeble.... He dissertates!

CYRANO. And writes?...

ROXANE. Still better! Listen now to this... (*Declaiming.*) "*The more of my heart you steal from me, the more heart I have!*" (*Triumphantly to* CYRANO.) Well?...

CYRANO. Pooh!

ROXANE. And to this: "*Since you have stolen my heart, and since I must suffer, to suffer with send me your own!*"

CYRANO. Now he has too much heart, now he has not enough,... just what does he want, in the matter of quantity?

ROXANE. You vex me! You are eaten up with jealousy...

CYRANO (*starting*). *Hein?*

ROXANE. Author's jealousy! And this, could anything be more exquisitely tender? "*Unanimously, believe it, my heart cries out to you, and if kisses could be sent in writing, Love, you should read my letter with your lips...*"

CYRANO (*in spite of himself smiling with satisfaction*). Ha! Ha! Those particular lines seem to me... ho!... ho!... (*remembering himself, disdainfully*)... puny, pretty...

ROXANE. This, then...

CYRANO (*delighted*). You know his letters by heart?

ROXANE. All!

CYRANO. It is flattering, one cannot deny.

ROXANE. In this art of expressing love he is a master!

CYRANO (*modest*). Oh,... a master!

ROXANE (*peremptory*). A master!

CYRANO. As you please, then... a master!

THE DUENNA (*who had gone toward the back, coming quickly forward*). Monsieur de Guiche! (*To* CYRANO, *pushing him toward the house.*) Go in! It is perhaps better that he should not see you here! it might put him on the scent...

ROXANE (*to* CYRANO). Yes, of my dear secret! He loves me, he is powerful,... he must not find out! He might cut in sunder our loves... with an axe!

CYRANO (*going into the house*). Very well, very well.

(DE GUICHE *appears*.)

ROXANE (*to* DE GUICHE, *with a curtsey*). I was leaving the house.

DE GUICHE. I have come to bid you farewell.

ROXANE. You are going away?

DE GUICHE. To war.

ROXANE. Ah!

DE GUICHE. I have my orders. Arras is besieged.

ROXANE. Ah!... it is besieged?

DE GUICHE. Yes.... I see that my departure does not greatly affect you.

ROXANE. Oh!...

DE GUICHE. As for me, I own it wrings my heart. Shall I see you again?... When?... You know that I am made commander-in-general?

ROXANE (*uninterested*). I congratulate you.

DE GUICHE. Of the Guards.

ROXANE (*starting*). Ah,... of the Guards?

DE GUICHE. Among whom your cousin serves,... the man of the boasts and tirades. I shall have opportunity in plenty to retaliate upon him down there.

ROXANE (*suffocating*). What? The Guards are going down there?

DE GUICHE. Surely. It is my regiment.

ROXANE (*falls sitting upon the bench; aside*). Christian!

DE GUICHE. What is it troubles you?

ROXANE (*greatly moved*). This departure... grieves me mortally. When one cares for a person... to know him away at the war!

DE GUICHE (*surprised and charmed*). For the first time you utter a kind and feeling word, when I am leaving!

ROXANE (*in a different tone, fanning herself*). So... you are thinking of revenge upon my cousin?

DE GUICHE (*smiling*). You side with him?

ROXANE. No... against him.

DE GUICHE. Do you see much of him?

ROXANE. Very little.

DE GUICHE. He is everywhere to be met with one of the cadets... (*trying to remember*) that Neu... villen... viller...

ROXANE. A tall man?

DE GUICHE. Light-haired.

ROXANE. Red-haired.

DE GUICHE. Good-looking.

ROXANE. Pooh!

DE GUICHE. But a fool!

ROXANE. He looks like one. (*In a different tone.*) Your vengeance upon Cyrano is then to place him within reach of shot, which is the thing of all he loves!... A miserable vengeance!... I know, I do, what would more seriously concern him!

DE GUICHE. And that is?

ROXANE. Why... that the regiment should march, and leave him behind, with his beloved cadets, arms folded, the whole war through, in Paris! That is the only way to cast down a man like him. You wish to punish him? Deprive him of danger.

DE GUICHE. A woman! A woman! None but a woman could devise a vengeance of the sort!

ROXANE. His friends will gnaw their fists, and he his very soul, with chagrin at not being under fire; and you will be abundantly avenged!

DE GUICHE (*coming nearer*). Then you do love me a little? (ROXANE *smiles.*) I wish to see in this fact of your espousing my grudge a proof of affection, Roxane...

ROXANE. ... You may!

DE GUICHE (*showing several folded papers*). I have here upon me the orders to be transmitted at once to each of the companies... except... (*he takes one from among the others.*) This one!... the company of the cadets... (*He puts it in his pocket.*) This, I will keep. (*Laughing.*) Ah, ah, ah! Cyrano! his belligerent humor! ... So you sometimes play tricks upon people, you?...

ROXANE. Sometimes.

DE GUICHE (*very near her*). I love you to distraction! This evening ... listen,... it is true that I must be gone. But to go when I feel that it is a matter for your caring! Listen!... There is, not far from here, in Rue Orléans, a convent founded by the Capuchins. Father Athanasius. A layman may not enter. But the good fathers... I fear no difficulty with them! They will hide me up their sleeve... their sleeve is wide. They are the Capuchins that serve Richelieu at home. Fearing the uncle, they proportionately fear the nephew. I shall be thought to have left. I will come to you masked. Let me delay by a single day, wayward enchantress!

ROXANE. But if it should transpire... your fame...

DE GUICHE. Bah!

ROXANE. But... the siege... Arras!...

DE GUICHE. Must wait! Allow me, I beg...

ROXANE. No!

DE GUICHE. I beseech!

ROXANE (*tenderly*). No! Love itself bids me forbid you!

DE GUICHE. Ah!

ROXANE. You must go! (*Aside.*) Christian will stay! (*Aloud.*) For my sake, be heroic... Antony!

DE GUICHE. Ah, heavenly word upon your lips!... Then you love the one who...

ROXANE. Who shall have made me tremble for his sake...

DE GUICHE (*in a transport of joy*). Ah, I will go! (*He kisses her hand.*) Are you satisfied with me?

ROXANE. My friend, I am. (*Exit* DE GUICHE.)

THE DUENNA (*dropping a mocking curtsey toward his back*). My friend, we are!

ROXANE (*to the* DUENNA). Not a word of what I have done: Cyrano would never forgive me for defrauding him of his war! (*She calls toward the house.*) Cousin! (CYRANO *comes out.*) We are going to Clomire's. (*She indicates the house opposite.*) Alcandre has engaged to speak, and so has Lysimon.

THE DUENNA (*putting her little finger to her ear*). Yes, but my little finger tells me that we shall be too late to hear them!

CYRANO (*to* ROXANE). Of all things do not miss the trained monkeys! (*They have reached* CLOMIRE'S *door.*)

THE DUENNA. See!... See! they have muffled the door-knocker! (*To the door-knocker.*) You have been gagged, that your voice should not disturb the beautiful lecture,... little brutal disturber! (*She lifts it with infinite care and knocks softly.*)

ROXANE (*seeing the door open*). Come! (*From the threshold to* CYRANO.) If Christian should come, as probably he will, say he must wait!

CYRANO (*hurriedly, as she is about to disappear*). Ah! (*She turns.*)
Upon what shall you, according to your custom, question him
today?

ROXANE. Upon...

CYRANO (*eagerly*). Upon?...

ROXANE. But you will be silent...

CYRANO. As that wall!

ROXANE. Upon nothing! I will say: Forward! Free rein! No
curb! Improvise! Talk of love! Be magnificent!

CYRANO (*smiling*). Good.

ROXANE. Hush!

CYRANO. Hush!

ROXANE. Not a word!   (*She goes in and closes the door.*)

CYRANO (*bowing, when the door is closed*). A thousand thanks!

(*The door opens again and* ROXANE *looks out.*)

ROXANE. He might prepare his speeches...

CYRANO. Ah, no!... the devil, no!

BOTH (*together*). Hush!...   (*The door closes.*)

CYRANO (*calling*). Christian! (*Enter* CHRISTIAN.) I know all that
we need to. Now make ready your memory. This is your
chance to cover yourself with glory. Let us lose no time. Do
not look sullen, like that. Quick! Let us go to your lodgings and
I will rehearse you...

CHRISTIAN. No!

CYRANO. What?

CHRISTIAN. No, I will await Roxane here.

CYRANO. What insanity possesses you? Come quickly and
learn...

CHRISTIAN. No, I tell you! I am weary of borrowing my letters, my
words... of playing a part, and living in constant fear.... It was
very well at first, but now I feel that she loves me. I thank you
heartily. I am no longer afraid. I will speak for myself...

CYRANO. *Ouais?*...

CHRISTIAN. And what tells you that I shall not know how? I am
not such an utter blockhead, after all! You shall see! Your
lessons have not been altogether wasted. I can shift to speak
without your aid! And, that failing, by Heaven! I shall still
know enough to take her in my arms! (*Catching sight of* ROXANE

who is coming out from CLOMIRE'S.) She is coming! Cyrano, no, do not leave me!...

CYRANO (*bowing to him*). I will not meddle, monsieur.

(*He disappears behind the garden wall.*)

ROXANE (*coming from Clomire's house with a number of people from whom she is taking leave. Curtseys and farewells.*) Barthénoïde!... Alcandre!... Grémione!...

THE DUENNA (*comically desperate*). We missed the disquisition upon the Softer Sentiments! (*She goes into* ROXANE'S *house.*)

ROXANE (*still taking leave of this one and that.*) Urimédonte!... Good-bye!

(*All bow to* ROXANE, *to one another, separate and go off by the various streets.* ROXANE *sees* CHRISTIAN.)

ROXANE. You are here! (*She goes to him.*) Evening is closing round.... Wait!... They have all gone.... The air is so mild.... Not a passer in sight.... Let us sit here.... Talk!... I will listen.

CHRISTIAN (*sits beside her, on the bench. Silence.*) I love you.

ROXANE (*closing her eyes*). Yes. Talk to me of love.

CHRISTIAN. I love you.

ROXANE. Yes. That is the theme. Play variations upon it.

CHRISTIAN. I love...

ROXANE. Variations!

CHRISTIAN. I love you so much...

ROXANE. I do not doubt it. What further?...

CHRISTIAN. And further... I should be so happy if you loved me! Tell me, Roxane, that you love me...

ROXANE (*pouting*). You proffer cider to me when I was hoping for champagne!... Now tell me a little *how* you love me?

CHRISTIAN. Why... very, very much.

ROXANE. Oh!... unravel, disentangle your sentiments!

CHRISTIAN. Your throat!... I want to kiss it!...

ROXANE. Christian!

CHRISTIAN. I love you!...

ROXANE (*attempting to rise*). Again!...

CHRISTIAN (*hastily, holding her back*). No, I do not love you!...

ROXANE (*sitting down again*). That is fortunate!

CHRISTIAN. I adore you!

ROXANE (*rising and moving away*). Oh!...

CHRISTIAN. Yes,... love makes me into a fool!

ROXANE (*drily*). And I am displeased at it! as I should be displeased at your no longer being handsome.

CHRISTIAN. But...

ROXANE. Go, and rally your routed eloquence!

CHRISTIAN. I...

ROXANE. You love me. I have heard it. Good-evening.

> (*She goes toward the house.*)

CHRISTIAN. No, no, not yet!... I wish to tell you...

ROXANE (*pushing open the door to go in*). That you adore me. Yes, I know. No! No! Go away!... Go!... Go!...

CHRISTIAN. But I...   (*She closes the door in his face.*)

CYRANO (*who has been on the scene a moment, unnoticed*). Unmistakably a success.

CHRISTIAN. Help me!

CYRANO. No, sir, no.

CHRISTIAN. I will go kill myself if I am not taken back into favor at once... at once!

CYRANO. And how can I... how, the devil?... make you learn on the spot...

CHRISTIAN (*seizing him by the arm*). Oh, there!... Look!... See!

> (*Light has appeared in the balcony window.*)

CYRANO (*with emotion*). Her window!

CHRISTIAN. Oh, I shall die!

CYRANO. Not so loud!

CHRISTIAN (*in a whisper*). I shall die!

CYRANO. It is a dark night....

CHRISTIAN. Well?

CYRANO. All may be mended. But you do not deserve... There! stand there, miserable boy!... in front of the balcony! I will stand under it and prompt you.

CHRISTIAN. But...

CYRANO. Do as I bid you!

THE PAGES (*reappearing at the back, to* CYRANO). Hey!

CYRANO. Hush!   (*He signs to them to lower their voices.*)

FIRST PAGE (*in a lower voice*). We have finished serenading Mont-fleury!

CYRANO (*low, quickly*). Go and stand out of sight. One at this street corner, the other at that; and if any one comes near, play!...

SECOND PAGE. What sort of tune, Monsieur the Gassendist?

CYRANO. Merry if it be a woman, mournful if it be a man. (*The* PAGES *disappear, one at each street corner. To* CHRISTIAN.) Call her!

CHRISTIAN. Roxane!

CYRANO (*picking up pebbles and throwing them at the window-pane*). Wait! A few pebbles...

ROXANE (*opening the window*). Who is calling me?

CHRISTIAN. It is I...

ROXANE. Who is... I?

CHRISTIAN. Christian!

ROXANE (*disdainfully*). Oh, you!

CHRISTIAN. I wish to speak with you.

CYRANO (*under the balcony, to* CHRISTIAN). Speak low!...

ROXANE. No, your conversation is too common. You may go home!

CHRISTIAN. In mercy!...

ROXANE. No... you do not love me any more!

CHRISTIAN (*whom* CYRANO *is prompting*). You accuse me... just Heaven! of loving you no more... when I can love you no more!

ROXANE (*who was about to close her window, stopping*). Ah, that is a little better!

CHRISTIAN (*same business*). To what a... size has Love grown in my ... sigh-rocked soul which the... cruel cherub has chosen for his cradle!

ROXANE (*stepping nearer to the edge of the balcony*). That is distinctly better!... But, since he is so cruel, this Cupid, you were unwise not to smother him in his cradle!

CHRISTIAN (*same business*). I tried to, but, madame, the... attempt was futile. This... new-born Love is... a little Hercules...

ROXANE. Much, much better!

CHRISTIAN (*same business*).... Who found it merest baby-play to... strangle the serpents... twain, Pride and... Mistrust.

ROXANE (*leaning her elbows on the balcony-rail*). Ah, that is very good indeed!... But why do you speak so slowly and stintedly? Has your imagination gout in its wings?

CYRANO (*drawing* CHRISTIAN *under the balcony, and taking his place*). Hush! It is becoming too difficult!

ROXANE. Tonight your words come falteringly.... Why is it?

CYRANO (*talking low like* CHRISTIAN). Because of the dark. They have to grope to find your ear.

ROXANE. My words do not find the same difficulty.

CYRANO. They reach their point at once? Of course they do! That is because I catch them with my heart. My heart, you see, is very large, your ear particularly small.... Besides, your words drop... that goes quickly; mine have to climb... and that takes longer!

ROXANE. They have been climbing more nimbly, however, in the last few minutes.

CYRANO. They are becoming used to this gymnastic feat!

ROXANE. It is true that I am talking with you from a very mountain top!

CYRANO. It is sure that a hard word dropped from such a height upon my heart would shatter it!

ROXANE (*with the motion of leaving*). I will come down.

CYRANO (*quickly*). Do not!

ROXANE (*pointing at the bench at the foot of the balcony*). Then do you get up on the seat!...

CYRANO (*drawing away in terror*). No!

ROXANE. How do you mean... no?

CYRANO (*with ever-increasing emotion*). Let us profit a little by this chance of talking softly together without seeing each other...

ROXANE. Without seeing each other?...

CYRANO. Yes, to my mind, delectable! Each guesses at the other, and no more. You discern but the trailing blackness of a mantle, and I a dawn-gray glimmer which is a summer gown. I am a shadow merely, a pearly phantom are you! You can never know what these moments are to me! If ever I was eloquent...

ROXANE. You were!

CYRANO. My words never till now surged from my very heart...

ROXANE. And why?

CYRANO. Because, till now, they must strain to reach you through...

ROXANE. What?

CYRANO. Why, the bewildering emotion a man feels who sees you, and whom you look upon!... But this evening, it seems to me that I am speaking to you for the first time!

ROXANE. It is true that your voice is altogether different.

CYRANO (*coming nearer, feverishly*). Yes, altogether different, because, protected by the dark, I dare at last to be myself. I dare ... (*He stops, and distractedly.*) What was I saying?... I do not know.... All this... forgive my incoherence!... is so delicious... is so new to me!

ROXANE. So new?...

CYRANO (*in extreme confusion, still trying to mend his expressions*). So new... yes, new, to be sincere; the fear of being mocked always constrains my heart...

ROXANE. Mocked... for what?

CYRANO. Why,... for its impulses, its flights!... Yes, my heart always cowers behind the defence of my wit. I set forth to capture a star... and then, for dread of laughter, I stop and pick a flower ... of rhetoric!

ROXANE. That sort of flower has its pleasing points...

CYRANO. But yet, tonight, let us scorn it!

ROXANE. Never before had you spoken as you are speaking!...

CYRANO. Ah, if far from Cupid-darts and quivers, we might seek a place of somewhat fresher things! If instead of drinking, flat sip by sip, from a chiselled golden thimble, drops distilled and dulcified, we might try the sensation of quenching the thirst of our souls by stooping to the level of the great river, and setting our lips to the stream!

ROXANE. But yet, wit... fancy... delicate conceits...

CYRANO. I gave my fancy leave to frame conceits, before, to make you linger,... but now it would be an affront to this balm-breathing night, to Nature and the hour, to talk like characters in a pastoral performed at Court!... Let us give Heaven leave, looking at us with all its earnest stars, to strip us of disguise and artifice: I fear,... oh, fear!... lest in our mistaken alchemy sentiment should be subtilized to evaporation; lest the life of the heart should waste in these empty pastimes, and the final refinement of the fine be the undoing of the refined!

ROXANE. But yet, wit,... aptness,... ingenuity...

CYRANO. I hate them in love! Criminal, when one loves, to prolong overmuch that paltry thrust and parry! The moment, however, comes inevitably, — and I pity those for whom it never comes! — in which, we apprehending the noble depth of the love we harbor, a shallow word hurts us to utter!

ROXANE. If... if, then, that moment has come for us two, what words will you say to me?

CYRANO. All those, all those, all those that come to me! Not in formal nosegay order,... I will throw them you in a wild sheaf! I love you, choke with love, I love you, dear.... My brain reels, I can bear no more, it is too much.... Your name is in my heart the golden clapper in a bell; and as I know no rest, Roxane, always the heart is shaken, and ever rings your name!... Of you, I remember all, all have I loved! Last year, one day, the twelfth of May, in going out at morning you changed the fashion of your hair.... I have taken the light of your hair for my light, and as having stared too long at the sun, on everything one sees a scarlet wheel, on everything when I come from my chosen light, my dazzled eye sets swimming golden blots!...

ROXANE (*in a voice unsteady with emotion*). Yes... this is love...

CYRANO. Ah, verily! The feeling which invades me, terrible and jealous, is love... with all its mournful frenzy! It is love, yet self-forgetting more than the wont of love! Ah, for your happiness now readily would I give mine, though you should never know it, might I but, from a distance, sometimes, hear the happy laughter bought by my sacrifice! Every glance of yours breeds in me new strength, new valor! Are you beginning to understand? Tell me, do you grasp my love's measure? Does some little part of my soul make itself felt of you there in the darkness?... Oh, what is happening to me this evening is too sweet, too deeply dear! I tell you all these things, and you listen to me, you! Not in my least modest hoping did I ever hope so much! I have now only to die! It is because of words of mine that she is trembling among the dusky branches! For you are trembling, like a flower among leaves! Yes, you tremble,... for whether you will or no, I have felt the worshipped trembling of your hand all along this thrilled and blissful jasmine-bough!

(*He madly kisses the end of a pendent bough.*)

ROXANE. Yes, I tremble... and weep... and love you... and am yours!... For you have carried me away... away!...

CYRANO. Then, let death come! I have moved you, I!... There is but one thing more I ask...

CHRISTIAN (*under the balcony*). A kiss!

ROXANE (*drawing hastily back*). What?

CYRANO. Oh!

ROXANE. You ask?...

CYRANO. Yes... I... (*To* CHRISTIAN.) You are in too great haste!

CHRISTIAN. Since she is so moved, I must take advantage of it!

CYRANO (*to* ROXANE). I... Yes, it is true I asked... but, merciful heavens!... I knew at once that I had been too bold.

ROXANE (*a shade disappointed*). You insist no more than so?

CYRANO. Indeed, I insist... without insisting! Yes! yes! but your modesty shrinks!... I insist, but yet... the kiss I begged... refuse it me!

CHRISTIAN (*to* CYRANO, *pulling at his mantle*). Why?

CYRANO. Hush, Christian!

ROXANE (*bending over the balcony-rail*). What are you whispering?

CYRANO. Reproaches to myself for having gone too far; I was saying "Hush, Christian!" (*The theorbos are heard playing.*) Your pardon!... a second!... Some one is coming!

(ROXANE *closes the window.* CYRANO *listens to the theorbos, one of which plays a lively, and the other a lugubrious tune.*)

CYRANO. A dance?... A dirge?... What do they mean? Is it a man or a woman?... Ah, it is a monk!

(*Enter a* CAPUCHIN MONK, *who goes from house to house, with a lantern, examining the doors.*)

CYRANO (*to the* CAPUCHIN). What are you looking for, Diogenes?

THE CAPUCHIN. I am looking for the house of Madame...

CHRISTIAN. He is in the way!

THE CAPUCHIN. Magdeleine Robin...

CYRANO (*pointing up one of the streets*). This way!... Straight ahead ... go straight ahead...

THE CAPUCHIN. I thank you. I will say ten Aves for your peace.

(*Exit.*)

CYRANO. My good wishes speed your cowl!

(*He comes forward toward* CHRISTIAN.)

CHRISTIAN. Insist upon the kiss!...

CYRANO. No, I will not!

CHRISTIAN. Sooner or later...

CYRANO. It is true! It must come, the moment of inebriation when your lips shall imperiously be impelled toward each other, because the one is fledged with youthful gold and the other is so soft a pink!... (*To himself.*) I had rather it should be because...

(*Sound of the window reopening;* CHRISTIAN *hides under the balcony.*)

ROXANE (*stepping forward on the balcony*). Are you there? We were speaking of... of... of a...

CYRANO. Kiss. The word is sweet. Why does your fair lip stop at it? If the mere word burns it, what will be of the thing itself? Do not make it into a fearful matter, and then fear! Said you not a moment ago insensibly leave playfulness behind and slip without trepidation from a smile to a sigh, from a sigh to a tear? Slip but a little further in the same blessed direction: from a tear to a kiss there is scarcely a dividing shiver!

ROXANE. Say no more!

CYRANO. A kiss! When all is said, what is a kiss? An oath of allegiance taken in closer proximity, a promise more precise, a seal on a confession, a rose-red dot upon the letter i in loving; a secret which elects the mouth for ear; an instant of eternity murmuring like a bee; balmy communion with a flavor of flowers; a fashion of inhaling each other's heart, and of tasting, on the brink of the lips, each other's soul!

ROXANE. Say no more... no more!

CYRANO. A kiss, madame, is a thing so noble that the Queen of France, on the most fortunate of lords, bestowed one, did the queen herself!

ROXANE. If that be so...

CYRANO (*with increasing fervor*). Like Buckingham I have suffered in long silence, like him I worship a queen, like him I am sorrowful and unchanging...

ROXANE. Like him you enthrall through the eyes the heart that follows you!

CYRANO (*to himself, sobered*). True, I am handsome... I had forgotten!

ROXANE. Come then and gather it, the supreme flower...

CYRANO (*pushing* CHRISTIAN *toward the balcony*). Go!

ROXANE. ... tasting of the heart.

CYRANO. Go!...

ROXANE. ... murmuring like a bee...

CYRANO. Go!

CHRISTIAN (*hesitating*). But now I feel as if I ought not!

ROXANE. ... making Eternity an instant...

CYRANO (*pushing* CHRISTIAN). Scale the balcony, you donkey!

> (CHRISTIAN *springs toward the balcony, and climbs by means of the bench, the vine, the posts and balusters.*)

CHRISTIAN. Ah, Roxane! (*He clasps her to him, and bends over her lips.*)

CYRANO. Ha!... What a turn of the screw to my heart!... Kiss, banquet of Love at which I am Lazarus, a crumb drops from your table even to me, here in the shade.... Yes, in my outstretched heart a little falls, as I feel that upon the lip pressing her lip Roxane kisses the words spoken by me!... (*The theorbos are heard.*) A merry tune... a mournful one... The monk! (*He goes through the pretence of arriving on the spot at a run, as if from a distance; calling.*) Ho, there!

ROXANE. What is it?

CYRANO. It is I. I was passing this way. Is Christian there?

CHRISTIAN (*astonished*). Cyrano!

ROXANE. Good-evening, cousin!

CYRANO. Cousin, good-evening!

ROXANE. I will come down.　　　　(ROXANE *disappears in the house.*)

(CAPUCHIN *re-enters at the back.*)

CHRISTIAN (*seeing him*). Oh, again!　　　　(*He follows* ROXANE.)

THE CAPUCHIN. It is here she lives, I am certain... Magdeleine Robin.

CYRANO. You said Ro-lin.

THE CAPUCHIN. No, bin,... b, i, n, bin!

ROXANE (*appearing upon the threshold, followed by* RAGUENEAU *carrying a lantern, and* CHRISTIAN). What is it?

THE CAPUCHIN. A letter.

CHRISTIAN. What?

THE CAPUCHIN (*to* ROXANE). Oh, the contents can be only of a sacred character! It is from a worthy nobleman who...

ROXANE (*to* CHRISTIAN). It is from De Guiche!

CHRISTIAN. He dares to...?

ROXANE. Oh, he will not trouble me much longer! (*Opening the letter.*) I love you, and if... (*By the light of* RAGUENEAU'S *lantern she reads, aside, low.*) Mademoiselle: The drums are beating. My regiment is buckling on its corselet. It is about to leave. I am thought to have left already, but lag behind. I am disobeying you. I am in the convent here. I am coming to you, and send you word by a friar, silly as a sheep, who has no suspicion of the import of this letter. You smiled too sweetly upon me an hour ago: I must see you smile again. Provide to be alone, and deign graciously to receive the audacious worshipper, forgiven already, I can but hope, who signs himself your — etc.... (*To the* CAPUCHIN.) Father, this is what the letter tells me... Listen: (*All draw nearer; she reads aloud.*) Mademoiselle: The wishes of the cardinal may not be disregarded, however hard compliance with them prove. I have therefore chosen as bearer of this letter a most reverend, holy, and sagacious Capuchin; it is our wish that he should at once, in your own dwelling, pronounce the nuptial blessing over you. Christian must secretly become your husband. I send him to you. You dislike him. Bow to Heaven's will in resignation, and be sure that it will bless your zeal, and sure, likewise, mademoiselle, of the respect of him who is and will be ever your most humble and... etc.

THE CAPUCHIN (*beaming*). The worthy gentleman!... I knew it! You remember that I said so: The contents of that letter can be only of a sacred character!

ROXANE (*low, to* CHRISTIAN). I am a fluent reader, am I not?

CHRISTIAN. Hm!

ROXANE (*with feigned despair*). Ah... it is horrible!

THE CAPUCHIN (*who has turned the light of his lantern upon* CYRANO). You are the one?

CHRISTIAN. No, I am.

THE CAPUCHIN (*turning the light upon him, and as if his good looks aroused suspicion*). But...

ROXANE (*quickly*). Postscript: You will bestow upon the convent two hundred and fifty crowns.

THE CAPUCHIN. The worthy, worthy gentleman! (*To* ROXANE.) Be reconciled!

ROXANE (*with the expression of a martyr*). I will endeavor! (*While* RAGUENEAU *opens the door for the* CAPUCHIN, *whom* CHRISTIAN *is showing into the house,* ROXANE *says low to* CYRANO.) De Guiche is coming!... Keep him here! Do not let him enter until...

CYRANO. I understand! (*To the* CAPUCHIN.) How long will it take to marry them?

THE CAPUCHIN. A quarter of an hour.

CYRANO (*pushing all toward the house*). Go in! I shall be here!

ROXANE (*to* CHRISTIAN). Come! (*They go in.*)

CYRANO. How can I detain De Guiche for a quarter of an hour? (*He jumps upon the bench, climbs the wall toward the balcony-rail.*) So! ... I climb up here!... I know what I will do!... (*The theorbos play a melancholy tune.*) Ho, it is a man! (*The tune quavers lugubriously.*) Ho, ho, this time there is no mistake! (*He is on the balcony; he pulls the brim of his hat over his eyes, takes off his sword, wraps his cloak about him, and bends over the balcony-rail.*) No, it is not too far! (*He climbs over the balcony-rail, and reaching for a long bough that projects beyond the garden wall, holds on to it with both hands, ready to let himself drop.*) I shall make a slight commotion in the atmosphere!

DE GUICHE (*enters masked, groping in the dark*). What can that thrice-damned Capuchin be about?

CYRANO. The devil! if he should recognize my voice? (*Letting go with one hand, he makes show of turning a key.*) Cric! crac! (*Solemnly.*) Cyrano, resume the accent of Bergerac!

DE GUICHE (*looking at* ROXANE'S *house*). Yes, that is it. I can scarcely see. This mask bothers my eyes!

(*He is about to enter* ROXANE'S *house;* CYRANO *swings from the balcony, holding on to the bough, which bends and lets him down between the door and* DE GUICHE. *He intentionally drops very heavily, to give the effect of dropping from a great height, and lies flattened upon the ground, motionless, as if stunned.*)

DE GUICHE. What is it? (*When he looks up, the bough has swung into place; he sees nothing but the sky.*) Where did this man drop from?

CYRANO (*rising to a sitting posture*). From the moon!

DE GUICHE. From the...?

CYRANO (*in a dreamy voice*). What time is it?

DE GUICHE. Is he mad?

CYRANO. What time? What country? What day? What season?

DE GUICHE. But...

CYRANO. I am dazed!

DE GUICHE. Monsieur...

CYRANO. I have dropped from the moon like a bomb!

DE GUICHE (*impatiently*). What are you babbling about?

CYRANO (*rising, in a terrible voice*). I tell you I have dropped from the moon!

DE GUICHE (*backing a step*). Very well. You have dropped from the moon!... He is perhaps a lunatic!

CYRANO (*walking up close to him*). Not metaphorically, mind that!

DE GUICHE. But...

CYRANO. A hundred years ago, or else a minute, — for I have no conception how long I have been falling, — I was up there, in that saffron-colored ball!

DE GUICHE (*shrugging his shoulders*). You were. Now, let me pass!

CYRANO (*standing in his way*). Where am I? Be frank with me! Keep nothing from me! In what region, among what people, have I been shot like an aerolite?

DE GUICHE. I wish to pass!

CYRANO. While falling I could not choose my way, and have no notion where I have fallen! Is it upon a moon, or is it upon an earth, I have been dragged by my posterior weight?

DE GUICHE. I tell you, sir...

CYRANO (*with a scream of terror at which* DE GUICHE *starts backward a step*). Great God!... In this country men's faces are soot-black!

DE GUICHE (*lifting his hand to his face*). What does he mean?

CYRANO (*still terrified*). Am I in Algeria? Are you a native?...

DE GUICHE (*who has felt his mask*). Ah, my mask!

CYRANO (*pretending to be easier*). So I am in Venice!... Or am I in Genoa?

DE GUICHE (*attempting to pass*). A lady is expecting me!

CYRANO (*completely reassured*). Ah, then I am in Paris.

DE GUICHE (*smiling in spite of himself*). The rogue is not far from amusing!

CYRANO. Ah, you are laughing!

DE GUICHE. I laugh... but intend to pass!

CYRANO (*beaming*).   To think I should strike Paris!   (*Quite at his ease, laughing, brushing himself, bowing.*)   I arrived — pray, pardon my appearance! — by the last whirlwind.   I am rather unpresentable — Travel, you know!   My eyes are still full of star-dust. My spurs are clogged with bristles off a planet.   (*Appearing to pick something off his sleeve.*)   See, on my sleeve, a comet's hair!
(*He makes a feint of blowing it away.*)

DE GUICHE (*beside himself*).   Sir...

CYRANO (*as* DE GUICHE *is about to pass, stretching out his leg as if to show something on it, thereby stopping him*).   Embedded in my calf, I have brought back one of the Great Bear's teeth... and as, falling too near the Trident, I strained aside to clear one of its prongs, I landed sitting in Libra,... yes, one of the scales!... and now my weight is registered up there!   (*Quickly preventing* DE GUICHE *from passing, and taking hold of a button on his doublet.*)   And if, monsieur, you should take my nose between your fingers and compress it... milk would result!

DE GUICHE.   What are you saying?   Milk?...

CYRANO.   Of the Milky Way.

DE GUICHE.   Go to the devil!

CYRANO.   No!   I am sent from Heaven, literally.   (*Folding his arms.*)   Will you believe — I discovered it in passing — that Sirius at night puts on a night-cap?   (*Confidentially.*)   The lesser Bear is too little yet to bite.... (*Laughing.*)   I tumbled plump through Lyra, and snapped a string!... (*Magnificent.*)   But I intend setting all this down in a book, and the golden stars I have brought back caught in my shaggy mantle, when the book is printed, will be seen serving as asterisks!

DE GUICHE.   I have stood this long enough!   I want...

CYRANO.   I know perfectly what you want!

DE GUICHE.   Man...

CYRANO.   You want to know, from me, at first hand, what the moon is made of, and whether that monumental pumpkin is inhabited?

DE GUICHE (*shouting*).   Not in the very least!   I want...

CYRANO.   To know how I got there?   I got there by a method of my own invention.

DE GUICHE (*discouraged*). He is mad!... stark!

CYRANO (*disdainfully*). Do not imagine that I resorted to anything so absurd as Regiomontanus's eagle, or anything so lacking in enterprise as Archytas's pigeon!...

DE GUICHE. The madman is erudite...

CYRANO. I drew up nothing that had ever been thought of before! (DE GUICHE *has succeeded in getting past* CYRANO, *and is nearing* ROXANE'S *door;* CYRANO *follows him, ready to buttonhole him.*) I invented no less than six ways of storming the blue fort of Heaven!

DE GUICHE (*turning around*). Six, did you say?

CYRANO (*volubly*). One way was to stand naked in the sunshine, in a harness thickly studded with glass phials, each filled with morning dew. The sun in drawing up the dew, you see, could not have helped drawing me up too!

DE GUICHE (*surprised, taking a step toward* CYRANO). True. That is one!

CYRANO (*taking a step backward, with a view to drawing* DE GUICHE *away from the door*). Or else, I could have let the wind into a cedar coffer, then rarefied the imprisoned element by means of cunningly adjusted burning-glasses, and soared up with it!

DE GUICHE (*taking another step toward* CYRANO). Two!

CYRANO (*backing*). Or else, mechanic as well as artificer, I could have fashioned a giant grasshopper, with steel joints, which, impelled by successive explosions of saltpeter, would have hopped with me to the azure meadows where graze the starry flocks!

DE GUICHE (*unconsciously following* CYRANO, *and counting on his fingers*). That makes three!

CYRANO. Since smoke by its nature ascends, I could have blown into an appropriate globe a sufficient quantity to ascend with me!

DE GUICHE (*as above, more and more astonished*). Four!

CYRANO. Since Phœbe, the moon-goddess, when she is at wane, is greedy, O beeves! of your marrow,... with that marrow have I besmeared myself!

DE GUICHE (*amazed*). Five!

CYRANO (*who while talking has backed, followed by* DE GUICHE, *to the further side of the square, near a bench*). Or else, I could have placed myself upon an iron plate, have taken a magnet of suitable size, and thrown it in the air! That way is a very good one! The magnet flies upward, the iron instantly after; the magnet no sooner overtaken than you fling it up again.... The rest is clear! You can go upward indefinitely.

DE GUICHE. Six!... But here are six excellent methods! Which of the six, my dear sir, did you select?

CYRANO. A seventh!

DE GUICHE. Did you, indeed? And what was that?

CYRANO. I give you a hundred guesses!

DE GUICHE. I must confess that I should like to know!

CYRANO (*imitating the noise of the surf, and making great mysterious gestures*). Hoo-ish! hoo-ish!

DE GUICHE. Well! What is that?

CYRANO. Cannot you guess?

DE GUICHE. No!

CYRANO. The tide!... At the hour in which the moon attracts the deep, I lay down upon the sands, after a sea-bath... and, my head being drawn up first — the reason of this, you see, that the hair will hold a quantity of water in its mop! — I rose in the air, straight, beautifully straight, like an angel. I rose... I rose softly... without an effort... when, suddenly, I felt a shock. Then...

DE GUICHE (*lured on by curiosity, taking a seat on the bench*). Well,... then?

CYRANO. Then... (*resuming his natural voice.*) The time is up, monsieur, and I release you. They are married.

DE GUICHE (*getting to his feet with a leap*). I am dreaming or drunk! That voice? (*The door of* ROXANE's *house opens; lackeys appear carrying lighted candelabra.* CYRANO *removes his hat.*) And that nose!... Cyrano!

CYRANO (*bowing*). Cyrano. They have exchanged rings within the quarter of the hour.

DE GUICHE. Who have? (*He turns round. Tableau. Behind the lackey stand* ROXANE *and* CHRISTIAN *holding hands. The* CAPUCHIN *follows them smiling.* RAGUENEAU *holds high a flambeau. The* DUENNA *closes the procession, bewildered, in her bedgown.*) Heavens! (*To* ROXANE.) You! (*Recognizing* CHRISTIAN *with amazement.*) He? (*Bowing to* ROXANE.) Your astuteness compels my admiration! (*To* CYRANO.) My compliments to you, ingenious inventor of flying machines. Your experiences would have beguiled a saint on the threshold of Paradise! Make a note of them.... They can be used again, with profit, in a book!

CYRANO (*bowing*). I will confidently follow your advice.

THE CAPUCHIN (*to* DE GUICHE, *pointing at the lovers, and wagging his great white beard with satisfaction*). A beautiful couple, my son, brought together by you!

DE GUICHE (*eyeing him frigidly*). As you say! (*To* ROXANE.) And now proceed, Madame, to take leave of your husband.

ROXANE. What?

DE GUICHE (*to* CHRISTIAN). The regiment is on the point of starting. You are to join it!

ROXANE. To go to war?

DE GUICHE. Of course!

ROXANE. But the cadets are not going!

DE GUICHE. They are! (*Taking out the paper which he had put in his pocket.*) Here is the order. (*To* CHRISTIAN.) I beg you will take it to the Captain, baron, yourself.

ROXANE (*throwing herself in* CHRISTIAN's *arms*). Christian!

DE GUICHE (*to* CYRANO, *with a malignant laugh*). The wedding night is somewhat far as yet!

CYRANO (*aside*). He thinks that he is giving me great pain!

CHRISTIAN (*to* ROXANE). Oh, once more, dear!... Once more!

CYRANO. Be reasonable... Come!... Enough!

CHRISTIAN (*still clasping* ROXANE). Oh, it is hard to leave her.... You cannot know...

CYRANO (*trying to draw him away*). I know.

(*Drums are heard in the distance sounding a march.*)

DE GUICHE (*at the back*). The regiment is on its way!

ROXANE (*to* CYRANO, *while she clings to* CHRISTIAN *whom he is trying to draw away*). Oh!... I entrust him to your care! Promise that under no circumstance shall his life be placed in danger!

CYRANO. I will endeavor... but obviously cannot promise...

ROXANE (*same business*). Promise that he will be careful of himself!

CYRANO. I will do my best, but...

ROXANE (*as above*). That during this terrible siege he shall not take harm from the cold!

CYRANO. I will try, but...

ROXANE (*as above*).   That he will be true to me!

CYRANO. Of course, but yet, you see...

ROXANE (*as above*).   That he will write to me often!

CYRANO (*stopping*).   Ah, that... I promise freely!

CURTAIN

ACT FOURTH

THE GASCONY CADETS

The post occupied at the siege of Arras by the company of CARBON DE CASTEL-JALOUX. *At the back, across the whole stage, sloping earthwork. Beyond this is seen a plain stretching to the horizon; the country is covered with constructions relating to the siege. In the distance, against the sky, the outlines of the walls and roofs of Arras. Tents; scattered arms; drums, etc. It is shortly before sunrise. The East is yellow. Sentinels at even intervals. Camp-fires. The* GASCONY CADETS *lie asleep, rolled in their cloaks.* CARBON DE CASTEL-JALOUX *and* LE BRET *are watching. All are very pale and gaunt.* CHRISTIAN *lies sleeping among the others, in his military cape, in the foreground, his face lighted by one of the camp-fires. Silence.*

LE BRET. It is dreadful!

CARBON. Yes. Nothing left.

LE BRET. *Mordious!*

CARBON (*warning him by a gesture to speak lower*).   Curse in a whisper! You will wake them!... (*To the* CADETS.)   Hush! Go to sleep! (*To* LE BRET.)   Who sleeps dines.

LE BRET. Who lies awake misses two good things... What a situation!   (*A few shots are heard in the distance.*)

CARBON. The devil take their popping! They will wake my young ones!... (*To the* CADETS *who lift their heads.*)   Go to sleep!
                  (*The* CADETS *lie down again. Other shots are heard, nearer.*)

ONE OF THE CADETS (*stirring*).   The devil! Again?

CARBON. It is nothing. It is Cyrano getting home.
                          (*The heads which had started up, go down again.*)

A SENTINEL (*outside*). *Ventrebleu!* Who goes there?

CYRANO'S VOICE. Bergerac!

THE SENTINEL (*upon the embankment*). *Ventrebleu!* Who goes there?

CYRANO (*appearing at the top of the embankment*). Bergerac, blockhead! (*He comes down.* LE BRET *goes to him, uneasy.*)

LE BRET. Ah, thank God!

CYRANO (*warning him by a sign to wake no one*). Hush!

LE BRET. Wounded?

CYRANO. Do you not know that it has become a habit with them to miss me?

LE BRET. To me, it seems a little excessive that you should, every morning, for the sake of taking a letter, risk...

CYRANO (*stopping in front of* CHRISTIAN). I promised that he would write often. (*He looks at* CHRISTIAN.) He sleeps. He has grown pale. If the poor little girl could know that he is starving.... But handsome as ever!

LE BRET. Go at once and sleep.

CYRANO. Le Bret, do not grumble! Learn this: I nightly cross the Spanish lines at a point where I know beforehand every one will be drunk.

LE BRET. You ought some time to bring us back some victuals!

CYRANO. I must be lightly burdened to flit through!... But I know that there will be events before the evening. The French, unless I am much mistaken, will eat or die.

LE BRET. Oh, tell us!

CYRANO. No, I am not certain... You will see!

CARBON. What a shameful reversal of the order of things, that the besieger should be starved!

LE BRET. Alas! never was more complicated siege than this of Arras: We besieged Arras, and, caught in a trap, are ourselves besieged by the Cardinal-prince of Spain....

CYRANO. Some one now ought to come and besiege him.

LE BRET. I am not joking!

CYRANO. Oh, oh!

LE BRET. To think, ungrateful boy, that every day you risk a life precious as yours, solely to carry... (CYRANO *goes toward one of the tents.*) Where are you going?

CYRANO. I am going to write another.

> (*He lifts the canvas flap, and disappears in the tent.   Daybreak has brightened.   Rosy flush.   The city of Arras at the horizon catches a golden light.   The report of a cannon is heard, followed at once by a drum-call, very far away, at the left.   Other drums beat, nearer.   The drum-calls answer one another, come nearer, come very near, and go off, decreasing, dying in the distance, toward the right, having made the circuit of the camp.   Noise of general awakening. Voices of officers in the distance.*)

CARBON (*with a sigh*). The réveillé ... Ah, me! ... (*The* CADETS *stir in their cloaks, stretch.*) An end to the succulent slumbers! I know but too well what their first word will be!

ONE OF THE CADETS (*sitting up*). I am famished!

OTHER CADET. I believe I am dying!

ALL. Oh!...

CARBON. Get up!

THIRD CADET. I cannot go a step!

FOURTH CADET. I have not strength to stir!

FIRST CADET (*looking at himself in a bit of armor*). My tongue is coated: it must be the weather that is indigestible!

OTHER CADET. Any one who wants them, can have all my titles of nobility for a Chester cheese... or part of one!

OTHER CADET. If my stomach does not have something put into it to take up the attention of my gastric juice, I shall retire into my tent before long... like Achilles!

OTHER CADET. Yes, they ought to provide us with bread!

CARBON (*going to the tent into which* CYRANO *has retired; low*). Cyrano!

OTHER CADETS. We cannot stand this much longer!

CARBON (*as above, at the door of the tent*). To the rescue, Cyrano! You who succeed so well always in cheering them, come and make them pluck up spirits!

SECOND CADET (*falling upon* FIRST CADET *who is chewing something*). What are you chewing, man?

FIRST CADET. A bit of gun-tow fried in axle-grease... using a burganet as frying pan. The suburbs of Arras are not precisely rich in game....

OTHER CADET (*entering*). I have been hunting!

OTHER CADET (*the same*). I have been fishing!

ALL (*rising and falling upon the newcomers*). What? — what did you catch? — A pheasant? — A carp? — Quick! quick!... Let us see!

THE HUNTSMAN. A sparrow!

THE ANGLER. A gudgeon!

ALL (*exasperated*). Enough of this! Let us revolt!

CARBON. To the rescue, Cyrano! (*It is now broad daylight.*)

CYRANO (*coming out of the tent, tranquil, a pen behind his ear, a book in his hand*). What is the matter? (*Silence. To* FIRST CADET.) Why do you go off like that, with that slouching gait?

THE CADET. I have something away down in my heels which inconveniences me.

CYRANO. And what is that?

THE CADET. My stomach.

CYRANO. That is where mine is, too.

THE CADET. Then you too must be inconvenienced.

CYRANO. No. The size of the hollow within me merely increases my sense of my size.

SECOND CADET. I happen to have teeth, long ones!

CYRANO. The better will you bite... in good time!

THIRD CADET. I reverberate like a drum!

CYRANO. You will be of use... to sound the charge!

OTHER CADET. I have a buzzing in my ears!

CYRANO. A mistake. Empty belly, no ears. You hear no buzzing.

OTHER CADET. Ah, a trifling article to eat... and a little oil upon it!

CYRANO (*taking off the* CADET's *morion and placing it in his hand*). That is seasoned.

OTHER CADET. What is there we could devour?

CYRANO (*tossing him the book he has been holding*). Try the Iliad!

OTHER CADET. The minister, in Paris, makes his four meals a day!

CYRANO. You feel it remiss in him not to send you a bit of partridge?

THE SAME. Why should he not? And some wine!

CYRANO. Richelieu, some Burgundy, if you please?

THE SAME. He might, by one of his Capuchins!

CYRANO. By his Eminence, perhaps, in sober gray?

OTHER CADET. No ogre was ever so hungry!

CYRANO. You may have your fill yet of humble-pie!

FIRST CADET (*shrugging his shoulders*). Forever jests!... puns!... *mots!*

CYRANO. *Le mot* forever, indeed! And I would wish to die, on a fine evening, under a rose-flushed sky, delivering myself of a good *mot* in a good cause!... Ah, yes, the best were indeed, far from fever-bed and potion, pierced with the only noble weapon, by an adversary worthy of oneself, to fall upon a glorious field, the point of a sword through his heart, the point of a jest on his lips!...

ALL (*in a wail*). I am hungry!

CYRANO (*folding his arms*). God ha' mercy! can you think of nothing but eating?... Come here, Bertrandou the fifer, once the shepherd! Take from the double case one of your fifes: breathe into it, play to this pack of guzzlers and of gluttons our homely melodies, of haunting rhythm, every note of which appeals like a little sister, through whose every strain are heard strains of beloved voices... mild melodies whose slowness brings to mind the slowness of the smoke upcurling from our native hamlet hearths... melodies that seem to speak to a man in his native dialect!... (*The old fifer sits down and makes ready his fife.*) Today let the fife, martial unwillingly, be reminded, while your fingers upon its slender stem flutter like birds in a delicate minuet, that before being ebony it was reed; surprise itself by what you make it sing, ... let it feel restored to it the soul of its youth, rustic and peaceable! (*The old man begins playing Languedoc tunes.*) Listen, Gascons! It is no more, beneath his fingers, the shrill fife of the camp, but the soft flute of the woodland! It is no more, between his lips, the whistling note of battle, but the lowly lay of goatherds leading their flocks to feed!... Hark!... It sings of the valley, the heath, the forest!... of the little shepherd, sunburned under his crimson cap!... the green delight of evening on the river!... Hark, Gascons all! It sings of Gascony!

(*Every head has drooped; all eyes have grown dreamy; tears are furtively brushed away with a sleeve, the hem of a cloak.*)

CARBON (*to* CYRANO, *low*). You are making them weep!

CYRANO. With homesickness!... a nobler pain than hunger... not physical: mental! I am glad the seat of their suffering should have removed... that the gripe should now afflict their hearts!

CARBON. But you weaken them, making them weep!

CYRANO (*beckoning to a drummer*). Never fear! The hero in their veins is quickly roused. It is enough to...

(*He signs to the drummer who begins drumming.*)

ALL (*starting to their feet and snatching up their arms*). Hein?... What?
... What is it?

CYRANO (*smiling*). You see?... The sound of the drum was enough!
Farewell dreams, regrets, old homestead, love... What comes
with the fife with the drum may go...

ONE OF THE CADETS (*looking off at the back*). Ah! ah!... Here comes
Monsieur de Guiche!

ALL THE CADETS (*grumbling*). Hoo...

CYRANO (*smiling*). Flattering murmur...

ONE OF THE CADETS. He bores us!...

OTHER CADET. Showing himself off, with his broad point collar on
top of his armor!...

OTHER CADET. As if lace were worn with steel!

FIRST CADET. Convenient, if you have a boil on your neck to cover...

SECOND CADET. There is another courtier for you!

OTHER CADET. His uncle's own nephew!

CARBON. He is a Gascon, nevertheless!

FIRST CADET. Not genuine!... Never trust him. For a Gascon,
look you, must be something of a madman: nothing is so deadly
to deal with as a Gascon who is completely rational!

LE BRET. He is pale!

OTHER CADET. He is hungry, as hungry as any poor devil of us!
But his corselet being freely embellished with gilt studs, his
stomach-ache is radiant in the sun!

CYRANO (*eagerly*). Let us not appear to suffer, either! You, your
cards, your pipes, your dice... (*All briskly set themselves to playing
with cards and dice, on the heads of drums, on stools, on cloaks spread over
the ground. They light long tobacco pipes.*) And I will be reading
Descartes....

> (*He walks to and fro, forward and backward, reading a small book
> which he has taken from his pocket. Tableau.*)

(*Enter* DE GUICHE. *Every one appears absorbed and satisfied.* DE GUICHE
is very pale. He goes toward CARBON.)

DE GUICHE (*to* CARBON). Ah, good-morning. (*They look at each
other attentively. Aside, with satisfaction.*) He is pale as plaster.

CARBON (*same business*). His eyes are all that is left of him.

DE GUICHE (*looking at the* CADETS). So here are the wrongheaded rascals?... Yes, gentlemen, it is reported to me on every side that I am your scoff and derision; that the cadets, highland nobility, Béarn clodhoppers, Périgord baronets, cannot express sufficient contempt for their colonel; call me intriguer, courtier, find it irksome to their taste that I should wear, with my cuirass, a collar of Genoese point, and never cease to air their wondering indignation that a man should be a Gascon without being a vagabond! (*Silence. The* CADETS *continue smoking and playing.*) Shall I have you punished by your captain?... I do not like to.

CARBON. Did you otherwise, however,... I am free, and punish only...

DE GUICHE. Ah?...

CARBON. My company is paid by myself, belongs to me. I obey no orders but such as relate to war.

DE GUICHE. Ah, is it so? Enough, then. I will treat your taunts with simple scorn. My fashion of deporting myself under fire is well known. You are not unaware of the manner in which yesterday, at Bapaume, I forced back the columns of the Comte de Bucquoi; gathering my men together to plunge forward like an avalanche, three times I charged him....

CYRANO (*without lifting his nose from his book*). And your white scarf?

DE GUICHE (*surprised and self-satisfied*). You heard of that circumstance?... In fact, it happened that as I was wheeling about to collect my men for the third charge, I was caught in a stream of fugitives which bore me onward to the edge of the enemy. I was in danger of being captured and cut off with an arquebuse, when I had the presence of mind to untie and let slip to the ground the white scarf which proclaimed my military grade. Thus was I enabled, undistinguished, to withdraw from among the Spaniards, and thereupon returning with my reinspirited men, to defeat them. Well?... What do you say to the incident?

(*The* CADETS *have appeared not to be listening; at this point, however, hands with cards and dice-boxes remain suspended in the air; no pipe-smoke is ejected; all express expectation.*)

CYRANO. That never would Henry the Fourth, however great the number of his opponents, have consented to diminish his presence by the size of his white plume.

(*Silent joy. Cards fall, dice rattle, smoke upwreathes.*)

DE GUICHE. The trick was successful, however!

> (*As before, expectation suspends gambling and smoking.*)

CYRANO. Very likely. But one should not resign the honor of being a target. (*Cards, dice, smoke, fall, rattle, and upwreathe, as before, in expression of increasing glee.*) Had I been at hand when you allowed your scarf to drop — the quality of our courage, monsieur, shows different in this — I would have picked it up and worn it....

DE GUICHE. Ah, yes — more of your Gascon bragging!...

CYRANO. Bragging?... Lend me the scarf. I engage to mount, ahead of all, to the assault, wearing it crosswise upon my breast!

DE GUICHE. A Gascon's offer, that too! You know that the scarf was left in the enemy's camp, by the banks of the Scarpe, where bullets since then have hailed... whence no one can bring it back!

CYRANO (*taking a white scarf from his pocket and handing it to DE GUICHE*). Here it is.

> (*Silence. The CADETS smother their laughter behind cards and in dice-boxes. DE GUICHE turns around, looks at them; instantly they become grave; one of them, with an air of unconcern, whistles the tune played earlier by the fifer.*)

DE GUICHE (*taking the scarf*). I thank you. I shall be able with this shred of white to make a signal... which I was hesitating to make.... (*He goes to the top of the bank and waves the scarf.*)

ALL. What now?... What is this?

THE SENTINEL (*at the top of the bank*). A man... over there... running off...

DE GUICHE (*coming forward again*). It is a supposed Spanish spy. He is very useful to us. The information he carries to the enemy is that which I give him — so that their decisions are influenced by us.

CYRANO. He is a scoundrel!!

DE GUICHE (*coolly tying on his scarf*). He is a convenience. We were saying?... Ah, I was about to tell you. Last night, having resolved upon a desperate stroke to obtain supplies, the Marshal secretly set out for Dourlens. The royal sutlers are encamped there. He expects to join them by way of the tilled fields; but, to provide against interference, he took with him troops in such number that, certainly, if we were now attacked, the enemy would find easy work. Half of the army is absent from the camp.

CARBON. If the Spaniards knew that, it might be serious. But they do not know.

DE GUICHE. They do. And are going to attack us.

CARBON. Ah!

DE GUICHE. My pretended spy came to warn me of their intention. He said, moreover: I can direct the attack. At what point shall it be? I will lead them to suppose it the least strong, and they will centre their efforts against it. I answered: Very well. Go from the camp. Look down the line. Let them attack at the point I signal from.

CARBON (*to the* CADETS). Gentlemen, get ready!

(*All get up. Noise of swords and belts being buckled on.*)

DE GUICHE. They will be here in an hour.

FIRST CADET. Oh!... if there is a whole hour!...

(*All sit down again, and go on with their games.*)

DE GUICHE (*to* CARBON). The main object is to gain time. The Marshal is on his way back.

CARBON. And to gain time?

DE GUICHE. You will be so obliging as to keep them busy killing you.

CYRANO. Ah, this is your revenge!

DE GUICHE. I will not pretend that if I had been fond of you, I would have thus singled out you and yours; but, as your bravery is unquestionably beyond that of others, I am serving my King at the same time as my inclination.

CYRANO. Suffer me, monsieur, to express my gratitude.

DE GUICHE. I know that you affect fighting one against a hundred. You will not complain of lacking opportunity.

(*He goes toward the back with* CARBON.)

CYRANO (*to the* CADETS). We shall now be able, gentlemen, to add to the Gascon escutcheon, which bears, as it is, six chevrons, or and azure, the chevron that was wanting to complete it — blood-red!

(DE GUICHE *at the back speaks low with* CARBON. *Orders are given. All is made ready to repel an attack.* CYRANO *goes toward* CHRISTIAN, *who stands motionless, with folded arms.*)

CYRANO (*laying his hand on* CHRISTIAN's *shoulder*). Christian?

CHRISTIAN (*shaking his head*). Roxane!

CYRANO. Ah me!

CHRISTIAN. I wish I might at least put my whole heart's last blessing in a beautiful letter!

CYRANO. I mistrusted that it would come today... (*he takes a letter from his doublet*) and I have written your farewells.

CHRISTIAN. Let me see!

CYRANO. You wish to see it?...

CHRISTIAN (*taking the letter*). Yes! (*He opens the letter, begins to read, stops short.*) Ah?...

CYRANO. What?

CHRISTIAN. That little round blister?

CYRANO (*hurriedly taking back the letter, and looking at it with an artless air*). A blister?

CHRISTIAN. It is a tear!

CYRANO. It looks like one, does it not?... A poet, you see, is sometimes caught in his own snare — that is what constitutes the interest, the charm!... This letter, you must know, is very touching. In writing it I apparently made myself shed tears.

CHRISTIAN. Shed tears?...

CYRANO. Yes, because... well, to die is not terrible at all... but never to see her again,... never!... that, you know, is horrible beyond all thinking.... And, things having taken the turn they have, I shall not see her... (CHRISTIAN *looks at him*) we shall not see her... (*hastily*) you will not see her....

CHRISTIAN (*snatching the letter from him*). Give me the letter!

(*Noise in the distance.*)

VOICE OF A SENTINEL. *Ventrebleu*, who goes there?

(*Shots. Noise of voices, tinkling of bells.*)

CARBON. What is it?

THE SENTINEL (*on the top of the bank*). A coach! (*All run to see.*) (*Noisy exclamations.*) What? — In the camp? — It is driving into the camp! — It comes from the direction of the enemy! — The devil! Fire upon it! — No! the coachman is shouting something! — What does he say? — He shouts: Service of the King!

DE GUICHE. What? Service of the King?

(*All come down from the bank and fall into order.*)

CARBON. Hats off, all!

DE GUICHE (*at the corner*). Service of the King! Stand back, low rabble, and give it room to turn around with a handsome sweep!

(*The coach comes in at a trot. It is covered with mud and dust. The curtains are drawn. Two lackeys behind. It comes to a standstill.*)

CARBON (*shouting*). Salute! (*Drums roll. All the* CADETS *uncover.*)

DE GUICHE. Let down the steps!

(*Two men hurry forward. The coach door opens.*)

ROXANE (*stepping from the carriage*). Good-morning!

(*At the sound of a feminine voice, all the men, in the act of bowing low, straighten themselves. Consternation.*)

DE GUICHE. Service of the King! You?

ROXANE. Of the only King!... of Love!

CYRANO. Ah, great God!

CHRISTIAN (*rushing to her*). You! Why are you here?

ROXANE. This siege lasted too long!

CHRISTIAN. Why have you come?

ROXANE. I will tell you!

CYRANO (*who at the sound of her voice has started, then stood motionless without venturing to look her way*). God!... can I trust myself to look at her?

DE GUICHE. You cannot remain here.

ROXANE. But I can — I can, indeed! Will you favor me with a drum? (*She seats herself upon a drum brought forward for her.*) There! I thank you! (*She laughs.*) They fired upon my carriage. (*Proudly.*) A patrol! — It does look rather as if it were made out of a pumpkin, does it not? like Cinderella's coach! and the footmen made out of rats! (*Blowing a kiss to* CHRISTIAN.) How do you do? (*Looking at them all.*) You do not look overjoyed!... Arras is a long way from Paris, do you know it? (*Catching sight of* CYRANO.) Cousin, delighted!

CYRANO (*coming toward her*). But how did you...?

ROXANE. How did I find the army? Dear me, cousin, that was simple: I followed straight along the line of devastation.... Ah, I should never have believed in such horrors had I not seen them! Gentlemen, if that is the service of your King, I like mine better!

CYRANO. But this is mad!... By what way did you come?

ROXANE. Way?... I drove through the Spaniards' camp.

FIRST CADET. Ah, what will keep lovely woman from her way!

DE GUICHE. But how did you contrive to get through their lines?

LE BRET. That must have been difficult...

ROXANE. No, not very. I simply drove through them, in my coach, at a trot. If a hidalgo, with arrogant front, showed likely to stop us, I put my face at the window, wearing my sweetest smile, and, those gentlemen being — let the French not grudge my saying so! — the most gallant in the world.... I passed!

CARBON. Such a smile is a passport, certainly!... But you must have been not unfrequently bidden to stand and deliver where you were going?

ROXANE. Not unfrequently, you are right. Whereupon I would say, "I am going to see my lover!" At once, the fiercest looking Spaniard of them all would gravely close my carriage door; and, with a gesture the King might emulate, motion aside the musket-barrels levelled at me; and, superb at once for grace and haughtiness, bringing his spurs together, and lifting his plumed hat, bow low and say, "Pass, señorita, pass!"

CHRISTIAN. But, Roxane...

ROXANE. I said, "My lover!" yes, forgive me! — You see, if I had said, "My husband!" they would never have let me by!

CHRISTIAN. But...

ROXANE. What troubles you?

DE GUICHE. You must leave at once.

ROXANE. I?

CYRANO. At once!

LE BRET. As fast as you can.

CHRISTIAN. Yes, you must.

ROXANE. But why?

CHRISTIAN (*embarrassed*). Because...

CYRANO (*embarrassed too*). In three quarters of an hour...

DE GUICHE (*the same*). Or an hour...

CARBON (*the same*). You had much better...

LE BRET (*the same*). You might...

ROXANE. I shall remain. You are going to fight.

ALL. Oh, no!... No!

ROXANE. He is my husband!   (*She throws herself in* CHRISTIAN'S *arms.*)   Let me be killed with you!

CHRISTIAN. How your eyes shine!

ROXANE. I will tell you why they shine!

DE GUICHE (*desperately*). It is a post of horrible probabilities!

ROXANE (*turning toward him*). What — of horrible?...

CYRANO. In proof of which he appointed us to it!...

ROXANE. Ah, you wish me made a widow?

DE GUICHE. I swear to you...

ROXANE. No! Now I have lost all regard.... Now I will surely not go.... Besides, I think it fun!

CYRANO. What? The précieuse contained a heroine?

ROXANE. Monsieur de Bergerac, I am a cousin of yours!

ONE OF THE CADETS. Never think but that we will take good care of you!

ROXANE (*more and more excited*). I am sure you will, my friends!

OTHER CADET. The whole camp smells of iris!

ROXANE. By good fortune I put on a hat that will look well in battle! (*Glancing toward* DE GUICHE.) But perhaps it is time the Count should go. — The battle might begin.

DE GUICHE. Ah, it is intolerable! — I am going to inspect my guns, and coming back. — You still have time: think better of it!

ROXANE. Never!   (*Exit* DE GUICHE.)

CHRISTIAN (*imploring*). Roxane!

ROXANE. No!

FIRST CADET. She is going to stay!

ALL (*hurrying about, pushing one another, snatching things from one another*). A comb! — Soap! — My jacket is torn, a needle! — A ribbon! — Lend me your pocket-mirror! — My cuffs! — Curling-irons! — A razor!

ROXANE (*to* CYRANO, *who is still pleading with her*). No! Nothing shall prevail upon me to stir from this spot!

CARBON (*after having, like the others, tightened his belt, dusted himself, brushed his hat, straightened his feather, pulled down his cuffs, approaches* ROXANE, *and ceremoniously*). It is, perhaps, proper, since you are going to stay, that I should present to you a few of the gentlemen about to have the honor of dying in your presence... (ROXANE *bows, and stands waiting, with her arm through* CHRISTIAN'S.)
Baron Peyrescous de Colignac!

THE CADET (*bowing*). Madame!

CARBON (*continuing to present the* CADETS). Baron de Casterac de Cahuzac — Vidame de Malgouyre Estressac Lesbas d'Escara-biot — Chevalier d'Antignac-Juzet — Baron Hillot de Blagnac-Saléchan de Castel Crabioules...

ROXANE. But how many names have you apiece?

BARON HILLOT. Innumerable!

CARBON (*to* ROXANE). Open your hand with the handkerchief!

ROXANE (*opens her hand; the handkerchief drops*). Why?

       (*The whole company starts forward to pick it up.*)

CARBON (*instantly catching it*). My company had no flag! Now, my word, it will have the prettiest one in the army!

ROXANE (*smiling*). It is rather small!

CARBON (*fastening the handkerchief on the staff of his captain's spear*). But it is lace!

ONE OF THE CADETS (*to the others*). I could die without a murmur, having looked upon that beautiful face, if I had so much as a walnut inside me!...

CARBON (*who has overheard, indignant*). Shame!... to talk of food when an exquisite woman...

ROXANE. But the air of the camp is searching, and I myself am hungry: Patties, jellied meat, light wine... are what I should like best! Will you kindly bring me some? (*Consternation.*)

ONE OF THE CADETS. Bring you some?

OTHER CADET. And where, great God, shall we get them?

ROXANE (*quietly*). In my coach.

ALL. What?

ROXANE. But there is much to be done, carving and boning and serving. Look more closely at my coachman, gentlemen, and you will recognize a precious individual: the sauces, if we wish, can be warmed over...

THE CADETS (*springing toward the coach*). It is Ragueneau! (*Cheers.*) Oh! Oh!

ROXANE (*watching them*). Poor fellows!

CYRANO (*kissing her hand*). Kind fairy!

RAGUENEAU (*standing upon the box-seat like a vender at a public fair*). Gentlemen! (*Enthusiasm.*)

THE CADETS. Bravo! Bravo!

RAGUENEAU. How should the Spaniards, when so much beauty passed, suspect the repast? (*Applause.*)

CYRANO (*low to* CHRISTIAN). Hm! Hm! Christian!

RAGUENEAU. Absorbed in gallantry, no heed took they... (*he takes a dish from the box-seat*) ... of galantine!

(*Applause. The galantine is passed from hand to hand.*)

CYRANO (*low to* CHRISTIAN). A word with you....

RAGUENEAU. Venus kept their eyes fixed upon herself, while Diana slipped past with the... (*he brandishes a joint*) game!

(*Enthusiasm. The joint is seized by twenty hands at once.*)

CYRANO (*low to* CHRISTIAN). I must speak with you.

ROXANE (*to the* CADETS *who come forward, their arms full of provisions*). Spread it all upon the ground!

(*Assisted by the two imperturbable footmen who were on the back of the coach, she arranges everything on the grass.*)

ROXANE (*to* CHRISTIAN *whom* CYRANO *is trying to draw aside*). Make yourself useful, sir!

(CHRISTIAN *comes and helps her.* CYRANO *gives evidence of uneasiness.*)

RAGUENEAU. A truffled peacock!

FIRST CADET (*radiant, comes forward cutting off a large slice of ham*). Praise the pigs, we shall not go to our last fight with nothing in our b... (*correcting himself at sight of* ROXANE) hm... stomachs!

RAGUENEAU (*flinging the carriage cushions*). The cushions are stuffed with snipe!

(*Tumult. The cushions are ripped open. Laughter. Joy.*)

RAGUENEAU (*flinging bottles of red wine*). Molten ruby! (*Bottles of white wine.*) Fluid topaz!

ROXANE (*throwing a folded tablecloth to* CYRANO). Unfold the cloth: Hey!... be nimble!

RAGUENEAU (*waving one of the coach lanterns*). Each lantern is a little larder!

CYRANO (*low to* CHRISTIAN, *while together they spread the cloth*). I must speak with you before you speak with her...

RAGUENEAU. The handle of my whip, behold, is a sausage!

ROXANE (*pouring wine, dispensing it*). Since we are the ones to be killed, *morbleu*, we will not fret ourselves about the rest of the army! Everything for the Gascons!... And if De Guiche comes, nobody must invite him! (*Going from one to the other.*) Gently! You have time... You must not eat so fast! There, drink. What are you crying about?

FIRST CADET. It is too good!

ROXANE. Hush! White wine or red? — Bread for Monsieur de Carbon! — A knife! — Pass your plate! — You prefer crust? — A little more? — Let me help you. — Champagne? — A wing?—

CYRANO (*following* ROXANE, *his hands full of dishes, helping her*). I adore her!

ROXANE (*going to* CHRISTIAN). What will you take?

CHRISTIAN. Nothing!

ROXANE. Oh, but you must take something! This biscuit — in a little Muscatel — just a little?

CHRISTIAN (*trying to keep her from going*). Tell me what made you come?

ROXANE. I owe myself to those poor fellows... Be patient,... By and by...

LE BRET (*who had gone toward the back to pass a loaf of bread on the end of a pike to the* SENTINEL *upon the earthwork*). De Guiche!

CYRANO. Presto! Vanish basket, flagon, platter and pan! Hurry! Let us look as if nothing were! (*To* RAGUENEAU.) Take a flying leap on to your box! — Is everything hidden?

    (*In a wink, all the eatables have been pushed into the tents, or hidden under clothes, cloaks, hats.*)

(*Enter* DE GUICHE, *hurriedly; he stops short, sniffing the air. Silence.*)

DE GUICHE. What a good smell!

ONE OF THE CADETS (*singing, with effect of mental abstraction*). To lo lo lo....

DE GUICHE (*stopping and looking at him closely*). What is the matter with you — you, there? You are red as a crab.

THE CADET. I? Nothing... It is just my blood.... We are going to fight: it tells...

OTHER CADET. Poom... poom... poom...

DE GUICHE (*turning*). What is this?

THE CADET (*slightly intoxicated*). Nothing... A song... just a little song.

DE GUICHE. You look in good spirits, my boy!

THE CADET. Danger affects me that way!

DE GUICHE (*calling* CARBON DE CASTEL-JALOUX *to give an order*). Captain, I... (*He stops at sight of his face.*) *Peste!* You look in good spirits, too.

CARBON (*flushed, holding a bottle behind him; with an evasive gesture*). Oh!...

DE GUICHE. I had a cannon left over, which I have ordered them to place (*he points in the wing*) there, in that corner, and which your men can use, if necessary...

ONE OF THE CADETS (*swaying from one foot to the other*). Charming attention!

OTHER CADET (*smiling sugarily*). Our thanks for your gracious thoughtfulness!

DE GUICHE. Have they gone mad?... (*Drily.*) As you are not accustomed to handling a cannon, look out for its kicking...

FIRST CADET. Ah, pfft!...

DE GUICHE (*going toward him, furious*). But...

THE CADET. A cannon knows better than to kick a Gascon!

DE GUICHE (*seizing him by the arm and shaking him*). You are all tipsy: on what?

THE CADET (*magnificently*). The smell of powder!

DE GUICHE (*shrugs his shoulders, pushes aside the* CADET, *and goes rapidly toward* ROXANE). Quick, Madame! what have you condescended to decide?

ROXANE. I remain.

DE GUICHE. Retire, I beseech you!

ROXANE. No.

DE GUICHE. If you are determined, then... Let me have a musket!

CARBON. What do you mean?

DE GUICHE. I, too, will remain.

CYRANO. At last, monsieur, an instance of pure and simple bravery!

FIRST CADET. Might you be a Gascon, lace collar notwithstanding?

DE GUICHE. I do not leave a woman in danger.

SECOND CADET (*to* FIRST CADET). Look here! I think he might be given something to eat! (*All the food reappears, as if by magic.*)

DE GUICHE (*his eyes brightening*). Provisions?

THIRD CADET. Under every waistcoat!

DE GUICHE (*mastering himself, haughtily*). Do you imagine that I will eat your leavings?

CYRANO (*bowing*). You are improving!

DE GUICHE (*proudly, falling at the last of the sentence into a slightly* GASCON *accent*). I will fight before I eat!

FIRST CADET (*exultant*). Fight! Eat!... He spoke with an accent!

DE GUICHE (*laughng*). I did?

THE CADET. He is one of us! (*All fall to dancing.*)

CARBON (*who a moment before disappeared behind the earthworks, reappearing at the top*). I have placed my pikemen. They are a determined troop...

(*He points at a line of pikes projecting above the bank.*)

DE GUICHE (*to* ROXANE, *bowing*). Will you accept my hand and pass them in review?

(*She takes his hand; they go toward the bank. Every one uncovers and follows.*)

CHRISTIAN (*going to* CYRANO, *quickly*). Speak! Be quick!

(*As* ROXANE *appears at the top of the bank, the pikes disappear, lowered in a salute, and a cheer goes up;* ROXANE *bows.*)

PIKEMEN (*outside*). · Vivat!

CHRISTIAN. What did you want to tell me?

CYRANO. In case Roxane...

CHRISTIAN. Well?

CYRANO. Should speak to you of the letters...

CHRISTIAN. Yes, the letters. I know!

CYRANO. Do not commit the blunder of appearing surprised...

CHRISTIAN. At what?

CYRANO. I must tell you ... It is quite simple, and merely comes into my mind today because I see her. You have...

CHRISTIAN. Hurry!

CYRANO. You... you have written to her oftener than you suppose...

CHRISTIAN. Oh, have I?

CYRANO. Yes. It was my business, you see. I had undertaken to interpret your passion, and sometimes I wrote without having told you I should write.

CHRISTIAN. Ah?

CYRANO. It is very simple.

CHRISTIAN. But how did you succeed since we have been so closely surrounded, in...?

CYRANO. Oh, before daybreak I could cross the lines...

CHRISTIAN (*folding his arms*). Ah, that is very simple, too?... And how many times a week have I been writing? Twice? Three times? Four?...

CYRANO. More.

CHRISTIAN. Every day?

CYRANO. Yes, every day... twice.

CHRISTIAN (*violently*). And you cared so much about it that you were willing to brave death....

CYRANO (*seeing* ROXANE *who returns*). Be still... Not before her!

(*He goes quickly into his tent.* CADETS *come and go at the back.* CARBON *and* DE GUICHE *give orders.*)

ROXANE (*running to* CHRISTIAN). And now, Christian...

CHRISTIAN (*taking her hands*). And now, you shall tell me why, over these fearful roads, through these ranks of rough soldiery, you risked your dear self to join me?

ROXANE. Because of the letters!

CHRISTIAN. The...? What did you say?

ROXANE. It is through your fault that I have been exposed to such and so many dangers. It is your letters that have gone to my head! Ah, think how many you have written me in a month, each one more beautiful...

CHRISTIAN. What?... Because of a few little love letters...

ROXANE. Say nothing! You cannot understand! Listen: The truth is that I took to idolizing you one evening, when, below my window, in a voice I did not know before, your soul began to reveal itself.... Think then what the effect should be of your letters, which have been like your voice heard constantly for one month, your voice of that evening, so tender, caressing... You must bear it as you can, I have come to you! Prudent Penelope would not have stayed at home with her eternal tapestry, if Ulysses, her lord, had written as you write... but, impulsive as Helen, have tossed aside her yarns, and flown to join him!

CHRISTIAN. But...

ROXANE. I read them, I re-read them, in reading I grew faint... I became your own indeed! Each fluttering leaf was like a petal of your soul wafted to me... In every word of those letters, love is felt as a flame would be felt — love, compelling, sincere, profound...

CHRISTIAN. Ah, sincere, profound?... You say that it can be felt, Roxane?

ROXANE. He asks me!

CHRISTIAN. And so you came?...

ROXANE. I came — oh Christian, my own, my master! If I were to kneel at your feet you would lift me, I know. It is my soul therefore which kneels, and never can you lift it from that posture! — I came to implore your pardon — as it is fitting, for we are both perhaps about to die! — your pardon for having done you the wrong, at first, in my shallowness, of loving you... for mere looking!

CHRISTIAN (*in alarm*). Ah, Roxane!...

ROXANE. Later, dear one, grown less shallow — similar to a bird which flutters before it can fly — your gallant exterior appealing to me still, but your soul appealing equally, I loved you for both!...

CHRISTIAN. And now?

ROXANE. Now at last yourself are vanquished by yourself: I love you for your soul alone...

CHRISTIAN (*drawing away*). Ah, Roxane!

ROXANE. Rejoice! For to be loved for that wherewith we are clothed so fleetingly must put a noble heart to torture.... Your dear thought at last casts your dear face in shadow: the harmonious lineaments whereby at first you pleased me, I do not see them, now my eyes are open!

CHRISTIAN. Oh!

ROXANE. You question your own triumph?

CHRISTIAN (*sorrowfully*). Roxane!

ROXANE. I understand, you cannot conceive of such a love in me?

CHRISTIAN. I do not wish to be loved like that! I wish to be loved quite simply...

ROXANE. For that which other women till now have loved in you? Ah, let yourself be loved in a better way.

CHRISTIAN. No... I was happier before!...

ROXANE. Ah, you do not understand! It is now that I love you

most, that I truly love you. It is that which makes you, you —
can you not grasp it? — that I worship... And did you no longer
walk our earth like a young martial Apollo...

CHRISTIAN. Say no more!

ROXANE. Still would I love you!... Yes, though a blight should
have fallen upon your face and form...

CHRISTIAN. Do not say it!

ROXANE. But I do say it,... I do!

CHRISTIAN. What? If I were ugly, distinctly, offensively?

ROXANE. If you were ugly, dear, I swear it!

CHRISTIAN. God!

ROXANE. And you are glad, profoundly glad?

CHRISTIAN (*in a smothered voice*). Yes...

ROXANE. What is it?

CHRISTIAN (*pushing her gently away*). Nothing. I have a word or
two to say to some one: your leave, for a second...

ROXANE. But...

CHRISTIAN (*pointing at a group of* CADETS *at the back*). In my selfish
love, I have kept you from those poor brothers.... Go, smile on
them a little, before they die, dear... go!

ROXANE (*moved*). Dear Christian!

(*She goes toward the* GASCONS *at the back; they respectfully gather
around her.*)

CHRISTIAN (*calling toward* CYRANO'S *tent*). Cyrano!

CYRANO (*appears, armed for battle*). What is it?... How pale you are!

CHRISTIAN. She does not love me any more!

CYRANO. What do you mean?

CHRISTIAN. She loves you.

CYRANO. No!

CHRISTIAN. She only loves my soul!

CYRANO. No!

CHRISTIAN. Yes! Therefore it is you she loves... and you love
her...

CYRANO. I...

CHRISTIAN. I know it!

CYRANO. It is true.

CHRISTIAN. To madness!

CYRANO. More.

CHRISTIAN. Tell her then.

CYRANO. No!

CHRISTIAN. Why not?

CYRANO. Look at me!

CHRISTIAN. She would love me grown ugly.

CYRANO. She told you so?

CHRISTIAN. With the utmost frankness!

CYRANO. Ah! I am glad she should have told you that! But, believe me, believe me, place no faith in such a mad asseveration! Dear God, I am glad such a thought should have come to her, and that she should have spoken it — but believe me, do not take her at her word: Never cease to be the handsome fellow you are. ... She would not forgive me!

CHRISTIAN. That is what I wish to discover.

CYRANO. No! no!

CHRISTIAN. Let her choose between us! You shall tell her everything.

CYRANO. No... No... I refuse the ordeal!

CHRISTIAN. Shall I stand in the way of your happiness because my outside is not so much amiss?

CYRANO. And I? shall I destroy yours, because, thanks to the hazard that sets us upon earth, I have the gift of expressing... what you perhaps feel?

CHRISTIAN. You shall tell her everything!

CYRANO. He persists in tempting me... It is a mistake... and cruel!

CHRISTIAN. I am weary of carrying about, in my own self, a rival!

CYRANO. Christian!

CHRISTIAN. Our marriage... contracted without witnesses... can be annulled... if we survive!

CYRANO. He persists!...

CHRISTIAN. Yes. I will be loved for my sole self, or not at all! — I am going to see what they are about. Look! I will walk to the end of the line and back... Tell her, and let her pronounce between us.

CYRANO. She will pronounce for you.

CHRISTIAN. I can but hope she will! (*calling*) Roxane!

CYRANO. No! No!

ROXANE (*coming forward*). What is it?

CHRISTIAN. Cyrano has something to tell you... something important! (ROXANE *goes hurriedly to* CYRANO. *Exit* CHRISTIAN.)

ROXANE. Something important?

CYRANO (*distracted*). He is gone!... (*To* ROXANE.) Nothing whatever! He attaches — but you must know him of old! — he attaches importance to trifles...

ROXANE (*quickly*). He did not believe what I told him a moment ago?... I saw that he did not believe...

CYRANO (*taking her hand*). But did you in very truth tell him the truth?

ROXANE. Yes. Yes. I should love him even...

(*She hesitates a second.*)

CYRANO (*smiling sadly*). You do not like to say it before me?

ROXANE. But...

CYRANO. I shall not mind!... Even if he were ugly?

ROXANE. Yes... Ugly. (*Musket shots outside.*) They are firing!

CYRANO (*ardently*). Dreadfully ugly?

ROXANE. Dreadfully.

CYRANO. Disfigured?

ROXANE. Disfigured!

CYRANO. Grotesque?

ROXANE. Nothing could make him grotesque... to me.

CYRANO. You would love him still?

ROXANE. I believe that I should love him more... if that were possible!

CYRANO (*losing his head, aside*). My God, perhaps she means it... perhaps it is true... and that way is happiness! (*To* ROXANE.) I... Roxane... listen!

LE BRET (*comes in hurriedly; calls softly*). Cyrano!

CYRANO (*turning*). Hein?

LE BRET. Hush! (*He whispers a few words to* CYRANO.)

CYRANO (*letting* ROXANE's *hand drop, with a cry*). Ah!...

ROXANE. What ails you?

CYRANO (*to himself, in consternation*). It is finished!

(*Musket reports.*)

ROXANE. What is it? What is happening? Who is firing?

(*She goes to the back to look off.*)

CYRANO. It is finished.... My lips are sealed forevermore!

(CADETS *come in, attempting to conceal something they carry among them; they surround it, preventing* ROXANE'S *seeing it.*)

ROXANE. What has happened?

CYRANO (*quickly stopping her as she starts toward them*). Nothing!

ROXANE. These men?...

CYRANO (*drawing her away*). Pay no attention to them!

ROXANE. But what were you about to say to me before?

CYRANO. What was I about to say?... Oh, nothing!... Nothing whatever, I assure you. (*Solemnly.*) I swear that Christian's spirit, that his soul, were... (*in terror, correcting himself*) are the greatest that...

ROXANE. Were?... (*With a great cry.*) Ah!...

(*Runs to the group of* CADETS, *and thrusts them aside.*)

CYRANO. It is finished!

ROXANE (*seeing* CHRISTIAN *stretched out in his cloak*). Christian!

LE BRET (*to* CYRANO). At the enemy's first shot!

(ROXANE *throws herself on* CHRISTIAN'S *body. Musket reports. Clashing of swords. Tramping. Drums.*)

CARBON (*sword in hand*). The attack! To your muskets!

(*Followed by the* CADETS *he goes to the further side of the earthworks.*)

ROXANE. Christian!

CARBON'S VOICE (*beyond the earthworks*). Make haste!

ROXANE. Christian!

CARBON. Fall into line!

ROXANE. Christian!

CARBON. Measure... match!

(RAGUENEAU *has come running in with water in a steel cap.*)

CHRISTIAN (*in a dying voice*). Roxane!

CYRANO (*quick, low in* CHRISTIAN'S *ear, while* ROXANE, *distracted, dips into the water a fragment of linen torn from her breast to bind his wound*). I have told her everything!... You are still the one she loves!

(CHRISTIAN *closes his eyes.*)

ROXANE. What, dear love?

CARBON. Muzzle... high!

ROXANE (*to* CYRANO). He is not dead?...

CARBON. Open charge... with teeth!

ROXANE. I feel his cheek grow cold against my own!

CARBON. Take aim!

ROXANE. A letter on his breast.... (*She opens it.*)   To me!

CYRANO (*aside*). My letter!

CARBON. Fire!   (*Musket shots.   Cries.   Roar of battle.*)

CYRANO (*trying to free his hand which* ROXANE *clasps kneeling*).   But, Roxane, they are fighting.

ROXANE (*clinging*).   No!... Stay with me a little!... He is dead. You are the only one that truly knew him.... (*She cries subduedly.*) Was he not an exquisite being,... an exceptional, marvellous being?...

CYRANO (*standing bareheaded*).   Yes, Roxane!

ROXANE. A poet without his peer,... one verily to reverence?

CYRANO. Yes, Roxane.

ROXANE. A sublime spirit?

CYRANO. Yes, Roxane.

ROXANE. A profound heart, such as the profane could never have understood... a soul as noble as it was charming?...

CYRANO (*firmly*).   Yes, Roxane.

ROXANE (*throwing herself on* CHRISTIAN'*s body*).   And he is dead!

CYRANO (*aside, drawing his sword*).   And I have now only to die, since, without knowing it, she mourns my death in his!

               (*Trumpets in the distance.*)

DE GUICHE (*reappears on the top of the bank, bareheaded, his forehead bloody; in a thundering voice*).   The signal they promised!   The flourish of trumpets!... The French are entering the camp with supplies!... Stand fast a little longer!

ROXANE. Upon his letter... blood,... tears!

A VOICE (*outside, shouting*).   Surrender!

VOICES OF THE CADETS. No!

RAGUENEAU (*who from the top of the coach is watching the battle beyond the bank*).   The conflict rages hotter!...

CYRANO (*to* DE GUICHE *pointing at* ROXANE).   Take her away!... I am going to charge.

ROXANE (*kissing the letter, in a dying voice*).   His blood!... his tears!

RAGUENEAU (*leaping from the coach and running to* ROXANE).   She is fainting!

DE GUICHE (*at the top of the bank, to the* CADETS, *madly*).   Stand fast!

VOICE (*outside*).   Surrender!

VOICES OF THE CADETS.   No!

CYRANO (*to* DE GUICHE).   Your courage none will question...
(*Pointing at* ROXANE.)   Fly for the sake of saving her!

DE GUICHE (*runs to* ROXANE *and lifts her in his arms*).   So be it!   But
we shall win the day if you can hold out a little longer...

CYRANO.   We can.   (*To* ROXANE, *whom* DE GUICHE, *helped by*
RAGUENEAU, *is carrying off insensible*.)   Good-bye, Roxane!

> (*Tumult.   Cries.* CADETS *reappear, wounded, and fall upon the
> stage.* CYRANO *dashing forward to join the combatants is
> stopped on the crest of the bank by* CARBON *covered with
> blood*.)

CARBON.   We are losing ground... I have got two halberd
wounds...

CYRANO (*yelling to the* GASCONS).   Steadfast!... Never give them an
inch!... Brave boys!   (*To* CARBON.)   Fear nothing!   I have
various deaths to avenge: Christian's and all my hopes'!   (*They
come down.* CYRANO *brandishes the spear at the head of which*
ROXANE's *handkerchief is fastened*.)   Float free, little cobweb flag,
embroidered with her initials!   (*He drives the spear-staff into the
earth; shouts to the* CADETS.)   Fall on them, boys!... Crush them!
(*To the fifer*.)   Fifer, play!

> (*The fifer plays.   Some of the wounded get to their feet again.
> Some of the* CADETS, *coming down the bank, group themselves
> around* CYRANO *and the little flag.   The coach, filled and covered
> with men, bristles with muskets and becomes a redoubt*.)

ONE OF THE CADETS (*appears upon the top of the bank backing while he
fights; he cries*).   They are coming up the slope!   (*Falls dead*.)

CYRANO.   We will welcome them!

(*Above the bank suddenly rises a formidable array of enemies.   The great
banners of the Imperial Army appear*.)

CYRANO.   Fire!   (*General discharge*.)

CRY (*among the hostile ranks*).   Fire!

> (*Shots returned.* CADETS *drop on every side*.)

A SPANISH OFFICER (*taking off his hat*).   What are these men, so determined all to be killed?

CYRANO (*declaiming, as he stands in the midst of flying bullets*).

> They are the Gascony Cadets
> Of Carbon de Castel-Jaloux;
> Famed fighters, liars, desperates...
> 　　(*He leaps forward, followed by a handful of survivors.*)
> They are the Gascony Cadets!...
> 　　　　(*The rest is lost in the confusion of battle.*)

CURTAIN

ACT FIFTH

CYRANO'S GAZETTE

Fifteen years later, 1655. The park belonging to the convent of the Sisters of the Cross, in Paris.

Superb shade-trees. At the left, the house; several doors opening on to broad terrace with steps. In the centre of the stage, huge trees standing alone in a clear oval space. At the right, first wing, a semicircular stone seat, surrounded by large box-trees.

All along the back of the stage, an avenue of chestnut-trees, which leads, at the right, fourth wing, to the door of a chapel seen through trees. Through the double row of trees overarching the avenue are seen lawns, other avenues, clumps of trees, the further recesses of the park, the sky.

The chapel opens by a small side-door into a colonnade, overrun by a scarlet creeper; the colonnade comes forward and is lost to sight behind the box-trees at the right.

It is Autumn. The leaves are turning, above the still fresh grass. Dark patches of evergreens, box and yew. Under each tree a mat of yellow leaves. Fallen leaves litter the whole stage, crackle underfoot, lie thick on the terrace and the seats.

Between the seat at the right and the tree in the centre, a large embroidery frame, in front of which a small chair. Baskets full of wools, in skeins and balls. On the frame, a piece of tapestry, partly done.

At the rise of the curtain, nuns come and go in the park; a few are seated on the stone seat around an older nun; leaves are falling.

SISTER MARTHA (*to* MOTHER MARGARET). Sister Claire, after putting on her cap went back to the mirror, to see herself again.

MOTHER MARGARET (*to* SISTER CLAIRE). It was unbecoming, my child.

SISTER CLAIRE. But Sister Martha, today, after finishing her portion, went back to the tart for a plum. I saw her!

MOTHER MARGARET (*to* SISTER MARTHA). My child, it was ill done.

SISTER CLAIRE. I merely glanced!...

SISTER MARTHA. The plum was about so big!...

MOTHER MARGARET. This evening, when Monsieur Cyrano comes, I will tell him.

SISTER CLAIRE (*alarmed*). No! He will laugh at us!

SISTER MARTHA. He will say that nuns are very vain!

SISTER CLAIRE. And very greedy!

MOTHER MARGARET. And really very good.

SISTER CLAIRE. Mother Margaret, is it not true that he has come here every Saturday in the last ten years?

MOTHER MARGARET. Longer! Ever since his cousin brought among our linen coifs her coif of crape, the worldly symbol of her mourning, which settled like a sable bird amidst our flock of white some fourteen years ago.

SISTER MARTHA. He alone, since she took her abode in our cloister, has art to dispel her never-lessening sorrow.

ALL THE NUNS. He is so droll! — It is merry when he comes! — He teases us! — He is delightful! — We are greatly attached to him! — We are making Angelica paste to offer him!

SISTER MARTHA. He is not, however, a very good Catholic!

SISTER CLAIRE. We will convert him.

THE NUNS. We will! We will!

MOTHER MARGARET. I forbid your renewing that attempt, my children. Do not trouble him: he might not come so often!

SISTER MARTHA. But... God!

MOTHER MARGARET. Set your hearts at rest: God must know him of old!

SISTER MARTHA. But every Saturday, when he comes, he says to me as soon as he sees me, "Sister, I ate meat, yesterday!"

MOTHER MARGARET. Ah, that is what he says?... Well, when he last said it, he had eaten nothing for two days.

SISTER MARTHA. Mother!

MOTHER MARGARET. He is poor.

SISTER MARTHA. Who told you?

MOTHER MARGARET. Monsieur Le Bret.

SISTER MARTHA. Does no one offer him assistance?

MOTHER MARGARET. No, he would take offence.

(*In one of the avenues at the back, appears* ROXANE, *in black, wearing a widow's coif and long mourning veil;* DE GUICHE, *markedly older, magnificently dressed, walks beside her. They go very slowly.* MOTHER MARGARET *gets up.*)

MOTHER MARGARET. Come, we must go within. Madame Magdeleine is walking in the park with a visitor.

SISTER MARTHA (*low to* SISTER CLAIRE). Is not that the Marshalduke de Grammont?

SISTER CLAIRE (*looking*). I think it is!

SISTER MARTHA. He has not been to see her in many months!

THE NUNS. He is much engaged! — The Court! — The Camp! —

SISTER CLAIRE. Cares of this world!

(*Exeunt.* DE GUICHE *and* ROXANE *come forward silently, and stop near the embroidery frame. A pause.*)

DE GUICHE. And so you live here, uselessly fair, always in mourning?

ROXANE. Always.

DE GUICHE. As faithful as of old?

ROXANE. As faithful.

DE GUICHE (*after a time*). Have you forgiven me?

ROXANE. Since I am here.   (*Other silence.*)

DE GUICHE. And he was really such a rare being?

ROXANE. To understand, one must have known him!

DE GUICHE. Ah, one must have known him!... Perhaps I did not know him well enough. And his last letter, still and always, against your heart?

ROXANE. I wear it on this velvet, as a more holy scapular.

DE GUICHE. Even dead, you love him?

ROXANE. It seems to me sometimes he is but half dead, that our hearts have not been severed, that his love still wraps me round, no less than ever living!

DE GUICHE (*after another silence*). Does Cyrano come here to see you?

ROXANE. Yes, often. That faithful friend fulfils by me the office of gazette. His visits are regular. He comes: when the weather is fine, his armchair is brought out under the trees. I wait for him here with my work; the hour strikes; on the last stroke, I hear — I do not even turn to see who comes! — his cane upon the steps; he takes his seat; he rallies me upon my never-ending tapestry; he tells off the events of the week, and... (LE BRET *appears on the steps.*) Ah, Le Bret! (LE BRET *comes down the steps.*) How does your friend?

LE BRET. Ill.

THE DUKE. Oh!

ROXANE. He exaggerates!...

LE BRET. All is come to pass as I foretold: neglect! poverty! his writings ever breeding him new enemies! Fraud he attacks in every embodiment: usurpers, pious pretenders, plagiarists, asses in lions' skins... all! He attacks all!

ROXANE. No one, however, but stands in profound respect of his sword. They will never succeed in silencing him.

DE GUICHE (*shaking his head*). Who knows?

LE BRET. What I fear is not the aggression of man; what I fear is loneliness and want and winter creeping upon him like stealthy wolves in his miserable attic; they are the insidious foes that will have him by the throat at last!... Every day he tightens his belt by an eyelet; his poor great nose is pinched, and turned the sallow of old ivory; the worn black serge you see him in is the only coat he has!

DE GUICHE. Ah, there is one who did not succeed!... Nevertheless, do not pity him too much.

LE BRET (*with a bitter smile*). Marshal!...

DE GUICHE. Do not pity him too much: he signed no bonds with the world; he has lived free in his thought as in his actions.

LE BRET (*as above*). Duke...

DE GUICHE (*haughtily*). I know, yes: I have everything, he has nothing.... But I should like to shake hands with him. (*Bowing to* ROXANE.) Good-bye.

ROXANE. I will go with you to the door.

(DE GUICHE *bows to* LE BRET *and goes with* ROXANE *toward the terrace steps.*)

DE GUICHE (*stopping, while she goes up the steps*). Yes, sometimes I envy him. You see, when a man has succeeded too well in life, he is not unlikely to feel — dear me! without having committed any very serious wrong! — a multitudinous disgust of himself, the sum of which does not constitute a real remorse, but an obscure uneasiness; and a ducal mantle, while it sweeps up the stairs of greatness, may trail in its furry lining a rustling of sere illusions and regrets, as, when you slowly climb toward those doors, your black gown trails the withered leaves.

ROXANE (*ironical*). Are you not unusually pensive?...

DE GUICHE. Ah, yes! (*As he is about to leave, abruptly.*) Monsieur Le Bret! (*To* ROXANE.) Will you allow me? A word. (*He goes to* LE BRET, *and lowering his voice.*) It is true that no one will dare overtly to attack your friend, but many have him in particular disrelish; and some one was saying to me yesterday, at the Queen's, "It seems not unlikely that this Cyrano will meet with an accident."

LE BRET. Ah?...

DE GUICHE. Yes. Let him keep indoors. Let him be cautious.

LE BRET (*lifting his arms toward Heaven*). Cautious!... He is coming here. I will warn him. Warn him!... Yes, but...

ROXANE (*who has been standing at the head of the steps, to a nun who comes toward her*). What is it?

THE NUN. Ragueneau begs to see you, Madame.

ROXANE. Let him come in. (*To* DE GUICHE *and* LE BRET.) He comes to plead distress. Having determined one day to be an author, he became in turn precentor...

LE BRET. Bath-house keeper...

ROXANE. Actor...

LE BRET. Beadle...

ROXANE. Barber...

LE BRET. Arch-lute teacher...

ROXANE. I wonder what he is now!

RAGUENEAU (*entering precipitately*). Ah, madame! (*He sees* LE BRET.) Monsieur!

ROXANE (*smiling*). Begin telling your misfortunes to Le Bret. I am coming back.

RAGUENEAU. But, madame...

ROXANE *leaves without listening, with the* DUKE. RAGUENEAU
goes to LE BRET.)

RAGUENEAU. It is better so. Since you are here, I had liefer not
tell her! Less than half an hour ago, I was going to see your
friend. I was not thirty feet from his door, when I saw him
come out. I hurried to catch up with him. He was about to
turn the corner. I started to run, when from a window below
which he was passing — was it pure mischance? It may have
been! — a lackey drops a block of wood...

LE BRET. Ah, the cowards!... Cyrano!

RAGUENEAU. I reach the spot, and find him...

LE BRET. Horrible!

RAGUENEAU. Our friend, monsieur, our poet, stretched upon the
ground, with a great hole in his head!

LE BRET. He is dead?

RAGUENEAU. No, but... God have mercy! I carried him to his
lodging... Ah, his lodging! You should see that lodging of his!

LE BRET. Is he in pain?

RAGUENEAU. No, monsieur, he is unconscious.

LE BRET. Has a doctor seen him?

RAGUENEAU. One came... out of good nature.

LE BRET. My poor, poor Cyrano!... We must not tell Roxane out-
right. And the doctor?...

RAGUENEAU. He talked... I hardly grasped... of fever... cerebral
inflammation! Ah, if you should see him, with his head done up
in cloths!... Let us hurry... No one is there to tend him... And
he might die if he attempted to get up!

LE BRET (*dragging* RAGUENEAU *off at the right*). This way. Come, it
is shorter through the chapel.

ROXANE (*appearing at the head of the steps, catching sight of* LE BRET
hurrying off through the colonnade which leads to the chapel side-door).
Monsieur Le Bret! (LE BRET *and* RAGUENEAU *make their escape
without answering.*) Le Bret not turning back when he is called?
... Poor Ragueneau must be in some new trouble! (*She comes
down the steps.*) How beautiful... how beautiful, this golden-
hazy waning day of September at its wane! My sorrowful mood,
which the exuberant gladness of April offends, Autumn, the

dreamy and subdued, lures on to smile... (*She sits down at her embroidery frame. Two* NUNS *come from the house bringing a large armchair which they place under the tree.*) Ah, here comes the classic armchair in which my old friend always sits!

SISTER MARTHA. The best in the convent parlor!

ROXANE. I thank you, sister. (*The nuns withdraw.*) He will be here in a moment. (*She adjusts the embroidery frame before her.*) There! The clock is striking... My wools!... The clock has struck?... I wonder at this!... Is it possible that for the first time he is late?... It must be that the sister who keeps the door... my thimble? ah, here it is!... is detaining him to exhort him to repentance... (*A pause.*) She exhorts him at some length!... He cannot be much longer... A withered leaf! (*She brushes away the dead leaf which has dropped on the embroidery.*) Surely nothing could keep... My scissors?... in my workbag!... could keep him from coming!

A NUN (*appearing at the head of the steps*). Monsieur de Bergerac!

ROXANE (*without turning round*). What was I saying?... (*She begins to embroider.* CYRANO *appears, exceedingly pale, his hat drawn down over his eyes. The* NUN *who has shown him into the garden, withdraws. He comes down the steps very slowly, with evident difficulty to keep on his feet, leaning heavily on his cane.* ROXANE *proceeds with her sewing.*) Ah, these dull soft shades!... How shall I match them? (*To* CYRANO, *in a tone of friendly chiding.*) After fourteen years, for the first time you are late!

CYRANO (*who has reached the armchair and seated himself, in a jolly voice which contrasts with his face*). Yes, it seems incredible! I am savage at it. I was detained, spite of all I could do!...

ROXANE. By?...

CYRANO. A somewhat inopportune call.

ROXANE (*absent-minded, sewing*). Ah, yes... some troublesome fellow!

CYRANO. Cousin, it was a troublesome Madam.

ROXANE. You excused yourself?

CYRANO. Yes. I said, "Your pardon, but this is Saturday, on which day I am due in certain dwelling. On no account do I ever fail. Come back in an hour!"

ROXANE (*lightly*). Well, she will have to wait some time to see you. I shall not let you go before evening.

CYRANO. Perhaps... I shall have to go a little earlier.

(He closes his eyes and is silent a moment. SISTER MARTHA is seen crossing the park from the chapel to the terrace. ROXANE sees her and beckons to her by a slight motion of her head.)

ROXANE *(to CYRANO)*. Are you not going to tease Sister Martha today?

CYRANO *(quickly, opening his eyes)*. I am indeed! *(In a comically gruff voice.)* Sister Martha, come nearer! *(The NUN demurely comes toward him.)* Ha! ha! ha! Beautiful eyes, ever studying the ground!

SISTER MARTHA *(lifting her eyes and smiling)*. But... *(She sees his face and makes a gesture of surprise.)* Oh!

CYRANO *(low, pointing at ROXANE)*. Hush!... It is nothing! *(In a swaggering voice, aloud.)* Yesterday, I ate meat!

SISTER MARTHA. I am sure you did! *(Aside.)* That is why he is so pale! *(Quickly, low.)* Come to the refectory presently. I shall have ready for you there a good bowl of broth... You will come!

CYRANO. Yes, yes, yes.

SISTER MARTHA. Ah, you are more reasonable today!

ROXANE *(hearing them whisper)*. She is trying to convert you?

SISTER MARTHA. Indeed I am not!

CYRANO. It is true, you, usually almost discursive in the holy cause, are reading me no sermon! You amaze me! *(With comical fury.)* I will amaze you, too! Listen, you are authorized... *(With the air of casting about in his mind, and finding the jest he wants.)* Ah, now I shall amaze you! to... pray for me, this evening... in the chapel.

ROXANE. Oh! oh!

CYRANO *(laughing)*. Sister Martha... lost in amazement!

SISTER MARTHA *(gently)*. I did not wait for your authorization.

(She goes in.)

CYRANO *(turning to ROXANE, who is bending over her embroidery)*. The devil, tapestry... the devil, if I hope to live to see the end of you!

ROXANE. I was waiting for that jest.

(A slight gust of wind makes the leaves fall.)

CYRANO. The leaves!

ROXANE *(looking up from her work and gazing off toward the avenues)*.

They are the russet gold of a Venetian beauty's hair... Watch them fall!

CYRANO. How consummately they do it! In that brief fluttering from bough to ground, how they contrive still to put beauty! And though foredoomed to moulder upon the earth that draws them, they wish their fall invested with the grace of a free bird's flight!

ROXANE. Serious, you?

CYRANO (*remembering himself*). Not at all, Roxane!

ROXANE. Come, never mind the falling leaves! Tell me the news, instead... Where is my budget?

CYRANO. Here it is!

ROXANE. Ah!

CYRANO (*growing paler and paler, and struggling with pain*). Saturday, the nineteenth: The king having filled his dish eight times with Cette preserves, and emptied it, was taken with a fever; his distemper, for high treason, was condemned to be let blood, and now the royal pulse is rid of febriculosity! On Sunday: at the Queen's great ball, were burned seven hundred and sixty-three wax candles; our troops, it is said, defeated Austrian John; four sorcerers were hanged; Madame Athis's little dog had a distressing turn, the case called for a...

ROXANE. Monsieur de Bergerac, leave out the little dog!

CYRANO. Monday,... nothing, or next to it: Lygdamire took a fresh lover.

ROXANE. Oh!

CYRANO (*over whose face is coming a change more and more marked*). Tuesday: the whole Court assembled at Fontainebleau. Wednesday, the fair Monglat said to Count Fiesco "No!" Thursday, Mancini, Queen of France,... or little less. Twenty-fifth, the fair Monglat said to Count Fiesco "Yes!" And Saturday, the twenty-sixth...

(*He closes his eyes. His head drops on his breast. Silence.*)

ROXANE (*surprised at hearing nothing further, turns, looks at him and starts to her feet in alarm*). Has he fainted? (*She runs to him, calling.*) Cyrano!

CYRANO (*opening his eyes, in a faint voice*). What is it?... What is the matter! (*He sees* ROXANE *bending over him, hurriedly readjusts his hat, pulling it more closely over his head, and shrinks back in his armchair in terror.*) No! no! I assure you, it is nothing!... Do not mind me!

ROXANE. But surely...

CYRANO. It is merely the wound I received at Arras... Sometimes ... you know... even now...

ROXANE. Poor friend!

CYRANO. But it is nothing... It will pass... (*He smiles with effort.*) It has passed.

ROXANE. Each one of us has his wound: I too have mine. It is here, never to heal, that ancient wound... (*She places her hand on her breast.*) It is here, beneath the yellowing letter on which are still faintly visible tear-drops and drops of blood!

(*The light is beginning to grow less.*)

CYRANO. His letter?... Did you not once say that some day... you might show it to me?

ROXANE. Ah!... Do you wish?... His letter?

CYRANO. Yes... today... I wish to...

ROXANE (*handing him the little bag from her neck*). Here!

CYRANO. I may open it?

ROXANE. Open it... read!

(*She goes back to her embroidery frame, folds it up, orders her wools.*)

CYRANO. "Good-bye, Roxane! I am going to die!"

ROXANE (*stopping in astonishment*). You are reading it aloud?

CYRANO (*reading*). "It is fated to come this evening, beloved, I believe! My soul is heavy, oppressed with love it had not time to utter... and now Time is at end! Never again, never again shall my worshipping eyes..."

ROXANE. How strangely you read his letter!

CYRANO (*continuing*). "... whose passionate revel it was, kiss in its fleeting grace your every gesture. One, usual to you, of tucking back a little curl, comes to my mind... and I cannot refrain from crying out..."

ROXANE. How strangely you read his letter!...

(*The darkness gradually increases.*)

CYRANO. "and I cry out: Good-bye!"

ROXANE. You read it...

CYRANO. "my dearest, my darling,... my treasure..."

ROXANE. ... in a voice...

CYRANO. "... my love!..."

ROXANE. ... in a voice... a voice which I am not hearing for the first time!

> (ROXANE *comes quietly nearer to him, without his seeing it; she steps behind his armchair, bends noiselessly over his shoulder, looks at the letter. The darkness deepens.*)

CYRANO. "... My heart never desisted for a second from your side ... and I am and shall be in the world that has no end, the one who loved you without measure, the one..."

ROXANE (*laying her hand on his shoulder*). How can you go on reading? It is dark. (CYRANO *starts, and turns round; sees her close to him, makes a gesture of dismay and hangs his head. Then, in the darkness which has completely closed round them, she says slowly, clasping her hands.*) And he, for fourteen years, has played the part of the comical old friend who came to cheer me!

CYRANO. Roxane!

ROXANE. So it was you.

CYRANO. No, no, Roxane!

ROXANE. I ought to have divined it, if only by the way in which he speaks my name!

CYRANO. No, it was not I!

ROXANE. So it was you!

CYRANO. I swear to you..."

ROXANE. Ah, I detect at last the whole generous imposture: The letters... were yours!

CYRANO. No!

ROXANE. The tender fancy, the dear folly,... yours!

CYRANO. No!

ROXANE. The voice in the night, was yours!

CYRANO. I swear to you that it was not!

ROXANE. The soul... was yours!

CYRANO. I did not love you, no!

ROXANE. And you loved me!

CYRANO. Not I... it was the other!

ROXANE. You loved me!

CYRANO. No!

ROXANE. Already your denial comes more faintly!

CYRANO. No, no, my darling love, I did not love you!

ROXANE. Ah, how many things within the hour have died... how many have been born! Why, why have... been silent these long years, when on this letter, in which he had no part, the tears were yours?

CYRANO (*handing her the letter*). Because... the blood was his.

ROXANE. Then why let the sublime bond of this silence be loosed today?

CYRANO. Why?

(LE BRET *and* RAGUENEAU *enter running.*)

LE BRET. Madness! Monstrous madness!... Ah, I was sure of it! There he is!

CYRANO (*smiling and straightening himself*). *Tiens!* Where else?

LE BRET. Madame, he is likely to have got his death by getting out of bed!

ROXANE. Merciful God! A moment ago, then... that faintness... that...?

CYRANO. It is true. I had not finished telling you the news. And on Saturday, the twenty-sixth, an hour after sundown, Monsieur de Bergerac died of murder done upon him.

(*He takes off his hat; his head is seen wrapped in bandages.*)

ROXANE. What is he saying?... Cyrano?... Those bandages about his head?... Ah, what have they done to you? Why?...

CYRANO. "Happy who falls, cut off by a hero, with an honest sword through his heart!" I am quoting from myself!... Fate will have his laugh at us!... Here am I killed, in a trap, from behind, by a lackey, with a log! Nothing could be completer! In my whole life I shall have not had anything I wanted... not even a decent death!

RAGUENEAU. Ah, monsieur!...

CYRANO. Ragueneau, do not sob like that! (*Holding out his hand to him.*) And what is the news with you, these latter days, fellow-poet?

RAGUENEAU (*through his tears*). I am candle-snuffer at Molière's theatre.

CYRANO. Molière!

RAGUENEAU. But I intend to leave no later than tomorrow. Yes, I

am indignant! Yesterday, they were giving Scapin, and I saw
that he has appropriated a scene of yours.

LE BRET. A whole scene?

RAGUENEAU. Yes, monsieur. The one in which occurs the famous
"What the devil was he doing in..."

LE BRET. Molière has taken that from you!

CYRANO. Hush! hush! He did well to take it! (*To* RAGUENEAU.)
The scene was very effective, was it not?

RAGUENEAU. Ah, monsieur, the public laughed... laughed!

CYRANO. Yes, to the end, I shall have been the one who prompted
... and was forgotten! (*To* ROXANE.) Do you remember that
evening on which Christian spoke to you from below the balcony?
There was the epitome of my life: while I have stood below in
darkness, others have climbed to gather the kiss and glory! It is
well done, and on the brink of my grave I approve it: Molière has
genius... Christian was a fine fellow! (*At this moment, the chapel
bell having rung, the* NUNS *are seen passing at the back, along the
avenue, on their way to service.*) Let them hasten to their prayers...
the bell is summoning them...

ROXANE (*rising and calling*). Sister! Sister!

CYRANO (*holding her back*). No! No! do not leave me to fetch anybody! When you come back I might not be here to rejoice...
(*The* NUNS *have gone into the chapel; the organ is heard.*) I longed for
a little music... it comes in time!

ROXANE. I love you... you shall live!

CYRANO. No! for it is only in the fairytale that the shy and awkward
prince when he hears the beloved say "I love you!" feels his un-
gainliness melt and drop from him in the sunshine of those
words!... But you would always know full well, dear Heart, that
there had taken place in your poor slave no beautifying change!

ROXANE. I have hurt you... I have wrecked your life, I!... I!

CYRANO. You?... The reverse! Woman's sweetness I had never
known. My mother... thought me unflattering. I had no
sister. Later, I shunned Love's crossroad in fear of mocking
eyes. To you I owe having had, at least, among the gentle and
fair, a friend. Thanks to you there was passed across my life the
rustle of a woman's gown.

LE BRET (*calling his attention to the moonlight peering through the branches*). Your other friend, among the gentle and fair, is there ... she comes to see you!

CYRANO (*smiling to the moon*). I see her!

ROXANE. I never loved but one... and twice I lose him!

CYRANO. Le Bret, I shall ascend into the opalescent moon, without need this time of a flying-machine!

ROXANE. What are you saying?

CYRANO. Yes, it is there, you may be sure, I shall be sent for my Paradise. More than one soul of those I have loved must be apportioned there... There I shall find Socrates and Galileo!

LE BRET (*in revolt*). No! No! It is too senseless, too cruel, too unfair! So true a poet! So great a heart! To die... like this! To die!...

CYRANO. As every... Le Bret is grumbling!

LE BRET (*bursting into tears*). My friend! My friend!

CYRANO (*lifting himself, his eyes wild*). They are the Gascony Cadets!... Man in the gross... Eh, yes!... the weakness of the weakest point...

LE BRET. Learned... even in his delirium!...

CYRANO. Copernicus said...

ROXANE. Oh!

CYRANO. But what the devil was he doing... and what the devil was he doing in that galley?

> Philosopher and physicist,
> Musician, rhymester, duellist,
> Explorer of the upper blue,
> Retorter apt with point and point,
> Lover as well — not for his peace!
> Here lies Hercule Savinien
> De Cyrano de Bergerac,
> Who was everything... but of account!

But, your pardons, I must go... I wish to keep no one waiting... See, a moonbeam, come to take me home! (*He has dropped in his chair;* ROXANE's *weeping calls him back to reality; he looks at her and gently stroking her mourning veil.*) I do not wish... indeed, I do not wish... that you should sorrow less for Christian, the comely and the kind! Only I wish that when the everlasting cold shall have seized upon my fibres, this funereal veil should have a twofold meaning, and the mourning you wear for him be worn for me too ... a little!

ROXANE. I promise...

CYRANO (*seized with a great shivering, starts to his feet*). Not there! No! Not in an elbow-chair! (*All draw nearer to help him.*) Let no one stay me! No one! (*He goes and stands against the tree.*) Nothing but this tree! (*Silence.*) She comes, Mors, the indiscriminate Madam!... Already I am booted with marble... gauntleted with lead! (*He stiffens himself.*) Ah, since she is on her way, I will await her standing... (*He draws his sword.*) Sword in hand!

LE BRET. Cyrano!

ROXANE (*swooning*). Cyrano!   (*All start back, terrified.*)

CYRANO. I believe she is looking at me... that she dares to look at my nose, the bony baggage who has none! (*He raises his sword.*) What are you saying? That it is no use?... I know it! But one does not fight because there is hope of winning! No!... no!... it is much finer to fight when it is no use!... What are all those? You are a thousand strong?... Ah, I know you now... all my ancient enemies!... Hypocrisy?... (*He beats with his sword, in the vacancy.*) Take this! and this! Ha! Ha! Compromises?... and Prejudices? and dastardly Expedients? (*He strikes.*) That I should come to terms, I?... Never! Never!... Ah, you are there too, you, bloated and pompous Silliness! I know full well that you will lay me low at last... No matter: whilst I have breath, I will fight you, I will fight you, I will fight you! (*He waves his sword in great sweeping circles, and stops, panting.*) Yes, you have wrested from me everything, laurel as well as rose... Work your wills!... Spite of your worst, something will still be left me to take whither I go... and tonight when I enter God's house, in saluting, broadly will I sweep the azure threshold with what despite of all I carry forth unblemished and unbent... (*He starts forward, with lifted sword.*)... and that is...

> (*The sword falls from his hands, he staggers, drops in the arms of* LE LRET *and* RAGUENEAU.)

ROXANE (*bending over him and kissing his forehead*). That is?...

CYRANO (*opens his eyes again, recognizes her and says with a smile*).... My plume!

CURTAIN

STRIFE

A DRAMA IN THREE ACTS

By JOHN GALSWORTHY

PERSONS OF THE PLAY

JOHN ANTHONY, *Chairman of the Trenartha Tin Plate Works.*

EDGAR ANTHONY, *his son,*
FREDERIC H. WILDER,
WILLIAM SCANTLEBURY, } *Directors of the same.*
OLIVER WANKLIN,

HENRY TENCH, *Secretary of the same.*

FRANCIS UNDERWOOD, C.E., *Manager of the same.*

SIMON HARNESS, *a Trades Union Official.*

DAVID ROBERTS,
JAMES GREEN,
JOHN BULGIN, } *The workmen's committee.*
HENRY THOMAS,
GEORGE ROUS,

HENRY ROUS,
LEWIS,
JAGO,
EVANS,
A BLACKSMITH, } *workmen at the Trenartha Tin Plate Works.*
DAVIES,
A RED-HAIRED YOUTH,
BROWN,

FROST, *valet to John Anthony.*

ENID UNDERWOOD, *wife of Francis Underwood, daughter of John Anthony.*

ANNIE ROBERTS, *wife of David Roberts.*

MADGE THOMAS, *daughter of Henry Thomas.*

MRS. ROUS, *mother of George and Henry Rous.*

MRS. BULGIN, *wife of John Bulgin.*

MRS. YEO, *wife of a workman.*

A PARLORMAID *to the Underwoods.*

JAN, *Madge's brother, a boy of ten.*

A CROWD OF MEN ON STRIKE.

ACT   I. THE DINING-ROOM OF THE MANAGER'S HOUSE
ACT II. SCENE I. THE KITCHEN OF THE ROBERTS'S COTTAGE
             NEAR THE WORKS
          SCENE II. A SPACE OUTSIDE THE WORKS
ACT III. THE DRAWING-ROOM OF THE MANAGER'S HOUSE

*The action takes place on February 7 between the hours of noon and six in the
     afternoon, close to the Trenartha Tin Plate Works, on the borders of
     England and Wales, where a strike has been in progress throughout the
     winter.*

ACT I

It is noon. In the Underwoods' dining-room a bright fire is burning. On one side of the fireplace are double doors leading to the drawing-room, on the other side a door leading to the hall. In the center of the room a long dining-table without a cloth is set out as a Board table. At the head of it, in the Chairman's seat, sits JOHN ANTHONY, *an old man, big, clean-shaven, and high-colored, with thick white hair, and thick dark eyebrows. His movements are rather slow and feeble, but his eyes are very much alive. There is a glass of water by his side. On his right sits his son* EDGAR, *an earnest-looking man of thirty, reading a newspaper. Next him* WANKLIN, *a man with jutting eyebrows, and silver-streaked light hair, is bending over transfer papers.* TENCH, *the Secretary, a short and rather humble, nervous man, with side whiskers, stands helping him. On* WANKLIN'S *right sits* UNDERWOOD, *the Manager, a quiet man, with a long, stiff jaw, and steady eyes. Back to the fire is* SCANTLEBURY, *a very large, pale, sleepy man, with gray hair, rather bald. Between him and the Chairman are two empty chairs.*

WILDER (*who is lean, cadaverous, and complaining, with drooping gray mustaches, stands before the fire*). I say, this fire's the devil! Can I have a screen, Tench?

SCANTLEBURY. A screen, ah!

TENCH. Certainly, Mr. Wilder. (*He looks at* UNDERWOOD.) That is — perhaps the Manager — perhaps Mr. Underwood —

SCANTLEBURY. These fireplaces of yours, Underwood —

UNDERWOOD (*roused from studying some papers*). A screen? Rather! I'm sorry. (*He goes to the door with a little smile.*) We're not accustomed to complaints of too much fire down here just now.

> (*He speaks as though he holds a pipe between his teeth, slowly, ironically.*)

WILDER (*in an injured voice*). You mean the men. H'm!

> (UNDERWOOD *goes out.*)

SCANTLEBURY. Poor devils!

WILDER. It's their own fault, Scantlebury.

EDGAR (*holding out his paper*). There's great distress among them, according to the "Trenartha News."

WILDER. Oh, that rag! Give it to Wanklin. Suit his Radical views. They call us monsters, I suppose. The editor of that rubbish ought to be shot.

EDGAR (*reading*). "If the Board of worthy gentlemen who control the Trenartha Tin Plate Works from their armchairs in London would condescend to come and see for themselves the conditions prevailing amongst their workpeople during this strike ——"

WILDER. Well, we *have* come.

EDGAR (*continuing*). "We cannot believe that even their leg-of-mutton hearts would remain untouched."

(WANKLIN *takes the paper from him.*)

WILDER. Ruffian! I remember that fellow when he hadn't a penny to his name; little snivel of a chap that's made his way by blackguarding everybody who takes a different view to himself.

(ANTHONY *says something that is not heard.*)

WILDER. What does your father say?

EDGAR. He says "The kettle and the pot."

WILDER. H'm! (*He sits down next to* SCANTLEBURY.)

SCANTLEBURY (*blowing out his cheeks*). I shall boil if I don't get that screen.

(UNDERWOOD *and* ENID *enter with a screen, which they place before the fire.* ENID *is tall; she has a small, decided face, and is twenty-eight years old.*)

ENID. Put it closer, Frank. Will that do, Mr. Wilder? It's the highest we've got.

WILDER. Thanks, capitally.

SCANTLEBURY (*turning with a sigh of pleasure*). Ah! Merci, madame!

ENID. Is there anything else you want, father? (ANTHONY *shakes his head.*) Edgar — anything?

EDGAR. You might give me a "J" nib, old girl.

ENID. There are some down there by Mr. Scantlebury.

SCANTLEBURY (*handing a little box of nibs*). Ah! your brother uses "J's." What does the manager use? (*With expansive politeness.*) What does your husband use, Mrs. Underwood?

UNDERWOOD. A quill!

SCANTLEBURY. The homely product of the goose.

(*He holds out quills.*)

UNDERWOOD (*dryly*). Thanks, if you can spare me one. (*He takes a quill.*) What about lunch, Enid?

ENID (*stopping at the double doors and looking back*). We're going to have lunch here, in the drawing-room, so you needn't hurry with your meeting.

(WANKLIN *and* WILDER *bow, and she goes out.*)

SCANTLEBURY (*rousing himself, suddenly*). Ah! Lunch! That hotel — Dreadful! Did you try the whitebait last night? Fried fat!

WILDER. Past twelve! Aren't you going to read the minutes, Tench?

TENCH (*looking for the* CHAIRMAN'S *assent, reads in a rapid and monotonous voice*). "At a Board Meeting held the 31st of January at the Company's Offices, 512 Cannon Street, E.C. Present — Mr. Anthony in the chair, Messrs. F. H. Wilder, William Scantlebury, Oliver Wanklin, and Edgar Anthony. Read letters from the Manager dated January 20th, 23d, 25th, 28th, relative to the strike at the Company's Works. Read letters to the Manager of January 21st, 24th, 26th, 29th. Read letter from Mr. Simon Harness, of the Central Union, asking for an interview with the Board. Read letter from the Men's Committee, signed David Roberts, James Green, John Bulgin, Henry Thomas, George Rous, desiring conference with the Board; and it was resolved that a special Board Meeting be called for February 7th at the house of the Manager, for the purpose of discussing the situation with Mr. Simon Harness and the Men's Committee on the spot. Passed twelve transfers, signed and sealed nine certificates and one balance certificate."

(*He pushes the book over to the* CHAIRMAN.)

ANTHONY (*with a heavy sigh*). If it's your pleasure, sign the same.

(*He signs, moving the pen with difficulty.*)

WANKLIN. What's the Union's game, Tench? They haven't made up their split with the men. What does Harness want this interview for?

TENCH. Hoping we shall come to a compromise, I think, sir; he's having a meeting with the men this afternoon.

WILDER. Harness! Ah! He's one of those cold-blooded, cool-headed chaps. I distrust them. I don't know that we didn't make a mistake to come down. What time'll the men be here?

UNDERWOOD. Any time now.

WILDER. Well, if we're not ready, they'll have to wait — won't do them any harm to cool their heels a bit.

SCANTLEBURY (*slowly*). Poor devils! It's snowing. *What* weather!

UNDERWOOD (*with meaning slowness*). This house'll be the warmest place they've been in this winter.

WILDER. Well, I hope we're going to settle this business in time for me to catch the 6.30. I've got to take my wife to Spain to-morrow. (*Chattily.*) My old father had a strike at his works in '69; just such a February as this. They wanted to shoot him.

WANKLIN. What! In the close season?

WILDER. By George, there was no close season for employers then! He used to go down to his office with a pistol in his pocket.

SCANTLEBURY (*faintly alarmed.*) Not seriously?

WILDER (*with finality*). Ended in his shootin' one of 'em in the legs.

SCANTLEBURY (*unavoidably feeling his thigh*). No? Which?

ANTHONY (*lifting the agenda paper*). To consider the policy of the Board in relation to the strike. (*There is a silence.*)

WILDER. It's this infernal three-cornered duel — the Union, the men, and ourselves.

WANKLIN. We needn't consider the Union.

WILDER. It's my experience that you've always got to consider the Union, confound them! If the Union were going to withdraw their support from the men, as they've done, why did they ever allow them to strike at all?

EDGAR. We've had that over a dozen times.

WILDER. Well, I've never understood it! It's beyond me. They talk of the engineers' and furnacemen's demands being excessive — so they are — but that's not enough to make the Union withdraw their support. What's behind it?

UNDERWOOD. Fear of strikes at Harper's and Tinewell's.

WILDER (*with triumph*). Afraid of other strikes — now, that's a reason! Why couldn't we have been told that before?

UNDERWOOD. You were.

TENCH. You were absent from the Board that day, sir.

SCANTLEBURY. The men must have seen they had no chance when the Union gave them up. It's madness.

UNDERWOOD. It's Roberts!

WILDER. Just our luck, the men finding a fanatical firebrand like Roberts for leader. (*A pause.*)

WANKLIN (*looking at* ANTHONY). Well?

WILDER (*breaking in fussily*). It's a regular mess. I don't like the position we're in; I don't like it; I've said so for a long time. (*Looking at* WANKLIN.) When Wanklin and I came down here before Christmas it looked as if the men must collapse. You thought so too, Underwood.

UNDERWOOD. Yes.

WILDER. Well, they haven't! Here we are, going from bad to worse — losing our customers — shares going down!

SCANTLEBURY (*shaking his head*). M'm! M'm!

WANKLIN. What loss have we made by this strike, Tench?

TENCH. Over fifty thousand, sir!

SCANTLEBURY (*pained*). You don't say!

WILDER. We shall never get it back.

TENCH. No, sir.

WILDER. Who'd have supposed the men were going to stick out like this — nobody suggested that. (*Looking angrily at* TENCH.)

SCANTLEBURY (*shaking his head*). I've never liked a fight — never shall.

ANTHONY. No surrender! (*All look at him.*)

WILDER. Who wants to surrender? (ANTHONY *looks at him.*) I — I want to act reasonably. When the men sent Roberts up to the Board in December — then was the time. We ought to have humored him; instead of that the Chairman — (*dropping his eyes before* ANTHONY'S) — er — we snapped his head off. We could have got them in then by a little tact.

ANTHONY. No compromise!

WILDER. There we are! This strike's been going on now since October, and as far as I can see it may last another six months. Pretty mess we shall be in by then. The only comfort is, the men'll be in a worse!

EDGAR. (*To* UNDERWOOD.) What sort of state are they really in, Frank?

UNDERWOOD (*without expression*). Damnable!

WILDER. Well, who on earth would have thought they'd have held on like this without support!

UNDERWOOD. Those who know them.

WILDER. I defy any one to know them! And what about tin? Price going up daily. When we do get started we shall have to work off our contracts at the top of the market.

WANKLIN. What do you say to that, Chairman?

ANTHONY. Can't be helped!

WILDER. Shan't pay a dividend till goodness knows when!

SCANTLEBURY (*with emphasis*). We ought to think of the shareholders. (*Turning heavily.*) Chairman, I say we ought to think of the shareholders. (ANTHONY *mutters.*) What's that?

TENCH. The Chairman says he *is* thinking of you, sir.

SCANTLEBURY (*sinking back into torpor*). Cynic!

WILDER. It's past a joke. *I* don't want to go without a dividend for years if the Chairman does. We can't go on playing ducks and drakes with the Company's prosperity.

EDGAR (*rather ashamedly*). I think we ought to consider the men.

(*All but* ANTHONY *fidget in their seats.*)

SCANTLEBURY (*with a sigh*). We mustn't think of our private feelings, young man. That'll never do.

EDGAR (*ironically*). I'm not thinking of our feelings. I'm thinking of the men's.

WILDER. As to that — we're men of business.

WANKLIN. That *is* the little trouble.

EDGAR. There's no necessity for pushing things so far in the face of all this suffering — it's — it's cruel.

(*No one speaks, as though* EDGAR *had uncovered something whose existence no man prizing his self-respect could afford to recognize.*)

WANKLIN (*with an ironical smile*). I'm afraid we mustn't base our policy on luxuries like sentiment.

EDGAR. I detest this state of things.

ANTHONY. We didn't seek the quarrel.

EDGAR. I know that sir, but surely we've gone far enough.

ANTHONY. No. (*All look at one another.*)

WANKLIN. Luxuries apart, Chairman, we must look out what we're doing.

ANTHONY. Give way to the men once and there'll be no end to it.

WANKLIN. I quite agree, but — (ANTHONY *shakes his head.*)   You make it a question of bedrock principle?   (ANTHONY *nods.*) Luxuries again, Chairman!   The shares are below par.

WILDER. Yes, and they'll drop to a half when we pass the next dividend.

SCANTLEBURY (*with alarm*).   Come, come!   Not so bad as that.

WILDER (*grimly*).   You'll see!   (*Craning forward to catch* ANTHONY'S *speech.*)   I didn't catch —

TENCH (*hesitating*).   The Chairman says, sir, "Fais que — que — devra —

EDGAR (*sharply*).   My father says: "Do what we ought — and let things rip."

WILDER. Tcha!

SCANTLEBURY (*throwing up his hands*).   The Chairman's a Stoic — I always said the Chairman was a Stoic.

WILDER. Much good that'll do us.

WANKLIN (*suavely*).   Seriously, Chairman, are you going to let the ship sink under you, for the sake of — a principle?

ANTHONY. She won't sink.

SCANTLEBURY (*with alarm*).   Not while I'm on the Board I hope.

ANTHONY (*with a twinkle*).   Better rat, Scantlebury.

SCANTLEBURY. What a man!

ANTHONY. I've always fought them; I've never been beaten yet.

WANKLIN. We're with you in theory, Chairman.   But we're not all made of cast-iron.

ANTHONY. We've only to hold on.

WILDER (*rising and going to the fire*).   And go to the devil as fast as we can!

ANTHONY. Better go to the devil than give in!

WILDER (*fretfully*).   That may suit you, sir, but it doesn't suit me, or any one else I should think.

(ANTHONY *looks him in the face — a silence.*)

EDGAR. I don't see how we can get over it that to go on like this means starvation to the men's wives and families.

(WILDER *turns abruptly to the fire, and* SCANTLEBURY *puts out a hand to push the idea away.*)

WANKLIN. I'm afraid again that sounds a little sentimental.

EDGAR. Men of business are excused from decency, you think?

WILDER. Nobody's more sorry for the men than I am, but if they (*lashing himself*) choose to be such a pig-headed lot, it's nothing to do with us; we've quite enough on *our* hands to think of ourselves and the shareholders.

EDGAR (*irritably*). It won't kill the shareholders to miss a dividend or two; I don't see that *that's* reason enough for knuckling under.

SCANTLEBURY (*with grave discomfort*). You talk very lightly of your dividends, young man; I don't know where we are.

WILDER. There's only one sound way of looking at it. We can't go on ruining *ourselves* with this strike.

ANTHONY. No caving in!

SCANTLEBURY (*with a gesture of despair*). Look at him!

(ANTHONY *is leaning back in his chair. They do look at him.*)

WILDER (*returning to his seat*). Well, all I can say is, if that's the Chairman's view, I don't know what we've come down here for.

ANTHONY. To tell the men that we've got nothing for them — (*Grimly.*) They won't believe it till they hear it spoken in plain English.

WILDER. H'm! Shouldn't be a bit surprised if that brute Roberts hadn't got us down here with the very same idea. I hate a man with a grievance.

EDGAR (*resentfully*). We didn't pay him enough for his discovery. I always said that at the time.

WILDER. We paid him five hundred and a bonus of two hundred three years later. If that's not enough! What does he want, for goodness' sake?

TENCH (*complainingly*). Company made a hundred thousand out of his brains, and paid him seven hundred — that's the way he goes on, sir.

WILDER. The man's a rank agitator! Look here, I hate the Unions. But now we've got Harness here let's get him to settle the whole thing.

ANTHONY. No! (*Again they look at him.*)

UNDERWOOD. Roberts won't let the men assent to that.

SCANTLEBURY. Fanatic! Fanatic!

WILDER (*looking at* ANTHONY). And not the only one!

(FROST *enters from the hall.*)

FROST (*To* ANTHONY.) Mr. Harness from the Union, waiting, sir. The men are here too, sir.

> (ANTHONY *nods.* UNDERWOOD *goes to the door, returning with* HARNESS, *a pale, clean-shaven man with hollow cheeks, quick eyes, and lantern jaw* — FROST *has retired.*)

UNDERWOOD (*pointing to* TENCH's *chair*). Sit there next the Chairman, Harness, won't you?

> (*At* HARNESS's *appearance, the Board have drawn together, as it were, and turned a little to him, like cattle at a dog.*)

HARNESS (*with a sharp look round, and a bow*). Thanks! (*He sits — his accent is slightly nasal.*) Well, gentlemen, we're going to do business at last, I hope.

WILDER. Depends on what you *call* business, Harness. Why don't you make the men come in?

HARNESS (*sardonically*). The men are far more in the right than you are. The question with us is whether we shan't begin to support them again.

> (*He ignores them all, except* ANTHONY, *to whom he turns in speaking.*)

ANTHONY. Support them if you like; we'll put in free labor and have done with it.

HARNESS. That won't do, Mr. Anthony. You can't get free labor, and you know it.

ANTHONY. We shall see that.

HARNESS. I'm quite frank with you. We were forced to withold our support from your men because some of their demands are in excess of current rates. I expect to make them withdraw those demands today: if they do, take it straight from me, gentlemen, we shall back them again at once. Now, I want to see something fixed upon before I go back tonight. Can't we have done with this old-fashioned tug-of-war business? What good's it doing you? Why don't you recognize once for all that these people are men like yourselves, and want what's good for them just as you want what's good for you — (*Bitterly.*) Your motor-cars, and champagne, and eight-course dinners.

ANTHONY. If the men will come in, we'll do something for them.

HARNESS (*ironically*). Is that your opinion too, sir — and yours —

and yours? (*The Directors do not answer.*) Well, all I can say is: it's a kind of high and mighty aristocratic tone I thought we'd grown out of — seems I was mistaken.

ANTHONY. It's the tone the men use. Remains to be seen which can hold out longest — they without us, or we without them.

HARNESS. As business men, I wonder you're not ashamed of this waste of force, gentlemen. You know what it'll all end in.

ANTHONY. What?

HARNESS. Compromise — it always does.

SCANTLEBURY. Can't you persuade the men that their interests are the same as ours?

HARNESS (*turning, ironically*). I could persuade them of that, sir, if they were.

WILDER. Come, Harness, you're a clever man, you don't believe all the Socialistic claptrap that's talked nowadays. There's no real difference between their interests and ours.

HARNESS. There's just one very simple question I'd like to put to you. Will you pay your men one penny more than they force you to pay them? (WILDER *is silent.*)

WANKLIN (*chiming in*). I humbly thought that not to pay more than was necessary was the A B C of commerce.

HARNESS (*with irony*). Yes, that seems to be the A B C of commerce, sir; and the A B C of commerce is between your interests and the men's.

SCANTLEBURY (*whispering*). We ought to arrange something.

HARNESS (*dryly*). Am I to understand then, gentlemen, that your Board is going to make no concessions?

(WANKLIN *and* WILDER *bend forward as if to speak, but stop.*)

ANTHONY (*nodding*). None.

(WANKLIN *and* WILDER *again bend forward, and* SCANTLEBURY *gives an unexpected grunt.*)

HARNESS. You were about to say something, I believe?

(*But* SCANTLEBURY *says nothing.*)

EDGAR (*looking up suddenly*). We're sorry for the state of the men.

HARNESS (*icily*). The men have no use for your pity, sir. What they want is justice.

ANTHONY. Then let *them* be just.

HARNESS. For that word "just" read "humble," Mr. Anthony.

Why should they be humble? Barring the accident of money, aren't they as good as you?

ANTHONY. Cant!

HARNESS. Well, I've been five years in America. It colors a man's notions.

SCANTLEBURY (*suddenly, as though avenging his uncompleted grunt*). Let's have the men in and hear what they've got to say!

(ANTHONY *nods, and* UNDERWOOD *goes out by the single door.*)

HARNESS (*dryly*). As I'm to have an interview with them this afternoon, gentlemen, I'll ask you to postpone your final decision till that's over.

(*Again* ANTHONY *nods, and taking up his glass drinks.* UNDERWOOD *comes in again, followed by* ROBERTS, GREEN, BULGIN, THOMAS, ROUS. *They file in, hat in hand, and stand silent in a row.* ROBERTS *is lean, of middle height, with a slight stoop. He has a little rat-gnawed, brown-gray beard, mustaches, high cheekbones, hollow cheeks, small fiery eyes. He wears an old and grease-stained blue serge suit, and carries an old bowler hat. He stands nearest the Chairman.* GREEN, *next to him, has a clean, worn face, with a small gray goatee beard and drooping mustaches, iron spectacles, and mild, straightforward eyes. He wears an overcoat, green with age, and a linen collar. Next to him is* BULGIN, *a tall, strong man, with a dark mustache, and fighting jaw, wearing a red muffler, who keeps changing his cap from one hand to the other. Next to him is* THOMAS, *an old man with a gray mustache, full beard, and weatherbeaten, bony face, whose overcoat discloses a lean, plucked-looking neck. On his right,* ROUS, *the youngest of the five, looks like a soldier; he has a glitter in his eyes.*)

UNDERWOOD (*pointing*). There are some chairs there against the wall, Roberts; won't you draw them up and sit down?

ROBERTS. Thank you, Mr. Underwood — we'll stand — in the presence of the Board. (*He speaks in a biting and staccato voice, rolling his r's, pronouncing his a's like an Italian a, and his consonants short and crisp.*) How are you, Mr. Harness? Didn't expect to have the pleasure of seeing you till this afternoon.

HARNESS (*steadily*). We shall meet again then, Roberts.

ROBERTS. Glad to hear that; we shall have some news for you to take to your people.

ANTHONY. What do the men want?

ROBERTS (*acidly*). Beg pardon, I don't quite catch the Chairman's remark.

TENCH (*from behind the Chairman's chair*). The Chairman wishes to know what the men have to say.

ROBERTS. It's what the Board has to say we've come to hear. It's for the Board to speak first.

ANTHONY. The Board has nothing to say.

ROBERTS (*looking along the line of men*). In that case we're wasting the Directors' time. We'll be taking our feet off this pretty carpet.

(*He turns, the men move slowly, as though hypnotically influenced.*)

WANKLIN (*suavely*). Come, Roberts, you didn't give us this long cold journey for the pleasure of saying that.

THOMAS (*A pure Welshman.*) No, sir, an' what I say iss ——

ROBERTS (*bitingly*). Go on, Henry Thomas, go on. You're better able to speak to the — Directors than me. (THOMAS *is silent.*)

TENCH. The Chairman means, Roberts, that it was the men who asked for the conference, the Board wish to hear what they have to say.

ROBERTS. Gad! If I was to begin to tell ye all they have to say, I wouldn't be finished today. And there'd be some that'd wish they'd never left their London palaces.

HARNESS. What's your proposition, man? Be reasonable.

ROBERTS. You want reason, Mr. Harness? Take a look round this afternoon before the meeting. (*He looks at the men; no sound escapes them.*) You'll see some very pretty scenery.

HARNESS. All right, my friend; you won't put me off.

ROBERTS (*To the men.*) We shan't put Mr. Harness off. Have some champagne with your lunch, Mr. Harness; you'll want it, sir.

HARNESS. Come, get to business, man!

THOMAS. What we're asking, look you, is just simple justice.

ROBERTS (*venomously*). Justice from London? What are you talking about, Henry Thomas? Have you gone silly? (THOMAS *is silent.*) We know very well what we are — discontented dogs — never satisfied. What did the Chairman tell me up in London? That I didn't know what I was talking about. I was a foolish, uneducated man, that knew nothing of the wants of the men I spoke for.

EDGAR. Do please keep to the point.

ANTHONY (*holding up his hand*). There can only be one master, Roberts.

ROBERTS. Then, be Gad, it'll be us.

(*There is a silence;* ANTHONY *and* ROBERTS *stare at one another.*)

UNDERWOOD. If you've nothing to say to the Directors, Roberts, perhaps you'll let Green or Thomas speak for the men.

(GREEN *and* THOMAS *look anxiously at* ROBERTS, *at each other, and the other men.*)

GREEN. (*An Englishman.*) If I'd been listened to, gentlemen ——

THOMAS. What I'fe got to say iss what we'fe all got to say ——

ROBERTS. Speak for yourself, Henry Thomas.

SCANTLEBURY (*with a gesture of deep spiritual discomfort*). Let the poor men call their souls their own!

ROBERTS. Aye, they shall keep their souls, for it's not much body that you've left them, Mr. (*with biting emphasis, as though the word were an offense*) Scantlebury! (*To the men.*) Well, will you speak, or shall I speak for you?

ROUS (*suddenly*). Speak out, Roberts, or leave it to others.

ROBERTS (*ironically*). Thank you, George Rous. (*Addressing himself to* ANTHONY.) The Chairman and Board of Directors have honored us by leaving London and coming all this way to hear what we've got to say; it would not be polite to keep them any longer waiting.

WILDER. Well, thank God for that!

ROBERTS. Ye will not dare to thank Him when I have done, Mr. Wilder, for all your piety. May be your God up in London has no time to listen to the working man. I'm told He is a wealthy God; but if he listens to what I tell Him, He will know more than ever He learned in Kensington.

HARNESS. Come, Roberts, you have your own God. Respect the God of other men.

ROBERTS. That's right, sir. We have another God down here; I doubt He is rather different to Mr. Wilder's. Ask Henry Thomas; he will tell you whether his God and Mr. Wilder's are the same.

(THOMAS *lifts his hand, and cranes his head as though to prophesy.*)

WANKLIN. For goodness' sake, let's keep to the point, Roberts.

ROBERTS. I rather think it is the point, Mr. Wanklin. If you can get the God of Capital to walk through the streets of Labor, and pay attention to what he sees, you're a brighter man than I take you for, for all that you're a Radical.

ANTHONY. Attend to me, Roberts! (ROBERTS *is silent.*) You are here to speak for the men, as I am here to speak for the Board. (*He looks slowly round.* WILDER, WANKLIN, *and* SCANTLEBURY *make movements of uneasiness, and* EDGAR *gazes at the floor. A faint smile comes on* HARNESS's *face.*) Now then, what is it?

ROBERTS. Right, sir! (*Throughout all that follows, he and* ANTHONY *look fixedly upon each other. Men and Directors show in their various ways suppressed uneasiness, as though listening to words that they themselves would not have spoken.*) The men can't afford to travel up to London; and they don't trust you to believe what they say in black and white. They know what the post is (*he darts a look at* UNDERWOOD *and* TENCH), and what Directors' meetings are: "Refer it to the manager — let the manager advise us on the men's condition. Can we squeeze them a little more?"

UNDERWOOD (*in a low voice*). Don't hit below the belt, Roberts!

ROBERTS. Is it below the belt, Mr. Underwood? The men know. When I came up to London, I told you the position straight. An' what came of it? I was told I didn't know what I was talkin' about. I can't afford to travel up to London to be told that again.

ANTHONY. What have you to say for the men?

ROBERTS. I have this to say — and first as to their condition. Ye shall 'ave no need to go and ask your manager. Ye can't squeeze them any more. Every man of us is well-nigh starving. (*A surprised murmur rises from the men.* ROBERTS *looks round.*) Ye wonder why I tell ye that? Every man of us is going short. We can't be no worse off than we've been these weeks past. Ye needn't think that by waiting ye'll drive us to come in. We'll die first, the whole lot of us. The men have sent for ye to know, once and for all, whether ye are going to grant them their demands. I see the sheet of paper in the Secretary's hand. (TENCH *moves nervously.*) That's it, I think, Mr. Tench. It's not very large.

TENCH (*nodding*).   Yes.

ROBERTS.   There's not one sentence of writing on that paper that we can do without.   (*A movement amongst the men.*   ROBERTS *turns on them sharply.*)   Isn't that so?   (*The men assent reluctantly.*   ANTHONY *takes from* TENCH *the paper and peruses it.*)   Not one single sentence.   All those demands are fair.   We have not asked anything that we are not entitled to ask.   What I said up in London, I say again now: there is not anything on that piece of paper that a just man should not ask, and a just man give.   (*A pause.*)

ANTHONY.   There is not one single demand on this paper that we will grant.

> (*In the stir that follows on these words,* ROBERTS *watches the Directors and* ANTHONY *the men.* WILDER *gets up abruptly and goes over to the fire.*)

ROBERTS.   D'ye mean that?

ANTHONY.   I do.

> (WILDER *at the fire makes an emphatic movement of disgust.*)

ROBERTS (*noting it, with dry intensity*).   Ye best know whether the condition of the Company is any better than the condition of the men.   (*Scanning the Directors' faces.*)   Ye best know whether ye can afford your tyranny — but this I tell ye: If ye think the men will give way the least part of an inch, ye're making the worst mistake ye ever made.   (*He fixes his eyes on* SCANTLEBURY.)   Ye think because the Union is not supporting us — more shame to it! — that we'll be coming on our knees to you one fine morning. Ye think because the men have got their wives an' families to think of — that it's just the question of a week or two ——

ANTHONY.   It would be better if you did not speculate so much on what we think.

ROBERTS.   Aye!   It's not much profit to us!   I will say this for you, Mr. Anthony — ye know your own mind!   (*Staring at* ANTHONY.) I can reckon on ye!

ANTHONY (*ironically*).   I am obliged to you!

ROBERTS.   And I know mine.   I tell ye this: The men will send their wives and families where the country will have to keep them; an' they will starve sooner than give way.   I advise ye, Mr. Anthony, to prepare yourself for the worst that can happen to your Company.   We are not so ignorant as you might suppose.   We know

the way the cat is jumping.   Your position is not all that it might
be — not exactly

ANTHONY.   Be good enough to allow us to judge of our position for
ourselves.   Go back, and reconsider your own.

ROBERTS (*stepping forward*).   Mr. Anthony, you are not a young man
now; from the time I remember anything ye have been an enemy
to every man that has come into your works.   I don't say that
ye're a mean man, or a cruel man, but ye've grudged them the
say of any word in their own fate.   Ye've fought them down four
times.   I've heard ye say ye love a fight — mark my words —
ye're fighting the last fight ye'll ever fight ——

> (TENCH *touches* ROBERTS'S *sleeve.*)

UNDERWOOD.   Roberts!   Roberts!

ROBERTS.   Roberts! Roberts! I mustn't speak my mind to the Chairman, but the Chairman may speak his mind to me!

WILDER.   What are things coming to?

ANTHONY (*with a grim smile at* WILDER).   Go on, Roberts; say what
you like!

ROBERTS (*after a pause*).   I have no more to say.

ANTHONY.   The meeting stands adjourned to five o'clock.

WANKLIN (*in a low voice to* UNDERWOOD).   We shall never settle anything like this.

ROBERTS (*bitingly*).   We thank the Chairman and Board of Directors for their gracious hearing.

> (*He moves towards the door; the men cluster together stupefied; then*
> ROUS, *throwing up his head, passes* ROBERTS *and goes out.   The*
> *others follow.*)

ROBERTS (*with his hand on the door — maliciously*).   Good-day,
gentlemen!   (*He goes out.*)

HARNESS (*ironically*).   I congratulate you on the conciliatory spirit
that's been displayed.   With your permission, gentlemen, I'll be
with you again at half-past five.   Good-morning!

> (*He bows slightly, rests his eyes on* ANTHONY, *who returns his stare*
> *unmoved, and, followed by* UNDERWOOD, *goes out.   There is a*
> *moment of uneasy silence.*   UNDERWOOD *reappears in the door-*
> *way.*)

WILDER (*with emphatic disgust*).   Well!   (*The double doors are opened.*)

ENID (*standing in the doorway*).   Lunch is ready.

> (EDGAR, *getting up abruptly, walks out past his sister.*)

WILDER. Coming to lunch, Scantlebury?

SCANTLEBURY (*rising heavily*). I suppose so, I suppose so. It's the only thing we can do.   (*They go out through the double doors.*)

WANKLIN (*in a low voice*). Do you really mean to fight to a finish, Chairman?   (ANTHONY *nods.*)

WANKLIN. Take care! The essence of things is to know when to stop.   (ANTHONY *does not answer.*)

WANKLIN (*very gravely*). This way disaster lies. The ancient Trojans were fools to your father, Mrs. Underwood.

(*He goes out through the double doors.*)

ENID. I want to speak to father, Frank.

(UNDERWOOD *follows* WANKLIN *out.* TENCH, *passing round the table, is restoring order to the scattered pens and papers.*)

ENID. Aren't you coming, Dad?

(ANTHONY *shakes his head.* ENID *looks meaningly at* TENCH.)

ENID. Won't you go and have some lunch, Mr. Tench?

TENCH (*with papers in his hand*). Thank you, ma'am, thank you!
(*He goes slowly, looking back.*)

ENID (*shutting the doors*). I do hope it's settled, father!

ANTHONY. No!

ENID (*very disappointed*). Oh! Haven't you done anything?
(ANTHONY *shakes his head.*)

ENID. Frank says they all want to come to a compromise, really, except that man Roberts.

ANTHONY. *I* don't.

ENID. It's such a horrid position for us. If you were the wife of the manager, and lived down here, and saw it all. You can't realize, Dad!

ANTHONY. Indeed?

ENID. We see *all* the distress. You remember my maid Annie, who married Roberts? (ANTHONY *nods.*) It's so wretched, her heart's weak; since the strike began, she hasn't even been getting proper food. I know it for a fact, father.

ANTHONY. Give her what she wants, poor woman!

ENID. Roberts won't let her take anything from *us*.

ANTHONY (*staring before him*). I can't be answerable for the men's obstinacy.

ENID. They're all suffering, Father! Do stop it, for my sake!

ANTHONY (*with a keen look at her*). You don't understand, my dear.

ENID. If I were on the Board, I'd do something.

ANTHONY. What would you do?

ENID. It's because you can't bear to give way. It's so —

ANTHONY. Well?

ENID. So unnecessary.

ANTHONY. What do *you* know about necessity? Read your novels, play your music, talk your talk, but don't try and tell *me* what's at the bottom of a struggle like this.

ENID. I live down here and see it.

ANTHONY. What do you imagine stands between you and your class and these men that you're so sorry for?

ENID (*coldly*). I don't know what you mean, father.

ANTHONY. In a few years you and your children would be down in the condition they're in, but for those who have the eyes to see things as they are and the backbone to stand up for themselves.

ENID. You don't know the state the men are in.

ANTHONY. I know it well enough.

ENID. You don't, father; if you did, you wouldn't ——

ANTHONY. It's you who don't know the simple facts of the position. What sort of mercy do you suppose you'd get if no one stood between you and the continual demands of labor? This sort of mercy — (*He puts his hand up to his throat and squeezes it.*) First would go your sentiments, my dear; then your culture, and your comforts would be going all the time!

ENID. I don't believe in barriers between classes.

ANTHONY. You — don't — believe — in — barriers — between the classes?

ENID (*coldly*). And I don't know what that has to do with this question.

ANTHONY. It will take a generation or two for you to understand.

ENID. It's only you and Roberts, father, and you know it! (AN-THONY *thrusts out his lower lip.*) It'll ruin the Company.

ANTHONY. Allow me to judge of that.

ENID (*resentfully*). I won't stand by and let poor Annie Roberts suffer like this! And think of the children, father! I warn you.

ANTHONY (*with a grim smile*). What do you propose to do?

ENID. That's my affair.   (ANTHONY *only looks at her.*)

ENID (*in a changed voice, stroking his sleeve*). Father, you *know* you oughtn't to have this strain on you — you know what Dr. Fisher said!

ANTHONY. No old man can afford to listen to old women.

ENID. But you *have* done enough, even if it really is such a matter of principle with you.

ANTHONY. Do you think so?

ENID. Don't, Dad! (*Her face works.*) You — you might think of *us!*

ANTHONY. I am.

ENID. It'll break you down.

ANTHONY (*slowly*). My dear, I am not going to funk; on that you may rely.

(*Reënter* TENCH *with papers; he glances at them, then plucking up courage.*)

TENCH. Beg pardon, madam, I think I'd rather see these papers were disposed of before I get my lunch.

    (ENID, *after an impatient glance at him, looks at her father, turns suddenly, and goes into the drawing-room.*)

TENCH (*holding the papers and a pen to* ANTHONY, *very nervously*). Would you sign these for me, please, sir?

                        (ANTHONY *takes the pen and signs.*)

TENCH (*standing with a sheet of blotting-paper behind* EDGAR's *chair, begins speaking nervously*). I owe my position to you, sir.

ANTHONY. Well?

TENCH. I'm obliged to see everything that's going on, sir; I — I depend upon the Company entirely. If anything were to happen to it, it'd be disastrous for me. (ANTHONY *nods.*) And, of course, my wife's just had another; and so it makes me doubly anxious just now. And the rates are really terrible down our way.

ANTHONY (*with grim amusement*). Not more terrible than they are up mine.

TENCH. No, sir? (*Very nervously.*) I know the Company means a great deal to you, sir.

ANTHONY. It does; I founded it.

TENCH. Yes, sir. If the strike goes on it'll be very serious. I think the Directors are beginning to realize that, sir.

ANTHONY (*ironically*). Indeed?

TENCH. I know you hold very strong views, sir, and it's always your habit to look things in the face; but I don't think the Directors — like it, sir, now they — they see it.

ANTHONY (*grimly*). Nor you, it seems.

TENCH (*with the ghost of a smile*). No, sir; of course I've got my children, and my wife's delicate; in my position I *have* to think of these things. (ANTHONY *nods.*) It wasn't *that* I was going to say, sir, if you'll excuse me —— (*Hesitates.*)

ANTHONY. Out with it, then!

TENCH. I know — from my own father, sir, that when you get on in life you do feel things dreadfully —

ANTHONY (*almost paternally*). Come, out with it, Tench!

TENCH. I don't like to say it, sir.

ANTHONY (*stonily*). You must.

TENCH (*after a pause, desperately bolting it out*). I think the Directors are going to throw you over, sir.

ANTHONY. (*Sits in silence.*) Ring the bell!

(TENCH *nervously rings the bell and stands by the fire.*)

TENCH. Excuse me for saying such a thing. I was *only* thinking of you, sir.

(FROST *enters from the hall, he comes to the foot of the table, and looks at* ANTHONY; TENCH *covers his nervousness by arranging papers.*)

ANTHONY. Bring me a whiskey and soda.

FROST. Anything to eat, sir?

(ANTHONY *shakes his head.* FROST *goes to the sideboard, and prepares the drink.*)

TENCH (*in a low voice, almost supplicating.*) If you *could* see your way, sir, it would be a great relief to my mind, it would indeed. (*He looks up at* ANTHONY, *who has not moved.*) It does make me so very anxious. I haven't slept properly for weeks, sir, and that's a fact.

(ANTHONY *looks in his face, then slowly shakes his head.*)

TENCH (*disheartened*). No, sir?

(*He goes on arranging papers.* FROST *places the whiskey and soda on a salver and puts it down by* ANTHONY's *right hand. He stands away, looking gravely at* ANTHONY.)

FROST. *Nothing* I can get you, sir? (ANTHONY *shakes his head.*) You're aware, sir, of what the doctor said, sir?

ANTHONY. I am.

> (*A pause.* FROST *suddenly moves closer to him, and speaks in a low voice.*)

FROST. This strike, sir; puttin' all this strain on you. Excuse me, sir, is it — is it worth it, sir? (ANTHONY *mutters some words that are inaudible.*) Very good, sir!

> (*He turns and goes out into the hall.* TENCH *makes two attempts to speak; but meeting his Chairman's gaze he drops his eyes, and, turning dismally, he too goes out.* ANTHONY *is left alone. He grips the glass, tilts it, and drinks deeply; then sets it down with a deep and rumbling sigh and leans back in his chair.*)

ACT II

SCENE I

It is half past three. In the kitchen of ROBERTS'S *cottage a meager little fire is burning. The room is clean and tidy, very barely furnished, with a brick floor and white-washed walls, much stained with smoke. There is a kettle on the fire. A door opposite the fireplace opens inward from a snowy street. On the wooden table are a cup and saucer, a teapot, knife, and plate of bread and cheese. Close to the fireplace in an old armchair, wrapped in a rug, sits* MRS. ROBERTS, *a thin and dark-haired woman about thirty-five, with patient eyes. Her hair is not done up, but tied back with a piece of ribbon. By the fire, too, is* MRS. YEO; *a red-haired, broad-faced person. Sitting near the table is* MRS. ROUS, *an old lady, ashen-white, with silver hair; by the door, standing, as if about to go, is* MRS. BULGIN, *a little, pale, pinched-up woman. In a chair, with her elbows resting on the table, and her face resting in her hands, sits* MADGE THOMAS, *a good-looking girl of twenty-two, with high cheekbones, deepset eyes, and dark untidy hair. She is listening to the talk, but she neither speaks nor moves.*

MRS. YEO. So he give me a sixpence, and that's the first bit o' money *I* seen this week. There an't much 'eat to this fire. Come and warm yerself, Mrs. Rous, you're lookin' as white as the snow, you are.

MRS. ROUS (*shivering — placidly*). Ah! but the winter my old man was took was the proper winter. Seventy-nine that was, when none of you was hardly born — not Madge Thomas, nor Sue Bulgin. (*Looking at them in turn.*) Annie Roberts, 'ow old were you, dear?

MRS. ROBERTS. Seven, Mrs. Rous.

MRS. ROUS. Seven — well, ther'! A tiny little thing!

MRS. YEO (*aggressively*). Well, I was ten myself, I remembers it.

MRS. ROUS (*placidly*). The Company hadn't been started three years. Father was workin' on the acid, that's 'ow he got 'is pisoned leg. I kep' sayin' to 'im, "Father, you've got a pisoned leg." "Well," 'e said, "mother, pison or no pison, I can't afford to go a-layin' up." An' two days after, he was on 'is back, and never got up again. It was Providence! There wasn't none o' these Compensation Acts then.

MRS. YEO. Ye hadn't no strike that winter! (*With grim humor.*) This winter's 'ard enough for me. Mrs. Roberts, you don't want no 'arder winter, do you? Wouldn't seem natural to 'ave a dinner, would it, Mrs. Bulgin?

MRS. BULGIN. We've had bread and tea last four days.

MRS. YEO. You got that Friday's laundry job?

MRS. BULGIN (*dispiritedly*). They said they'd give it me, but when I went last Friday, they were full up. I got to go again next week.

MRS. YEO. Ah! There's too many after that. I send Yeo out on the ice to put on the gentry's skates an' pick up what 'e can. Stops 'im from broodin' about the 'ouse.

MRS. BULGIN (*in a desolate, matter-of-fact voice*). Leavin' out the men — it's bad enough with the children. I keep 'em in bed, they don't get so hungry when they're not running about; but they're that restless in bed they worry your life out.

MRS. YEO. You're lucky they're all so small. It's the goin' to school that makes 'em 'ungry. Don't Bulgin give you *any*thin'?

MRS. BULGIN. (*Shakes her head, then, as though by afterthought.*) Would if he could, I s'pose.

MRS. YEO (*sardonically*). What! 'Aven't 'e got no shares in the Company?

MRS. ROUS (*rising with tremulous cheerfulness*). Well, good-bye, Annie Roberts, I'm going along home.

MRS. ROBERTS. Stay an' have a cup of tea, Mrs. Rous?

MRS. ROUS (*with the faintest smile*). Roberts'll want 'is tea when he comes in. I'll just go an' get to bed; it's warmer there than anywhere. (*She moves very shakily towards the door.*)

MRS. YEO (*rising and giving her an arm*). Come on, mother, take my arm; we're all goin' the same way.

MRS. ROUS (*taking the arm*). Thank you, my dearies!

(THEY *go out, followed by* MRS. BULGIN.)

MADGE (*moving for the first time*). There, Annie, you see that! I told George Rous, "Don't think to have my company till you've made an end of all this trouble. You ought to be ashamed," I said, "with your own mother looking like a ghost, and not a stick to put on the fire. So long as you're able to fill your pipes, you'll let us starve." "I'll take my oath, Madge," he said, "I've not had smoke nor drink these three weeks!" "Well, then, why do you go on with it?" "I can't go back on Roberts!" "... That's it! Roberts, always Roberts!" They'd all drop it but for him. When *he* talks it's the devil that comes into them. (*A silence.* MRS. ROBERTS *makes a movement of pain.*) Ah! *You* don't want him beaten! He's your man. With everybody like their own shadows! (*She makes a gesture towards* MRS. ROBERTS.) If Rous wants me he must give up Roberts. If *he* gave him up — they all would. They're only waiting for a lead. Father's against him — they're all against him in their hearts.

MRS. ROBERTS. You won't beat Roberts!

(*They look silently at each other.*)

MADGE. Won't I? The cowards — when their own mothers and their own children don't know where to turn.

MRS. ROBERTS. Madge!

MADGE (*looking searchingly at* MRS. ROBERTS). I wonder he can look *you* in the face. (*She squats before the fire, with her hands out to the flame.*) Harness is here again. They'll have to make up their minds today.

MRS. ROBERTS (*in a soft, slow voice, with a slight West-country burr*). Roberts will never give up the furnacemen and engineers. 'Twouldn't be right.

MADGE. You can't deceive me. It's just his pride.

(*A tapping at the door is heard, the women turn as* ENID *enters. She wears a round fur cap, and a jacket of squirrel's fur. She closes the door behind her.*)

ENID. Can I come in, Annie?

MRS. ROBERTS (*flinching*). Miss Enid! Give Mrs. Underwood a chair, Madge!

(MADGE *gives* ENID *the chair she has been sitting on.*)

ENID. Thank you! (*To* MRS. ROBERTS.) Are you any better?

MRS. ROBERTS. Yes, m'm; thank you, m'm.

ENID (*looking at the sullen* MADGE *as though requesting her departure*). Why did you send back the jelly? I call that really wicked of you!

MRS. ROBERTS. Thank you, m'm, I'd no need for it.

ENID. Of course! It was Roberts's doing, wasn't it? How can he let all this suffering go on amongst you?

MADGE (*suddenly*). What suffering?

ENID (*surprised*). I beg your pardon!

MADGE. Who said there was suffering?

MRS. ROBERTS. Madge!

MADGE (*throwing her shawl over her head*). Please to let us keep ourselves to ourselves. We don't want you coming here and spying on us.

ENID (*confronting her, but without rising*). I didn't speak to *you.*

MADGE (*in a low, fierce voice*). Keep your kind feelings to yourself. You think you can come amongst us, but you're mistaken. Go back and tell the Manager that.

ENID (*stonily*). This is not your house.

MADGE (*turning to the door*). No, it is not my house; keep clear of my house, Mrs. Underwood.

(*She goes out.* ENID *taps her fingers on the table.*)

MRS. ROBERTS. Please to forgive Madge Thomas, m'm; she's a bit upset today. (*A pause.*)

ENID (*looking at her*). Oh, I think they're so *stupid,* all of them.

MRS. ROBERTS (*with a faint smile*). Yes, m'm.

ENID. Is Roberts out?

MRS. ROBERTS. Yes, m'm.

ENID. It is *his doing* that they don't come to an agreement. Now isn't it, Annie?

MRS. ROBERTS (*softly, with her eyes on* ENID, *and moving the fingers of one hand continually on her breast*). They do say that your father, m'm ——

ENID. My father's getting an old man, and you know what old men are.

MRS. ROBERTS. I am sorry, m'm.

ENID (*more softly*). I don't expect *you* to feel sorry, Annie. I know it's his fault as well as Roberts's.

MRS. ROBERTS. I'm sorry for any one that gets old, m'm; it's dreadful to get old, and Mr. Anthony was such a fine old man I always used to think.

ENID (*impulsively*). He always liked you, don't you remember? Look here, Annie, what can I do? I do so want to know. You don't get what you ought to have. (*Going to the fire, she takes the kettle off, and looks for coals.*) And you're so naughty sending back the soup and things!

MRS. ROBERTS (*with a faint smile*). Yes, m'm?

ENID (*resentfully*). Why, you haven't even got coals?

MRS. ROBERTS. If you please, m'm, to put the kettle on again; Roberts won't have long for his tea when he comes in. He's got to meet the men at four.

ENID (*putting the kettle on*). That means he'll lash them into a fury again. Can't you stop his going, Annie? (MRS. ROBERTS *smiles ironically.*) Have you tried? (*A silence.*) Does he know how ill you are?

MRS. ROBERTS. It's only my weak 'eart, m'm.

ENID. You used to be so well when you were with us.

MRS. ROBERTS (*stiffening*). Roberts is always good to me.

ENID. But you ought to have everything you want, and you have nothing!

MRS. ROBERTS (*appealingly*). They tell me I don't look like a dyin' woman?

ENID. Of course you don't; if you could only have proper —— Will you see my doctor if I send him to you? I'm sure he'd do you good.

MRS. ROBERTS (*with faint questioning*). Yes, m'm.

ENID. Madge Thomas oughtn't to come here; she only excites you. As if I didn't know what suffering there is amongst the men!

I do feel for them dreadfully, but you know they *have* gone too far.

MRS. ROBERTS (*continually moving her fingers*).   They say there's no other way to get better wages, m'm.

ENID (*earnestly*).   But, Annie, that's why the Union won't help them. My husband's very sympathetic with the men, but he says they're not underpaid.

MRS. ROBERTS.   No, m'm?

ENID.   They never think how the Company could go on if we paid the wages they want.

MRS. ROBERTS (*with an effort*).   But the dividends having been so big, m'm.

ENID (*taken aback*).   You all seem to think the shareholders are rich men, but they're not — most of them are really no better off than working men.   (MRS. ROBERTS *smiles.*)   They have to keep up appearances.

MRS. ROBERTS.   Yes, m'm?

ENID.   You don't have to pay rates and taxes, and a hundred other things that they do.   If the men didn't spend such a lot in drink and betting they'd be quite well off!

MRS. ROBERTS.   They say, workin' so hard, they must have some pleasure.

ENID.   But surely not low pleasure like that.

MRS. ROBERTS (*a little resentfully*).   Roberts never touches a drop; and he's never had a bet in his life.

ENID.   Oh! but he's not a com — I mean he's an engineer — a superior man.

MRS. ROBERTS.   Yes, m'm.   Roberts says they've no chance of other pleasures.

ENID (*musing*).   Of course, I know it's hard.

MRS. ROBERTS (*with a spice of malice*).   And they say gentlefolk's just as bad.

ENID (*with a smile*).   I go as far as most people, Annie, but you know, yourself, that's nonsense.

MRS. ROBERTS (*with painful effort*).   A lot o' the men never go near the Public; but even they don't save but very little, and that goes if there's illness.

ENID.   But they've got their clubs, haven't they?

MRS. ROBERTS. The clubs only give up to eighteen shillin's a week, m'm, and it's not much amongst a family. Roberts says workin' folk have always lived from hand to mouth. Sixpence today is worth more than a shillin' tomorrow, that's what they say.

ENID. But that's the spirit of gambling.

MRS. ROBERTS (*with a sort of excitement*). Roberts says a working man's life is all a gamble, from the time 'e's born to the time 'e dies. (ENID *leans forward, interested.* MRS. ROBERTS *goes on with a growing excitement that culminates in the personal feeling of the last words.*) He says, m'm, that when a working man's baby is born, it's a toss-up from breath to breath whether it ever draws another, and so on all 'is life; an' when he comes to be old, it's the work-house or the grave. He says that without a man is very near, and pinches and stints 'imself and 'is children to save, there can't be neither surplus nor security. That's why he wouldn't have no children (*she sinks back*), not though I *wanted* them.

ENID. Yes, yes, I know!

MRS. ROBERTS. No you don't, m'm. You've got your children, and you'll never need to trouble for them.

ENID (*gently*). You oughtn't to be talking so much, Annie. (*Then, in spite of herself.*) But Roberts was paid a lot of money, wasn't he, for discovering that process?

MRS. ROBERTS (*on the defensive*). All Roberts's savin's have gone. He's always looked forward to this strike. He says he's no right to a farthing when the others are suffering. 'Tisn't so with all of them! Some don't seem to care no more than that — so long as they get their own.

ENID. I don't see how they can be expected to when they're suffer-ing like this. (*In a changed voice.*) But Roberts ought to think of *you!* It's all terrible! The kettle's boiling. Shall I make the tea? (*She takes the teapot, and, seeing tea there, pours water into it.*) Won't you have a cup?

MRS. ROBERTS. No, thank you, m'm. (*She is listening, as though for footsteps.*) I'd sooner you didn't see Roberts, m'm, he gets so wild.

ENID. Oh! but I must, Annie; I'll be quite calm, I promise.

MRS. ROBERTS. It's life an' death to him, m'm.

ENID (*very gently*). I'll get him to talk to me outside, we won't excite you.

MRS. ROBERTS (*faintly*). No, m'm.

> (*She gives a violent start.* ROBERTS *has come in, unseen.*)

ROBERTS (*removing his hat — with subtle mockery*). Beg pardon for coming in; you're engaged with a lady, I see.

ENID. Can I speak to you, Mr. Roberts?

ROBERTS. Whom have I the pleasure of addressing, ma'am?

ENID. But surely you know me! I'm Mrs. Underwood.

ROBERTS (*with a bow of malice*). The daughter of our Chairman.

ENID (*earnestly*). I've come on purpose to speak to you; will you come outside a minute? (*She looks at* MRS. ROBERTS.)

ROBERTS (*hanging up his hat*). I have nothing to say, ma'am.

ENID. But I *must* speak to you, please. (*She moves towards the door.*)

ROBERTS (*with sudden venom*). I have not the time to listen!

MRS. ROBERTS. David!

ENID. Mr. Roberts, *please!*

ROBERTS (*taking off his overcoat*). I am sorry to disoblige a lady — Mr. Anthony's daughter.

ENID (*wavering, then with sudden decision*). Mr. Roberts, I know you've another meeting of the men. (ROBERTS *bows.*) I came to appeal to you. Please, please, try to come to some compromise; give way a little, if it's only for your own sakes!

ROBERTS (*speaking to himself*). The daughter of Mr. Anthony begs me to give way a little, if it's only for our own sakes!

ENID. For everybody's sake; for your wife's sake.

ROBERTS. For my wife's sake, for everybody's sake — for the sake of Mr. Anthony.

ENID. Why are you so bitter against my father? He has never done anything to you.

ROBERTS. Has he not?

ENID. He can't help his views, any more than you can help yours.

ROBERTS. I really didn't know that I had a right to views!

ENID. He's an old man, and you ——

> (*Seeing his eyes fixed on her, she stops.*)

ROBERTS (*without raising his voice*). If I saw Mr. Anthony going to die, and I could save him by lifting my hand, I would not lift the little finger of it.

ENID. You — you —— (*She stops again, biting her lips.*)

ROBERTS. I would not, and that's flat!

ENID (*coldly*).   You don't mean what you say, and you know it!

ROBERTS. I mean every word of it.

ENID. But why?

ROBERTS (*with a flash*).   Mr. Anthony stands for tyranny! That's why!

ENID. Nonsense!

(MRS. ROBERTS *makes a movement as if to rise, but sinks back in her chair.*)

ENID (*with an impetuous movement*).   Annie!

ROBERTS. Please not to touch my wife!

ENID (*recoiling with a sort of horror*).   I believe — you are mad.

ROBERTS. The house of a madman then is not the fit place for a lady.

ENID. I'm not afraid of you.

ROBERTS (*bowing*).   I would not expect the daughter of Mr. Anthony to be afraid. Mr. Anthony is not a coward like the rest of them.

ENID (*suddenly*).   I suppose you think it brave, then, to go on with the struggle.

ROBERTS. Does Mr. Anthony think it brave to fight against women and children? Mr. Anthony is a rich man, I believe; does he think it brave to fight against those who haven't a penny? Does he think it brave to set children crying with hunger, an' women shivering with cold?

ENID (*putting up her hand, as though warding off a blow*).   My father is acting on his principles, and you know it!

ROBERTS. And so am I!

ENID. You hate us; and you can't bear to be beaten!

ROBERTS. Neither can Mr. Anthony, for all that he may say.

ENID. At any rate you might have pity on your wife.

(MRS. ROBERTS *who has her hand pressed to her heart, takes it away, and tries to calm her breathing.*)

ROBERTS. Madam, I have no more to say.

(*He takes up the loaf. There is a knock at the door, and* UNDERWOOD *comes in. He stands looking at them.* ENID *turns to him, then seems undecided.*)

UNDERWOOD. Enid!

ROBERTS (*ironically*). Ye were not needing to come for your wife, Mr. Underwood. We are not rowdies.

UNDERWOOD. I know that, Roberts. I hope Mrs. Roberts is better. (ROBERTS *turns away without answering*.) Come, Enid!

ENID. I make one more appeal to you, Mr. Roberts, for the sake of your wife.

ROBERTS (*with polite malice*). If I might advise ye, ma'am — make it for the sake of your husband and your father.

> (ENID, *suppressing a retort, goes out*. UNDERWOOD *opens the door for her and follows*. ROBERTS, *going to the fire, holds out his hands to the dying glow*.)

ROBERTS. How goes it, my girl? Feeling better, are you? (MRS. ROBERTS *smiles faintly*. *He brings his overcoat and wraps it round her*. *Looking at his watch*.) Ten minutes to four! (*As though inspired*.) I've seen their faces, there's no fight in them, except for that one old robber.

MRS. ROBERTS. Won't you stop and eat, David? You've 'ad nothing all day!

ROBERTS (*putting his hand to his throat*). Can't swallow till those old sharks are out o' the town. (*He walks up and down*.) I shall have a bother with the men — there's no heart in them, the cowards. Blind as bats, they are — can't see a day before their noses.

MRS. ROBERTS. It's the women, David.

ROBERTS. Ah! So they say! They can remember the women when their own bellies speak! The women never stop them from the drink; but from a little suffering to themselves in a sacred cause, the women stop them fast enough.

MRS. ROBERTS. But think o' the children, David.

ROBERTS. Ah! If they will go breeding themselves for slaves, without a thought o' the future o' them they breed ——

MRS. ROBERTS (*gasping*). That's enough, David; don't begin to talk of that — I won't — I can't ——

ROBERTS (*staring at her*). Now, now, my girl!

MRS. ROBERTS (*breathlessly*). No, no, David — I won't!

ROBERTS. There, there! Come, come! That's right! (*Bitterly*.) Not one penny will they put by for a day like this. Not they! Hand to mouth — Gad! — I know them! They've broke my heart. There was no holdin' them at the start, but now the pinch 'as come.

MRS. ROBERTS. How can you expect it, David? They're not made of iron.

ROBERTS. Expect it? Wouldn't I expect what I would do meself? Wouldn't I starve an' rot rather than give in? What one man can do, another can.

MRS. ROBERTS. And the women?

ROBERTS. This is not women's work.

MRS. ROBERTS (*with a flash of malice*). No, the women may die for all you care. That's their work.

ROBERTS (*averting his eyes*). Who talks of dying? No one will die till we have beaten these — (*He meets her eyes again, and again turns his away. Excitedly.*) This is what I've been waiting for all these months. To get the old robbers down, and send them home again without a farthin's worth o' change. I've seen their faces, I tell you, in the valley of the shadow of defeat.

(*He goes to the peg and takes down his hat.*)

MRS. ROBERTS (*following with her eyes — softly*). Take your overcoat, David; it must be bitter cold.

ROBERTS (*coming up to her — his eyes are furtive*). No, no! There, there, stay quiet and warm. I won't be long, my girl.

MRS. ROBERTS. (*with soft bitterness*). You'd better take it.

(*She lifts the coat. But ROBERTS puts it back, and wraps it round her. He tries to meet her eyes, but cannot. MRS. ROBERTS stays huddled in the coat, her eyes, that follow him about, are half malicious, half yearning. He looks at his watch again, and turns to go. In the doorway he meets JAN THOMAS, a boy of ten in clothes too big for him, carrying a penny whistle.*)

ROBERTS. Hallo, boy!

(*He goes. JAN stops within a yard of MRS. ROBERTS, and stares at her without a word.*)

MRS. ROBERTS. Well, Jan!

JAN. Father's coming; sister Madge's coming.

(*He sits at the table, and fidgets with his whistle; he blows three vague notes; then imitates a cuckoo. There is a tap on the door. Old THOMAS comes in.*)

THOMAS. A very coot tay to you, ma'am. It is petter that you are.

MRS. ROBERTS. Thank you, Mr. Thomas.

THOMAS (*nervously*).   Roberts in?

MRS. ROBERTS. Just gone on to the meeting, Mr. Thomas.

THOMAS (*with relief, becoming talkative*).   This is fery unfortunate, look you! I came to tell him that we must make terms with London. It is a fery great pity he is gone to the meeting. He will be kicking against the pricks, I am thinking.

MRS. ROBERTS (*half rising*).   He'll never give in, Mr. Thomas.

THOMAS. You must not be fretting, that is very pat for you. Look you, there iss hartly any mans for supporting him now, but the engineers and George Rous. (*Solemnly.*) This strike is no longer coing with Chapel, look you! I have listened carefully, an' I have talked with her. (JAN *blows.*) Sst! I don't care what th' others say, I say that *Chapel means us* to be stopping the trouple, that is what I make of her; and it is my opinion that this is the fery best thing for all of us. If it wasn't my opinion, I ton't say — but it is my opinion, look you.

MRS. ROBERTS (*trying to suppress her excitement*).   I don't know what'll come to Roberts, if you give in.

THOMAS. It iss no disgrace whateffer! All that a mortal man coult do he hass tone. It iss against human nature he hass gone; fery natural — any man may do that; but Chapel has spoken and he must not go against her. (JAN *imitates the cuckoo.*) Ton't make that squeaking! (*Going to the door.*) Here iss my daughter come to sit with you. A fery goot day, ma'am — no fretting — rememper!

(MADGE *comes in and stands at the open door, watching the street.*)

MADGE. You'll be late, father; they're beginning. (*She catches him by the sleeve.*) For the love of God, stand up to him, father — this time!

THOMAS (*detaching his sleeve with dignity*).   Leave me to do what's proper, girl!

(*He goes out.* MADGE *in the center of the open doorway, slowly moves in, as though before the approach of some one.*)

ROUS (*appearing in the doorway*).   Madge!

(MADGE *stands with her back to* MRS. ROBERTS, *staring at him with her head up and her hands behind her.*)

ROUS (*who has a fierce distracted look*). Madge! I'm going to the meeting. (MADGE, *without moving, smiles contemptuously*.) D'ye hear me?
(*They speak in quick low voices.*)

MADGE. I hear! Go, and kill your own mother, if you must.

(ROUS *seizes her by both her arms. She stands rigid, with her head bent back. He releases her, and he too stands motionless.*)

ROUS. I swore to stand by Roberts. I swore that! Ye want me to go back on what I've sworn.

MADGE (*with slow soft mockery*). You are a pretty lover!

ROUS. Madge!

MADGE (*smiling*). I've heard that lovers do what their girls ask them — (JAN *sounds the cuckoo's notes*) — but that's not true, it seems!

ROUS. You'd make a blackleg of me!

MADGE (*with her eyes half closed*). Do it for me!

ROUS (*dashing his hand across his brow*). Damn! I can't!

MADGE (*swiftly*). Do it for me!

ROUS (*through his teeth*). Don't play the wanton with me!

MADGE (*with a movement of her hand towards* JAN — *quick and low*). I would be *that* for the children's sake!

ROUS (*in a fierce whisper*). Madge! Oh, Madge!

MADGE (*with soft mockery*). But *you* can't break your word for me!

ROUS (*with a choke*). Then, begod, I can!

(*He turns and rushes off.* MADGE *stands, with a faint smile on her face, looking after him. She turns to* MRS. ROBERTS.)

MADGE. I have done for Roberts!

MRS. ROBERTS (*scornfully*). Done for my man, with that ——
(*She sinks back.*)

MADGE (*running to her, and feeling her hands*). You're as cold as a stone! You want a drop of brandy. Jan, run to the "Lion"; say I sent you for Mrs. Roberts.

MRS. ROBERTS (*with a feeble movement*). I'll just sit quiet, Madge. Give Jan — his — tea.

MADGE (*giving* JAN *a slice of bread*). There, ye little rascal. Hold your piping. (*Going to the fire, she kneels.*) It's going out.

MRS. ROBERTS (*with a faint smile*). 'Tis all the same!
(JAN *begins to blow his whistle.*)

MADGE. Tsht! Tsht! — you ——
(JAN *stops.*)

MRS. ROBERTS (*smiling*). Let 'im play, Madge.

MADGE (*on her knees at the fire, listening*). Waiting an' waiting. I've no patience with it; waiting an' waiting — that's what a woman has to do! Can you hear them at it — I can!

> (JAN *begins to play his whistle;* MADGE *gets up; half tenderly she ruffles his hair; then, sitting, leans her elbows on the table, and her chin on her hands. Behind her, on* MRS. ROBERTS'S *face the smile has changed to horrified surprise. She makes a sudden movement, sitting forward, pressing her hands against her breast. Then slowly she sinks back; slowly her face loses the look of pain, the smile returns. She fixes her eyes again on* JAN, *and moves her lips and finger to the tune.*)

SCENE II

It is past four. In a gray, failing light, an open muddy space is crowded with workmen. Beyond, divided from it by a barbed wire fence, is the raised towing-path of a canal, on which is moored a barge. In the distance are marshes and snow-covered hills. The "Works" high wall runs from the canal across the open space, and in the angle of this wall is a rude platform of barrels and boards. On it, HARNESS *is standing.* ROBERTS, *a little apart from the crowd, leans his back against the wall. On the raised towing-path two bargemen lounge and smoke indifferently.*

HARNESS (*holding out his hand*). Well, I've spoken to you straight. If I speak till tomorrow I can't say more.

JAGO. (*A dark, sallow, Spanish-looking man with a short, thin beard.*) Mister, want to ask you! Can they get blacklegs?

BULGIN (*menacing*). Let 'em try.

> (*There are savage murmurs from the crowd.*)

BROWN. (*A round-faced man.*) Where could they get 'em then?

EVANS. (*A small, restless, harassed man, with a fighting face.*) There's always blacklegs; it's the nature of 'em. There's always men that'll save their own skins.

> (*Another savage murmur. There is a movement, and old* THOMAS, *joining the crowd, takes his stand in front.*)

HARNESS (*holding up his hand*). They can't get them. But that won't help you. Now men, be reasonable. Your demands would have brought on us the burden of a dozen strikes at a time when we were not prepared for them. The Unions live by Justice, not to one but all. Any fair man will tell you — you were ill-advised! I don't say you go too far for that which you're entitled to, but you're going too far for the moment; you've dug a pit for yourselves. Are you to stay there, or are you to climb out? Come!

LEWIS. (*A clean-cut Welshman with a dark mustache.*) You've hit it, mister! Which is it to be?

> (*Another movement in the crowd, and* ROUS, *coming quickly, takes his stand next* THOMAS.)

HARNESS. Cut your demands to the right pattern, and we'll see you through; refuse, and don't expect me to waste my time coming down here again. I'm not the sort that speaks at random, as you ought to know by this time. If you're the sound men I take you for — no matter who advises you against it — (*he fixes his eyes on* ROBERTS) you'll make up your minds to come in, and trust to us to get your terms. Which is it to be? Hands together, and victory — or — the starvation you've got now.

> (*A prolonged murmur from the crowd.*)

JAGO (*sullenly*). Talk about what you know.

HARNESS (*lifting his voice above the murmur*). Know? (*With cold passion.*) All that you've been through, my friend, I've been through — I was through it when I was no bigger than (*pointing to a youth*) that shaver there; the Unions then weren't what they are now. What's made them strong? It's hands together that's made them strong. I've been through it all, I tell you, the brand's on my soul yet. I know what you've suffered — there's nothing you can tell me that I don't know; but the whole is greater than the part, and you are only the part. Stand by us, and we will stand by you.

> (*Quartering them with his eyes, he waits. The murmuring swells; the men form little groups.* GREEN, BULGIN, *and* LEWIS *talk together.*)

LEWIS. Speaks very sensible, the Union chap.

GREEN (*quietly*). Ah! if I'd 'a' been *listened* to, you'd 'ave 'eard sense these two months past. (*The bargemen are seen laughing.*)

LEWIS (*pointing*). Look at those two blanks over the fence there!

BULGIN (*with gloomy violence*). They'd best stop their cackle, or I'll break their jaws.

JAGO (*suddenly*). You say the furnace men's paid enough?

HARNESS. I did not say they were paid enough; I said they were paid as much as the furnace men in similar works elsewhere.

EVANS. That's a lie! (*Hubbub.*) What about Harper's?

HARNESS (*with cold irony*). You may look at home for lies, my man. Harper's shifts are longer, the pay works out the same.

HENRY ROUS. (*A dark edition of his brother George.*) Will ye support us in double pay overtime Saturdays?

HARNESS. Yes, we will.

JAGO. What have ye done with our subscriptions?

HARNESS (*coldly*). I have told you what we *will* do with them.

EVANS. Ah! *will*, it's always will! Ye'd have our mates desert us.
(*Hubbub.*)

BULGIN (*shouting*). Hold your row! (EVANS *looks round angrily.*)

HARNESS (*lifting his voice*). Those who know their right hands from their lefts know that the Unions are neither thieves nor traitors. I've said my say. Figure it out, my lads; when you want me you know where I shall be.

> (*He jumps down, the crowd gives way, he passes through them, and goes away.* A BARGEMAN *looks after him jerking his pipe with a derisive gesture. The men close up in groups, and many looks are cast at* ROBERTS, *who stands alone against the wall.*)

EVANS. He wants ye to turn blacklegs, that's what he wants. He wants ye to go back on us. Sooner than turn blackleg — I'd starve, I would.

BULGIN. Who's talkin' o' blacklegs — mind what you're saying, will you?

BLACKSMITH (*A youth with yellow hair and huge arms*). What about the women?

EVANS. They can stand what we can stand, I suppose, can't they?

BLACKSMITH. Ye've no wife?

EVANS. An' don't want one!

THOMAS (*raising his voice*). Aye! Give us the power to come to terms with London, lads.

DAVIES. (*A dark, slow-fly, gloomy man.*) Go up the platform, if you got anything to say, go up an' say it.

> (*There are cries of "Thomas!" He is pushed towards the plat-*

form; he ascends it with difficulty, and bares his head, waiting for silence. A hush.)

RED-HAIRED YOUTH (*suddenly*). Coot old Thomas!

(*A hoarse laugh; the bargemen exchange remarks; a hush again, and* THOMAS *begins speaking.*)

THOMAS. We are all in the tepth together, and it iss Nature that has put us there.

HENRY ROUS. It's London put us there!

EVANS. It's the Union.

THOMAS. It iss not Lonton; nor it iss not the Union — it iss Nature. It iss no disgrace whateffer to a potty to give in to Nature. For this Nature iss a fery pig thing; it is pigger than what a man is. There iss more years to my hett than to the hett of any one here. It is fery pat, look you, this coing against Nature. It is pat to make other potties suffer, when there is nothing to pe cot py it. (*A laugh.* THOMAS *angrily goes on.*) What are ye laughing at? It is pat, I say! We are fighting for a principle; there is no potty that shall say I am not a peliever in principle. Putt when Nature says "No further," then it is no coot snapping your fingers in her face. (*A laugh from* ROBERTS, *and murmurs of approval.*) This Nature must pe humort. It is a man's pisiness to pe pure, honest, just, and merciful. That's what Chapel tells you. (*To* ROBERTS, *angrily.*) And, look you, David Roberts, Chapel tells you ye can do that without coing against Nature.

JAGO. What about the Union?

THOMAS. I ton't trust the Union; they haf treated us like tirt. "Do what we tell you," said they. I haf peen captain of the furnace men twenty years, and I say to the Union — (*excitedly*) — "Can you tell me then, as well as I can tell you, what iss the right wages for the work that these men do?" For fife and twenty years I haf paid my moneys to the Union and — (*with great excitement*) — for nothings! What iss that but roguery, for all that this Mr. Harness says! (*Murmurs.*)

EVANS. Hear, hear.

HENRY ROUS. Get on with you! Cut on with it then!

THOMAS. Look you, if a man toes not trust me, am I coing to trust him?

JAGO. That's right.

THOMAS. Let them alone for rogues, and act for ourselves.

(*Murmurs.*)

BLACKSMITH. That's what we been doin', haven't we?

THOMAS (*with increased excitement*). I wass brought up to do for me-self. I wass brought up to go without a thing if I hat not moneys to puy it. There iss too much, look you, of doing things with other people's moneys. We haf fought fair, and if we haf peen beaten, it iss no fault of ours. Gif us the power to make terms with Lonton for ourself; if we ton't succeed, I say it iss petter to take our peating like men, than to tie like togs, or hang on to others' coat-tails to make them do our pisiness for us!

EVANS (*muttering*). Who wants to?

THOMAS (*craning*). What's that? If I stand up to a potty, and he knocks me town, I am not to go hollering to other potties to help me; I am to stand up again; and if he knocks me town properly, I am to stay there, isn't that right? (*Laughter.*)

JAGO. No Union!

HENRY ROUS. Union! (*Others take up the shout.*)

EVANS. Blacklegs!

(BULGIN *and the* BLACKSMITH *shake their fists at* EVANS.)

THOMAS (*with a gesture*). I am an olt man, look you.

(*A sudden silence, then murmurs again.*)

LEWIS. Olt fool, with his "No Union!"

BULGIN. Them furnace chaps! For twopence I'd smash the faces o' the lot of them.

GREEN. If I'd 'a' been listened to at the first ——

THOMAS (*wiping his brow*). I'm comin' now to what I was coing to say ——

DAVIES (*muttering*). An' time too!

THOMAS (*solemnly*). Chapel says: Ton't carry on this strife! Put an end to it.

JAGO. That's a lie! Chapel says go on!

THOMAS (*scornfully*). Inteet! I haf ears to my head.

RED-HAIRED YOUTH. Ah! long ones! (*A laugh.*)

JAGO. Your ears have misbeled you then.

THOMAS (*excitedly*). Ye cannot be right if I am, ye cannot haf it both ways.

RED-HAIRED YOUTH. Chapel can though!

("*The Shaver*" *laughs; there are murmurs from the crowd.*)

THOMAS (*fixing his eyes on "The Shaver"*). Ah! ye're coing the roat to tamnation. An' so I say to all of you. If ye co against Chapel I will not pe with you, nor will any other Got-fearing man.

> (*He steps down from the platform.* JAGO *makes his way towards it. There are cries of "Don't let 'im go up!"*)

JAGO. Don't let him go up? That's free speech, that is. (*He goes up.*) I ain't got much to say to you. Look at the matter plain; ye've come the road this far, and now you want to chuck the journey. We've all been in one boat; and now you want to pull in two. We engineers have stood by you; ye're ready now, are ye, to give us the go-by? If we'd 'a' known that before, we'd not 'a' started out with you so early one bright morning! That's all I've got to say. Old man Thomas ain't got his Bible lesson right. If you give up to London, or to Harness, now, it's givin' us the chuck — to save your skins — you won't get over that, my boys; it's a dirty thing to do.

> (*He gets down; during his little speech, which is ironically spoken, there is a restless discomfort in the crowd.* ROUS, *stepping forward, jumps on the platform. He has an air of fierce distraction. Sullen murmurs of disapproval from the crowd.*)

ROUS (*speaking with great excitement*). I'm no blanky orator, mates, but wot I say is drove from me. What I say is yuman nature. Can a man set an' see 'is mother starve? Can 'e now?

ROBERTS (*starting forward*). Rous!

ROUS (*staring at him fiercely*). Sim 'Arness said fair! I've changed my mind!

ROBERTS. Ah! Turned your coat you mean!

> (*The crowd manifests a great surprise.*)

LEWIS (*apostrophizing* ROUS). Hallo! What's turned him round?

ROUS (*speaking with intense excitement*). 'E said fair. "Stand by us," 'e said, "and we'll stand by you." That's where we've been makin' our mistake this long time past; and who's to blame for 't? (*He points at* ROBERTS.) That man there! "No," 'e said, "fight the robbers," 'e said, "squeeze the breath out o' them!" But it's not the breath out o' them that's being squeezed; it's the breath out of *us* and *ours*, and that's the book of truth. I'm no orator, mates, it's the flesh and blood in me that's speakin', it's the heart o' me. (*With a menacing, yet half-ashamed movement towards* ROB-

ERTS.)   He'll speak to you again, mark my words, but don't ye
listen.   (*The crowd groans.*)   It's hell fire that's on that man's
tongue.   (ROBERTS *is seen laughing.*)   Sim 'Arness is right.   What
are we without the Union — handful o' parched leaves — a
puff o' smoke.   I'm no orator, but I say: Chuck it up!   Chuck
it up!   Sooner than go on starving the women and the children.
> (*The murmurs of acquiescence almost drown the murmurs of dissent.*)

EVANS.   What's turned *you* to blacklegging?

ROUS (*with a furious look*).   Sim 'Arness knows what he's talking
about.   Give us power to come to terms with London; I'm no
orator, but I say — have done wi' this black misery!

> (*He gives his muffler a twist, jerks his head back, and jumps off the*
> *platform.   The crowd applauds and surges forward.   Amid cries*
> *of "That's enough!"   "Up Union!"   "Up Harness!"*
> ROBERTS *quietly ascends the platform.   There is a moment of*
> *silence.*)

BLACKSMITH.   We don't want to hear you.   Shut it!

HENRY ROUS.   Get down!

> (*Amid such cries they surge towards the platform.*)

EVANS (*fiercely*).   Let 'im speak!   Roberts!   Roberts!

BULGIN (*muttering*).   He's better look out that I don't crack his skull.

> (ROBERTS *faces the crowd, probing them with his eyes, till they*
> *gradually become silent.   He begins speaking.   One of the barge-*
> *men rises and stands.*)

ROBERTS.   You don't want to hear me, then?   You'll listen to Rous
and to that old man, but not to me.   You'll listen to Sim Harness
of the Union that's treated you *so fair;* maybe you'll listen to those
men from London?   Ah!   You groan!   What for?   You love
their feet on your necks, don't you?   (*Then as* BULGIN *elbows his*
way towards the platform, with calm pathos.)   You'd like to break
my jaw, John Bulgin.   Let me speak, then do your smashing, if
it gives you pleasure.   (BULGIN *stands motionless and sullen.*)   Am I
a liar, a coward, a traitor?   If only I were, ye'd listen to me, I'm
sure.   (*The murmurings cease, and there is now dead silence.*)   Is there
a man of you here that has less to gain by striking?   Is there a
man of you that had more to lose?   Is there a man of you that
has given up *eight hundred* pounds since this trouble here began?
Come now, is there?   How much has Thomas given up — ten

pounds or five, or what? You listened to him, and what had he to say? "None can pretend," he said, "that I'm not a believer in principle — (*with biting irony*) — but when Nature says: 'No further, 't es going agenst Nature.' " *I* tell you if a man cannot say to Nature: "Budge me from this if ye can!" — (*with a sort of exaltation*) — his principles are but his belly. "Oh, but," Thomas says, "a man can be pure and honest, just and merciful, and take off his hat to Nature!" *I* tell you Nature's neither pure nor honest, just nor merciful. You chaps that live over the hill, an' go home dead beat in the dark on a snowy night — don't ye fight your way every inch of it? Do ye go lyin' down an' trustin' to the tender mercies of this merciful Nature? Try it and you'll soon know with what ye've got to deal. 'Tes only by that — (*he strikes a blow with his clenched fist*) — in Nature's face that a man can be a man. "Give in," says Thomas, "go down on your knees; throw up your foolish fight, an' perhaps," he said, "perhaps your enemy will chuck you down a crust."

JAGO. Never!

EVANS. Curse them!

THOMAS. I nefer said that.

ROBERTS (*bitingly*). If ye did not say it, man, ye meant it. An' what did ye say about Chapel? "Chapel's against it," ye said. "She's against it!" Well, if Chapel and Nature go hand in hand, it's the first I've ever heard of it. That young man there — (*pointing to* ROUS) — said I 'ad 'ell fire on my tongue. If I had I would use it all to scorch and wither this talking of surrender. Surrendering's the work of cowards and traitors.

HENRY ROUS (*as* GEORGE ROUS *moves forward*). Go for him, George — don't stand his lip!

ROBERTS (*flinging out his finger*). Stop there, George Rous, it's no time this to settle personal matters. (ROUS *stops*.) But there was one other spoke to you — Mr. Simon Harness. We have not much to thank Mr. Harness and the Union for. They said to us "Desert your mates, or we'll desert you." An' they did desert us.

EVANS. They did.

ROBERTS. Mr. Simon Harness is a clever man, but he has come too late. (*With intense conviction.*) For all that Mr. Simon Harness says, for all that Thomas, Rous, for all that any man present here can say — *We've won the fight!* (*The crowd sags nearer, looking eagerly up. With withering scorn.*) You've felt the pinch o't in your bellies. You've forgotten what that fight 'as been; many times I have told you; I will tell you now this once again. The fight o' the country's body and blood against a blood-sucker. The fight of those that spend themselves with every blow they strike and every breath they draw, against a thing that fattens on them, and grows and grows by the law of *merciful* Nature. That thing is Capital! A thing that buys the sweat o' men's brows, and the tortures o' their brains, at its own price. *Don't* I know that? Wasn't the work o' *my* brains bought for seven hundred pounds, and hasn't one hundred thousand pounds been gained them by that seven hundred without the stirring of a finger. It is a thing that will take as much and give you as little as it can. That's *Capital!* A thing that will say — "I'm very sorry for you, poor fellows — you have a cruel time of it, I know," but will not give one sixpence of its dividends to help you have a better time. That's Capital! Tell me, for all their talk, is there one of them that will consent to another penny on the Income Tax to help the poor? That's Capital! A white-faced, stony-hearted monster! Ye have got it on its knees; are ye to give up at the last minute to save your miserable bodies pain? When I went this morning to these old men from London, I looked into their very 'earts. One of them was sitting there — Mr. Scantlebury, a mass of flesh nourished on us: sittin' there for all the world like the shareholders in this Company, that sit not moving tongue nor finger, takin' dividends — a great dumb ox that can only be roused when its food is threatened. I looked into his eyes and I saw *he was afraid* — afraid for himself and his dividends, afraid for his fees, afraid of the very shareholders he stands for; and all but one of them's afraid — like children that get into a wood at night, and start at every rustle of the leaves. I ask you, men — (*he pauses, holding out his hand till there is utter silence*) — give me a free hand to tell them: "Go you back to London. The men have nothing for you!" (*A murmuring.*) Give me that, an' I swear to you, within a week you shall have from London all you want.

EVANS, JAGO, and OTHERS. A free hand! Give him a free hand! Bravo — bravo!

ROBERTS. 'Tis not for this little moment of time we're fighting (*the murmuring dies*), not for ourselves, our own little bodies, and their wants, 'tis for all those that come after throughout all time. (*With intense sadness.*) Oh! men — for the love o' them, don't roll up another stone upon their heads, don't help to blacken the sky, an' let the bitter sea in over them. They're welcome to the worst that can happen to me, to the worst that can happen to us all, aren't they — aren't they? If we can shake (*passionately*) that white-faced monster with the bloody lips, that has sucked the life out of ourselves, our wives, and children, since the world began. (*Dropping the note of passion, but with the utmost weight and intensity.*) If we have not the hearts of men to stand against it breast to breast, and eye to eye, and force it backward till it cry for mercy, it will go on sucking life; and we shall stay forever what we are (*in almost a whisper*), less than the very dogs.

(*An utter stillness, and* ROBERTS *stands rocking his body slightly, with his eyes burning the faces of the crowd.*)

EVANS and JAGO (*suddenly*). Roberts!

(*The shout is taken up. There is a slight movement in the crowd, and* MADGE *passing below the towing-path, stops by the platform, looking up at* ROBERTS. *A sudden doubting silence.*)

ROBERTS. "Nature," says that old man, "give in to Nature." I tell you, strike your blow in Nature's face — an' let it do its worst!

(*He catches sight of* MADGE, *his brows contract, he looks away.*)

MADGE (*in a low voice — close to the platform*). Your wife's dying!

(ROBERTS *glares at her as if torn from some pinnacle of exaltation.*)

ROBERTS (*trying to stammer on*). I say to you — answer them — answer them —— (*He is drowned by the murmur in the crowd.*)

THOMAS (*stepping forward*). Ton't you hear her, then?

ROBERTS. What is it? (*A dead silence.*)

THOMAS. Your wife, man!

(ROBERTS *hesitates, then with a gesture, he leaps down, and goes away below the towing-path, the men making way for him. The standing bargeman opens and prepares to light a lantern. Daylight is fast failing.*)

MADGE. He needn't have hurried! Annie Roberts is dead. (*Then in the silence, passionately.*) You pack of blinded hounds! How many more women are you going to let to die?

(*The crowd shrinks back from her, and breaks up in groups, with a*

confused, uneasy movement. MADGE *goes quickly away below
the towing-path. There is a hush as they look after her.*)

LEWIS. There's a spitfire for ye!

BULGIN (*growling*). I'll smash 'er jaw.

GREEN. If I'd 'a' been listened to, that poor woman ——

THOMAS. It's a judgment on him for coing against Chapel. I tolt
him how 'twould be!

EVANS. All the more reason for sticking by 'im. (*A cheer.*) Are
you goin' to desert him now 'e's down? Are you goin' to chuck
him over, now 'e's lost 'is wife?

> (*The crowd is murmuring and cheering all at once.*)

ROUS (*stepping in front of platform*). Lost his wife! Aye! Can't ye
see? Look at home, look at your own wives! What's to save
them? You'll have the same in all your houses before long!

LEWIS. Aye, aye!

HENRY ROUS. Right! George, right! (*There are murmurs of assent.*)

ROUS. It's not us that's blind, it's Roberts. How long will ye put
up with 'im!

HENRY ROUS, BULGIN, DAVIES. Give 'im the chuck!

> (*The cry is taken up.*)

EVANS (*fiercely*). Kick a man that's down? Down?

HENRY ROUS. Stop his jaw there!

> (EVANS *throws up his arm at a threat from* BULGIN. *The barge-
> man, who has lighted the lantern, holds it high above his head.*)

ROUS (*springing on to the platform*). What brought him down then,
but 'is own black obstinacy? Are ye goin' to follow a man that
can't see better than that where he's goin'?

EVANS. He's lost 'is wife.

ROUS. An' who's fault's that but his own. 'Ave done with 'im,
I say, before he's killed your own wives and mothers.

DAVIES. Down 'im!

HENRY ROUS. He's finished!

BROWN. We've had enough of 'im!

BLACKSMITH. Too much!

> (*The crowd takes up these cries, excepting only* EVANS, JAGO, *and*
> GREEN, *who is seen to argue mildly with the* BLACKSMITH.)

ROUS (*above the hubbub*). We'll make terms with the Union, lads.

> (*Cheers.*)

EVANS (*fiercely*). Ye blacklegs!

BULGIN (*savagely — squaring up to him*). Who are ye callin' blacklegs, Rat?

> (EVANS *throws up his fists, parries the blow, and returns it. They fight. The bargemen are seen holding up the lantern and enjoying the sight. Old* THOMAS *steps forward and holds out his hands.*)

THOMAS. Shame on your strife!

> (*The* BLACKSMITH, BROWN, LEWIS, *and the* RED-HAIRED YOUTH *pull* EVANS *and* BULGIN *apart. The stage is almost dark.*)

ACT III

It is five o'clock. In the UNDERWOODS' *drawing-room, which is artistically furnished,* ENID *is sitting on the sofa working at a baby's frock.* EDGAR, *by a little spindle-legged table in the center of the room, is fingering a china box. His eyes are fixed on the double doors that lead into the dining-room.*

EDGAR (*putting down the china box, and glancing at his watch*). Just on five, they're all in there waiting, except Frank. Where's he?

ENID. He's had to go down to Gasgoyne's about a contract. Will you want him?

EDGAR. He can't help us. This is a director's job. (*Motioning towards a single door half hidden by a curtain.*) Father in his room?

ENID. Yes.

EDGAR. I wish he'd stay there, Enid. (ENID *looks up at him.*) This is a beastly business, old girl!

> (*He takes up the little box again and turns it over and over.*)

ENID. I went to the Roberts's this afternoon, Ted.

EDGAR. That wasn't very wise.

ENID. He's simply killing his wife.

EDGAR. We are, you mean.

ENID (*suddenly*). Roberts *ought* to give way!

EDGAR. There's a lot to be said on the men's side.

ENID. I don't feel half so sympathetic with them as I did before I went. They just set up class feeling against you. Poor Annie was looking dreadfully bad — fire going out, and nothing fit for her to eat. (EDGAR *walks to and fro.*) But she would stand up for Roberts. When you see all this wretchedness going on and feel you can do nothing, you have to shut your eyes to the whole thing.

EDGAR. If you can.

ENID. When I went I was all on their side, but as soon as I got there I began to feel quite different at once. People talk about sympathy with the working classes, they don't know what it means to try and put it into practice. It seems hopeless.

EDGAR. Ah! well.

ENID. It's dreadful going on with the men in this state. I do hope the Dad will make concessions.

EDGAR. He won't. (*Gloomily.*) It's a sort of religion with him. Curse it! I know what's coming! He'll be voted down.

ENID. They wouldn't dare!

EDGAR. They will — they're in a funk.

ENID (*indignantly*). He'd never stand it!

EDGAR (*with a shrug*). My dear girl, if you're beaten in a vote, you've got to stand it.

ENID. Oh! (*She gets up in alarm.*) But would he resign?

EDGAR. Of course! It goes to the roots of his beliefs.

ENID. But he's so *wrapped up in this company*, Ted! There'd be nothing left for him! It'd be dreadful! (EDGAR *shrugs his shoulders.*) Oh, Ted, he's so old now! You mustn't let them!

EDGAR (*hiding his feelings in an outburst*). My sympathies in this strike are all on the side of the men.

ENID. He's been Chairman for more than thirty years! He made the whole thing! And think of the bad times they've had; it's always been he who pulled them through. Oh, Ted, you must —

EDGAR. What is it you want? You said just now you hoped he'd make concessions. Now you want me to back him in not making them. This isn't a game, Enid!

ENID (*hotly*). It isn't a game to *me* that the Dad's in danger of losing all he cares about in life. If he won't give way, and he's beaten, it'll simply break him down!

EDGAR. Didn't you say it was dreadful going on with the men in this state?

ENID. But can't you see, Ted, father'll never get over it! You must stop them somehow. The others are afraid of him. If you back him up ——

EDGAR (*putting his hand to his head*). Against my convictions — against yours! The moment it begins to pinch one personally —

ENID. It isn't personal, it's the Dad!

EDGAR. Your family or yourself, and over goes the show!

ENID (*resentfully*). If you don't take it seriously, I do.

EDGAR. I am as fond of him as you are; that's nothing to do with it.

ENID. We can't tell about the men; it's all guess-work. But we know the Dad might have a stroke any day. D'you mean to say that he isn't more to you than ——

EDGAR. Of course he is.

ENID. I don't understand you then.

EDGAR. H'm!

ENID. If it were for one's self it would be different, but for our own father! You don't seem to realize.

EDGAR. I realize perfectly.

ENID. It's your first duty to save him.

EDGAR. I wonder.

ENID (*imploring*). Oh, Ted! It's the only interest he's got left; it'll be like a death-blow to him!

EDGAR (*restraining his emotion*). I know.

ENID. Promise!

EDGAR. I'll do what I can.

> (*He turns to the double doors. The curtained door is opened, and* ANTHONY *appears.* EDGAR *opens the double doors and passes through.* SCANTLEBURY's *voice is faintly heard: "Past five; we shall never get through — have to eat another dinner at that hotel!" The doors are shut.* ANTHONY *walks forward.*)

ANTHONY. You've been seeing Roberts, I hear.

ENID. Yes.

ANTHONY. Do you know what trying to bridge such a gulf as this is like? (ENID *puts her work on the little table, and faces him.*) Filling a sieve with sand!

ENID. Don't!

ANTHONY. You think with your gloved hands you can cure the trouble of the century. (*He passes on.*)

ENID. Father! (ANTHONY *stops at the double doors.*) I'm only thinking of you!

ANTHONY (*more softly*). I can take care of myself, my dear.

ENID. Have you thought what'll happen if you're beaten — (*she points*) — in there?

ANTHONY. I don't mean to be.

ENID. Oh! father, don't give them a chance. You're not well; need you go to the meeting at all?

ANTHONY (*with a grim smile*). Cut and run?

ENID. But they'll out-vote you!

ANTHONY (*putting his hand on the doors*). We shall see!

ENID. I beg you, Dad! (ANTHONY *looks at her softly.*) Won't you?

> (ANTHONY *shakes his head. He opens the doors. A buzz of voices comes in.*)

SCANTLEBURY. Can one get dinner on that 6.30 train up?

TENCH. No, sir, I believe not, sir.

WILDER. Well, I shall speak out; I've had enough of this.

EDGAR (*sharply*). What?

> (*It ceases instantly.* ANTHONY *passes through, closing the doors behind him.* ENID *springs to them with a gesture of dismay. She puts her hand on the knob, and begins turning it; then goes to the fireplace, and taps her foot on the fender. Suddenly she rings the bell.* FROST *comes in by the door that leads into the hall.*)

FROST. Yes, m'm?

ENID. When the men come, Frost, please show them in here; the hall's cold.

FROST. I could put them in the pantry, m'm.

ENID. No. I don't want to — to offend them; they're so touchy.

FROST. Yes, m'm. (*Pause.*) Excuse me, Mr. Anthony's 'ad nothing to eat all day.

ENID. I know, Frost.

FROST. Nothin' but two whiskies and sodas, m'm.

ENID. Oh! you oughtn't to have let him have those.

FROST (*gravely*). Mr. Anthony is a little difficult, m'm. It's not as if he were a younger man, an' knew what was good for 'im; he will have his own way.

ENID. I suppose we all want that.

FROST. Yes, m'm. (*Quietly.*) Excuse me speakin' about the strike.

I'm sure if the other gentlemen were to give up to Mr. Anthony, and quietly let the men 'ave what they want, afterwards, that'd be the best way. I find that very useful with him at times, m'm. (ENID *shakes her head.*) If he's crossed, it makes him violent (*with an air of discovery*), and I've noticed in my own case, when I'm violent I'm always sorry for it afterwards.

ENID (*with a smile*). Are *you* ever violent, Frost?

FROST. Yes, m'm; oh! sometimes very violent.

ENID. I've never seen you.

FROST (*impersonally*). No, m'm; that is so. (ENID *fidgets towards the back of the door.*) (*With feeling.*) Bein' with Mr. Anthony, as you know, m'm, ever since I was fifteen, it worries me to see him crossed like this at this age. I've taken the liberty to speak to Mr. Wanklin (*dropping his voice*) — seems to be the most sensible of the gentlemen — but 'e said to me: "That's all very well, Frost, but this strike's a very serious thing," 'e said. "Serious for all parties, no doubt," I said, "but yumor 'im, sir," I said, "yumor 'im. It's like this, if a man comes to a stone wall, 'e doesn't drive 'is 'ead against it, 'e gets over it." "Yes," 'e said, "you'd better tell your master that." (FROST *looks at his nails.*) That's where it is, m'm. I said to Mr. Anthony this morning: "Is it worth it, sir?" "Damn it," he said to me, "Frost! Mind your own business, or take a month's notice!" Beg pardon, m'm, for using such a word.

ENID (*moving to the double doors, and listening*). Do you know that man Roberts, Frost?

FROST. Yes, m'm; that's to say, not to speak to. But to *look* at 'im you can tell what *he's* like.

ENID (*stopping*). Yes?

FROST. He's not one of these 'ere ordinary 'armless Socialists. 'E's violent; got a fire inside 'im. What I call "personal." A man may 'ave what opinions 'e likes, so long as 'e's not personal; when 'e's that 'e's *not* safe.

ENID. I think that's what my father feels about Roberts.

FROST. No doubt, m'm, Mr. Anthony has a feeling against him. (ENID *glances at him sharply, but finding him in perfect earnest, stands biting her lips, and looking at the double doors.*) It's a regular right down struggle between the two. I've no patience with this

Roberts, from what I 'ear he's just an ordinary workin' man like the rest of 'em. If he did invent a thing he's no worse off than 'undreds of others. My brother invented a new kind o' dumb-waiter — nobody gave *him* anything for it, an' there it is, bein' used all over the place. (ENID *moves closer to the double doors.*) There's a kind o' man that never forgives the world, because 'e wasn't born a gentleman. What I say is — no man that's a gentleman looks down on another because 'e 'appens to be a class or two above 'im, no more than if 'e 'appens to be a class or two below.

ENID (*with slight impatience*). Yes, I know, Frost, of course. Will you please go in and ask if they'll have some tea; say I sent you.

FROST. Yes, m'm.

> (*He opens the doors gently and goes in. There is a momentary sound of earnest, rather angry talk.*)

WILDER. I don't agree with you.

WANKLIN. We've had this over a dozen times.

EDGAR (*impatiently*). Well, what's the proposition?

SCANTLEBURY. Yes, what does your father say? Tea? Not for the, not for me!

WANKLIN. What I understand the Chairman to say is this ——

> (FROST *reënters closing the door behind him.*)

ENID (*moving from the door*). Won't they have any tea, Frost?

> (*She goes to the little table, and remains motionless, looking at the baby's frock.*)

> (*A* Parlormaid *enters from the hall.*)

PARLORMAID. A Miss Thomas, m'm.

ENID (*raising her head*). Thomas? What Miss Thomas — d'you mean a ——?

PARLORMAID. Yes, m'm.

ENID (*blankly*). Oh! Where is she?

PARLORMAID. In the porch.

ENID. I don't want —— (*She hesitates.*)

FROST. Shall I dispose of her, m'm?

ENID. I'll come out. No, show her in here, Ellen.

> (*The* PARLORMAID *and* FROST *go out.* ENID *pursing her lips, sits*

at the little table, taking up the baby's frock. The PARLORMAID
ushers in MADGE THOMAS *and goes out;* MADGE *stands by the
door.*)

ENID. Come in. What is it? What have you come for, please?

MADGE. Brought a message from Mrs. Roberts.

ENID. A message? Yes?

MADGE. She asks you to look after her mother.

ENID. I don't understand.

MADGE (*sullenly*). That's the message.

ENID. But — what — why?

MADGE. Annie Roberts is dead. (*There is a silence.*)

ENID (*horrified*). But it's only a little more than an hour since I saw
her.

MADGE. Of cold and hunger.

ENID (*rising*). Oh! that's not true! the poor thing's heart — What
makes you look at me like that? I tried to help her.

MADGE (*with suppressed savagery*). I thought you'd like to know.

ENID (*passionately*). It's so unjust! Can't you see that I wanted to
help you all?

MADGE. I never harmed any one that hadn't harmed me first.

ENID (*coldly*). What harm have I done you? Why do you speak to
me like that?

MADGE (*with the bitterest intensity*). You come out of your comfort to
spy on us! A week of hunger, that's what *you* want?

ENID (*standing her ground*). Don't talk nonsense!

MADGE. I saw her die; her hands were blue with the cold.

ENID (*with a movement of grief*). Oh! why wouldn't she let me help
her? It's such senseless pride!

MADGE. Pride's better than nothing to keep your body warm.

ENID (*passionately*). I won't talk to you! How can you tell what I
feel? It's not my fault that I was born better off than you.

MADGE. We don't want your money.

ENID. You don't understand, and you don't want to; please to go
away!

MADGE (*balefully*). You've killed her, for all your soft words, you
and your father ——

ENID (*with rage and emotion*). That's wicked! My father is suffering
himself through this wretched strike.

MADGE (*with somber triumph*).   Then tell him Mrs. Roberts is dead. That'll make him better.

ENID.   Go away!

MADGE.   When a person hurts us we get it back on them.

> (*She makes a sudden and swift movement towards* ENID, *fixing her eyes on the child's frock lying across the little table.* ENID *snatches the frock up, as though it were the child itself. They stand a yard apart, crossing glances.*)

MADGE (*pointing to the frock with a little smile*).   Ah!   You felt *that!* Lucky it's her mother — not her children — you've to look after, isn't it.   *She* won't trouble you long!

ENID.   Go away!

MADGE.   I've given you the message.

> (*She turns and goes out into the hall.* ENID, *motionless till she has gone, sinks down at the table, bending her head over the frock, which she is still clutching to her. The double doors are opened, and* ANTHONY *comes slowly in; he passes his daughter, and lowers himself into an armchair. He is very flushed.*)

ENID (*hiding her emotion — anxiously*).   What is it, Dad?   (ANTHONY *makes a gesture, but does not speak.*)   Who was it?   (ANTHONY *does not answer.* ENID *going to the double doors meets* EDGAR *coming in. They speak together in low tones.*)   What is it, Ted?

EDGAR.   That fellow Wilder!   Taken to personalities!   He was downright insulting.

ENID.   What did he say?

EDGAR.   Said father was too old and feeble to know what he was doing!   The Dad's worth six of him!

ENID.   Of course he is.

> (*They look at* ANTHONY. *The doors open wider,* WANKLIN *appears with* SCANTLEBURY.)

SCANTLEBURY (*sotto voce*).   I don't like the look of this!

WANKLIN (*going forward*).   Come, Chairman!   Wilder sends you his apologies.   A man can't do more.

> (WILDER, *followed by* TENCH, *comes in, and goes to* ANTHONY.)

WILDER (*glumly*).   I withdraw my words, sir.   I'm sorry.

> (ANTHONY *nods to him.*)

ENID.   You haven't come to a decision, Mr. Wanklin?

> (WANKLIN *shakes his head.*)

WANKLIN. We're all here, Chairman; what do you say? Shall we get on with the business, or shall we go back to the other room?

SCANTLEBURY. Yes, yes; let's get on. We must settle something.

(*He turns from a small chair, and settles himself suddenly in the largest chair with a sigh of comfort.* WILDER *and* WANKLIN *also sit; and* TENCH, *drawing up a straight-backed chair close to his chairman, sits on the edge of it with the minute-book and a stylographic pen.*)

ENID (*whispering*). I want to speak to you a minute, Ted.

(*They go out through the double doors.*)

WANKLIN. Really, Chairman, it's no use soothing ourselves with a sense of false security. If this strike's not brought to an end before the General Meeting, the shareholders will certainly haul us over the coals.

SCANTLEBURY (*stirring*). What — what's that?

WANKLIN. I know it for a fact.

ANTHONY. Let them!

WILDER. And get turned out?

WANKLIN. (*To* ANTHONY.) I don't mind martyrdom for a policy in which I believe, but I object to being burnt for some one else's principles.

SCANTLEBURY. Very reasonable — you must see that, Chairman.

ANTHONY. We owe it to other employers to stand firm.

WANKLIN. There's a limit to that.

ANTHONY. You were all full of fight at the start.

SCANTLEBURY (*with a sort of groan*). We thought the men would give in, but they — haven't!

ANTHONY. They will!

WILDER (*rising and pacing up and down*). I can't have my reputation as a man of business destroyed for the satisfaction of starving the men out. (*Almost in tears.*) I can't have it. How can we meet the shareholders with things in the state they are?

SCANTLEBURY. Hear, hear — hear, hear!

WILDER (*lashing himself*). If any one expects me to say to them I've lost you fifty thousand pounds and sooner than put my pride in my pocket I'll lose you another. (*Glancing at* ANTHONY.) It's — it's unnatural! *I don't want* to go against you, sir ——

WANKLIN (*persuasively*). Come Chairman, we're *not* free agents. We're part of a machine. Our only business is to see the Company earns as much profit as it safely can.   If you blame me for want of principle; I say that we're trustees.   Reason tells us we shall never get back in the saving of wages what we shall lose if we continue this struggle — really, Chairman, we *must* bring it to an end, on the best terms we can make.

ANTHONY. No.   (*There is a pause of general dismay.*)

WILDER. It's a deadlock then.   (*Letting his hands drop with a sort of despair.*)   Now I shall never get off to Spain!

WANKLIN (*retaining a trace of irony*).   You hear the consequences of your victory, Chairman?

WILDER (*with a burst of feeling*).   My wife's *ill!*

SCANTLEBURY. Dear, dear!   You don't say so.

WILDER. If I don't get her out of this cold, I won't answer for the consequences.

(*Through the double doors* EDGAR *comes in looking very grave.*)

EDGAR (*to his father*).   Have you heard this, sir?   Mrs. Roberts is dead!   (*Every one stares at him, as if trying to gauge the importance of this news.*)   Enid saw her this afternoon, she had no coals, or food, or anything.   It's enough!

(*There is a silence, every one avoiding the other's eyes, except* ANTHONY, *who stares hard at his son.*)

SCANTLEBURY. You don't suggest that we could have helped the poor thing?

WILDER (*flustered*).   The woman was in bad health.   Nobody can say there's any responsibility on us.   At least — not on me.

EDGAR (*hotly*).   I say that we *are* responsible.

ANTHONY. War is war!

EDGAR. Not on women!

WANKLIN. It not infrequently happens that women are the greatest sufferers.

EDGAR. If we knew that, all the more responsibility rests on us.

ANTHONY. This is no matter for amateurs.

EDGAR. Call me what you like, sir.   It's sickened me.   We had no right to carry things to such a length.

WILDER. I don't like this business a bit — that Radical rag will twist it to their own ends; see if they don't!   They'll get up some cock and bull story about the poor woman's dying from starvation.   I wash my hands of it.

EDGAR. You can't. None of us can.

SCANTLEBURY (*striking his fist on the arm of his chair*). But I protest against this ——

EDGAR. Protest as you like, Mr. Scantlebury, it won't alter facts.

ANTHONY. That's enough.

EDGAR (*facing him angrily*). No, sir. I tell you exactly what I think. If we pretend the men are not suffering, it's humbug; and if they're suffering, we know enough of human nature to know the women are suffering more, and as to the children — well — it's damnable! (SCANTLEBURY *rises from his chair*.) I don't say that we meant to be cruel, I don't say anything of the sort; but I do say it's criminal to shut our eyes to the facts. We employ these men, and we can't get out of it. I don't care so much about the men, but I'd sooner resign my position on the Board than go on starving women in this way.

> (*All except* ANTHONY *are now upon their feet*, ANTHONY *sits grasping the arms of his chair and staring at his son*.)

SCANTLEBURY. I don't — I don't like the way you're putting it, young sir.

WANKLIN. You're rather overshooting the mark.

WILDER. I should think so indeed!

EDGAR (*losing control*). It's no use blinking things! If *you* want to have the death of women on your hands — *I* don't!

SCANTLEBURY. Now, now, young man!

WILDER. On *our* hands? Not on *mine*, I won't have it!

EDGAR. We are five members of this Board; if we were four against it, why did we let it drift till it came to this? You know perfectly well why — because we hoped we should starve the men out. Well, all we've done is to starve one woman out!

SCANTLEBURY (*almost hysterically*). I protest, I protest! I'm a humane man — we're all humane men!

EDGAR (*scornfully*). There's nothing wrong with our *humanity*. It's our imaginations, Mr. Scantlebury.

WILDER. Nonsense! My imagination's as good as yours.

EDGAR. If so, it isn't good enough.

WILDER. I foresaw this!

EDGAR. Then why didn't you put your foot down!

WILDER. Much good that would have done.

(*He looks at* ANTHONY.)

EDGAR. If you, and I, and each one of us here who say that our imaginations are so good ——

SCANTLEBURY (*flurried*). I never said so.

EDGAR (*paying no attention*). — Had put our feet down, the thing would have been ended long ago, and this poor woman's life wouldn't have been crushed out of her like this. For all we can tell there may be a dozen other starving women.

SCANTLEBURY. For God's sake, sir, don't use that word at a — at a Board meeting; it's — it's monstrous.

EDGAR. I *will* use it, Mr. Scantlebury.

SCANTLEBURY. Then I shall not listen to you. I shall not listen! It's painful to me. (*He covers his ears.*)

WANKLIN. None of us are opposed to a settlement, except your father.

EDGAR. I'm certain that if the shareholders knew ——

WANKLIN. I don't think you'll find their imaginations are any better than ours. Because a woman happens to have a weak heart ——

EDGAR. A struggle like this finds out the weak spots in everybody. Any child knows that. If it hadn't been for this cut-throat policy, she needn't have died like this; and there wouldn't be all this misery that any one who isn't a fool can see is going on. (*Throughout the foregoing* ANTHONY *has eyed his son; he now moves as though to rise, but stops as* EDGAR *speaks again.*) I don't defend the men, or myself, or anybody.

WANKLIN. You may have to! A coroner's jury of disinterested sympathizers may say some very nasty things. We mustn't lose sight of our position.

SCANTLEBURY (*without uncovering his ears*). Coroner's jury! No, no, it's not a case for that!

EDGAR. I've had enough of cowardice.

WANKLIN. Cowardice is an unpleasant word, Mr. Edgar Anthony. It will look very like cowardice if we suddenly concede the men's demands when a thing like this happens; we must be careful!

WILDER. Of course we must. We've no knowledge of this matter, except a rumor. The proper course is to put the whole thing into the hands of Harness to settle for us; that's natural, that's what we *should* have come to any way.

SCANTLEBURY (*with dignity*). Exactly! (*Turning to* EDGAR.) And as to you, young sir, I can't sufficiently express my — my distaste for the way you've treated the whole matter. You ought to withdraw! Talking of starvation, talking of cowardice! Considering what our views are! Except your own father — we're all agreed the only policy is — is one of good will — it's most irregular, it's most improper, and all I can say is it's — it's given me pain —— (*He places his hand over his heart.*)

EDGAR (*stubbornly*). I withdraw nothing.

> (*He is about to say more when* SCANTLEBURY *once more covers up his ears.* TENCH *suddenly makes a demonstration with the minute-book. A sense of having been engaged in the unusual comes over all of them, and one by one they resume their seats.* EDGAR *alone remains on his feet.*)

WILDER (*with an air of trying to wipe something out*). I pay no attention to what young Mr. Anthony has said. Coroner's jury! The idea's preposterous. I — I move this amendment to the Chairman's motion: that the dispute be placed at once in the hands of Mr. Simon Harness for settlement, on the lines indicated by him this morning. Any one second that?

> (TENCH *writes in his book.*)

WANKLIN. I do.

WILDER. Very well, then; I ask the Chairman to put it to the Board.

ANTHONY (*with a great sigh — slowly*). We have been made the subject of an attack. (*Looking round at* WILDER *and* SCANTLEBURY *with ironical contempt.*) I take it on *my* shoulders. I am seventy-six years old. I have been Chairman of this Company since its inception two-and-thirty years ago. I have seen it pass through good and evil report. My connection with it began in the year that this young man was born. (EDGAR *bows his head.* ANTHONY, *gripping his chair, goes on.*) I have had to do with "men" for fifty years; I've always stood up to them; I have never been beaten yet. I have fought the men of this Company four times, and four times I have beaten them. It has been said that I am not the man I was. (*He looks at* WILDER.) However that may be, I am man enough to stand to my guns. (*His voice grows stronger. The double doors are opened.* ENID *slips in, followed by* UNDERWOOD, *who restrains her.*) The men have been treated justly, they have had fair wages, we have always been ready to listen to complaints. It has been said that times have changed; if they have, I have not changed with them. Neither will I. It has been said that masters and men are equal! Cant! There can only be one master in a house! Where two men meet the better man will rule. It has been said that Capital and Labor have the same interests. Cant! Their interests are as wide asunder as the poles. It has been said that the Board is only part of a machine. Cant! We *are* the machine; its brains and sinews; it is for us to lead and to determine what is to be done, and to do it without fear or favor. Fear of the men! Fear of the shareholders! Fear of our own shadows! Before I am like that, I hope to die. (*He pauses, and meeting his son's eyes, goes on.*) There is only one way of treating "men" — with *the iron hand*. This half and half business, the half and half manners of this generation, has brought all this upon us. Sentiment and softness, and what this young man, no doubt, would call his social policy. You can't eat cake and have it! This middle-class sentiment, or socialism, or whatever it may be, is rotten. Masters are masters, men are men! Yield one demand, and they will make it six. They are (*he smiles grimly*) like Oliver Twist, asking for more. If I were in *their* place I should be the same. But I am not in their place. Mark my words: one fine morning, when you have given way here, and given way there — you will find you have parted with the ground beneath your feet, and are deep in the bog of bankruptcy; and with you, floundering in that bog, will be the very men you have given way to. I have been accused of being a domineering tyrant, thinking only of my pride — I am thinking of the future of this country, threatened with the black waters of confusion, threatened with mob government, threatened with what I cannot see. If by any conduct of mine I help to bring this on us, I shall be ashamed to look my fellows in the face.

(ANTHONY *stares before him, at what he cannot see, and there is perfect stillness.* FROST *comes in from the hall, and all but* ANTHONY *look round at him uneasily.*)

FROST (*to his master*). The men are here, sir. (ANTHONY *makes a gesture of dismissal.*) Shall I bring them in, sir?

ANTHONY. Wait! (FROST *goes out,* ANTHONY *turns to face his son.*) I come to the attack that has been made upon me. (EDGAR, *with a gesture of deprecation, remains motionless with his head a little bowed.*) A woman has died. I am told that her blood is on my hands; I am told that on my hands is the starvation and the suffering of other women and of children.

EDGAR. I said "on *our* hands," sir.

ANTHONY. It is the same. (*His voice grows stronger and stronger, his feeling is more and more made manifest.*) I am not aware that if my adversary suffer in a fair fight not sought by me, it is *my* fault. If I fall under *his* feet — as fall I may — I shall not complain. That will be *my* lookout — and this is — his. I cannot separate, as I would, these men from their women and children. A fair fight is a fair fight! Let them learn to think before they pick a quarrel!

EDGAR (*in a low voice*). But is it a fair fight, father? Look at them, and look at us! They've only this one weapon!

ANTHONY (*grimly*). And you're weak-kneed enough to teach them how to use it! It seems the fashion nowadays for men to take their enemy's side. I have not learned that art. Is it my fault that they quarreled with their Union too?

EDGAR. There is such a thing as mercy.

ANTHONY. And justice comes before it.

EDGAR. What seems just to one man, sir, is injustice to another.

ANTHONY (*with suppressed passion*). You accuse me of injustice — of what amounts to inhumanity — of cruelty ——

(EDGAR *makes a gesture of horror — a general frightened movement.*)

WANKLIN. Come, come, Chairman.

ANTHONY (*in a grim voice*). These are the words of my own son. They are the words of a generation that I don't understand; the words of a soft breed.

(*A general murmur. With a violent effort* ANTHONY *recovers his control.*)

EDGAR (*quietly*). I said it of *myself*, too, father.

(*A long look is exchanged between them, and* ANTHONY *puts out his hand with a gesture as if to sweep the personalities away; then places it against his brow, swaying as though from giddiness. There is a movement towards him. He moves them back.*)

ANTHONY. Before I put this amendment to the Board, I have one more word to say. (*He looks from face to face.*) If it is carried, it means that we shall fail in what we set ourselves to do. It means that we shall fail in the duty that we owe to all Capital. It means that we shall fail in the duty that we owe ourselves. It means that we shall be open to constant attack to which we as constantly shall have to yield. Be under no misapprehension — run this time, and you will never make a stand again! You will have to fly like curs before the whips of your own men. If that is the lot you wish for, you will vote for this amendment. (*He looks again, from face to face, finally resting his gaze on* EDGAR; *all sit with their eyes on the ground.* ANTHONY *makes a gesture, and* TENCH *hands him the book. He reads.*) "Moved by Mr. Wilder, and seconded by Mr. Wanklin: 'That the men's demands be placed at once in the hands of Mr. Simon Harness for settlement on the lines indicated by him this morning.'" (*With sudden vigor.*) Those in favor: Signify the same in the usual way! (*For a minute no one moves; then hastily just as* ANTHONY *is about to speak,* WILDER's *hand and* WANKLIN's *are held up, then* SCANTLEBURY's, *and last* EDGAR's *who does not lift his head.*) Contrary? (ANTHONY *lifts his own hand. In a clear voice.*) The amendment is carried. I resign my position on this Board. (ENID *gasps, and there is dead silence.* ANTHONY *sits motionless, his head slowly drooping; suddenly he heaves as though the whole of his life had risen up within him.*) Fifty years! You have disgraced me, gentlemen. Bring in the men!

(*He sits motionless, staring before him. The Board draws hurriedly together, and forms a group.* TENCH *in a frightened manner speaks into the hall.* UNDERWOOD *almost forces* ENID *from the room.*)

WILDER (*hurriedly*). What's to be said to them? Why isn't Harness here? Ought we to see the men before he comes? I don't ——

TENCH. Will you come in, please?

(*Enter* THOMAS, GREEN, BULGIN, *and* ROUS, *who file up in a row past the little table.* TENCH *sits down and writes. All eyes are fixed on* ANTHONY, *who makes no sign.*)

WANKLIN (*stepping up to the little table, with nervous cordiality*). Well, Thomas, how's it to be? What's the result of your meeting?

ROUS. Sim Harness has our answer. He'll tell you what it is. We're waiting for him. He'll speak for us.

WANKLIN. Is that so, Thomas?

THOMAS (*sullenly*). Yes. Roberts will not be coming, his wife is dead.

SCANTLEBURY. Yes, yes! Poor woman! Yes! Yes!

FROST (*entering from the hall*). Mr. Harness, sir!

(*As* HARNESS *enters he retires.* HARNESS *has a piece of paper in his hand, he bows to the Directors, nods toward the men, and takes his stand behind the little table in the very center of the room.*)

HARNESS. Good-evening, gentlemen.

(TENCH, *with the paper he has been writing, joins him; they speak together in low tones.*)

WILDER. We've been waiting for you, Harness. Hope we shall come to some ——

FROST (*entering from the hall*). Roberts!

(*He goes.* ROBERTS *comes hastily in, and stands staring at* ANTHONY. *His face is drawn and old.*)

ROBERTS. Mr. Anthony, I am afraid I am a little late, I would have been here in time but for something that — has happened. (*To the men.*) Has anything been said?

THOMAS. No! But, man, what made ye come?

ROBERTS. Ye told us this morning, gentlemen, to go away and re-consider our position. We have reconsidered it; we are here to bring you the men's answer. (*To* ANTHONY.) Go ye back to London. We have nothing for you. By no jot or tittle do we abate our demands, nor will we until the whole of those demands are yielded.

(ANTHONY *looks at him but does not speak. There is a movement amongst the men as though they were bewildered.*)

HARNESS. Roberts!

ROBERTS (*glancing fiercely at him, and back to* ANTHONY). Is that clear enough for ye? Is it short enough and to the point? Ye made a mistake to think that we would come to heel. Ye may break the body, but ye cannot break the spirit. Get back to London, the men have nothing for ye?

(*Pausing uneasily he takes a step towards the unmoving* ANTHONY.)

EDGAR. We're all sorry for you, Roberts, but ——

ROBERTS. Keep your sorrow, young man. Let your father speak!

HARNESS (*with the sheet of paper in his hand, speaking from behind the little table*). Roberts!

ROBERTS (*to* ANTHONY, *with passionate intensity*). Why don't ye answer?

HARNESS. Roberts!

ROBERTS (*turning sharply*). What is it?

HARNESS (*gravely*). You're talking without the book; things have travelled past you. (*He makes a sign to* TENCH, *who beckons the Directors. They quickly sign his copy of the terms.*) Look at this man! (*Holding up his sheet of paper.*) "Demands conceded, *with the exception of those relating to the engineers and furnace men. Double wages for Saturday's overtime. Night-shifts as they are.*" These terms have been agreed. The men go back to work again tomorrow. The strike is at an end.

ROBERTS (*reading the paper, and turning on the men. They shrink back from him, all but* ROUS, *who stands his ground. With deadly stillness*). Ye have gone back on me? I stood by ye to the death; ye waited for *that* to throw me over!

(*The men answer, all speaking together.*)

ROUS. It's a lie!

THOMAS. Ye were past endurance, man.

GREEN. If ye'd listen to me ——

BULGIN (*under his breath*). Hold your jaw!

ROBERTS. Ye waited for *that!*

HARNESS (*taking the Directors' copy of the terms, and handing his own to* TENCH). That's enough, men. You had better go.

(*The men shuffle slowly, awkwardly away.*)

WILDER (*in a low, nervous voice*). There's nothing to stay for now, I suppose. (*He follows to the door.*) I shall have a try for that train! Coming, Scantlebury?

SCANTLEBURY (*following with* WANKLIN). Yes, yes; wait for me.

(*He stops as* ROBERTS *speaks.*)

ROBERTS (*to* ANTHONY).   But *ye* have not signed them terms!   They can't make terms without their Chairman!   Ye would never sign them terms!   (ANTHONY *looks at him without speaking.*)   Don't tell me ye have! for the love o' God!   (*With passionate appeal.*)   I reckoned on ye!

HARNESS (*holding out the Directors' copy of the terms*).   *The Board* has signed!

> (ROBERTS *looks dully at the signatures — dashes the paper from him, and covers up his eyes.*)

SCANTLEBURY (*behind his hand to* TENCH).   Look after the Chairman! He's not well; he's not well — he had no lunch.   If there's any fund started for the women and children, put me down for — for twenty pounds.

> (*He goes out into the hall, in cumbrous haste; and* WANKLIN, *who has been staring at* ROBERTS *and* ANTHONY *with twitchings of his face, follows.* EDGAR *remains seated on the sofa, looking at the ground;* TENCH, *returning to the bureau, writes in his minute-book.* HARNESS *stands by the little table, gravely watching* ROBERTS.)

ROBERTS.   Then you're no longer Chairman of this Company! (*Breaking into half-mad laughter.*)   Ah! ha — ah, ha, ha!   They've thrown ye over — thrown over their Chairman!   Ah — ha — ha!   (*With a sudden dreadful calm.*)   So — they've done us both down, Mr. Anthony?

> (ENID, *hurrying through the double doors, comes quickly to her father.*)

ANTHONY.   Both broken men, my friend Roberts!

HARNESS (*coming down and laying his hands on* ROBERTS's *sleeve*).   For shame, Roberts!   Go home quietly, man; go home!

ROBERTS (*tearing his arm away*).   Home?   (*Shrinking together — in a whisper.*)   Home!

ENID (*quietly to her father*).   Come away, dear!   Come to your room!

> (ANTHONY *rises with an effort.   He turns to* ROBERTS *who looks at him.   They stand several seconds, gazing at each other fixedly;* ANTHONY *lifts his hand, as though to salute, but lets it fall.   The expression of* ROBERTS's *face changes from hostility to wonder.   They bend their heads in token of respect.* ANTHONY *turns, and slowly walks towards the curtained door.   Suddenly he sways as though about to fall, recovers himself, and is assisted out*

by EDGAR *and* ENID; UNDERWOOD *follows, but stops at the
door.* ROBERTS *remains motionless for several seconds, staring
intently after* ANTHONY, *then goes out into the hall.*)

TENCH (*approaching* HARNESS). It's a great weight off my mind, Mr.
Harness? But what a painful scene, sir! (*He wipes his brow.*
HARNESS, *pale and resolute, regards, with a grim half-smile the quavering*
TENCH.) It's all been so violent! What did he mean by: "Done
us both down"? If he has lost his wife, poor fellow, he oughtn't
to have spoken to the Chairman like that!

HARNESS. A woman dead; and the two best men both broken!

TENCH (*staring at him — suddenly excited*). D'you know, sir — these
terms, they're the *very same* we drew up together, you and I, and
put to both sides before the fight began? All this — all this —
and — and what for?

HARNESS (*in a slow grim voice*). That's where the fun comes in!

(UNDERWOOD *without turning from the door makes a gesture of
assent.*)

RIDERS TO THE SEA

A PLAY IN ONE ACT

By JOHN MILLINGTON SYNGE

PERSONS

MAURYA, *an old woman.*
BARTLEY, *her son.*
CATHLEEN, *her daughter.*
NORA, *a younger daughter.*
MEN AND WOMEN.

RIDERS TO THE SEA

SCENE. — *An Island off the west of Ireland.*

Cottage kitchen, with nets, oil-skins, spinning-wheel, some new boards standing by the wall, etc. CATHLEEN, *a girl of about twenty, finishes kneading cake, and puts it down in the pot-oven by the fire; then wipes her hands, and begins to spin at the wheel.* NORA, *a young girl, puts her head in at the door.*

NORA (*in a low voice*). Where is she?

CATHLEEN. She's lying down, God help her, and may be sleeping, if she's able.

(NORA *comes in softly, and takes a bundle from under her shawl.*)

CATHLEEN (*spinning the wheel rapidly*). What is it you have?

NORA. The young priest is after bringing them. It's a shirt and a plain stocking were got off a drowned man in Donegal.

    (CATHLEEN *stops her wheel with a sudden movement, and leans out to listen.*)

NORA. We're to find out if it's Michael's they are, some time herself will be down looking by the sea.

CATHLEEN. How would they be Michael's, Nora? How would he go the length of that way to the far north?

NORA. The young priest says he's known the like of it. "If it's Michael's they are," says he, "you can tell herself he's got a clean burial by the grace of God, and if they're not his, let no one say a word about them, for she'll be getting her death," says he, "with crying and lamenting."

    (*The door which* NORA *half closed is blown open by a gust of wind.*)

CATHLEEN (*looking out anxiously*). Did you ask him would he stop Bartley going this day with the horses to the Galway fair?

NORA. "I won't stop him," says he, "but let you not be afraid. Herself does be saying prayers half through the night, and the Almighty God won't leave her destitute," says he, "with no son living."

CATHLEEN. Is the sea bad by the white rocks, Nora?

NORA. Middling bad, God help us. There's a great roaring in the west, and it's worse it'll be getting when the tide's turned to the wind. (*She goes over to the table with the bundle.*) Shall I open it now?

CATHLEEN. Maybe she'd wake up on us, and come in before we'd done. (*Coming to the table.*) It's a long time we'll be, and the two of us crying.

NORA (*goes to the inner door and listens*). She's moving about on the bed. She'll be coming in a minute.

CATHLEEN. Give me the ladder, and I'll put them up in the turf-loft, the way she won't know of them at all, and maybe when the tide turns she'll be going down to see would he be floating from the east.

(*They put the ladder against the gable of the chimney; CATHLEEN goes up a few steps and hides the bundle in the turf-loft. MAURYA comes from the inner room.*)

MAURYA (*looking up at CATHLEEN and speaking querulously*). Isn't it turf enough you have for this day and evening?

CATHLEEN. There's a cake baking at the fire for a short space (*throwing down the turf*) and Bartley will want it when the tide turns if he goes to Connemara.

(*NORA picks up the turf and puts it round the pot-oven.*)

MAURYA (*sitting down on a stool at the fire*). He won't go this day with the wind rising from the south and west. He won't go this day, for the young priest will stop him surely.

NORA. He'll not stop him, mother, and I heard Eamon Simon and Stephen Pheety and Colum Shawn saying he would go.

MAURYA. Where is he itself?

NORA. He went down to see would there be another boat sailing in the week, and I'm thinking it won't be long till he's here now, for the tide's turning at the green head, and the hooker's tacking from the east.

CATHLEEN. I hear some one passing the big stones.

NORA (*looking out*). He's coming now, and he in a hurry.

BARTLEY (*comes in and looks round the room; speaking sadly and quietly*). Where is the bit of new rope, Cathleen, was bought in Connemara?

CATHLEEN (*coming down*). Give it to him, Nora; it's on a nail by the white boards. I hung it up this morning, for the pig with the black feet was eating it.

NORA (*giving him a rope*). Is that it, Bartley?

MAURYA. You'd do right to leave that rope, Bartley, hanging by the boards. (BARTLEY *takes the rope*.) It will be wanting in this place, I'm telling you, if Michael is washed up tomorrow morning, or the next morning, or any morning in the week, for it's a deep grave we'll make him by the grace of God.

BARTLEY (*beginning to work with the rope*). I've no halter the way I can ride down on the mare, and I must go now quickly. This is the one boat going for two weeks or beyond it, and the fair will be a good fair for horses I heard them saying below.

MAURYA. It's a hard thing they'll be saying below if the body is washed up and there's no man in it to make the coffin, and I after giving a big price for the finest white boards you'd find in Connemara.   (*She looks round at the boards*).

BARTLEY. How would it be washed up, and we after looking each day for nine days, and a strong wind blowing a while back from the west and south?

MAURYA. If it wasn't found itself, that wind is raising the sea, and there was a star up against the moon, and it rising in the night. If it was a hundred horses, or a thousand horses you had itself, what is the price of a thousand horses against a son where there is one son only?

BARTLEY (*working at the halter, to* CATHLEEN). Let you go down each day, and see the sheep aren't jumping in on the rye, and if the jobber comes you can sell the pig with the black feet if there is a good price going.

MAURYA. How would the like of her get a good price for a pig?

BARTLEY (*to* CATHLEEN). If the west wind holds with the last bit of the moon let you and Nora get up weed enough for another cock for the kelp. It's hard set we'll be from this day with no one in it but one man to work.

MAURYA. It's hard set we'll be surely the day you're drownd'd with the rest. What way will I live and the girls with me, and I an old woman looking for the grave?

(BARTLEY *lays down the halter, takes off his old coat, and puts on a newer one of the same flannel.*)

BARTLEY (*to* NORA). Is she coming to the pier?

NORA (*looking out*). She's passing the green head and letting fall her sails.

BARTLEY (*getting his purse and tobacco*). I'll have half an hour to go down, and you'll see me coming again in two days, or in three days, or maybe in four days if the wind is bad.

MAURYA (*turning round to the fire, and putting her shawl over her head*). Isn't it a hard and cruel man won't hear a word from an old woman, and she holding him from the sea?

CATHLEEN. It's the life of a young man to be going on the sea, and who would listen to an old woman with one thing and she saying it over?

BARTLEY (*taking the halter*). I must go now quickly. I'll ride down on the red mare, and the gray pony'll run behind me.... The blessing of God on you. (*He goes out.*)

MAURYA (*crying out as he is in the door*). He's gone now, God spare us, and we'll not see him again. He's gone now, and when the black night is falling I'll have no son left me in the world.

CATHLEEN. Why wouldn't you give him your blessing and he looking round in the door? Isn't it sorrow enough is on every one in this house without your sending him out with an unlucky word behind him, and a hard word in his ear?

(MAURYA *takes up the tongs and begins raking the fire aimlessly without looking round.*)

NORA (*turning toward her*). You're taking away the turf from the cake.

CATHLEEN (*crying out*). The Son of God forgive us, Nora, we're after forgetting his bit of bread. (*She comes over to the fire.*)

NORA. And it's destroyed he'll be going till dark night, and he after eating nothing since the sun went up.

CATHLEEN (*turning the cake out of the oven*). It's destroyed he'll be, surely. There's no sense left on any person in a house where an old woman will be talking forever.

(MAURYA *sways herself on her stool.*)

CATHLEEN (*cutting off some of the bread and rolling it in a cloth; to* MAURYA). Let you go down now to the spring well and give him this and he passing. You'll see him then and the dark word will be broken, and you can say "God speed you," the way he'll be easy in his mind.

MAURYA (*taking the bread*). Will I be in it as soon as himself?

CATHLEEN. If you go now quickly.

MAURYA (*standing up unsteadily*). It's hard set I am to walk.

CATHLEEN (*looking at her anxiously*). Give her the stick, Nora, or maybe she'll slip on the big stones.

NORA. What stick?

CATHLEEN. The stick Michael brought from Connemara.

MAURYA (*taking a stick* NORA *gives her*). In the big world the old people do be leaving things after them for their sons and children, but in this place it is the young men do be leaving things behind for them that do be old.

(*She goes out slowly.* NORA *goes over to the ladder.*)

CATHLEEN. Wait, Nora, maybe she'd turn back quickly. She's that sorry, God help her, you wouldn't know the thing she'd do.

NORA. Is she gone round by the bush?

CATHLEEN (*looking out*). She's gone now. Throw it down quickly, for the Lord knows when she'll be out of it again.

NORA (*getting the bundle from the loft*). The young priest said he'd be passing tomorrow, and we might go down and speak to him below if it's Michael's they are surely.

CATHLEEN (*taking the bundle*). Did he say what way they were found?

NORA (*coming down*). "There were two men," says he, "and they rowing round with poteen before the cocks crowed, and the oar of one of them caught the body, and they passing the black cliffs of the north."

CATHLEEN (*trying to open the bundle*). Give me a knife, Nora, the string's perished with the salt water, and there's a black knot on it you wouldn't loosen in a week.

NORA (*giving her a knife*). I've heard tell it was a long way to Donegal.

CATHLEEN (*cutting the string*). It is surely. There was a man in here a while ago — the man sold us that knife — and he said if you set off walking from the rocks beyond, it would be seven days you'd be in Donegal.

NORA. And what time would a man take, and he floating?

(CATHLEEN *opens the bundle and takes out a bit of a stocking. They look at them eagerly.*)

CATHLEEN (*in a low voice*). The Lord spare us, Nora! isn't it a queer hard thing to say if it's his they are surely?

NORA. I'll get his shirt off the hook the way we can put the one flannel on the other. (*She looks through some clothes hanging in the corner.*) It's not with them, Cathleen, and where will it be?

CATHLEEN. I'm thinking Bartley put it on him in the morning, for his own shirt was heavy with the salt in it (*pointing to the corner*). There's a bit of a sleeve was of the same stuff. Give me that and it will do.

(NORA *brings it to her and they compare the flannel.*)

CATHLEEN. It's the same stuff, Nora; but if it is itself aren't there great rolls of it in the shops of Galway, and isn't it many another man may have a shirt of it as well as Michael himself?

NORA (*who has taken up the stocking and counted the stitches, crying out*). It's Michael, Cathleen, it's Michael; God spare his soul, and what will herself say when she hears this story, and Bartley on the sea?

CATHLEEN (*taking the stocking*). It's a plain stocking.

NORA. It's the second one of the third pair I knitted, and I put up threescore stitches, and I dropped four of them.

CATHLEEN (*counts the stitches*). It's that number is in it (*crying out*). Ah, Nora, isn't it a bitter thing to think of him floating that way to the far north, and no one to keen him but the black hags that do be flying on the sea?

NORA (*swinging herself round, and throwing out her arms on the clothes*). And isn't it a pitiful thing when there is nothing left of a man who was a great rower and fisher, but a bit of an old shirt and a plain stocking?

CATHLEEN (*after an instant*). Tell me is herself coming, Nora? I hear a little sound on the path.

NORA (*looking out*). She is, Cathleen. She's coming up to the door.

CATHLEEN. Put these things away before she'll come in. Maybe it's easier she'll be after giving her blessing to Bartley, and we won't let on we've heard anything the time he's on the sea.

NORA (*helping* CATHLEEN *to close the bundle*). We'll put them here in the corner.

(*They put them into a hole in the chimney corner.* CATHLEEN *goes back to the spinning-wheel.*)

NORA. Will she see it was crying I was?

CATHLEEN. Keep your back to the door the way the light'll not be on you.

(NORA *sits down at the chimney corner, with her back to the door.* MAURYA *comes in very slowly, without looking at the girls, and goes over to her stool at the other side of the fire. The cloth with the bread is still in her hand. The girls look at each other, and* NORA *points to the bundle of bread.*)

CATHLEEN (*after spinning for a moment*). You didn't give him his bit of bread? (MAURYA *begins to keen softly, without turning round.*)

CATHLEEN. Did you see him riding down?

(MAURYA *goes on keening.*)

CATHLEEN (*a little impatiently*). God forgive you; isn't it a better thing to raise your voice and tell what you seen, than to be making lamentation for a thing that's done? Did you see Bartley, I'm saying to you.

MAURYA (*with a weak voice*). My heart's broken from this day.

CATHLEEN (*as before*). Did you see Bartley?

MAURYA. I seen the fearfulest thing.

CATHLEEN (*leaves her wheel and looks out*). God forgive you; he's riding the mare now over the green head, and the gray pony behind him.

MAURYA (*starts, so that her shawl falls back from her head and shows her white tossed hair. With a frightened voice*). The gray pony behind him.

CATHLEEN (*coming to the fire*). What is it ails you, at all?

MAURYA (*speaking very slowly*). I've seen the fearfulest thing any person has seen, since the day Bride Dara seen the dead man with a child in his arms.

CATHLEEN AND NORA. Uah.

(*They crouch down in front of the old woman at the fire.*)

NORA. Tell us what it is you seen.

MAURYA. I went down to the spring well, and I stood there saying a prayer to myself. Then Bartley came along, and he riding on the red mare with the gray pony behind him. (*She puts up her hands, as if to hide something from her eyes.*) The Son of God spare us, Nora!

CATHLEEN. What is it you seen?

MAURYA. I seen Michael himself.

CATHLEEN (*speaking softly*). You did not, mother; it wasn't Michael you seen, for his body is after being found in the Far North, and he's got a clean burial by the grace of God.

MAURYA (*a little defiantly*). I'm after seeing him this day, and he riding and galloping. Bartley came first on the red mare; and I tried to say, "God speed you," but something choked the words in my throat. He went by quickly; and "the blessing of God on you," says he, and I could say nothing. I looked up then, and I crying, at the gray pony, and there was Michael upon it — with fine clothes on him, and new shoes on his feet.

CATHLEEN (*begins to keen*). It's destroyed we are from this day. It's destroyed, surely.

NORA. Didn't the young priest say the Almighty God wouldn't leave her destitute with no son living?

MAURYA (*in a low voice, but clearly*). It's little the like of him knows of the sea.... Bartley will be lost now, and let you call in Eamon and make me a good coffin out of the white boards, for I won't live after them. I've had a husband, and a husband's father, and six sons in this house — six fine men, though it was a hard birth I had with every one of them and they coming to the world — and some of them were found and some of them were not found, but they're gone now the lot of them.... There were Stephen, and Shawn, were lost in the great wind, and found after in the Bay of Gregory of the Golden Mouth, and carried up the two of them on the one plank, and in by that door.

> (*She pauses for a moment, the girls start as if they heard something through the door that is half open behind them.*)

NORA (*in a whisper*). Did you hear that, Cathleen? Did you hear a noise in the northeast?

CATHLEEN (*in a whisper*). There's some one after crying out by the seashore.

MAURYA (*continues without hearing anything*). There was Sheamus and his father, and his own father again, were lost in a dark night, and not a stick or sign was seen of them when the sun went up. There was Patch after was drowned out of a curagh that turned over. I was sitting here with Bartley, and he a baby, lying on my two knees, and I seen two women, and three women, and four women coming in, and they crossing themselves, and not saying a word. I looked out then, and there were men coming after them, and they holding a thing in the half of a red sail, and water dripping out of it — it was a dry day, Nora — and leaving a track to the door.

> (*She pauses again with her hand stretched out toward the door. It opens softly and old women begin to come in, crossing themselves on the threshold, and kneeling down in front of the stage with red petticoats over their heads.*)

MAURYA (*half in a dream, to* CATHLEEN). Is it Patch, or Michael, or what is it at all?

CATHLEEN. Michael is after being found in the Far North, and when he is found there how could he be here in this place?

MAURYA. There does be a power of young men floating round in the sea, and what way would they know if it was Michael they had, or another man like him, for when a man is nine days in the sea, and the wind blowing, it's hard set his own mother would be to say what man was it.

CATHLEEN. It's Michael, God spare him, for they're after sending us a bit of his clothes from the Far North.

> (*She reaches out and hands* MAURYA *the clothes that belonged to* MICHAEL. MAURYA *stands up slowly, and takes them in her hands.* NORA *looks out.*)

NORA. They're carrying a thing among them and there's water dripping out of it and leaving a track by the big stones.

CATHLEEN (*in a whisper to the women who have come in*). Is it Bartley it is?

ONE OF THE WOMEN. It is surely, God rest his soul.

> (*Two younger women come in and pull out the table. Then men carry in the body of* BARTLEY, *laid on a plank, with a bit of a sail over it, and lay it on the table.*)

CATHLEEN (*to the women, as they are doing so*). What way was he drowned?

ONE OF THE WOMEN. The gray pony knocked him into the sea, and he was washed out where there is a great surf on the white rocks.

> (MAURYA *has gone over and knelt down at the head of the table. The women are keening softly and swaying themselves with a slow movement.* CATHLEEN *and* NORA *kneel at the other end of the table. The men kneel near the door.*)

MAURYA (*raising her head and speaking as if she did not see the people around her*). They're all gone now, and there isn't anything more the sea can do to me.... I'll have no call now to be up crying and praying when the wind breaks from the south, and you can hear the surf is in the east, and the surf is in the west, making a great stir with the two noises, and they hitting one on the other. I'll have no call now to be going down and getting Holy Water in the dark nights after Samhain, and I won't care what way the sea is when the other women will be keening. (*To* NORA.) Give me the Holy Water, Nora, there's a small sup still on the dresser.

(NORA *gives it to her.*)

MAURYA (*drops* MICHAEL'S *clothes across* BARTLEY'S *feet, and sprinkles the Holy Water over him*). It isn't that I haven't prayed for you, Bartley, to the Almighty God. It isn't that I haven't said prayers in the dark night till you wouldn't know what I'd be saying; but it's a great rest I'll have now, and it's time surely. It's a great rest I'll have now, and great sleeping in the long nights after Samhain, if it's only a bit of wet flour we do have to eat, and maybe a fish that would be stinking.

(*She kneels down again, crossing herself, and saying prayers under her breath.*)

CATHLEEN (*to an old man*). Maybe yourself and Eamon would make a coffin when the sun rises. We have fine white boards herself bought, God help her, thinking Michael would be found, and I have a new cake you can eat while you'll be working.

THE OLD MAN (*looking at the boards*). Are there nails with them?

CATHLEEN. There are not, Colum; we didn't think of the nails.

ANOTHER MAN. It's a great wonder she wouldn't think of the nails, and all the coffins she's seen made already.

CATHLEEN. It's getting old she is, and broken.

(MAURYA *stands up again very slowly and spreads out the pieces of* MICHAEL'S *clothes beside the body, sprinkling them with the last of the Holy Water.*)

NORA (*in a whisper to* CATHLEEN). She's quiet now and easy; but the day Michael was drowned you could hear her crying out from this to the spring well. It's fonder she was of Michael, and would any one have thought that?

CATHLEEN (*slowly and clearly*). An old woman will be soon tired with anything she will do, and isn't it nine days herself is after crying and keening, and making great sorrow in the house?

MAURYA (*puts the empty cup mouth downwards on the table, and lays her hands together on* BARTLEY's *feet*). They're all together this time, and the end is come. May the Almighty God have mercy on Bartley's soul, and on Michael's soul, and on the souls of Sheamus and Patch, and Stephen and Shawn (*bending her head*); and may He have mercy on my soul, Nora, and on the soul of every one is left living in the world.

> (*She pauses, and the keen rises a little more loudly from the women, then sinks away.*)

MAURYA (*continuing*). Michael has a clean burial in the Far North, by the grace of the Almighty God. Bartley will have a fine coffin out of the white boards, and a deep grave surely. What more can we want than that? No man at all can be living forever, and we must be satisfied.

> (*She kneels down again and the curtain falls slowly.*)

BEYOND THE HORIZON

A PLAY IN THREE ACTS

By EUGENE O'NEILL

CHARACTERS

JAMES MAYO, *a farmer.*

KATE MAYO, *his wife.*

CAPTAIN DICK SCOTT, *of the bark* Sunda, *her brother.*

ANDREW MAYO ⎱ *sons of* JAMES MAYO.
ROBERT MAYO ⎰

RUTH ATKINS.

MRS. ATKINS, *her widowed mother.*

MARY.

BEN, *a farm hand.*

DOCTOR FAWCETT.

ACT I

Scene I: The Road.   Sunset of a day in Spring.
Scene II: The Farm House.   The same night.

ACT II

(Three years later)

Scene I: The Farm House.   Noon of a Summer day.
Scene II: The top of a hill on the farm overlooking the sea.   The
following day.

ACT III

(Five years later)

Scene I: The Farm House.   Dawn of a day in late Fall.
Scene II: The Road.   Sunrise.

ACT ONE

Scene One

A section of country highway. The road runs diagonally from the left, forward, to the right, rear, and can be seen in the distance winding toward the horizon like a pale ribbon between the low, rolling hills with their freshly plowed fields clearly divided from each other, checkerboard fashion, by the lines of stone walls and rough snake fences.

The forward triangle cut off by the road is a section of a field from the dark earth of which myriad bright-green blades of fall-sown rye are sprouting. A straggling line of piled rocks, too low to be called a wall, separates this field from the road.

To the rear of the road is a ditch with a sloping, grassy bank on the far side. From the center of this an old, gnarled apple tree, just budding into leaf, strains its twisted branches heavenwards, black against the pallor of distance. A snake fence sidles from left to right along the top of the bank, passing beneath the apple tree.

The hushed twilight of a day in May is just beginning. The horizon hills are still rimmed by a faint line of flame, and the sky above them glows with the crimson flush of the sunset. This fades gradually as the action of the scene progresses.

At the rise of the curtain, ROBERT MAYO *is discovered sitting on the fence. He is a tall, slender young man of twenty-three. There is a touch of the poet about him expressed in his high forehead and wide, dark eyes. His features are delicate and refined, leaning to weakness in the mouth and chin. He is dressed in gray corduroy trousers pushed into high laced boots, and a blue flannel shirt with a bright colored tie. He is reading a book by the fading sunset light. He shuts this, keeping a finger in to mark the place, and turns his head toward the horizon, gazing out over the fields and hills. His lips move as if he were reciting something to himself.*

His brother ANDREW *comes along the road from the right, returning from his work in the fields. He is twenty-seven years old, an opposite type to* ROBERT — *husky, sun-bronzed, handsome in a large-featured, manly fashion — a son of the soil, intelligent in a shrewd way, but with nothing of the intellectual about him. He wears overalls, leather boots, a gray flannel*

shirt open at the neck, and a soft, mud-stained hat pushed back on his head.
He stops to talk to ROBERT, *leaning on the hoe he carries.*

ANDREW (*seeing* ROBERT *has not noticed his presence — in a loud shout*).
Hey there! (ROBERT *turns with a start. Seeing who it is, he smiles.*)
Gosh, you do take the prize for daydreaming! And I see you've
toted one of the old books along with you. (*He crosses the ditch
and sits on the fence near his brother.*) What is it this time — poetry,
I'll bet. (*He reaches for the book.*) Let me see.

ROBERT (*handing it to him rather reluctantly*). Look out you don't get
it full of dirt.

ANDREW (*glancing at his hands*). That isn't dirt — it's good clean
earth. (*He turns over the pages. His eyes read something and he gives
an exclamation of disgust.*) Hump! (*With a provoking grin at his
brother he reads aloud in a doleful, sing-song voice.*) "I have loved
wind and light and the bright sea. But holy and most sacred
night, not as I love and have loved thee." (*He hands the book
back.*) Here! Take it and bury it. I suppose it's that year in
college gave you a liking for that kind of stuff. I'm darn glad I
stopped at High School, or maybe I'd been crazy too. (*He grins
and slaps* ROBERT *on the back affectionately.*) Imagine me reading
poetry and plowing at the same time! The team'd run away,
I'll bet.

ROBERT (*laughing*). Or picture me plowing.

ANDREW. You should have gone back to college last fall, like I know
you wanted to. You're fitted for that sort of thing — just as I
ain't.

ROBERT. You know why I didn't go back, Andy. Pa didn't like
the idea, even if he didn't say so; and I know he wanted the
money to use improving the farm. And besides, I'm not keen on
being a student, just because you see me reading books all the
time. What I want to do now is keep on moving so that I won't
take root in any one place.

ANDREW. Well, the trip you're leaving on tomorrow will keep you
moving all right. (*At this mention of the trip they both fall silent.
There is a pause. Finally* ANDREW *goes on, awkwardly, attempting to
speak casually.*) Uncle says you'll be gone three years.

ROBERT. About that, he figures.

ANDREW (*moodily*).   That's a long time.

ROBERT.   Not so long when you come to consider it.   You know the *Sunda* sails around the Horn for Yokohama first, and that's a long voyage on a sailing ship; and if we go to any of the other places Uncle Dick mentions — India, or Australia, or South Africa, or South America — they'll be long voyages, too.

ANDREW.   You can have all those foreign parts for all of me.   (*After a pause.*)   Ma's going to miss you a lot, Rob.

ROBERT.   Yes — and I'll miss her.

ANDREW.   And Pa ain't feeling none too happy to have you go — though he's been trying not to show it.

ROBERT.   I can see how he feels.

ANDREW.   And you can bet that I'm not giving any cheers about it.
                    (*He puts one hand on the fence near* ROBERT.)

ROBERT (*putting one hand on top of* ANDREW's *with a gesture almost of shyness*).   I know that, too, Andy.

ANDREW.   I'll miss you as much as anybody, I guess.   You see, you and I ain't like most brothers — always fighting and separated a lot of the time, while we've always been together — just the two of us.   It's different with us.   That's why it hits so hard, I guess.

ROBERT (*with feeling*).   It's just as hard for me, Andy — believe that!   I hate to leave you and the old folks — but — I feel I've got to.   There's something calling me —— (*He points to the horizon.*)   Oh, I can't just explain it to you, Andy.

ANDREW.   No need to, Rob.   (*Angry at himself.*)   Hell!   You want to go — that's all there is to it; and I wouldn't have you miss this chance for the world.

ROBERT.   It's fine of you to feel that way, Andy.

ANDREW.   Huh!   I'd be a nice son-of-a-gun if I didn't, wouldn't I?   When I know how you need this sea trip to make a new man of you — in the body, I mean — and give you your full health back.

ROBERT (*a trifle impatiently*).   All of you seem to keep harping on my health.   You were so used to seeing me lying around the house in the old days that you never will get over the notion that I'm a chronic invalid.   You don't realize how I've bucked up in the past few years.   If I had no other excuse for going on Uncle Dick's ship but just my health, I'd stay right here and start in plowing.

ANDREW. Can't be done. Farming ain't your nature. There's all the difference shown in just the way us two feel about the farm. You — well, you like the home part of it, I expect; but as a place to work and grow things, you hate it. Ain't that right?

ROBERT. Yes, I suppose it is. For you it's different. You're a Mayo through and through. You're wedded to the soil. You're as much a product of it as an ear of corn is, or a tree. Father is the same. This farm is his life-work, and he's happy in knowing that another Mayo, inspired by the same love, will take up the work where he leaves off. I can understand your attitude, and Pa's; and I think it's wonderful and sincere. But I — well, I'm not made that way.

ANDREW. No, you ain't; but when it comes to understanding, I guess I realize that you've got your own angle of looking at things.

ROBERT (*musingly*). I wonder if you do, really.

ANDREW (*confidently*). Sure I do. You've seen a bit of the world, enough to make the farm seem small, and you've got the itch to see it all.

ROBERT. It's more than that, Andy.

ANDREW. Oh, of course. I know you're going to learn navigation, and all about a ship, so's you can be an officer. That's natural, too. There's a fair pay in it, I expect, when you consider that you've always got a home and grub thrown in; and if you're set on traveling, you can go anywhere you're a mind to without paying fare.

ROBERT (*with a smile that is half sad*). It's more than that, Andy.

ANDREW. Sure it is. There's always a chance of a good thing coming your way in some of those foreign ports or other. I've heard there are great opportunities for a young fellow with his eyes open in some of those new countries that are just being opened up. (*Jovially.*) I'll bet that's what you've been turning over in your mind under all your quietness! (*He slaps his brother on the back with a laugh.*) Well, if you get to be a millionaire all of a sudden, call 'round once in a while and I'll pass the plate to you. We could use a lot of money right here on the farm without hurting it any.

ROBERT (*forced to laugh*). I've never considered that practical side of it for a minute, Andy.

ANDREW. Well, you ought to.

ROBERT. No, I oughtn't. (*Pointing to the horizon — dreamily.*) Supposing I was to tell you that it's just Beauty that's calling me, the beauty of the far off and unknown, the mystery and spell of the East which lures me in the books I've read, the need of the freedom of great wide spaces, the joy of wandering on and on — in quest of the secret which is hidden over there, beyond the horizon? Suppose I told you that was the one and only reason for my going?

ANDREW. I should say you were nutty.

ROBERT (*frowning*). Don't, Andy. I'm serious.

ANDREW. Then you might as well stay here, because we've got all you're looking for right on this farm. There's wide space enough, Lord knows; and you can have all the sea you want by walking a mile down to the beach; and there's plenty of horizon to look at, and beauty enough for anyone, except in the winter. (*He grins.*) As for the mystery and spell, I haven't met 'em yet, but they're probably lying around somewheres. I'll have you understand this is a first class farm with all the fixings. (*He laughs.*)

ROBERT (*joining in the laughter in spite of himself*). It's no use talking to you, you chump!

ANDREW. You'd better not say anything to Uncle Dick about spells and things when you're on the ship. He'll likely chuck you overboard for a Jonah. (*He jumps down from the fence.*) I'd better run along. I've got to wash up some as long as Ruth's Ma is coming over for supper.

ROBERT (*pointedly — almost bitterly*). And Ruth.

ANDREW (*confused — looking everywhere except at* ROBERT — *trying to appear unconcerned*). Yes, Ruth'll be staying too. Well, I better hustle, I guess, and ——

        (*He steps over the ditch to the road while he is talking.*)

ROBERT (*who appears to be fighting some strong inward emotion — impulsively*). Wait a minute, Andy! (*He jumps down from the fence.*) There is something I want to ——

        (*He stops abruptly, biting his lips, his face coloring.*)

ANDREW (*facing him; half-defiantly*). Yes?

ROBERT (*confusedly*). No —— never mind —— it doesn't matter, it was nothing.

ANDREW (*after a pause, during which he stares fixedly at* ROBERT'S *averted face*).   Maybe I can guess — what you were going to say — but I guess you're right not to talk about it.   (*He pulls* ROBERT'S *hand from his side and grips it tensely; the two brothers stand looking into each other's eyes for a minute.*)   We can't help those things, Rob.   (*He turns away, suddenly releasing* ROBERT'S *hand.*)   You'll be coming along shortly, won't you?

ROBERT (*dully*).   Yes.

ANDREW.   See you later, then.

(*He walks off down the road to the left.* ROBERT *stares after him for a moment; then climbs to the fence rail again, and looks out over the hills, an expression of deep grief on his face. After a moment or so,* RUTH *enters hurriedly from the left. She is a healthy, blonde, out-of-door girl of twenty, with a graceful, slender figure. Her face, though inclined to roundness, is undeniably pretty, its large eyes of a deep blue set off strikingly by the sun-bronzed complexion. Her small, regular features are marked by a certain strength — an underlying, stubborn fixity of purpose hidden in the frankly-appealing charm of her fresh youthfulness. She wears a simple white dress but no hat.*)

RUTH (*seeing him*).   Hello, Rob!

ROBERT (*startled*).   Hello, Ruth!

RUTH (*jumps the ditch and perches on the fence beside him*).   I was looking for you.

ROBERT (*pointedly*).   Andy just left here.

RUTH.   I know.   I met him on the road a second ago.   He told me you were here.   (*Tenderly playful.*)   I wasn't looking for Andy, Smarty, if that's what you mean.   I was looking for *you*.

ROBERT.   Because I'm going away tomorrow?

RUTH.   Because your mother was anxious to have you come home and asked me to look for you.   I just wheeled Ma over to your house.

ROBERT (*perfunctorily*).   How is your mother?

RUTH (*a shadow coming over her face*).   She's about the same.   She never seems to get any better or any worse.   Oh, Rob, I do wish she'd try to make the best of things that can't be helped.

ROBERT.   Has she been nagging at you again?

RUTH (*nods her head, and then breaks forth rebelliously*).   She never stops nagging. No matter what I do for her she finds fault. If only Pa was still living —— (*She stops as if ashamed of her outburst.*) I suppose I shouldn't complain this way. (*She sighs.*) Poor Ma, Lord knows it's hard enough for her. I suppose it's natural to be cross when you're not able ever to walk a step. Oh, I'd like to be going away some place — like you!

ROBERT. It's hard to stay — and equally hard to go, sometimes.

RUTH. There! If I'm not the stupid body! I swore I wasn't going to speak about your trip — until after you'd gone; and there I go, first thing!

ROBERT. Why didn't you want to speak of it?

RUTH. Because I didn't want to spoil this last night you're here. Oh, Rob, I'm going to — we're all going to miss you so awfully. Your mother is going around looking as if she'd burst out crying any minute. You ought to know how I feel. Andy and you and I — why it seems as if we'd always been together.

ROBERT (*with a wry attempt at a smile*). You and Andy will still have each other. It'll be harder for me without anyone.

RUTH. But you'll have new sights and new people to take your mind off; while we'll be here with the old, familiar place to remind us every minute of the day. It's a shame you're going — just at this time, in spring, when everything is getting so nice. (*With a sigh.*) I oughtn't to talk that way when I know going's the best thing for you. You're bound to find all sorts of opportunities to get on, your father says.

ROBERT (*heatedly*). I don't give a damn about that! I wouldn't take a voyage across the road for the best opportunity in the world of the kind Pa thinks of. (*He smiles at his own irritation.*) Excuse me, Ruth, for getting worked up over it; but Andy gave me an overdose of the practical considerations.

RUTH (*slowly, puzzled*). Well, then, if it isn't —— (*With sudden intensity.*) Oh, Rob, why *do* you want to go?

ROBERT (*turning to her quickly, in surprise — slowly*). Why do you ask that, Ruth?

RUTH (*dropping her eyes before his searching glance*). Because —— (*Lamely*). It seems such a shame.

ROBERT (*insistently*). Why?

RUTH. Oh, because — everything.

ROBERT. I could hardly back out now, even if I wanted to.   **And** I'll be forgotten before you know it.

RUTH (*indignantly*).   You won't!   I'll never forget ——
                        (*She stops and turns away to hide her confusion.*)

ROBERT (*softly*).   Will you promise me that?

RUTH (*evasively*).   Of course.   It's mean of you to think that any of us would forget so easily.

ROBERT (*disappointedly*).   Oh!

RUTH (*with an attempt at lightness*).   But you haven't told me your reason for leaving yet?

ROBERT (*moodily*).   I doubt if you'll understand.   It's difficult to explain, even to myself.   Either you feel it, or you don't.   I can remember being conscious of it first when I was only a kid — you haven't forgotten what a sickly specimen I was then, in those days, have you?

RUTH (*with a shudder*).   Let's not think about them.

ROBERT. You'll have to, to understand.   Well, in those days, when Ma was fixing meals, she used to get me out of the way by pushing my chair to the west window and telling me to look out and be quiet.   That wasn't hard.   I guess I was always quiet.

RUTH (*compassionately*).   Yes, you always were — and you suffering so much, too!

ROBERT (*musingly*).   So I used to stare out over the fields to the hills, out there — (*he points to the horizon*) and somehow after a time I'd forget any pain I was in, and start dreaming.   I knew the sea was over beyond those hills — the folks had told me — and I used to wonder what the sea was like, and try to form a picture of it in my mind.   (*With a smile.*)   There was all the mystery in the world to me then about that — far-off sea — and there still is!   It called to me then just as it does now.   (*After a slight pause.*)   And other times my eyes would follow this road, winding off into the distance, towards the hills, as if it, too, was searching for the sea.   And I'd promise myself that when I grew up and was strong, I'd follow that road, and it and I would find the sea together.   (*With a smile.*)   You see, my making this trip is only keeping that promise of long ago.

RUTH (*charmed by his low, musical voice telling the dreams of his childhood.*)   Yes, I see.

ROBERT. Those were the only happy moments of my life then, dreaming there at the window. I liked to be all alone — those times. I got to know all the different kinds of sunsets by heart. And all those sunsets took place over there — (*he points*) beyond the horizon. So gradually I came to believe that all the wonders of the world happened on the other side of those hills. There was the home of the good fairies who performed beautiful miracles. I believed in fairies then. (*With a smile.*) Perhaps I still do believe in them. Anyway, in those days they were real enough, and sometimes I could actually hear them calling to me to come out and play with them, dance with them down the road in the dusk in a game of hide-and-seek to find out where the sun was hiding himself. They sang their little songs to me, songs that told of all the wonderful things they had in their home on the other side of the hills; and they promised to show me all of them, if I'd only come, come! But I couldn't come then, and I used to cry sometimes and Ma would think I was in pain. (*He breaks off suddenly with a laugh.*) That's why I'm going now, I suppose. For I can still hear them calling. But the horizon is as far away and as luring as ever. (*He turns to her — softly.*) Do you understand now, Ruth?

RUTH (*spellbound, in a whisper*). Yes.

ROBERT. You feel it then?

RUTH. Yes, yes, I do! (*Unconsciously she snuggles close against his side. His arm steals about her as if he were not aware of the action.*) Oh, Rob, how could I help feeling it? You tell things so beautifully!

ROBERT (*suddenly realizing that his arm is around her, and that her head is resting on his shoulder, gently takes his arm away. RUTH, brought back to herself, is overcome with confusion*). So now you know why I'm going. It's for that reason — that and one other.

RUTH. You've another? Then you must tell me that, too.

ROBERT (*looking at her searchingly. She drops her eyes before his gaze*). I wonder if I ought to! You'll promise not to be angry — whatever it is?

RUTH (*softly, her face still averted*). Yes, I promise.

ROBERT (*simply*). I love you. That's the other reason.

RUTH (*hiding her face in her hands*). Oh, Rob!

ROBERT. I wasn't going to tell you, but I feel I have to. It can't matter now that I'm going so far away, and for so long — perhaps forever. I've loved you all these years, but the realization never came 'til I agreed to go away with Uncle Dick. Then I thought of leaving you, and the pain of that thought revealed to me in a flash — that I loved you, had loved you as long as I could remember. (*He gently pulls one of* RUTH's *hands away from her face.*) You mustn't mind my telling you this, Ruth. I realize how impossible it all is — and I understand; for the revelation of my own love seemed to open my eyes to the love of others. I saw Andy's love for you — and I knew that you must love him.

RUTH (*breaking out stormily*). I don't! I don't love Andy! I don't! (ROBERT *stares at her in stupid astonishment.* RUTH *weeps hysterically.*) Whatever — put such a fool notion into — into your head? (*She suddenly throws her arms about his neck and hides her head on his shoulder.*) Oh, Rob! Don't go away! Please! You mustn't, now! You can't! I won't let you! It'd break my — my heart!

ROBERT (*the expression of stupid bewilderment giving way to one of overwhelming joy. He presses her close to him — slowly and tenderly*). Do you mean that — that you love me?

RUTH (*sobbing*). Yes, yes — of course I do — what d'you s'pose? (*She lifts up her head and looks into his eyes with a tremulous smile.*) You stupid thing! (*He kisses her.*) I've loved you right along.

ROBERT (*mystified*). But you and Andy were always together!

RUTH. Because you never seemed to want to go any place with me. You were always reading an old book, and not paying any attention to me. I was too proud to let you see I cared because I thought the year you had away to college had made you stuck-up, and you thought yourself too educated to waste any time on me.

ROBERT (*kissing her*). And I was thinking —— (*With a laugh.*) What fools we've both been!

RUTH (*overcome by a sudden fear*). You won't go away on the trip, will you, Rob? You'll tell them you can't go on account of me, won't you? You can't go now! You can't!

ROBERT (*bewildered*). Perhaps — you can come too.

RUTH. Oh, Rob, don't be so foolish. You know I can't. Who'd take care of ma? Don't you see I couldn't go — on her account? (*She clings to him imploringly.*) Please don't go — not now. Tell them you've decided not to. They won't mind. I know your

mother and father'll be glad. They'll all be. They don't want
you to go so far away from them. Please, Rob! We'll be so
happy here together where it's natural and we know things.
Please tell me you won't go!

ROBERT (*face to face with a definite, final decision, betrays the conflict going
on within him*). But — Ruth — I — Uncle Dick ——

RUTH. He won't mind when he knows it's for your happiness to
stay. How could he? (*As* ROBERT *remains silent she bursts into
sobs again.*) Oh, Rob! And you said — you loved me!

ROBERT (*conquered by this appeal — an irrevocable decision in his voice*). I
won't go, Ruth. I promise you. There! Don't cry! (*He
presses her to him, stroking her hair tenderly. After a pause he speaks
with happy hopefulness.*) Perhaps after all Andy was right —
righter than he knew — when he said I could find all the things I
was seeking for here, at home on the farm. I think love must
have been the secret — the secret that called to me from over the
world's rim — the secret beyond every horizon; and when I did
not come, it came to me. (*He clasps* RUTH *to him fiercely.*) Oh,
Ruth, our love is sweeter than any distant dream!

> (*He kisses her passionately and steps to the ground, lifting* RUTH *in
> his arms and carrying her to the road where he puts her down.*)

RUTH (*with a happy laugh*). My, but you're strong!

ROBERT. Come! We'll go and tell them at once.

RUTH (*dismayed*). Oh, no, don't, Rob, not 'til after I've gone.
There'd be bound to be such a scene with them all together.

ROBERT (*kissing her — gayly*). As you like — little Miss Common
Sense!

RUTH. Let's go, then.

> (*She takes his hand, and they start to go off left.* ROBERT *suddenly
> stops and turns as though for a last look at the hills and the dying
> sunset flush.*)

ROBERT (*looking upward and pointing*). See! The first star. (*He
bends down and kisses her tenderly.*) Our star!

RUTH (*in a soft murmur*). Yes. Our very own star. (*They stand for
a moment looking up at it, their arms around each other. Then* RUTH
takes his hand again and starts to lead him away.) Come, Rob, let's
go. (*His eyes are fixed again on the horizon as he half turns to follow
her.* RUTH *urges.*) We'll be late for supper, Rob.

ROBERT (*shakes his head impatiently, as though he were throwing off some disturbing thought — with a laugh*). All right. We'll run then. Come on! (*They run off laughing as*

(*The Curtain Falls*)

ACT ONE

SCENE TWO

The sitting-room of the Mayo farm house about nine o'clock the same night. On the left, two windows looking out on the fields. Against the wall between the windows, an old-fashioned walnut desk. In the left corner, rear, a sideboard with a mirror. In the rear wall to the right of the sideboard, a window looking out on the road. Next to the window, a door leading out into the yard. Farther right, a black horse-hair sofa, and another door opening on a bedroom. In the corner, a straight-backed chair. In the right wall, near the middle, an open doorway leading to the kitchen. Farther forward a double-heater stove with coal scuttle, etc. In the center of the newly carpeted floor, an oak dining-room table with a red cover. In the center of the table, a large oil reading lamp. Four chairs, three rockers with crocheted tidies on their backs, and one straight-backed, are placed about the table. The walls are papered a dark red with a scrolly-figured pattern.

Everything in the room is clean, well-kept, and in its exact place, yet there is no suggestion of primness about the whole. Rather the atmosphere is one of the orderly comfort of a simple, hard-earned prosperity, enjoyed and maintained by the family as a unit.

JAMES MAYO, *his wife, her brother,* CAPTAIN DICK SCOTT, *and* ANDREW *are discovered.* MAYO *is his son* ANDREW *over again in body and face — an* ANDREW *sixty-five years old with a short, square, white beard.* MRS. MAYO *is a slight, round-faced, rather prim-looking woman of fifty-five who had once been a school teacher. The labors of a farmer's wife have bent but not broken her, and she retains a certain refinement of movement and expression foreign to the* MAYO *part of the family. Whatever of resemblance* ROBERT *has to his parents may be traced to her. Her brother, the* CAPTAIN, *is short and stocky, with a weather-beaten, jovial face and a white mustache — a typical old salt, loud of voice and given to gesture. He is fifty-eight years old.*

JAMES MAYO *sits in front of the table.* *He wears spectacles, and a farm journal which he has been reading lies in his lap.* THE CAPTAIN *leans forward from a chair in the rear, his hands on the table in front of him.* ANDREW *is tilted back on the straight-backed chair to the left, his chin sunk forward on his chest, staring at the carpet, preoccupied and frowning.*

As the Curtain rises the CAPTAIN *is just finishing the relation of some sea episode.* *The others are pretending an interest which is belied by the absent-minded expressions on their faces.*

THE CAPTAIN (*chuckling*). And that mission woman, she hails me on the dock as I was acomin' ashore, and she says — with her silly face all screwed up serious as judgment — "Captain," she says, "would you be so kind as to tell me where the sea-gulls sleeps at nights?" Blow me if them warn't her exact words! (*He slaps the table with the palm of his hands and laughs loudly.* *The others force smiles.*) Ain't that just like a fool woman's question? And I looks at her serious as I could, "Ma'am," says I, "I couldn't rightly answer that question. I ain't never seed a sea-gull in his bunk yet. The next time I hears one snorin'," I says, "I'll make a note of where he's turned in, and write you a letter 'bout it." And then she calls me a fool real spiteful and tacks away from me quick. (*He laughs again uproariously.*) So I got rid of her that way. (*The others smile but immediately relapse into expressions of gloom again.*)

MRS. MAYO (*absent-mindedly — feeling that she has to say something.*) But when it comes to that, where *do* sea-gulls sleep, Dick?

SCOTT (*slapping the table*). Ho! Ho! Listen to her, James. 'Nother one! Well, if that don't beat all hell — 'scuse me for cussin', Kate.

MAYO (*with a twinkle in his eyes*). They unhitch their wings, Katey, and spread 'em out on a wave for a bed.

SCOTT. And then they tells the fish to whistle to 'em when it's time to turn out. Ho! Ho!

MRS. MAYO (*with a forced smile*). You men folks are too smart to live, aren't you?

> (*She resumes her knitting.* MAYO *pretends to read his paper;* ANDREW *stares at the floor.*)

SCOTT (*looks from one to the other of them with a puzzled air. Finally he is unable to bear the thick silence a minute longer, and blurts out*): You folks look as if you was settin' up with a corpse. (*With exaggerated concern.*) God A'mighty, there ain't anyone dead, be there?

MAYO (*sharply.*) Don't play the dunce, Dick! You know as well as we do there ain't no great cause to be feelin' chipper.

SCOTT (*argumentatively*). And there ain't no cause to be wearin' mourning, either, I can make out.

MRS. MAYO (*indignantly*). How can you talk that way, Dick Scott, when you're taking our Robbie away from us, in the middle of the night, you might say, just to get on that old boat of yours on time! I think you might wait until morning when he's had his breakfast.

SCOTT (*appealing to the others hopelessly*). Ain't that a woman's way o' seein' things for you? God A'mighty, Kate, I can't give orders to the tide that it's got to be high just when it suits me to have it. I ain't gettin' no fun out o' missin' sleep and leavin' here at six bells myself. (*Protestingly.*) And the *Sunda* ain't an old ship — leastways, not very old — and she's good's she ever was.

MRS. MAYO (*her lips trembling*). I wish Robbie weren't going.

MAYO (*looking at her over his glasses — consolingly*). There, Katey!

MRS. MAYO (*rebelliously*). Well, I *do* wish he wasn't!

SCOTT. You shouldn't be taking it so hard, 's far as I kin see. This vige'll make a man of him. I'll see to it he learns how to navigate, 'n' study for a mate's c'tificate right off — and it'll give him a trade for the rest of his life, if he wants to travel.

MRS. MAYO. But I don't want him to travel all his life. You've got to see he comes home when this trip is over. Then he'll be all well, and he'll want to — to marry — (ANDREW *sits forward in his chair with an abrupt movement*) — and settle down right here. (*She stares down at the knitting in her lap — after a pause.*) I never realized how hard it was going to be for me to have Robbie go — or I wouldn't have considered it a minute.

SCOTT. It ain't no good goin' on that way, Kate, now it's all settled.

MRS. MAYO (*on the verge of tears*). It's all right for *you* to talk. You've never had any children. You don't know what it means to be parted from them — and Robbie my youngest, too.

(ANDREW *frowns and fidgets in his chair.*)

ANDREW (*suddenly turning to them*). There's one thing none of you

seem to take into consideration — that Rob wants to go. He's
dead set on it. He's been dreaming over this trip ever since it
was first talked about. It wouldn't be fair to him not to have
him go. (*A sudden uneasiness seems to strike him.*) At least, not if
he still feels the same way about it he did when he was talking to
me this evening.

MAYO (*with an air of decision*). Andy's right, Katey. That ends all
argyment, you can see that. (*Looking at his big silver watch.*)
Wonder what's happened to Robert? He's been gone long
enough to wheel the widder to home, certain. He can't be out
dreamin' at the stars his last night.

MRS. MAYO (*a bit reproachfully*). Why didn't you wheel Mrs. Atkins
back tonight, Andy? You usually do when she and Ruth come
over.

ANDREW (*avoiding her eyes*). I thought maybe Robert wanted to
tonight. He offered to go right away when they were leaving.

MRS. MAYO. He only wanted to be polite.

ANDREW (*gets to his feet*). Well, he'll be right back, I guess. (*He
turns to his father.*) Guess I'll go take a look at the black cow, Pa
— see if she's ailing any.

MAYO. Yes — better had, son.

(ANDREW *goes into the kitchen on the right.*)

SCOTT (*as he goes out — in a low tone*). There's the boy that would
make a good, strong sea-farin' man — if he'd a mind to.

MAYO (*sharply*). Don't you put no such fool notions in Andy's head,
Dick — or you 'n' me's goin' to fall out. (*Then he smiles.*) You
couldn't tempt him, no ways. Andy's a Mayo bred in the bone,
and he's a born farmer, and a damn good one, too. He'll live
and die right here on this farm, like I expect to. (*With proud
confidence.*) And he'll make this one of the slickest, best-payin'
farms in the state, too, afore he gits through!

SCOTT. Seems to me it's a pretty slick place right now.

MAYO (*shaking his head*). It's too small. We need more land to
make it amount to much, and we ain't got the capital to buy it.

(ANDREW *enters from the kitchen. His hat is on, and he carries a lighted
lantern in his hand. He goes to the door in the rear leading out.*)

ANDREW (*opens the door and pauses*). Anything else you can think of
to be done, Pa?

MAYO. No, nothin' I know of. (ANDREW *goes out, shutting the door.*)

MRS. MAYO (*after a pause*). What's come over Andy tonight, I wonder? He acts so strange.

MAYO. He does seem sort o' glum and out of sorts. It's 'count o' Robert leavin', I s'pose. (*To* SCOTT.) Dick, you wouldn't believe how them boys o' mine sticks together. They ain't like most brothers. They've been thick as thieves all their lives, with nary a quarrel I kin remember.

SCOTT. No need to tell me that. I can see how they take to each other.

MRS. MAYO (*pursuing her train of thought*). Did you notice, James, how queer everyone was at supper? Robert seemed stirred up about something; and Ruth was so flustered and giggly; and Andy sat there dumb, looking as if he'd lost his best friend; and all of them only nibbled at their food.

MAYO. Guess they was all thinkin' about tomorrow, same as us.

MRS. MAYO (*shaking her head*). No. I'm afraid somethin's happened — somethin' else.

MAYO. You mean — 'bout Ruth?

MRS. MAYO. Yes.

MAYO (*after a pause frowning*). I hope her and Andy ain't had a serious fallin'-out. I always sorter hoped they'd hitch up together sooner or later. What d'you say, Dick? Don't you think them two'd pair up well?

SCOTT (*nodding his head approvingly*). A sweet, wholesome couple they'd make.

MAYO. It'd be a good thing for Andy in more ways than one. I ain't what you'd call calculatin' generally, and I b'lieve in lettin' young folks run their affairs to suit themselves; but there's advantages for both o' them in this match you can't overlook in reason. The Atkins farm is right next to ourn. Jined together they'd make a jim-dandy of a place, with plenty o' room to work in. And bein' a widder with only a daughter, and laid up all the time to boot, Mrs. Atkins can't do nothin' with the place as it ought to be done. She needs a man, a first-class farmer, to take hold o' things; and Andy's just the one.

MRS. MAYO (*abruptly*). I don't think Ruth loves Andy.

MAYO. You don't? Well, maybe a woman's eyes is sharper in such things, but — they're always together. And if she don't love him now, she'll likely come around to it in time. (*As* MRS. MAYO *shakes her head.*) You seem mighty fixed in your opinion, Katey. How d'you know?

MRS. MAYO. It's just — what I feel.

MAYO (*a light breaking over him*). You don't mean to say — (MRS. MAYO *nods.* MAYO *chuckles scornfully.*) Shucks! I'm losin' my respect for your eyesight, Katey. Why, Robert ain't got no time for Ruth, 'cept as a friend!

MRS. MAYO (*warningly*). Sss-h-h!

(*The door from the yard opens, and* ROBERT *enters. He is smiling happily, and humming a song to himself, but as he comes into the room an undercurrent of nervous uneasiness manifests itself in his bearing.*)

MAYO. So here you be at last! (ROBERT *comes forward and sits on* ANDY'S *chair.* MAYO *smiles slyly at his wife.*) What have you been doin' all this time — countin' the stars to see if they all come out right and proper?

ROBERT. There's only one I'll ever look for any more, Pa.

MAYO (*reproachfully*). You might've even not wasted time lookin' for that one — your last night.

MRS. MAYO (*as if she were speaking to a child*). You ought to have worn your coat a sharp night like this, Robbie.

SCOTT (*disgustedly*). God A'mighty, Kate, you treat Robert as if he was one year old!

MRS. MAYO (*notices* ROBERT'S *nervous uneasiness*). You look all worked up over something, Robbie. What is it?

ROBERT (*swallowing hard, looks quickly from one to the other of them — then begins determinedly.*) Yes, there *is* something — something I must tell you — all of you. (*As he begins to talk* ANDREW *enters quietly from the rear, closing the door behind him, and setting the lighted lantern on the floor. He remains standing by the door, his arms folded, listening to* ROBERT *with a repressed expression of pain on his face.* ROBERT *is so much taken up with what he is going to say that he does not notice* ANDREW'S *presence.*) Something I discovered only this evening — very beautiful and wonderful — something I did not take into consideration previously because I hadn't dared to hope that such happiness could ever come to me. (*Appealingly.*) You must all remember that fact, won't you?

MAYO (*frowning*). Let's get to the point, son.

ROBERT (*with a trace of defiance*). Well, the point is this, Pa: I'm not going — I mean — I can't go tomorrow with Uncle Dick — or at any future time, either.

MRS. MAYO (*with a sharp sigh of joyful relief*). Oh, Robbie, I'm so glad!

MAYO (*astounded*). You ain't serious, be you, Robert? (*Severely.*) Seems to me it's a pretty late hour in the day for you to be up-settin' all your plans so sudden!

ROBERT. I asked you to remember that until this evening I didn't know myself. I had never dared to dream ——

MAYO (*irritably*). What is this foolishness you're talkin' of?

ROBERT (*flushing*). Ruth told me this evening that — she loved me. It was after I'd confessed I loved her. I told her I hadn't been conscious of my love until after the trip had been arranged, and I realized it would mean — leaving her. That was the truth. I *didn't* know until then. (*As if justifying himself to the others.*) I hadn't intended telling her anything but — suddenly — I felt I must. I didn't think it would matter, because I was going away. And I thought she loved — someone else. (*Slowly — his eyes shining.*) And then she cried and said it was I she'd loved all the time, but I hadn't seen it.

MRS. MAYO (*rushes over and throws her arms about him*). I knew it! I was just telling your father when you came in — and, oh, Robbie, I'm so happy you're not going!

ROBERT (*kissing her*). I knew you'd be glad, Ma.

MAYO (*bewilderedly*). Well, I'll be damned! You do beat all for gettin' folks' minds all tangled up, Robert. And Ruth too! Whatever got into her of a sudden? Why, I was thinkin' ——

MRS. MAYO (*hurriedly — in a tone of warning*). Never mind what you were thinking, James. It wouldn't be any use telling us that now. (*Meaningly.*) And what you were hoping for turns out just the same almost, doesn't it?

MAYO (*thoughtfully — beginning to see this side of the argument*). Yes; I suppose you're right, Katey. (*Scratching his head in puzzlement.*) But how it ever come about! It do beat anything ever I heard. (*Finally he gets up with a sheepish grin and walks over to* ROBERT.) We're glad you ain't goin', your Ma and I, for we'd have missed you terrible, that's certain and sure; and we're glad you've found happiness. Ruth's a fine girl and'll make a good wife to you.

ROBERT (*much moved*). Thank you, Pa. (*He grips his father's hand in his.*)

ANDREW (*his face tense and drawn comes forward and holds out his hand, forcing a smile*). I guess it's my turn to offer congratulations, isn't it?

ROBERT (*with a startled cry when his brother appears before him so suddenly*). Andy! (*Confused.*) Why — I — I didn't see you. Were you here when ——

ANDREW. I heard everything you said; and here's wishing you every happiness, you and Ruth. You both deserve the best there is.

ROBERT (*taking his hand*). Thanks, Andy, it's fine of you to ——
            (*His voice dies away as he sees the pain in* ANDREW's *eyes.*)

ANDREW (*giving his brother's hand a final grip*). Good luck to you both!

        (*He turns away and goes back to the rear where he bends over the lantern, fumbling with it to hide his emotion from the others.*)

MRS. MAYO (*to the* CAPTAIN, *who has been too flabbergasted by* ROBERT's *decision to say a word*). What's the matter, Dick? Aren't you going to congratulate Robbie?

SCOTT (*embarrassed*). Of course I be! (*He gets to his feet and shakes* ROBERT's *hand, muttering a vague.*) Luck to you, boy.

        (*He stands beside* ROBERT *as if he wanted to say something more but doesn't know how to go about it.*)

ROBERT. Thanks, Uncle Dick.

SCOTT. So you're not acomin' on the *Sunda* with me?
                            (*His voice indicates disbelief.*)

ROBERT. I can't, Uncle — not now. I wouldn't miss it for anything else in the world under any other circumstances. (*He sighs unconsciously.*) But you see I've found — a bigger dream. (*Then with joyous high spirits.*) I want you all to understand one thing — I'm not going to be a loafer on your hands any longer. This means the beginning of a new life for me in every way. I'm going to settle right down and take a real interest in the farm, and do my share. I'll prove to you, Pa, that I'm as good a Mayo as you are — or Andy, when I want to be.

MAYO (*kindly but skeptically*). That's the right spirit, Robert. Ain't none of us doubts your willin'ness, but you ain't never learned——

ROBERT. Then I'm going to start learning right away, and you'll teach me, won't you?

MAYO (*mollifyingly*). Of course I will, boy, and be glad to, only you'd best go easy at first.

SCOTT (*who has listened to this conversation in mingled consternation and amazement*). You don't mean to tell me you're goin' to let him stay, do you, James?

MAYO. Why, things bein' as they be, Robert's free to do as he's a mind to.

MRS. MAYO. *Let him!* The very idea!

SCOTT (*more and more ruffled*). Then all I got to say is, you're a soft, weak-willed critter to be permittin' a boy — and women, too — to be layin' your course for you wherever they damn pleases.

MAYO (*slyly amused*). It's just the same with me as 'twas with you, Dick. You can't order the tides on the seas to suit you, and I ain't pretendin' I can reg'late love for young folks.

SCOTT (*scornfully*). Love! They ain't old enough to know love when they sight it! Love! I'm ashamed of you, Robert, to go lettin' a little huggin' and kissin' in the dark spile your chances to make a man out o' yourself. It ain't common sense — no siree, it ain't — not by a hell of a sight!

> (*He pounds the table with his fists in exasperation.*)

MRS. MAYO (*laughing provokingly at her brother*). A fine one you are to be talking about love, Dick — an old cranky bachelor like you. Goodness sakes!

SCOTT (*exasperated by their joking*). I've never been a damn fool like most, if that's what you're steerin' at.

MRS. MAYO (*tauntingly*). Sour grapes, aren't they, Dick? (*She laughs.* ROBERT *and his father chuckle.* SCOTT *sputters with annoyance.*) Good gracious, Dick, you do act silly, flying into a temper over nothing.

SCOTT (*indignantly*). Nothin'! You talk as if I wasn't concerned nohow in this here business. Seems to me I've got a right to have my say. Ain't I made all arrangements with the owners and stocked up with some special grub all on Robert's account?

ROBERT. You've been fine, Uncle Dick; and I appreciate it. Truly.

MAYO. 'Course; we all does, Dick.

SCOTT (*unplacated*). I've been countin' sure on havin' Robert for company on this vige — to sorta talk to and show things to, and teach, kinda, and I got my mind so set on havin' him I'm goin' to be double lonesome this vige. (*He pounds on the table, attempting to cover up this confession of weakness.*) Darn all this silly lovin' business, anyway. (*Irritably.*) But all this talk ain't tellin' me what I'm to do with that sta'b'd cabin I fixed up. It's all painted white, an' a bran new mattress on the bunk, 'n' new sheets 'n' blankets 'n' things. And Chips built in a book-case so's Robert could take his books along — with a slidin' bar fixed across't it, mind, so's they couldn't fall out no matter how she rolled. (*With excited consternation.*) What d'you suppose my officers is goin' to think when there's no one comes aboard to occupy that sta'b'd cabin? And the men what did the work on it — what'll *they* think? (*He shakes his finger indignantly.*) They're liable as not to suspicion it was a *woman* I'd planned to ship along, and that she gave me the go-by at the last moment! (*He wipes his perspiring brow in anguish at this thought.*) Gawd A'mighty! They're only lookin' to have the laugh on me for something like that. They're liable to b'lieve anything, those fellers is!

MAYO (*with a wink*). Then there's nothing to it but for you to get right out and hunt up a wife somewheres for that spick 'n' span cabin. She'll have to be a pretty one, too, to match it. (*He looks at his watch with exaggerated concern.*) You ain't got much time to find her, Dick.

SCOTT (*as the others smile — sulkily*). You kin go to thunder, Jim Mayo!

ANDREW (*comes forward from where he has been standing by the door, rear, brooding. His face is set in a look of grim determination*). You needn't worry about that spare cabin, Uncle Dick, if you've a mind to take me in Robert's place.

ROBERT (*turning to him quickly*). Andy! (*He sees at once the fixed resolve in his brother's eyes, and realizes immediately the reason for it — in consternation.*) Andy, you mustn't!

ANDREW. You've made your decision, Rob, and now I've made mine. You're out of this, remember.

ROBERT (*hurt by his brother's tone*). But Andy ——

ANDREW. Don't interfere, Rob — that's all I ask. (*Turning to his uncle.*) You haven't answered my question, Uncle Dick.

SCOTT (*clearing his throat, with an uneasy side glance at* JAMES MAYO *who is staring at his elder son as if he thought he had suddenly gone mad*). O' course, I'd be glad to have you, Andy.

ANDREW. It's settled then. I can pack the little I want to take in a few minutes.

MRS. MAYO. Don't be a fool, Dick. Andy's only joking you.

SCOTT (*disgruntedly*). It's hard to tell who's jokin' and who's not in this house.

ANDREW (*firmly*). I'm not joking, Uncle Dick. (*As* SCOTT *looks at him uncertainly.*) You needn't be afraid I'll go back on my word.

ROBERT (*hurt by the insinuation he feels in* ANDREW'S *tone*). Andy! That isn't fair!

MAYO (*frowning*). Seems to me this ain't no subject to joke over — not for Andy.

ANDREW (*facing his father*). I agree with you, Pa, and I tell you again, once and for all, that I've made up my mind to go.

MAYO (*dumbfounded — unable to doubt the determination in* ANDREW'S *voice — helplessly*). But why, son? Why?

ANDREW (*evasively*). I've always wanted to go.

ROBERT. Andy!

ANDREW (*half angrily*). You shut up, Rob! (*Turning to his father again.*) I didn't ever mention it because as long as Rob was going I knew it was no use; but now Rob's staying on here, there isn't any reason for me not to go.

MAYO (*breathing hard*). No reason? Can you stand there and say that to me, Andrew?

MRS. MAYO (*hastily — seeing the gathering storm*). He doesn't mean a word of it, James.

MAYO (*making a gesture to her to keep silence*). Let me talk, Katey. (*In a more kindly tone.*) What's come over you so sudden, Andy? You know's well as I do that it wouldn't be fair o' you to run off at a moment's notice right now when we're up to our necks in hard work.

ANDREW (*avoiding his eyes*). Rob'll hold his end up as soon as he learns.

MAYO. Robert was never cut out for a farmer, and you was.

ANDREW. You can easily get a man to do my work.

MAYO (*restraining his anger with an effort*). It sounds strange to hear you, Andy, that I always thought had good sense, talkin' crazy like that. (*Scornfully.*) Get a man to take your place! You ain't been workin' here for no hire, Andy, that you kin give me your notice to quit like you've done. The farm is your'n as well as mine. You've always worked on it with that understanding; and what you're sayin' you intend doin' is just skulkin' out o' your rightful responsibility.

ANDREW (*looking at the floor — simply*). I'm sorry, Pa. (*After a slight pause.*) It's no use talking any more about it.

MRS. MAYO (*in relief*). There! I knew Andy'd come to his senses!

ANDREW. Don't get the wrong idea, Ma. I'm not backing out.

MAYO. You mean you're goin' in spite of — everythin'?

ANDREW. Yes. I'm going. I've got to. (*He looks at his father defiantly.*) I feel I oughtn't to miss this chance to go out into the world and see things, and — I want to go.

MAYO (*with bitter scorn*). So — you want to go out into the world and see thin's! (*His voice raised and quivering with anger.*) I never thought I'd live to see the day when a son o' mine'd look me in the face and tell a bare-faced lie! (*Bursting out.*) You're a liar, Andy Mayo, and a mean one to boot!

MRS. MAYO. James!

ROBERT. Pa!

SCOTT. Steady there, Jim!

MAYO (*waving their protests aside*). He is and he knows it.

ANDREW (*his face flushed*). I won't argue with you, Pa. You can think as badly of me as you like.

MAYO (*shaking his finger at* ANDY, *in a cold rage*). You know I'm speakin' truth — that's why you're afraid to argy! You lie when you say you want to go 'way — and see thin's! You ain't got no likin' in the world to go. I've watched you grow up, and I know your ways, and they're my ways. You're runnin' against your own nature, and you're goin' to be a 'mighty sorry for it if you do. 'S if I didn't know your real reason for runnin' away! And runnin' away's the only words to fit it. You're runnin' away 'cause you're put out and riled 'cause your own brother's got Ruth 'stead o' you, and ——

ANDREW (*his face crimson — tensely*). Stop, Pa! I won't stand hearing that — not even from you!

MRS. MAYO (*rushing to* ANDY *and putting her arms about him protectingly*). Don't mind him, Andy dear. He don't mean a word he's saying!

(ROBERT *stands rigidly, his hands clenched, his face contracted by pain.* SCOTT *sits dumbfounded and open-mouthed.* ANDREW *soothes his mother who is on the verge of tears.*)

MAYO (*in angry triumph*). It's the truth, Andy Mayo! And you ought to be bowed in shame to think of it!

ROBERT (*protestingly*). Pa!

MRS. MAYO (*coming from* ANDREW *to his father; puts her hands on his shoulders as though to try and push him back in the chair from which he has risen*). Won't you be still, James? Please won't you?

MAYO (*looking at* ANDREW *over his wife's shoulder — stubbornly*). The truth — God's truth!

MRS. MAYO. Sh-h-h!

(*She tries to put a finger across his lips, but he twists his head away.*)

ANDREW (*who has regained control over himself*). You're wrong, Pa, it isn't truth. (*With defiant assertiveness.*) I don't love Ruth. I never loved her, and the thought of such a thing never entered my head.

MAYO (*with an angry snort of disbelief*). Hump! You're pilin' lie on lie!

ANDREW (*losing his temper — bitterly*). I suppose it'd be hard for you to explain anyone's wanting to leave this blessed farm except for some outside reason like that. But I'm sick and tired of it — whether you want to believe me or not — and that's why I'm glad to get a chance to move on.

ROBERT. Andy! Don't! You're only making it worse.

ANDREW (*sulkily*). I don't care. I've done my share of work here. I've earned my right to quit when I want to. (*Suddenly overcome with anger and grief; with rising intensity.*) I'm sick and tired of the whole damn business. I hate the farm and every inch of ground in it. I'm sick of digging in the dirt and sweating in the sun like a slave without getting a word of thanks for it. (*Tears of rage starting to his eyes — hoarsely.*) I'm through, through for good and all; and if Uncle Dick won't take me on his ship, I'll find another. I'll get away somewhere, somehow.

MRS. MAYO (*in a frightened voice*). Don't you answer him, James. He doesn't know what he's saying. Don't say a word to him 'til he's in his right senses again. Please James, don't ——

MAYO (*pushes her away from him; his face is drawn and pale with the violence of his passion. He glares at* ANDREW *as if he hated him*). You dare to — you dare to speak like that to me? You talk like that 'bout this farm — the Mayo farm — where you was born — you — you —— (*He clenches his fist above his head and advances threateningly on* ANDREW.) You damned whelp!

MRS. MAYO (*with a shriek*). James!

> (*She covers her face with her hands and sinks weakly into* MAYO's *chair.* ANDREW *remains standing motionless, his face pale and set.*)

SCOTT (*starting to his feet and stretching his arms across the table toward* MAYO). Easy there, Jim!

ROBERT (*throwing himself between father and brother*). Stop! Are you mad?

MAYO (*grabs* ROBERT's *arm and pushes him aside — then stands for a moment gasping for breath before* ANDREW. *He points to the door with a shaking finger*). Yes — go! — go! — You're no son o' mine — no son o' mine! You can go to hell if you want to! Don't let me find you here — in the mornin' — or — or — I'll *throw* you out!

ROBERT. Pa! For God's sake!

> (MRS. MAYO *bursts into noisy sobbing.*)

MAYO (*he gulps convulsively and glares at* ANDREW). You go — to-morrow mornin' — and by God — don't come back — don't dare come back — by God, not while I'm livin' — or I'll — I'll ——

> (*He shakes over his muttered threat and strides toward the door rear, right.*)

MRS. MAYO (*rising and throwing her arms around him — hysterically*). James! James! Where are you going?

MAYO (*incoherently*). I'm goin' — to bed, Katey. It's late, Katey — it's late. (*He goes out.*)

MRS. MAYO (*following him, pleading hysterically*). James! Take back what you've said to Andy. James!

> (*She follows him out.* ROBERT *and the* CAPTAIN *stare after them with horrified eyes.* ANDREW *stands rigidly looking straight in front of him, his fists clenched at his sides.*)

SCOTT (*the first to find his voice — with an explosive sigh*). Well, if he ain't the devil himself when he's roused! You oughtn't to have talked to him that way, Andy 'bout the damn farm, knowin' how touchy he is about it. (*With another sigh.*) Well, you won't mind what he's said in anger. He'll be sorry for it when he's calmed down a bit.

ANDREW (*in a dead voice*). You don't know him. (*Defiantly.*) What's said is said and can't be unsaid; and I've chosen.

ROBERT (*with violent protest*). Andy! You can't go! This is all so stupid — and terrible!

ANDREW (*coldly*). I'll talk to you in a minute, Rob.

    (*Crushed by his brother's attitude* ROBERT *sinks down into a chair, holding his head in his hands.*)

SCOTT (*comes and slaps* ANDREW *on the back*). I'm damned glad you're shippin' on, Andy. I like your spirit, and the way you spoke up to him. (*Lowering his voice to a cautious whisper.*) The sea's the place for a young feller like you that isn't half dead 'n' alive. (*He gives* ANDY *a final approving slap.*) You 'n' me'll get along like twins, see if we don't. I'm goin' aloft to turn in. Don't forget to pack your dunnage. And git some sleep, if you kin. We'll want to sneak out extra early b'fore they're up. It'll do away with more argyments. Robert can drive us down to the town, and bring back the team. (*He goes to the door in the rear, left.*) Well, good night.

ANDREW. Good night. (SCOTT *goes out. The two brothers remain silent for a moment. Then* ANDREW *comes over to his brother and puts a hand on his back. He speaks in a low voice, full of feeling.*) Buck up, Rob. It ain't any use crying over spilt milk; and it'll all turn out for the best — let's hope. It couldn't be helped — what's happened.

ROBERT (*wildly*). But it's a lie, Andy, a lie!

ANDREW. Of course it's a lie. You know it and I know it — but that's all ought to know it.

ROBERT. Pa'll never forgive you. Oh, the whole affair is so senseless and tragic. Why did you think you must go away?

ANDREW. You know better than to ask that. You know why. (*Fiercely.*) I can wish you and Ruth all the good luck in the world, and I do, and I mean it; but you can't expect me to stay around here and watch you two together, day after day — and me alone. I couldn't stand it — not after all the plans I'd made to happen on this place thinking —— (*his voice breaks*) thinking she cared for me.

ROBERT (*putting a hand on his brother's arm*). God! It's horrible! I feel so guilty — to think that I should be the cause of your suffering, after we've been such pals all our lives. If I could have foreseen what'd happen, I swear to you I'd have never said a word to Ruth. I swear I wouldn't have, Andy! .

ANDREW. I know you wouldn't; and that would've been worse, for Ruth would've suffered then. (*He pats his brother's shoulder.*) It's best as it is. It had to be, and I've got to stand the gaff, that's all. Pa'll see how I felt — after a time. (*As* ROBERT *shakes his head.*) — and if he don't — well, it can't be helped.

ROBERT. But think of Ma! God, Andy, you can't go! You can't!

ANDREW (*fiercely*). I've got to go — to get away! I've got to, I tell you. I'd go crazy here, bein' reminded every second of the day what a fool I'd made of myself. I've got to get away and try and forget, if I can. And I'd hate the farm if I stayed, hate it for bringin' things back. I couldn't take interest in the work any more, work with no purpose in sight. Can't you see what a hell it'd be? You love her too, Rob. Put yourself in my place, and remember I haven't stopped loving her, and couldn't if I was to stay. Would that be fair to you or to her? Put yourself in my place. (*He shakes his brother fiercely by the shoulder.*) What'd you do then? Tell me the truth! You love her. What'd you do?

ROBERT (*chokingly*). I'd — I'd go, Andy! (*He buries his face in his hands with a shuddering sob.*) God!

ANDREW (*seeming to relax suddenly all over his body — in a low, steady voice*). Then you know why I got to go; and there's nothing more to be said.

ROBERT (*in a frenzy of rebellion*). Why did this have to happen to us? It's damnable!

(*He looks about him wildly, as if his vengeance were seeking the responsible fate.*)

ANDREW (*soothingly — again putting his hands on his brother's shoulder*). It's no use fussing any more, Rob. It's done. (*Forcing a smile.*) I guess Ruth's got a right to have who she likes. She made a good choice — and God bless her for it!

ROBERT. Andy! Oh, I wish I could tell you half I feel of how fine you are!

ANDREW (*interrupting him quickly*). Shut up! Let's go to bed. I've got to be up long before sun-up. You, too, if you're going to drive us down.

ROBERT. Yes. Yes.

ANDREW (*turning down the lamp*). And I've got to pack yet. (*He yawns with utter weariness.*) I'm as tired as if I'd been plowing twenty-four hours at a stretch. (*Dully.*) I feel — dead. (ROBERT *covers his face again with his hands.* ANDREW *shakes his head as if to get rid of his thoughts, and continues with a poor attempt at cheery briskness.*) I'm going to douse the light. Come on. (*He slaps his brother on the back.* ROBERT *does not move.* ANDREW *bends over and blows out the lamp. His voice comes from the darkness.*) Don't sit there mourning, Rob. It'll all come out in the wash. Come on and get some sleep. Everything'll turn out all right in the end.

> (ROBERT *can be heard stumbling to his feet, and the dark figures of the two brothers can be seen groping their way toward the doorway in the rear as*

> (*The Curtain Falls*)

ACT TWO

SCENE ONE

Same as Act One, Scene Two. Sitting room of the farm house about half past twelve in the afternoon of a hot, sun-baked day in mid-summer, three years later. All the windows are open, but no breeze stirs the soiled white curtains. A patched screen door is in the rear. Through it the yard can be seen, its small stretch of lawn divided by the dirt path leading to the door from the gate in the white picket fence which borders the road.

The room has changed, not so much in its outward appearance as in its general atmosphere. Little significant details give evidence of carelessness, of inefficiency, of an industry gone to seed. The chairs appear shabby from lack of paint; the table cover is spotted and askew; holes show in the curtains; a child's doll, with one arm gone, lies under the table; a hoe stands in a corner;

a man's coat is flung on the couch in the rear; the desk is cluttered up with odds and ends; a number of books are piled carelessly on the sideboard. The noon enervation of the sultry, scorching day seems to have penetrated indoors, causing even inanimate objects to wear an aspect of despondent exhaustion.

A place is set at the end of the table, left, for someone's dinner. Through the open door to the kitchen comes the clatter of dishes being washed, interrupted at intervals by a woman's irritated voice and the peevish whining of a child.

At the rise of the curtain MRS. MAYO *and* MRS. ATKINS *are discovered sitting facing each other,* MRS. MAYO *to the rear,* MRS. ATKINS *to the right of the table.* MRS. MAYO'S *face has lost all character, disintegrated, become a weak mask wearing a helpless, doleful expression of being constantly on the verge of comfortless tears. She speaks in an uncertain voice, without assertiveness, as if all power of willing had deserted her.* MRS. ATKINS *is in her wheel chair. She is a thin, pale-faced, unintelligent looking woman of about forty-eight, with hard, bright eyes. A victim of partial paralysis for many years, condemned to be pushed from day to day of her life in a wheel chair, she has developed the selfish, irritable nature of the chronic invalid. Both women are dresse*l *in black.* MRS. ATKINS *knits nervously as she talks. A ball of unused yarn, with needles stuck through it, lies on the table before* MRS. MAYO.

MRS. ATKINS (*with a disapproving glance at the place set on the table*). Robert's late for his dinner again, as usual. I don't see why Ruth puts up with it, and I've told her so. Many's the time I've said to her "It's about time you put a stop to his nonsense. Does he suppose you're runnin' a hotel — with no one to help with things?" But she don't pay no attention. She's as bad as he is, a'most — thinks she knows better than an old, sick body like me.

MRS. MAYO (*dully*). Robbie's always late for things. He can't help it, Sarah.

MRS. ATKINS (*with a snort*). Can't help it! How you do go on, Kate, findin' excuses for him! Anybody can help anything they've a mind to — as long as they've got health, and ain't rendered helpless like me — (*she adds as a pious afterthought*) — through the will of God.

MRS. MAYO. Robbie can't.

MRS. ATKINS. Can't! It do make me mad, Kate Mayo, to see folks that God gave all the use of their limbs to potterin' round and wastin' time doin' everything the wrong way — and me powerless to help and at their mercy, you might say. And it ain't that I haven't pointed the right way to 'em. I've talked to Robert thousands of times and told him how things ought to be done. You know that, Kate Mayo. But d'you s'pose he takes any notice of what I say? Or Ruth, either — my own daughter? No, they think I'm a crazy, cranky old woman, half dead a'ready, and the sooner I'm in the grave and out o' their way the better it'd suit them.

MRS. MAYO. You mustn't talk that way, Sarah. They're not as wicked as that. And you've got years and years before you.

MRS. ATKINS. You're like the rest, Kate. You don't know how near the end I am. Well, at least I can go to my eternal rest with a clear conscience. I've done all a body could do to avert ruin from this house. On their heads be it!

MRS. MAYO (*with hopeless indifference*). Things might be worse. Robert never had any experience in farming. You can't expect him to learn in a day.

MRS. ATKINS (*snappily*). He's had three years to learn, and he's gettin' worse 'stead of better. Not on'y your place but mine too is driftin' to rack and ruin, and I can't do nothin' to prevent.

MRS. MAYO (*with a spark of assertiveness*). You can't say but Robbie works hard, Sarah.

MRS. ATKINS. What good's workin' hard if it don't accomplish anythin', I'd like to know?

MRS. MAYO. Robbie's had bad luck against him.

MRS. ATKINS. Say what you've a mind to, Kate, the proof of the puddin's in the eatin'; and you can't deny that things have been goin' from bad to worse ever since your husband died two years back.

MRS. MAYO (*wiping tears from her eyes with her handkerchief*). It was God's will that he should be taken.

MRS. ATKINS (*triumphantly*). It was God's punishment on James Mayo for the blasphemin' and denyin' of God he done all his sinful life! (MRS. MAYO *begins to weep softly*.) There, Kate, I shouldn't be remindin' you, I know. He's at peace, poor man, and forgiven, let's pray.

MRS. MAYO (*wiping her eyes — simply*). James was a good man.

MRS. ATKINS (*ignoring this remark*). What I was sayin' was that since Robert's been in charge things've been goin' down hill steady. You don't know *how* bad they are. Robert don't let on to you what's happenin'; and you'd never see it yourself if 'twas under your nose. But, thank the Lord, Ruth still comes to me once in a while for advice when she's worried near out of her senses by his goin's-on. Do you know what she told me last night? But I forgot, she said not to tell you — still I think you've got a right to know, and it's my duty not to let such things go on behind your back.

MRS. MAYO (*wearily*). You can tell me if you want to.

MRS. ATKINS (*bending over toward her — in a low voice*). Ruth was almost crazy about it. Robert told her he'd have to mortage the farm — said he didn't know how he'd pull through 'til harvest without it, and he can't get money any other way. (*She straightens up — indignantly.*) Now what do you think of your Robert?

MRS. MAYO (*resignedly*). If it has to be ——

MRS. ATKINS. You don't mean to say you're goin' to sign away your farm, Kate Mayo — after me warnin' you?

MRS. MAYO. — I'll do what Robbie says is needful.

MRS. ATKINS (*holding up her hands*). Well, of all the foolishness! — well, it's your farm, not mine, and I've nothin' more to say.

MRS. MAYO. Maybe Robbie'll manage till Andy gets back and sees to things. It can't be long now.

MRS. ATKINS (*with keen interest*). Ruth says Andy ought to turn up any day. When does Robert figger he'll get here?

MRS. MAYO. He says he can't calculate exactly on account o' the *Sunda* being a sail boat. Last letter he got was from England, the day they were sailing for home. That was over a month ago, and Robbie thinks they're overdue now.

MRS. ATKINS. We can give praise to God then that he'll be back in the nick o' time. He ought to be tired of travelin' and anxious to get home and settle down to work again.

MRS. MAYO. Andy *has* been working. He's head officer on Dick's boat, he wrote Robbie. You know that.

MRS. ATKINS. That foolin' on ships is all right for a spell, but he must be right sick of it by this.

MRS. MAYO (*musingly*). I wonder if he's changed much. He used to be so fine-looking and strong. (*With a sigh.*) Three years! It seems more like three hundred. (*Her eyes filling — piteously.*) Oh, if James could only have lived 'til he came back — and forgiven him!

MRS. ATKINS. He never would have — not James Mayo! Didn't he keep his heart hardened against him till the last in spite of all you and Robert did to soften him?

MRS. MAYO (*with a feeble flash of anger*). Don't you dare say that! (*Brokenly.*) Oh, I know deep down in his heart he forgave Andy, though he was too stubborn ever to own up to it. It was that brought on his death — breaking his heart just on account of his stubborn pride. (*She wipes her eyes with her handkerchief and sobs.*)

MRS. ATKINS (*piously*). It was the will of God. (*The whining crying of the child sounds from the kitchen.* MRS. ATKINS *frowns irritably.*) Drat that young one! Seems as if she cries all the time on purpose to set a body's nerves on edge.

MRS. MAYO (*wiping her eyes*). It's the heat upsets her. Mary doesn't feel any too well these days, poor little child!

MRS. ATKINS. She gets it right from her Pa — bein' sickly all the time. You can't deny Robert was always ailin' as a child. (*She sighs heavily.*) It was a crazy mistake for them two to get married. I argyed against it at the time, but Ruth was so spelled with Robert's wild poetry notions she wouldn't listen to sense. Andy was the one would have been the match for her.

MRS. MAYO. I've often thought since it might have been better the other way. But Ruth and Robbie seem happy enough together.

MRS. ATKINS. At any rate it was God's work — and His will be done.

(*The two women sit in silence for a moment.* RUTH *enters from the kitchen, carrying in her arms her two year old daughter,* MARY, *a pretty but sickly and anæmic looking child with a tear-stained face.* RUTH *has aged appreciably. Her face has lost its youth and freshness. There is a trace in her expression of something hard and spiteful. She sits in the rocker in front of the table and sighs wearily. She wears a gingham dress with a soiled apron tied around her waist.*)

RUTH. Land sakes, if this isn't a scorcher! That kitchen's like a furnace. Phew! (*She pushes the damp hair back from her forehead.*)

MRS. MAYO. Why didn't you call me to help with the dishes?

RUTH (*shortly*). No. The heat in there'd kill you.

MARY (*sees the doll under the table and struggles on her mother's lap*). Dolly, Mama! Dolly!

RUTH (*pulling her back*). It's time for your nap. You can't play with Dolly now.

MARY (*commencing to cry whiningly*). Dolly!

MRS. ATKINS (*irritably*). Can't you keep that child still? Her racket's enough to split a body's ears. Put her down and let her play with the doll if it'll quiet her.

RUTH (*lifting* MARY *to the floor*). There! I hope you'll be satisfied and keep still. (MARY *sits down on the floor before the table and plays with the doll in silence.* RUTH *glances at the place set on the table*). It's a wonder Rob wouldn't try to get to meals on time once in a while.

MRS. MAYO (*dully*). Something must have gone wrong again.

RUTH (*wearily*). I s'pose so. Something's always going wrong these days, it looks like.

MRS. ATKINS (*snappily*). It wouldn't if you possessed a bit of spunk. The idea of you permittin' him to come in to meals at all hours — and you doin' the work! I never heard of such a thin'. You're too easy goin', that's the trouble.

RUTH. Do stop your nagging at me, Ma! I'm sick of hearing you. I'll do as I please about it; and thank you for not interfering. (*She wipes her moist forehead — wearily.*) Phew! It's too hot to argue. Let's talk of something pleasant. (*Curiously.*) Didn't I hear you speaking about Andy a while ago?

MRS. MAYO. We were wondering when he'd get home.

RUTH (*brightening*). Rob says any day now he's liable to drop in and surprise us — him and the Captain. It'll certainly look natural to see him around the farm again.

MRS. ATKINS. Let's hope the farm'll look more natural, too, when he's had a hand at it. The way thin's are now!

RUTH (*irritably*). Will you stop harping on that, Ma? We all know things aren't as they might be. What's the good of your complaining all the time?

MRS. ATKINS. There, Kate Mayo! Ain't that just what I told you? I can't say a word of advice to my own daughter even, she's that stubborn and self-willed.

RUTH (*putting her hands over her ears — in exasperation*). For goodness sakes, Ma!

MRS. MAYO (*dully*). Never mind. Andy'll fix everything when he comes.

RUTH (*hopefully*). Oh, yes, I know he will. He always did know just the right thing ought to be done. (*With weary vexation.*) It's a shame for him to come home and have to start in with things in such a topsy-turvy.

MRS. MAYO. Andy'll manage.

RUTH (*sighing*). I s'pose it isn't Rob's fault things go wrong with him.

MRS. ATKINS (*scornfully*). Hump! (*She fans herself nervously.*) Land o' Goshen, but it's bakin' in here! Let's go out in under the trees in back where there's a breath of fresh air. Come, Kate. (MRS. MAYO *gets up obediently and starts to wheel the invalid's chair toward the screen door.*) You better come too, Ruth. It'll do you good. Learn him a lesson and let him get his own dinner. Don't be such a fool.

RUTH (*going and holding the screen door open for them — listlessly*). He wouldn't mind. He doesn't eat much. But I can't go anyway. I've got to put baby to bed.

MRS. ATKINS. Let's go, Kate. I'm boilin' in here.

(MRS. MAYO *wheels her out and off left.* RUTH *comes back and sits down in her chair.*)

RUTH (*mechanically*). Come and let me take off your shoes and stockings, Mary, that's a good girl. You've got to take your nap now.

(*The child continues to play as if she hadn't heard, absorbed in her doll. An eager expression comes over* RUTH'S *tired face. She glances toward the door furtively — then gets up and goes to the desk. Her movements indicate a guilty fear of discovery. She takes a letter from a pigeon-hole and retreats swiftly to her chair with it. She opens the envelope and reads the letter with great interest, a flush of excitement coming to her cheeks.* ROBERT *walks up the path and opens the screen door quietly and comes into the room. He, too, has aged. His shoulders are stooped as if under too great a burden. His eyes are dull and lifeless, his face burned by the sun and unshaven for days. Streaks of sweat have smudged the layer of dust on his cheeks. His lips drawn down at the corners, give him a hopeless, resigned expression. The three years have accentuated the weakness of his mouth and chin. He is dressed in overalls, laced boots, and a flannel shirt open at the neck.*)

ROBERT (*throwing his hat over on the sofa — with a great sigh of exhaustion*). Phew! The sun's hot today!

    (RUTH *is startled. At first she makes an instinctive motion as if to hide the letter in her bosom. She immediately thinks better of this and sits with the letter in her hands looking at him with defiant eyes. He bends down and kisses her.*)

RUTH (*feeling of her cheek — irritably*). Why don't you shave? You look awful.

ROBERT (*indifferently*). I forgot — and it's too much trouble this weather.

MARY (*throwing aside her doll, runs to him with a happy cry*). Dada! Dada!

ROBERT (*swinging her up above his head — lovingly*). And how's this little girl of mine this hot day, eh?

MARY (*screeching happily*). Dada! Dada!

RUTH (*in annoyance*). Don't do that to her! You know it's time for her nap and you'll get her all waked up; then I'll be the one that'll have to sit beside her till she falls asleep.

ROBERT (*sitting down in the chair on the left of table and cuddling MARY on his lap*). You needn't bother. I'll put her to bed.

RUTH (*shortly*). You've got to get back to your work, I s'pose.

ROBERT (*with a sigh*). Yes, I was forgetting. (*He glances at the open letter on* RUTH'S *lap.*) Reading Andy's letter again? I should think you'd know it by heart by this time.

RUTH (*coloring as if she'd been accused of something — defiantly*). I've got a right to read it, haven't I? He says it's meant for all of us.

ROBERT (*with a trace of irritation*). Right? Don't be so silly. There's no question of right. I was only saying that you must know all that's in it after so many readings.

RUTH. Well, I don't. (*She puts the letter on the table and gets wearily to her feet.*) I s'pose you'll be wanting your dinner now.

ROBERT (*listlessly*). I don't care. I'm not hungry.

RUTH. And here I been keeping it hot for you!

·

ROBERT (*irritably*). Oh, all right then. Bring it in and I'll try to eat.

RUTH. I've got to get her to bed first. (*She goes to lift* MARY *off his lap.*) Come, dear. It's after time and you can hardly keep your eyes open now.

MARY (*crying*). No, no! (*Appealing to her father.*) Dada! No!

RUTH (*accusingly to* ROBERT). There! Now see what you've done! I told you not to ——

ROBERT (*shortly*). Let her alone, then. She's all right where she is. She'll fall asleep on my lap in a minute if you'll stop bothering her.

RUTH (*hotly*). She'll not do any such thing! She's got to learn to mind me! (*Shaking her finger at* MARY.) You naughty child! Will you come with Mama when she tells you for your own good?

MARY (*clinging to her father*). No, Dada!

RUTH (*losing her temper*). A good spanking's what you need, my young lady — and you'll get one from me if you don't mind better, d'you hear? (MARY *starts to whimper frightenedly.*)

ROBERT (*with sudden anger*). Leave her alone! How often have I told you not to threaten her with whipping? I won't have it. (*Soothing the wailing* MARY.) There! There, little girl! Baby mustn't cry. Dada won't like you if you do. Dada'll hold you and you must promise to go to sleep like a good little girl. Will you when Dada asks you?

MARY (*cuddling up to him*). Yes, Dada.

RUTH (*looking at them, her pale face set and drawn*). A fine one you are to be telling folks how to do things! (*She bites her lips. Husband and wife look into each other's eyes with something akin to hatred in their expressions; then* RUTH *turns away with a shrug of affected indifference.*) All right, take care of her then, if you think it's so easy.

(*She walks away into the kitchen.*)

ROBERT (*smoothing* MARY's *hair — tenderly*). We'll show Mama you're a good little girl, won't we?

MARY (*crooning drowsily*). Dada, Dada.

ROBERT. Let's see: Does your mother take off your shoes and stockings before your nap?

MARY (*nodding with half-shut eyes*). Yes, Dada.

ROBERT (*taking off her shoes and stockings*). We'll show Mama we know how to do those things, won't we? There's one old shoe off — and there's the other old shoe — and here's one old stocking — and there's the other old stocking. There we are, all nice and cool and comfy. (*He bends down and kisses her.*) And now will you promise to go right to sleep if Dada takes you to bed? (MARY *nods sleepily.*) That's the good little girl.

(*He gathers her up in his arms carefully and carries her into the bedroom. His voice can be heard faintly as he lulls the child to sleep. RUTH comes out of the kitchen and gets the plate from the table. She hears the voice from the room and tiptoes to the door to look in. Then she starts for the kitchen but stands for a moment thinking, a look of ill-concealed jealousy on her face. At a noise from inside she hurriedly disappears into the kitchen. A moment later ROBERT reënters. He comes forward and picks up the shoes and stockings which he shoves carelessly under the table. Then, seeing no one about, he goes to the sideboard and selects a book. Coming back to his chair, he sits down and immediately becomes absorbed in reading. RUTH returns from the kitchen bringing his plate heaped with food, and a cup of tea. She sets those before him and sits down in her former place. ROBERT continues to read, oblivious to the food on the table.*)

RUTH (*after watching him irritably for a moment*). For heaven's sakes, put down that old book! Don't you see your dinner's getting cold?

ROBERT (*closing his book*). Excuse me, Ruth. I didn't notice.

(*He picks up his knife and fork and begins to eat gingerly, without appetite.*)

RUTH. I should think you might have some feeling for me, Rob, and not always be late for meals. If you think it's fun sweltering in that oven of a kitchen to keep things warm for you, you're mistaken.

ROBERT. I'm sorry, Ruth, really I am. Something crops up every day to delay me. I mean to be here on time.

RUTH (*with a sigh*). Mean-tos don't count.

ROBERT (*with a conciliating smile*). Then punish me, Ruth. Let the food get cold and don't bother about me.

RUTH. I'd have to wait just the same to wash up after you.

ROBERT. But I can wash up.

RUTH. A nice mess there'd be then!

ROBERT (*with an attempt at lightness*). The food is lucky to be able to get cold this weather.

 (*As* RUTH *doesn't answer or smile he opens his book and resumes his reading, forcing himself to take a mouthful of food every now and then.* RUTH *stares at him in annoyance.*)

RUTH. And besides, you've got your own work that's got to be done.

ROBERT (*absent-mindedly, without taking his eyes from the book*). Yes, of course.

RUTH (*spitefully*). Work you'll never get done by reading books all the time.

ROBERT (*shutting the book with a snap*). Why do you persist in nagging at me for getting pleasure out of reading? Is it because ——

 (*He checks himself abruptly.*)

RUTH (*coloring*). Because I'm too stupid to understand them, I s'pose you were going to say.

ROBERT (*shame-facedly*). No — no. (*In exasperation.*) Why do you goad me into saying things I don't mean? Haven't I got my share of troubles trying to work this cursed farm without your adding to them? You know how hard I've tried to keep things going in spite of bad luck ——

RUTH (*scornfully*). Bad luck!

ROBERT. And my own very apparent unfitness for the job, I was going to add; but you can't deny there's been bad luck to it, too. Why don't you take things into consideration? Why can't we pull together? We used to. I know it's hard on you also. Then why can't we help each other instead of hindering?

RUTH (*sullenly*). I do the best I know how.

ROBERT (*gets up and puts his hand on her shoulder*). I know you do. But let's both of us try to do better. We can both improve. Say a word of encouragement once in a while when things go wrong, even if it is my fault. You know the odds I've been up against since Pa died. I'm not a farmer. I've never claimed to be one. But there's nothing else I can do under the circumstances, and I've got to pull things through somehow. With your help, I can do it. With you against me —— (*He shrugs his shoulders. There is a pause. Then he bends down and kisses her hair — with an attempt at cheerfulness.*) So you promise that; and I'll promise to be here when the clock strikes — and anything else you tell me to. Is it a bargain?

RUTH (*dully*). I s'pose so. (*They are interrupted by the sound of a loud knock at the kitchen door.*) There's someone at the kitchen door. (*She hurries out. A moment later she reappears.*) It's Ben.

ROBERT (*frowning*). What's the trouble now, I wonder? (*In a loud voice.*) Come on in here, Ben. (*BEN slouches in from the kitchen. He is a hulking, awkward young fellow with a heavy, stupid face and shifty, cunning eyes. He is dressed in overalls, boots, etc., and wears a broad-brimmed hat of coarse straw pushed back on his head.*) Well, Ben, what's the matter?

BEN (*drawlingly*). The mowin' machine's bust.

ROBERT. Why, that can't be. The man fixed it only last week.

BEN. It's bust just the same.

ROBERT. And can't you fix it?

BEN. No. Don't know what's the matter with the goll-darned thing. 'Twon't work, anyhow.

ROBERT (*getting up and going for his hat*). Wait a minute and I'll go look it over. There can't be much the matter with it.

BEN (*impudently*). Don't make no diff'rence t' me whether there be or not. I'm quittin'.

ROBERT (*anxiously*). You don't mean you're throwing up your job here?

BEN. That's what! My month's up today and I want what's owin' t' me.

ROBERT. But why are you quitting now, Ben, when you know I've so much work on hand? I'll have a hard time getting another man at such short notice.

BEN. That's for you to figger. I'm quittin'.

ROBERT. But what's your reason? You haven't any complaint to make about the way you've been treated, have you?

BEN. No. 'Tain't that. (*Shaking his finger.*) Look-a-here. I'm sick o' being made fun at, that's what; an' I got a job up to Timms' place; an' I'm quittin' here.

ROBERT. Being made fun of? I don't understand you. Who's making fun of you?

BEN. They all do. When I drive down with the milk in the mornin' they all laughs and jokes at me — that boy up to Harris' and the new feller up to Slocum's, and Bill Evans down to Meade's, and all the rest on 'em.

ROBERT. That's a queer reason for leaving me flat. Won't they laugh at you just the same when you're working for Timms?

BEN. They wouldn't dare to. Timms is the best farm hereabouts. They was laughin' at me for workin' for *you*, that's what! "How're things up to the Mayo place?" they hollers every mornin'. "What's Robert doin' now — pasturin' the cattle in the cornlot? Is he seasonin' his hay with rain this year, same as last?" they shouts. "Or is he inventin' some 'lectrical milkin' engine to fool them dry cows o' his into givin' hard cider?" (*Very much ruffled.*) That's like they talks; and I ain't goin' to put up with it no longer. Everyone's always knowed me as a first-class hand hereabouts, and I ain't wantin' 'em to get no different notion. So I'm quittin' you. And I wants what's comin' to me.

ROBERT (*coldly*). Oh, if that's the case, you can go to the devil. You'll get your money tomorrow when I get back from town — not before!

BEN (*turning to doorway to kitchen*). That suits me. (*As he goes out he speaks back over his shoulder.*) And see that I do get it, or there'll be trouble.

(*He disappears and the slamming of the kitchen door is heard.*)

ROBERT (*as* RUTH *comes from where she has been standing by the doorway and sits down dejectedly in her old place*). The stupid damn fool! And now what about the haying? That's an example of what I'm up against. No one can say I'm responsible for that.

RUTH. He wouldn't dare act that way with anyone else! (*Spitefully with a glance at* ANDREW'S *letter on the table.*) It's lucky Andy's coming back.

ROBERT (*without resentment*). Yes, Andy'll see the right thing to do in a jiffy. (*With an affectionate smile.*) I wonder if the old chump's changed much? He doesn't seem to from his letters, does he? (*Shaking his head.*) But just the same I doubt if he'll want to settle down to a hum-drum farm life, after all he's been through.

RUTH (*resentfully*). Andy's not like you. He likes the farm.

ROBERT (*immersed in his own thoughts — enthusiastically*). Gad, the things he's seen and experienced! Think of the places he's been!

All the wonderful far places I used to dream about! God, how I envy him! What a trip!

> (*He springs to his feet and instinctively goes to the window and stares out at the horizon.*)

RUTH (*bitterly*). I s'pose you're sorry now you didn't go?

ROBERT (*too occupied with his own thoughts to hear her — vindictively*). Oh, those cursed hills out there that I used to think promised me so much! How I've grown to hate the sight of them! They're like the walls of a narrow prison yard shutting me in from all the freedom and wonder of life! (*He turns back to the room with a gesture of loathing.*) Sometimes I think if it wasn't for you, Ruth, and — (*his voice softening*) — little Mary, I'd chuck everything up and walk down the road with just one desire in my heart — to put the whole rim of the world between me and those hills, and be able to breathe freely once more! (*He sinks down into his chair and smiles with bitter self-scorn.*) There I go dreaming again — my old fool dreams.

RUTH (*in a low, repressed voice — her eyes smoldering*). You're not the only one!

ROBERT (*buried in his own thoughts — bitterly*). And Andy, who's had the chance — what has he got out of it? His letters read like the diary of a — of a farmer! "We're in Singapore now. It's a dirty hole of a place and hotter than hell. Two of the crew are down with fever and we're short-handed on the work. I'll be damn glad when we sail again, although tacking back and forth in these blistering seas is a rotten job too!" (*Scornfully.*) That's about the way he summed up his impressions of the East.

RUTH (*her repressed voice trembling*). You needn't make fun of Andy.

ROBERT. When I think — but what's the use? You know I wasn't making fun of Andy personally, but his attitude toward things is ——

RUTH (*her eyes flashing — bursting into uncontrollable rage*). You was too making fun of him! And I ain't going to stand for it! You ought to be ashamed of yourself! (ROBERT *stares at her in amazement. She continues furiously.*) A fine one to talk about anyone else — after the way you've ruined everything with your lazy loafing! — and the stupid way you do things!

ROBERT (*angrily*). Stop that kind of talk, do you hear?

RUTH. You findin' fault — with your own brother who's ten times the man you ever was or ever will be! You're jealous, that's what! Jealous because he's made a man of himself, while you're nothing but a — but a ——

(*She stutters incoherently, overcome by rage.*)

ROBERT. Ruth! Ruth! You'll be sorry for talking like that.

RUTH. I won't! I won't never be sorry! I'm only saying what I've been thinking for years.

ROBERT (*aghast*). Ruth! You can't mean that!

RUTH. What do you think — living with a man like you — having to suffer all the time because you've never been man enough to work and do things like other people. But no! You never own up to that. You think you're so much better than other folks, with your college education, where you never learned a thing, and always reading your stupid books instead of working. I s'pose you think I ought to be *proud* to be your wife — a poor, ignorant thing like me! (*Fiercely.*) But I'm not. I hate it! I hate the sight of you. Oh, if I'd only known! If I hadn't been such a fool to listen to your cheap, silly, poetry talk that you learned out of books! If I could have seen how you were in your true self — like you are now — I'd have killed myself before I'd have married you! I was sorry for it before we'd been together a month. I knew what you were really like — when it was too late.

ROBERT (*his voice raised loudly*). And now — I'm finding out what you're really like — what a — a creature I've been living with. (*With a harsh laugh.*) God! It wasn't that I haven't guessed how mean and small you are — but I've kept on telling myself that I must be wrong — like a fool! — like a damned fool!

RUTH. You were saying you'd go out on the road if it wasn't for me. Well, you can go, and the sooner the better! I don't care! I'll be glad to get rid of you! The farm'll be better off too. There's been a curse on it ever since you took hold. So go! Go and be a tramp like you've always wanted. It's all you're good for. I can get along without you, don't you worry. (*Exulting fiercely.*) Andy's coming back, don't forget that! He'll attend to things like they should be. He'll show what a man can do! I don't need you. Andy's coming!

ROBERT (*they are both standing.* ROBERT *grabs her by the shoulders and glares into her eyes*). What do you mean? (*He shakes her violently.*) What are you thinking of? What's in your evil mind, you — you —— (*His voice is a harsh shout.*)

RUTH (*in a defiant scream*). Yes I do mean it! I'd say it if you was to kill me! I do love Andy. I do! I do! I always loved him. (*Exultantly.*) And he loves me! He loves me! I know he does. He always did! And you know he did, too! So go! Go if you want to!

ROBERT (*throwing her away from him.* *She staggers back against the table — thickly*). You — you slut!

(*He stands glaring at her as she leans back, supporting herself by the table, gasping for breath. A loud frightened whimper sounds from the awakened child in the bedroom. It continues. The man and woman stand looking at one another in horror, the extent of their terrible quarrel suddenly brought home to them. A pause. The noise of a horse and carriage comes from the road before the house. The two, suddenly struck by the same premonition, listen to it breathlessly, as to a sound heard in a dream. It stops. They hear* ANDY's *voice from the road shouting a long hail —* "Ahoy there!")

RUTH (*with a strangled cry of joy*). Andy! Andy!

(*She rushes and grabs the knob of the screen door, about to fling it open.*)

ROBERT (*in a voice of command that forces obedience*). Stop! (*He goes to the door and gently pushes the trembling* RUTH *away from it. The child's crying rises to a louder pitch.*) I'll meet Andy. You better go in to Mary, Ruth.

(*She looks at him defiantly for a moment, but there is something in his eyes that makes her turn and walk slowly into the bedroom.*)

ANDY's VOICE (*in a louder shout*). Ahoy there, Rob!

ROBERT (*in an answering shout of forced cheeriness*). Hello, Andy!

(*He opens the door and walks out as*

(*The Curtain Falls*).

ACT TWO

Scene Two

The top of a hill on the farm. It is about eleven o'clock the next morning. The day is hot and cloudless. In the distance the sea can be seen.

The top of the hill slopes downward slightly toward the left. A big boulder stands in the center toward the rear. Further right, a large oak tree. The faint trace of a path leading upward to it from the left foreground can be detected through the bleached, sun-scorched grass.

ROBERT is discovered sitting on the boulder, his chin resting on his hands, staring out toward the horizon seaward. His face is pale and haggard, his expression one of utter despondency. MARY is sitting on the grass near him in the shade, playing with her doll, singing happily to herself. Presently she casts a curious glance at her father, and, propping her doll up against the tree, comes over and clambers to his side.

MARY (*pulling at his hand — solicitously*). Dada sick?

ROBERT (*looking at her with a forced smile*). No, dear. Why?

MARY. Play wif Mary.

ROBERT (*gently*). No, dear, not today. Dada doesn't feel like playing today.

MARY (*protestingly*). Yes, Dada!

ROBERT. No, dear. Dada does feel sick — a little. He's got a bad headache.

MARY. Mary see. (*He bends his head. She pats his hair.*) Bad head.

ROBERT (*kissing her — with a smile*). There! It's better now, dear, thank you. (*She cuddles up close against him. There is a pause during which each of them looks out seaward. Finally ROBERT turns to her tenderly.*) Would you like Dada to go away? — far, far away?

MARY (*tearfully*). No! No! No, Dada, no!

ROBERT. Don't you like Uncle Andy — the man that came yesterday — not the old man with the white mustache — the other?

MARY. Mary loves Dada.

ROBERT (*with fierce determination*). He won't go away, baby. He was only joking. He couldn't leave his little Mary.

(*He presses the child in his arms.*)

MARY (*with an exclamation of pain*). Oh! Hurt!

ROBERT. I'm sorry, little girl. (*He lifts her down to the grass.*) Go play with Dolly, that's a good girl; and be careful to keep in the shade.

> (*She reluctantly leaves him and takes up her doll again. A moment later she points down the hill to the left.*)

MARY. Mans, Dada.

ROBERT (*looking that way*). It's your Uncle Andy.

(*A moment later* ANDREW *comes up from the left, whistling cheerfully. He has changed but little in appearance, except for the fact that his face has been deeply bronzed by his years in the tropics; but there is a decided change in his manner. The old easy-going good-nature seems to have been partly lost in a breezy, business-like briskness of voice and gesture. There is an authoritative note in his speech as though he were accustomed to give orders and have them obeyed as a matter of course. He is dressed in the simple blue uniform and cap of a merchant ship's officer.*)

ANDREW. Here you are, eh?

ROBERT. Hello, Andy.

ANDREW (*going over to* MARY). And who's this young lady I find you all alone with, eh? Who's this pretty young lady? (*He tickles the laughing, squirming* MARY, *then lifts her up at arm's length over his head.*) Upsy — daisy! (*He sets her down on the ground again.*) And there you are! (*He walks over and sits down on the boulder beside* ROBERT *who moves to one side to make room for him.*) Ruth told me I'd probably find you up top-side here; but I'd have guessed it, anyway. (*He digs his brother in the ribs affectionately.*) Still up to your old tricks, you old beggar! I can remember how you used to come up here to mope and dream in the old days.

ROBERT (*with a smile*). I come up here now because it's the coolest place on the farm. I've given up dreaming.

ANDREW (*grinning*). I don't believe it. You can't have changed that much. (*After a pause — with boyish enthusiasm.*) Say, it sure brings back old times to be up here with you having a chin all by our lonesomes again. I feel great being back home.

ROBERT. It's great for us to have you back.

ANDREW (*after a pause — meaningly*). I've been looking over the old place with Ruth. Things don't seem to be ——

ROBERT (*his face flushing — interrupts his brother shortly*). Never mind the damn farm! Let's talk about something interesting. This is the first chance I've had to have a word with you alone. Tell me about your trip.

ANDREW. Why, I thought I told you everything in my letters.

ROBERT (*smiling*). Your letters were — sketchy, to say the least.

ANDREW. Oh, I know I'm no author. You needn't be afraid of hurting my feelings. I'd rather go through a typhoon again than write a letter.

ROBERT (*with eager interest*). Then you were through a typhoon?

ANDREW. Yes — in the China sea. Had to run before it under bare poles for two days. I thought we were bound down for Davy Jones, sure. Never dreamed waves could get so big or the wind blow so hard. If it hadn't been for Uncle Dick being such a good skipper we'd have gone to the sharks, all of us. As it was we came out minus a main top-mast and had to beat back to Hong-Kong for repairs. But I must have written you all this.

ROBERT. You never mentioned it.

ANDREW. Well, there was so much dirty work getting things ship-shape again I must have forgotten about it.

ROBERT (*looking at* ANDREW — *marveling*). Forget a typhoon? (*With a trace of scorn.*) You're a strange combination, Andy. And is what you've told me all you remember about it?

ANDREW. Oh, I could give you your bellyful of details if I wanted to turn loose on you. It was all-wool-and-a-yard-wide-Hell, I'll tell you. You ought to have been there. I remember thinking about you at the worst of it, and saying to myself: "This'd cure Rob of them ideas of his about the beautiful sea, if he could see it." And it would have too, you bet! (*He nods emphatically.*)

ROBERT (*dryly*). The sea doesn't seem to have impressed you very favorably.

ANDREW. I should say it didn't! I'll never set foot on a ship again if I can help it — except to carry me some place I can't get to by train.

ROBERT. But you studied to become an officer!

ANDREW. Had to do something or I'd gone mad. The days were like years. (*He laughs.*) And as for the East you used to rave about — well, you ought to see it, and *smell* it! One walk down one of their filthy narrow streets with the tropic sun beating on it would sicken you for life with the "wonder and mystery" you used to dream of.

ROBERT (*shrinking from his brother with a glance of aversion*).   So all you found in the East was a stench?

ANDREW. *A* stench!   Ten thousand of them!

ROBERT. But you did like some of the places, judging from your letters — Sydney, Buenos Aires ——

ANDREW. Yes, Sydney's a good town.   (*Enthusiastically.*)   But Buenos Aires — there's the place for you.   Argentine's a country where a fellow has a chance to make good.   You're right I like it.   And I'll tell you, Rob, that's right where I'm going just as soon as I've seen you folks a while and can get a ship.   I can get a berth as second officer, and I'll jump the ship when I get there.   I'll need every cent of the wages Uncle's paid me to get a start at something in B. A.

ROBERT (*staring at his brother — slowly*).   So you're not going to stay on the farm?

ANDREW. Why sure not!   Did you think I was?   There wouldn't be any sense.   One of us is enough to run this little place.

ROBERT. I suppose it does seem small to you now.

ANDREW (*not noticing the sarcasm in* ROBERT's *tone*).   You've no idea, Rob, what a splendid place Argentine is.   I had a letter from a marine insurance chap that I'd made friends with in Hong-Kong to his brother, who's in the grain business in Buenos Aires.   He took quite a fancy to me, and what's more important, he offered me a job if I'd come back there.   I'd have taken it on the spot, only I couldn't leave Uncle Dick in the lurch, and I'd promised you folks to come home.   But I'm going back there, you bet, and then you watch me get on!   (*He slaps* ROBERT *on the back.*)   But don't you think it's a big chance, Rob?

ROBERT. It's fine — for you, Andy.

ANDREW. We call this a farm—but you ought to hear about the farms down there — ten square miles where we've got an acre.   It's a new country where big things are opening up—and I want to get in on something big before I die.   I'm no fool when it comes to farming, and I know something about grain.   I've been reading up a lot on it, too, lately.   (*He notices* ROBERT's *absent-minded expression and laughs.*) Wake up, you old poetry bookworm, you! I know my talking about business makes you want to choke me, doesn't it?

ROBERT (*with an embarrassed smile*). No, Andy, I — I just happened to think of something else. (*Frowning.*) There've been lots of times lately that I've wished I had some of your faculty for business.

ANDREW (*soberly*). There's something I want to talk about, Rob — the farm. You don't mind, do you?

ROBERT. No.

ANDREW. I walked over it this morning with Ruth — and she told me about things —— (*Evasively.*) I could see the place had run down; but you mustn't blame yourself. When luck's against anyone ——

ROBERT. Don't, Andy! It *is* my fault. You know it as well as I do. The best I've ever done was to make ends meet.

ANDREW (*after a pause*). I've got over a thousand saved, and you can have that.

ROBERT (*firmly*). No. You need that for your start in Buenos Aires.

ANDREW. I don't. I can ——

ROBERT (*determinedly*). No, Andy! Once and for all, no! I won't hear of it!

ANDREW (*protestingly*). You obstinate old son of a gun!

ROBERT. Oh, everything'll be on a sound footing after harvest. Don't worry about it.

ANDREW (*doubtfully*). Maybe. (*After a pause.*) It's too bad Pa couldn't have lived to see things through. (*With feeling.*) It cut me up a lot — hearing he was dead. He never — softened up, did he — about me, I mean?

ROBERT. He never understood, that's a kinder way of putting it. He does now.

ANDREW (*after a pause*). You've forgotten all about what — caused me to go, haven't you, Rob? (ROBERT *nods but keeps his face averted.*) I was a slushier damn fool in those days than you were. But it was an act of Providence I did go. It opened my eyes to how I'd been fooling myself. Why, I'd forgotten all about — that — before I'd been at sea six months.

ROBERT (*turns and looks into* ANDREW'S *eyes searchingly*). You're speaking of — Ruth?

ANDREW (*confused*). Yes. I didn't want you to get false notions in your head, or I wouldn't say anything. (*Looking* ROBERT *squarely in the eyes.*) I'm telling you the truth when I say I'd forgotten long ago. It don't sound well for me, getting over things so easy, but I guess it never really amounted to more than a kid idea I was letting rule me. I'm certain now I never was in love — I was getting fun out of thinking I was — and being a hero to myself. (*He heaves a great sigh of relief.*) There! Gosh, I'm glad that's off my chest. I've been feeling sort of awkward ever since I've been home, thinking of what you two might think. (*A trace of appeal in his voice.*) You've got it all straight now, haven't you, Rob?

ROBERT (*in a low voice*). Yes, Andy.

ANDREW. And I'll tell Ruth, too, if I can get up the nerve. She must feel kind of funny having me round — after what used to be — and not knowing how I feel about it.

ROBERT (*slowly*). Perhaps — for her sake — you'd better not tell her.

ANDREW. For her sake? Oh, you mean she wouldn't want to be reminded of my foolishness? Still, I think it'd be worse if ——

ROBERT (*breaking out — in an agonized voice*). Do as you please, Andy; but for God's sake, let's not talk about it! (*There is a pause.* ANDREW *stares at* ROBERT *in hurt stupefaction.* ROBERT *continues after a moment in a voice which he vainly attempts to keep calm.*) Excuse me, Andy. This rotten headache has my nerves shot to pieces.

ANDREW (*mumbling*). It's all right, Rob — long as you're not sore at me.

ROBERT. Where did Uncle Dick disappear to this morning?

ANDREW. He went down to the port to see to things on the *Sunda*. He said he didn't know exactly when he'd be back. I'll have to go down and tend to the ship when he comes. That's why I dressed up in these togs.

MARY (*pointing down the hill to the left*). See! Mama! Mama!
  (*She struggles to her feet.* RUTH *appears at left. She is dressed in white, shows she has been fixing up. She looks pretty, flushed and full of life.*)

MARY (*running to her mother*).   Mama!

RUTH (*kissing her*).   Hello, dear!   (*She walks toward the rock and addresses* ROBERT *coldly*.)   Jake wants to see you about something. He finished working where he was.   He's waiting for you at the road.

ROBERT (*getting up — wearily*).   I'll go down right away.

(*As he looks at* RUTH, *noting her changed appearance, his face darkens with pain*.)

RUTH.   And take Mary with you, please.   (*To* MARY.)   Go with Dada, that's a good girl.   Grandma has your dinner most ready for you.

ROBERT (*shortly*).   Come, Mary!

MARY (*taking his hand and dancing happily beside him*).   Dada! Dada! (*They go down the hill to the left*.)

RUTH (*looks after them for a moment, frowning — then turns to* ANDY *with a smile*).   I'm going to sit down.   Come on, Andy.   It'll be like old times.   (*She jumps lightly to the top of the rock and sits down*.) It's so fine and cool up here after the house.

ANDREW (*half-sitting on the side of the boulder*).   Yes.   It's great.

RUTH.   I've taken a holiday in honor of your arrival.   (*Laughing excitedly*.)   I feel so free I'd like to have wings and fly over the sea.   You're a man.   You can't know how awful and stupid it is — cooking and washing dishes all the time.

ANDREW (*making a wry face*).   I can guess.

RUTH.   Besides, your mother just insisted on getting your first dinner to home, she's that happy at having you back.   You'd think I was planning to poison you the flurried way she shooed me out of the kitchen.

ANDREW.   That's just like Ma, bless her!

RUTH.   She's missed you terrible.   We all have.   And you can't deny the farm has, after what I showed you and told you when we was looking over the place this morning.

ANDREW (*with a frown*).   Things are run down, that's a fact!   It's too darn hard on poor old Rob.

RUTH (*scornfully*).   It's his own fault.   He never takes any interest in things.

ANDREW (*reprovingly*).   You can't blame him.   He wasn't born for it; but I know he's done his best for your sake and the old folks and the little girl.

RUTH (*indifferently*). Yes, I suppose he has. (*Gayly.*) But thank the Lord, all those days are over now. The "hard luck" Rob's always blaming won't last long when you take hold, Andy. All the farm's ever needed was someone with the knack of looking ahead and preparing for what's going to happen.

ANDREW. Yes, Rob hasn't got that. He's frank to own up to that himself. I'm going to try and hire a good man for him — an experienced farmer — to work the place on a salary and percentage. That'll take it off of Rob's hands, and he needn't be worrying himself to death any more. He looks all worn out, Ruth. He ought to be careful.

RUTH (*absent-mindedly*). Yes, I s'pose. (*Her mind is filled with premonitions by the first part of his statement.*) Why do you want to hire a man to oversee things? Seems as if now that you're back it wouldn't be needful.

ANDREW. Oh, of course I'll attend to everything while I'm here. I mean after I'm gone.

RUTH (*as if she couldn't believe her ears*). Gone!

ANDREW. Yes. When I leave for the Argentine again.

RUTH (*aghast*). You're going away to sea!

ANDREW. Not to sea, no; I'm through with the sea for good as a job. I'm going down to Buenos Aires to get in the grain business.

RUTH. But — that's far off — isn't it?

ANDREW (*easily*). Six thousand miles more or less. It's quite a trip (*With enthusiasm.*) I've got a peach of a chance down there, Ruth. Ask Rob if I haven't. I've just been telling him all about it.

RUTH (*a flush of anger coming over her face*). And didn't he try to stop you from going?

ANDREW (*in surprise*). No, of course not. Why?

RUTH (*slowly and vindictively*). That's just like him — not to.

ANDREW (*resentfully*). Rob's too good a chum to try and stop me when he knows I'm set on a thing. And he could see just as soon's I told him what a good chance it was.

RUTH (*dazedly*). And you're bound on going?

ANDREW. Sure thing. Oh, I don't mean right off. I'll have to wait for a ship sailing there for quite a while, likely. Anyway, I want to stay to home and visit with you folks a spell before I go.

RUTH (*dumbly*). I s'pose. (*With sudden anguish.*) Oh, Andy, you can't go! You can't. Why we've all thought — we've all been hoping and praying you was coming home to stay, to settle down on the farm and see to things. You mustn't go! Think of how your Ma'll take on if you go — and how the farm'll be ruined if you leave it to Rob to look after. You can see that.

ANDREW (*frowning*). Rob hasn't done so bad. When I get a man to direct things the farm'll be safe enough.

RUTH (*insistently*). But your Ma — think of her.

ANDREW. She's used to me being away. She won't object when she knows it's best for her and all of us for me to go. You ask Rob. In a couple of years down there I'll make my pile, see if I don't; and then I'll come back and settle down and turn this farm into the crackiest place in the whole state. In the meantime, I can help you both from down there. (*Earnestly.*) I tell you, Ruth, I'm going to make good right from the minute I land, if working hard and a determination to get on can do it; and I *know* they can! (*Excitedly — in a rather boastful tone.*) I tell you, I feel ripe for bigger things than settling down here. The trip did that for me, anyway. It showed me the world is a larger proposition than ever I thought it was in the old days. I couldn't be content any more stuck here like a fly in molasses. It all seems trifling, somehow. You ought to be able to understand what I feel.

RUTH (*dully*). Yes — I s'pose I ought. (*After a pause — a sudden suspicion forming in her mind.*) What did Rob tell you — about me?

ANDREW. Tell? About you? Why, nothing.

RUTH (*staring at him intensely*). Are you telling me the truth, Andy Mayo? Didn't he say — I —— (*She stops confusedly.*)

ANDREW (*surprised*). No, he didn't mention you, I can remember. Why? What made you think he did?

RUTH (*wringing her hands*). Oh, I wish I could tell if you're lying or not!

ANDREW (*indignantly*). What're you talking about? I didn't used to lie to you, did I? And what in the name of God is there to lie for?

RUTH (*still unconvinced*). Are you sure — will you swear — it isn't

the reason —— (*She lowers her eyes and half turns away from him.*)
The same reason that made you go last time that's driving you
away again? 'Cause if it is — I was going to say — you mustn't
go — on that account.

    (*Her voice sinks to a tremulous, tender whisper as she finishes.*)

ANDREW (*confused — forces a laugh*). Oh, is *that* what you're driving
at? Well, you needn't worry about that no more —— (*Soberly.*)
I don't blame you, Ruth, feeling embarrassed having me around
again, after the way I played the dumb fool about going away
last time.

RUTH (*her hope crushed — with a gasp of pain*). Oh, Andy!

ANDREW (*misunderstanding*). I know I oughtn't to talk about such
foolishness to you. Still I figure it's better to get it out of my
system so's we three can be together same's years ago, and not
be worried thinking one of us might have the wrong notion.

RUTH. Andy! Please! Don't!

ANDREW. Let me finish now that I've started. It'll help clear
things up. I don't want you to think once a fool always a fool,
and be upset all the time I'm here on my fool account. I want
you to believe I put all that silly nonsense back of me a long time
ago — and now — it seems — well — as if you'd always been
my sister, that's what, Ruth.

RUTH (*at the end of her endurance — laughing hysterically*). For God's
sake, Andy — won't you please stop talking!

    (*She again hides her face in her hands, her bowed shoulders trembling.*)

ANDREW (*ruefully*). Seem's if I put my foot in it whenever I open
my mouth today. Rob shut me up with almost the same words
when I tried speaking to him about it.

RUTH (*fiercely*). You told him — what you've told me?

ANDREW (*astounded*). Why sure! Why not?

RUTH (*shuddering*). Oh, my God!

ANDREW (*alarmed*). Why? Shouldn't I have?

RUTH (*hysterically*). Oh, I don't care what you do! I don't care!
Leave me alone!

    (ANDREW *gets up and walks down the hill to the left, embarrassed,
    hurt, and greatly puzzled by her behavior.*)

ANDREW (*after a pause — pointing down the hill*). Hello! Here they
come back — and the Captain's with them. How'd he come to

get back so soon, I wonder? That means I've got to hustle down to the port and get on board. Rob's got the baby with him. (*He comes back to the boulder.* RUTH *keeps her face averted from him.*) Gosh, I never saw a father so tied up in a kid as Rob is! He just watches every move she makes. And I don't blame him. You both got a right to feel proud of her. She's sure a little winner. .(*He glances at* RUTH *to see if this very obvious attempt to get back in her good graces is having any effect.*) I can see the likeness to Rob standing out all over her, can't you? But there's no denying she's your young one, either. There's something about her eyes ——

RUTH (*piteously*). Oh, Andy, I've a headache! I don't want to talk! Leave me alone, won't you please?

ANDREW (*stands staring at her for a moment — then walks away saying in a hurt tone*). Everybody hereabouts seems to be on edge today. I begin to fell as if I'm not wanted around.

> (*He stands near the path, left, kicking at the grass with the toe of his shoe. A moment later* CAPTAIN DICK SCOTT *enters, followed by* ROBERT *carrying* MARY. *The* CAPTAIN *seems scarcely to have changed at all from the jovial, booming person he was three years before. He wears a uniform similar to* ANDREW'S. *He is puffing and breathless from his climb and mops wildly at his perspiring countenance.* ROBERT *casts a quick glance at* ANDREW, *noticing the latter's discomfited look, and then turns his eyes on* RUTH *who, at their approach, has moved so her back is toward them, her chin resting on her hands as she stares out seaward.*)

MARY. Mama! Mama!

> (ROBERT *puts her down and she runs to her mother.* RUTH *turns and grabs her up in her arms with a sudden fierce tenderness, quickly turning away again from the others. During the following scene she keeps* MARY *in her arms.*)

SCOTT (*wheezily*). Phew! I got great news for you, Andy. Let me get my wind first. Phew! God A'mighty, mountin' this damned hill is worser'n goin' aloft to the skys'l yard in a blow. I got to lay to a while. (*He sits down on the grass, mopping his face.*)

ANDREW. I didn't look for you this soon, Uncle.

SCOTT. I didn't figger it, neither; but I run across a bit o' news down to the Seamen's Home made me 'bout ship and set all sail back here to find you.

ANDREW (*eagerly*). What is it, Uncle?

SCOTT. Passin' by the Home I thought I'd drop in an' let 'em know I'd be lackin' a mate next trip count o' your leavin'. Their man in charge o' the shippin' asked after you 'special curious. "Do you think he'd consider a berth as Second on a steamer, Captain?" he asks. I was goin' to say no when I thinks o' you wantin' to get back down south to the Plate agen; so I asks him: "What is she and where's she bound?" "She's the *El Paso*, a brand new tramp," he says, "and she's bound for Buenos Aires."

ANDREW (*his eyes lighting up — excitedly*). Gosh, that is luck! When does she sail?

SCOTT. Tomorrow mornin'. I didn't know if you'd want to ship away agen so quick an' I told him so. "Tell him I'll hold the berth open for him until late this afternoon," he says. So there you be, an' you can make your own choice.

ANDREW. I'd like to take it. There may not be another ship for Buenos Aires with a vacancy in months. (*His eyes roving from* ROBERT *to* RUTH *and back again — uncertainly.*) Still — damn it all — tomorrow morning *is* soon. I wish she wasn't leaving for a week or so. That'd give me a chance — it seems hard to go right away again when I've just got home. And yet it's a chance in a thousand —— (*Appealing to* ROBERT.) What do you think, Rob? What would you do?

ROBERT (*forcing a smile*). He who hesitates, you know. (*Frowning.*) It's a piece of good luck thrown in your way — and — I think you owe it to yourself to jump at it. But don't ask me to decide for you.

RUTH (*turning to look at* ANDREW — *in a tone of fierce resentment*). Yes, go, Andy!

(*She turns quickly away again. There is a moment of embarrassed silence.*)

ANDREW (*thoughtfully*). Yes, I guess I will. It'll be the best thing for all of us in the end, don't you think so, Rob?

(ROBERT *nods but remains silent.*)

SCOTT (*getting to his feet*). Then, that's settled.

ANDREW (*now that he has definitely made a decision his voice rings with hopeful strength and energy*). Yes, I'll take the berth. The sooner I go the sooner I'll be back, that's a certainty; and I won't come back with empty hands next time. You bet I won't!

SCOTT. You ain't got so much time, Andy.   To make sure you'd best leave here soon's you kin.   I got to get right back aboard.   You'd best come with me.

ANDREW. I'll go to the house and repack my bag right away.

ROBERT (*quietly*). You'll both be here for dinner, won't you?

ANDREW (*worriedly*). I don't know.   Will there be time?   What time is it now, I wonder?

ROBERT (*reproachfully*). Ma's been getting dinner especially for you, Andy.

ANDREW (*flushing — shamefacedly*). Hell!   And I was forgetting!   Of course I'll stay for dinner if I missed every damned ship in the world.   (*He turns to the* CAPTAIN — *briskly*.)   Come on, Uncle. Walk down with me to the house, and you can tell me more about this berth on the way.   I've got to pack before dinner.   (*He and the* CAPTAIN *start down to the left.* ANDREW *calls back over his shoulder.*)   You're coming soon, aren't you, Rob?

ROBERT. Yes.   I'll be right down.

> (ANDREW *and the* CAPTAIN *leave.* RUTH *puts* MARY *on the ground and hides her face in her hands.   Her shoulders shake as if she were sobbing.* ROBERT *stares at her with a grim, somber expression.* MARY *walks backward toward* ROBERT, *her wondering eyes fixed on her mother.*)

MARY (*her voice vaguely frightened, taking her father's hand*).   Dada, Mama's cryin', Dada.

ROBERT (*bending down and stroking her hair — in a voice he endeavors to keep from being harsh*).   No, she isn't, little girl.   The sun hurts her eyes, that's all.   Aren't you beginning to feel hungry, Mary?

MARY (*decidedly*). Yes, Dada.

ROBERT (*meaningly*). It must be your dinner time now.

RUTH (*in a muffled voice*). I'm coming, Mary.   (*She wipes her eyes quickly and, without looking at* ROBERT, *comes and takes* MARY's *hand — in a dead voice.*)   Come on and I'll get your dinner for you.

> (*She walks out left, her eyes fixed on the ground, the skipping* MARY *tugging at her hand.* ROBERT *waits a moment for them to get ahead and then slowly follows as*

(*The Curtain Falls*)

ACT THREE

Scene One

Same as Act Two, Scene One — The sitting room of the farm house about six o'clock in the morning of a day toward the end of October five years later. It is not yet dawn, but as the action progresses the darkness outside the windows gradually fades to gray.

The room, seen by the light of the shadeless oil lamp with a smoky chimney which stands on the table, presents an appearance of decay, of dissolution. The curtains at the windows are torn and dirty and one of them is missing. The closed desk is gray with accumulated dust as if it had not been used in years. Blotches of dampness disfigure the wall paper. Threadbare trails, leading to the kitchen and outer doors, show in the faded carpet. The top of the coverless table is stained with the imprints of hot dishes and spilt food. The rung of one rocker has been clumsily mended with a piece of plain board. A brown coating of rust covers the unblacked stove. A pile of wood is stacked up carelessly against the wall by the stove.

The whole atmosphere of the room, contrasted with that of former years, is one of an habitual poverty too hopelessly resigned to be any longer ashamed or even conscious of itself.

At the rise of the curtain RUTH *is discovered sitting by the stove, with hands outstretched to the warmth as if the air in the room were damp and cold. A heavy shawl is wrapped about her shoulders, half-concealing her dress of deep mourning. She has aged horribly. Her pale, deeply lined face has the stony lack of expression of one to whom nothing more can ever happen, whose capacity for emotion has been exhausted. When she speaks her voice is without timbre, low and monotonous. The negligent disorder of her dress, the slovenly arrangement of her hair, now streaked with gray, her muddied shoes run down at the heel, give full evidence of the apathy in which she lives.*

Her mother is asleep in her wheel chair beside the stove toward the rear, wrapped up in a blanket.

There is a sound from the open bedroom door in the rear as if someone were getting out of bed. RUTH *turns in that direction with a look of dull annoyance. A moment later* ROBERT *appears in the doorway, leaning weakly against it for support. His hair is long and unkempt, his face and body emaciated. There are bright patches of crimson over his cheek bones and his eyes are burning with fever. He is dressed in corduroy pants, a flannel shirt, and wears worn carpet slippers on his bare feet.*

RUTH (*dully*). S-s-s-h-! Ma's asleep.

ROBERT (*speaking with an effort*). I won't wake her.

> (*He walks weakly to a rocker by the side of the table and sinks down in it exhausted.*)

RUTH (*staring at the stove*). You better come near the fire where it's warm.

ROBERT. No. I'm burning up now.

RUTH. That's the fever. You know the doctor told you not to get up and move round.

ROBERT (*irritably*). That old fossil! He doesn't know anything. Go to bed and stay there — that's his only prescription.

RUTH (*indifferently*). How are you feeling now?

ROBERT (*buoyantly*). Better! Much better than I've felt in ages. Really I'm fine now — only very weak. It's the turning point, I guess. From now on I'll pick up so quick I'll surprise you — and no thanks to that old fool of a country quack, either.

RUTH. He's always tended to us.

ROBERT. Always helped us to die, you mean! He "tended" to Pa and Ma and — (*his voice breaks*) — and to — Mary.

RUTH (*dully*). He did the best he knew, I s'pose. (*After a pause.*) Well, Andy's bringing a specialist with him when he comes. That ought to suit you.

ROBERT (*bitterly*). Is that why you're waiting up all night?

RUTH. Yes.

ROBERT. For Andy?

RUTH (*without a trace of feeling*). Somebody had got to. It's only right for someone to meet him after he's been gone five years.

ROBERT (*with bitter mockery*). Five years! It's a long time.

RUTH. Yes.

ROBERT (*meaningly*). To *wait*!

RUTH (*indifferently*). It's past now.

ROBERT. Yes, it's past. (*After a pause.*) Have you got his two telegrams with you? (RUTH *nods.*) Let me see them, will you? My head was so full of fever when they came I couldn't make head or tail to them. (*Hastily.*) But I'm feeling fine now. Let me read them again.

> (RUTH *takes them from the bosom of her dress and hands them to him.*)

RUTH. Here. The first one's on top.

ROBERT (*opening it*). New York. "Just landed from steamer. Have important business to wind up here. Will be home as soon as deal is completed." (*He smiles bitterly.*) Business first was always Andy's motto. (*He reads.*) "Hope you are all well. Andy." (*He repeats ironically.*) "Hope you are all well!"

RUTH (*dully*). He couldn't know you'd been took sick till I answered that and told him.

ROBERT (*contritely*). Of course he couldn't. I'm a fool. I'm touchy about nothing lately. Just what did you say in your reply?

RUTH (*inconsequentially*). I had to send it collect.

ROBERT (*irritably*). What did you say was the matter with me?

RUTH. I wrote you had lung trouble.

ROBERT (*flying into a petty temper*). You *are* a fool! How often have I explained to you that it's *pleurisy* is the matter with me. You can't seem to get it in your head that the pleura is outside the lungs, not in them!

RUTH (*callously*). I only wrote what Doctor Smith told me.

ROBERT (*angrily*). He's a damned ignoramus!

RUTH (*dully*). Makes no difference. I had to tell Andy something, didn't I?

ROBERT (*after a pause, opening the other telegram*). He sent this last evening. Let's see. (*He reads.*) "Leave for home on midnight train. Just received your wire. Am bringing specialist to see Rob. Will motor to farm from Port." (*He calculates.*) What time is it now?

RUTH. Round six, must be.

ROBERT. He ought to be here soon. I'm glad he's bringing a doctor who knows something. A specialist will tell you in a second that there's nothing the matter with my lungs.

RUTH (*stolidly*). You've been coughing an awful lot lately.

ROBERT (*irritably*). What nonsense! For God's sake, haven't you ever had a bad cold yourself? (RUTH *stares at the stove in silence.* ROBERT *fidgets in his chair. There is a pause. Finally* ROBERT's *eyes are fixed on the sleeping* MRS. ATKINS.) Your mother is lucky to be able to sleep so soundly.

RUTH. Ma's tired. She's been sitting up with me most of the night.

ROBERT (*mockingly*).   Is she waiting for Andy, too?   (*There is a pause.   ROBERT sighs.*)   I couldn't get to sleep to save my soul.   I counted ten million sheep if I counted one.   No use!   I gave up trying finally and just laid there in the dark thinking.   (*He pauses, then continues in a tone of tender sympathy.*)   I was thinking about you, Ruth — of how hard these last years must have been for you.   (*Appealingly.*)   I'm sorry, Ruth.

RUTH (*in a dead voice*).   I don't know.   They're past now.   They were hard on all of us.

ROBERT.   Yes; on all of us but Andy.   (*With a flash of sick jealousy.*)   Andy's made a big success of himself — the kind he wanted.   (*Mockingly.*)   And now he's coming home to let us admire his greatness.   (*Frowning — irritably.*)   What am I talking about?   My brain must be sick, too.   (*After a pause.*)   Yes, these years have been terrible for both of us.   (*His voice is lowered to a trembling whisper.*)   Especially the last eight months since Mary — died.   (*He forces back a sob with a convulsive shudder — then breaks out in a passionate agony.*)   Our last hope of happiness!   I could curse God from the bottom of my soul — if there was a God!

> (*He is racked by a violent fit of coughing and hurriedly puts his handkerchief to his lips.*)

RUTH (*without looking at him*).   Mary's better off — being dead.

ROBERT (*gloomily*).   We'd all be better off for that matter.   (*With a sudden exasperation.*)   You tell that mother of yours she's got to stop saying that Mary's death was due to a weak constitution inherited from me.   (*On the verge of tears of weakness.*)   It's got to stop, I tell you!

RUTH (*sharply*).   S-h-h!   You'll wake her; and then she'll nag at me — not you.

ROBERT (*coughs and lies back in his chair weakly — a pause*).   It's all because your mother's down on me for not begging Andy for help.

RUTH (*resentfully*).   You might have.   He's got plenty.

ROBERT.   How can *you* of all people think of taking money from him?

RUTH (*dully*).   I don't see the harm.   He's your own brother.

ROBERT (*shrugging his shoulders*).   What's the use of talking to you?   Well, *I* couldn't.   (*Proudly.*)   And I've managed to keep things going, thank God.   You can't deny that without help I've succeeded in —— (*He breaks off with a bitter laugh.*) My God, what am I boasting of? Debts to this one and that, taxes, interest unpaid! I'm a fool! (*He lies back in his chair closing his eyes for a moment, then speaks in a low voice.*) I'll be frank, Ruth. I've been an utter failure, and I've dragged you with me. I couldn't blame you in all justice — for hating me.

RUTH (*without feeling*). I don't hate you. It's been my fault too, I s'pose.

ROBERT. No. You couldn't help loving — Andy.

RUTH (*dully*). I don't love anyone.

ROBERT (*waving her remark aside*). You needn't deny it. It doesn't matter. (*After a pause — with a tender smile.*) Do you know Ruth, what I've been dreaming back there in the dark? (*With a short laugh.*) I was planning our future when I get well. (*He looks at her with appealing eyes as if afraid she will sneer at him. Her expression does not change. She stares at the stove. His voice takes on a note of eagerness.*) After all, why shouldn't we have a future? We're young yet. If we can only shake off the curse of this farm! It's the farm that's ruined our lives, damn it! And now that Andy's coming back — I'm going to sink my foolish pride, Ruth! I'll borrow the money from him to give us a good start in the city. We'll go where people live instead of stagnating, and start all over again. (*Confidently.*) I won't be the failure there that I've been here, Ruth. You won't need to be ashamed of me there. I'll prove to you the reading I've done can be put to some use. (*Vaguely.*) I'll write, or something of that sort. I've always wanted to write. (*Pleadingly.*) You'll want to do that, won't you, Ruth?

RUTH (*dully*). There's Ma.

ROBERT. She can come with us.

RUTH. She wouldn't.

ROBERT (*angrily*). So that's your answer! (*He trembles with violent passion. His voice is so strange that* RUTH *turns to look at him in alarm.*) You're lying, Ruth! Your mother's just an excuse. You want to stay here. You think that because Andy's coming back that —— (*He chokes and has an attack of coughing.*)

RUTH (*getting up — in a frightened voice*). What's the matter? (*She goes to him.*) I'll go with you, Rob. Stop that coughing for goodness' sake! It's awful bad for you. (*She soothes him in dull tones.*) I'll go with you to the city — soon's you're well again. Honest I will, Rob, I promise! (ROB *lies back and closes his eyes. She stands looking down at him anxiously.*) Do you feel better now?

ROBERT. Yes. (RUTH *goes back to her chair. After a pause he opens his eyes and sits up in his chair. His face is flushed and happy.*) Then you *will* go, Ruth?

RUTH. Yes.

ROBERT (*excitedly*). We'll make a new start, Ruth — just you and I. Life owes us some happiness after what we've been through. (*Vehemently.*) It must! Otherwise our suffering would be meaningless — and that is unthinkable.

RUTH (*worried by his excitement*). Yes, yes, of course, Rob, but you mustn't ——

ROBERT. Oh, don't be afraid. I feel completely well, really I do — now that I can hope again. Oh if you knew how glorious it feels to have something to look forward to! Can't you feel the thrill of it, too — the vision of a new life opening up after all the horrible years?

RUTH. Yes, yes, but do be ——

ROBERT. Nonsense! I won't be careful. I'm getting back all my strength. (*He gets lightly to his feet.*) See! I feel light as a feather. (*He walks to her chair and bends down to kiss her smilingly.*) One kiss — the first in years, isn't it? — to greet the dawn of a new life together.

RUTH (*submitting to his kiss — worriedly*). Sit down, Rob, for goodness' sake!

ROBERT (*with tender obstinacy — stroking her hair*). I won't sit down. You're silly to worry. (*He rests one hand on the back of her chair.*) Listen. All our suffering has been a test through which we had to pass to prove ourselves worthy of a finer realization. (*Exultingly.*) And we did pass through it! It hasn't broken us! And now the dream is to come true! Don't you see?

RUTH (*looking at him with frightened eyes as if she thought he had gone mad*). Yes, Rob, I see; but won't you go back to bed now and rest?

ROBERT. No. I'm going to see the sun rise. It's an augury of good fortune. (*He goes quickly to the window in the rear left, and pushing the curtains aside, stands looking out.* RUTH *springs to her feet and comes quickly to the table, left, where she remains watching* ROBERT *in a tense, expectant attitude. As he peers out his body seems gradually to sag, to grow limp and tired. His voice is mournful as he speaks.*) No sun yet. It isn't time. All I can see is the black rim of the damned hills outlined against a creeping grayness. (*He turns around; letting the curtains fall back, stretching a hand out to the wall to support himself. His false strength of a moment has evaporated leaving his face drawn and hollow-eyed. He makes a pitiful attempt to smile.*) That's not a very happy augury, is it? But the sun'll come — soon.

(*He sways weakly.*)

RUTH (*hurrying to his side and supporting him*). Please go to bed, won't you, Rob? You don't want to be all wore out when the specialist comes, do you?

ROBERT (*quickly*). No. That's right. He mustn't think I'm sicker than I am. And I feel as if I could sleep now — (*cheerfully*) — a good, sound, restful sleep.

RUTH (*helping him to the bedroom door*). That's what you need most. (*They go inside. A moment later she reappears calling back.*) I'll shut this door so's you'll be quiet. (*She closes the door and goes quickly to her mother and shakes her by the shoulder.*) Ma! Ma! Wake up!

MRS. ATKINS (*coming out of her sleep with a start*). Glory be! What's the matter with you?

RUTH. It was Rob. He's just been talking to me out here. I put him back to bed. (*Now that she is sure her mother is awake her fear passes and she relapses into dull indifference. She sits down in her chair and stares at the stove — dully.*) He acted — funny; and his eyes looked so — so wild like.

MRS. ATKINS (*with asperity*). And is that all you woke me out of a sound sleep for, and scared me near out of my wits?

RUTH. I was afraid. He talked so crazy. I couldn't quiet him. I didn't want to be alone with him that way. Lord knows what he might do.

MRS. ATKINS (*scornfully*). Humph! A help I'd be to you and me not able to move a step! Why didn't you run and get Jake?

RUTH (*dully*). Jake isn't here. He quit last night. He hasn't been paid in three months.

MRS. ATKINS (*indignantly*). I can't blame him. What decent

person'd want to work on a place like this? (*With sudden exasperation.*) Oh, I wish you'd never married that man!

RUTH (*wearily*). You oughtn't to talk about him now when he's sick in his bed.

MRS. ATKINS (*working herself into a fit of rage*). You know very well, Ruth Mayo, if it wasn't for me helpin' you on the sly out of my savin's, you'd both been in the poor house — and all 'count of his pigheaded pride in not lettin' Andy know the state thin's were in. A nice thin' for me to have to support him out of what I'd saved for my last days — and me an invalid with no one to look to!

RUTH. Andy'll pay you back, Ma. I can tell him so's Rob'll never know.

MRS. ATKINS (*with a snort*). What'd Rob think you and him was livin' on, I'd like to know?

RUTH (*dully*). He didn't think about it, I s'pose. (*After a slight pause.*) He said he'd made up his mind to ask Andy for help when he comes. (*As a clock in the kitchen strikes six.*) Six o'clock. Andy ought to get here directly.

MRS. ATKINS. D'you think this special doctor'll do Rob any good?

RUTH (*hopelessly*). I don't know.

(*The two women remain silent for a time staring dejectedly at the stove.*)

MRS. ATKINS (*shivering irritably*). For goodness' sake put some wood on that fire. I'm most freezin'!

RUTH (*pointing to the door in the rear*). Don't talk so loud. Let him sleep if he can. (*She gets wearily from the chair and puts a few pieces of wood in the stove.*) This is the last of the wood. I don't know who'll cut more now that Jake's left. (*She sighs and walks to the window in the rear, left, pulls the curtains aside, and looks out.*) It's getting gray out. (*She comes back to the stove.*) Looks like it'd be a nice day. (*She stretches out her hands to warm them.*) Must've been a heavy frost last night. We're paying for the spell of warm weather we've been having.

(*The throbbing whine of a motor sounds from the distance outside.*)

MRS. ATKINS (*sharply*). S-h-h-! Listen! Ain't that an auto I hear?

RUTH (*without interest*). Yes. It's Andy, I s'pose.

MRS. ATKINS (*with nervous irritation*). Don't sit there like a silly goose. Look at the state of this room! What'll this strange doctor think

of us?   Look at that lamp chimney all smoke!   Gracious sakes,
Ruth ——

RUTH (*indifferently*).   I've got a lamp all cleaned up in the kitchen.

MRS. ATKINS (*peremptorily*).   Wheel me in there this minute.   I don't
want him to see me looking a sight.   I'll lay down in the room
the other side.   You don't need me now and I'm dead for sleep.

> (RUTH *wheels her mother off right.   The noise of the motor grows
> louder and finally ceases as the car stops on the road before the
> farmhouse.   RUTH returns from the kitchen with a lighted lamp
> in her hand which she sets on the table beside the other.   The
> sound of footsteps on the path is heard — then a sharp rap on the
> door.   RUTH goes and opens it.   ANDREW enters, followed by
> DOCTOR FAWCETT carrying a small black bag.   ANDREW has
> changed greatly.   His face seems to have grown highstrung,
> hardened by the look of decisiveness which comes from being
> constantly under a strain where judgments on the spur of the
> moment are compelled to be accurate.   His eyes are keener and
> more alert.   There is even a suggestion of ruthless cunning about
> them.   At present, however, his expression is one of tense anxiety.
> DOCTOR FAWCETT is a short, dark, middle-aged man with a
> Vandyke beard.   He wears glasses.*)

RUTH.   Hello, Andy!   I've been waiting ——

ANDREW (*kissing her hastily*).   I got here as soon as I could.   (*He
throws off his cap and heavy overcoat on the table, introducing* RUTH *and
the* DOCTOR *as he does so.   He is dressed in an expensive business suit and
appears stouter.*)   My sister-in-law, Mrs. Mayo — Doctor Fawcett.
(*They bow to each other silently.*   ANDREW *casts a quick glance about
the room.*)   Where's Rob?

RUTH (*pointing*).   In there.

ANDREW.   I'll take your coat and hat, Doctor.   (*As he helps the*
DOCTOR *with his things.*)   Is he very bad, Ruth?

RUTH (*dully*).   He's been getting weaker.

ANDREW.   Damn!   This way, Doctor.   Bring the lamp, Ruth.

> (*He goes into the bedroom, followed by the* DOCTOR *and* RUTH
> carrying the clean lamp.   RUTH reappears almost immediately
> closing the door behind her, and goes slowly to the outside door,
> which she opens, and stands in the doorway looking out.   The
> sound of* ANDREW'S *and* ROBERT'S *voices comes from the bed-*

room.   A moment later ANDREW *reënters, closing the door softly.   He comes forward and sinks down in the rocker on the right of table, leaning his head on his hand.   His face is drawn in a shocked expression of great grief.   He sighs heavily, staring mournfully in front of him.* RUTH *turns and stands watching him.   Then she shuts the door and returns to her chair by the stove, turning it so she can face him.*)

ANDREW (*glancing up quickly — in a harsh voice*).   How long has this been going on?

RUTH.   You mean — how long has he been sick?

ANDREW (*shortly*).   Of course!   What else?

RUTH.   It was last summer he had a bad spell first, but he's been ailin' ever since Mary died — eight months ago.

ANDREW (*harshly*).   Why didn't you let me know — cable me?   Do you want him to die, all of you?   I'm damned if it doesn't look that way!   (*His voice breaking.*)   Poor old chap!   To be sick in this out-of-the-way hole without anyone to attend to him but a country quack!   It's a damned shame!

RUTH (*dully*).   I wanted to send you word once, but he only got mad when I told him.   He was too proud to ask anything, he said.

ANDREW.   Proud?   To ask me?   (*He jumps to his feet and paces nervously back and forth.*)   I can't understand the way you've acted.   Didn't you see how sick he was getting?   Couldn't you realize — why, I nearly dropped in my tracks when I saw him!   He looks — (*he shudders*) — terrible!   (*With fierce scorn.*)   I suppose you're so used to the idea of his being delicate that you took his sickness as a matter of course.   God, if I'd only known!

RUTH (*without emotion*).   A letter takes so long to get where you were — and we couldn't afford to telegraph.   We owed everyone already, and I couldn't ask Ma.   She'd been giving me money out of her savings till she hadn't much left.   Don't say anything to Rob about it.   I never told him.   He'd only be mad at me if he knew.   But I had to, because — God knows how we'd have got on if I hadn't.

ANDREW.   You mean to say —— (*His eyes seem to take in the poverty-stricken appearance of the room for the first time.*)   You sent that telegram to me collect.   Was it because —— (RUTH *nods silently.* ANDREW *pounds on the table with his fist.*)   Good God!   And all this time I've been — why I've had everything! (*He sits down in his chair and pulls it close to* RUTH's — *impulsively.*) But — I can't get it through my head. Why? Why? What has happened? How did it ever come about? Tell me!

RUTH (*dully*). There's nothing much to tell. Things kept getting worse, that's all — and Rob didn't seem to care. He never took any interest since way back when your Ma died. After that he got men to take charge, and they nearly all cheated him — he couldn't tell — and left one after another. Then after Mary died he didn't pay no heed to anything any more — just stayed indoors and took to reading books again. So I had to ask Ma if she wouldn't help us some.

ANDREW (*surprised and horrified*). Why, damn it, this is frightful! Rob must be mad not to have let me know. Too proud to ask help of *me!* What's the matter with him in God's name? (*A sudden, horrible suspicion entering his mind.*) Ruth! Tell me the truth. His mind hasn't gone back on him, has it?

RUTH (*dully*). I don't know. Mary's dying broke him up terrible — but he's used to her being gone by this, I s'pose.

ANDREW (*looking at her queerly*). Do you mean to say *you're* used to it?

RUTH (*in a dead tone*). There's a time comes — when you don't mind any more — anything.

ANDREW (*looks at her fixedly for a moment — with great pity*). I'm sorry, Ruth — if I seemed to blame you. I didn't realize —— The sight of Rob lying in bed there, so gone to pieces — it made me furious at everyone. Forgive me, Ruth.

RUTH. There's nothing to forgive. It doesn't matter.

ANDREW (*springing to his feet again and pacing up and down*). Thank God I came back before it was too late. This doctor will know exactly what to do. That's the first thing to think of. When Rob's on his feet again we can get the farm working on a sound basis once more. I'll see to that — before I leave.

RUTH. You're going away again?

ANDREW. I've got to.

RUTH. You wrote Rob you was coming back to stay this time.

ANDREW. I expected to — until I got to New York. Then I learned certain facts that make it necessary. (*With a short laugh.*) To

be candid, Ruth, I'm not the rich man you've probably been led
to believe by my letters — not now. I was when I wrote them.
I made money hand over fist as long as I stuck to legitimate
trading; but I wasn't content with that. I wanted it to come
easier, so like all the rest of the idiots, I tried speculation. Oh, I
won all right! Several times I've been almost a millionaire — on
paper — and then come down to earth again with a bump.
Finally the strain was too much. I got disgusted with myself and
made up my mind to get out and come home and forget it and
really live again. (*He gives a harsh laugh.*) And now comes the
funny part. The day before the steamer sailed I saw what I
thought was a chance to become a millionaire again. (*He snaps
his fingers.*) That easy! I plunged. Then, before things broke,
I left — I was so confident I couldn't be wrong. But when I
landed in New York — I wired you I had business to wind up,
didn't I? Well, it was the business that wound me up!

(*He smiles grimly, pacing up and down, his hands in his pockets.*)

RUTH (*dully*). You found — you'd lost everything?

ANDREW (*sitting down again*). Practically. (*He takes a cigar from his
pocket, bites the end off, and lights it.*) Oh, I don't mean I'm dead
broke. I've saved ten thousand from the wreckage, maybe
twenty. But that's a poor showing for five years' hard work.
That's why I'll have to go back. (*Confidently.*) I can make it up
in a year or so down there — and I don't need but a shoestring
to start with. (*A weary expression comes over his face and he sighs
heavily.*) I wish I didn't have to. I'm sick of it all.

RUTH. It's too bad — things seem to go wrong so.

ANDREW (*shaking off his depression — briskly*). They might be much
worse. There's enough left to fix the farm O.K. before I go. I
won't leave 'til Rob's on his feet again. In the meantime I'll
make things fly around here. (*With satisfaction.*) I need a rest,
and the kind of rest I need is hard work in the open — just like I
used to do in the old days. (*Stopping abruptly and lowering his voice
cautiously.*) Not a word to Rob about my losing money! Remember that, Ruth! You can see why. If he's grown so touchy
he'd never accept a cent if he thought I was hard up; see?

RUTH. Yes, Andy.

(*After a pause, during which* ANDREW *puffs at his cigar abstractedly, his mind evidently busy with plans for the future, the bedroom door is opened and* DOCTOR FAWCETT *enters, carrying a bag. He closes the door quietly behind him and comes forward, a grave expression on his face.* ANDREW *springs out of his chair.*)

ANDREW. Ah, Doctor! (*He pushes a chair between his own and* RUTH'S.) Won't you have a chair?

FAWCETT (*glancing at his watch*). I must catch the nine o'clock back to the city. It's imperative. I have only a moment. (*Sitting down and clearing his throat — in a perfunctory, impersonal voice.*) The case of your brother, Mr. Mayo, is —— (*He stops and glances at* RUTH *and says meaningly to* ANDREW.) Perhaps it would be better if you and I ——

RUTH (*with dogged resentment*). I know what you mean, Doctor. (*Dully.*) Don't be afraid I can't stand it. I'm used to bearing trouble by this; and I can guess what you've found out. (*She hesitates for a moment — then continues in a monotonous voice.*) Rob's going to die.

ANDREW (*angrily*). Ruth!

FAWCETT (*raising his hand as if to command silence*). I am afraid my diagnosis of your brother's condition forces me to the same conclusion as Mrs. Mayo's.

ANDREW (*groaning*). But Doctor, surely ——

FAWCETT (*calmly*). Your brother hasn't long to live — perhaps a few days, perhaps only a few hours. It's a marvel that he's alive at this moment. My examination revealed that both of his lungs are terribly affected.

ANDREW (*brokenly*). Good God!

(RUTH *keeps her eyes fixed on her lap in a trance-like stare.*)

FAWCETT. I am sorry I have to tell you this. If there was anything that could be done ——

ANDREW. There isn't anything?

FAWCETT (*shaking his head*). It's too late. Six months ago there might have ——

ANDREW (*in anguish*). But if we were to take him to the mountains — or to Arizona — or ——

FAWCETT. That might have prolonged his life six months ago. (ANDREW *groans.*) But now ——

(*He shrugs his shoulders significantly.*)

ANDREW (*appalled by a sudden thought*). Good heavens, you haven't told him this, have you, Doctor?

FAWCETT. No. I lied to him. I said a change of climate —— (*He looks at his watch again nervously.*) I must leave you.

(*He gets up.*)

ANDREW (*getting to his feet — insistently*). But there must still be some chance ——

FAWCETT (*as if he were reassuring a child*). There is always that last chance — the miracle. (*He puts on his hat and coat — bowing to* RUTH.) Good-by, Mrs. Mayo.

RUTH (*without raising her eyes — dully*). Good-by.

ANDREW (*mechanically*). I'll walk to the car with you, Doctor. (*They go out of the door.* RUTH *sits motionlessly. The motor is heard starting and the noise gradually recedes into the distance.* ANDREW *re-enters, and sits down in his chair, holding his head in his hands.*) Ruth! (*She lifts her eyes to his.*) Hadn't we better go in and see him? God! I'm afraid to! I know he'll read it in my face. (*The bedroom door is noiselessly opened and* ROBERT *appears in the doorway. His cheeks are flushed with fever, and his eyes appear unusually large and brilliant.* ANDREW *continues with a groan.*) It can't be, Ruth. It can't be as hopeless as he said. There's always a fighting chance. We'll take Rob to Arizona. He's *got* to get well. There *must* be a chance!

ROBERT (*in a gentle tone*). Why must there, Andy?

(RUTH *turns and stares at him with terrified eyes.*)

ANDREW (*whirling around*). Rob! (*Scoldingly.*) What are you doing out of bed? (*He gets up and goes to him.*) Get right back now and obey the Doc, or you're going to get a licking from me!

ROBERT (*ignoring these remarks*). Help me over to the chair, please, Andy.

ANDREW. Like hell I will! You're going right back to bed, that's where you're going, and stay there!

(*He takes hold of* ROBERT'S *arm.*)

ROBERT (*mockingly*). Stay there 'til I die, eh, Andy? (*Coldly.*) Don't behave like a child. I'm sick of lying down. I'll be more rested sitting up. (*As* ANDREW *hesitates — violently.*) I swear I'll get out of bed every time you put me there. You'll have to sit on my chest, and that wouldn't help my health any. Come on, Andy. Don't play the fool. I want to talk to you, and I'm going to. (*With a grim smile.*) A dying man has some rights, hasn't he?

ANDREW (*with a shudder*). Don't talk that way, for God's sake! I'll only let you sit down if you'll promise that. Remember. (*He helps* ROBERT *to the chair between his own and* RUTH's.) Easy now! There you are! Wait, and I'll get a pillow for you. (*He goes into the bedroom.* ROBERT *looks at* RUTH *who shrinks away from him in terror.* ROBERT *smiles bitterly.* ANDREW *comes back with the pillow which he places behind* ROBERT's *back.*) How's that?

ROBERT (*with an affectionate smile*). Fine! Thank you! (*As* ANDREW *sits down.*) Listen, Andy. You've asked me not to talk — and I won't after I've made my position clear. (*Slowly.*) In the first place I know I'm dying.

> (RUTH *bows her head and covers her face with her hands. She remains like this all during the scene between the two brothers.*)

ANDREW. Rob! That isn't so!

ROBERT (*wearily*). It *is* so! Don't lie to me. After Ruth put me to bed before you came, I saw it clearly for the first time. (*Bitterly.*) I'd been making plans for our future — Ruth's and mine — so it came hard at first — the realization. Then when the doctor examined me, I knew — although he tried to lie about it. And then to make sure I listened at the door to what he told you. So don't mock me with fairy tales about Arizona, or any such rot as that. Because I'm dying is no reason you should treat me as an imbecile or a coward. Now that I'm sure what's happening I can say Kismet to it with all my heart. It was only the silly uncertainty that hurt.

> (*There is a pause.* ANDREW *looks around in impotent anguish, not knowing what to say.* ROBERT *regards him with an affectionate smile.*)

ANDREW (*finally blurts out*). It isn't foolish. You *have* got a chance. If you heard all the Doctor said that ought to prove it to you.

ROBERT. Oh, you mean when he spoke of the miracle? (*Dryly.*) I don't believe in miracles — in my case. Besides, I know more than any doctor on earth *could* know — because I *feel* what's coming. (*Dismissing the subject.*) But we've agreed not to talk of it. Tell me about yourself, Andy. That's what I'm interested in. Your letters were too brief and far apart to be illuminating.

ANDREW. I meant to write oftener.

ROBERT (*with a faint trace of irony*). I judge from them you've accomplished all you set out to do five years ago?

ANDREW. That isn't much to boast of.

ROBERT (*surprised*). Have you really, honestly reached that conclusion?

ANDREW. Well, it doesn't seem to amount to much now.

ROBERT. But you're rich, aren't you?

ANDREW (*with a quick glance at* RUTH). Yes, I s'pose so.

ROBERT. I'm glad. You can do to the farm all I've undone. But what did you do down there? Tell me. You went in the grain business with that friend of yours?

ANDREW. Yes. After two years I had a share in it. I sold out last year. (*He is answering* ROBERT's *questions with great reluctance.*)

ROBERT. And then?

ANDREW. I went in on my own.

ROBERT. Still in grain?

ANDREW. Yes.

ROBERT. What's the matter? You look as if I were accusing you of something.

ANDREW. I'm proud enough of the first four years. It's after that I'm not boasting of. I took to speculating.

ROBERT. In wheat?

ANDREW. Yes.

ROBERT. And you made money — gambling?

ANDREW. Yes.

ROBERT (*thoughtfully*). I've been wondering what the great change was in you. (*After a pause.*) You — a farmer — to gamble in a wheat pit with scraps of paper. There's a spiritual significance in that picture, Andy. (*He smiles bitterly.*) I'm a failure, and Ruth's another — but we can both justly lay some of the blame for our stumbling on God. But you're the deepest-dyed failure of the three, Andy. You've spent eight years running away from yourself. Do you see what I mean? You used to be a creator when you loved the farm. You and life were in harmonious partnership. And now —— (*He stops as if seeking vainly for words.*) My brain is muddled. But part of what I mean is that your gambling with the thing you used to love to create proves how far astray —— So you'll be punished. You'll have to suffer to win back —— (*His voice grows weaker and he sighs wearily.*) It's no use. I can't say it. (*He lies back and closes his eyes, breathing pantingly.*)

ANDREW (*slowly*). I think I know what you're driving at, Rob — and it's true, I guess.

(ROBERT *smiles gratefully and stretches out his hand, which* ANDREW *takes in his.*)

ROBERT. I want you to promise me to do one thing, Andy, after ——

ANDREW. I'll promise anything, as God is my Judge!

ROBERT. Remember, Andy, Ruth has suffered double her share. (*His voice faltering with weakness.*) Only through contact with suffering, Andy, will you — awaken. Listen. You must marry Ruth — afterwards.

RUTH (*with a cry*). Rob!

(ROBERT *lies back, his eyes closed, gasping heavily for breath.*)

ANDREW (*making signs to her to humor him — gently*). You're tired out, Rob. You better lie down and rest a while, don't you think? We can talk later on.

ROBERT (*with a mocking smile*). Later on! You always were an optimist, Andy! (*He sighs with exhaustion.*) Yes, I'll go and rest a while. (*As* ANDREW *comes to help him.*) It must be near sunrise, isn't it?

ANDREW. It's after six.

ROBERT (*as* ANDREW *helps him into the bedroom*). Shut the door, Andy. I want to be alone.

(ANDREW *reappears and shuts the door softly. He comes and sits down on his chair again, supporting his head on his hands. His face is drawn with the intensity of his dry-eyed anguish.*)

RUTH (*glancing at him — fearfully*). He's out of his mind now, isn't he?

ANDREW. He may be a little delirious. The fever would do that. (*With impotent rage.*) God, what a shame! And there's nothing we can do but sit and — wait!

(*He springs from his chair and walks to the stove.*)

RUTH (*dully*). He was talking — wild — like he used to — only this time it sounded — unnatural, don't you think?

ANDREW. I don't know. The things he said to me had truth in them — even if he did talk them way up in the air, like he always sees things. Still —— (*He glances down at* RUTH *keenly.*) Why do you suppose he wanted us to promise we'd —— (*Confusedly.*) You know what he said.

RUTH (*dully*). His mind was wandering, I s'pose.

ANDREW (*with conviction*). No — there was something back of it.

RUTH. He wanted to make sure I'd be all right — after he'd gone, I expect.

ANDREW. No, it wasn't that. He knows very well I'd naturally look after you without — anything like that.

RUTH. He might be thinking of — something happened five years back, the time you came home from the trip.

ANDREW. What happened? What do you mean?

RUTH (*dully*). We had a fight.

ANDREW. A fight? What has that to do with me?

RUTH. It was about you — in a way.

ANDREW (*amazed*). About *me?*

RUTH. Yes, mostly. You see I'd found out I'd made a mistake about Rob soon after we were married — when it was too late.

ANDREW. Mistake? (*Slowly.*) You mean — you found out you didn't love Rob?

RUTH. Yes.

ANDREW. Good God!

RUTH. And then I thought that when Mary came it'd be different, and I'd love him; but it didn't happen that way. And I couldn't bear with his blundering and book-reading — and I grew to hate him, almost.

ANDREW. Ruth!

RUTH. I couldn't help it. No woman could. It had to be because I loved someone else, I'd found out. (*She sighs wearily.*) It can't do no harm to tell you now — when it's all past and gone — and dead. *You* were the one I really loved — only I didn't come to the knowledge of it 'til too late.

ANDREW (*stunned*). Ruth! Do you know what you're saying?

RUTH. It was true — then. (*With sudden fierceness.*) How could I help it? No woman could.

ANDREW. Then — you loved me — that time I came home?

RUTH (*doggedly*). I'd known your real reason for leaving home the first time — everybody knew it — and for three years I'd been thinking ——

ANDREW. That I loved you?

RUTH. Yes. Then that day on the hill you laughed about what a fool you'd been for loving me once — and I knew it was all over.

ANDREW. Good God, but I never thought —— (*He stops, shuddering at his remembrance.*) And did Rob ——

RUTH. That was what I'd started to tell. We'd had a fight just before you came and I got crazy mad — and I told him all I've told you.

ANDREW (*gaping at her speechlessly for a moment*). You told Rob — you loved me?

RUTH. Yes.

ANDREW (*shrinking away from her in horror*). You — you — you mad fool, you! How could you do such a thing?

RUTH. I couldn't help it. I'd got to the end of bearing things — without talking.

ANDREW. Then Rob must have known every moment I stayed here! And yet he never said or showed — God, how he must have suffered! Didn't you know how much he loved you?

RUTH (*dully*). Yes. I knew he liked me.

ANDREW. Liked you! What kind of a woman are you? Couldn't you have kept silent? Did you have to torture him? No wonder he's dying! And you've lived together for five years with this between you?

RUTH. We've lived in the same house.

ANDREW. Does he still think ——

RUTH. I don't know. We've never spoke a word about it since that day. Maybe, from the way he went on, he s'poses I care for you yet.

ANDREW. But you don't. It's outrageous. It's stupid! You don't love me!

RUTH (*slowly*). I wouldn't know how to feel love, even if I tried, any more.

ANDREW (*brutally*). And I don't love you, that's sure! (*He sinks into his chair, his head between his hands.*) It's damnable such a thing should be between Rob and me. Why, I love Rob better'n anybody in the world and always did. There isn't a thing on God's green earth I wouldn't have done to keep trouble away from him. And I have to be the very one — it's damnable! How am I going to face him again? What can I say to him now? (*He groans with anguished rage. After a pause.*) He asked me to promise — what am I going to do?

RUTH. You can promise — so's it'll ease his mind — and not mean anything.

ANDREW. What? Lie to him now — when he's dying? (*Determinedly.*) No! It's *you* who'll have to do the lying, since it must be done. You've got a chance now to undo some of all the suffering you've brought on Rob. Go in to him! Tell him you never loved me — it was all a mistake. Tell him you only said so because you were mad and didn't know what you were saying! Tell him something, anything, that'll bring him peace!

RUTH (*dully*). He wouldn't believe me.

ANDREW (*furiously*). You've got to make him believe you, do you hear? You've got to — now — hurry — you never know when it may be too late. (*As she hesitates — imploringly.*) For God's sake, Ruth! Don't you see you owe it to him? You'll never forgive yourself if you don't.

RUTH (*dully*). I'll go. (*She gets wearily to her feet and walks slowly toward the bedroom.*) But it won't do any good. (ANDREW's *eyes are fixed on her anxiously. She opens the door and steps inside the room. She remains standing there for a minute. Then she calls in a frightened voice.*) Rob! Where are you? (*Then she hurries back, trembling with fright.*) Andy! Andy! He's gone!

ANDREW (*misunderstanding her — his face pale with dread*). He's not——

RUTH (*interrupting him — hysterically*). He's gone! The bed's empty. The window's wide open. He must have crawled out into the yard!

ANDREW (*springing to his feet. He rushes into the bedroom and returns immediately with an expression of alarmed amazement on his face*). Come! He can't have gone far! (*Grabbing his hat he takes* RUTH's *arm and shoves her toward the door.*) Come on! (*Opening the door.*) Let's hope to God —— (*The door closes behind them, cutting off his words as*

(*The Curtain Falls.*)

ACT THREE

SCENE TWO

Same as Act One, Scene One — A section of country highway. The sky to the east is already alight with bright color and a thin, quivering line of flame is spreading slowly along the horizon rim of the dark hills. The roadside, however, is still steeped in the grayness of the dawn, shadowy and vague. The field in the foreground has a wild uncultivated appearance as if it had been allowed to remain fallow the preceding summer. Parts of the snake-fence in the rear have been broken down. The apple tree is leafless and seems dead.

ROBERT staggers weakly in from the left. He stumbles into the ditch and lies there for a moment; then crawls with a great effort to the top of the bank where he can see the sun rise, and collapses weakly. RUTH and ANDREW come hurriedly along the road from the left.

ANDREW (*stopping and looking about him*). There he is! I knew it! I knew we'd find him here.

ROBERT (*trying to raise himself to a sitting position as they hasten to his side — with a wan smile*). I thought I'd given you the slip.

ANDREW (*with kindly bullying*). Well you didn't, you old scoundrel, and we're going to take you right back where you belong — in bed. (*He makes a motion to lift ROBERT.*)

ROBERT. Don't, Andy. Don't, I tell you!

ANDREW. You're in pain?

ROBERT (*simply*). No. I'm dying. (*He falls back weakly. RUTH sinks down beside him with a sob and pillows his head on her lap. ANDREW stands looking down at him helplessly. ROBERT moves his head restlessly on RUTH's lap.*) I couldn't stand it back there in the room. It seemed as if all my life — I'd been cooped in a room. So I thought I'd try to end as I might have — if I'd had the courage — alone — in a ditch by the open road — watching the sun rise.

ANDREW. Rob! Don't talk. You're wasting your strength. Rest a while and then we'll carry you ——

ROBERT. Still hoping, Andy? Don't. I know. (*There is a pause during which he breathes heavily, straining his eyes toward the horizon.*)

The sun comes so slowly. (*With an ironical smile.*) The doctor told me to go to the far-off places — and I'd be cured. He was right. That was always the cure for me. It's too late — for this life — but —— (*He has a fit of coughing which racks his body.*)

ANDREW (*with a hoarse sob*). Rob! (*He clenches his fists in an impotent rage against Fate.*) God! God!

(RUTH *sobs brokenly and wipes* ROBERT's *lips with her handkerchief.*)

ROBERT (*in a voice which is suddenly ringing with the happiness of hope*). You mustn't feel sorry for me. Don't you see I'm happy at last — free — free! — freed from the farm — free to wander on and on — eternally! (*He raises himself on his elbow, his face radiant, and points to the horizon.*) Look! Isn't it beautiful beyond the hills? I can hear the old voices calling me to come —— (*Exultantly.*) And this time I'm going! It isn't the end. It's a free beginning — the start of my voyage! I've won to my trip — the right of release — beyond the horizon! Oh, you ought to be glad — glad — for my sake! (*He collapses weakly.*) Andy! (ANDREW *bends down to him.*) Remember Ruth ——

ANDREW. I'll take care of her, I swear to you, Rob!

ROBERT. Ruth has suffered — remember, Andy — only through sacrifice — the secret beyond there —— (*He suddenly raises himself with his last remaining strength and points to the horizon where the edge of the sun's disc is rising from the rim of the hills.*) The sun! (*He remains with his eyes fixed on it for a moment. A rattling noise throbs from his throat. He mumbles.*) Remember! (*And falls back and is still.* RUTH *gives a cry of horror and springs to her feet, shuddering, her hands over her eyes.* ANDREW *bends on one knee beside the body, placing a hand over* ROBERT's *heart, then he kisses his brother reverentially on the forehead and stands up.*)

ANDREW (*facing* RUTH, *the body between them — in a dead voice*). He's dead. (*With a sudden burst of fury.*) God damn you, you never told him!

RUTH (*piteously*). He was so happy without my lying to him.

ANDREW (*pointing to the body — trembling with the violence of his rage*). This is your doing, you damn woman, you coward, you murderess!

RUTH (*sobbing*). Don't, Andy! I couldn't help it — and he knew how I'd suffered, too. He told you — to remember.

ANDREW (*stares at her for a moment, his rage ebbing away, an expression of deep pity gradually coming over his face. Then he glances down at his brother and speaks brokenly in a compassionate voice*). Forgive me, Ruth — for his sake — and I'll remember —— (RUTH *lets her hands fall from her face and looks at him uncomprehendingly. He lifts his eyes to hers and forces out falteringly.*) I — you — we've both made a mess of things! We must try to help each other — and — in time — we'll come to know what's right —— (*Desperately.*) And perhaps we ——

    (*But* RUTH, *if she is aware of his words, gives no sign. She remains silent, gazing at him dully with the sad humility of exhaustion, her mind already sinking back into that spent calm beyond the further troubling of any hope.*)

(*The Curtain Falls.*)

APPENDIX

APPENDIX

I

NOTES ON THE AUTHORS AND THE PLAYS

HENRIK IBSEN

HENRIK IBSEN was born March 20, 1828, at Skien, a little town on the south coast of Norway. His father was a well-to-do merchant who dispensed a generous hospitality during his days of prosperity. When Henrik was eight years old, a commercial panic swept away the elder Ibsen's entire fortune, and the family was compelled to retire to a poor little farm on the outskirts of the town. From that time on the father made but a meager income by doing odd jobs, and finally took to drink. When the boy was fifteen, he was taken from school, and apprenticed to an apothecary in the neighboring town of Grimstad. Here for several years he was wretchedly poor, and lived a lonely, introspective life.

He began his literary career as a contributor to newspapers, and in 1849 wrote his first play, *Catalina*, a revolutionary drama, which was published later at the expense of a friend. His ambition awakening, he set out the following year for Christiania (now Oslo) with the intention of entering the university. Here he fell in with a group of young radicals of a literary turn of mind (Björnson among the rest)who started a newspaper that succumbed after a feeble existence of nine months. The next year, Ibsen, through the influence of Ole Bull, the famous violinist, was made director of the Bergen Theater. In 1857 he returned to Christiania to direct the National Theater; he was not very successful, however, for five years of his management reduced it to bankruptcy.

Ibsen's satiric bent revealed itself unmistakably in his first important play, *Love's Comedy*, published in 1862. Two years after its appearance, embittered by the scant appreciation accorded to his works and by the unsettled political state of the country, he gladly accepted a small pension from the Norwegian Parliament, and set out for Rome. In the congenial atmosphere of the Eternal City his poetic genius expanded and burgeoned, and his imagination was kindled into new life. The first fruit of his exile was the dramatic poem, *Brand*. On its appearance it was at once hailed as a masterpiece, and achieved an extraordinary popularity. Riding triumphant on the wave of success, he soon brought to completion his poetic fantasy, *Peer Gynt*, which in some quarters is regarded as his most important contribution to literature.

In 1868, Ibsen removed to Dresden, and later settled down in Munich. By this time, through the publication of his prose dramas of social life, beginning with *Pillars of Society* (1877), his reputation as the foremost dramatist of the day was firmly established, and he was enjoying a comfortable revenue from his writings. Finally, in 1891, after a voluntary exile of twenty-seven years, he returned to Christiania. There he lived for the rest of his life. He died in 1906, full of years and honors.

One finds it well-nigh impossible to separate Ibsen the dramatist from Ibsen the man, so closely was his life bound up with the world of the theater. Probably no writer for the past two centuries has exerted so potent an influence on the drama of European countries. He greatly simplified the technique of the drama by achieving a unity and compactness of plot through the elimination of the paraphernalia of episodes, asides, monologues, disguises, and the like, which had hitherto encumbered it.

He was also the creator of the so-called drama of ideas. In the history of the modern drama his *The Doll's House* is of the utmost importance. While the first two acts are conventional enough, the third act marks a distinct break with the French tradition; in the scene where Nora and Helmer sit down and calmly talk over the shipwreck of their married life is born a new type of drama — one whose climax lies not so much in action as in the thoughts that are the motive force of action. In this and in the plays that followed, Ibsen demonstrated that there is ample material for effective drama in the everyday life of commonplace people without resorting to the violent and extravagant devices of melodrama. The merits of this method were so immediately apparent that it set a standard, and was widely adopted.

Ibsen was a pioneer, and hence in advance of his age. Certain of his ideas that seemed so radical and exciting to the audiences of his day are now but the merest commonplaces. He was always a sturdy individualist and non-conformist, crying out against "soul-destroying compromises, against hypocrisy, against the whole tribe of mediocre standards which the 'average spirit' takes refuge in." His ideas are invariably destructive and anarchistic; he was more inclined to tear down than to build up. Yet there is something tonic in his frank facing of the essential facts of life, in his stirring protest against spineless conformity to conventions and machinery that deaden and dull. Yet he satirized false ideals as a meliorist rather than as a pessimist. The central tenet of his philosophy of life is aptly summed up in a letter that he once wrote to Björnson: "So to conduct one's life as to realize one's self — this is the loftiest attainment of man."

In his dramatic career, Isben passed through three stages — he began as a romanticist, then became a realist, and ended as a symbolist. He was one of the first playwrights to employ "overtones" in order to indicate the more intangible soul-states that cannot be adequately conveyed by the ordinary means of expression. His employment of "overtones" has since his day been developed by Maeterlinck and other dramatists into a definite symbolistic technique. The realistic social plays have remained, however, the most popular of his works.

While Ibsen's keen interest in problems lent a polemical note to many of his plays, it may be maintained that he was more poet and artist than reformer, more concerned with character-drawing than with propaganda. The figures that people his dramas, particularly on the distaff side, form a rich gallery of portraits. It is likely that Hedda Gabler, Nora Helmer, Mrs. Alving, and Dr. Stockmann, to single out but four of the distinguished company, will be remembered long after the propaganda that weighs down certain of the plays will cease to have any validity.

March 20, 1928, marked the centenary of Ibsen's birth, and was the occasion of numerous appraisals of his work. It cannot be said that the estimates were uniformly favorable. Recent revivals of his plays show that some of them have aged not a little. It is likely, however, that certain of them, notably *The Wild Duck* and *Hedda Gabler*, possess sufficient vitality to keep them alive. Historically speaking, Ibsen's place is of course quite secure.

The Enemy of the People, which was published in November, 1882, was apparently inspired by Ibsen's indignation over the storm of protest aroused by the appearance of *Ghosts*. Yet the idea lying behind it must have been conceived some time before, since the germ of it is found in an oft-quoted letter of Ibsen's to Lorentz Dietrichson under date of December, 1879: "It appears to me doubtful whether better artistic conditions can be attained in Norway before the intellectual soil has been thoroughly turned up and cleansed, and the swamps drained off." In this play Ibsen describes, under a thinly veiled allegory, the rough treatment he received at the hands of the Norwegian public; though he deals ostensibly with the water-supply of the little Norwegian town, his attack is really directed at the moral water-supply, at the humbug and hypocrisy that gradually interpenetrate institutions. This theme is embodied in certain statements of Dr. Stockmann, who for the most part seems to serve as spokesman for Ibsen himself. He says to his brother, the hypocritical Burgomaster: "We live by trafficking in filth and corruption. The whole of our flourishing social life is rooted in a lie"; and again: "For now it's no mere question of water-works and sewers, you see. No, the whole community must be purged, disinfected ——"

The play involves the eternal conflict between the mob and the individual — a theme which has received eloquent treatment at the hands of living dramatists; in *The Weavers* of Hauptmann, *The Mob* of Galsworthy, *The Boss* of Edward Sheldon.

It would seem that Ibsen holds with Bernard Shaw that the minority might be right, but the majority is always wrong, for he allows Dr. Stockmann to say: "The most dangerous foe to truth and freedom in our midst is the compact majority. Yes, it's the confounded compact majority.... The majority is never right. Never, I say." His satire is sweeping, for he not only attacks the liberals, but the conservatives, as vested in the person of Aslaksen, the printer, whose motto is "Moderation in everything." The free press, "which is ruled by the subscribers," also comes in for a share of abuse.

The hero of *The Enemy of the People* is a sympathetic character. Although he is a muddle-headed idealist, stubborn, and vain as a child, we are won over by the good Doctor's geniality and enthusiasm, his whole-hearted devotion to the cause of righteousness, and above all by his indomitable fighting spirit. Though he may be discomfited and humiliated, he is never conquered. Opposition fails to dampen his moral ardor, and only serves to strengthen his power of resistance. We rejoice when he lets loose his pent-up indignation upon the crowd, in spite of the howling and jeers of the unregenerate; and we applaud when in the final scene of the play the Doctor, indomitable still, puts Hovstad and Aslaksen to flight wtih his umbrella. His brave fight against the forces of evil takes on inevitably a larger perspective. His arena is no longer a small Norwegian town, but the larger world of men. He becomes the incarnate champion of truth against falsehood, of right against wrong. And thus it comes to pass that his final discovery — that "the strongest man is he who stands most alone" — seems to us an eternal truth, of the greatest moment to mankind. Dr. Stockmann almost succeeds in making us willing to accept without question Ibsen's theory of individualism.

The Enemy of the People may be described as a straightforward satiric comedy dealing objectively with the prosaic life of every day. While there is in it little of poetry or imaginative beauty, it is unique among Ibsen's works by virtue of its carefully articulated plot, its abounding vitality, its spirit of geniality. From the day of its first presentation it has been exceedingly popular on the stage. Mr. Walter Hampden's successful revival of it in New York in 1927 bore abundant testimony to the robustness of the old play.

GERHART HAUPTMANN

In 1922 the German Republic, in a splendid commemoration of the sixtieth birthday of Gerhart Hauptmann, paid tribute to him as the foremost literary figure of modern Germany. His leadership in both the naturalistic and neo-romantic phases of the drama remains unchallenged, and his influence has extended far beyond the boundaries of the fatherland.

Hauptmann was born in Obersalzbrunn, Silesia, in 1862. His grandfather, who was at first a poor weaver, had later risen to the dignity of an innkeeper, and his father became the owner of a prosperous hotel. The boy received his early schooling in his native town and at the Realschule at Breslau. Later, when the family fortunes declined, he was taken from school, and worked for two years on the farm of a pious uncle. His artistic proclivity asserting itself, he entered the Royal Academy of Art in Breslau, and then took a special course at the University of Jena. At this period his ambition was to become a sculptor, and in 1884 he had a studio in Rome. Returning to Germany, he became an actor for a time, and then literature claimed him for her own. In 1885 he married Fräulein Thienemann and settled down with his young wife in Ekner, a suburb of Berlin. Here in his little cottage, half-hidden in trees, with far prospects over the fields and waters of Brandenburg, he gathered about himself a group of young writers, among others Arno Holz, whose naturalistic play, *Die Familie Selicke* (written in collaboration with Johannes Schlaf (inspired Hauptmann to compose his first drama, *Vor Sonnenaufgang* (*Before Sunrise*). This play was produced with great success at the Freie Buhne, Berlin, October 20, 1889, and Hauptmann was well launched upon his dramatic career. In 1891 he returned to Silesia. Many honors have been bestowed upon him: in 1905 he was given an LL.D. by Oxford University; in 1912 he was awarded the Nobel Prize.

Although Hauptmann is usually identified with the naturalistic movement, he is a dual artist with strongly romantic tendencies; some of his works are even tinged with symbolism and mysticism. He pays allegiance now to Zola, now to Ibsen, now to Maeterlinck. A constant experimenter, ever reaching out for new forms of expression, he is never content for long with any one particular medium. The wide range of his interests may be fairly indicated by a summary of the types which he has essayed: naturalistic tragedies and comedies, fantasies, folk plays, fairy plays, and historical dramas. Then there are some plays that do not fall under any definite category in which the strains of various moods are skillfully blended.

The naturalistic drama, although it originated elsewhere, probably reached its highest development in Germany; and while it has temporarily been superseded there by the current vogue of expressionism, it is likely to prove in the end Germany's most permanent contribution to the modern drama. The particular merit of the German brand, so Lewisohn believes, is "to have set down a vision of life that coincides remarkably with the humble truth."

Hauptmann is the most distinguished exponent of German naturalism, and *The Weavers*, his powerful study of a strike among the Silesian spinners, is usually regarded as the finest specimen of its genre, Tchekov's dramas alone excepted. It reveals unmistakably the basic principles of his method. He rejects the stereotyped formulas of the "well-made" play, and disdains to use the conventional devices ordinarily employed for unraveling an artificial plot. With him the plot is quite subordinate to the characters; he is apparently not much interested in problems, his aim being to present a picture of the life of ordinary human beings without distortion or exaggeration or any attempt at interpretation. In *The Weavers* the plot is not closely knit, but is presented in a series of somewhat unrelated episodes; yet the method, casual as it may seem, succeeds, through the cumulative power of the scenes, in creating a powerful impression of the wretchedness and suffering of the Silesian spinners. While his sympathies are evidently enlisted on the side of the poverty-stricken weavers, he does not allow the accuracy of the presentation to be imperiled by the intrusion of his own personality.

The Sunken Bell, although it has been frequently and successfully acted, conforms no more closely to the "well-made" play than does *The Weavers*. Yet in most respects the two plays are worlds apart, representing as they do the two antithetical tendencies of their author. While *The Weavers* is purely naturalistic, *The Sunken Bell* might best be described as a dramatic poem, touched with imagination, symbolism, and romantic feeling. Certain of the scenes are conceived in a realistic vein, to be sure, but they are not of sufficient weight seriously to affect the essential romanticism of the work.

One can hardly doubt that in *The Sunken Bell*, Hauptmann has embodied much of his own personal philosophy of life, since it is concerned with the difficulties that particularly beset the artist soul. In it he attempts to reconcile two warring doctrines — the Christian and the Nietzschean. The play relates the tragedy of Heinrich, a bell-founder, who sets out to be a superman and fails. Pursued by a burning desire to realize the dreams his imagination has conjured up, he forsakes his wife and children in the valley, and ascends to the heights, there to attempt to create the sun-bells under the inspiration of the elf-maid, Rautendelein. Yet he does not find it so easy to escape from duty to instinct; his strength does not prove equal to his ambition, moral obligations still torment him, and he finds himself miserably "wandering between two worlds" — to use Matthew Arnold's telling phrase — "the one dead, the other powerless to be born." Remorse seizes him as he hears the bell of conscience loudly toll, stirred by the dead hands of the wife he has wronged. Yet he still clings to his creative vision, and when death overtakes him, he cries out ecstatically that he hears the sun-bells' song.

The charm of *The Sunken Bell* lies not so much in its philosophy or its symbolism, which is at times not a little confusing, as in the richness of its poetry and the beauty of its fantastic world of nature peopled by the elfin-folk.

ANTON TCHEKOV

ANTON TCHEKOV, greatest of Russian dramatists and short-story writers, was born in 1860 in Tagarog, in South Russia. Although he came of a family of liberated serfs, he was patrician in intellect, sensibilities, and tastes. His upbringing was rigorous — so rigorous in fact that he afterwards said he had had no childhood. Educated in the Greek school and the high school in his native town, he entered in 1879 the University of Moscow, and took a degree in medicine. As in the case of Schnitzler, the study of medicine and familiarity with scientific methods exercised, according to his own confession, a considerable influence on his literary career, in the way of enlarging the range of his observation and of serving as a guiding force. No doubt it also tended to intensify the naturally analytical character of his mind. Although never robust, Tchekov had a tremendous capacity for hard work and was a prolific writer. He began his literary career as a contributor of humorous sketches to newspapers, and it was not long before he had established a reputation as the most accomplished of Russian short-story writers.

In 1885 he wrote his first play, *On the High Road*. Some years later, after the failure of *The Sea Gull* at St. Petersburg, Stanislavsky took it over and brought it to a notable success at the Moscow Art Theater. Thus was initiated Tchekov's connection with this famous organization — a relation which continued with mutual advantage until his death. In 1890 he paid a visit to the penal colony on the Island of Saghalin, preparatory to the writing of a book on the convict prisons. Some time later he contracted tuberculosis, and, at the advice of his physician, settled down in the warmer climate of the Crimea. In 1904, three years after he had married Olga Kneipper, a leading actress of the Moscow Art Theater, he died at Badenweiler, a small village in the Black Forest, Germany.

The *Letters of Anton Chekhov to his Family and Friends* reveals a singularly lovable and saintly character — generous, tender-hearted, fearless, sensitive, interested in social reforms, ever willing to put his financial resources and his medical knowledge at the service of needy Russians of all classes. A strong individualist, he succeeded, unlike Peer Gynt, in being himself all the days of his life. As Maxim Gorky has well phrased it: "All his life Tchekov lived on his own soul; he was always himself, inwardly free, and never troubled about what some people expected, and others — coarser people — demanded of him."

When one has termed a writer a naturalist he has by no means said all that need be said by way of classification. Tchekov is primarily a naturalist, but he does not dwell unduly on the sordidness of life; he is not heavy-handed in manner, and he not infrequently makes use of a sensitive symbolism. His art is one of great delicacy and beauty; at times it is so casual as to seem almost aimless, but one comes to believe that it is ever governed by a fine intelligence. While Tchekov is skillful in reproducing the surface texture of life, his chief concern is with the "moments in between," and his plays are rich in essential non-essentials, in nuances and overtones, in a "thousand nothings which together make up something vitally important." This method is wholly justified by the results, since Tchekov's characters under his magic touch come to life with an authenticity that is sometimes startling.

While Tchekov may have been somewhat influenced by his study of the French drama, he deliberately rejected the academic conventions of the well-made play — with its carefully articulated scenes, its obvious conflicts, its artificial climaxes — for a medium more individual and more flexible. His plots are lacking in action, and seem formless; but the formlessness is more apparent than real. It may well be, however, that Treplev, the playwright of *The Sea Gull*, voices the author's own conclusion as to the importance of form: "I come more and more to the conviction that it is not a question of new and old forms, but that what matters is that a man should write without thinking about forms at all, write because it springs freely from his soul."

As one reads the Russian drama, one wonders what makes these weary-hearted people, so weak of will, so lacking in self-control, so ineffectual when face to face with the necessity of doing something, cling so tenaciously to life, until the conviction is borne in upon one that Russians have an enormous capacity to suffer and endure. Conscious that their opportunities are slipping away, these characters still continue to hesitate and procrastinate, falling back upon that fatalism which oftentimes seems to be but a mere excuse for idleness.

Tchekov resembles Carlyle to this extent, that he had a wholesome respect for work, and he apparently regarded it as a panacea for most of the ills that beset his countrymen. His belief in work takes on sometimes the nature of a prophecy, as in the words of Tusenbach in *The Three Sisters*: "The time is at hand, an avalanche is moving down upon us, a mighty clearing storm which is coming, is already near, and will soon blow the laziness, the indifference, the distaste for work, the rotten boredom out of our society. I shall work, and in another twenty-five or thirty years every one will have to work."

This inspiring speech, together with other passages of like import, seems to give the lie to the commonly held opinion that his plays indicate a depressing outlook on life. It is not strange that an artist so sensitive and sympathetic as Tchekov should have been affected by the atmosphere of moral and political stagnation of his day. Yet, while he deals for the most part with the absurdities and misery of life, the gloom of his picture is not infrequently lighted up with flashes of humor. His natural optimism most often takes form in an expression of unbounded faith in human progress, in an idealistic vision of a happy future state. This spirit is most eloquently voiced by Trofimov, the perpetual student of *The Cherry Orchard*, in the oft-quoted lines: "All Russia is our garden. The earth is great and beautiful — there are many beautiful places in it.... It is clear that to begin to live in the present we must first expiate our past, we must break with it; and we can expiate it only by suffering, by extraordinary increasing labor.... Humanity progresses, perfecting its powers. Everything that is beyond our ken now will one day become familiar and comprehensible; only we must work, we must with all our powers aid the seeker after truth."

Tchekov's major plays (he wrote but fourteen in all) are *The Sea Gull*, *Three Sisters*, *The Cherry Orchard*, and *Uncle Vanya*. *The Cherry Orchard*, his last play, and perhaps the fullest revelation of his dramatic genius, was produced in Moscow in 1904, just a few months before his death, by the Moscow Art Theater, which later brought it to the United States. It has been frequently revived successfully in England and in this country.

The Cherry Orchard has sometimes been referred to as the "tragedy of nothing doing." It is in fact almost plotless, but for some at least the charm of its setting and the lifelikeness of its characters are ample compensation for any deficiency in action. What movement there is is largely in the flow of soul as the characters interact one upon the other, revealing themselves unmistakably through the sinuous and flexible dialogue.

The play deals with a group of gentry and their dependents in a small Russian town, and has for its theme the decay of the old régime and its replacement by a new order of practical, hard-headed business men. Madame Ranevsky and her brother Gaev are amiable people, with considerable charm of manner, sentimental and easy-going, and quite improvident and helpless in the practical world of affairs; but they have much to say about their dying hopes. Ineffectual, too, are most of the others, with the shining exception of the peasant-born Lopahin, the rich landowner who in the end buys the cherry orchard, the most cherished possession of the family.

There is much plain speaking. Lopahin denounces the so-called intellectuals, and Madame Ranevsky, recently returned from Paris, is critical of her old friends: "How gray your lives are. How much nonsense you talk." But the palm for frankness goes to Trofimov, the student, who, one suspects, not infrequently serves as Tchekov's mouthpiece. In this wise he speaks: "the majority of us — ninety-five per cent — live like savages, at the least thing fly to blows and abuse, sleep in filth and stuffiness, bugs everywhere, stench and damp and moral impurity." It is not a lovely picture that Tchekov paints here, but it must be said that elsewhere he retouches it with brighter colors.

The final scene is most effective, set as it is in a low key. After the sale of the old homestead, the family departs for the city, and the laborers from without close the heavy shutters of the windows. Old Firs, the eighty-seven-year-old servant, inadvertently left behind, wanders into the dimly lighted room, and finds the door locked. "They have gone," he mumbles. "They have forgotten me.... Life has slipped by as though I hadn't lived." So the old man lies down on the couch, and as his cane drops from his nerveless hand there is heard in the distance the sound of an axe on a tree that both signals the doom of the cherry orchard and symbolizes the passing of the old régime.

EDMOND ROSTAND

EDMOND ROSTAND, by common consent the leading romantic of the modern theater, was born in Marseilles, France, in 1868. He came of aristocratic lineage, his father being a distinguished economist, his mother the granddaughter of one of Napoleon's marshals. Educated in his native town, he went up to Paris, and entered the Collège Stanislas. He next studied law, which did not for long hold his interest, and then turned to the field of writing. In his early thirties, after fame had come to him, he built himself a villa in the Pyrenees and settled down to the life of a recluse. In 1901 he was elected to membership in the French Academy. His death occurred in 1918.

Rostand's literary work has all the warmth and color that one expects from a son of the Midi. A thoroughgoing romanticist he wrote to please himself, making not the slightest concession to the popular realistic tendencies of the day. His earlier works were cordially welcomed by a public surfeited with the sordid realistic plays then current on the French stage, and he was at once hailed as the initiator of a great romantic revival. This hope was never realized, however, for as it turned out Rostand's influence did not prove sufficiently robust to divert the realistic and naturalistic stream into the channel of poetry and romance. He had no imitators and he left no successors, and he must therefore be regarded as a more or less isolated figure. Perhaps it would be fairer to accept Lemaître's view, and regard Rostand's plays as backward-looking rather than forward-looking, representing the distilled essence of French romanticism from Pierre and Thomas Corneille, through Victor Hugo, Alfred de Musset, and the elder Dumas, down to Theodore de Boanville and Jean Richepin.

Rostand was a true poet, although not a major one, who achieved wonderful effects through his color and imagery and verbal magic. Of his immense popularity there can be no question. He has not, however, fared as well with the critics as with the *hoi polloi*; some of them are suspicious of his exuberance and regard him as merely a brilliant virtuoso who was at times a bit too conscious of his cleverness. To speak truth, even those who are favorably disposed toward him are not infrequently annoyed by his obvious artificialities and theatricalism.

Rostand was an exceedingly careful and conscientious workman, and always allowed plenty of time for the development of his dramatic ideas; hence his output was limited. In fact, nearly ten years elapsed between *L'Aiglon* and *Chantecler*. When the latter play, long awaited and long promised, finally appeared in 1910, the great Coquelin, for whom the rôle of the cock had originally been intended, had been dead a year.

The first play of Rostand's to earn recognition was *Les Romanesques*, first acted in 1894 at the Comédie Française. It is a graceful and delicate comedy, dealing with the loves of Percinet and Sylvette, who might indeed be regarded as first sketches of Cyrano and Roxane. This was followed by *La Princesse Lointaine*, which at its première had a notable cast in Coquelin, Sarah Bernhardt, and Lucien Guitry; then came *La Samaritaine*, *Cyrano de Bergerac*, *L'Aiglon* — embodying the career of the Duc de Reichstadt, the unfortunate little son of Napoleon — and finally *Chantecler*. This completes the list of Rostand's more important plays.

Chantecler, while in no sense as effective an acting play as *Cyrano*, is perhaps the most mature and modern of his works, and the most complete revelation of his poetic gift. The vagueness of it is due largely to its symbolism and its wealth of spiritual implication. Although its characters are birds and animals, it is really a thinly veiled satire on modern society — the "drama of human endeavor grappling with life," to use Rostand's own words. It is rich in poetry; the cock's "Hymn to the Sun" in particular is quite unsurpassed for the eloquence and lyric passion of its style.

Rostand's defects are obvious: his plots show little originality and are for the most part lacking in unity and compactness; he had difficulty in creating strong characters; his heroines in particular are superficial and shallow, exhibiting at times a surprising lack of common-sense. Moreover, his plays are full of improbabilities and inconsistencies that lay a heavy burden upon the actors, and make it difficult to create the illusion of reality.

Yet, when all is said in the way of censure, it must be admitted that Rostand's virtues go far to compensate for all deficiencies; his plays, with their Gallic wit and brilliancy of style and lyrical fervor, are an effective antidote to the sordid and sex-drenched realism of the day, and offer a delightful romantic escape when the world is too much with us.

Cyrano de Bergerac is unquestionably the most successful acting play of the age. Hailed as a masterpiece of dramatic construction at its première in Paris in 1897, it later met with enthusiastic approval in other lands, and few plays have been more frequently revived. The play was written for Coquelin, greatest of French comedians, in order to provide this master actor with a rôle that would permit him in a single evening to display all the rich resources of his art. The part, with its plethora of long speeches, so attractive to an actor who has a gift for impassioned declamation, has been a favorite with two of America's leading actors — Richard Mansfield and Walter Hampden.

Among the numerous reasons offered for the universal appeal of *Cyrano de Bergerac*, the most satisfactory is the perhaps oft-quoted statement of Madame Rostand: "Certain people exist who always inspire sympathy simply because they possess charm. Isn't it the same way with the mind and what it creates?"

Certainly one of the sources of this "charm" is to be found in the character of the hero. Cyrano, who traces his lineage back to a Gascon of the same name that actually lived in the days of Molière, is a pure idealist, who ever asserts the supremacy of the spirit over the flesh. With his fiery bravado and his quickness in sword-play, he is boon-brother of the immortal d'Artagnan. But there is this difference — that whereas d'Artagnan is a handsome and triumphant figure, Cyrano is cruelly grotesque, the possessor of a nose so huge that children laugh at him on the street. There is something of the bully and the braggart about him, but one feels convinced that his boasting is but a screen to cover up his sensitiveness of soul.

Clayton Hamilton says that Cyrano is guilty of the crime of self-sacrifice, and adds: "I call self-sacrifice a crime, for... the primary object of life is not self-sacrifice but self-fulfillment." The answer is that Cyrano was quite sincere in his renunciation of his love, and that no one can say he did not best fulfill himself through its renunciation and through his success in keeping his white plume unsullied.

Although the play ends in a death, it is rightly termed an heroic comedy — so filled with the gusto of life is it, so rich in purely comic scenes. Pathos there is in plenty, but little of the stuff out of which great tragedy is made. It may indeed be argued that Cyrano's death is not tragic, but rather the crowning event of his heroic, unselfish life.

Cyrano de Bergerac is a thoroughly romantic play — romantic in its theme, its characters, its setting, its poetry. Because of the universality of its theme, and its appeal to the primary emotions, it is sure to live long after most of the contemporary realistic plays have departed to the limbo of forgotten things.

It is easy to pick flaws in the play. For one thing the plot is lacking in unity. The five acts, while interesting individually, are somewhat inconsistent and episodic. What unity the play possesses is to be found in the persistence of the hero, who dominates the action as completely as does Hamlet in the Elizabethan play. Then, too, Cyrano's skill in composing a ballad during the duel is a bit too perfect; Roxane's sudden appearance in camp is not sufficiently motivated, and the death scene is so prolonged that the most experienced of actors finds great difficulty in preserving verisimilitude. (This Walter Hampden acknowledged in a recent letter.)

But these defects are many times outweighed by scenes and passages of great beauty: the dissertation on his nose — an amazing piece of verbal fireworks — the perfectly managed first entrance of Cyrano, the pure poetry of a balcony scene that even challenges comparison with the most famous of all balcony scenes, that of *Romeo and Juliet*. These and many more such make up a richness of texture such as few plays can boast.

JOHN GALSWORTHY

JOHN GALSWORTHY was fortunate in his family connections and in his upbringing. Born in 1867 at Combe, Surrey, son of a leading London lawyer of ancient Devonshire stock, he was educated first at Harrow and then at New College, Oxford, where he took an honor degree in law. Although he was later admitted to the bar, he found the profession of law uncongenial, and practiced it but little. In 1891 he set out on a trip around the world — the first of a series of journeyings that have taken him into the distant corners of the earth. Once on a voyage from Australia to South Africa he met Joseph Conrad, at that time a sailor, and cemented a firm friendship that was broken only by the death of the great Polish novelist in 1924. During the war Galsworthy served for a time as a masseur in a French hospital. At present he is living the quiet life of a literary man at Holly Brush Hill overlooking Hampstead Heath.

Secure in the possession of abundant means, Galsworthy took his time in deciding on his life-work. It was, in fact, not until the middle-nineties that he took up writing seriously. His first book, a volume of short stories, published in 1898, was followed by several novels, and he was then definitely launched on a literary career. That golden year, 1906, witnessed the publication of his first play, *The Silver Box*, and of *The Man of Property*, the initial volume of that splendid series of novels dealing with the Forsyte family, which constitutes perhaps his most solid and permanent work. Wholly apart from its merit as fiction, the Forsyte cycle is sure to endure as an intimate and searching study of social and commercial life among the English middle class. Its popularity is attested by the fact that the name Forsyte has come to stand for every member of that English class whose particular hallmark is its "sense of property." Soames Forsyte, the protagonist of the series, is drawn with extraordinary skill and sympathy and takes his place by right among the great characters of English fiction.

Galsworthy is a careful and conscientious workman who seems to have a clear understanding of the genesis of his works. His illuminating observations on the craft of writing form a valuable body of critical dogma, and make his purpose and method abundantly clear. "A drama," he asserts, "must be shaped so as to have a spire of meaning. Every grouping of life and character has its inherent moral; and the business of the dramatist is so to pose the group as to bring that moral poignantly to the light of day."

Apparently Galsworthy is little concerned with plays as mere entertainment, but rather as records of the "phenomena of life and character, selected and combined, *but not distorted*, by the dramatist's outlook, set down without fear, favor, or prejudice." While he is unquestionably a man of strong feeling, his effort to be absolutely impartial sometimes leads him to understatement and underemphasis; in fact so quietly does he speak at times that the earnestness of his plea might easily fail to impress the casual reader. The irony that pervades his works indicates a certain detachment and dispassionateness. His well-balanced mind rarely is betrayed into excesses by his emotions; now and then, however, the force of real feeling asserts itself to lend conviction to his words. In *The Silver Box*, for instance, he points an accusing finger at the law which makes a discrimination between the rich and the poor — the theme of which is so perfectly summed up in *King Lear*: "Plate sin with gold, and the strong lance of justice hurtless breaks. Arm it in rags, a pigmy's straw does pierce it." In *Justice* he brings to trial the prison system of England and proves it guilty.

In many of his plays he represents the clash of classes: in *The Mob*, the conflict between the mass and the individual; in *The Skin Game*, the strife between the aristocracy and the *nouveau riche*; in *Loyalties*, the friction resulting from a sense of loyalty on the part of various individuals toward their particular caste. In nearly every instance, it would seem, Galsworthy's sympathy is with the underdog — a distinctively English trait.

In casting about for words with which to sum up the qualities of Galsworthy's work, one inevitably hits upon the following: sincerity, sanity, moderation, tolerance, sympathy. These traits reveal themselves unmistakably in that refined style of his which has been so greatly admired. Nowhere has it been more aptly described than in the tribute of Joseph Conrad, who characterized it as "clear, direct, sane, illumined by a perfectly unaffected sincerity. It is the style of a man whose sympathy with mankind is too genuine to allow him the smallest gratification of his vanity at the cost of his fellow creatures ... sufficiently pointed to carry deep his remorseless irony and grave enough to be the dignified vehicle of his profound compassion."

The plays of Galsworthy constantly reveal his careful workmanship; his plots are well-built (perhaps at times a bit too strongly architectural) and his dialogue is unsurpassed for flexibility and beauty in the drama of the day. A certain thinness is, however, to be remarked in his imaginative work; a thoroughgoing realist, his touch seems surest in dealing with the things that have come out of his actual experiences.

While some of his minor characters seem a bit wooden, such major figures as Falder, Roberts, and Anthony are conceived from within, and possess an amazing vitality. Galsworthy apparently regards character-drawing as all-important in the drama, for he somewhere says: "Take care of character; action and dialogue will take care of themselves."

Lovers of Galsworthy have at times been fearful lest his interest in social problems might in the end undermine the integrity of his artistry. Apparently this fear is unwarranted, for thus far the artist in him has succeeded in keeping that reforming spirit in its proper place. This is as it should be. The world of letters could ill afford to lose an artist of the stature of John Galsworthy.

Strife, published in 1909, is one of Galsworthy's major dramas, and was the first of his plays to earn general favor. Its theme is the eternal conflict between labor and capital. While it has been often compared with Hauptmann's *The Weavers*, the two plays really have little in common save the likeness of theme. No play of Galsworthy's so clearly reveals at once his profound sympathy for suffering humanity and his eminent sense of fairness. While it is evident that his feelings are chiefly enlisted on the side of the workingmen, he makes it abundantly clear that the right is not all on one side. His training as a lawyer shows itself in the way he marshals his facts and presents his evidence pro and con. The struggle between the labor and capitalist parties is concentrated in a personal contest between two dominant characters — Roberts, the fiery labor leader, and Anthony, the hard-headed, stubborn manufacturer. Both leaders are honest and sincere in their convictions; Roberts is fanatical in his willingness to sacrifice himself and his family in his devotion to the cause he has espoused. He reveals his sincerity and selflessness in his eloquent speech to the crowd, as he assures them: "'Tis not for this little moment of time that we're fighting, not for ourselves... 'tis for all those that come after throughout all time.... They're welcome to the worst that can happen to me, to the worst that can happen to us all... if we can shake that white-faced monster with the bloody lips that has sucked the life out of ourselves, our wives and children, since the world began."

In the end both sides are defeated. In the absence of Roberts, called to the deathbed of his wife, the workingmen, out of fear of starvation, vote for conciliation; and the board of directors, impelled by fear of financial loss, carries over Anthony's protest a vote to leave the whole matter to the adjustment of Harness, the trades-union official. It remains for Harness and Tench to point out the underlying irony of the situation as the play ends:

HARNESS. A woman dead; and the two best men both broken!
TENCH (*staring at him — suddenly excited*). D'you know, sir — these terms, they're the very same we drew up together, you and I, and put to both sides before the fight began? All this — all this — and — and what for?
HARNESS (*in a slow grim voice*). That's where the fun comes in!

In this play, as elsewhere, Galsworthy raises the problem, but makes no attempt to solve it. In fact, the only remedies he ever proposes for the ills of humanity are greater understanding and sympathy. As for the conflict between labor and capital, he apparently regards it as quite futile.

Strife was first performed in London on March 9, 1909. Its first performance in America was at the New Theater, New York, November 19, 1909, with Louis Calvert, Albert Bruning, and Thais Lawton in the leading rôles.

JOHN MILLINGTON SYNGE

JOHN MILLINGTON SYNGE, the glory of the Irish National Theater, whose plays of peasant life constitute the most important contribution of Ireland to the drama of the day, was born at Newtown Little, near Dublin, 1871. After graduating from Trinity College, Dublin, in 1892, he sought to satisfy at once his taste for music and his wanderlust by traveling about Europe with his violin for two years or more, much as did Goldsmith over a century earlier. His love of the gypsy trail and his interest in the knights of the road revealed itself later in his sympathetic treatment of tramps and outlaws. In 1898, W. B. Yeats discovered him living in a garret in the Latin Quarter of Paris, preparing himself to be a literary critic. On the advice of Yeats, he returned to Ireland, and settled down on the Aran Islands, to study at first hand the life and speech of a primitive fisher-folk. The result of this contact was a series of dramas of contemporary peasant life, his most vital and enduring work, revealing not only a remarkable gift for reproducing the surface texture of life, but a successful probing into the subjective soul of these simple Aran people. Synge's single excursion into the field of Irish folk-lore, *Deirdre of the Sorrows*, while a poignant and telling rendering of the old legend, shows a less perfect mastery of his material, a touch somewhat less sure.

It is not at all certain that Synge really intended to satirize the Irish, but it is not strange that his searching, dispassionate, ironical treatment of Irish character should be resented by a race so sensitive, so quick to take offense. It is not to be wondered at that *The Shadow of the Glen* should be held in some quarters to be a slander on Irish womanhood, that *The Playboy of the Western World* should be regarded as a satire on the pugnacity and boastfulness of the race, on its tendency to elevate mere physical prowess into heroism. This latter play in fact created riots among the audiences in both Dublin and Philadelphia when it was presented by the famous Abbey Players.

While Synge chose prose as his medium and employed the method of the realist in his treatment of the Irish scene, the poet in him reveals itself unmistakably in the shaping power of his imagination and particularly in his unique style. This beautifully modulated prose — with its color, its lilt, and its haunting cadence — is his own creation, derived in part from his loving study of the Anglo-Irish idiom; in part from his admiration of certain French writers such as Anatole France and Pierre Loti. It has the flavor of the wild apple about it, the tang of peat smoke. The peculiar quality of it has nowhere been more aptly described than in the words of the late Stuart Sherman, who speaks of "the irresistibly quaint idiom, the drifting rhythm, the loose sentence structure, thought thrown out after thought as it were, without premeditation, and blossoming from phrase to phrase, the window opened upon a mist of vague and limitless emotion, the poignant and adorable Celtic wistfulness." It may well be that in time to come this individual and eloquent style of Synge's will be regarded as his greatest achievement.

The plays of Synge are a very far remove from the contemporary drama of ideas. He was in no sense a preacher, and was not particularly interested in problems. He avoided anything that smacked of the didactic, looking upon the drama as a thing to be enjoyed for its vivid treatment of real life.

While pathos is the most insistent note in his work — he often brings the eternal note of sadness in — he did possess the saving sense of humor, which gave a savor to his thought and softened the bitterness of his satire. Yet, with the exception of *The Tinker's Wedding*, his plays are not for laughter. Through them runs a spirit of disillusionment, and his laughter is apt to be a bit ironic — "homeless laughter," Stuart Sherman called it, "the laughter of men who have wandered all the highways of the world and have found no abiding city."

One of the hallmarks of Synge's genius is his gift of transmuting the small thing, the merely local or national happening, into an event of universal significance. This power is, I fancy, due largely to his sense of majesty, his apprehension of the dignity and unconscious heroism of simple and primitive people.

Some of Synge's faults are purely individual; others he shares with the Irish dramatists of his day. His plays at times seem a little thin, suggesting an incapacity for sustained effort. His fondness for certain stock expressions cannot but be regarded as an annoying mannerism. His fun tends to become extravagant and unrestrained, and his comedy tends to degenerate into farce.

The Playboy of the Western World is generally held to be the best of modern Irish comedies, *Riders to the Sea* the most perfect of Irish tragedies. The germ of *Riders to the Sea* occurs in a comment Synge once made on the finding of the body of a drowned seaman: "The loss of one man seems a slight catastrophe to all except the immediate relatives. Often when an accident happens a father is lost with his two eldest sons, or in some way all the active men of the household die together."

Riders to the Sea is usually termed a tragedy. It is a wonderfully poignant and moving little play, set in a minor key, and filled with the surge and thunder of the sea. The ending comes as surely and inevitably as the catastrophe of a Greek drama, prepared for by the skillful interplay of minute details. Yet it falls somewhat short of a great tragedy. For one thing it is brief, and therefore lacks the impressiveness of the fuller treatment of the theme permitted by a full-length play. The theme itself is painful rather than tragic, the pathos of the final scene interfering with the proper effect of the catharsis. There is in it no clash of human wills, only the revelation of the helplessness of man in the face of the power of the sea. Maurya, the poor old fisherwoman, shows an incapacity "to rise to tragic heights of feeling at the greatest crisis in a lifetime of numbing griefs." She accepts the loss of Bartley, her sixth and last son, with resignation, almost with a sense of relief. She speaks in a kind of reverie: "They're all gone now, and there isn't anything more the sea can do to me... it's a great rest I'll have now, and it's time surely. It's a great rest I'll have now, and great sleeping in the long nights after Samhain.... Michael has a clean burial in the Far North, by the grace of the Almighty God. Bartley will have a fine coffin out of the white boards, and a deep grave surely. What more can we want than that? No man at all can be living forever, and we must be satisfied."

Riders to the Sea may perhaps be regarded, then, as a tragic idyl, rather than a true tragedy. But in any event, by reason of the greatness of its theme, its successful creation of a mood, and the beauty of the style, it belongs by right to the province of high drama.

EUGENE O'NEILL

EUGENE O'NEILL is the only American dramatist of the present generation with an international reputation. His plays have been presented in London, Berlin, Paris, Vienna, Moscow, in Czech

countries, and even in Japan; and, while he is not always understood in lands beyond the sea, he is everywhere recognized as a
new and vital force in the dramatic world.   In America he stands
supreme: three of his plays have won the Pulitzer Prize, and in
some quarters *Strange Interlude* has been hailed as "the great
American drama."

Eugene O'Neill was born in New York City, October 16, 1888,
in the building at the corner of Broadway and Forty-Third Street,
then known as the Barrett House.   He was early accustomed to the
atmosphere of the theater.   His father, James O'Neill, the distinguished actor of *Monte Cristo* fame, on his annual tours dragged the
boy back and forth across the continent, until he was seven years
old.   He then attended various schools, and in 1906 matriculated
at Princeton.   For some boyish misdemeanor he was expelled in
the spring of his freshman year, and thus his formal education
ended.   At the age of twenty he entered upon an adventurous
career, the early chapters of which have the following headings:
secretary to a mail-order firm on lower Broadway, gold prospector
in Honduras, assistant manager for Viola Allen on a road tour,
sailor — journeying first to Buenos Aires, when he stayed for a
year and a half in the service of several American firms, then to
South Africa, and other lands — denizen of the docks along the
New York water-front, actor, and newspaper reporter.

These years of hardship and irregular living finally took their
toll; for in 1913 he contracted a lung weakness, and entered a
sanitarium.   This breakdown marked a turning-point in his
career.   The five months he spent in the sanitarium gave him for
the first time a chance to read and think, and to evaluate his impressions of life.   Then it was that he was seized with a burning
desire to express in the form of the drama his adventurings in the
world of men and in the realm of the imagination.   He had at
last found his life-work.   To be sure, restlessness still pursued him,
but from now on it spent itself in a ceaseless search for new and
untried modes of expression.

For a year or so he devoted himself chiefly to the building-up of
his health, and to the writing of plays; then followed a winter at
Harvard as a member of Professor Baker's "47" playwriting class;
after which he settled down to the life of a playwright, first at
Greenwich Village, and then at Provincetown, Massachusetts,
where he occupied a converted life-saving station at the very tip of
Cape Cod.   Here began his connection with the Provincetown
Players, who encouraged him to write and presented his earlier

plays, first in the Wharf Theater in Provincetown, and then at the tiny Provincetown Playhouse in New York. The connection was mutually advantageous, for O'Neill did much to establish the fame of the organization.

His earliest plays were one-act sea-plays. *Bound East for Cardiff* was the first of these to be produced at Provincetown, and O'Neill himself took the part of the second mate. In 1914 his first volume, *Thirst and Other One-Act Plays*, was published at his father's expense. However, it made no great stir in the literary world. With the appearance of his first important full-length play, *Beyond the Horizon*, in 1920, O'Neill's period of apprenticeship came to an end, and he became recognized as our leading dramatist — a position he has never since relinquished. In recent years the Theater Guild has sponsored the O'Neill plays, some of which have fully tested the rich resources of this organization. *Strange Interlude* proved the most successful of all the Guild productions, running for several years in New York, and playing before large audiences on the road. O'Neill's last play, *Mourning Becomes Electra*, on which he has been laboring for two years at his villa in France, is promised for the fall of 1931.

Eugene O'Neill is an interesting and baffling personality, who always succeeds in evading inclusion in a definite category. To quote Barrett Clark: "The man still refuses to stay put, and defies anything like final analysis." A constant experimenter, he often gives the impression of being too impatient to allow his dramatic ideas to ripen. There is something tentative and wavering about his work, as if he were continually being driven by a restless urge to search for new modes of expression. Often it seems that he begins with gusto, and then loses interest before the plot is far on its way, as if he were eager to be off to fresh fields and pastures new. This waning of interest may perhaps account for the splendid first act of *Anna Christie*, for instance, and the comparative weakness of the succeeding acts.

O'Neill's plays exhibit a considerable diversity of mood and form. While he acknowledges a certain indebtedness to Strindberg, whose plays he read while in the sanitarium, he apparently owed little or nothing to George Kaiser and the other German expressionists, since he wrote *The Hairy Ape* and *The Emperor Jones* before he became acquainted with their work. His interest in naturalism was short-lived, for, after he had made a popular success with *Anna Christie*, he declared he would never write another play of that ilk. Some of his plays, such as *The Great God Brown*,

are touched with symbolism. Once — in *The Fountain* — he wrote a pure romance. *Marco Millions*, while fundamentally a satire on commercialism, reveals an unexpected wealth of humor. The serious vein is manifestly more germane to his genius.

There is something admirable in O'Neill's frank acceptance of the essential facts of life, and in his effort to present these truths without distortion and exaggeration in all their stark reality. At times, it must be confessed, he carries this direct literalness a bit too far — to the point where beauty vanishes, as if in disgust at the sordidness and ugliness of life. It should be said, however, in fairness to O'Neill, that few writers of our day have so frequently succeeded in extracting beauty and poetry from the coarseness and ugliness of contemporary life.

This direct method was anathema to Hofmannsthal, the Austrian critic, who, I believe, laid his finger on one of O'Neill's chief weaknesses. He says, "The characters in Mr. O'Neill's plays seem to me a little too direct... they are not sufficiently drenched in the atmosphere of their own individual past." In other words, O'Neill's characters often seem to have been called into being merely for the purpose of the play, and to be lacking in that richness of background which one finds in the great dramas of the world.

The plays of O'Neill are for the most part unpleasant plays, wrought out of the agony and pain of life. His most successful characters are people of rather primitive instincts, misfits, suffering from disease, economic inhibitions, frustrations, from soul-destroying powers which they cannot understand. These poor souls are usually beaten in the battle of life by a force either within or outside themselves that makes for their confusion and ruin. In fact, few plays of our day have such a plethora of murders, violent deaths, suicides, and insanity. The dramatist's artistic sense is nowhere more clearly revealed than in the way in which he expresses this relentless, devastating force in a symbol — such as the "tom-tom-tom" of the drum in *The Emperor Jones*, the mountains that hem in the lonely farm in *Beyond the Horizon*, the telltale scales in *Thirst*, the humming of the motor in *Dynamo*, steel in *The Hairy Ape* — steel of ship's hull, steel of prison cell, steel of cage bars; these symbols set the tone of the plays and permeate the plots with the persistence of a *leit motif*.

O'Neill seems to find difficulty in writing in a natural way of aristocrats or well-bred people of the upper middle class. Witness the stilted and artificial dialogue between the girl and her aunt in

The Hairy Ape (the chief blemish in the play), and much of the speech in *The First Man,* a play dealing ostensibly with people of not a little culture.

O'Neill has undoubtedly a considerable gift for language; he loves the flavor of words, and uses with fine effect speech that smacks of the soil or has the tang of the sea in it. His tendency to interlard his pages with profanity has given offense in some quarters, and even his admirers have not always found it easy to justify its use. Clayton Hamilton's explanation has more than a modicum of truth in it: "It is, I think, his sense of literary style that accounts for his fondness for obscene phrases and profane ejaculations, more than any wish to shock the ladies in the audience or to assert his unconventionality. Most of the swearing is done from an obscure desire to revel in the sound of words." Yet, while it seems clear that O'Neill is using coarse, profane language as an artist to re-create the actual speech of his rough characters, one feels that such language could be properly indicated with a less generous supply of profanity.

In his more recent plays O'Neill has been attempting grandiose themes that some feel to be beyond the reach of his present capacity. As Barrett Clark puts it: "Just now he seems a bit off the track. Certainly O'Neill is worrying too much about God and his own soul." He is surer and more successful when he deals with material that is more objective, more nearly within the compass of his actual experiences.

O'Neill has an undoubted vein of originality, a fresh and unhackneyed point of view, the courage to do the unconventional thing, if it suits his purpose, and a style of considerable distinction. In spite of obvious defects — a tendency toward the violent, an occasional touch of "fine writing," a propensity for getting beyond his depth in philosophizings and abstractions — he must still be regarded as the figure that at present looms largest on the American dramatic horizon.

Beyond the Horizon was first presented at a special matinée at the Morosco Theater, New York, February 2, 1920, with Richard Bennett in the rôle of Robert Mayo. It was well received, enjoyed a successful run, and was awarded the Pulitzer Prize for that year. The germ of the play was an experience of O'Neill's on a British tramp steamer where he met a Norwegian sailor who expressed regret that he had not remained on the farm.

The play is the tragedy of Robert Mayo, a dreamy, imaginative youth, attracted by the lure of the far-horizons, who, thwarted of his ambition to venture into the world beyond the enfolding hills, is slowly choked to death in the stifling atmosphere of a New England farm. The hills become to him a symbol of a crushing, irresistible force. "Oh — those cursed hills — how I've grown to hate the sight of them. They're like the walls of a narrow prison yard shutting me in from all the freedom and wonder of life."

The theme is a gripping one, and in the acting version O'Neill with relentless logic carries it through to the bitter end. The final scene is unsparing in its realism. While Robert's lamp of life flickers and goes out in the sordid farmhouse, Andrew, the older brother, returned from abroad, curses the wife for not lying to the dying man. In its acting form the play cannot but be regarded as a study of futility and frustration, of moral and physical degeneration. Its one heartening note is the revelation of brother love, surpassing in its strength the love of man for woman. The written version is more cheerful in tone and ends on a note of hope. Robert, realizing his end is near, drags his painful way to his loved hilltop; when he is found there by Andrew and Ruth, his voice rings out with the happiness of hope: "Look, isn't it beautiful beyond the hills! I can hear the old voices, calling me to come — and this time I'm going — I'm free. It isn't the end. I've won to my trip — the right of release — beyond the horizon." And thus, to use the language of *King Lear*, "his heart burst smilingly."

It is likely that at its first appearance *Beyond the Horizon* was overpraised, as it was hailed as "the first great tragedy that has been contributed to the drama of the world by a native American." The historical estimate should not, however, blind us to its obvious defects. To some it has seemed a depressing and turgid drama, marked by occasional awkwardness of dialogue and crudities of plot. Certain it is that O'Neill's technique has since those early days developed immeasurably in firmness and finish. The play does, however, reveal (as Clayton Hamilton states it) "in the alternation of outdoor and indoor scenes... a striving for a rhythm and meaning which would break down the tight bounds of our current realism." In any event, it is a striking play by reason of its truth of characterization, its beauty of speech, and the gripping and cumulative power of its theme.

II

BIBLIOGRAPHY

WORKS ON THE MODERN DRAMA

Archer, William. *The Old Drama and the New.* Boston, 1923.

Baker, G. P. *Technique of the Drama.* Boston, 1919.

Bechofer, C. E. *The Literary Renaissance in America.* London, 1923.

Boyd, Ernest. *Ireland's Literary Renaissance.* New York, 1917.

Boyd, Ernest. *The Contemporary Drama of Ireland.* Boston, 1917.

Chandler, Frank W. *Aspects of Modern Drama.* New York, 1914.

Chandler, Frank W. *The Contemporary Drama of France.* Boston, 1920.

Clark, Barrett H. *The Continental Drama of Today.* New York, 1914.

Clark, Barrett H. *Contemporary French Dramatists.* Cincinnati, 1915.

Clark, Barrett H. *The British and American Drama of Today.* New York, 1915.

Clark, Barrett H. *A Study of the Modern Drama.* New York, 1925.

Coad, Oral S., and Mims, Edwin, Jr. *The American Stage.* New Haven, 1929.

Cunliffe, J. W. *English Literature During the Last Half-Century.* New York, 1923.

Cunliffe, J. W. *Modern English Playwrights.* New York, 1927.

Dickinson, T. H. *The Contemporary Drama of England.* Boston, 1920.

Dickinson, T. H. *Playwrights of the New American Theatre.* New York, 1925.

Dickinson, T. H. *Outline of Contemporary Drama.* Boston, 1927.

Dukes, Ashley. *Modern Dramatists.* Chicago, 1912.

Dukes, Ashley. *The Youngest Drama.* Chicago, 1921.

Eaton, W. P. *The Drama in English.* New York, 1930.

Filon, A. *Modern French Drama.* London, 1898.

Hale, E. E. *Dramatists of Today.* New York, 1911.

Hamilton, Clayton. *Conversations on Contemporary Dramatists.* New York, 1925.

Hamilton, Clayton. *The Theory of the Theatre.* New York, 1910.

Henderson, A. *The Changing Drama.* Cincinnati, 1919.

Henderson, A. *European Dramatists.* New York, 1926.

Huneker, James. *Iconoclasts*. New York, 1912.

Jameson, Storm. *The Modern Drama in Europe*. New York, 1920.

Jourdain, Eleanor. *The Drama in Europe*. New York, 1924.

Lewisohn, Ludwig. *The Modern Drama*. New York, 1915.

Lewisohn, Ludwig. *The Drama and the Stage*. New York, 1922.

MacClintock, L. *The Contemporary Drama in Italy*. Boston, 1920.

MacGowan, Kenneth. *The Theatre of Tomorrow*. New York, 1921.

Mantle, Burns. *American Playwrights of Today*. New York, 1929.

Mantle, Burns. *The Best Plays of 1919–1920*, and subsequent years. New York.

Matthews, Brander. *The Development of the Drama*. New York, 1908.

Matthews, Brander. *A Study of the Drama*. Boston 1910.

Morgan, A. E. *Tendencies of Modern English Drama*. New York, 1924.

Moses, M. J. *The American Dramatist*. Boston, 1925.

Nicoll, Allardyce. *British Drama*. New York, 1925.

Phelps, W. L. *Essays on Modern Dramatists*. New York, 1921.

Phelps, W. L. *The Twentieth Century Theatre*. New York, 1918.

Quinn, A. H. *A History of the American Drama from the Civil War to the Present Day*. Vol. II. New York, 1927.

Sayler, Oliver M. *Our American Theatre*. New York, 1923.

Shaw, Bernard. *Dramatic Opinions and Essays*. New York, 1910.

Smith, W. A. *Main Currents in Modern French Drama*. New York, 1925.

Stoeckius, A. *Naturalism in Recent German Drama*. New York, 1903.

Stuart, D. C. *The Development of Dramatic Art*. New York, 1928.

Thorndike, Ashley H. *English Comedy*. New York, 1929.

Wiener, Leo. *The Contemporary Drama of Russia*. Boston, 1924.

Witkowski, George. *German Drama of the Nineteenth Century*. New York, 1910.

Woollcott, Alexander. *Shouts and Murmurs*. New York, 1922.

HENRIK IBSEN

Archer, William. *Introduction to Ibsen's Collected Works*. New York, 1907.

Boyesen, H. H. *A Commentary on the Writings of Henrik Ibsen*. New York, 1894.

Brandès, Georg. *Creative Spirits of the Nineteenth Century.* New York, 1923.

Brandès, Georg. *Henrik Ibsen; Björnsterne Björnson: Critical Studies.* New York, 1899.

Firkins, I. T. E. *Henrik Ibsen: A Bibliography of Criticism and Biography.* New York, 1921.

Gosse, Edmund. *Ibsen.* London, 1907. New York, 1911.

Henderson, A. *European Dramatists.* Cincinnati, 1913.

Heller, Otto. *Henrik Ibsen: Plays and Problems.* Boston, 1912.

Huneker, J. G. *Iconoclasts.* New York, 1905.

Huneker, J. G. *Egoists.* New York, 1918.

Ibsen, Henrik. *Letters.* New York, 1905.

Lavrin, Janco. *Ibsen and His Creation.* London, 1921.

Lee, J. *The Ibsen Secret.* New York, 1907.

Litzmann, H. *Ibsen's Dramen.* Hamburg, 1921.

McFall, H. *Ibsen, the Man, His Art and His Significance.* New York and San Francisco, 1907.

Moses, M. J. *Henrik Ibsen: the Man and His Plays.* New York, 1918.

Roberts, R. E. *Henrik Ibsen: A Critical Study.* London, 1912.

Rose, Henry. *Henrik Ibsen: Poet, Mystic, and Moralist.* London, 1913.

Shaw, Bernard. *The Quintessence of Ibsenism.* London, 1915 (revised).

Weigand, N. J. *The Modern Ibsen.* New York, 1926.

Zucker, A. E. *Ibsen, the Master Builder.* New York, 1929.

GERHART HAUPTMANN

Bartels, A. *Gerhart Hauptmann.* Weimar, 1897.

Bytkowski, Sigmund. *Gerhart Hauptmanns Naturalismus und das Drama.* Hamburg, 1908.

Dukes, Ashley. *Modern Dramatists.* Chicago, 1912.

Fechter, Paul. *Gerhart Hauptmann.* Dresden, 1922.

Hale, E. E., Jr. *Dramatists of Today.* New York, 1911.

Holl, Karl. *Gerhart Hauptmann: His Life and His Work.* London, 1913. Chicago, 1914.

Huneker, James. *Iconoclasts.* New York, 1905.

Lewisohn, Ludwig. *Introductions to the Dramatic Works of Gerhart Hauptmann.* New York, 1914–1924.

Lewisohn, Ludwig. *The Modern Drama.* New York, 1915.

Roehr, J. *Gerhart Hauptmanns dramatisches Schaffen.* Dresden, 1912.

Hamilton, Clayton. *Conversations on Contemporary Dramatists.* New York, 1924.

MacGowan, Kenneth. *The Theatre of Tomorrow,* New York, 1921.

Mantle, Burns. *American Playwrights of Today.* New York, 1929.

Mickle, A. D. *Studies on Six Plays of O'Neill.* New York, 1929.

Quinn, A. H. *The History of the American Drama from the Civil War to the Present Day.* Vol. II. New York, 1927.

Sayler, Oliver M. *Our American Theatre.* New York, 1923.

Sutton, Graham. *Some Contemporary Dramatists.* London, 1924.

Van Doren, Carl. *American and British Literature Since 1890.* New York, 1925.

Whipple, Thomas K. *Spokesmen.* New York, 1928.

Woollcott, A. *Shouts and Murmurs.* New York, 1922.

III

PLAYS BY THE AUTHORS REPRESENTED IN THIS
VOLUME

(The dates are those of publication)

HENRIK IBSEN

Catilina (1850). *The Warriors Barrow* (1854). *Lady Inger of Ostrat* (1855). *The Feast at Solhoug* (1856). *Olaf Liljekrans* (1857). *The Vikings at Helgeland* (1858). *Love's Comedy* (1862). *The Pretenders* (1864). *Brand* (1866). *Peer Gynt* (1867). *The League of Youth* (1869). *Emperor and Galilean* (1873). *The Pillars of Society* (1877). *A Doll's House* (1879). *Ghosts* (1881). *An Enemy of the People* (1882). *The Wild Duck* (1884). *Rosmersholm* (1886). *The Lady from the Sea* (1888). *Hedda Gabler* (1890). *The Master Builder* (1892). *Little Eyolf* (1894). *John Gabriel Borkman* (1894). *When We Dead Awaken* (1899).

GERHART HAUPTMANN

Before Dawn (1889). *The Festival of Peace* (1890). *Lonely Lives* (1891). *The Weavers* (1892). *Colleague Crampton* (1892). *The Beaver Coat* (1893). *The Assumption of Hannele* (1893). *Florian Geyer* (1894). *Helios* (1896). *The Sunken Bell* (1896). *Elga* (1896). *Pastoral* (1898). *Drayman Henschel* (1898). *Schluck und Jau* (1899). *Michael Kramer* (1900). *The Red Cock* (1901). *Poor Heinrich* (1902). *Rose Bernd* (1903). *And Pippa Dances* (1906). *The Maidens of Bischofsberg* (1907). *Charlemagne's Hostage* (1908). *Griselda* (1909). *The Rats* (1911). *Gabriel Schilling's Flight* (1912). *The Festival Play* (1913). *The Bow of Odysseus* (1914). *Winter Ballad* (1917). *The White Savior* (1920). *Indipohdi* (1920). *Peter Brauer* (1921). *Veland* (1925). *Dorothea Angermann* (1926). *Till Eulenspiegel* (1927).

ANTON TCHEKOV

On the High Road (1884). *The Swan Song* (1886). *Ivanov* (1887). *The Wood Demon* (1888). *The Bear* (1888). *The Proposal* (1889). *The Wedding* (1890). *The Tragedian in Spite of Himself* (1890). *The Anniversary* (1892). *The Sea Gull* (1896). *Uncle Vanya* (1897). *Three Sisters* (1901). *The Cherry Orchard* (1903).

EDMOND ROSTAND

The Red Glove (1888). *The Two Pierrots* (1891). *The Romancers* (1894). *The Princess Faraway* (1895). *The Woman of Samaria* (1897). *Cyrano de Bergerac* (1897). *L'Aiglon* (1900). *Chantecler* (1910). *The Sacred Wood* (1910). *Don Juan's Last Night* (1921).

JOHN GALSWORTHY

The Silver Box (1906). *Joy* (1907). *Strife* (1909). *Justice* (1910). *The Little Dream* (1911). *The Pigeon* (1912). *The Eldest Son* (1912). *The Fugitive* (1913). *The Mob* (1914). *Hall-Marked* (1914). *A Bit of Love* (1915). *The Little Man* (1915). *The Foundations* (1917). *The Skin Game* (1920). *Defeat* (1920). *The First and the Last* (1921). *Punch and Go* (1921). *A Family Man* (1921). *The Sun* (1921). *Windows* (1922). *Loyalties* (1922). *The Forest* (1924). *Old English* (1924). *The Show* (1925). *Escape* (1926). *Exiled* (1929). *The Roof* (1929).

JOHN SYNGE

The Shadow of the Glen (1903). *Riders to the Sea* (1904). *The Well of the Saints* (1905). *The Playboy of the Western World* (1907). *The Tinker's Wedding* (1909). *Deidre of the Sorrows* (1910).

EUGENE O'NEILL

Thirst and Other One-Act Plays (contains *Thirst, The Web, Warnings, Fog,* and *Recklessness*) (1914). *Bound East for Cardiff* (1916). *Before Breakfast* (1916). *In the Zone* (1917). *The Long Voyage Home* (1917). *Ile* (1917). *The Rope* (1918). *Where the Cross is Made* (1918.) *The Moon of the Caribbees* (1918). *The Dreamy Kid* (1919). *Beyond the Horizon* (1920). *Chris Christopherson* (rewritten as *Anna Christie*) (1920). *The Emperor Jones* (1920). *Diff'rent* (1920). *Gold* (1921). *Anna Christie* (1921). *The Straw* (1921). *The First Man* (1922). *The Hairy Ape* (1922). *Welded* (1924). *The Ancient Mariner* (Not Published) (1924). *All God's Chillun Got Wings* (1924). *Desire Under the Elms* (1924). *S. S. Glencairn* (contains *The Moon of the Caribbees, The Long Voyage Home, In the Zone,* and *Bound East for Cardiff*) (1924). *The Fountain* (1925). *The Great God Brown* (1926). *Marco Millions* (1927). *Lazarus Laughed* (1927). *Strange Interlude* (1928). *Dynamo* (1929).